PLUS

PLUS

Expanding the frame

A fashion photography collection showcasing plus-size bodies

Lydia Hudgens

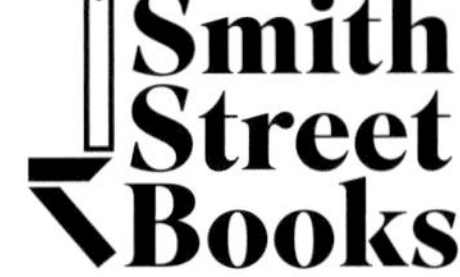

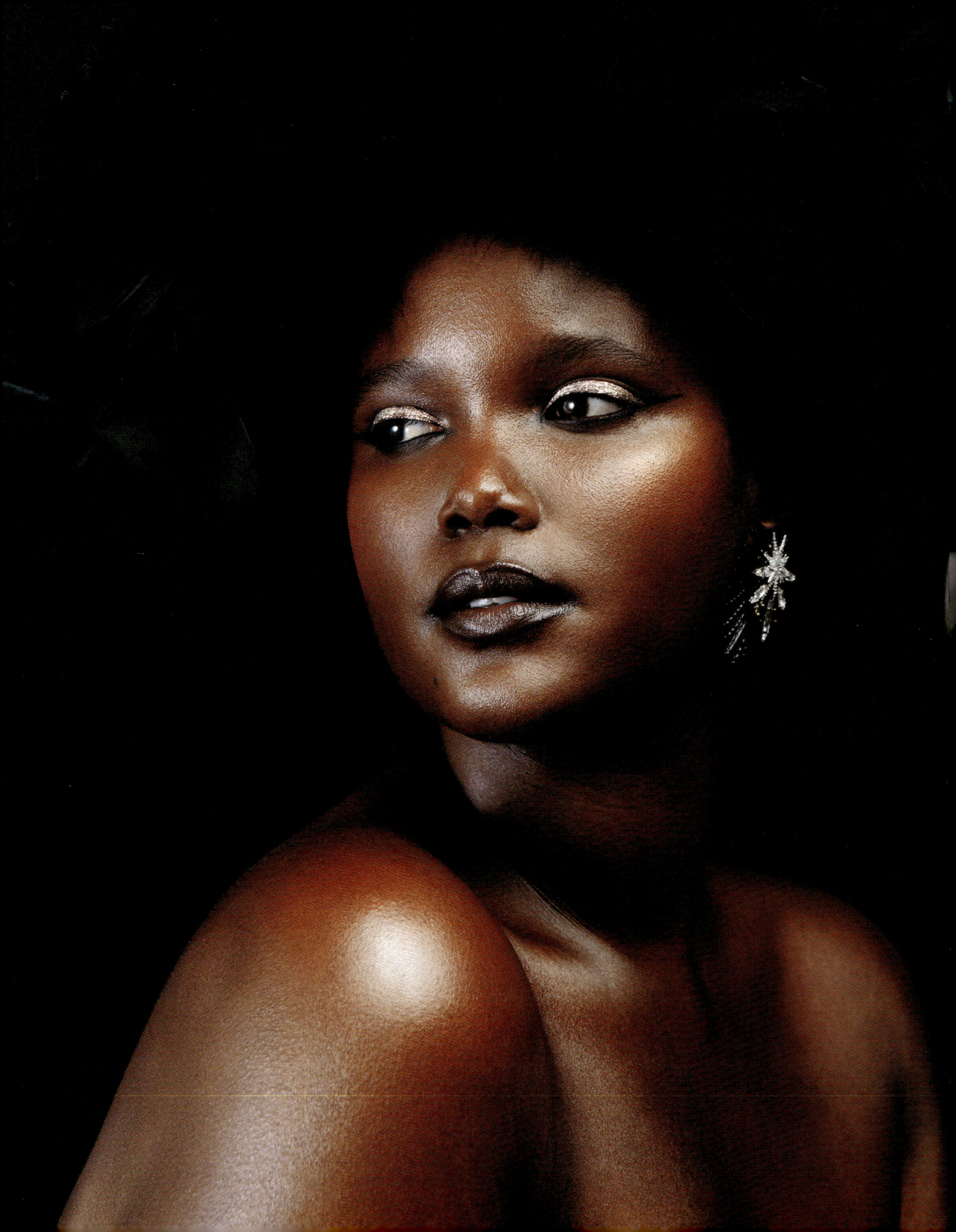

Contents

Sabey Dantsira wears Erickson Beamon headpiece and earrings.

Overleaf: Lydia Hudgens

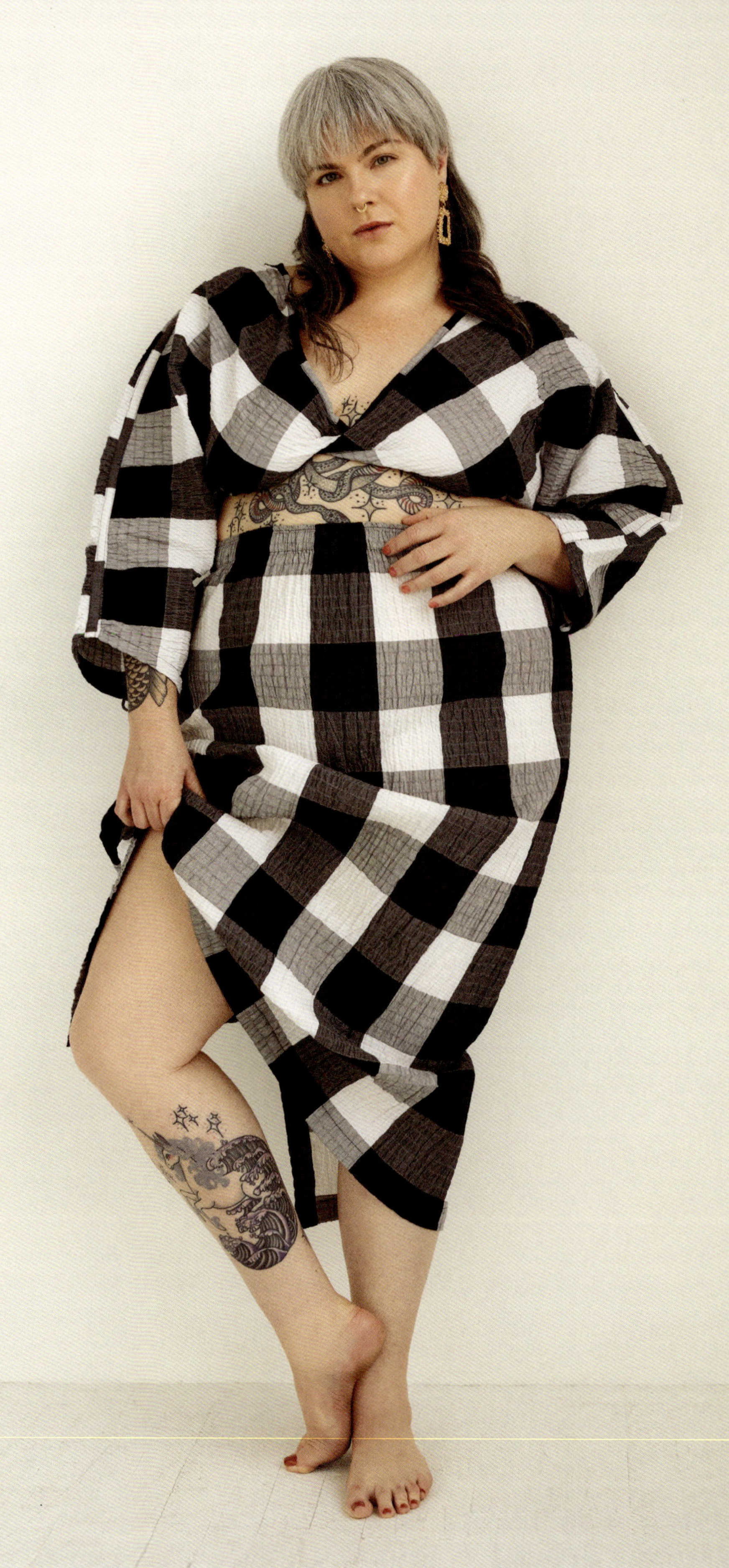

Introduction

Sitting down to write this book feels like revisiting a lifelong conversation—one shaped by my own experiences and the trailblazers who inspired me along the way, some of whom I have the honor of featuring in this book. I started *Plus* only a year ago, yet so much has shifted in that time. After years of progress, "thin is in" has reemerged, and brands are retreating from plus-size representation, labels that once championed inclusivity shrinking their extended sizing. For those of us in the plus-size community, this backslide into narrow beauty standards isn't just frustrating—it's personal.

Plus was born out of that frustration, but also out of hope. While this project is a celebration of beauty, it's also about resisting erasure, reclaiming space, and telling the stories that too often go untold in a time when this work feels more urgent than ever.

When I was approached to create *Plus*, I felt an overwhelming mix of emotions: joy, apprehension, and a deep sense of responsibility. I wanted to honor a community that has shaped me, welcomed me, and inspired me to think differently about bodies, art, and representation. This book is deeply personal—a reflection of my own journey toward self-acceptance. It's also an opportunity to highlight the beauty, artistry, and humanity of a space the fashion industry has long overlooked.

Growing up as a small, fat child, I was taught to hate my body before I even understood it. Doctors and family members ushered me into diets like WeightWatchers and Jenny Craig long before I grasped the concept of calories. The 1980s and '90s were brutal for bodies like mine: a time when beauty was defined by thinness, whether it belonged to the athletic supermodels or the heroin chic waifs. Every diet, every workout, every attempt to "fix" myself left me feeling more fractured. My self-worth felt conditional, tied to a number on the scale.

In my early 30s, I was at my thinnest, working full-time at a gym while maintaining a strict regimen of intense workouts and limited caloric intake. I'd achieved the goal society had always dangled before me, but I wasn't happy. Thinness didn't fulfill me—it left me feeling hollow.

But something in me started to shift during this period. I began shooting for plus-size influencers like Nicolette Mason and Kellie Brown—women who are unapologetic, experimental, and deeply creative. Their self-expression challenged everything I had internalized about beauty and value, forcing me to see myself through a different lens.

This shift became even more intentional when I started photographing myself. Turning the camera on my own body allowed me to confront years of shame and criticism. I wasn't just taking pictures—I was reclaiming a stolen narrative. Slowly, I began to see the body I had fought so hard to change as part of me, instead of as an enemy. This exploration wasn't easy, but it allowed me to embrace my natural self for the first time in decades: a journey countless activists made possible.

Body positivity didn't start as a hashtag or a marketing tool. Its origins are radical, planted in the fat acceptance and Black liberation movements of the 1960s and '70s by activists who were tired of being ignored, stigmatized, and mistreated. Their work was deeply rooted in the civil rights and feminist movements, drawing strength from the era's widespread calls for equity and inclusion.

In 1969, the National Association to Advance Fat Acceptance was created in the United States to push back against the pervasive discrimination fat individuals faced in employment, healthcare, and beyond. Around the same time, Los Angeles' Fat Underground emerged, reclaiming the word "fat" while rejecting the idea that fatness needed fixing. These activists called out diet culture and the medical system for profiting off people's insecurities while perpetuating harm. They weren't asking for acceptance—they were demanding change.

The body positivity movement we know today owes everything to these activists. While the movement has been commercialized and softened over time, its roots remain. Fat liberation wasn't about aesthetics; it was about dismantling systems of oppression. This vision still resonates today as we fight for representation that's meaningful, not just marketable.

The progress we have made in plus-size representation didn't happen by chance. It arose from the efforts of people who refused to accept exclusion—trailblazers who demanded better. In fashion, we can thank figures like Nicolette Mason, Kelly Augustine, Kellie Brown, Jessica Torres, Amanda Richards, and Emma Zack, who are all featured throughout this book. These women have not only influenced the industry, but have reshaped the conversation entirely.

Nicolette Mason has always been a trailblazer in plus-size fashion, using her platform during her time as a columnist for *Marie Claire* to push for inclusivity and challenge the industry's limitations. Her writing is about more than highlighting options for plus-size shoppers—it demands systemic change.

Kelly Augustine has made certain plus-size representation reaches the red carpet. Dressing stars like Danielle Brooks and Gabourey Sidibe, she's opened high fashion up to the larger bodies that it has long excluded. Her work blends accessibility with glamour, reminding everyone that luxury has no size limit.

Kellie Brown has demanded visibility where it didn't exist. Her viral #FatAtFashionWeek campaign more than a hashtag—it was a rallying cry. Kellie's time as a consultant helped brands create campaigns that felt authentic, centering plus-size voices in a way that wasn't performative.

Jessica Torres has reshaped plus-size representation by blending bold style with authentic storytelling to shift how we see beauty. As an influencer, she challenges industry standards, advocating for visibility and inclusion. Through her content, she inspires others to embrace themselves unapologetically, helping to create space in fashion for all bodies.

Amanda Richards has offered a vital voice, using sharp wit and incisive commentary to advocate for greater inclusivity in fashion. As a writer and editor, she created the first-ever street style gallery dedicated to plus-size individuals with *InStyle* in 2019. Her groundbreaking work is a powerful statement, showing that plus-size bodies not only belong in fashion but thrive within it.

And Emma Zack has helped to address the lack of size-inclusive options in independent fashion by founding Shop Berriez. By curating vintage and sustainable designs, Emma provides a platform for diverse bodies to express themselves. Her brand not only champions inclusivity but also challenges the industry's environmental impact, proving that fashion can be sustainable.

I've had the honor of speaking to and photographing each of these women for this book. Through their collective creativity and unwavering commitment to redefining what's possible, they've influenced fashion at large. Their presence in *Plus* is also personal, however, as they've all impacted me in ways that are present in every image I create. Over the years, I've had the privilege of witnessing their brilliance firsthand, and it has expanded my perspective on how photography and fashion can work together to tell richer, more meaningful stories.

Their voices have driven me to see past the surface of an image and understand the significance of what we create, how we create it, and who we create it with. This group has challenged, inspired, and collaborated with me to envision a world where beauty and creativity exist without limitation. I am the photographer I am today thanks to them, and it is my privilege to give them their flowers and to share a glimpse of their incredible work.

They represent, of course, a very small selection of the names that deserve recognition in the plus-size community. These creatives have worked alongside so many others, like Gabi Fresh, who changed how we see swimwear with the help of Kellie Brown. Her viral "fatkini" moment wasn't just about bikinis—it was about empowerment. Gabi's collaborations with Swimsuits for All and Fashion to Figure were unapologetic and vibrant, refusing the idea that swimwear for plus-size women had to be drab or "flattering." She made it clear: Everyone deserves fun, sexy, bold options.

Then there's Chastity Garner and CeCe Olisa, who founded CurvyCon, a space for plus-size individuals during New York Fashion Week—an event that historically excluded them. Similarly, *PLUS Model Mag*, founded by Madeline Jones and Valery Amador, gave plus-size models a platform long before the mainstream took notice.

These efforts created spaces where change could begin and where it continues to grow from. Like those featured in *Plus*, these women have worked to challenge the industry. Collectively, they've moved representation forward and onto the runway, where models like Ashley Graham and Precious Lee have taken the conversation mainstream.

No one could ignore Graham's *Sports Illustrated* cover in 2016; it was a win for every plus-size woman who had been told bikinis weren't for them. Her editorial work with *Vogue*, *Glamour*, and *Harper's Bazaar* further cemented her legacy, while her time as a judge on *America's Next Top Model* amplified her advocacy for aspiring models.

Precious Lee has brought sophistication and undeniable power to high fashion. She hit the ground running with her first *Vogue* cover in 2015 and appeared on the New York runway in 2017. She followed this in 2021 with an appearance walking for Versace: one of the first ever curve models to do so. Her editorials for *Vogue Italia* and *British Vogue* highlight her ability to balance avant-garde concepts with timeless beauty, proving that plus-size women can lead in high fashion.

However, for every household name, there are many models whose work goes unacknowledged but which is no less important. These are the e-commerce and campaign models—the ones we see on websites, in ads, and on social media. They're the ones showing consumers that plus-size fashion isn't just aspirational, but accessible.

Seeing someone with a body like yours wearing that dress or swimsuit? That's more than represenation—that's trust. Brands like Torrid, Eloquii, and Good American have relied on these models to redefine how plus-size fashion is marketed, proving that it doesn't have to be safe or subdued. In beauty, campaigns from Fenty Beauty and MAC have done the same, opening the door for size inclusivity in makeup ads.

These models, though often untagged and unnamed, are a vital part of this movement. Their work normalizes larger bodies in a way that feels tangible, reminding us that representation is about what's real.

Beauty exists in every fold, every curve, every roll. It exists simply because we do.

It is thanks to all these these trailblazers, and those like them, who refuse to wait for the industry to catch up, that representation will keep progressing.

Throughout my own journey as a photographer, I've drawn inspiration from artists who redefine how we see the body and who push boundaries. Two such creators, Lily Cummings and Michaela Stark, have deeply influenced my approach to this book. Their work embodies boldness, intimacy, and a refusal to conform to traditional beauty standards; each offers a unique perspective through which to celebrate the human form.

Lily Cummings' photography—particularly *Bodies on Paper*, her limited-edition series—offers a delicate yet defiant exploration of bodies often excluded from mainstream beauty narratives. Her work captures every curve, roll, and fold with tenderness, transforming what society deems as "imperfections" into visual poetry. What moves me most is her ability to reveal, not conceal. Her work reminds us that beauty lies in authenticity, and her approach to texture and negative space has profoundly shaped how I see and document plus-size bodies.

In contrast, Michaela Stark treats the body as a living sculpture. Her avant-garde use of corsetry, fabric, and exaggeration challenges traditional proportions and symmetry, reframing stretch marks, folds, and stomachs as elements of high art. Stark's creations provoke and inspire, reminding me that discomfort can be a powerful tool in redefining beauty. Her work has encouraged me to experiment more boldly, embracing the creative potential of the human form. She, like Cummings, has taught me to embrace duality: to capture raw, unfiltered intimacy while creating avant-garde imagery.

As I've worked, inspired by these women, my experiences with incredible female photographers like Emma Trim, Tayler Smith, and Youn Jung Kim have been equally transformative. Our collaborations have enriched my creative process and reminded me of the strength that comes from shared vision and mutual respect: of the power of community and its creative potential.

Emma Trim, with her focus on light and emotion, captures moments that feel timeless. Her ability to find intimacy within chaos has inspired me to bring more vulnerability into my own work. Similarly, Tayler Smith, who models in this book, taught me to love the studio again. During the pandemic, her guidance reignited my passion for working with controlled light and movement, helping me refine the technical aspects of my craft while giving me the space to explore freely. Youn Jung Kim's work, meanwhile, is a masterclass in storytelling. Her ability to weave narrative and culture into her photographs inspired me to think beyond aesthetics and connect more deeply with the stories behind each image.

Each of these artists, in their own way, has influenced how I approach my work, both as a photographer and as a collaborator and storyteller. Their impact is embedded in every page of this book, my experiences with them shaping this body of images that I hope feels expansive, emotional, and deeply intentional.

I wish that I had seen these types of photos when I was a child. A lot would have changed for me: the self-hatred, the baggy clothes, the years of hiding and shrinking myself. If you can take anything away from *Plus*, know that every person is deserving of fashion, of style, of feeling beautiful—no matter their size, race, religion, gender, or sexuality. The rise of diets is nipping at our heels again, and brands are slipping through our fingertips. But this is just part of a cycle, and as the body positivity movement achieved change before, I know it will again, thanks to the efforts of the amazing individuals who continue to progress the fashion industry and our culture.

Plus is a celebration, a reclamation, and a call to action. It's a love letter to the creatives and advocates who have made this moment possible.

To the incredible models featured in this book, thank you for trusting me with your vulnerability and power, for stepping in front of the camera to show the world what unapologetic beauty looks like. These images are testament to your talent and artistry.

To the stylists, hair and makeup teams, and collaborators like Kelly Mazzini and Auralis Flores, thank you for bringing these visions to life. Your creativity, care, and skill elevated this work beyond what I could have dreamed of.

To the readers who pick up this book, I hope it serves as a source of inspiration and reflection. Whether you're here as a fan of fashion, a supporter of body positivity, or simply someone seeking to see themselves in art, my greatest hope is that this book feels like home.

Let it remind us all: Beauty exists in every fold, every curve, every roll. It exists simply because we do.

Editorial

As a plus-size woman, fashion has always been a space of passion, frustration, and resilience for me. When I set out to create this book, I envisioned editorial looks that were bold, dramatic, and unapologetic—that captured the beauty and power of plus-size bodies. But the reality of producing this work was far more challenging than anticipated. From sourcing garments to working within budgetary constraints, it was a constant emotional struggle, punctuated by moments of deep frustration and creative triumph.

One of the biggest hurdles was the scarcity of options. Many of the design houses I admire—Vivienne Westwood, Alexander McQueen, Maison Margiela—don't produce clothing for larger bodies. While a few brands stepped up to support my vision, the broader industry is retreating from plus-size fashion. I didn't receive direct "no's" from designers: The pieces I needed simply didn't exist. As size ranges shrink and plus-size collections disappear, the resources available to create editorial moments are becoming increasingly rare.

That absence left me to rely on the creativity and dedication of my team. Kelly Augustine, Kingsley Osuji, and Yoko J (Jaquea Knuckles) worked tirelessly, sourcing unique pieces from independent designers I might never have discovered otherwise. Their contributions were invaluable, but there were still gaps to fill—gaps I had to address myself.

One of this book's most memorable images features a model wearing what looks like a dramatic, classic gown. In truth, the garment is paper—crumpled, pinned, and fashioned into a silhouette that's timeless and powerful. It's astonishing how such a simple material can have such impact, but it also speaks to the ingenuity that I and so many others require to create high-fashion moments when resources are so limited.

Similarly, I found myself draping models in fabric—a technique used frequently in plus-size styling. While I'm proud of the beauty and drama we achieved, these images also left me conflicted. Draping felt like falling into familiar habits: a reminder of how often plus-size bodies are left out of the conversation. I didn't want to settle for making something look beautiful out of necessity—I wanted bold, tailored, high-fashion pieces designed to celebrate the body.

That tension—between what I wanted to create and what was available—was a constant undercurrent throughout this project. I wanted this book to feel groundbreaking, to push beyond the tropes and compromises that so often define plus-size editorial fashion. And in many ways, I think I succeeded. But the process was also a reminder of how far we still have to go, and how much the industry needs to evolve.

The models themselves were central to this success. Plus-size models bring a level of energy and presence that is unmatched. They know, intimately, what it means to be "othered" in this industry, and they channel that into their work, transforming paper and draped fabric into moments of drama, elegance, and power. Their contributions elevated *Plus* beyond the materials and challenges into something deeply meaningful.

This chapter represents my take on plus-size editorial fashion: resourceful, daring, and full of heart. It reflects the challenges of working within a system that often excludes us, but also the beauty and power that can emerge from those limitations. Fashion should be for everyone, and this book is my small but determined step toward that vision.

Isabel Ebeid wears deconstructed Siri Studio coat.

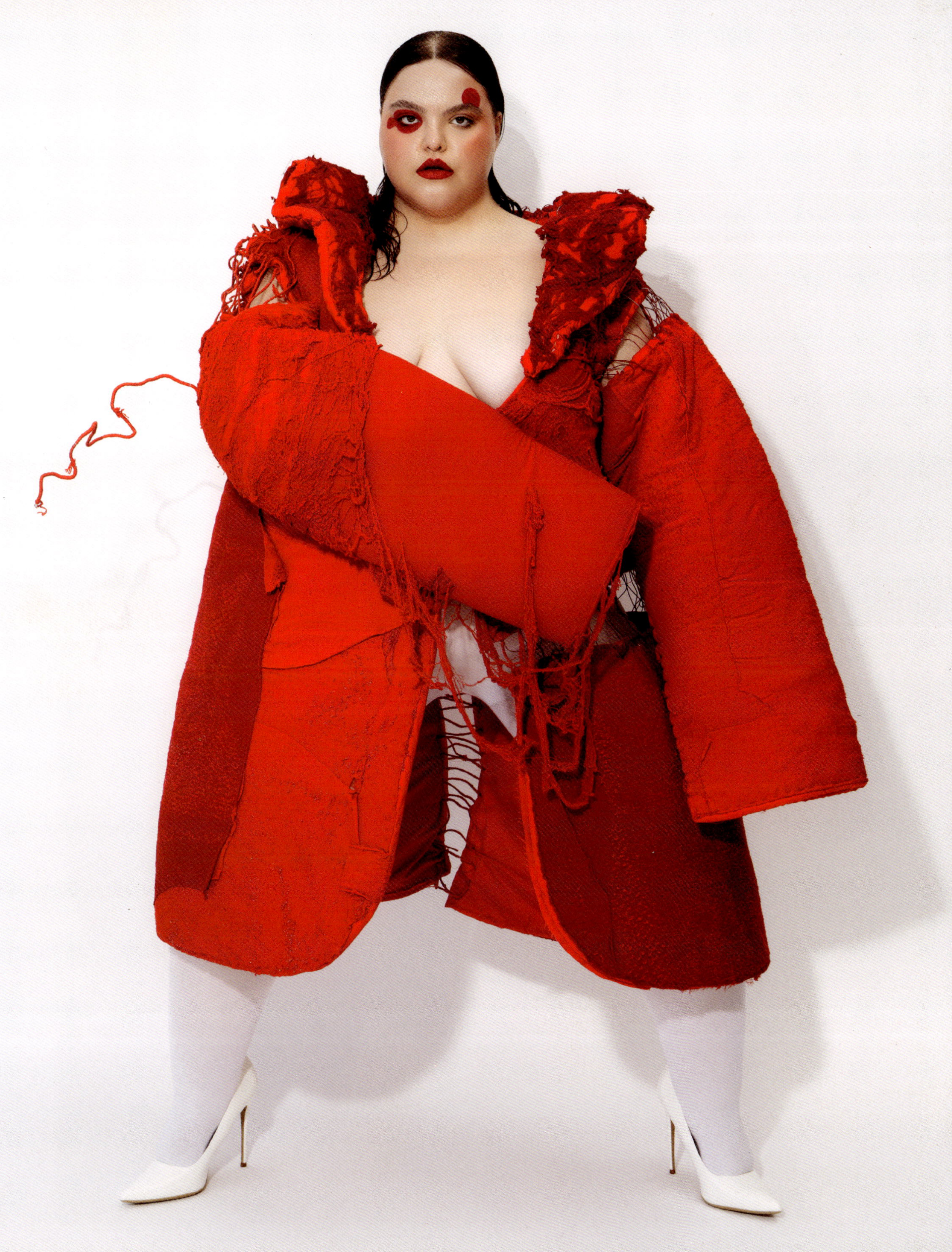

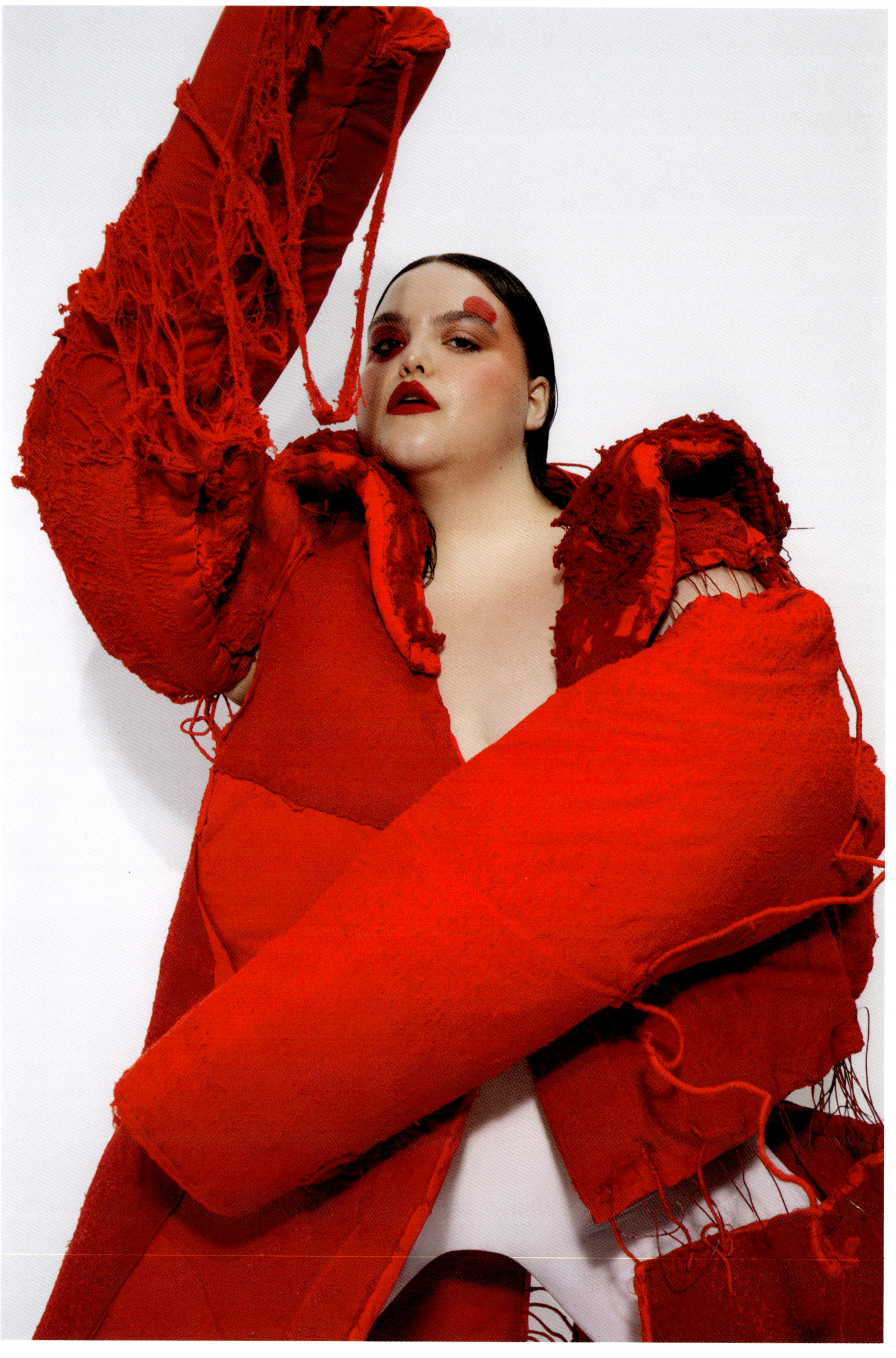

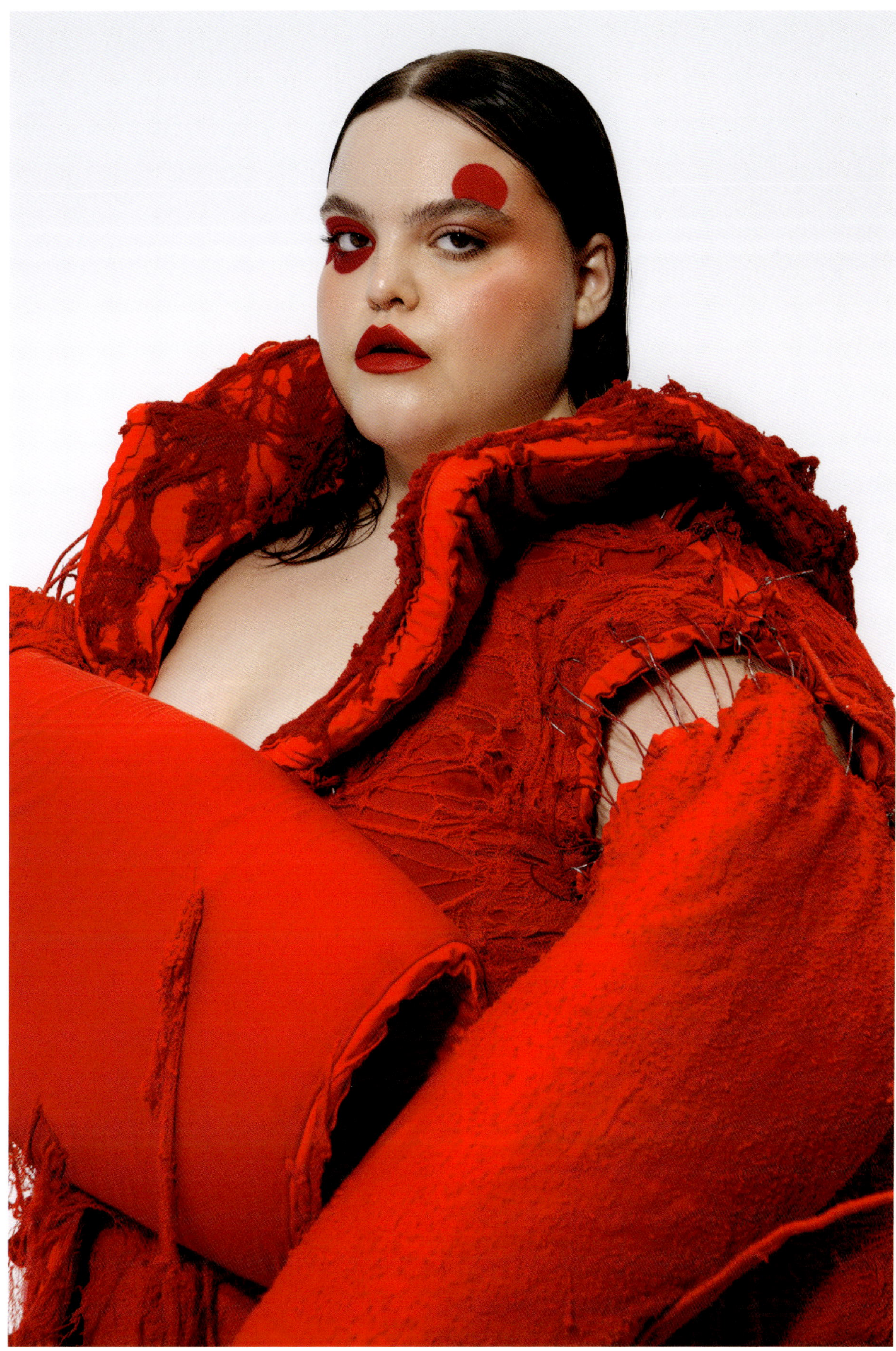

Cearah Peck wears Pipenco Lorena.

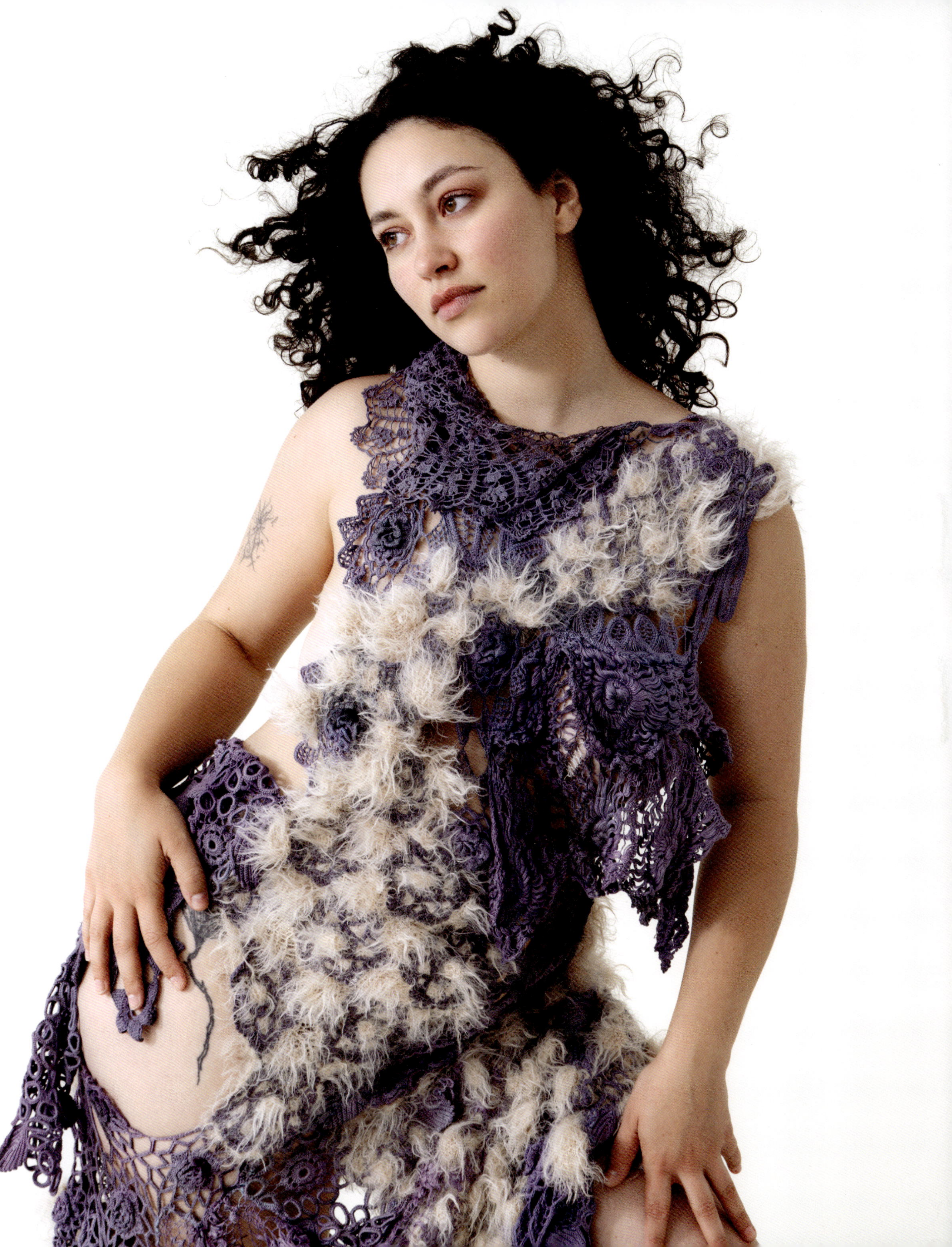

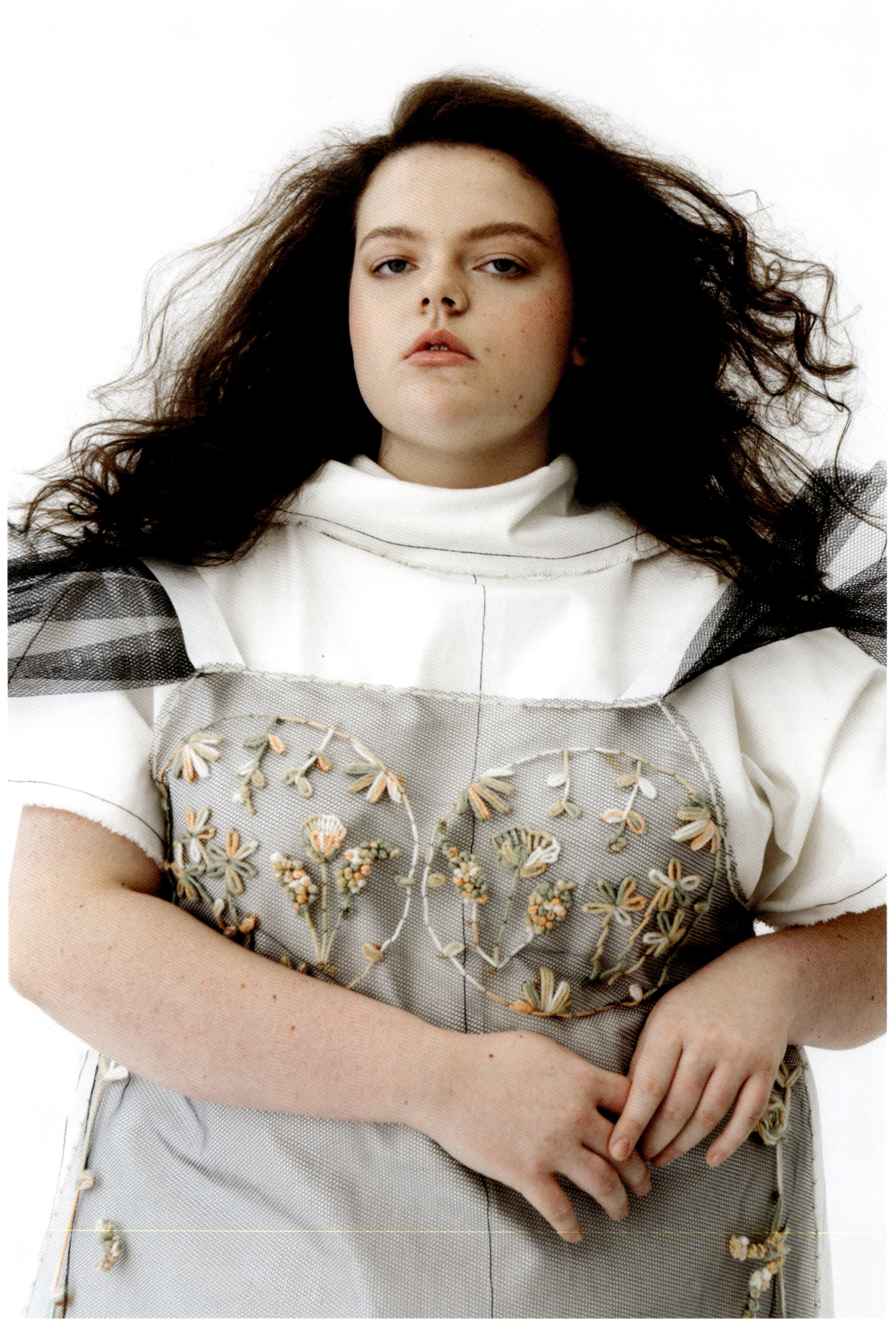

Zoey Hart wears Theo Banzon.

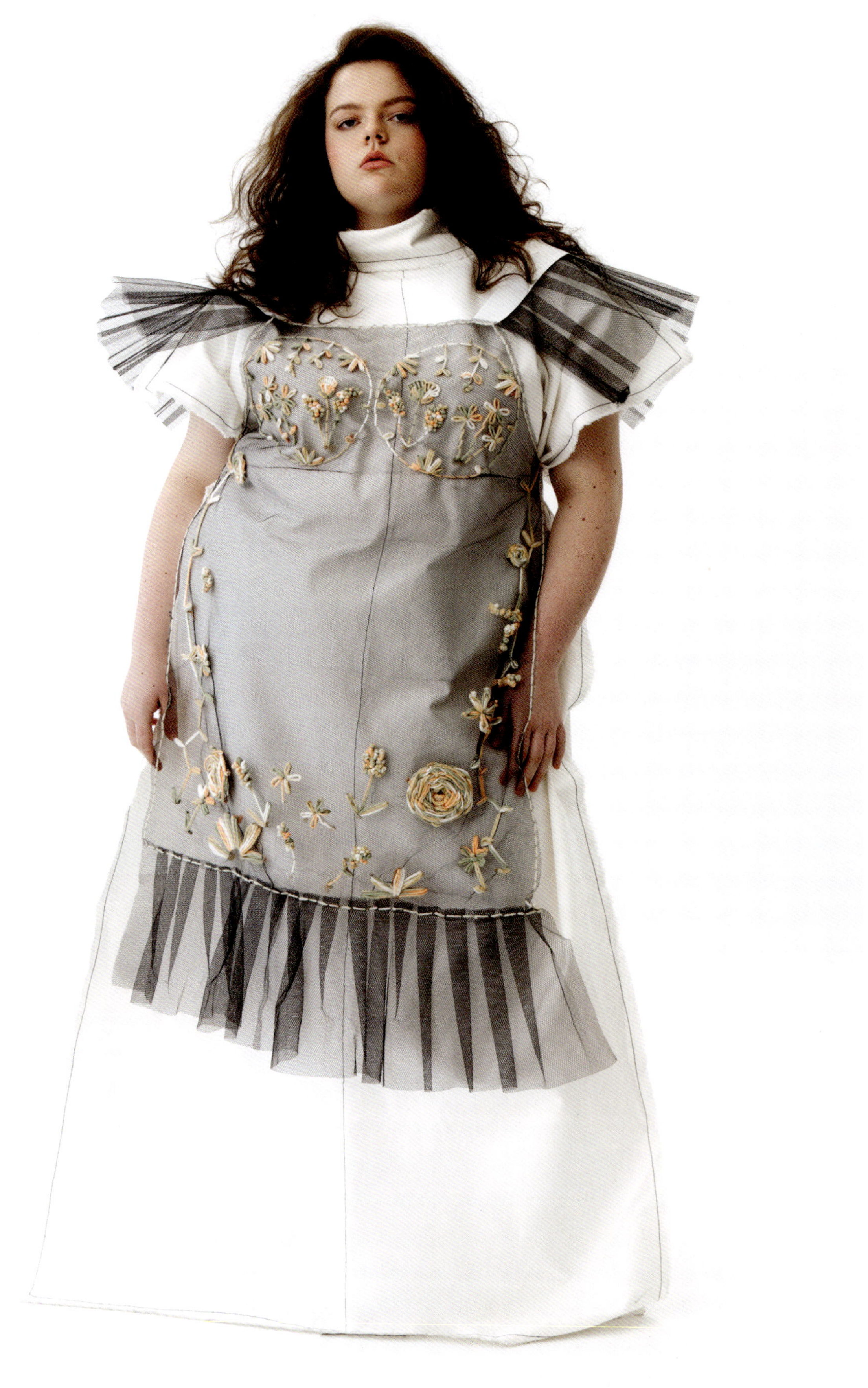

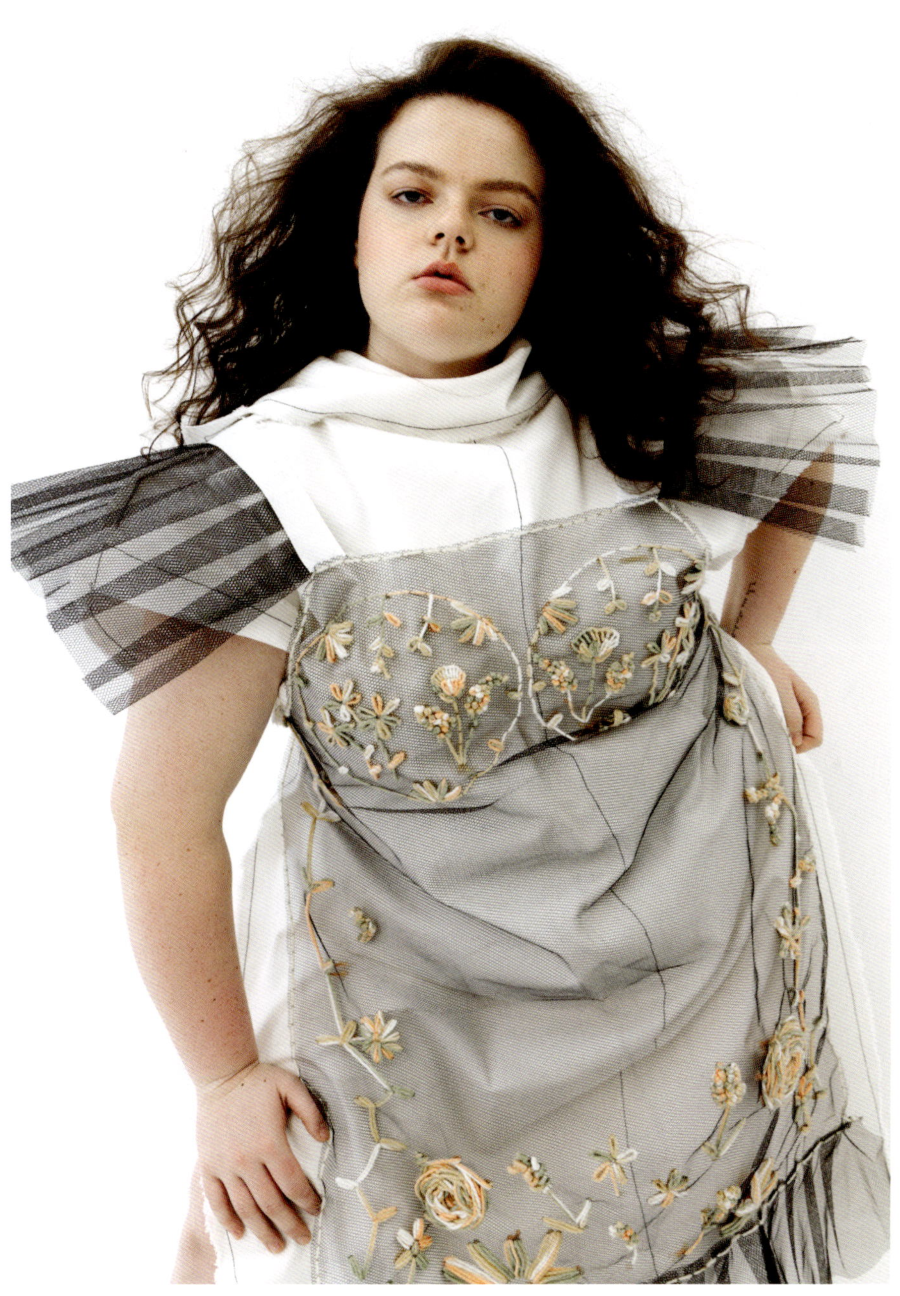

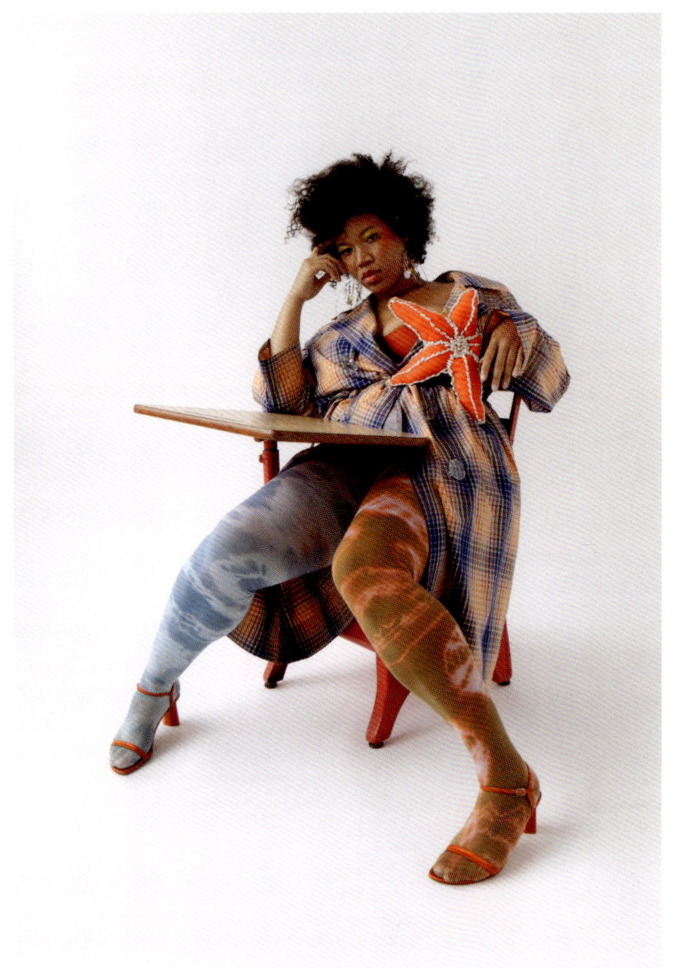

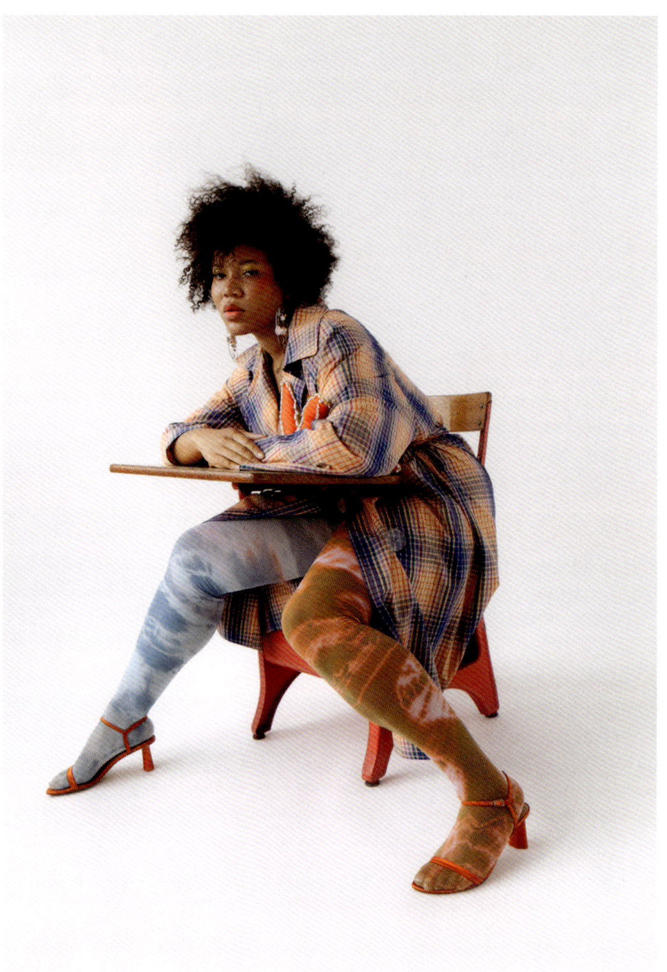

Noni Cyngor wears Simon Miller trench; Shop Journal tights; By Far shoes; Jazz by Jazz earrings and starfish.

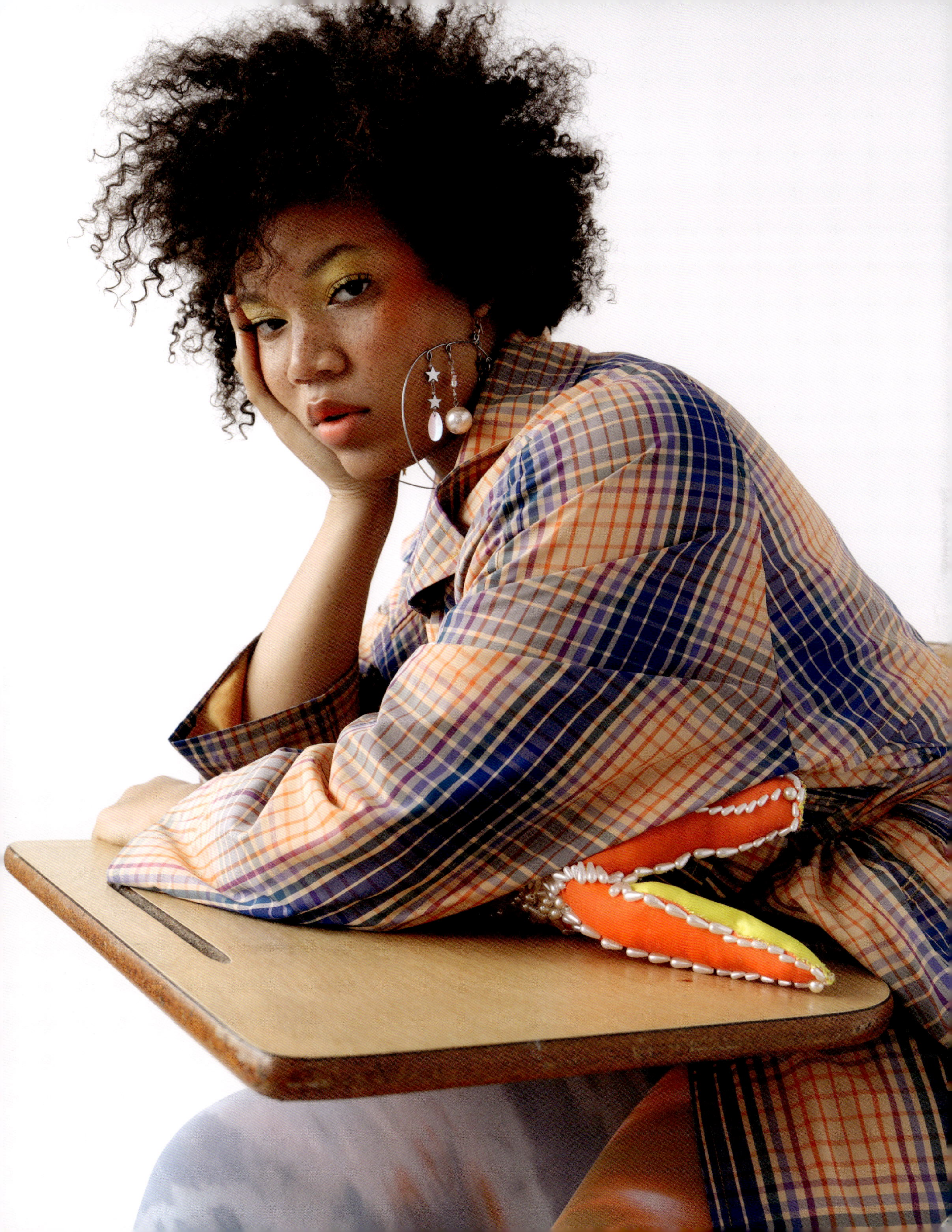

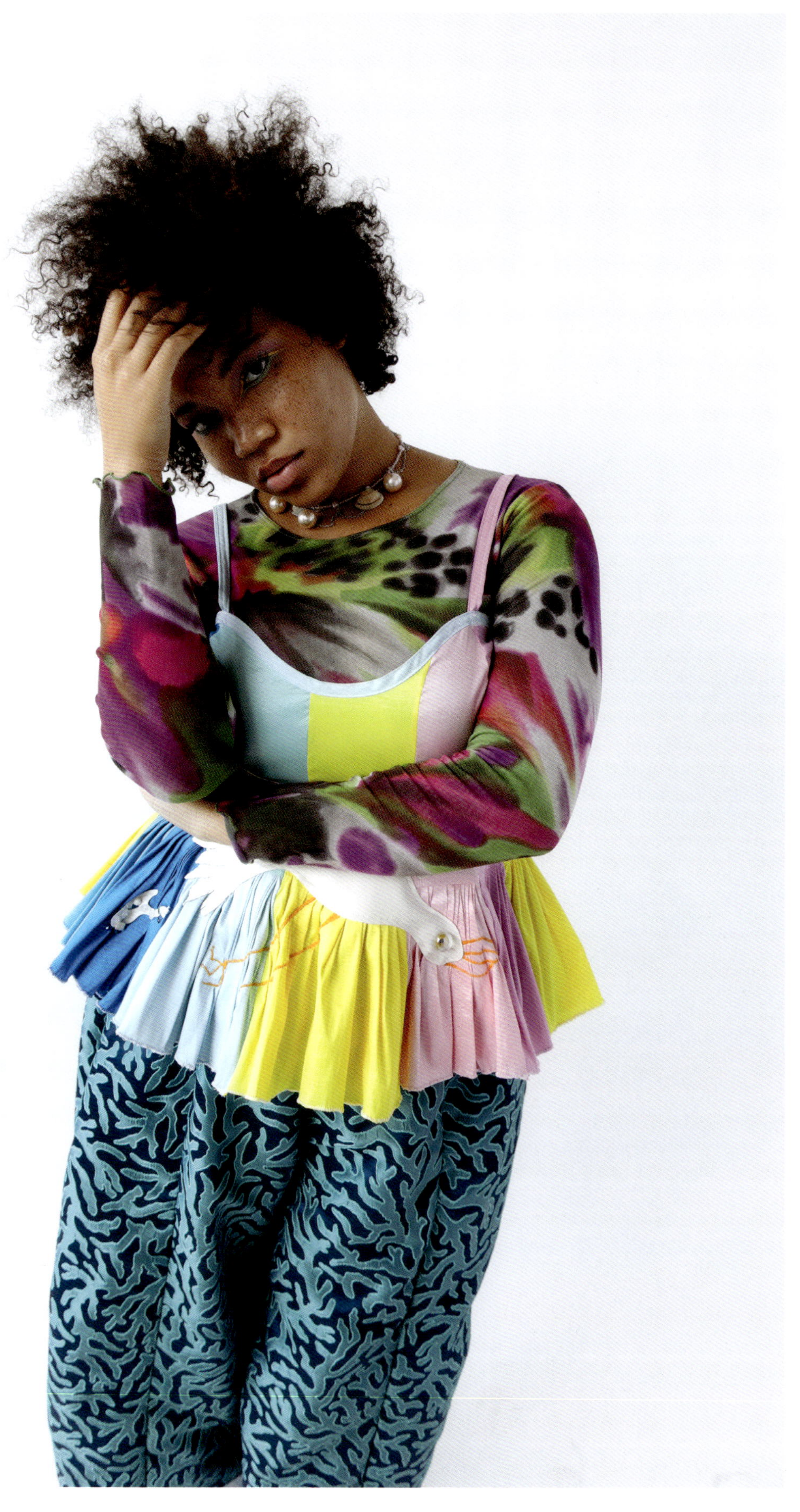

Jazz by Jazz blouse and pants;
vintage undershirt from Shop Berriez.

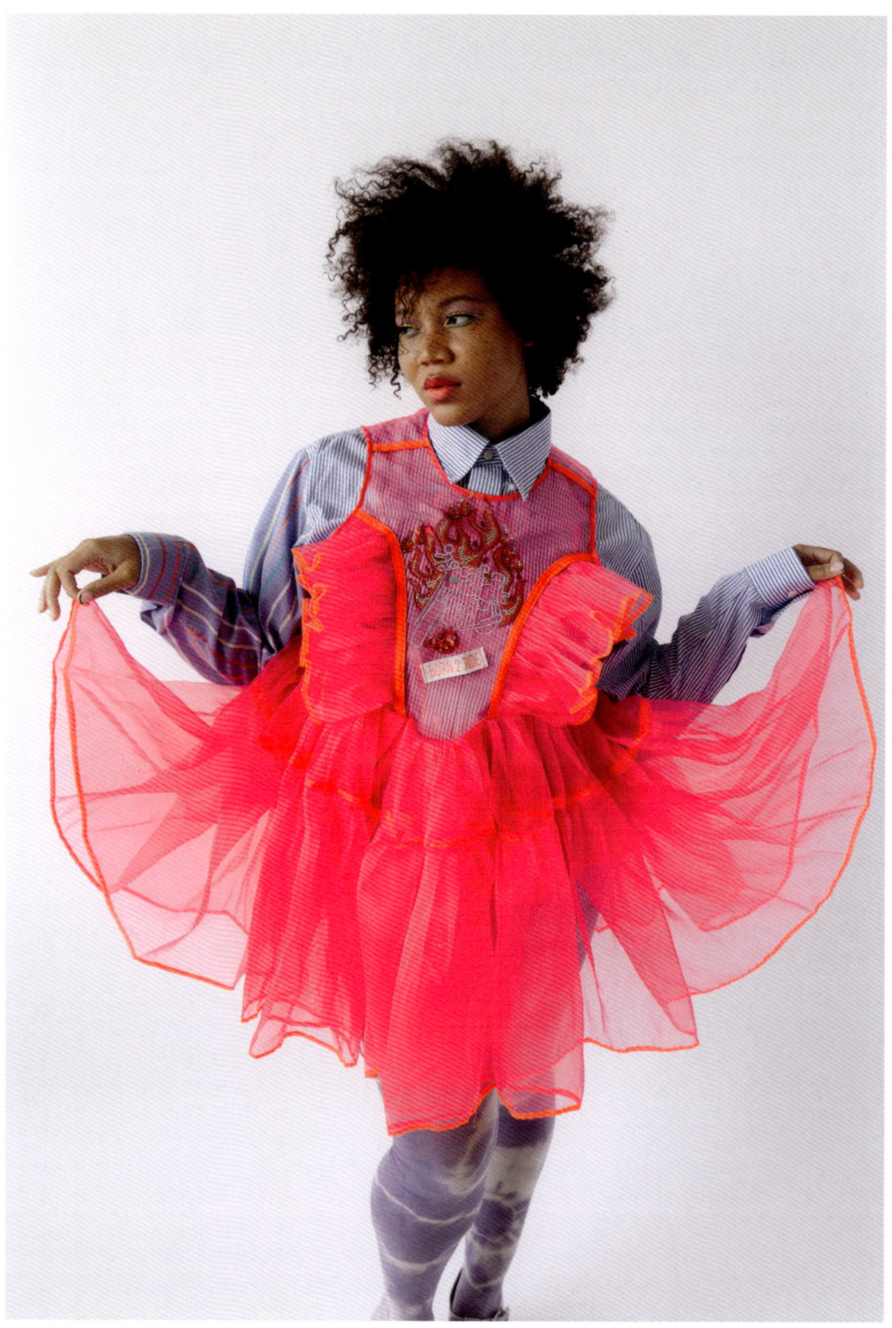

Jazz by Jazz dress; House of Tame shirt;
Shop Journal tights.

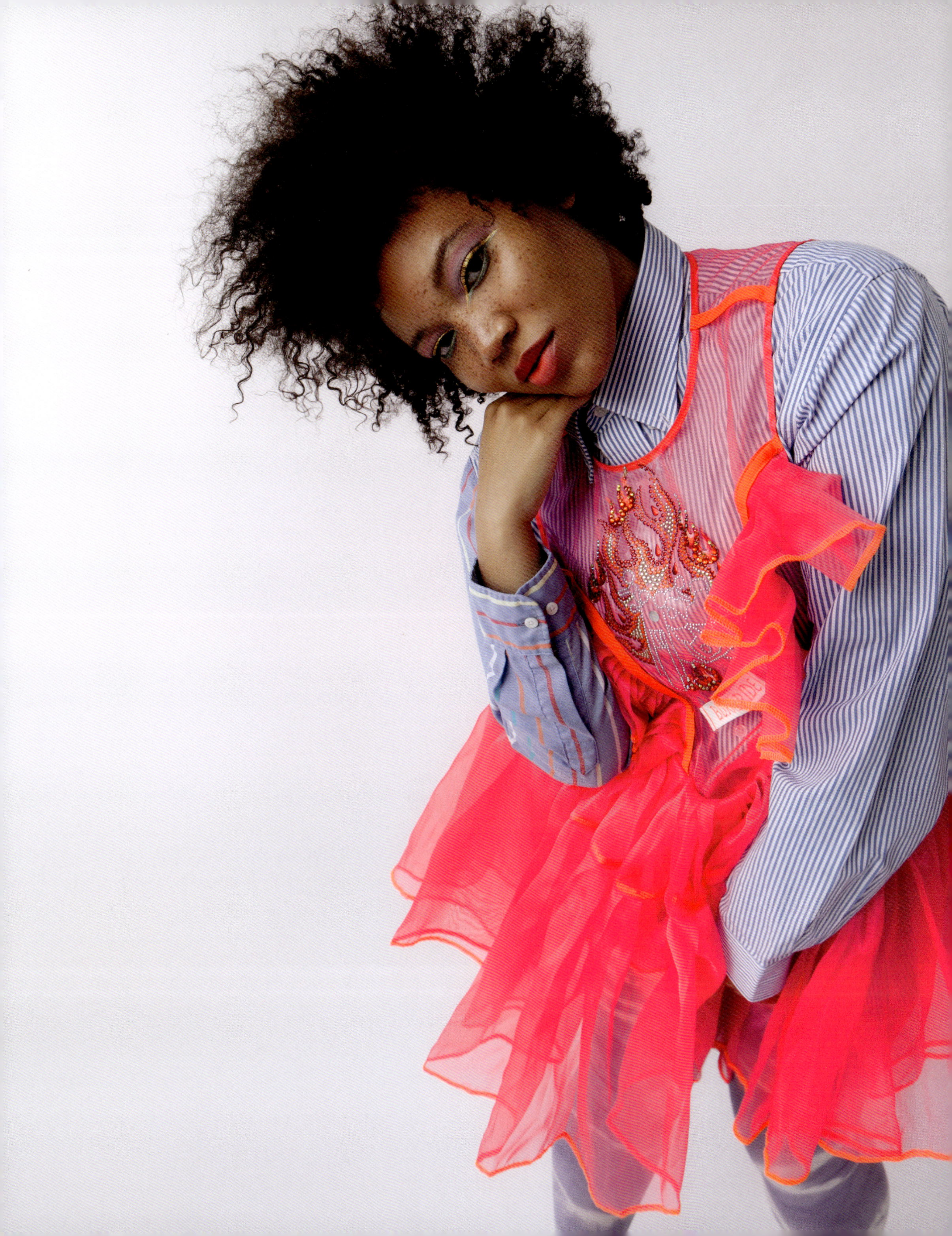

Madison Z. McNally wears Rick Owens dress;
Circus NY by Sam Edelman boots; CRZM necklace.

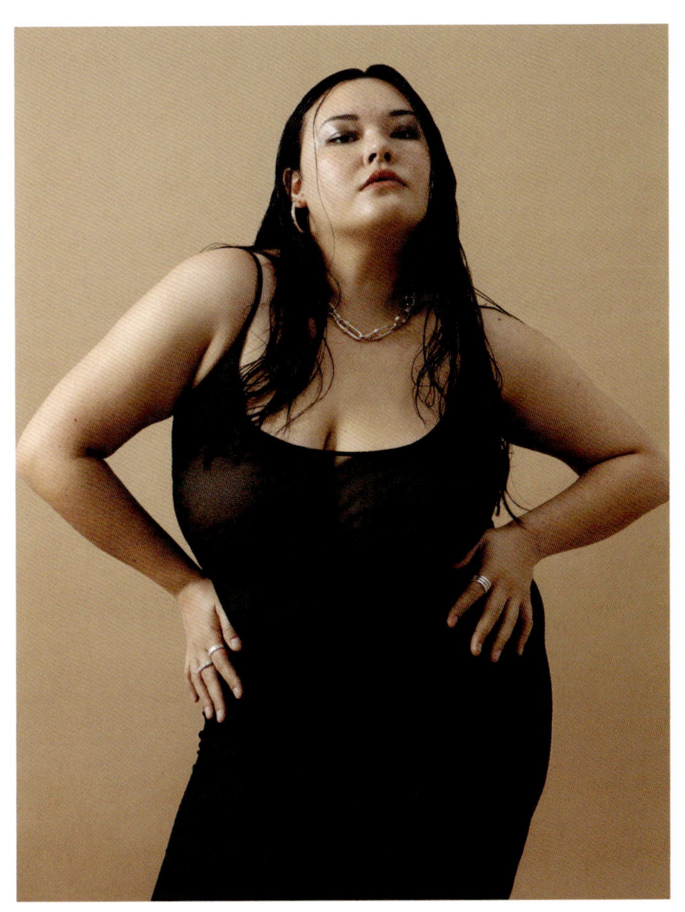
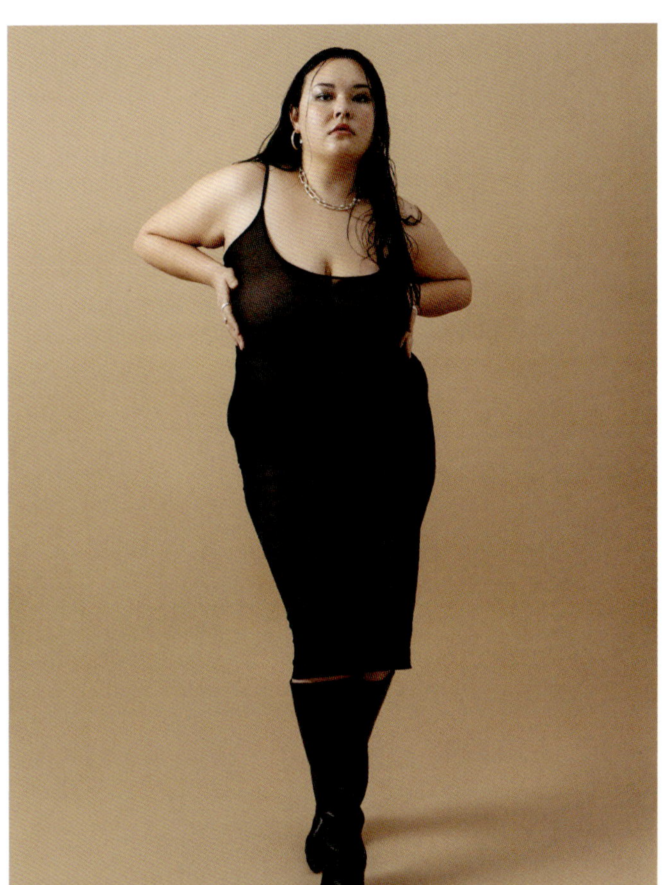
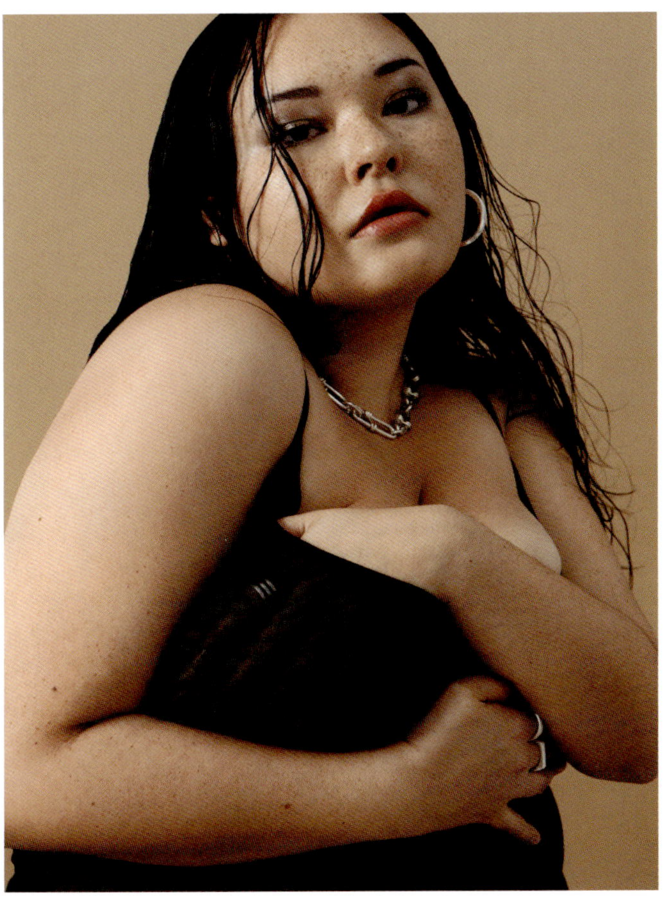
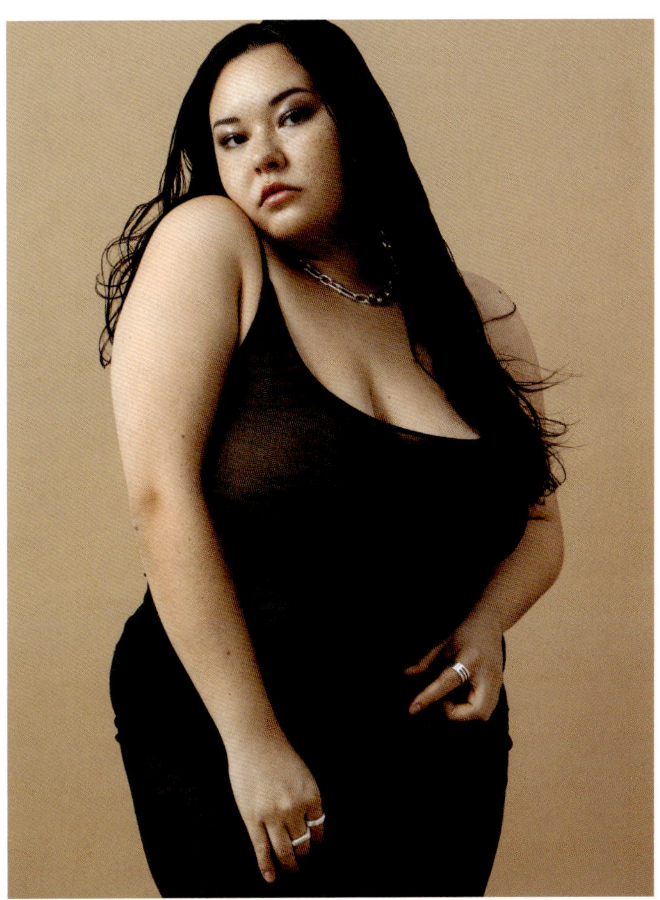

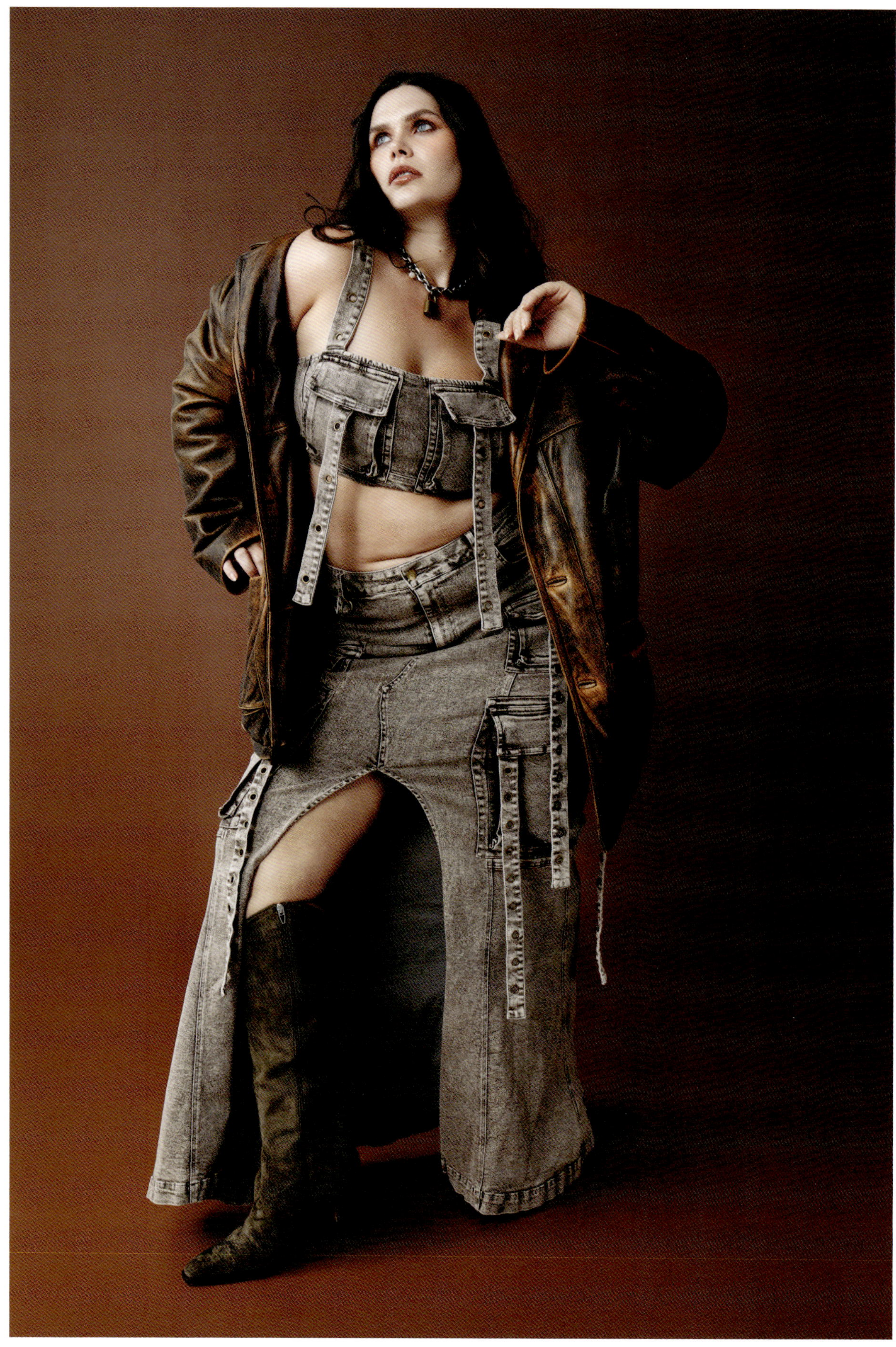

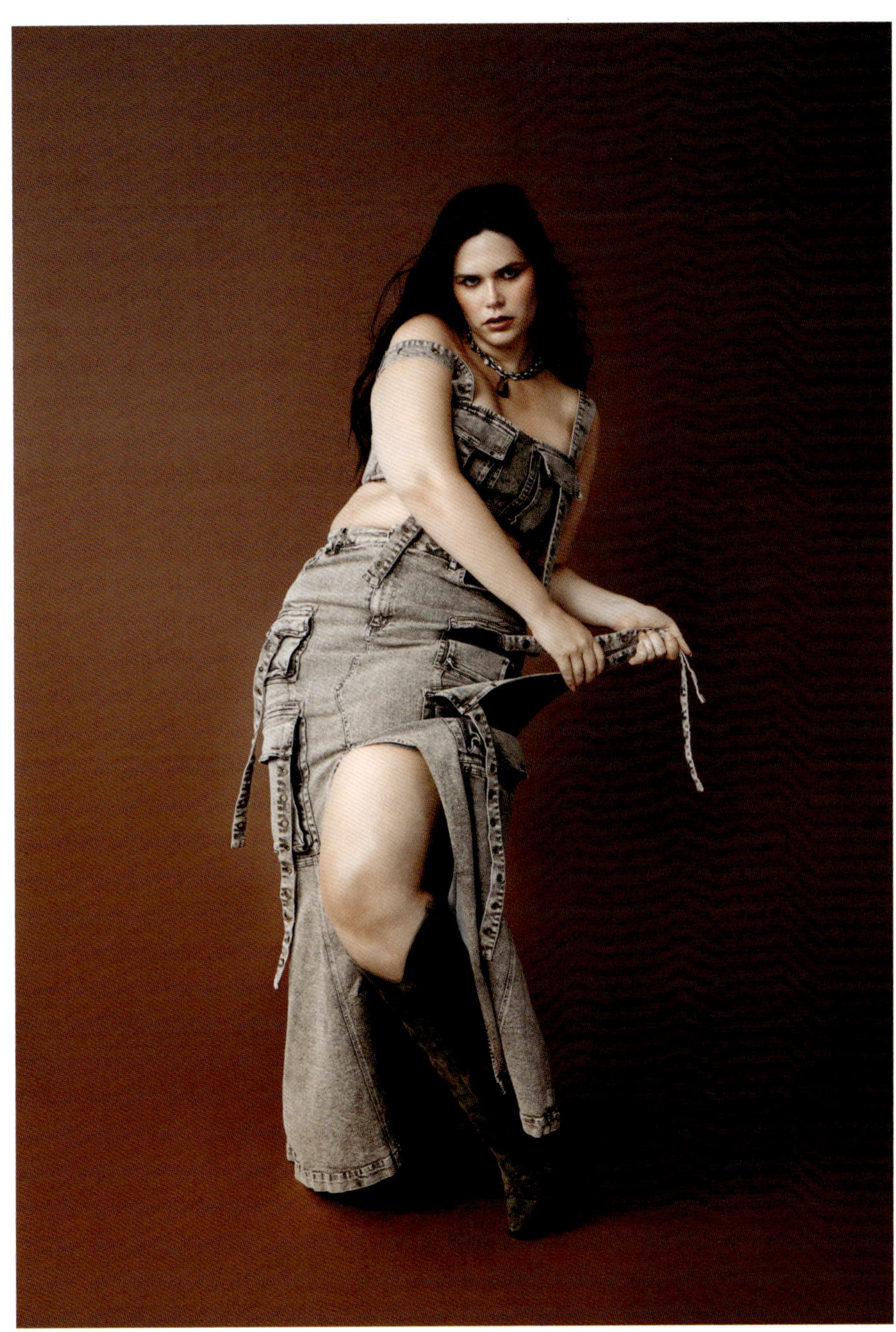

Chloe DeCleene wears vintage jacket from Shop Berriez; set from Lydia Hudgens' closet; Shop Journal necklace; Dolce Vita boots.

Overleaf: Madison Simone wears Abacaxi.

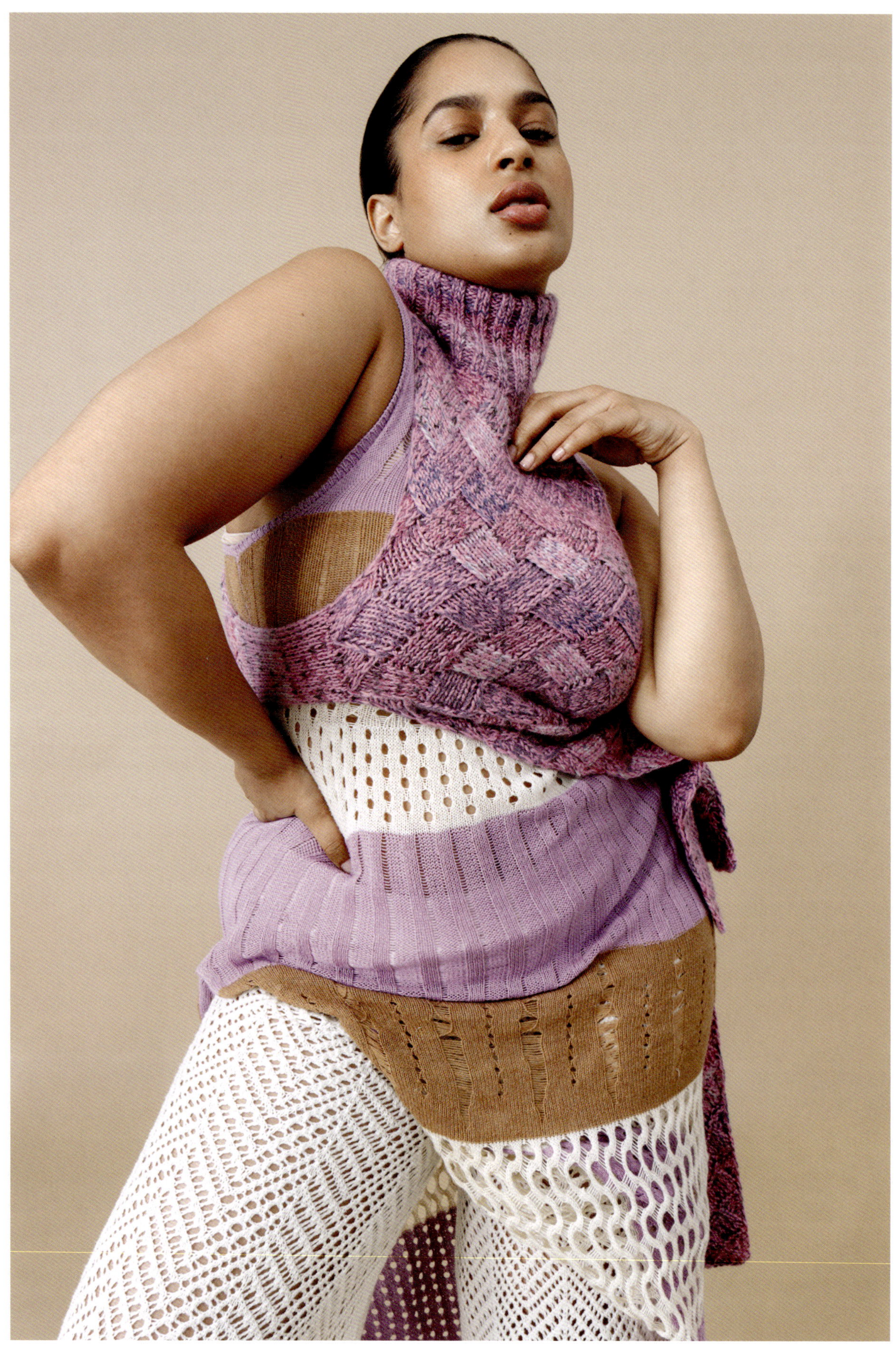

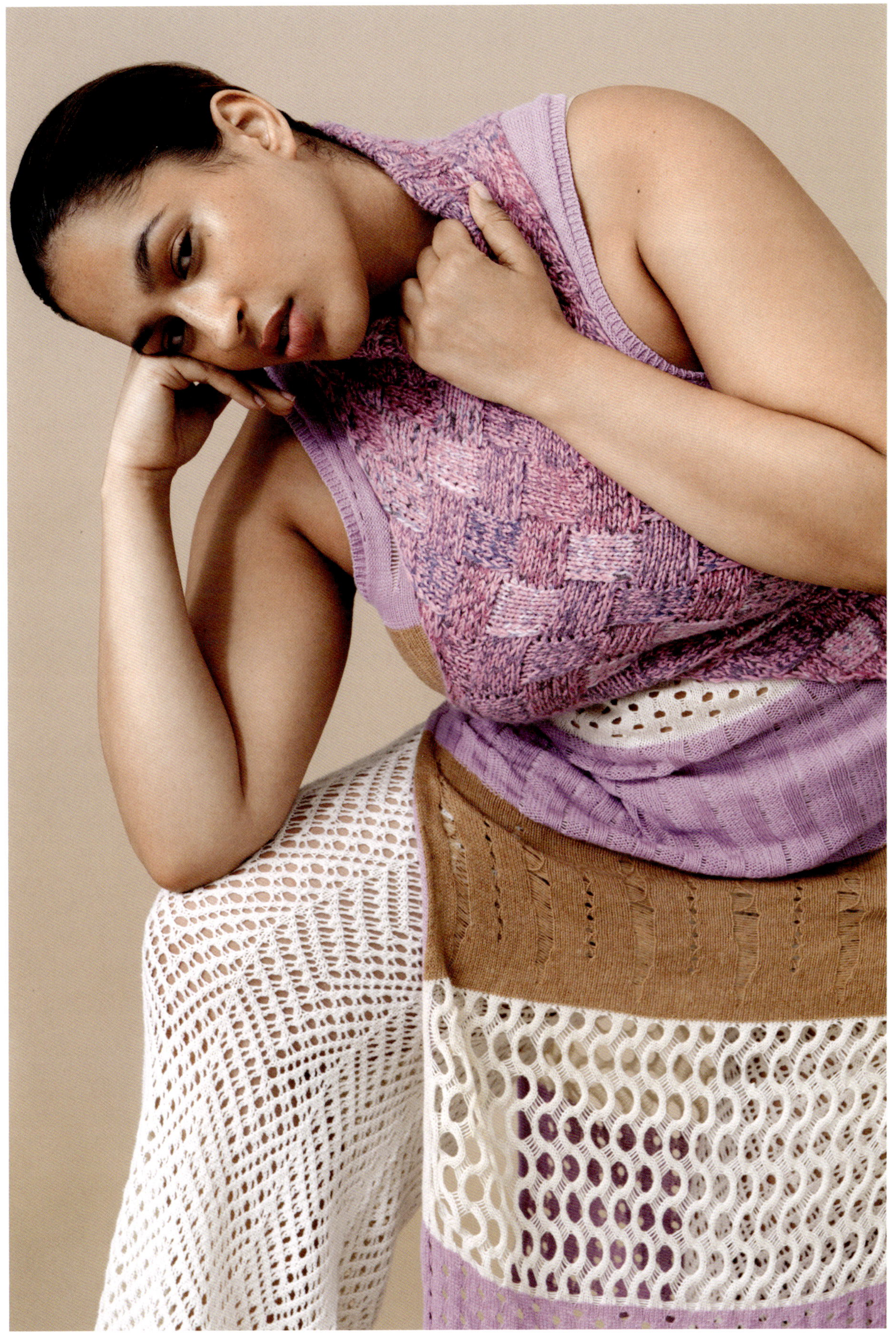

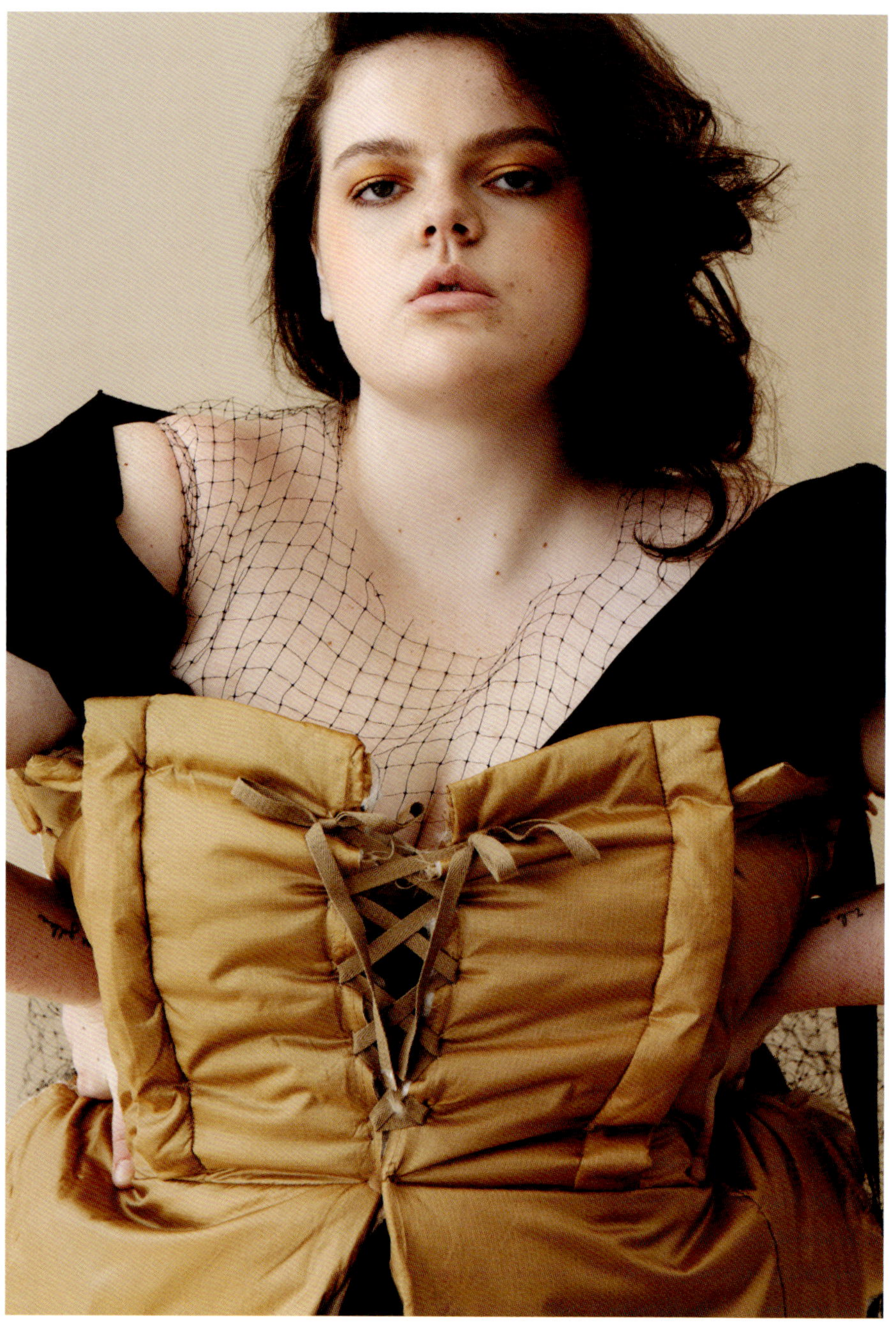

Zoey Hart wears Theo Banzon.

Overleaf: Manni Amoah wears crochet set from Lydia Hudgens' closet.

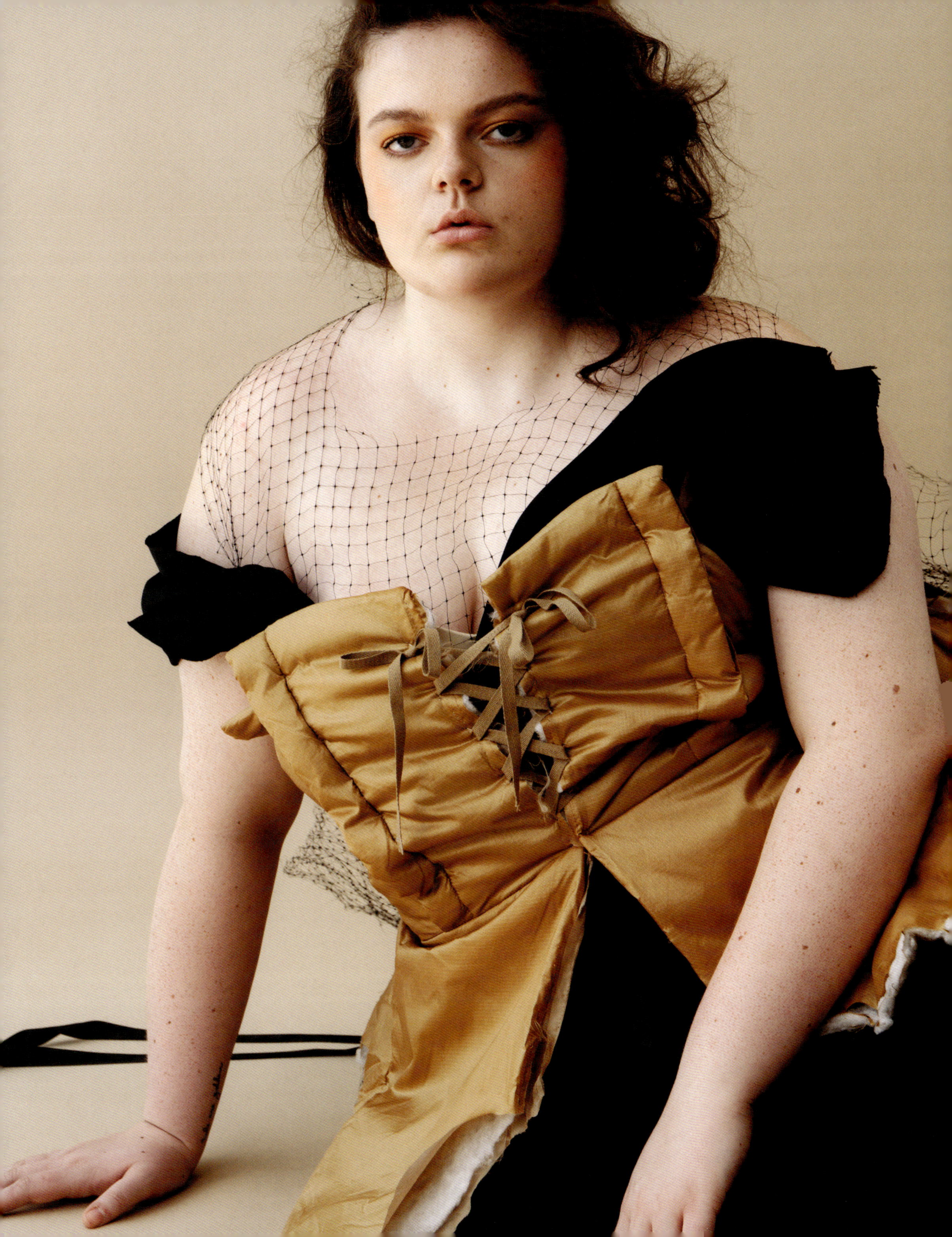

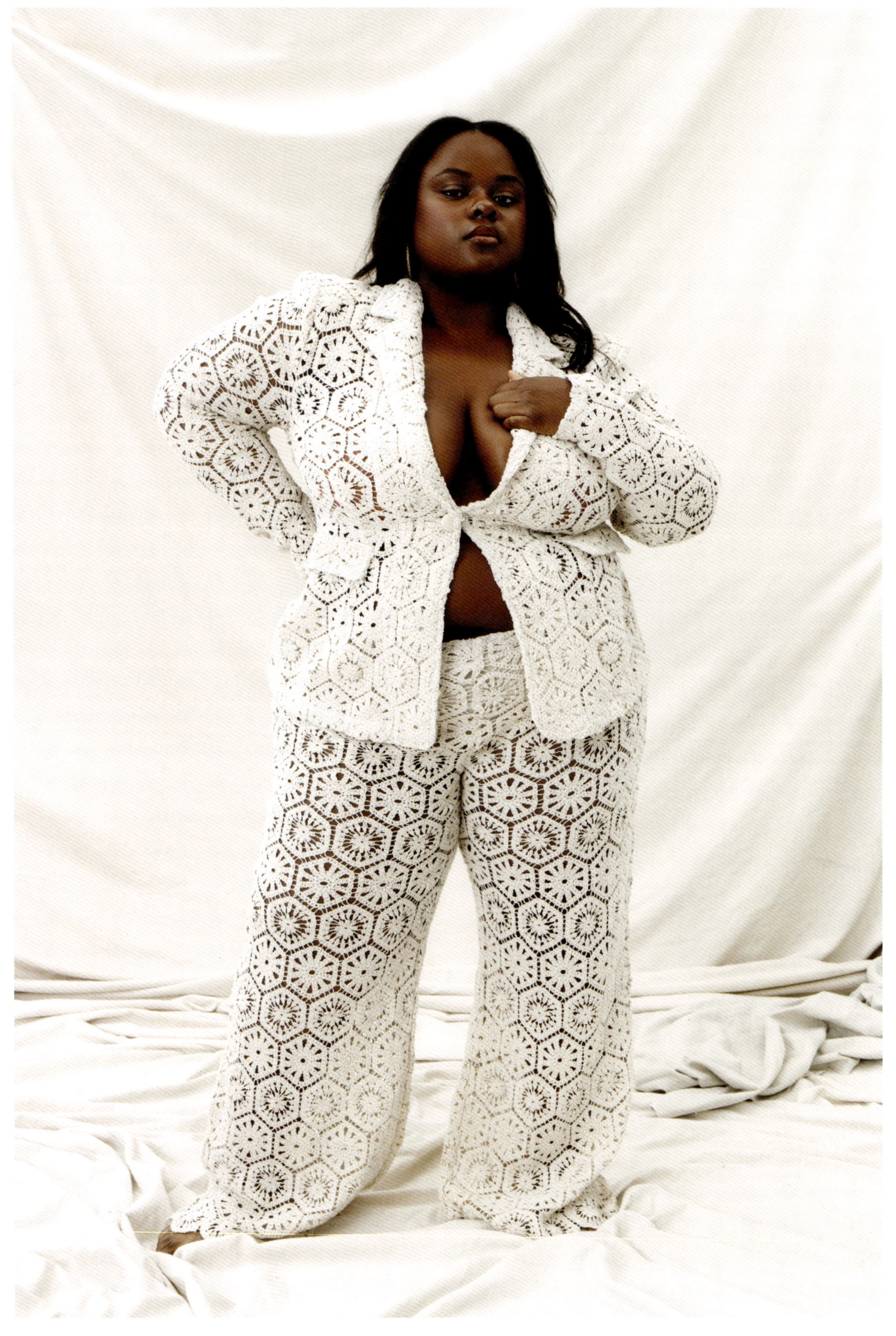

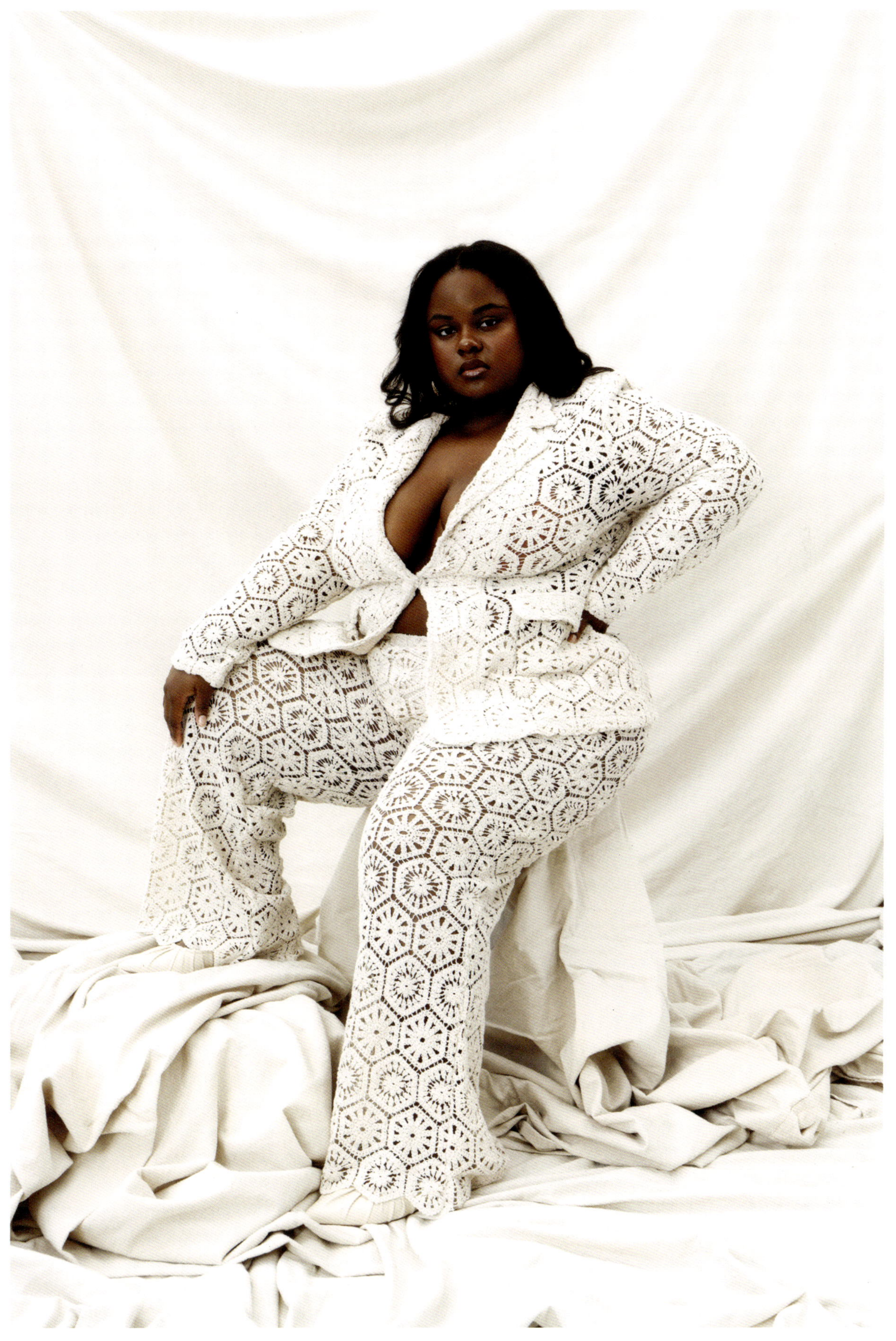

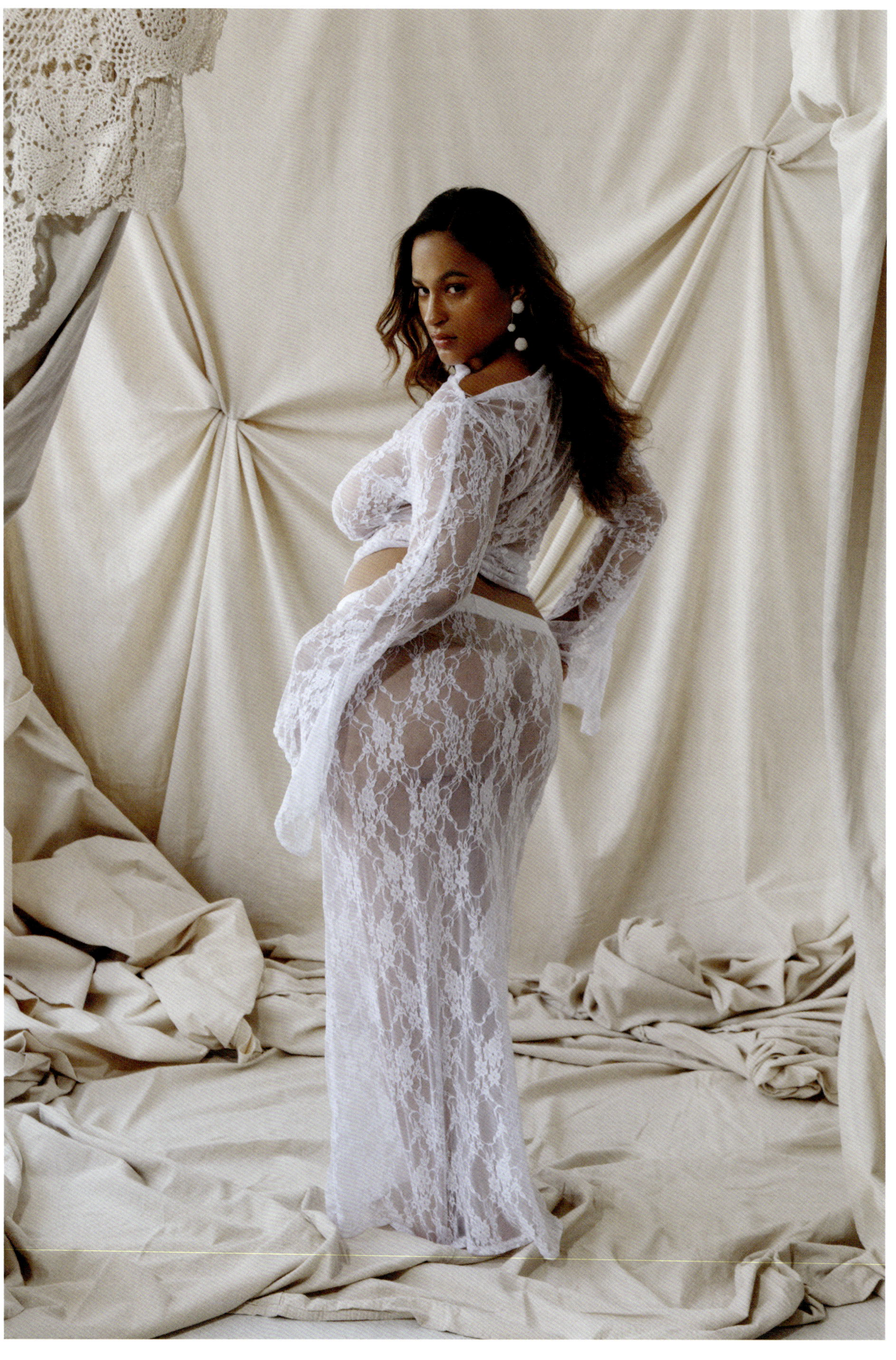

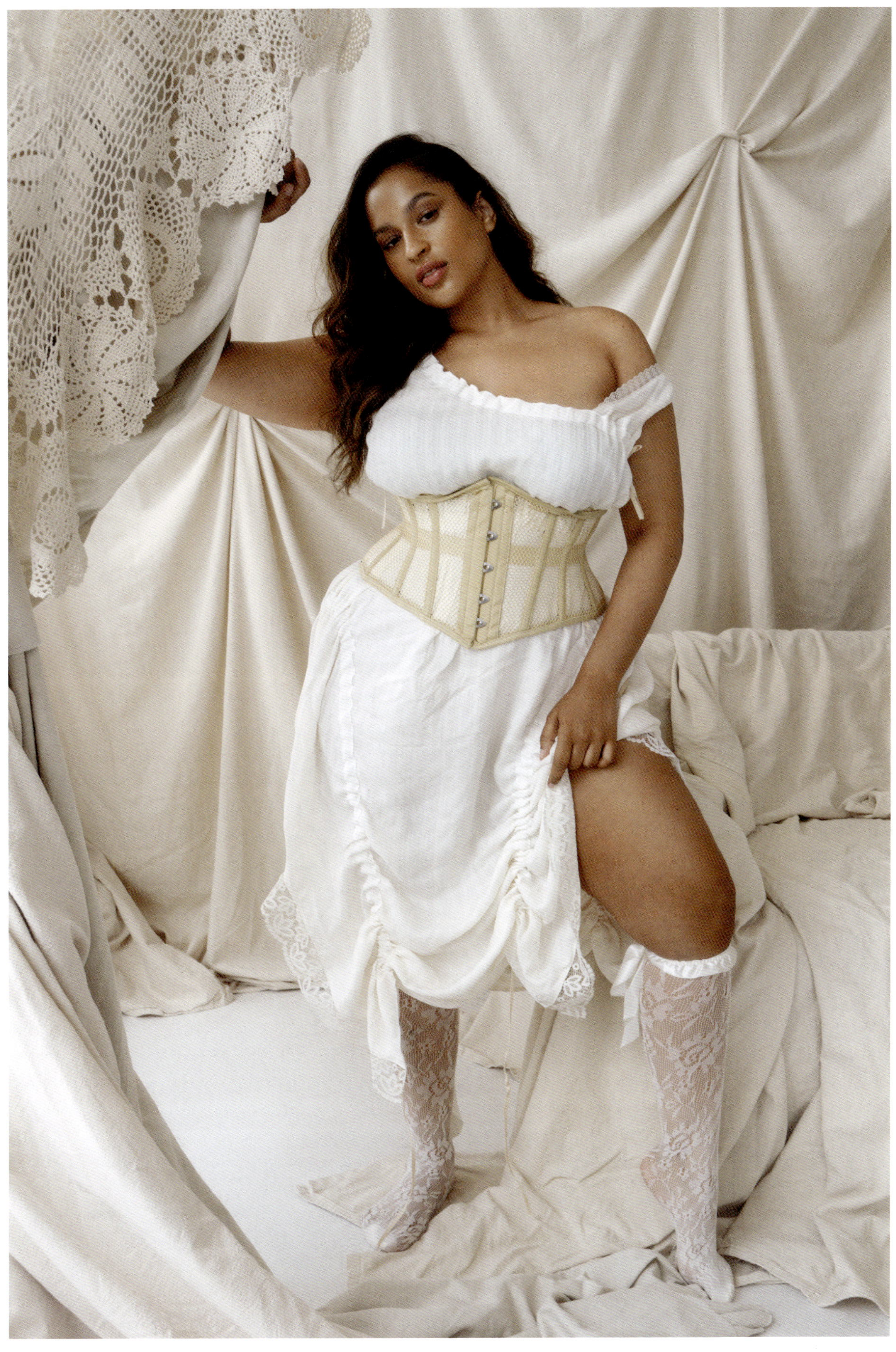

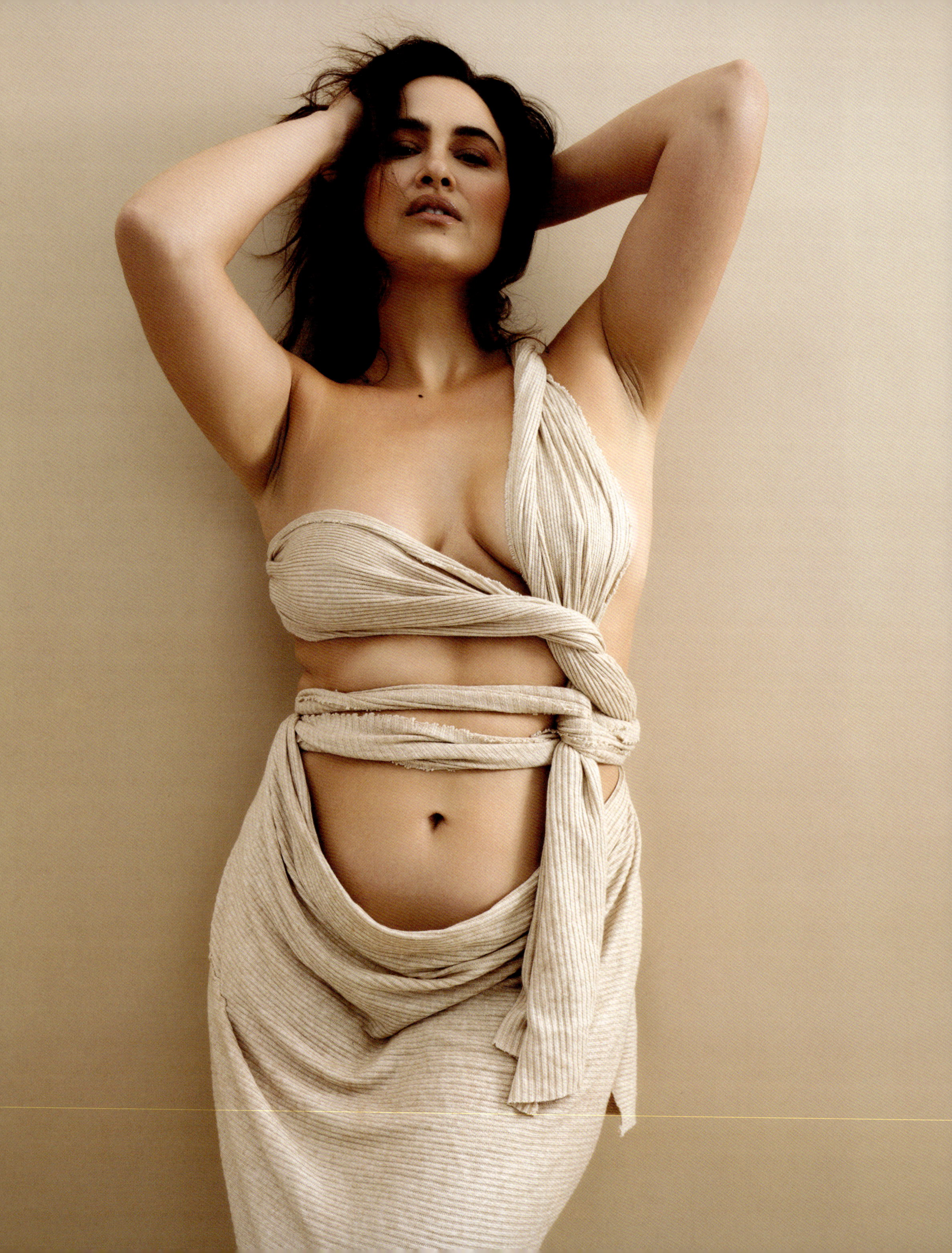

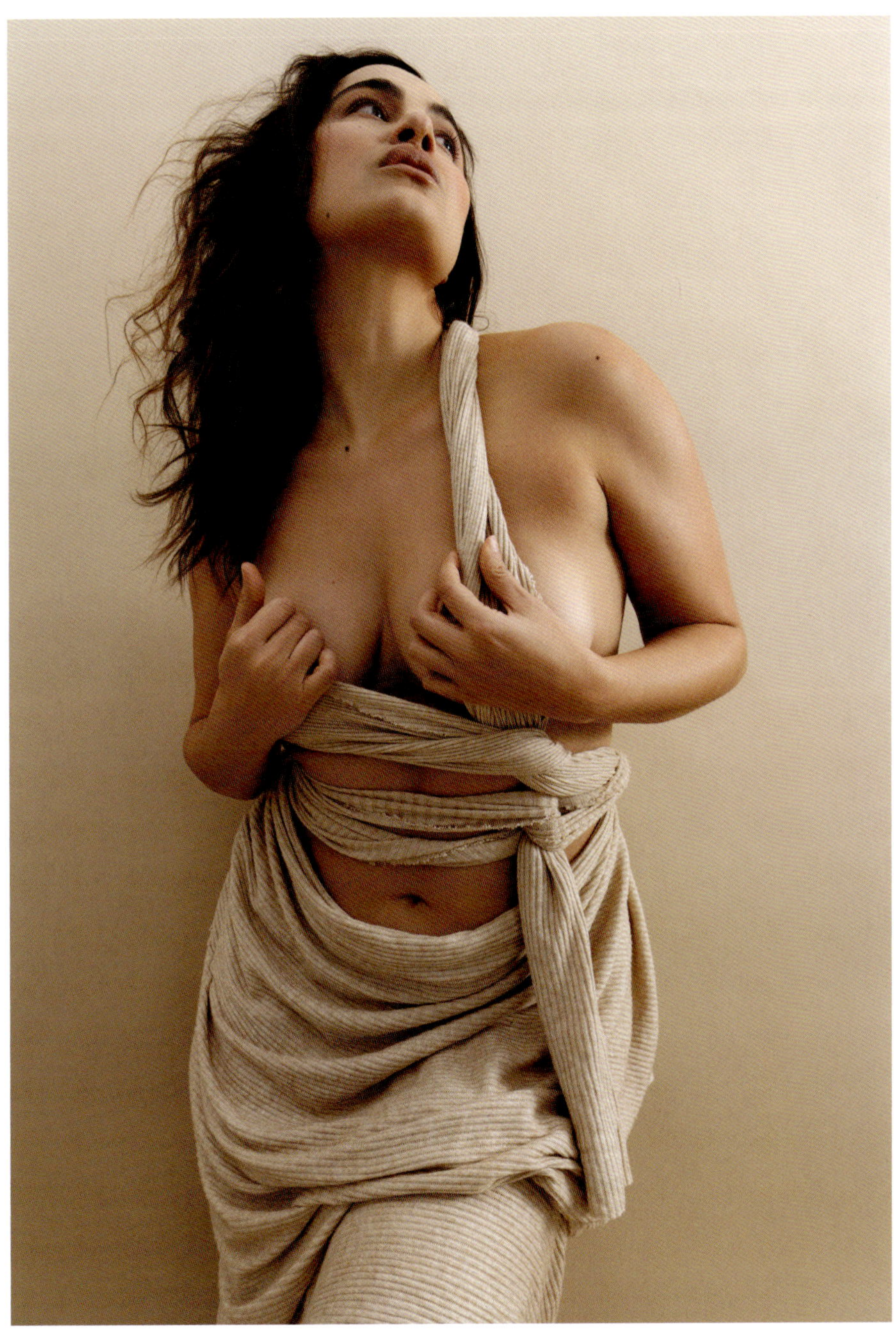

Previous pages: Madison Simone wears Lapoze lace set (left); Greta dress (right).

Denka Obradovic wears fabric draped by Yoko J.

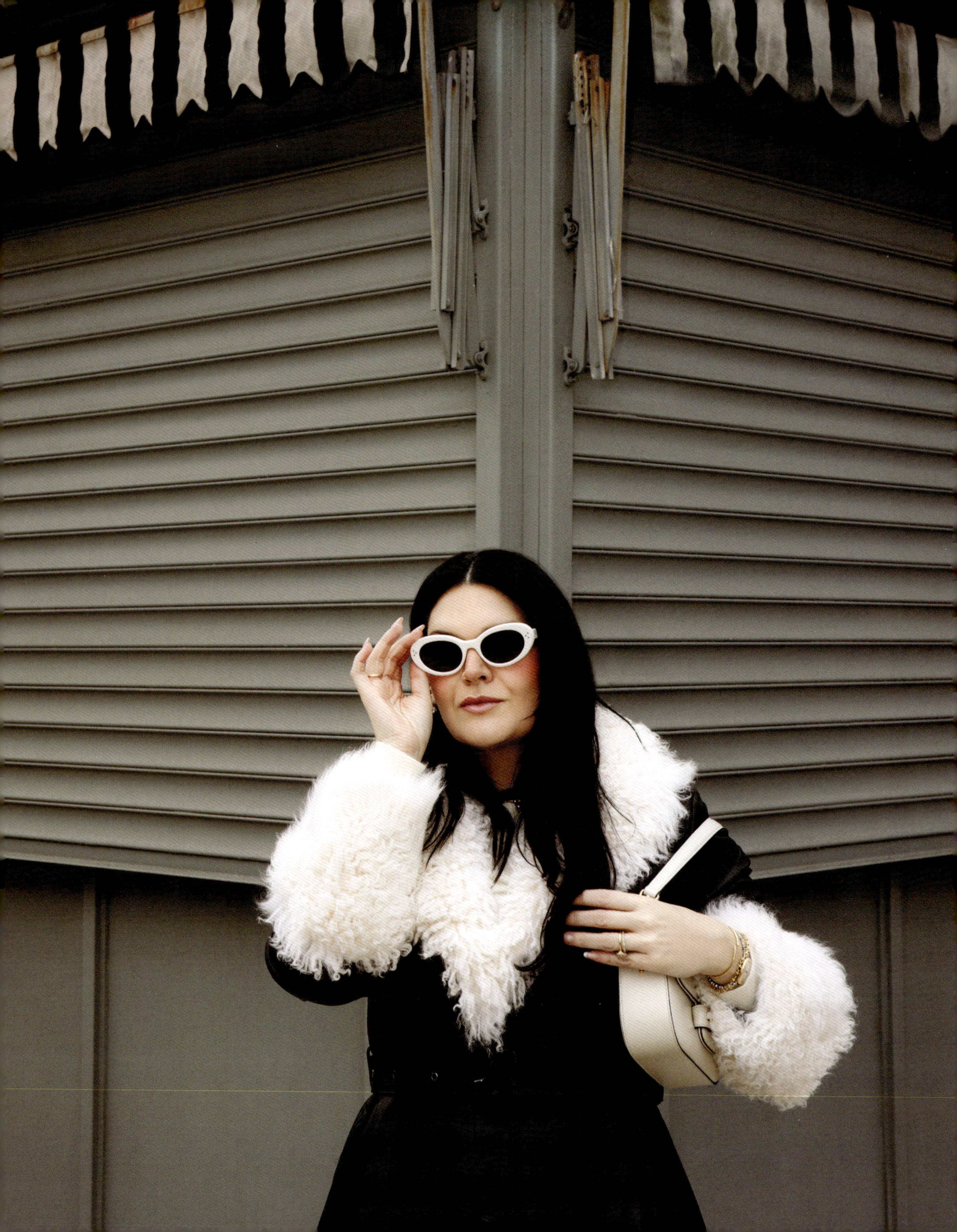

Nicolette Mason

A changemaker for beauty and body diversity

Nicolette Mason was one of the first plus-size influencers I collaborated with. We met when I photographed her for her blog over a decade ago, at a time when only a handful of plus-size influencers were making waves. Our work together introduced me to a vibrant realm of fashion and representation, which Nicolette has profoundly impacted through her work as an influencer, writer, entrepreneur and consultant.

Throughout her career, Nicolette has played a crucial role in the body positivity narrative and in shifting industry conversations. This is particularly true of her time at *Marie Claire*, where she contributed from 2016 to 2020. When discussing her work from this era and its impact, she states, "At the time, a lot of writing for or about plus-sizes in the mainstream fashion industry came from a very self-critical, apologetic tone—it wasn't about having fun with fashion, but about minimizing, disguising, and appealing. It was refreshing to take—and offer—a different approach." For Nicolette, writing on bodies and fashion from different perspectives is vital. "I love seeing incredible writing and theory on bodies from people like Tressie McMillan Cotton and Roxane Gay and Audrey Gordon and so many more. It's all part of the same ecosystem to me."

In 2017, alongside writing, Nicolette co-founded Premme with Gabi Fresh: a brand aimed at providing trendy plus-size clothing to fill a significant gap in the market. This initiative was groundbreaking, offering fashionable options for individuals who often felt overlooked by mainstream labels. "We knew that after years of working with other brands, there were still needs and wants of the plus-size customer that weren't being heard or delivered, and we thought, if they're not going to listen to us, why not do it ourselves? If nothing else, we wanted to prove that it was possible to approach plus-size fashion differently—that you could work with models that reflected the customer, that you could eschew the 'rules' of dressing

I think the most important thing brands need to understand is that body diversity shouldn't be a trend—it should be part of a long-term commitment to inclusivity.

larger bodies and play with bold colors, cut-outs, patterns, and trends, and that plus-size fashion could also be aspirational."

Premme not only expanded the market: It became a love letter to the community. Nicolette continues, "There are few feelings that rival seeing people in clothes you've created and having them express how much they feel like themselves and that they were finally given permission to dress in a way that felt true to them."

Nicolette's collaborations extend beyond Premme; her work with designers like Christian Siriano has been pivotal in advancing inclusivity in fashion. These partnerships have not only showcased diverse body types but helped bridge the gap between high fashion and the plus-size market.

In her role as a creative consultant, Nicolette's expertise spans the spectrum from creating the first pride campaign for a luxury beauty brand to partnering with top US retailers on developing inclusive sizing initiatives. In this role, she has worked to help brands navigate the challenges of authentically engaging with the plus-size community: a group whose unique needs many brands struggle to understand. With larger, well-resourced companies, Nicolette's found that "there's often an expectation of a quick return on investment, especially when launching new plus-size offshoots. But it takes time and requires a full 360-degree approach—investing in everything from accessible fit guides and accurate product measurements to marketing, customer experience, and casting reflective of the target market." She emphasizes that for brands to successfully engage the plus-size market, it's crucial to hire from the communities they wish to reach.

Throughout Nicolette's career as both an influencer and a consultant, brand messaging has shifted, with influencers serving an important role in shaping it—particularly in plus-size fashion. Today, influencers serve as vital advocates, using their platforms to challenge outdated beauty standards and promote diverse narratives. Nicolette's own journey underscores this evolution and highlights how the landscape continues to change and grow.

Looking to the future, Nicolette envisions a world where brands fully prioritize authentic representation. "I think the most important thing brands need to understand is that body diversity shouldn't be a trend—it should be part of a long-term commitment to inclusivity. There's no going back from this movement, and it's exciting to see how brands can play a role in shaping a more inclusive future."

As to today's landscape, she shares her excitement about the progress that is happening around us, especially among independent designers and in fashion shows: "I can't just pick one! But my god—every time I see a new fashion editorial or an independent designer emerging or a fashion show with incredible casting, I still get butterflies. I love what designers like Sinéad O'Dwyer and Karoline Vitto have been doing in their fashion week presentations. I love it every time a curve and plus model gets a sick fashion editorial in a print magazine. I love seeing people have fun with fashion. There are so many ebbs and flows and ups and downs—launches, shut downs, collapses, sunsets—I love reminders that it's all cyclical and inclusivity is not going anywhere."

As we look ahead, Nicolette's contributions to the industry and her commitment to diversity set an inspiring example. Her work has not only helped redefine beauty standards but also empowered individuals to embrace their unique styles and identities. Through her continued advocacy, writing, and collaborations, she remains a key figure in the ongoing dialogue about body positivity and representation.

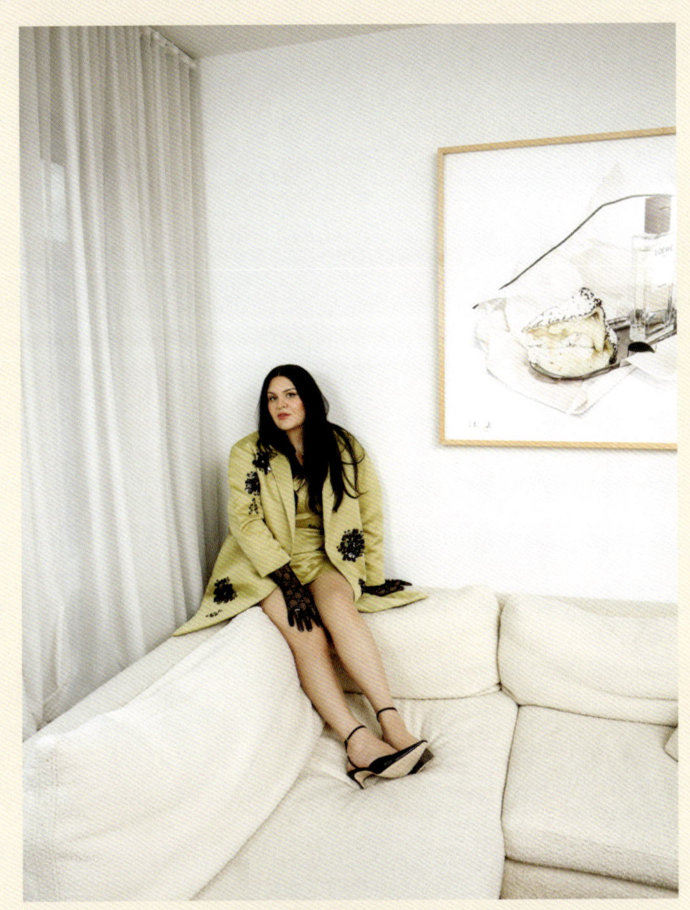
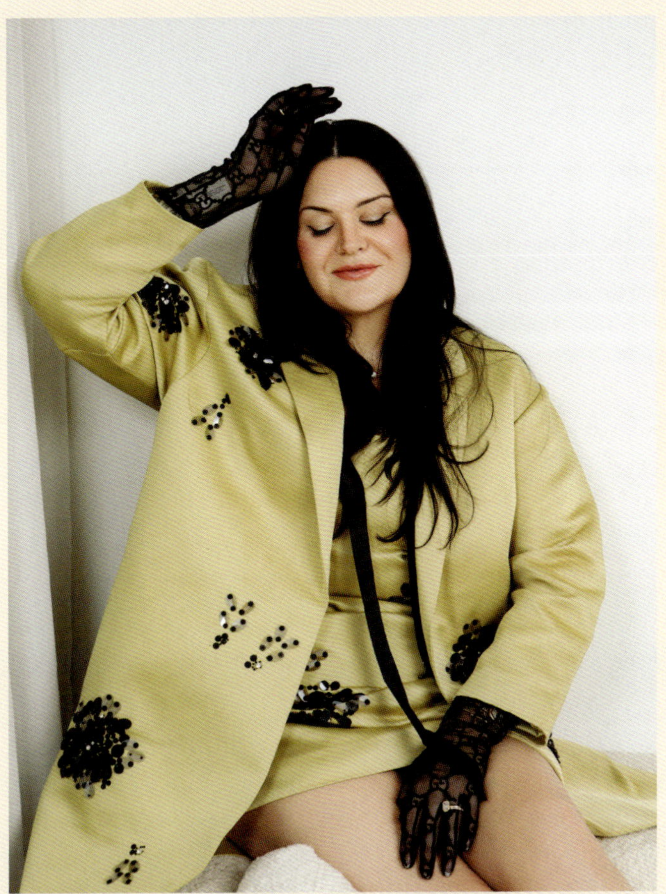
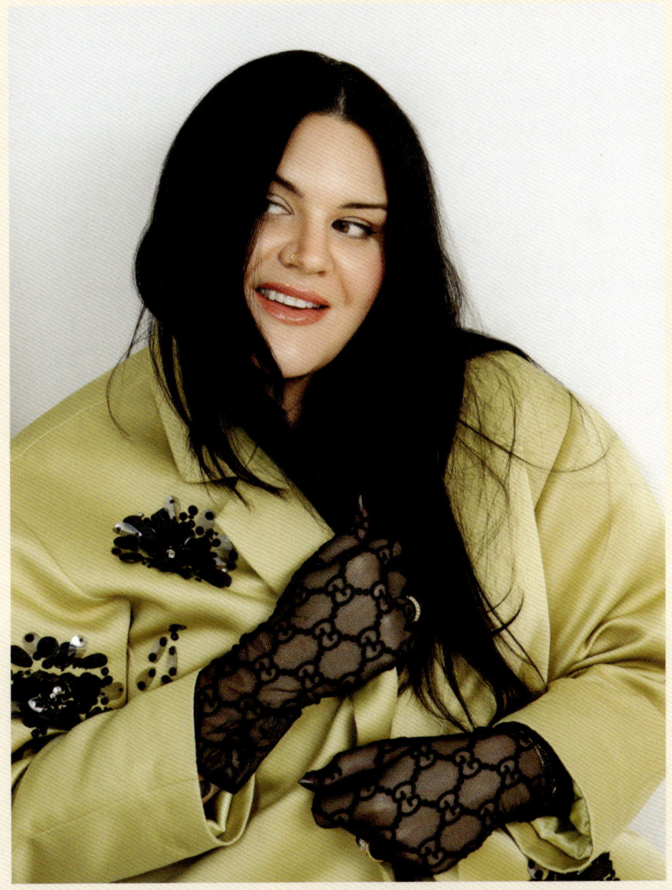
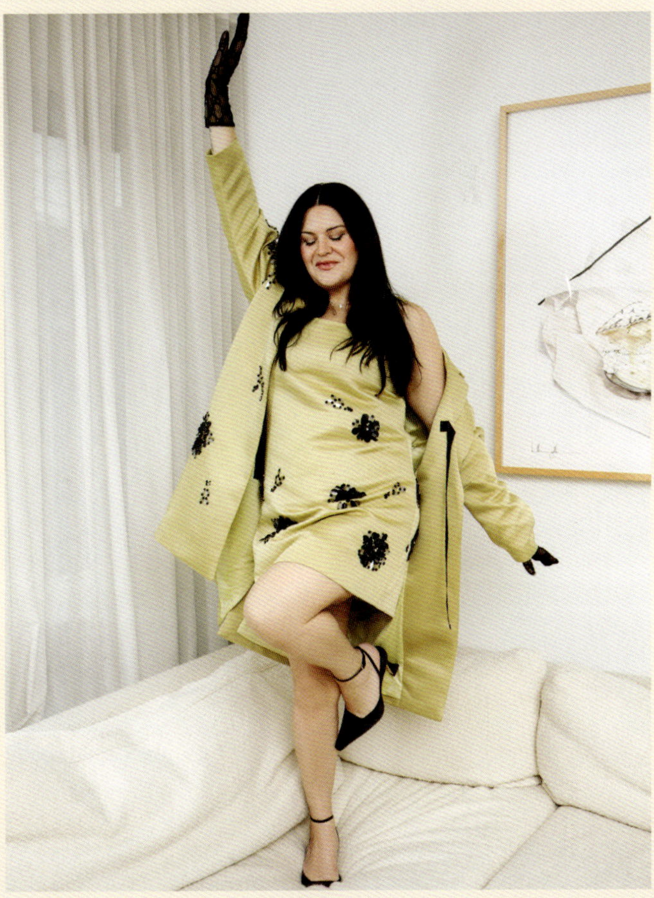

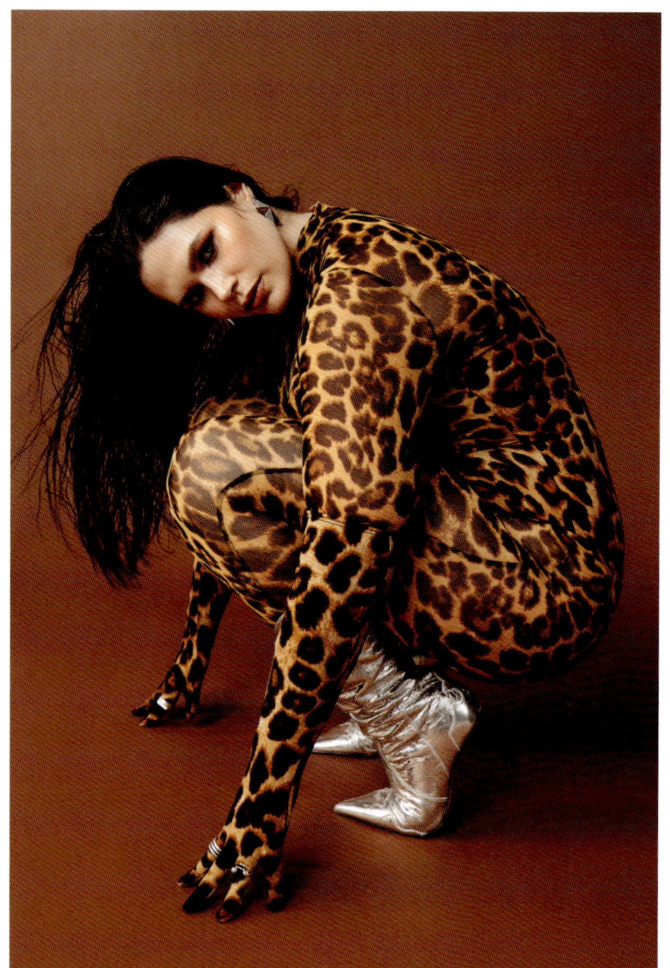

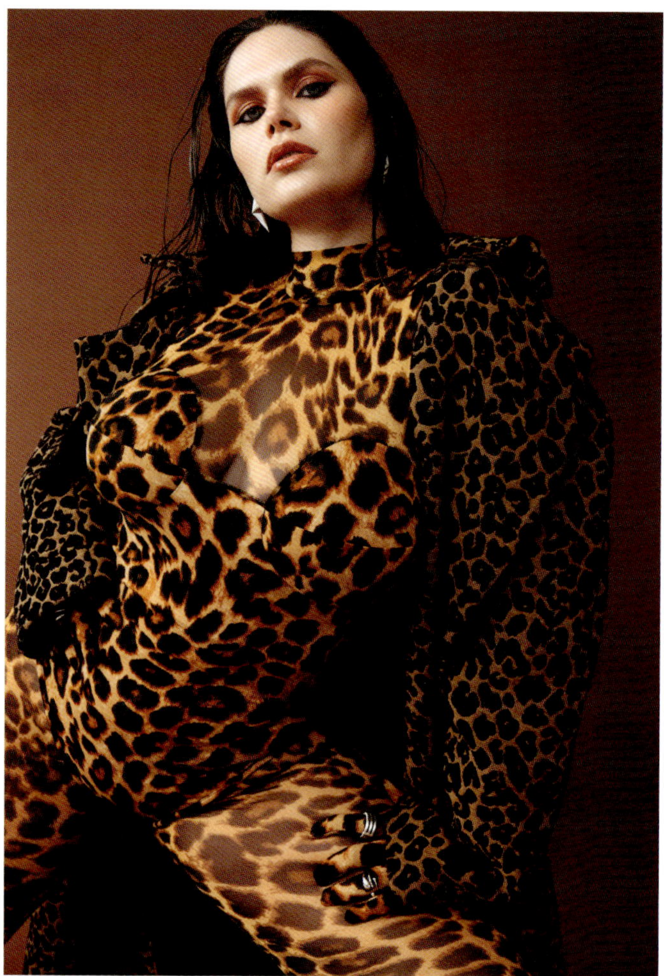

Chloe DeCleene wears vintage coat; jumpsuit from Lydia Hudgens' closet; Dolce Vita boots.

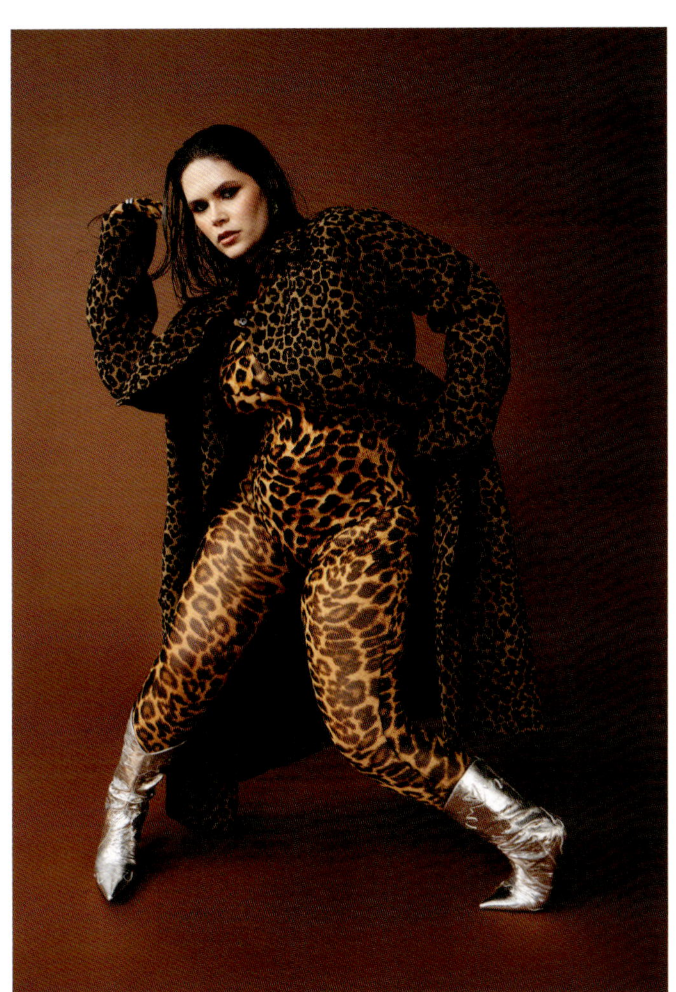

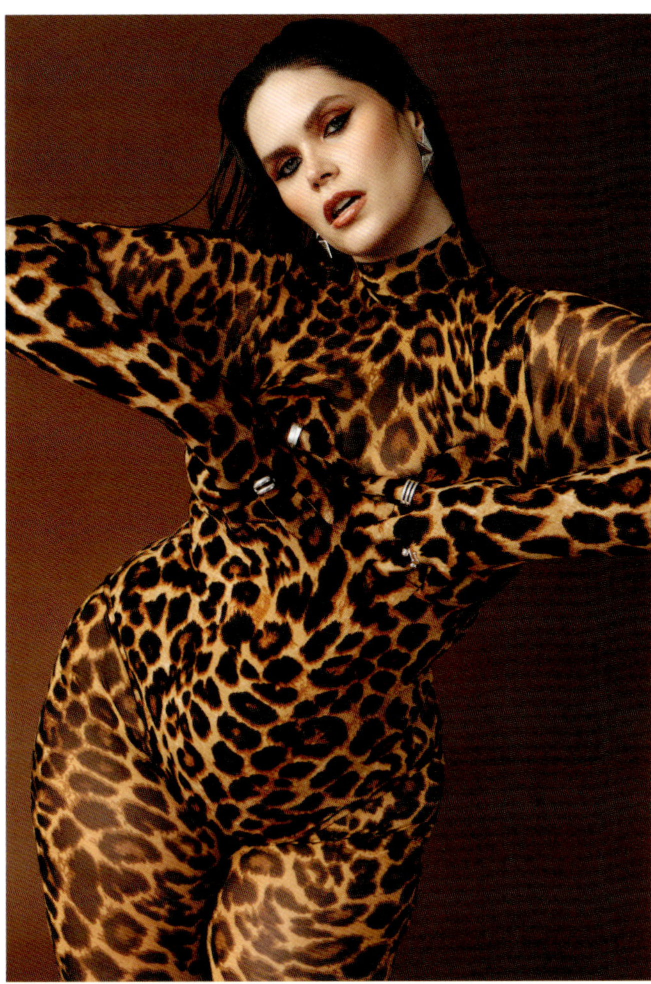

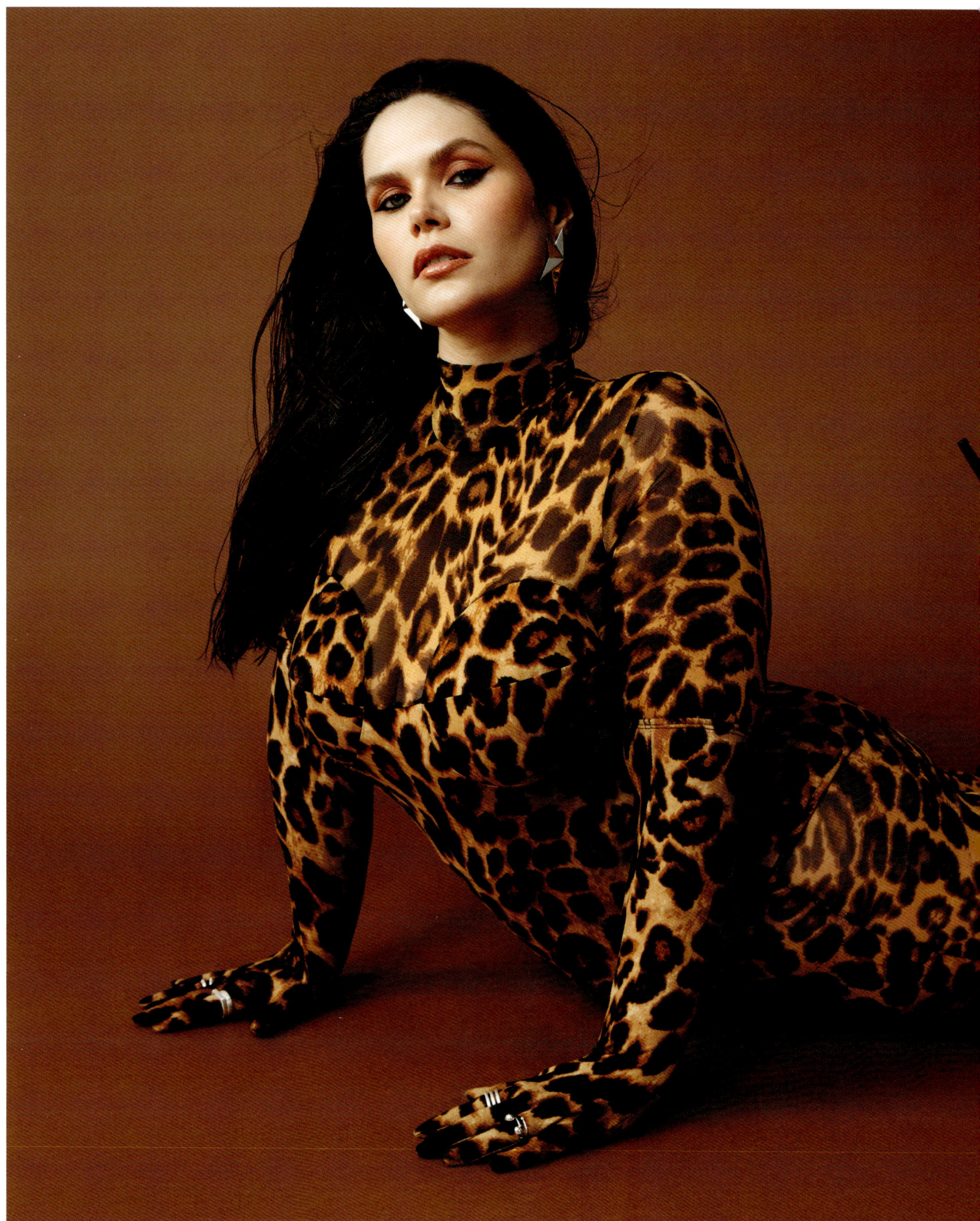

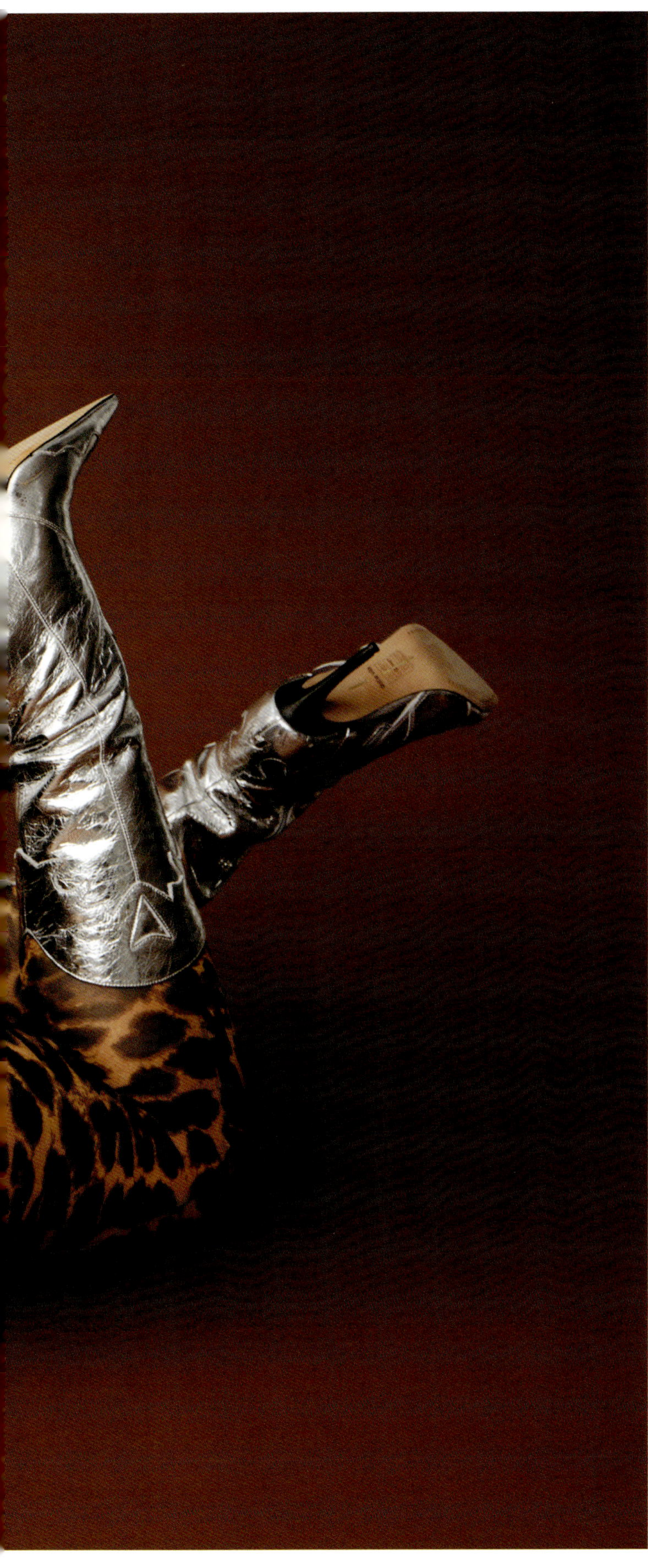

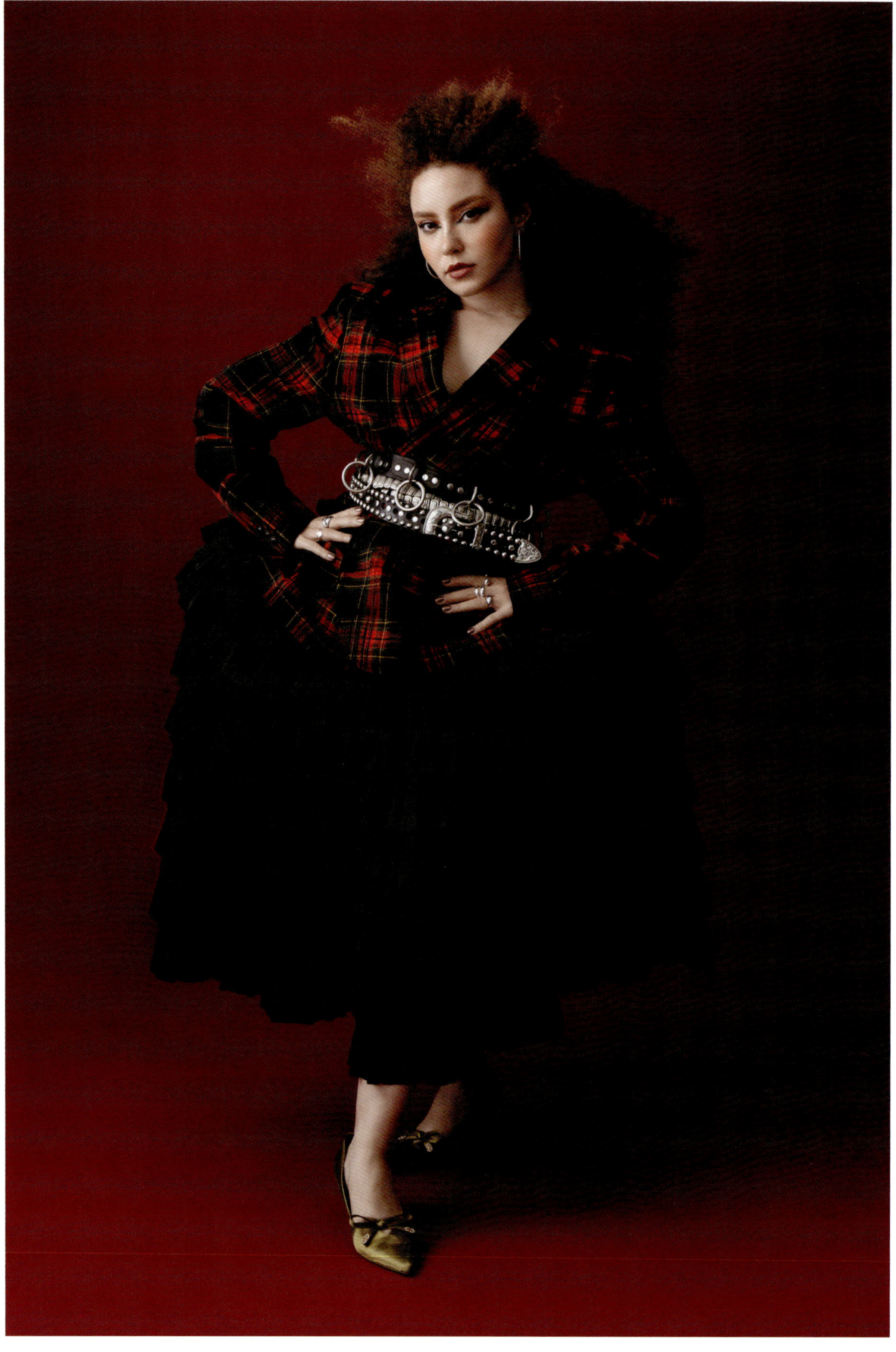

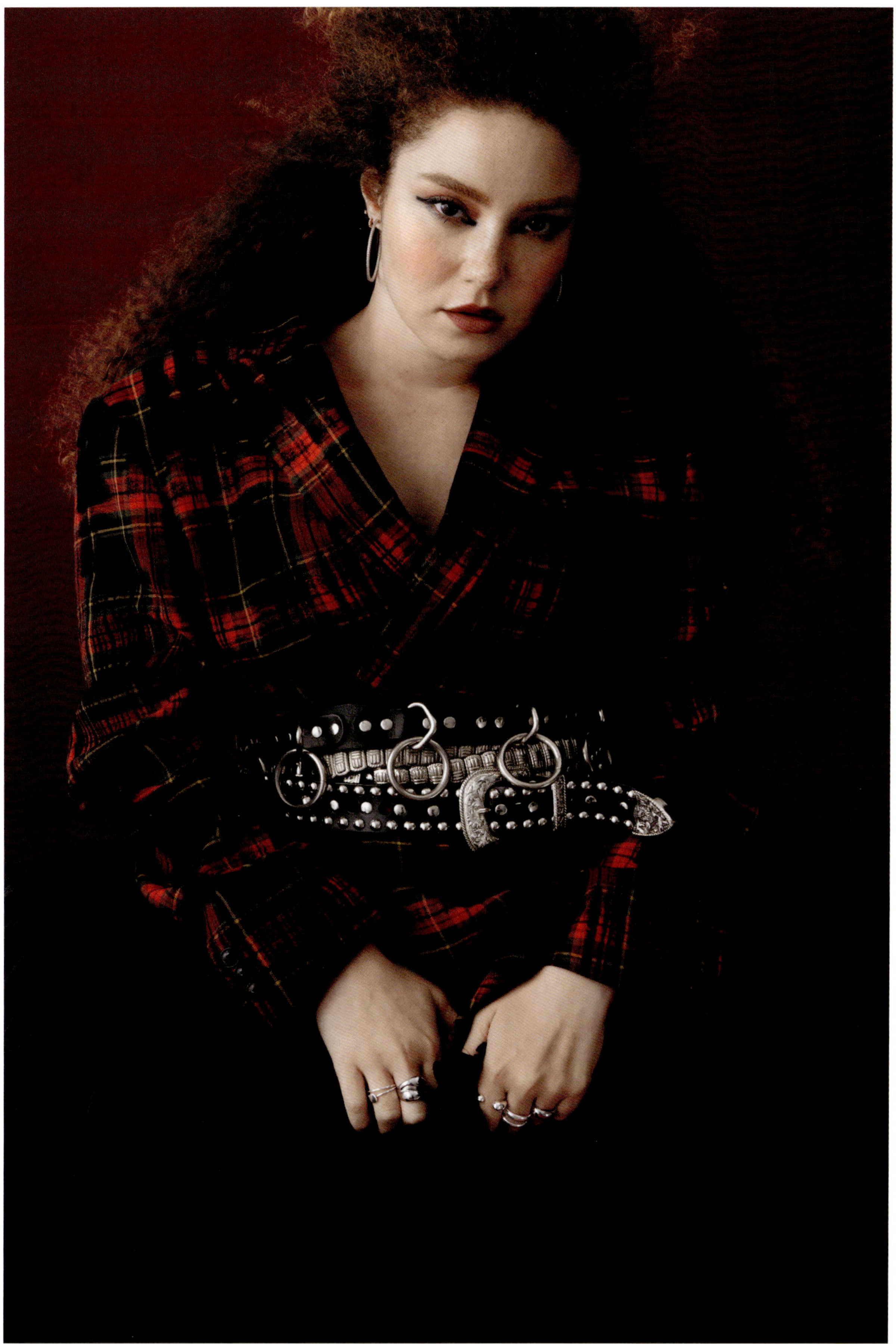

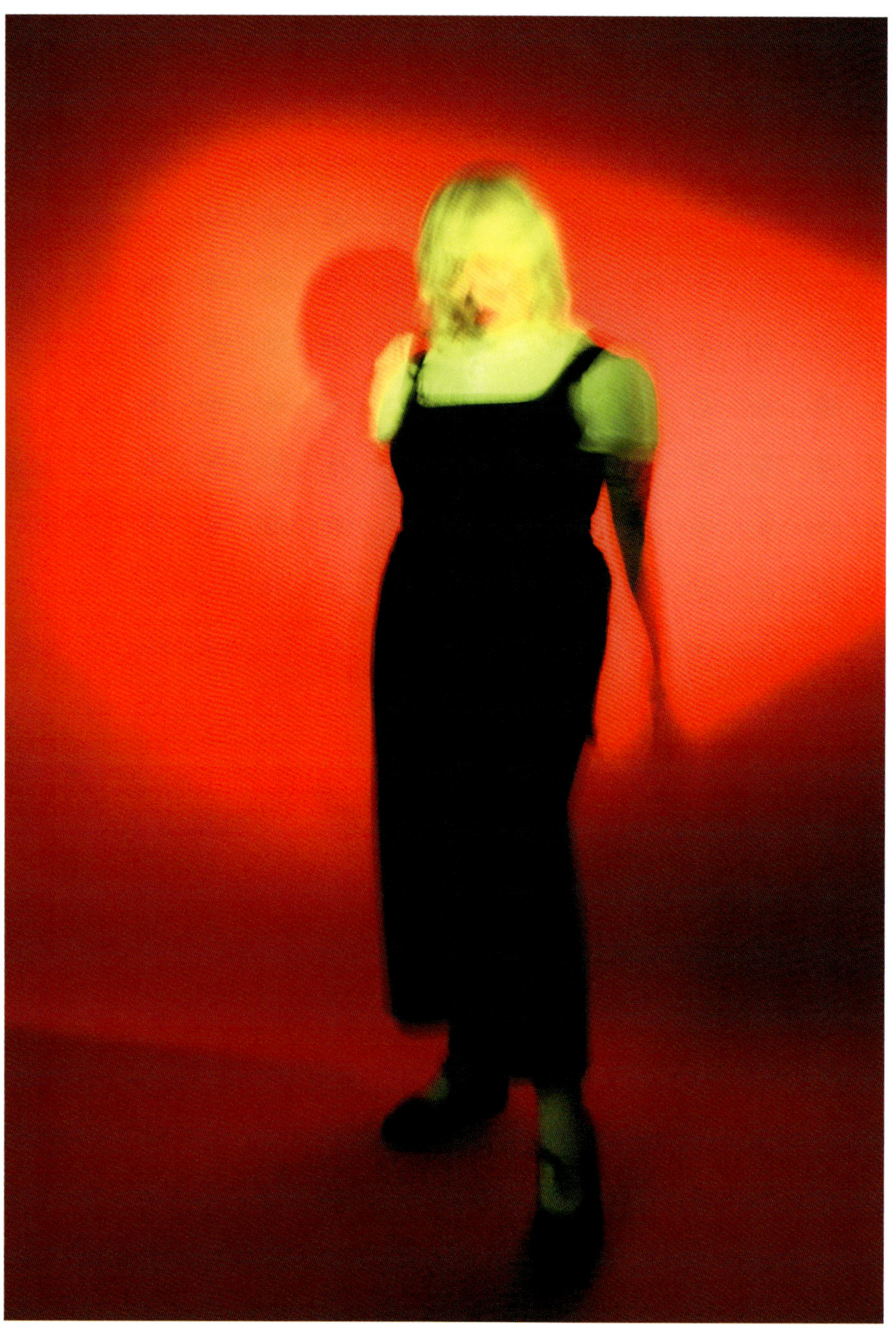

Previous pages: Katarina Tsokolati wears John Varvatos blazer; Ulla Johnson skirt; Circus NY by Sam Edelman shoes; Shop Berriez and Zana Bayne belts.

Tayler Smith wears dress from Lydia Hudgens' closet; Nicole Saldaña shoes.

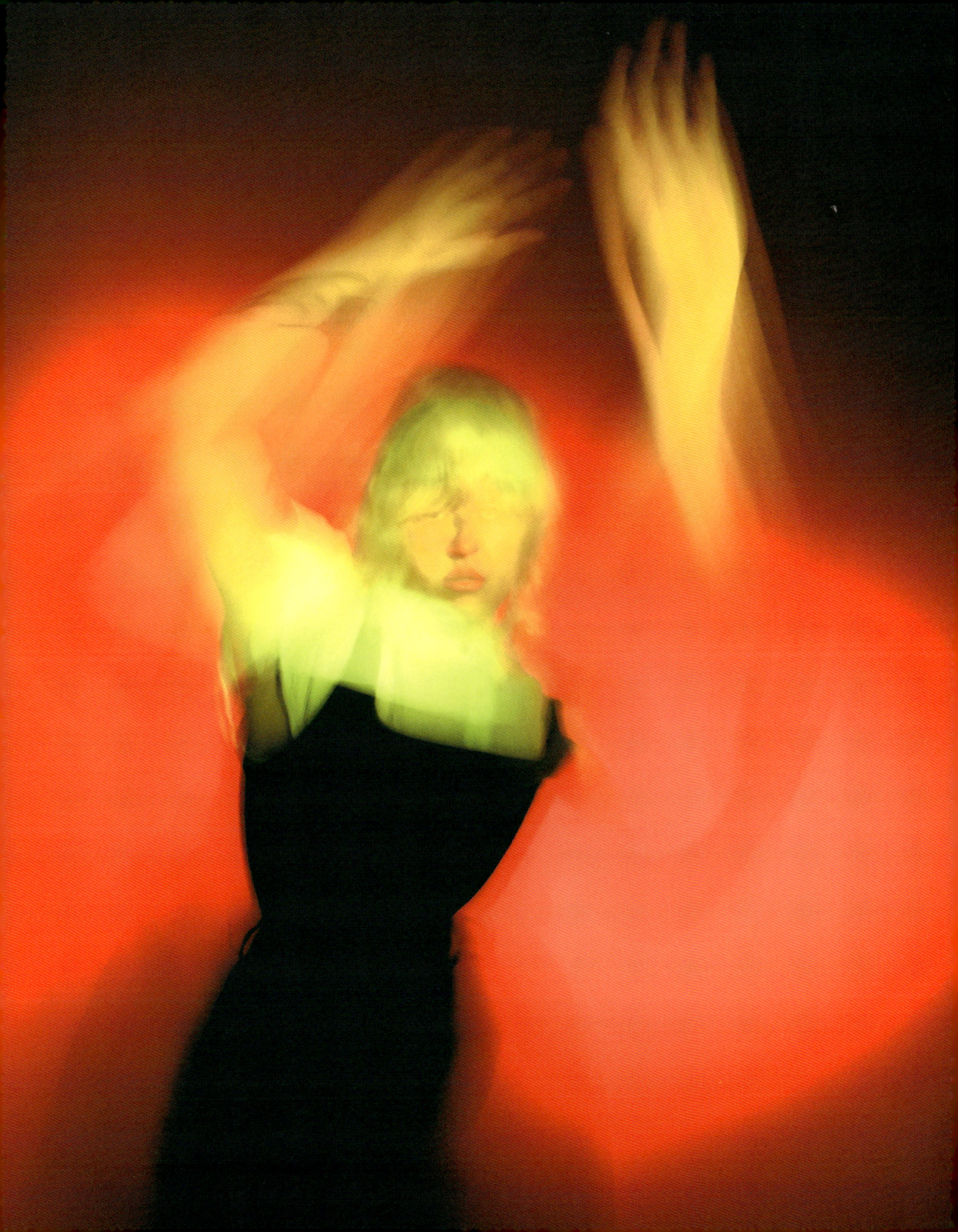

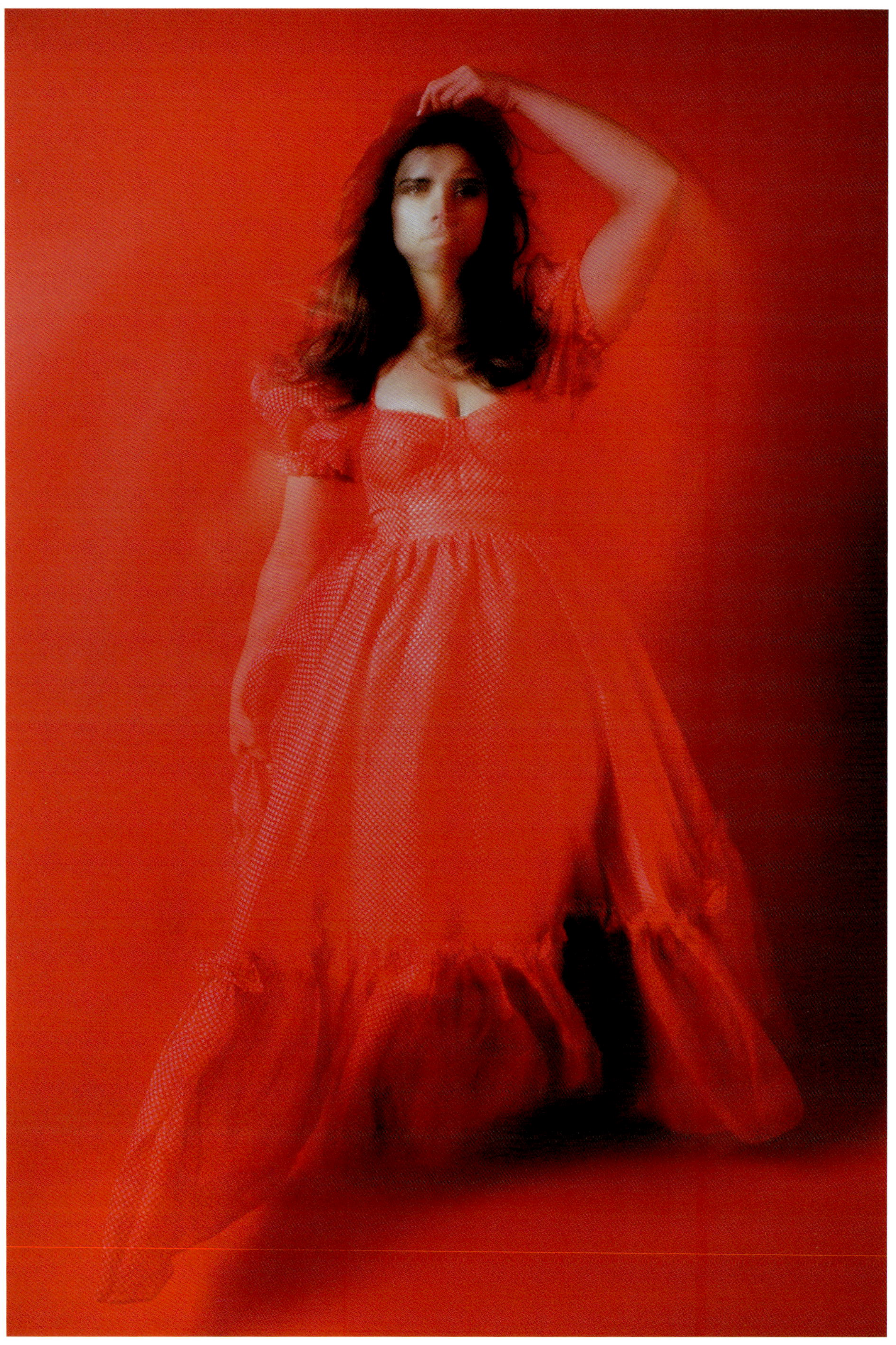

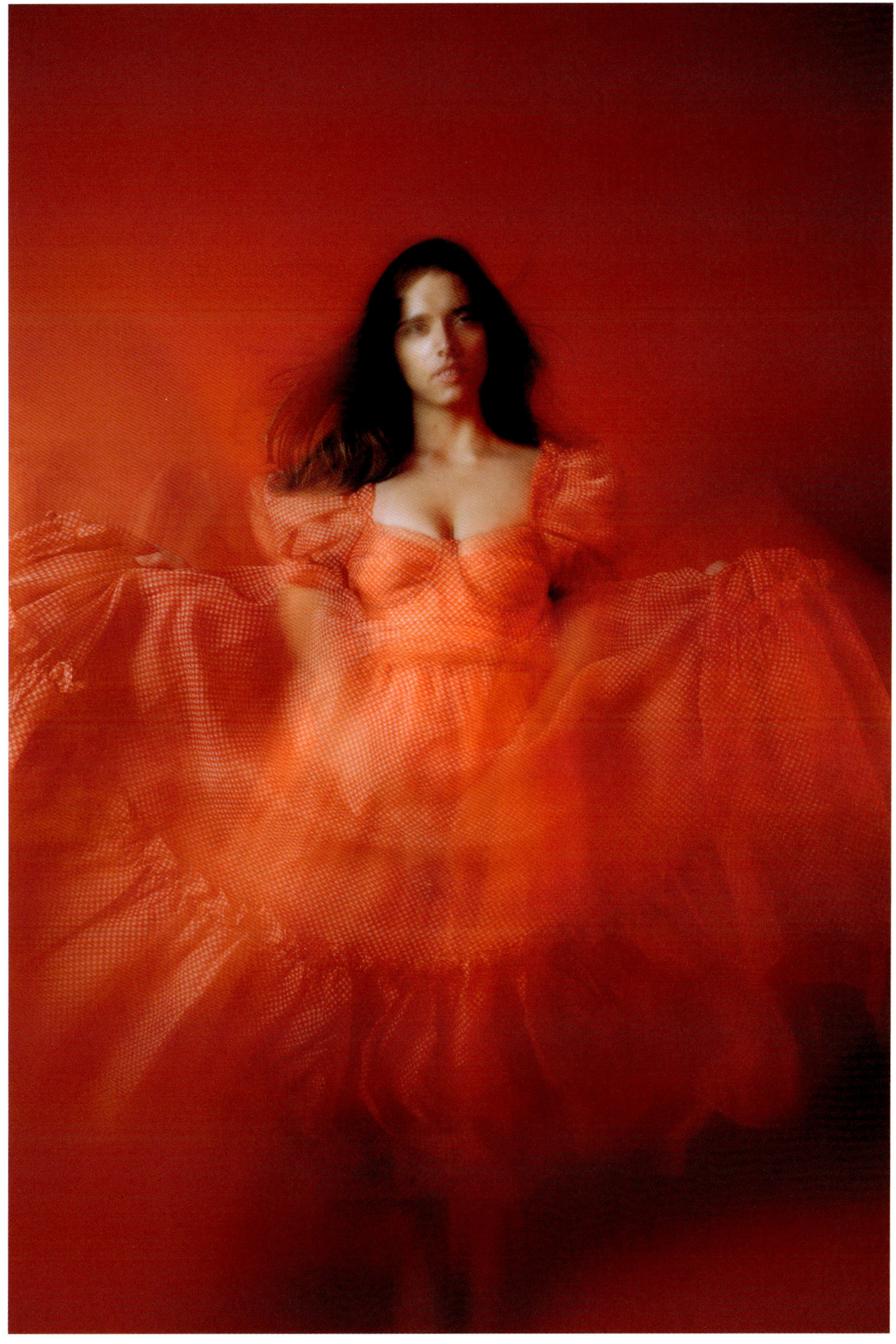

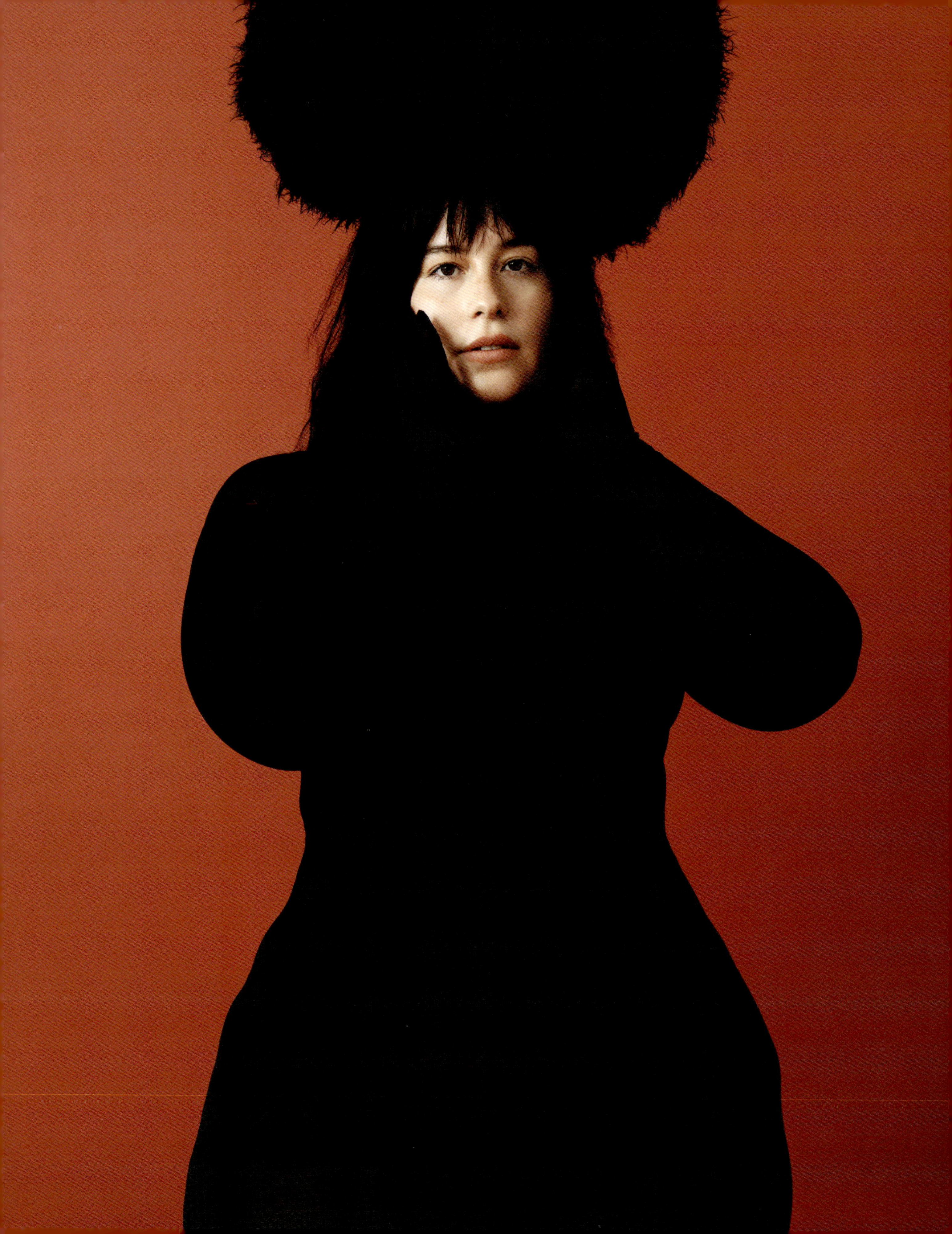

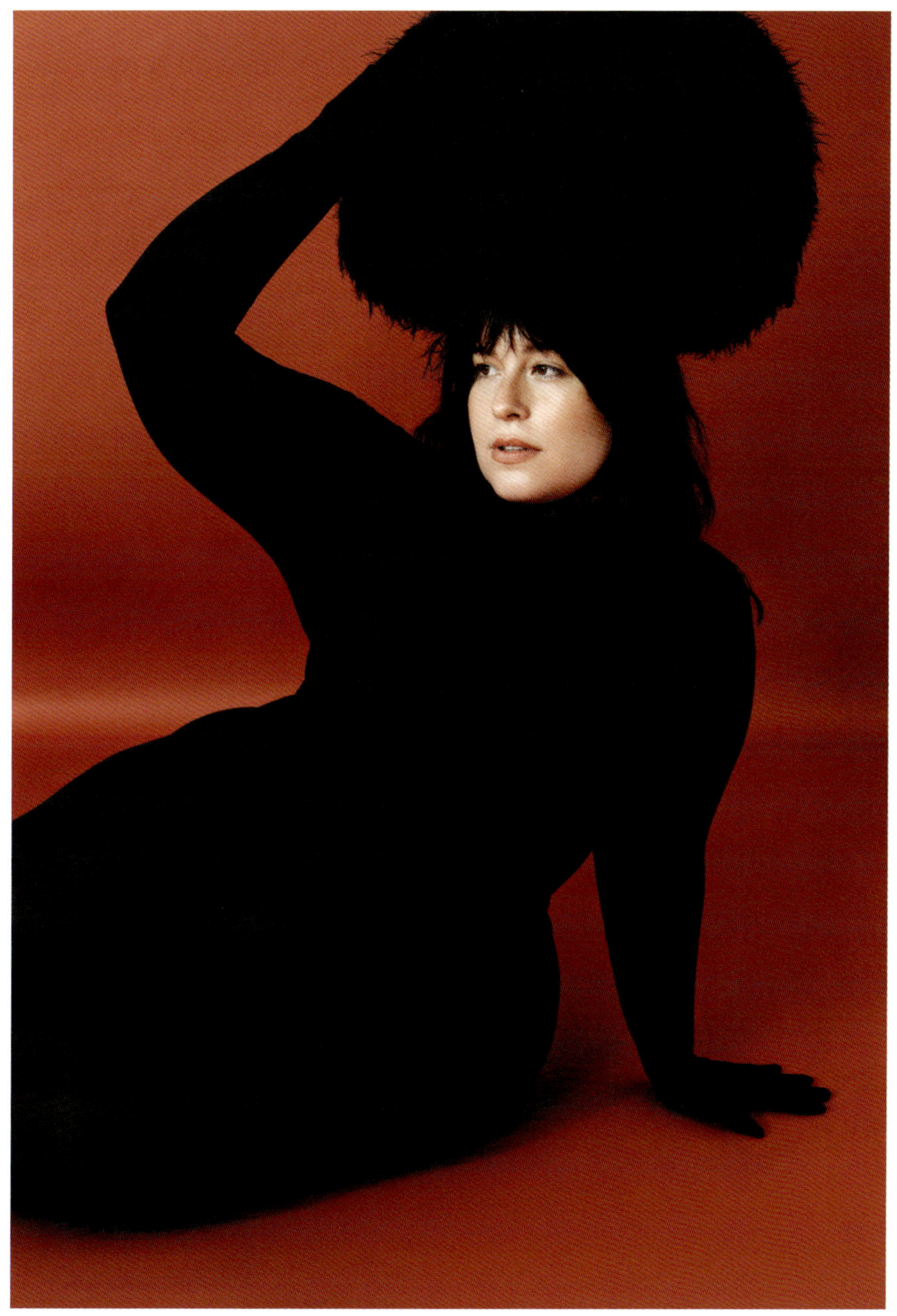

Previous pages: Wren Parker wears Selkie.

Maggie Rodriguez wears Pipenco Lorena headpiece; bodysuit from Kelly Augustine's closet.

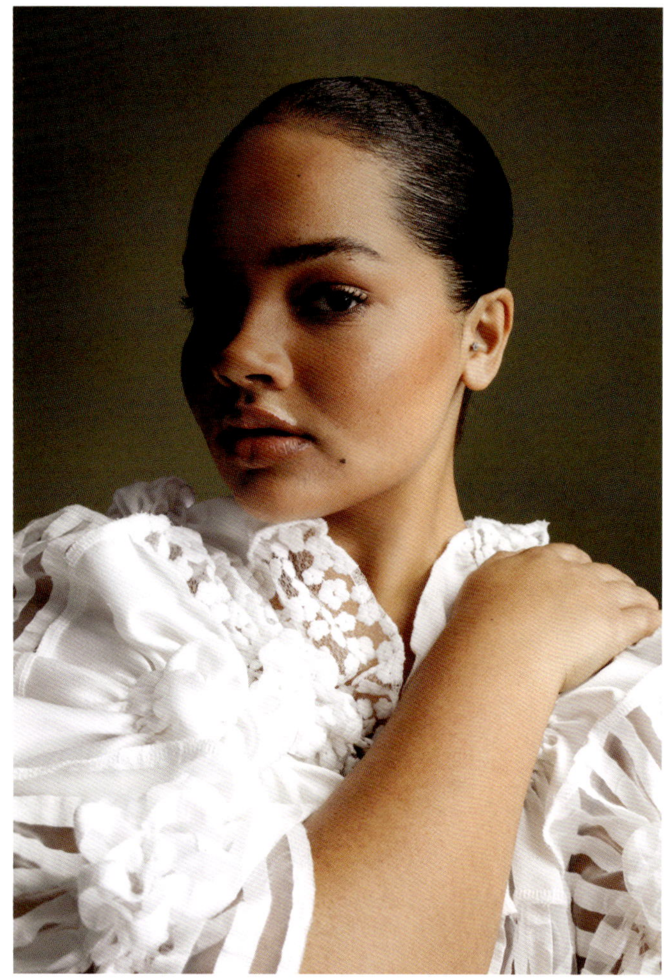

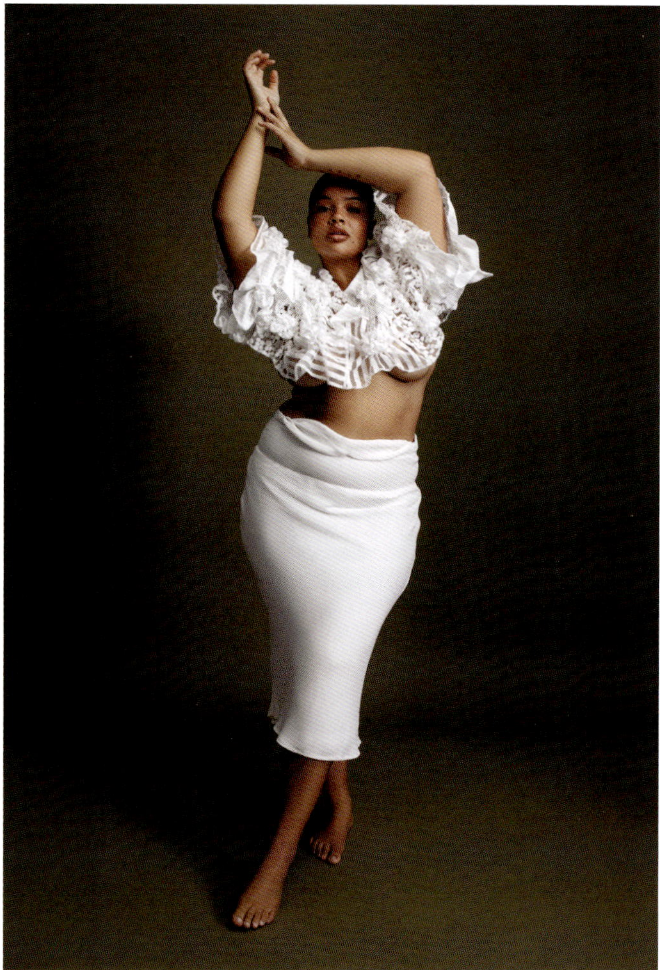

Aylah Karine wears Róisín Pierce.

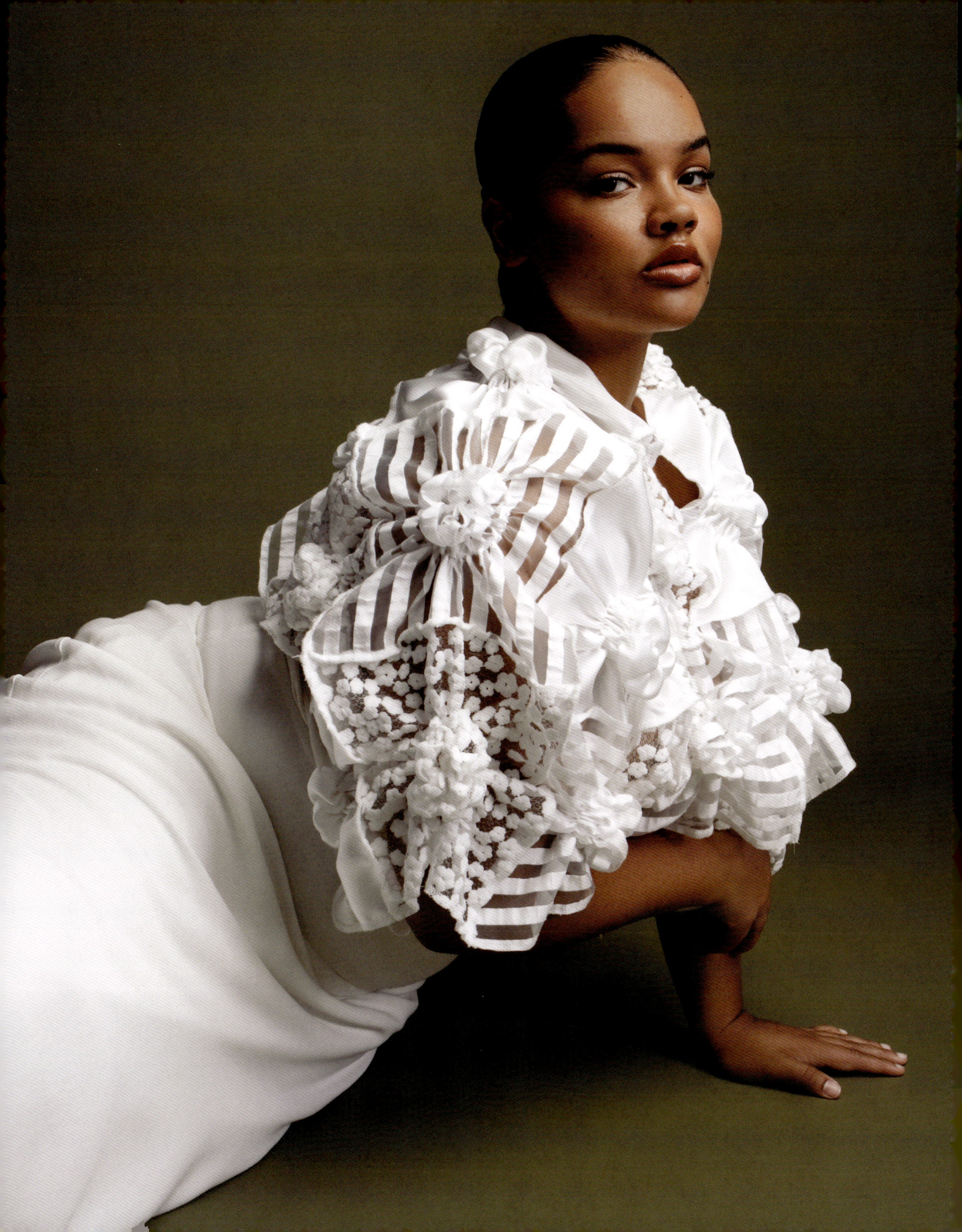

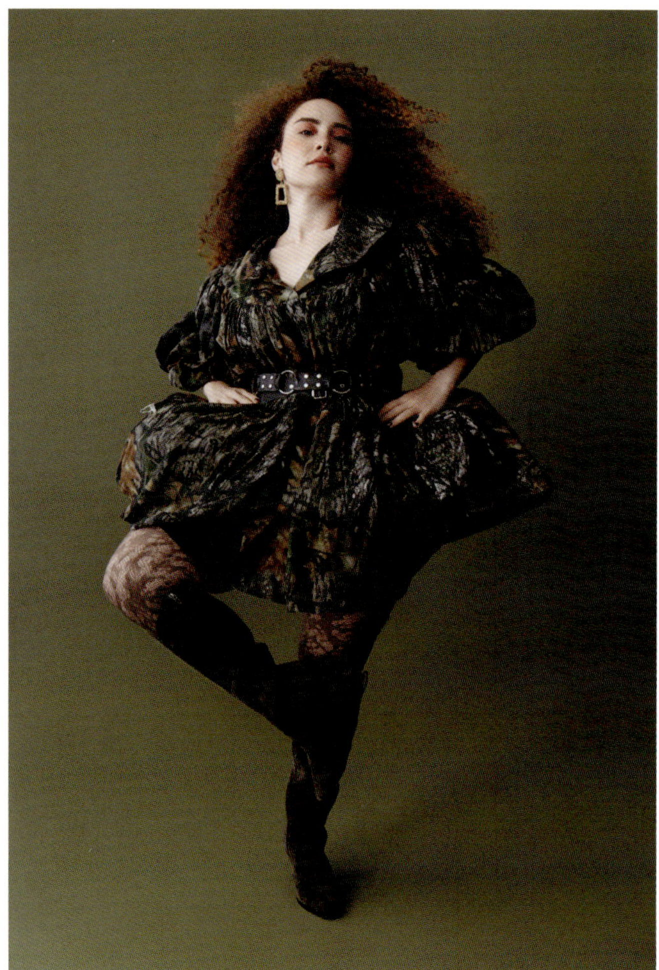

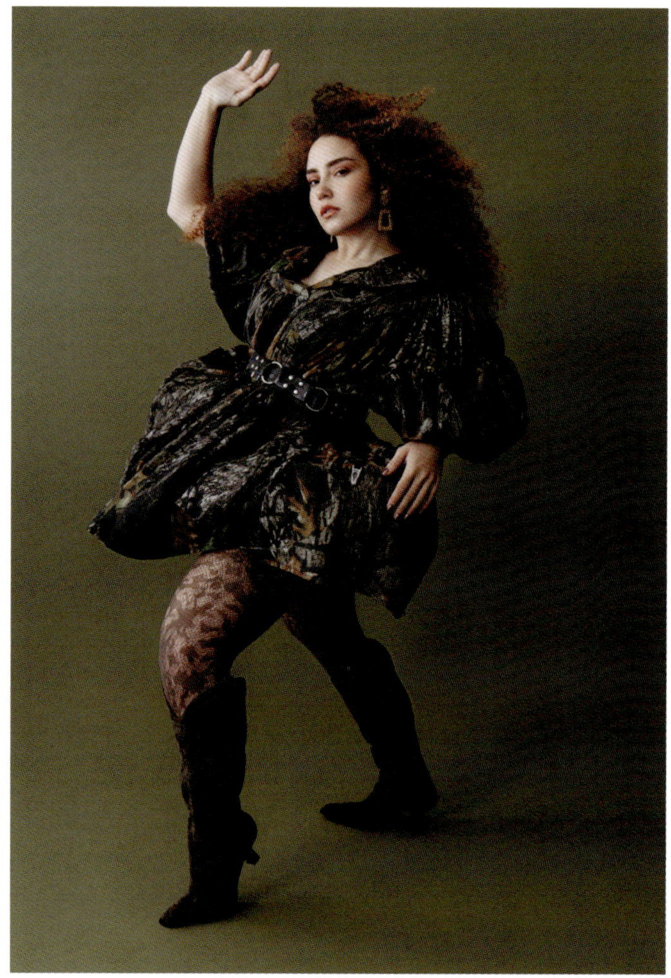

Katarina Tsokolati wears Lizzie Kidd dress;
Dolce Vita boots; vintage belt from Shop Berriez.

Pages 60–63: Delphine Clowe wears Theo Banzon.

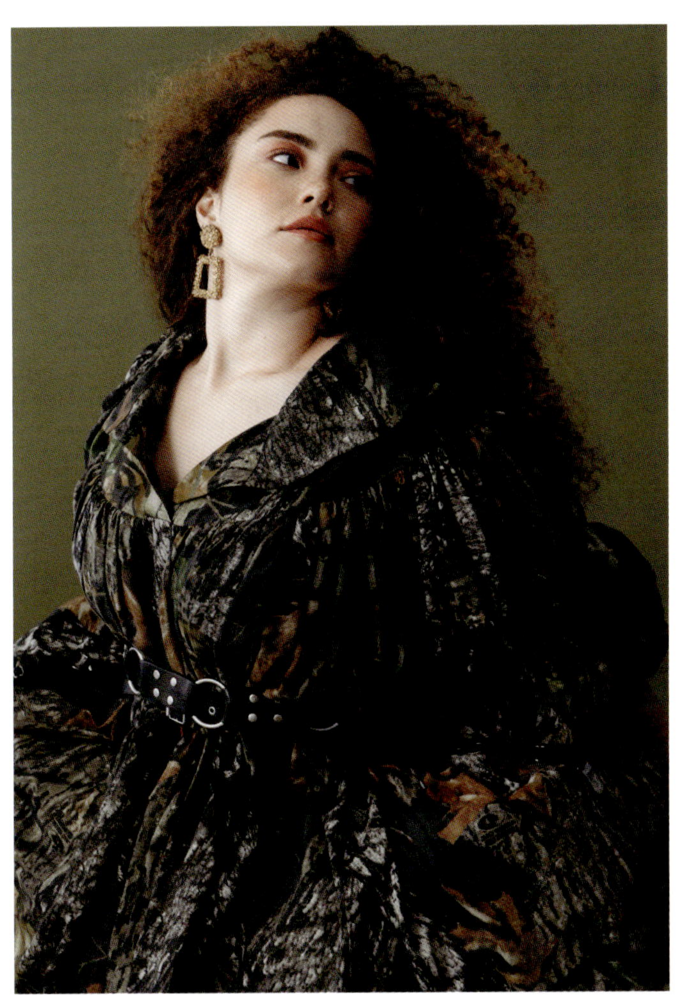

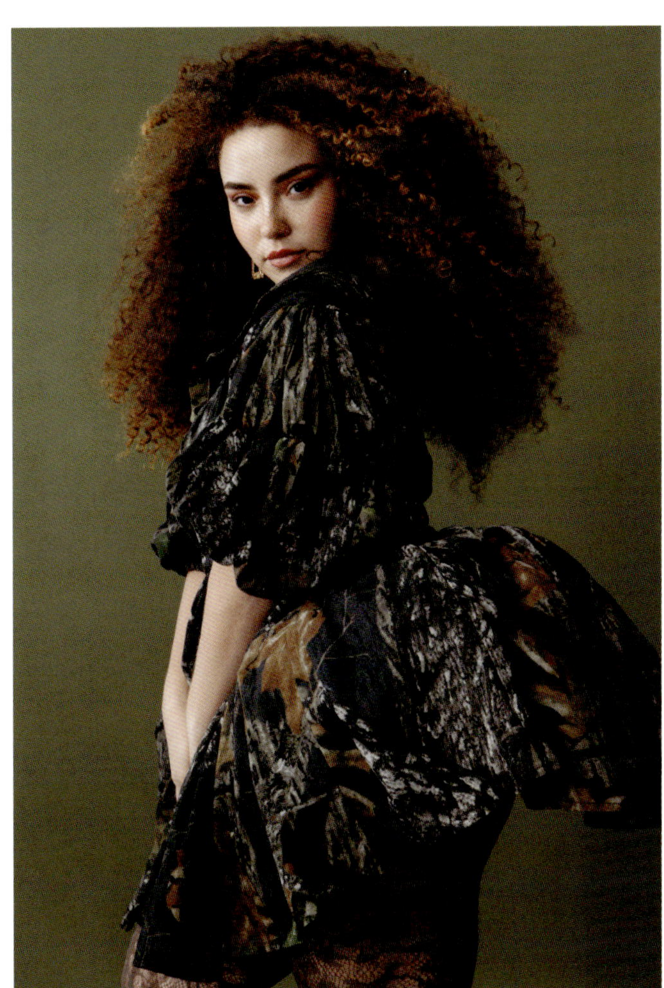

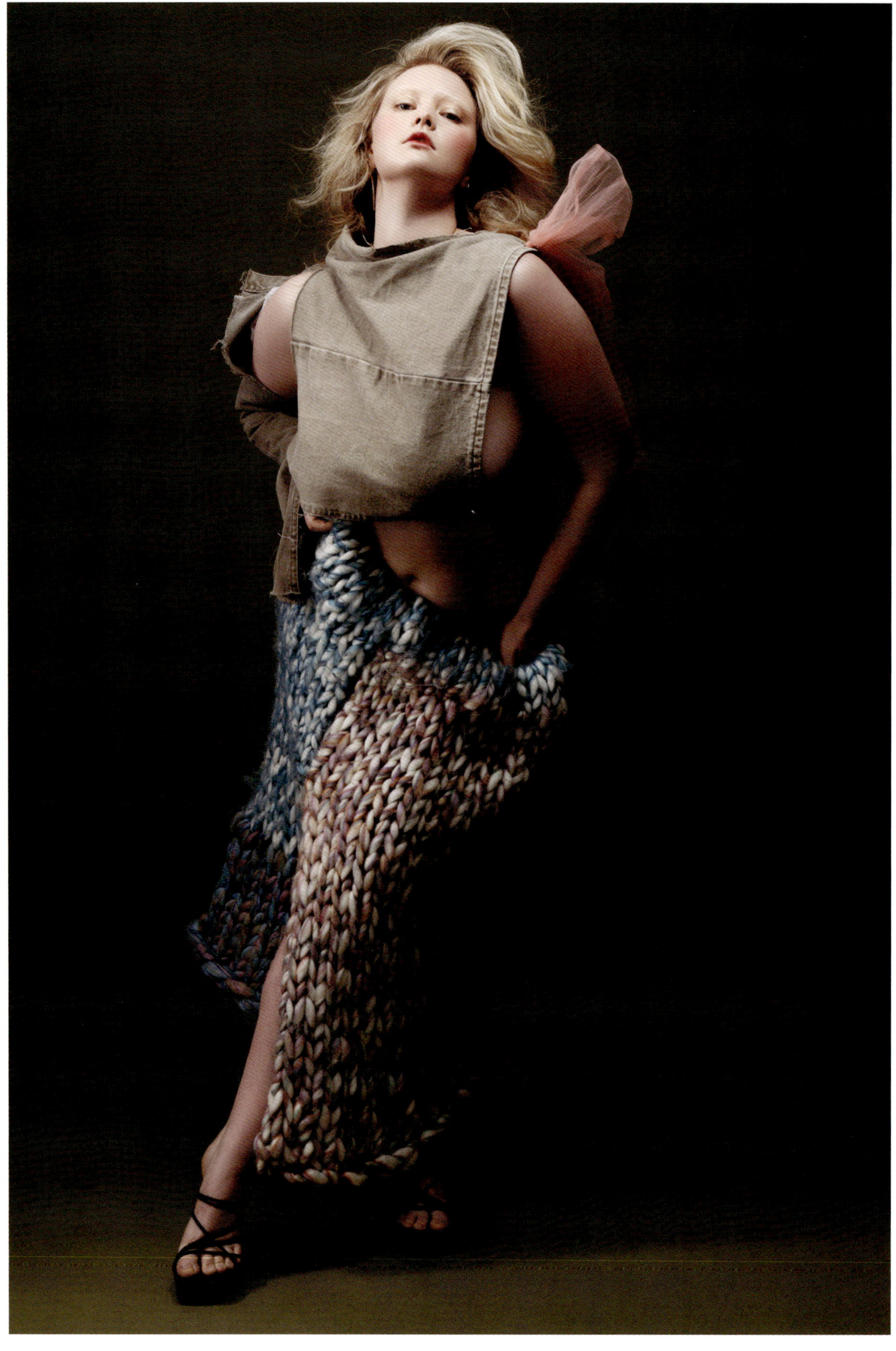

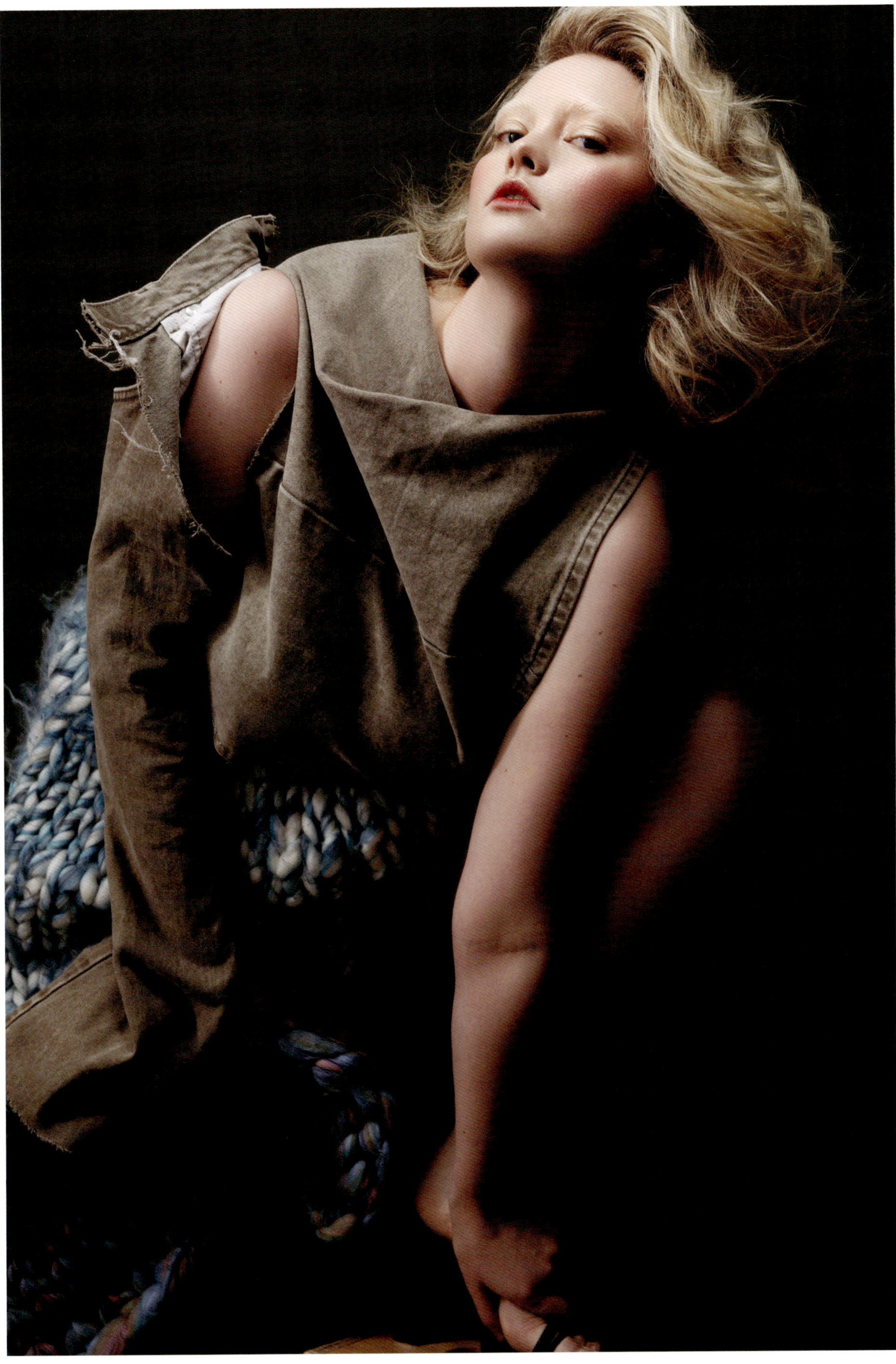

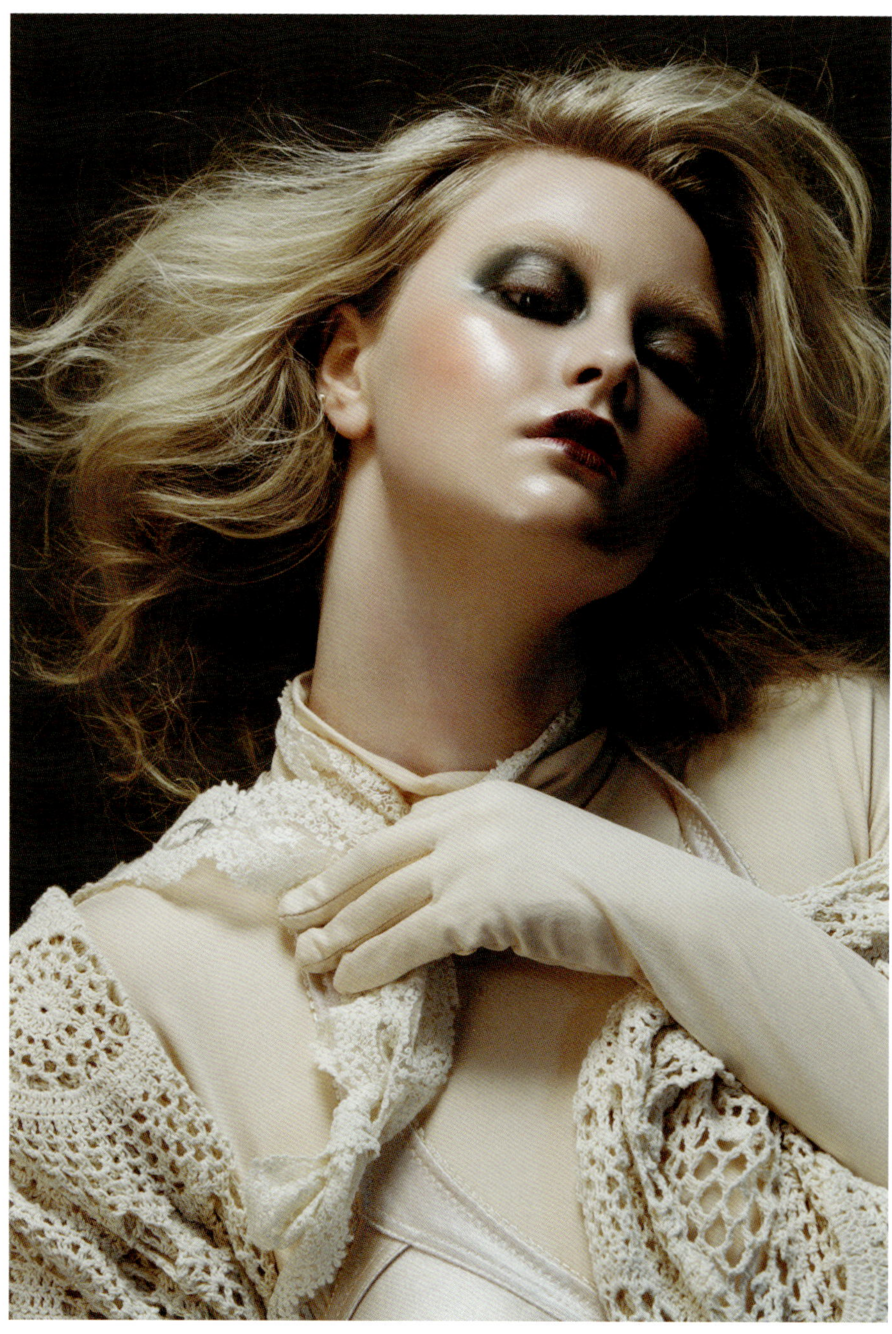

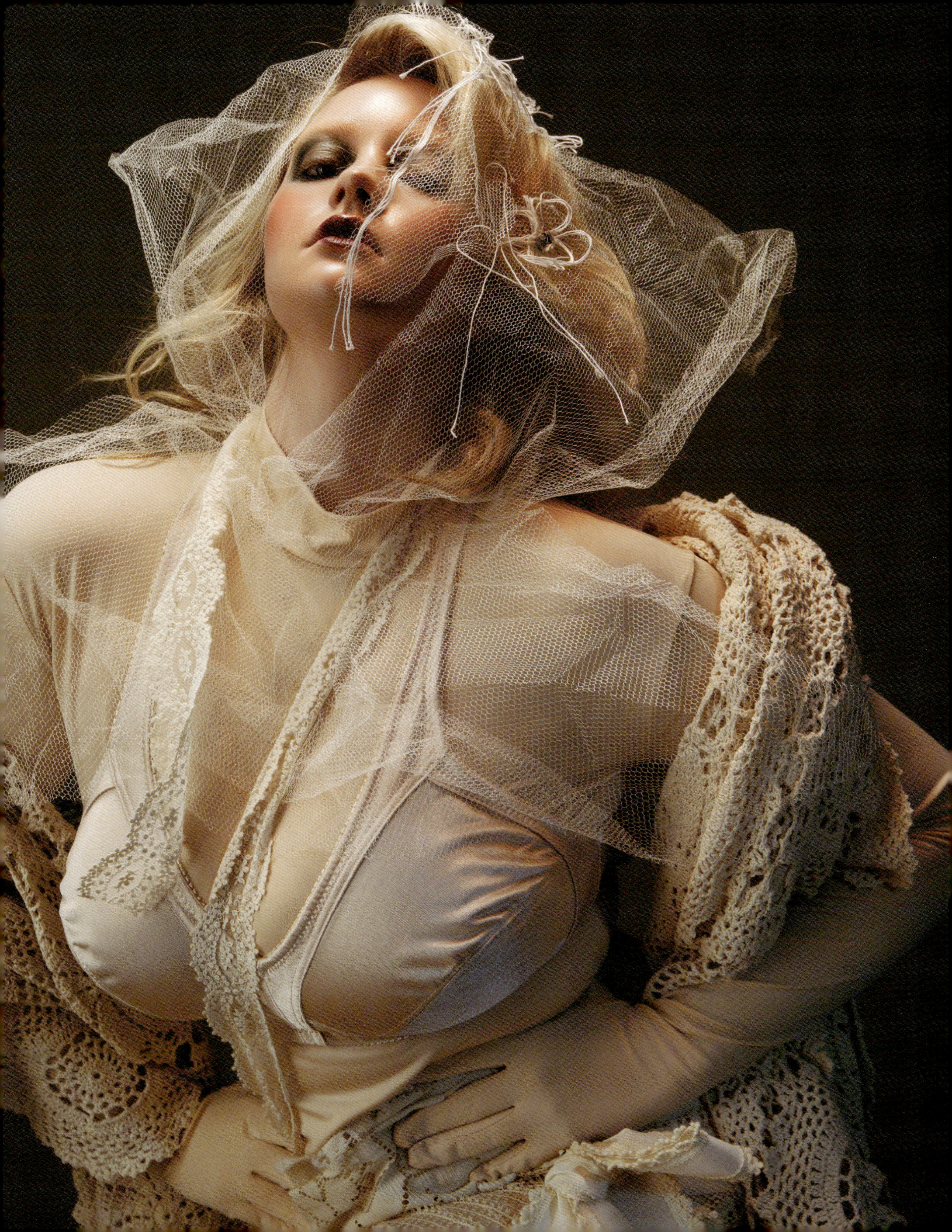

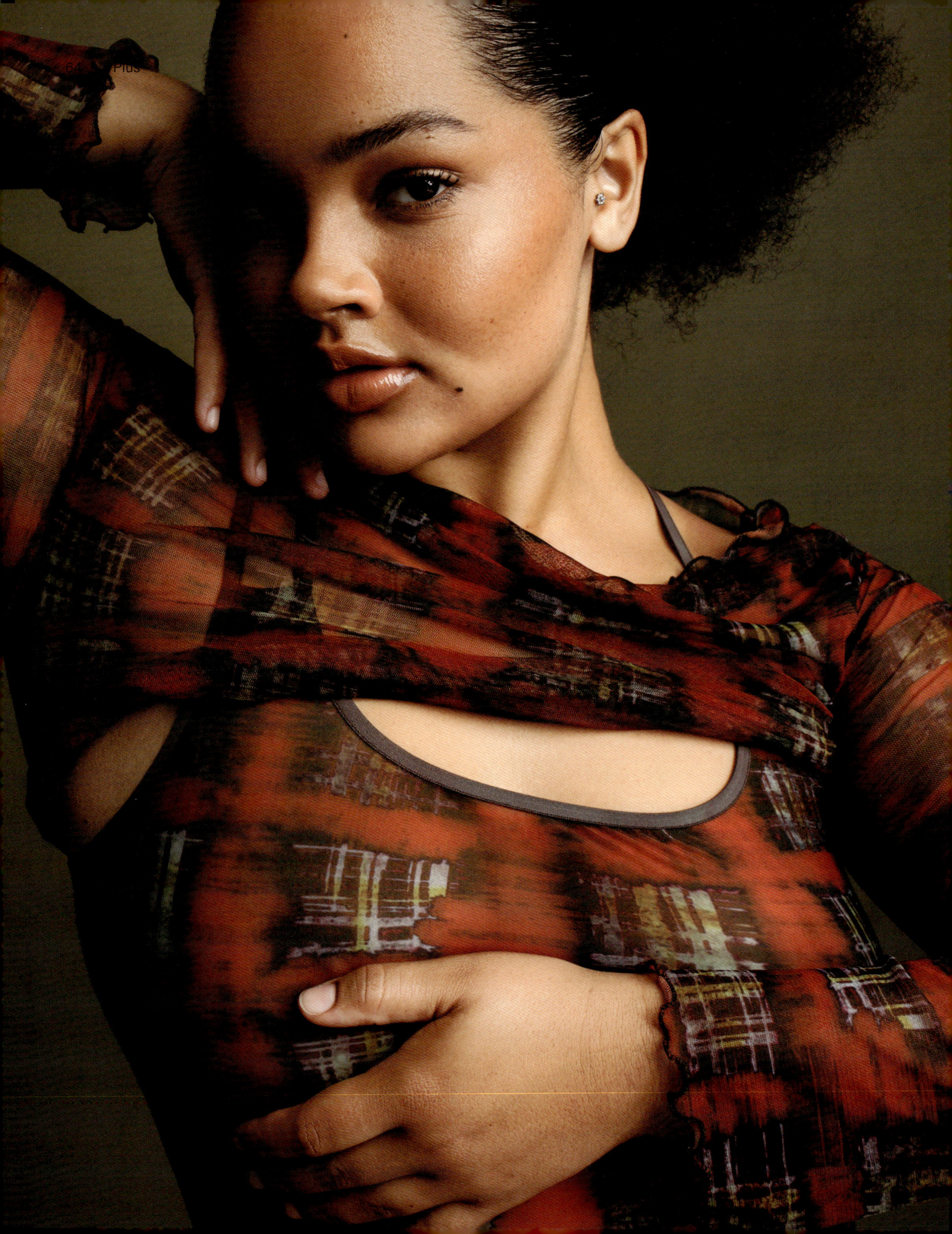

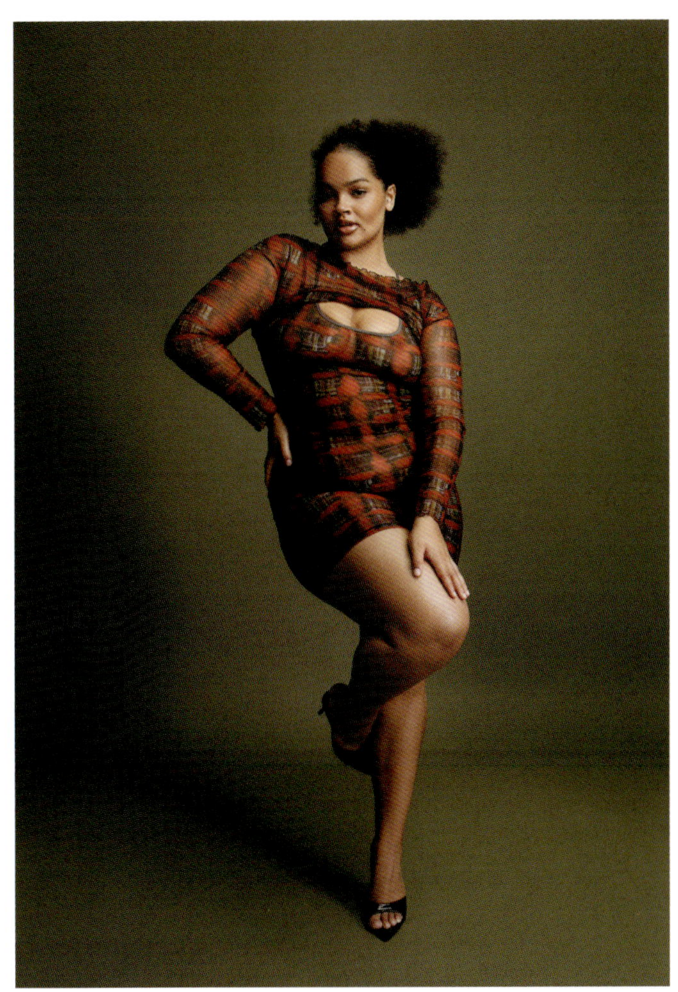

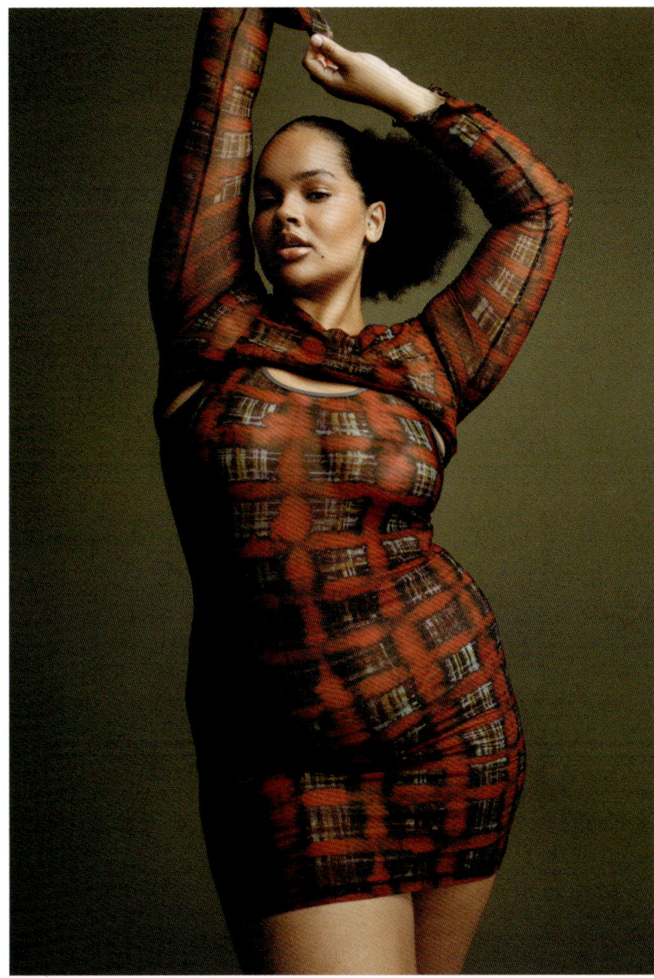

Aylah Karine wears KNWLS.

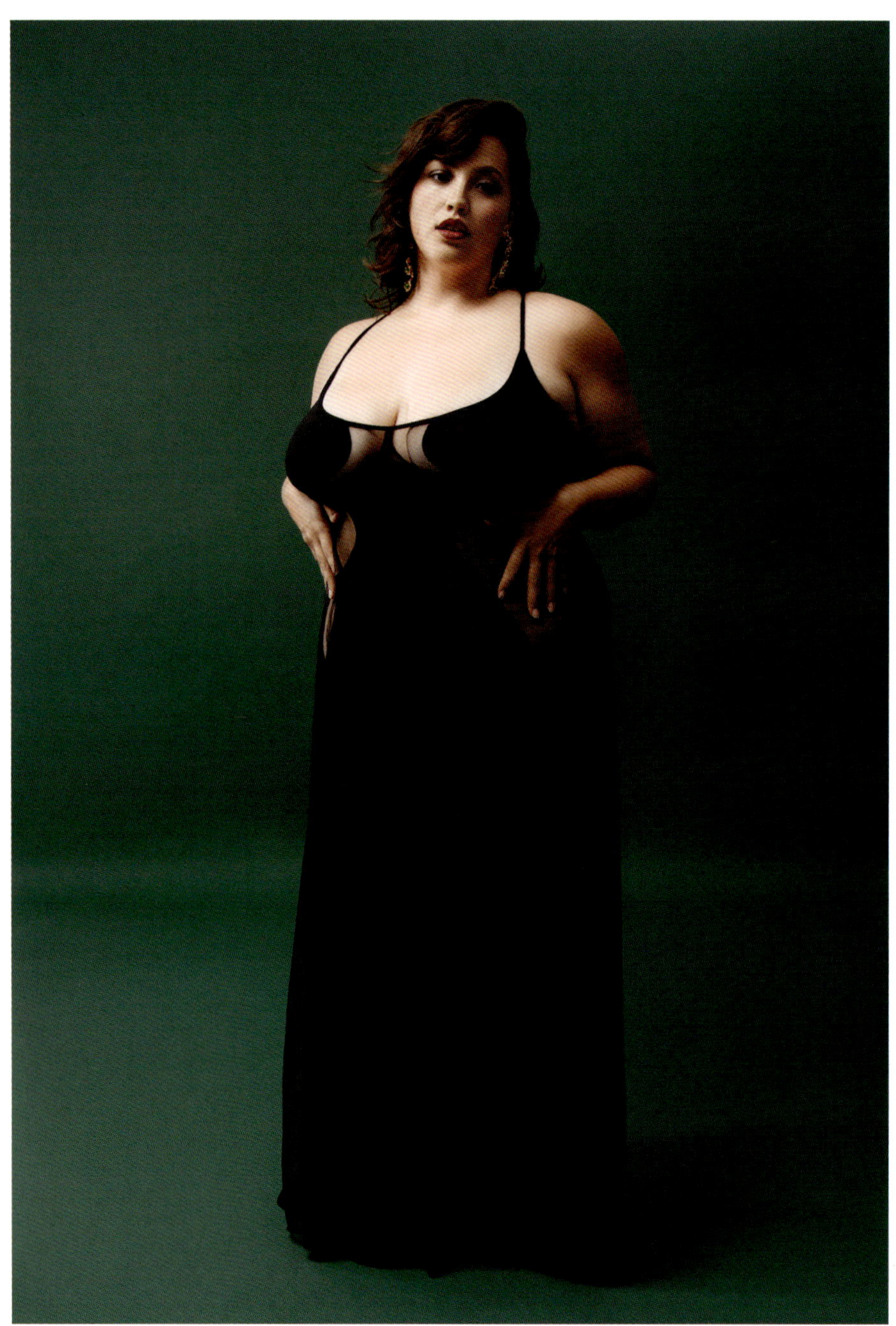

Sam Welsch wears Thistle and Spire dress; Alexis Bittar earrings.

Overleaf: Roseline Lawrence wears Never Fully Dressed dress.

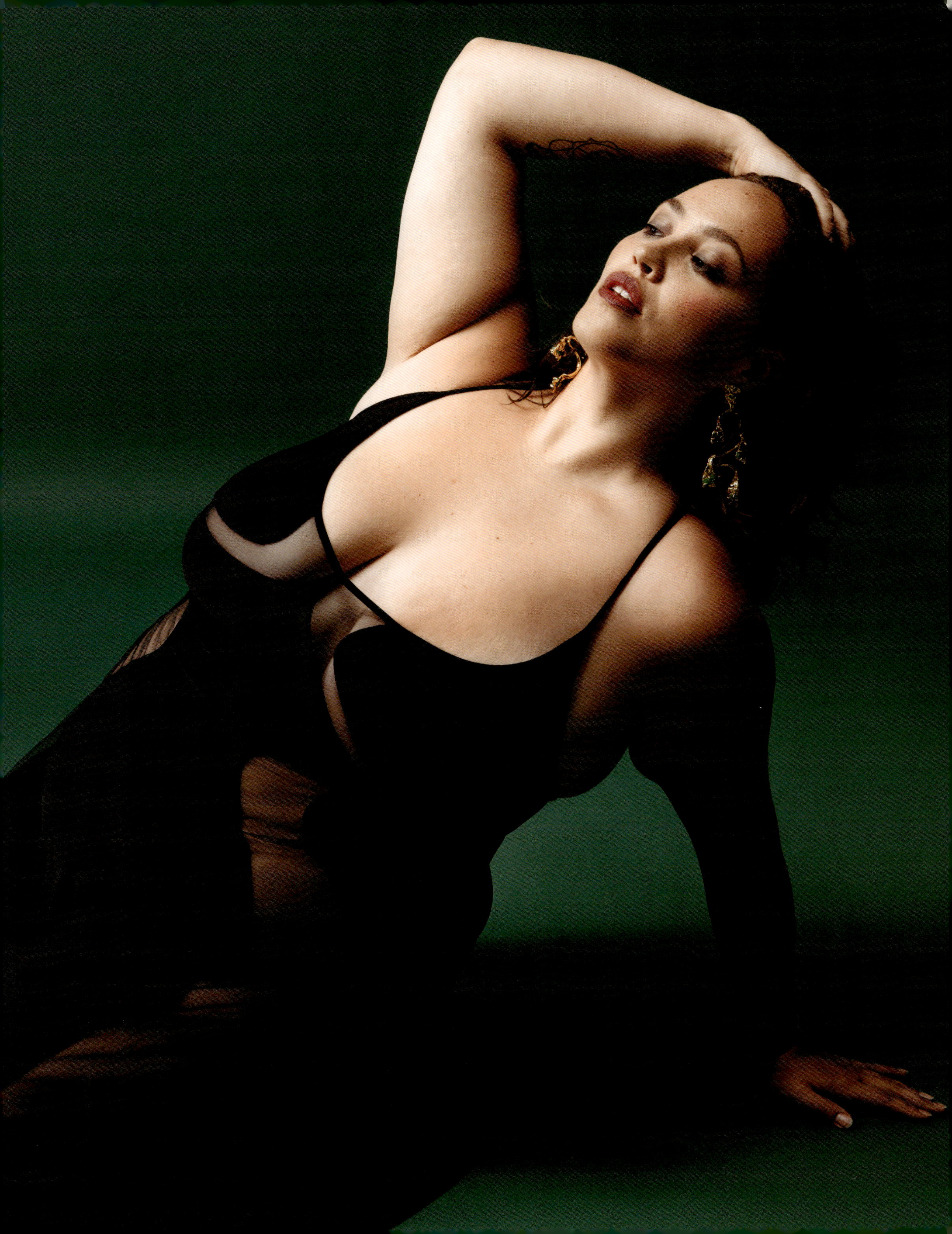

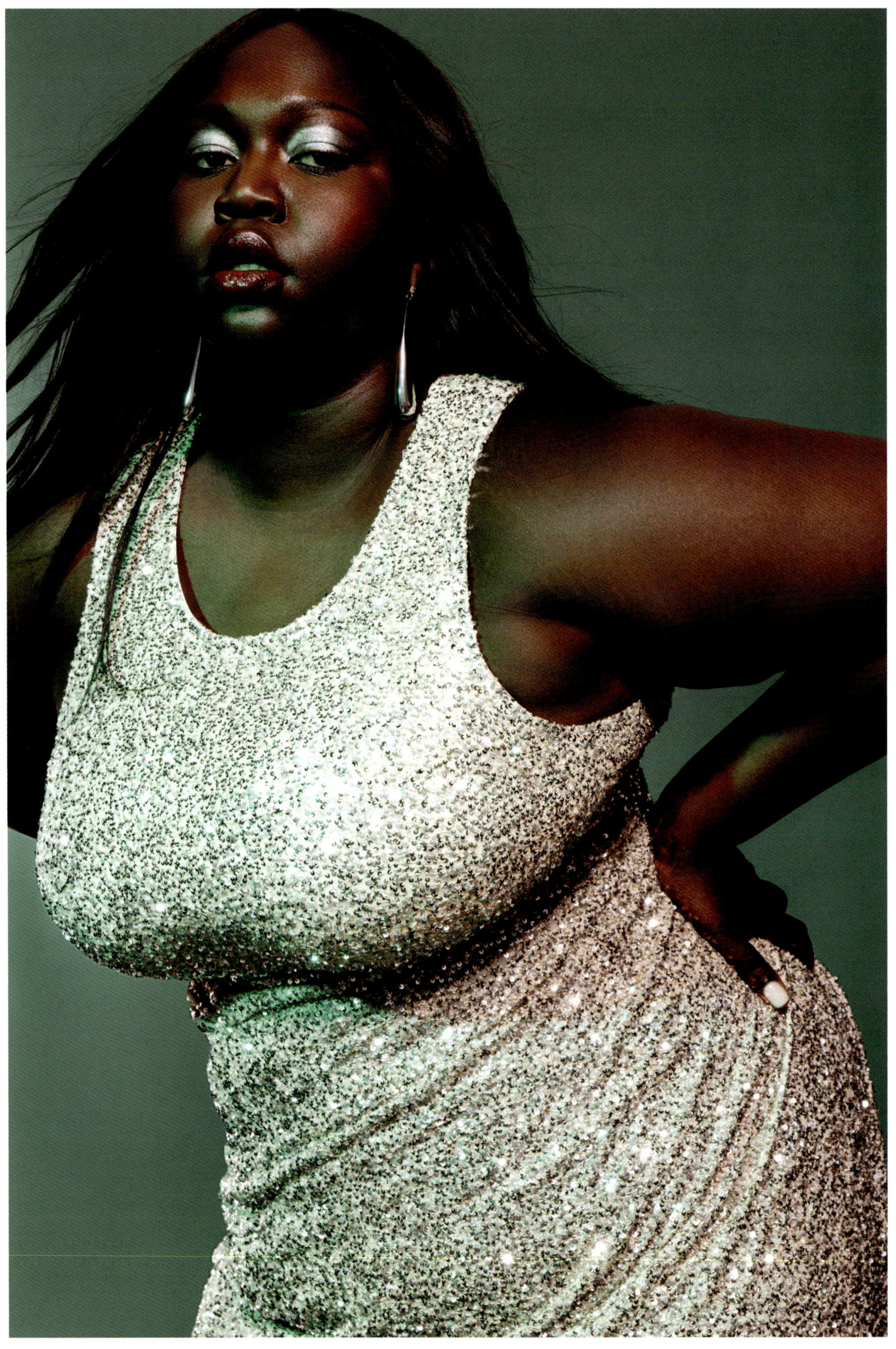

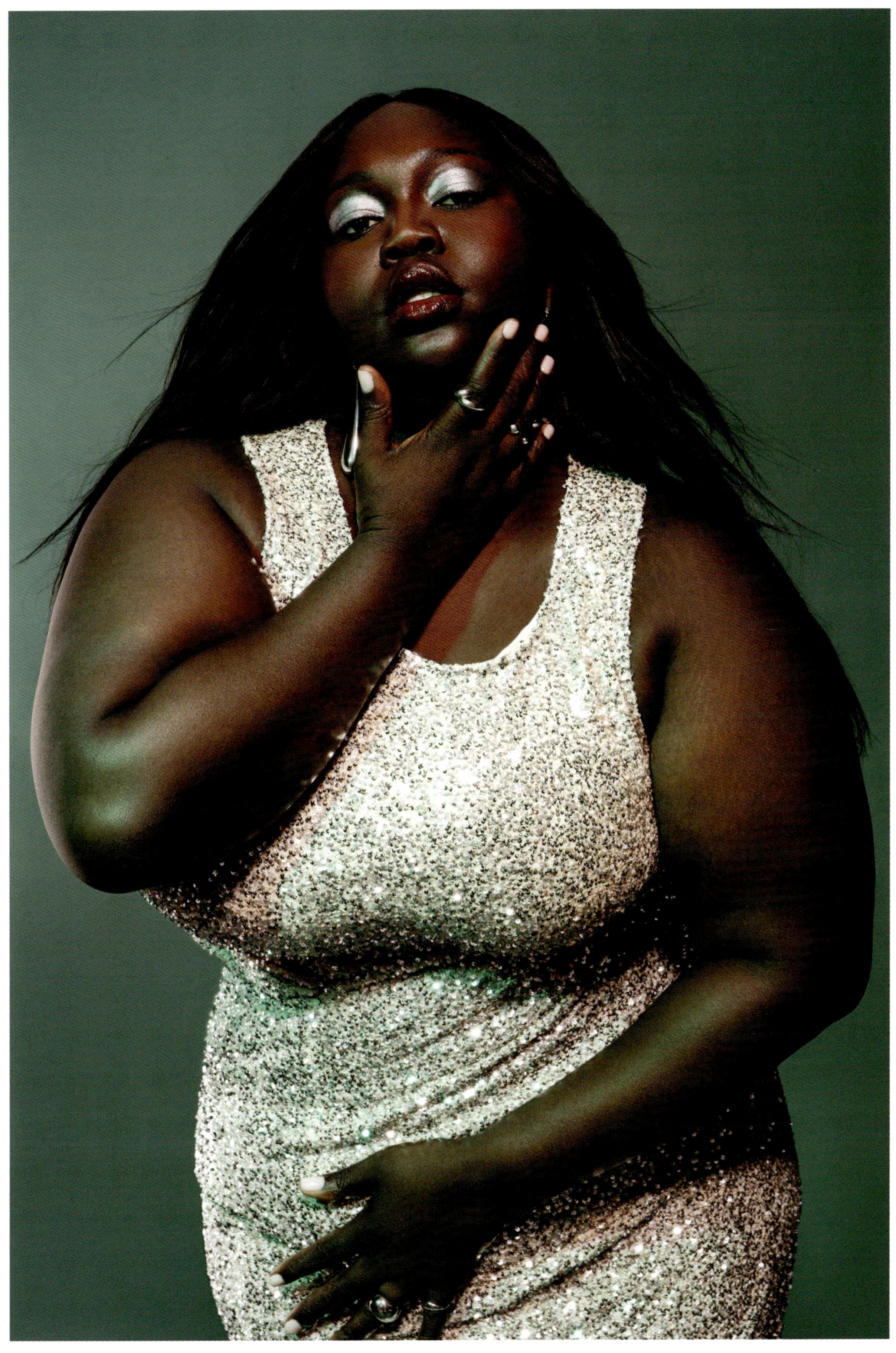

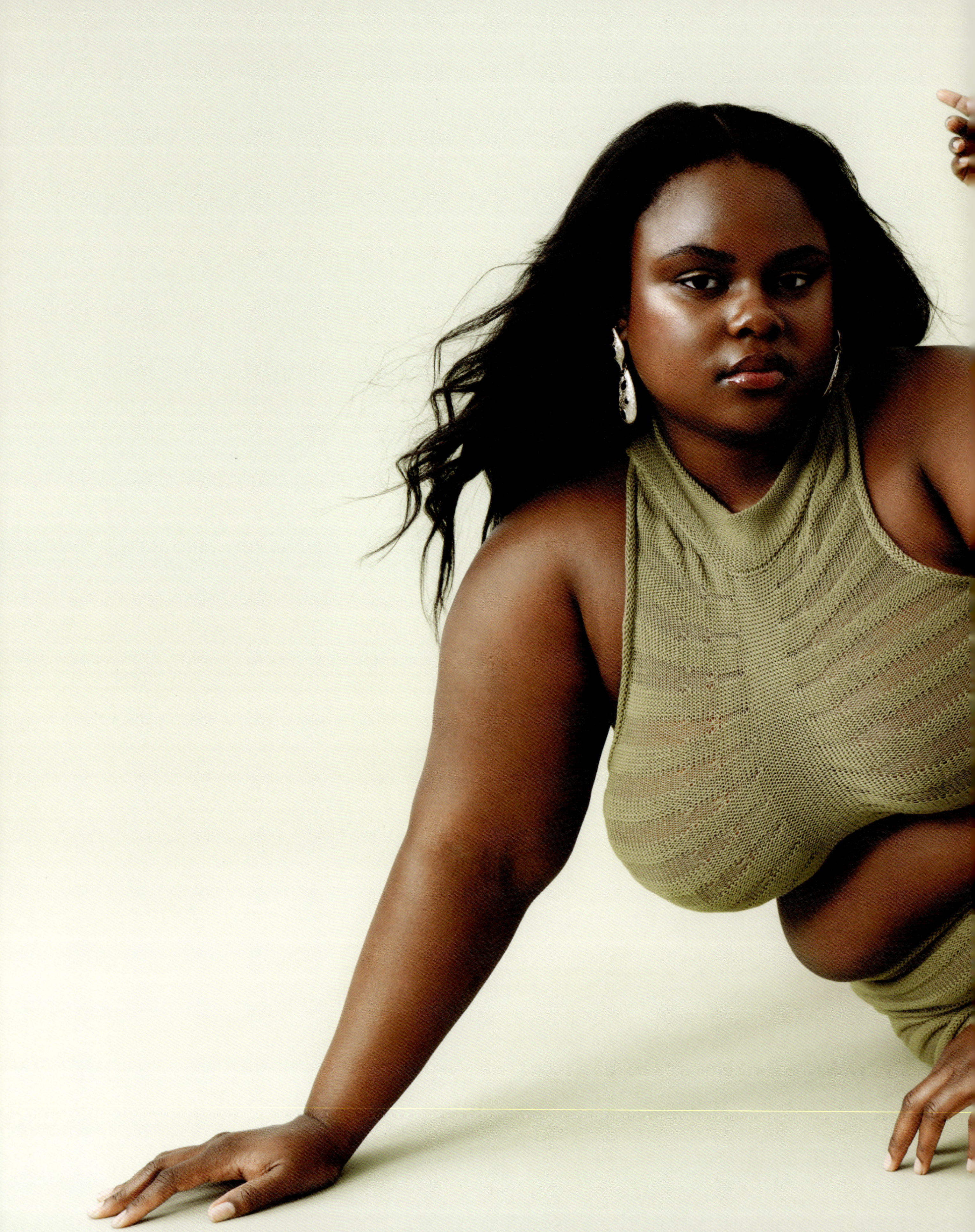

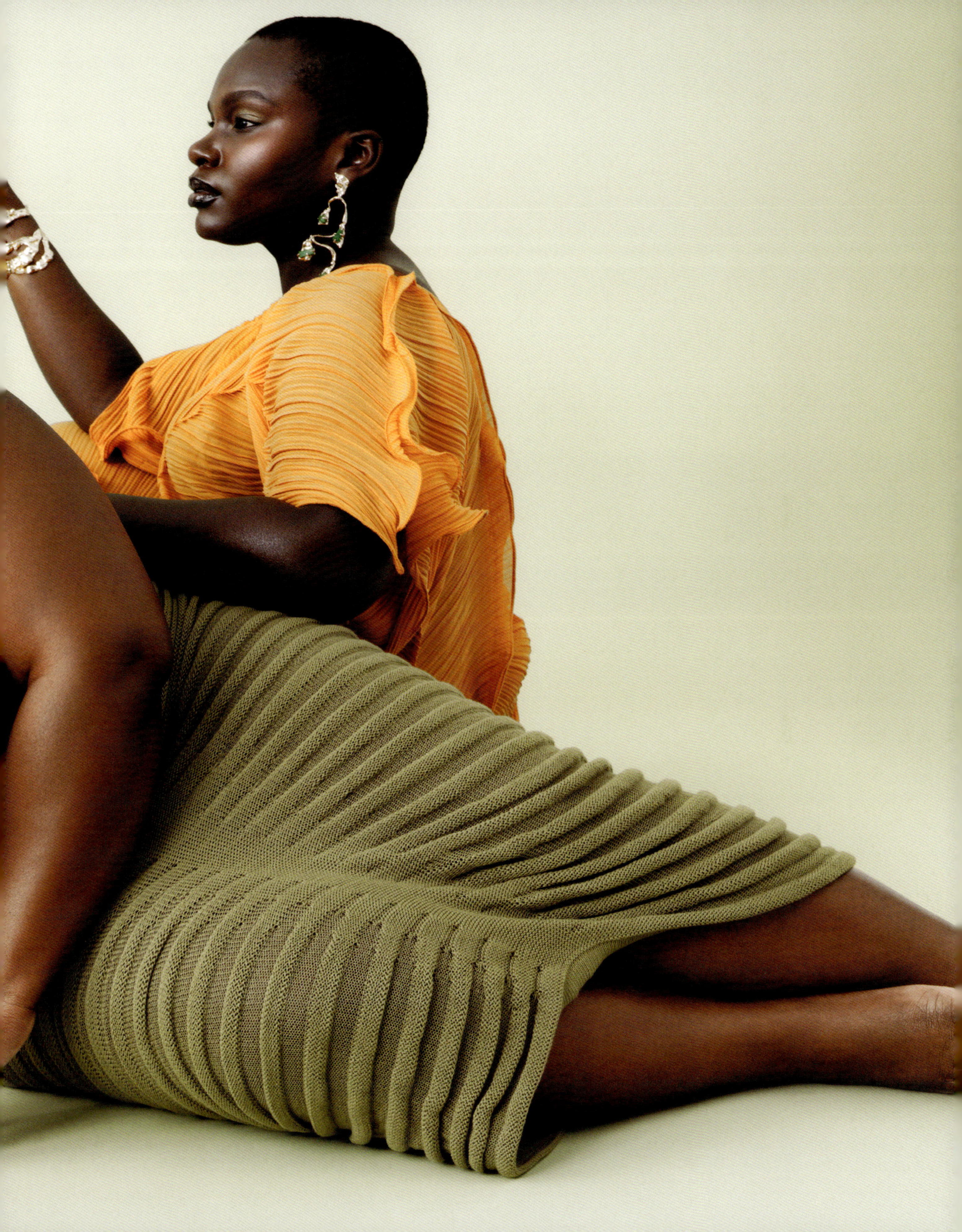

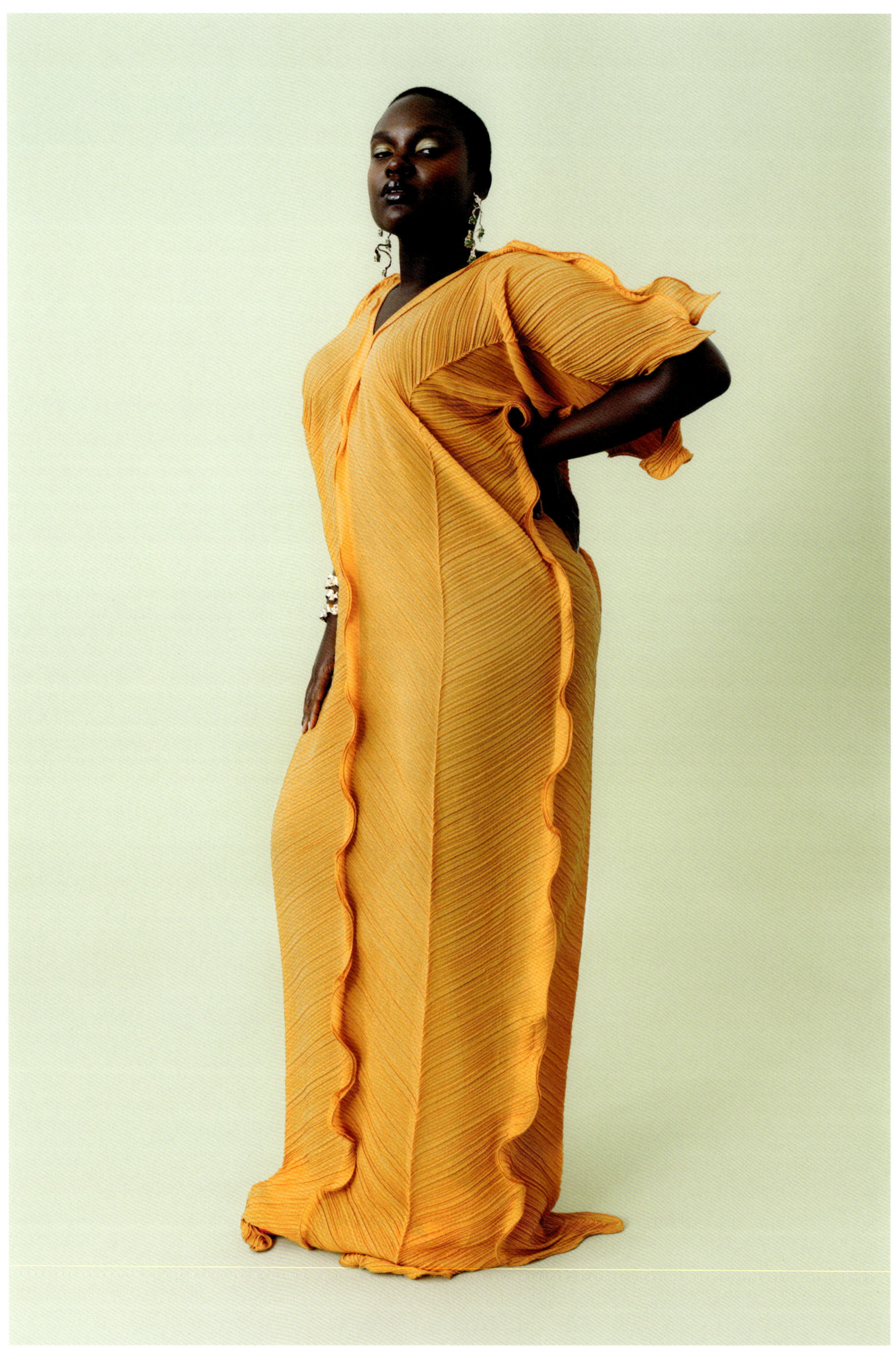

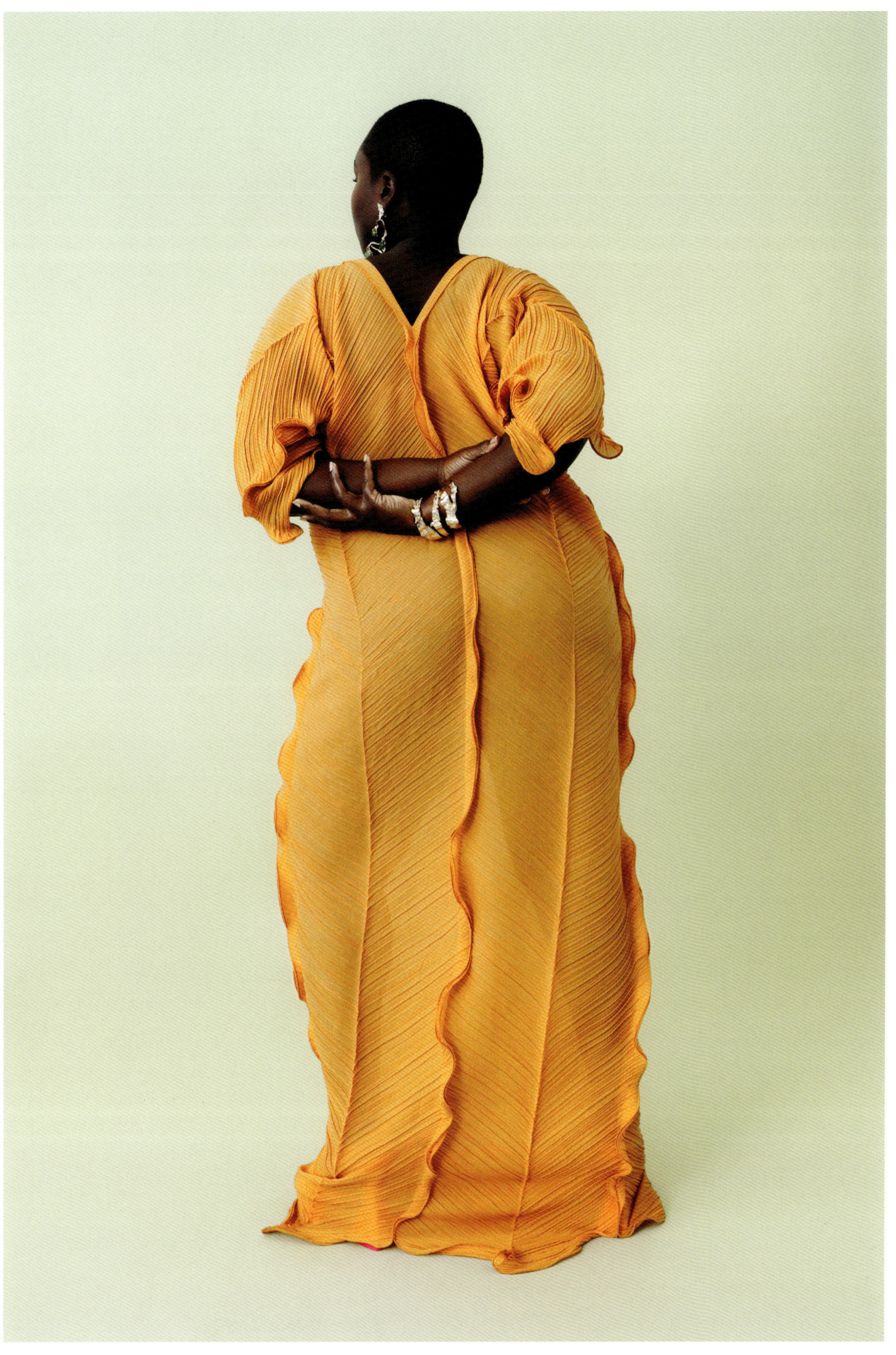

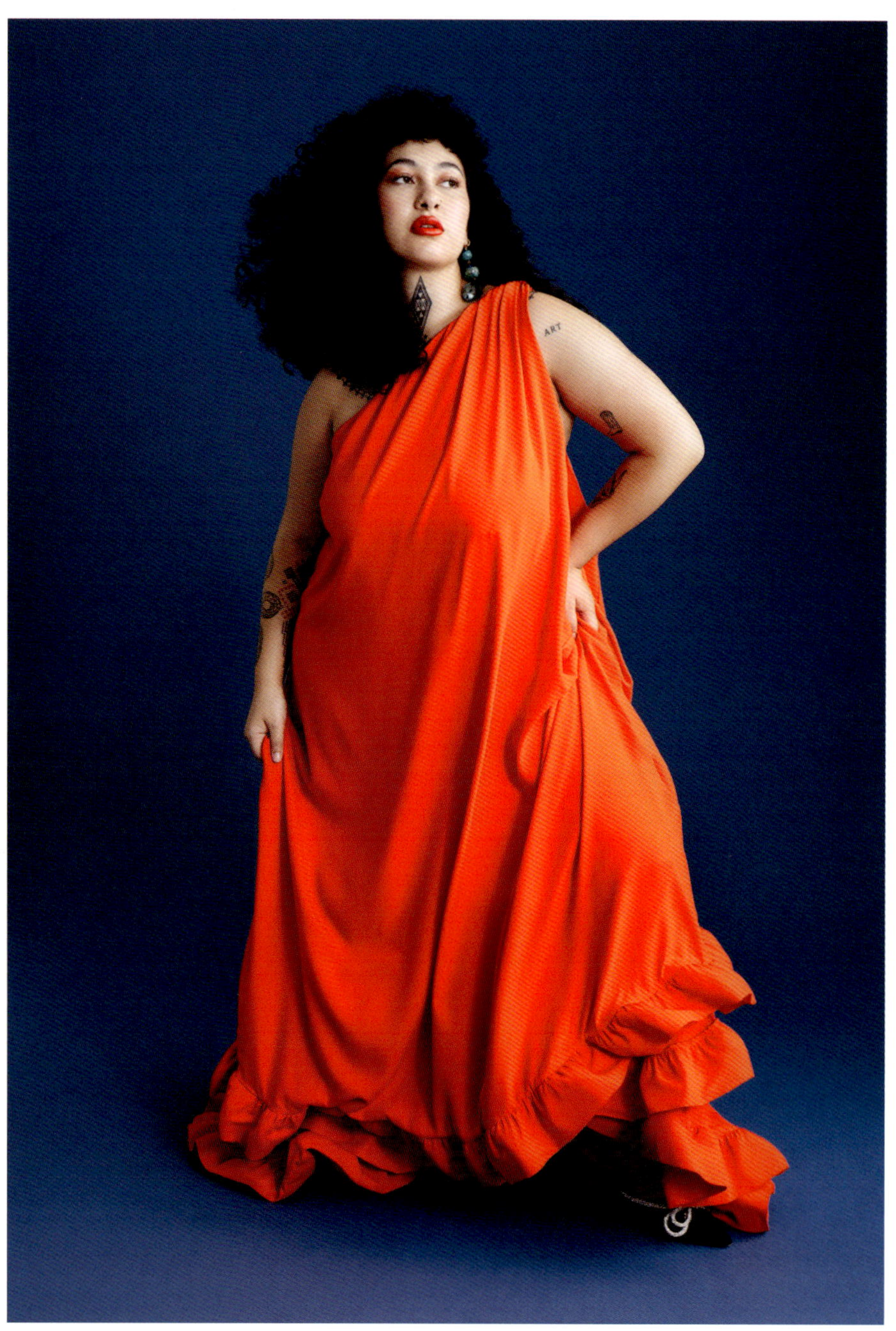

Pages 70–73: Manni Amoah (left) and PJ Nyambok (right) wear pieces from Lydia Hudgens' closet; PJ wears Alexis Bittar earrings.

Ashley Emiko wears Eloquii.

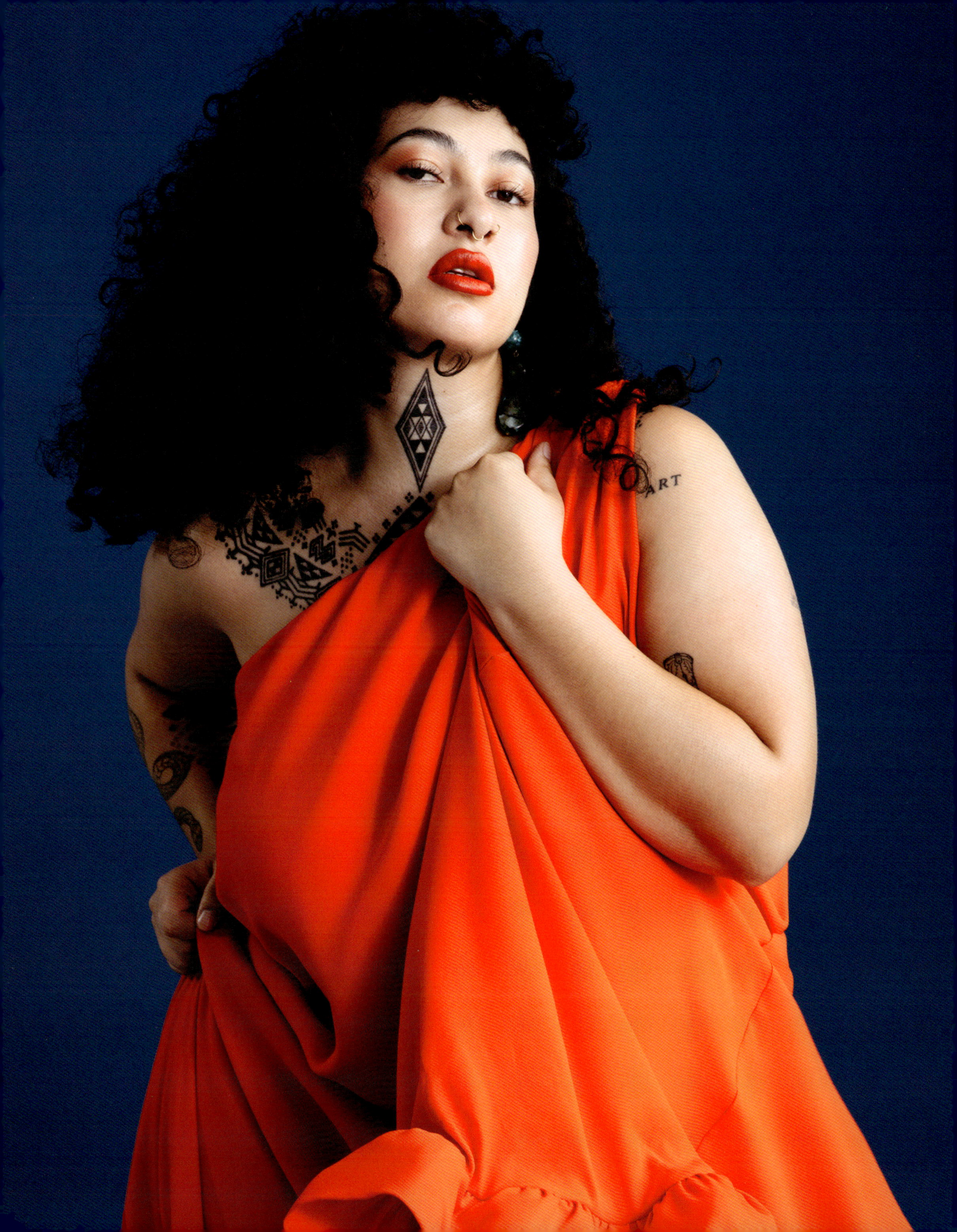

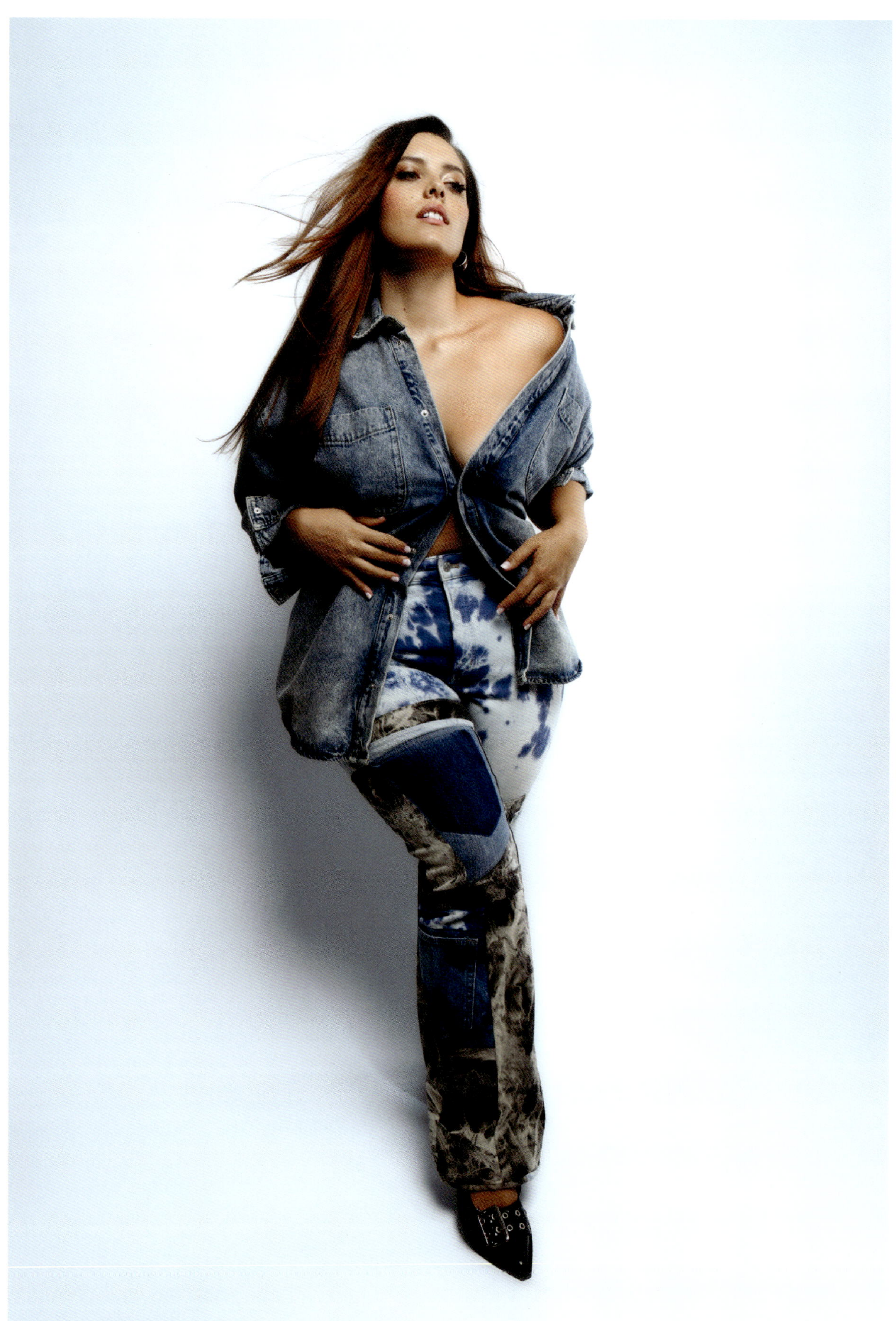

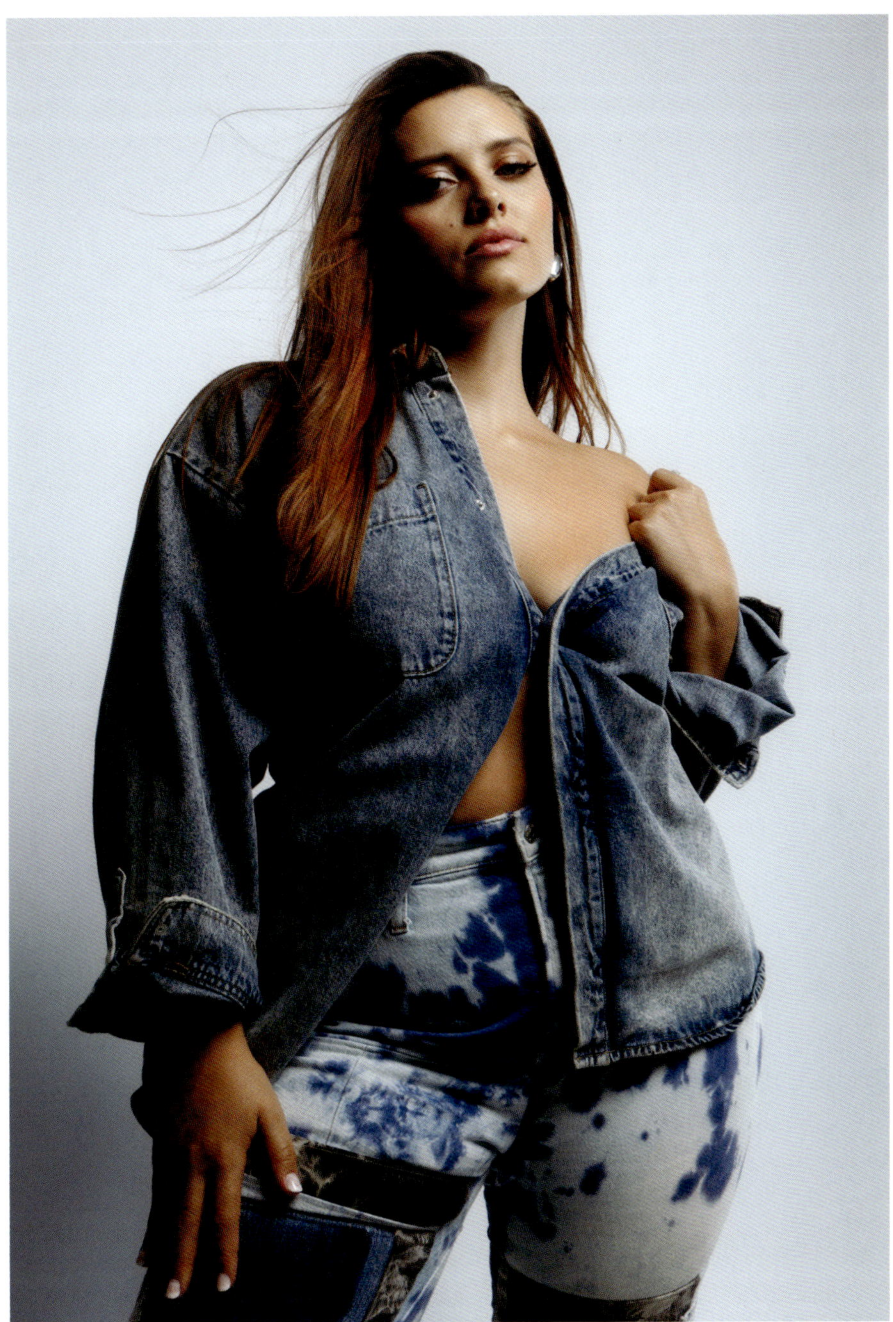

Wren Parker wears Good American jacket;
Syd Brisco jeans; Ganni shoes.

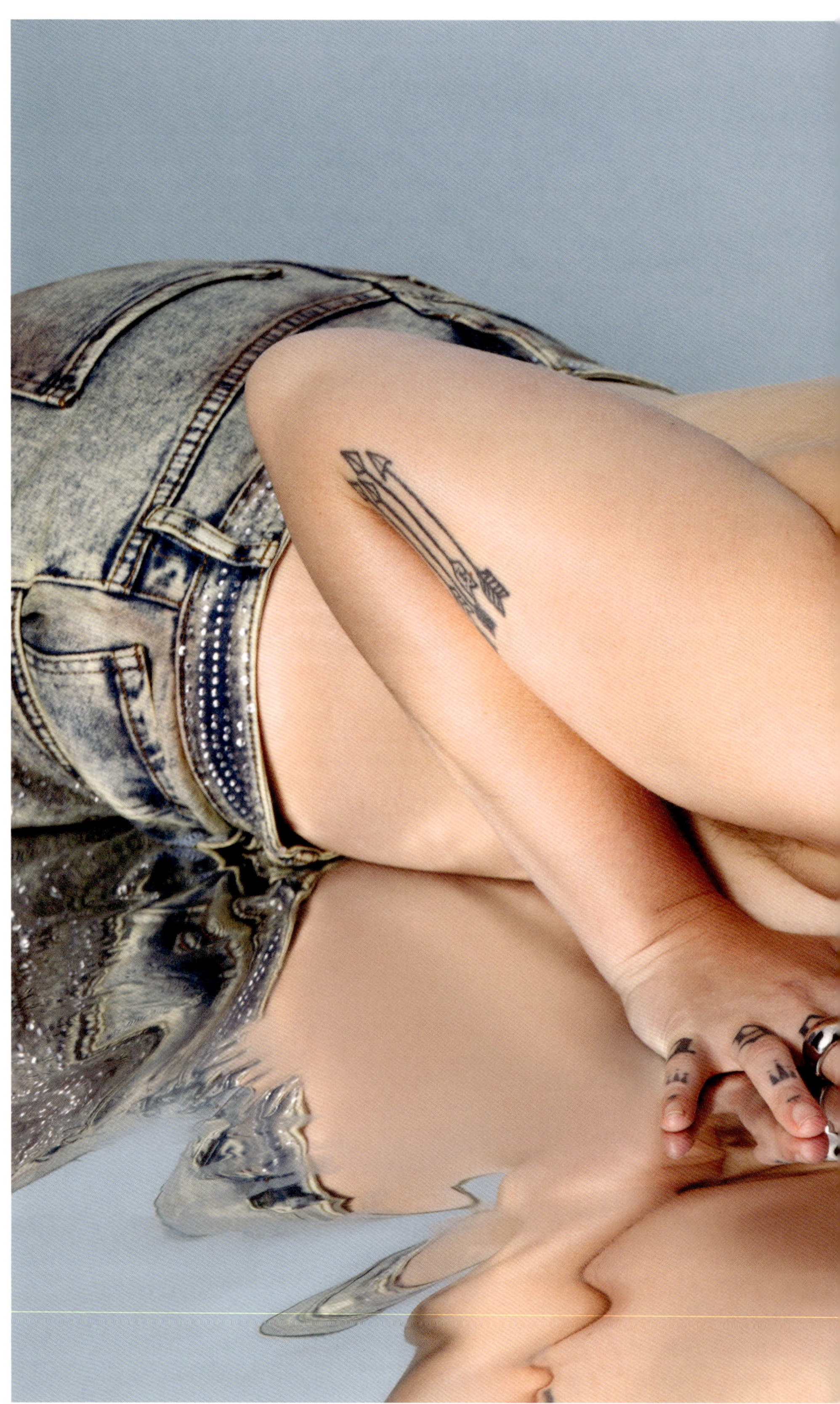

Apollo wears denim set from Lydia Hudgens' closet; AREA earrings.

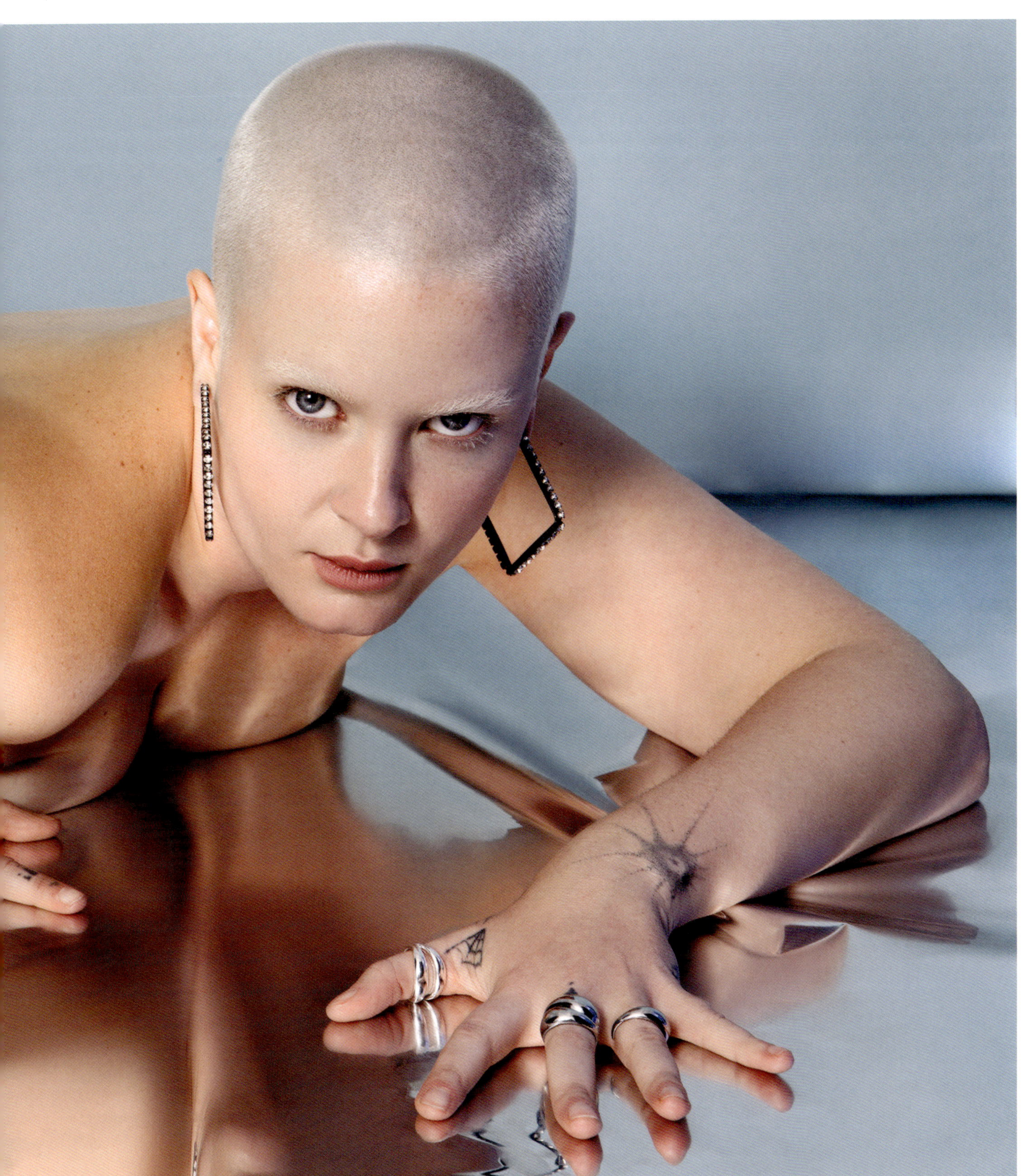

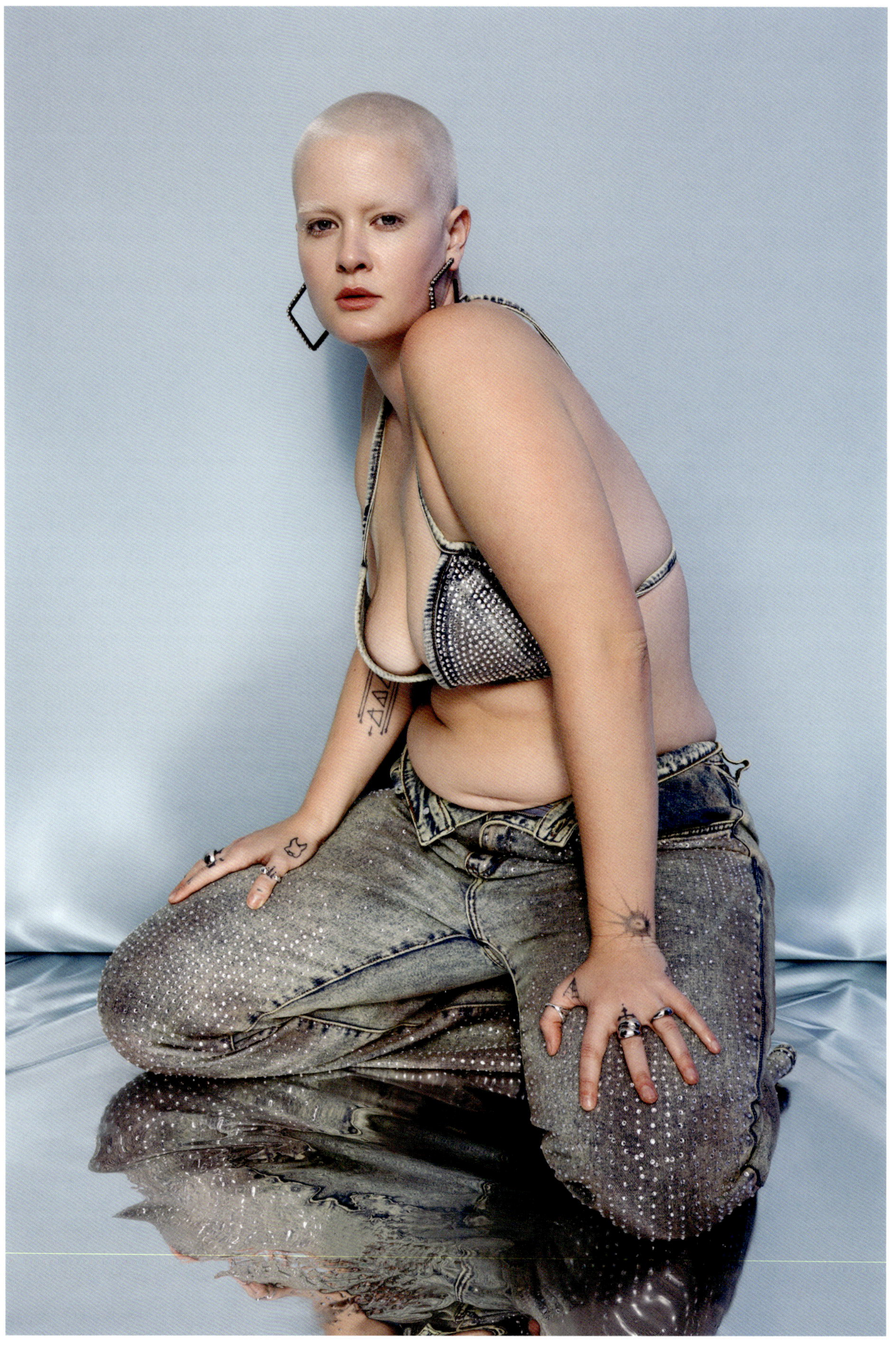

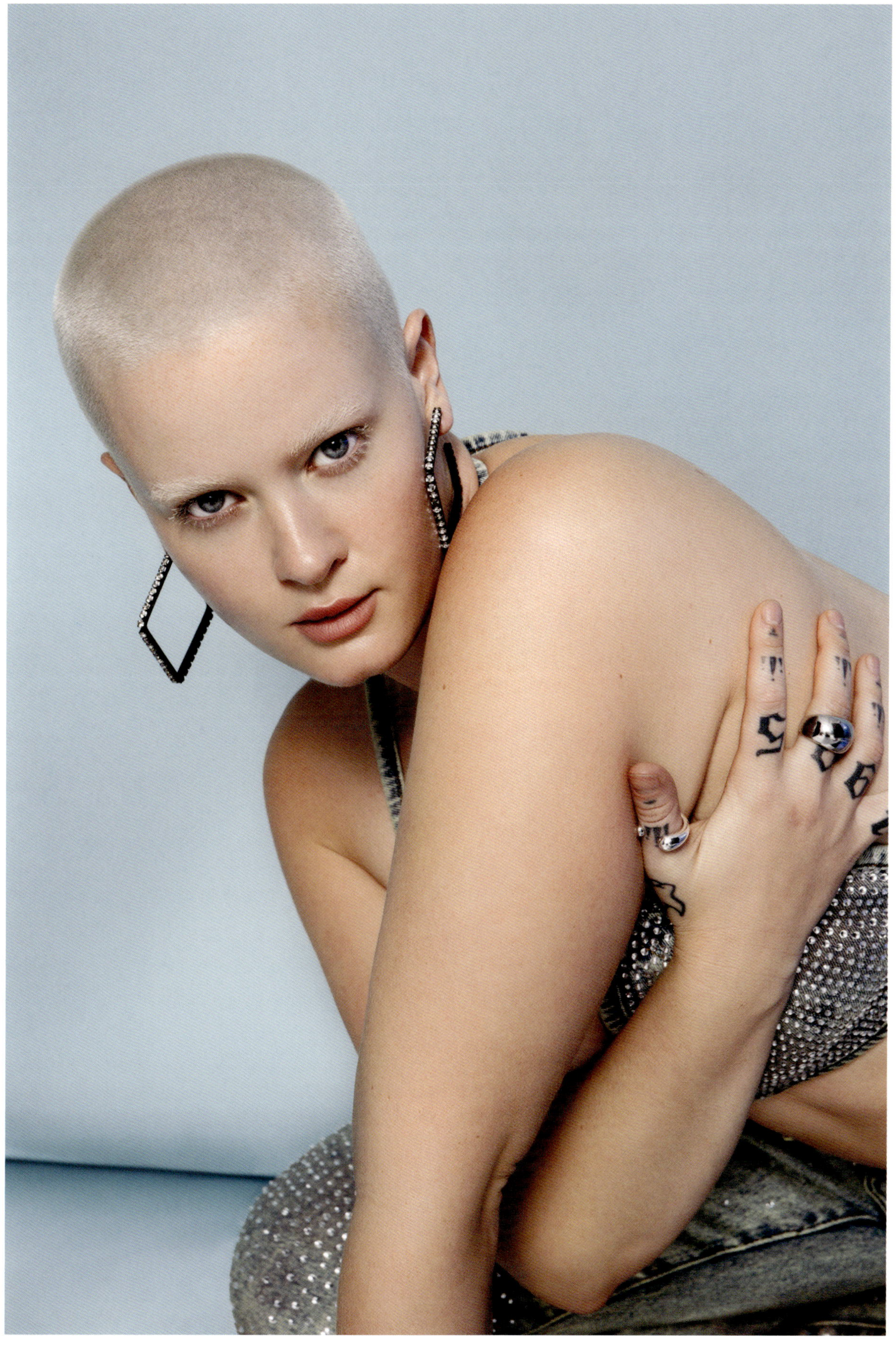

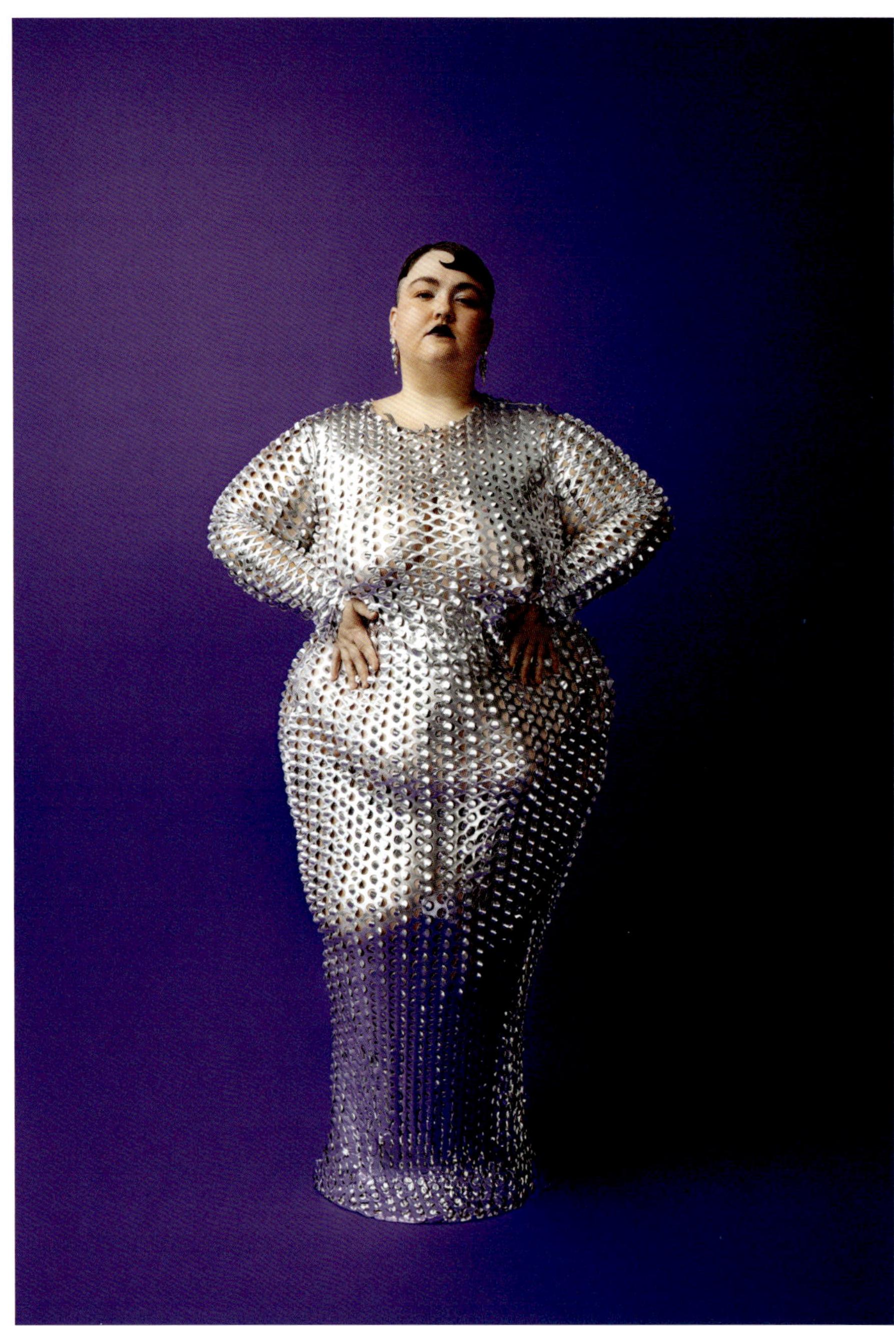

Jordan Underwood wears dress from Lydia Hudgens' closet.

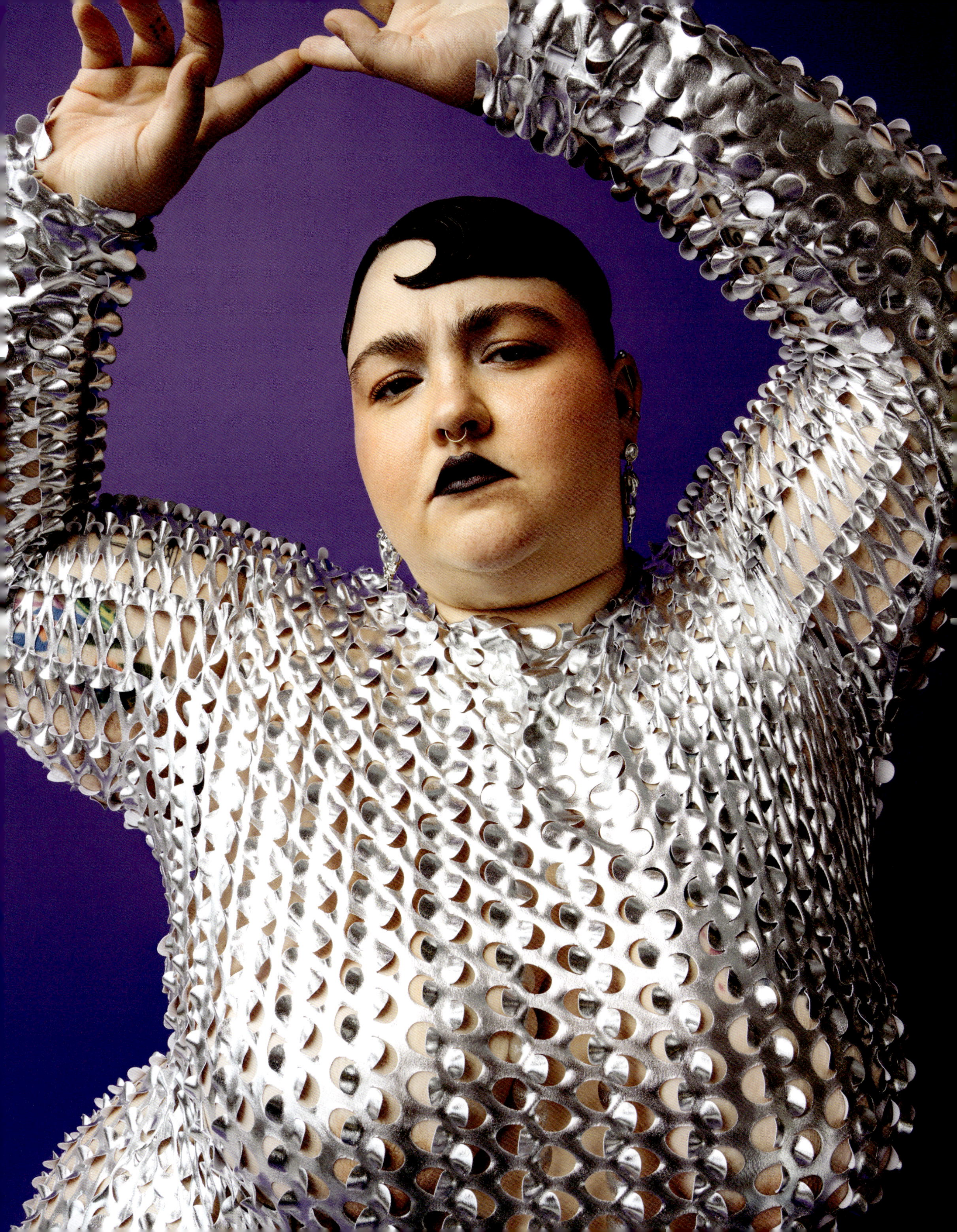

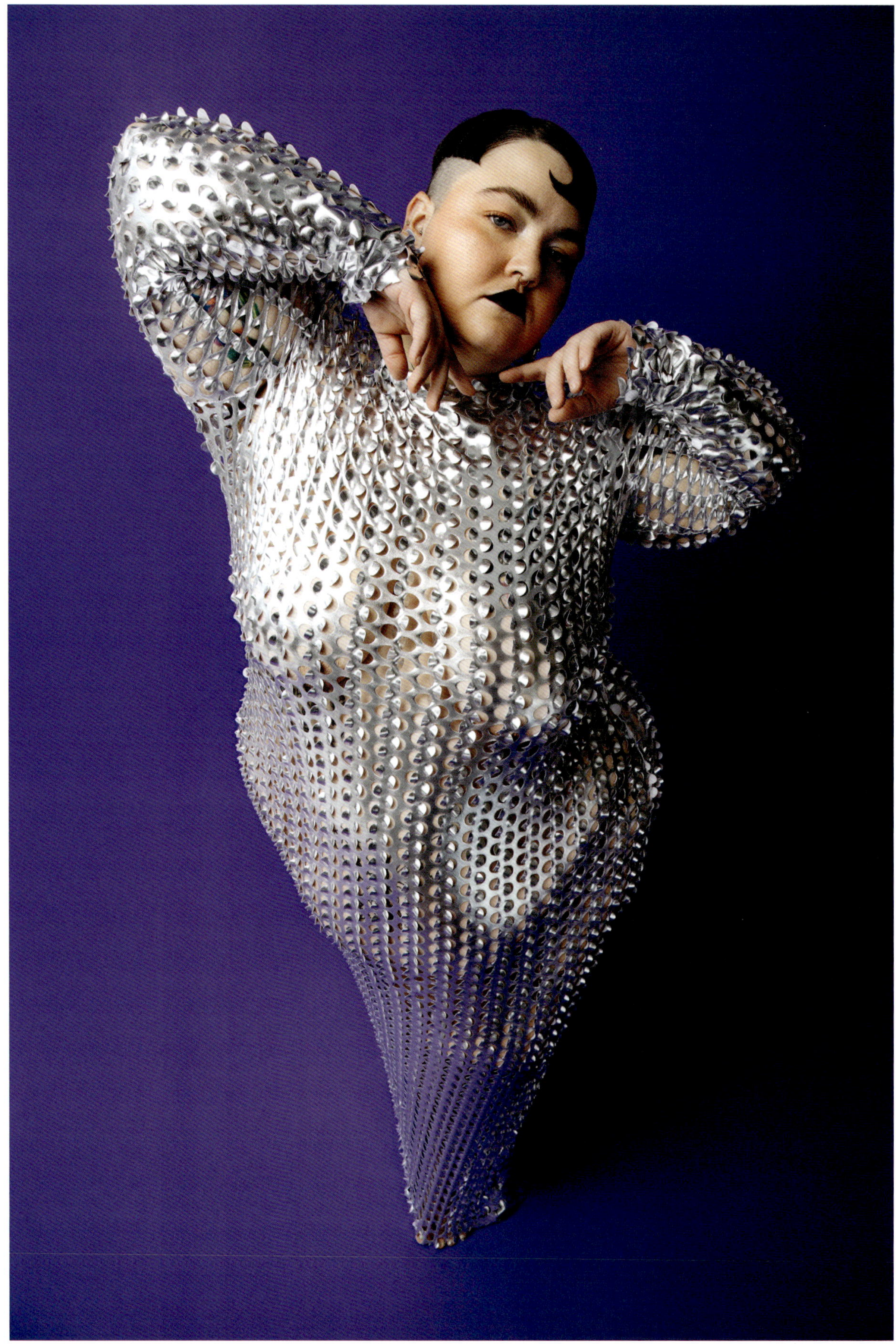

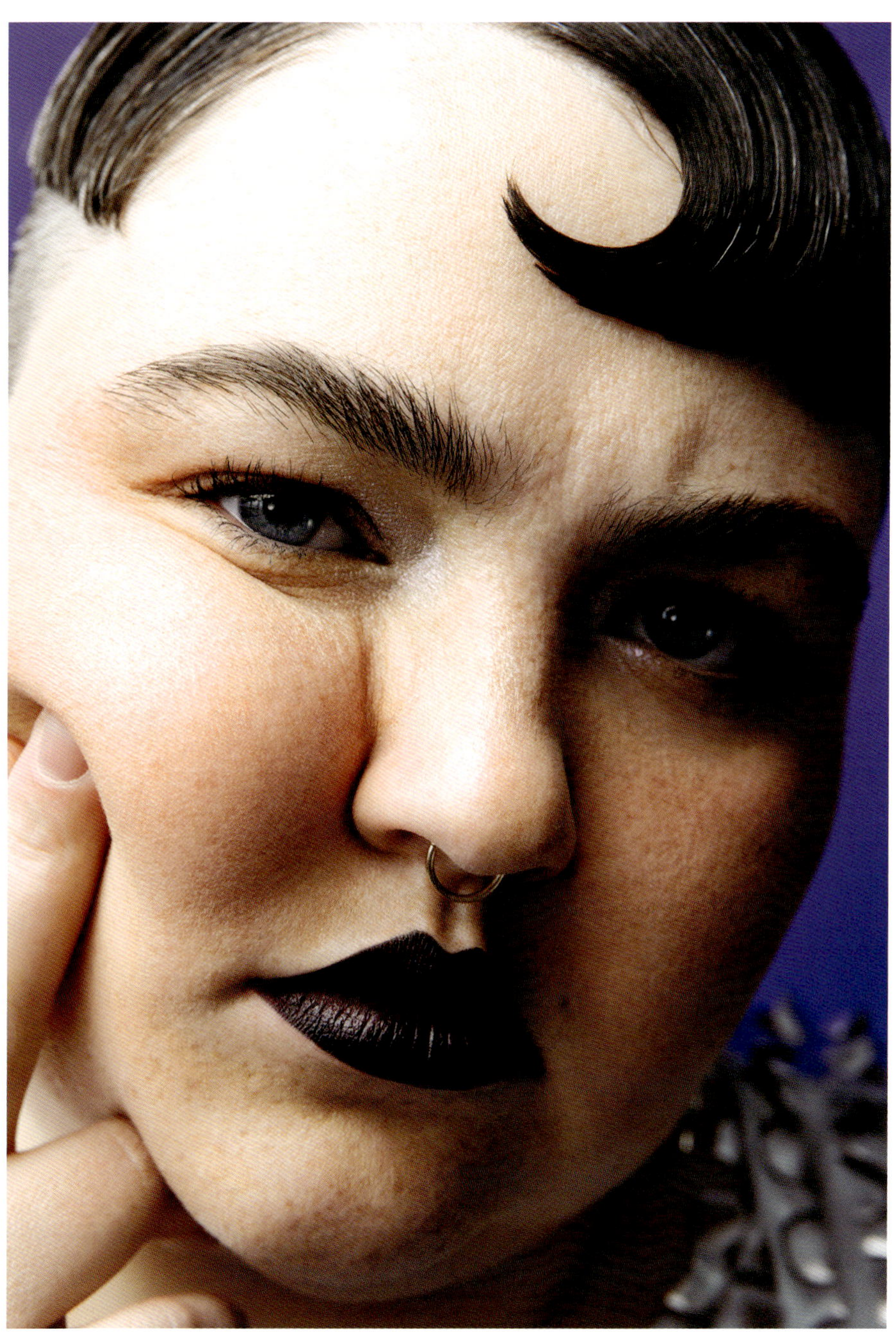

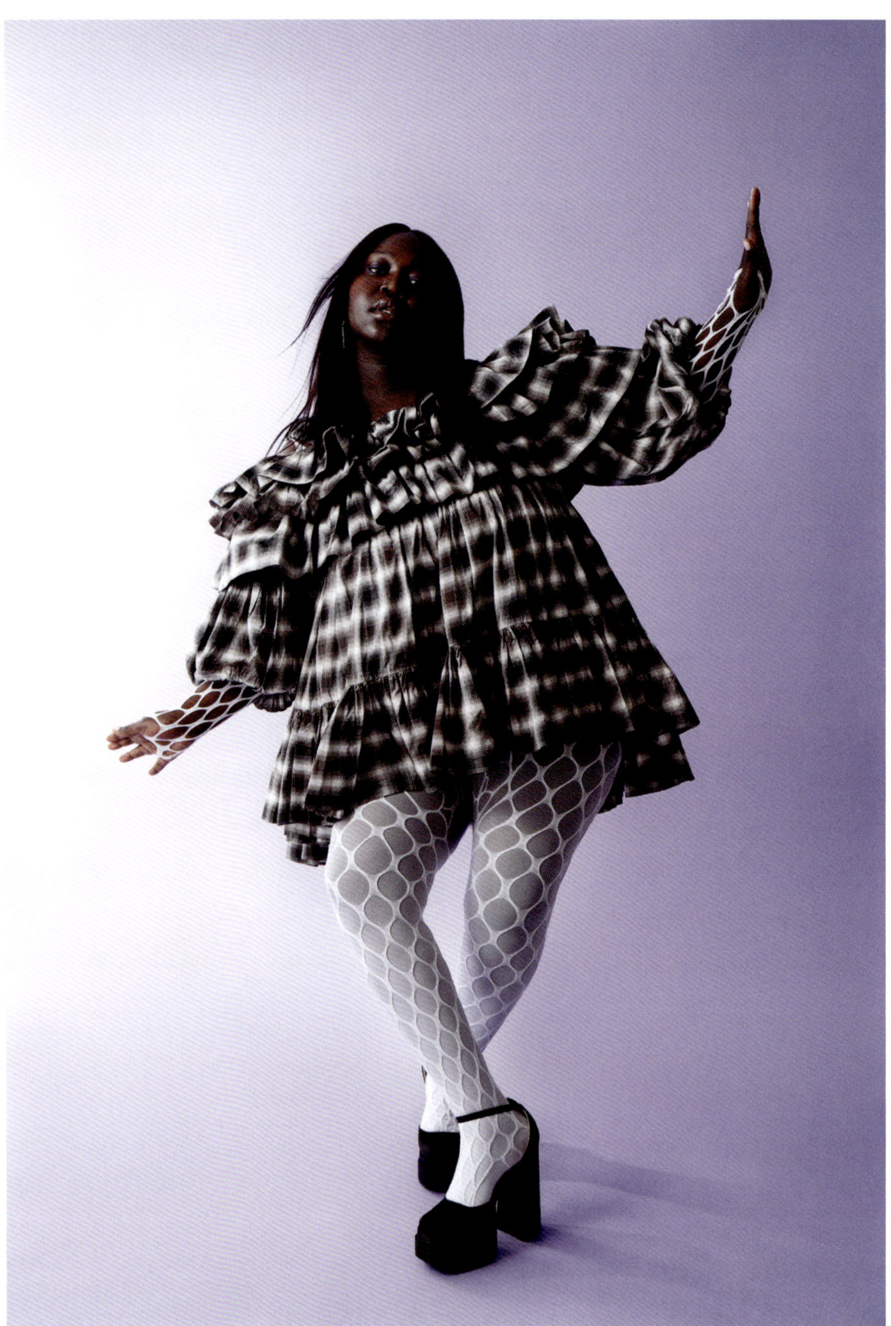

Roseline Lawrence wears Vaquera dress;
Area earrings.

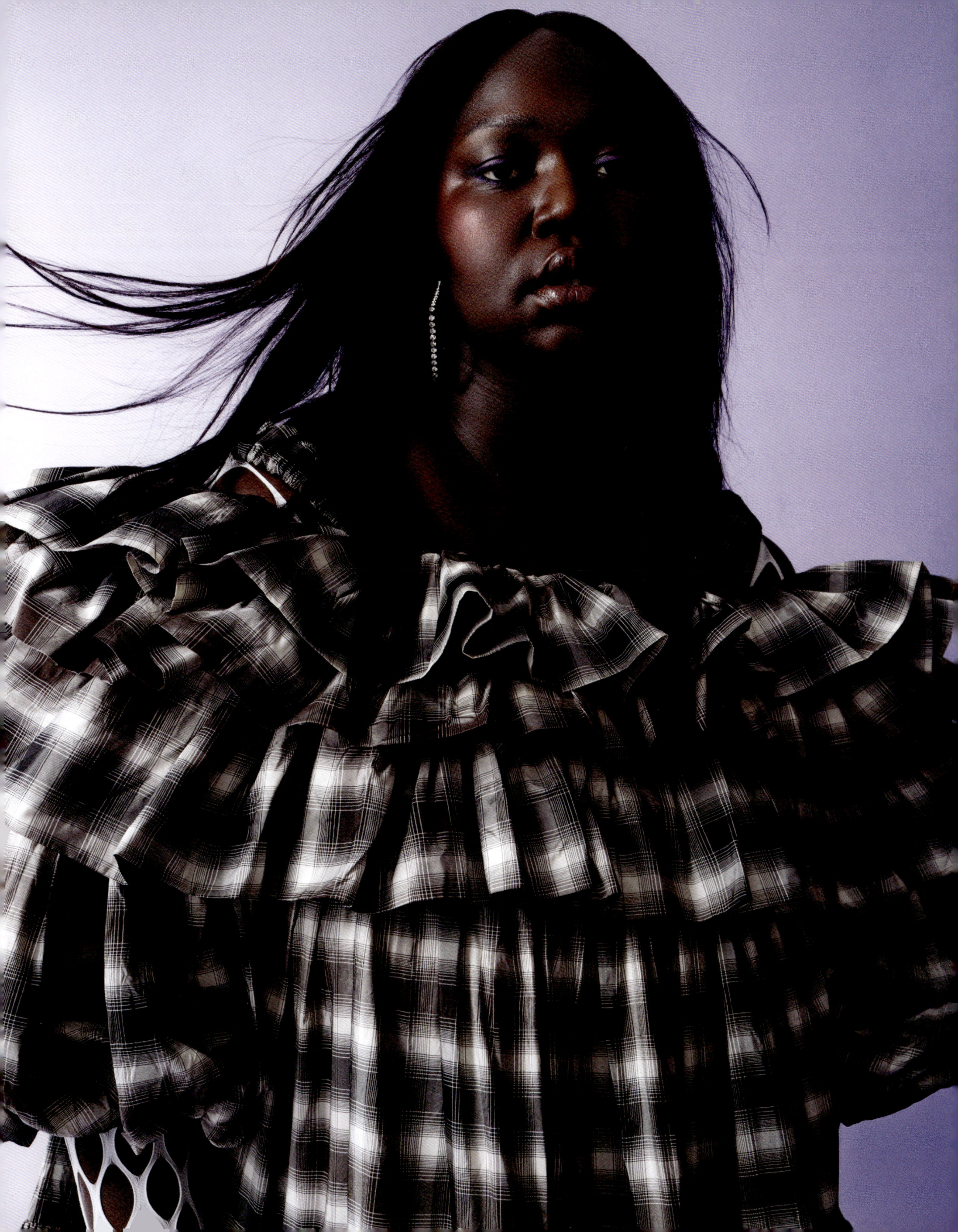

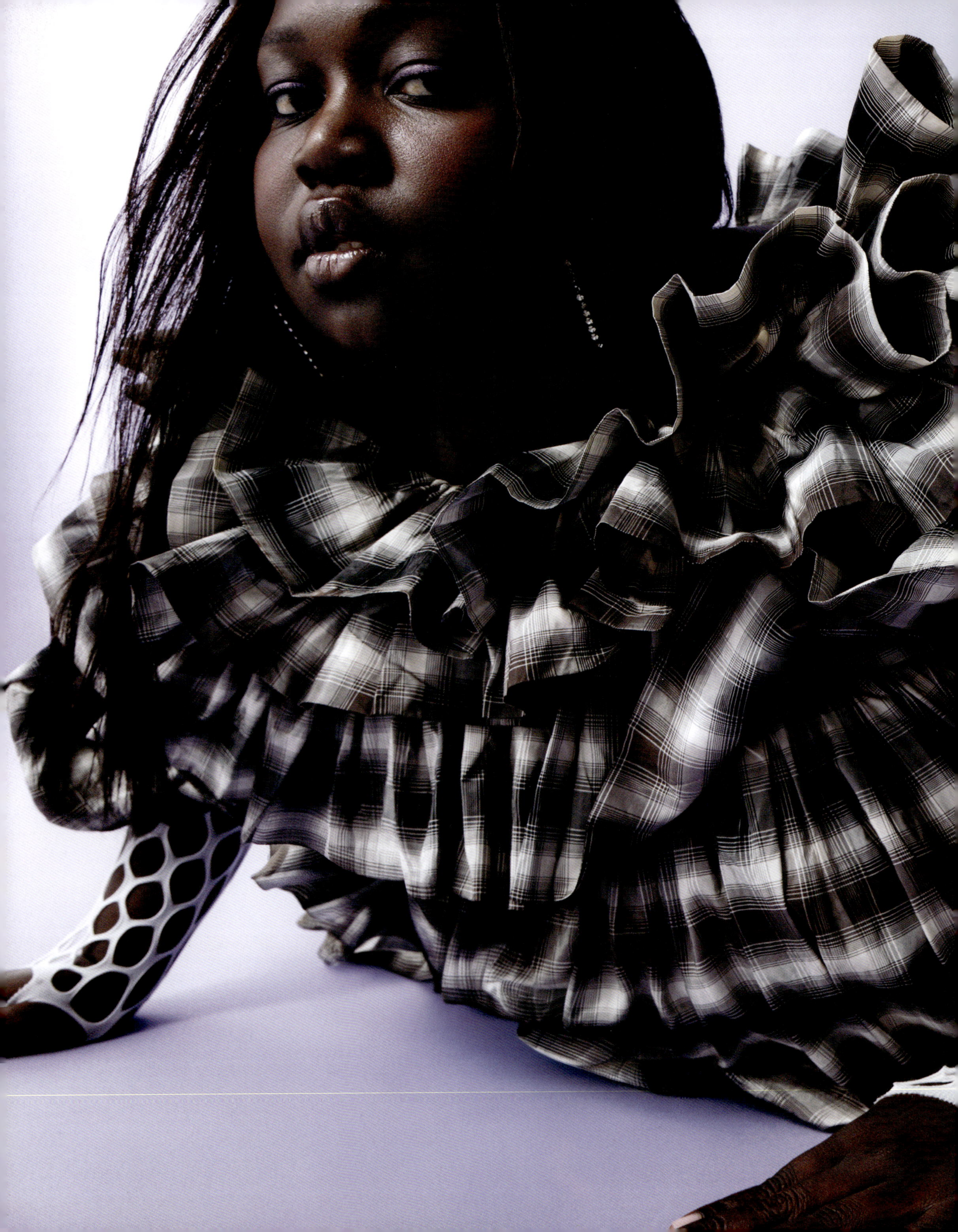

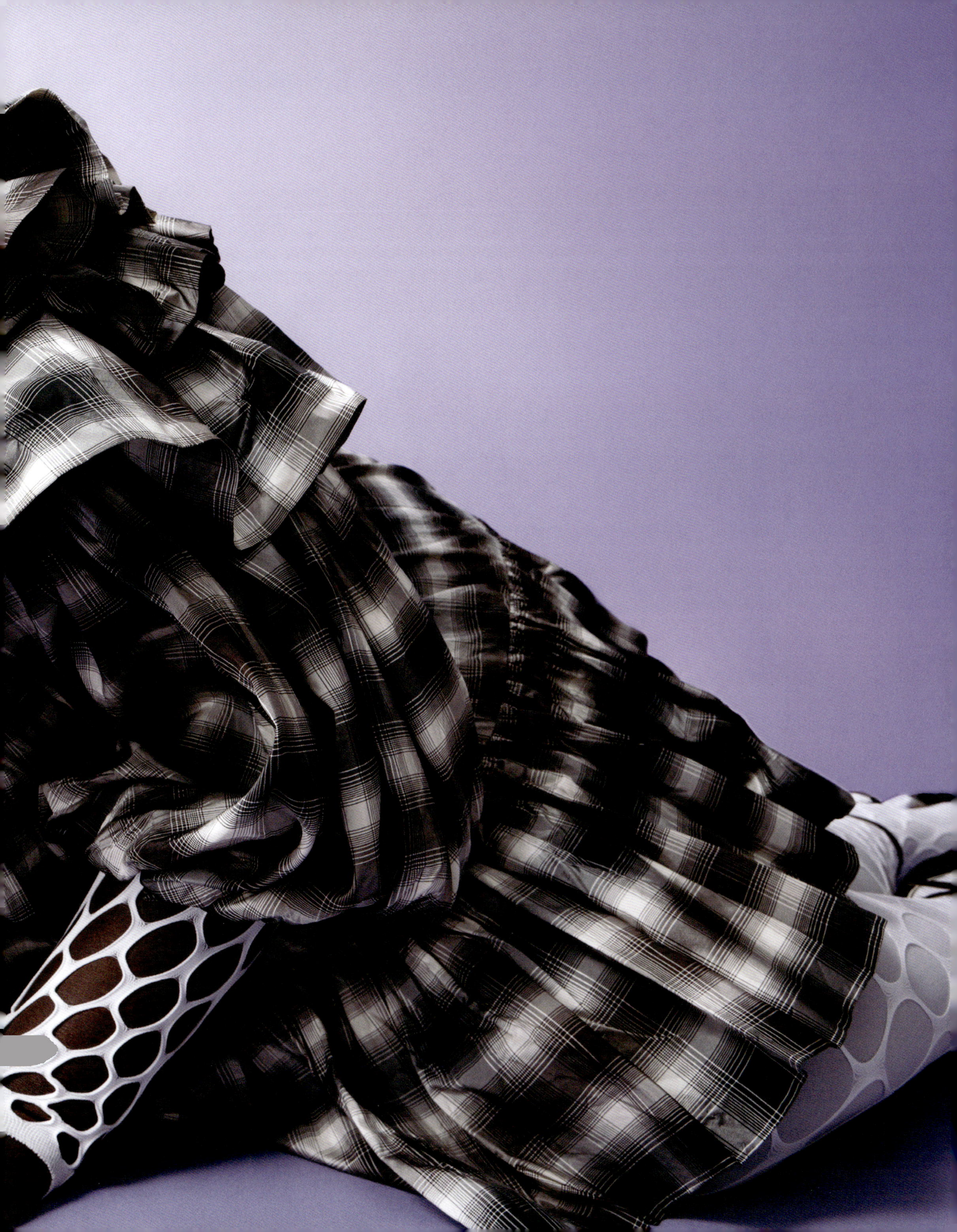

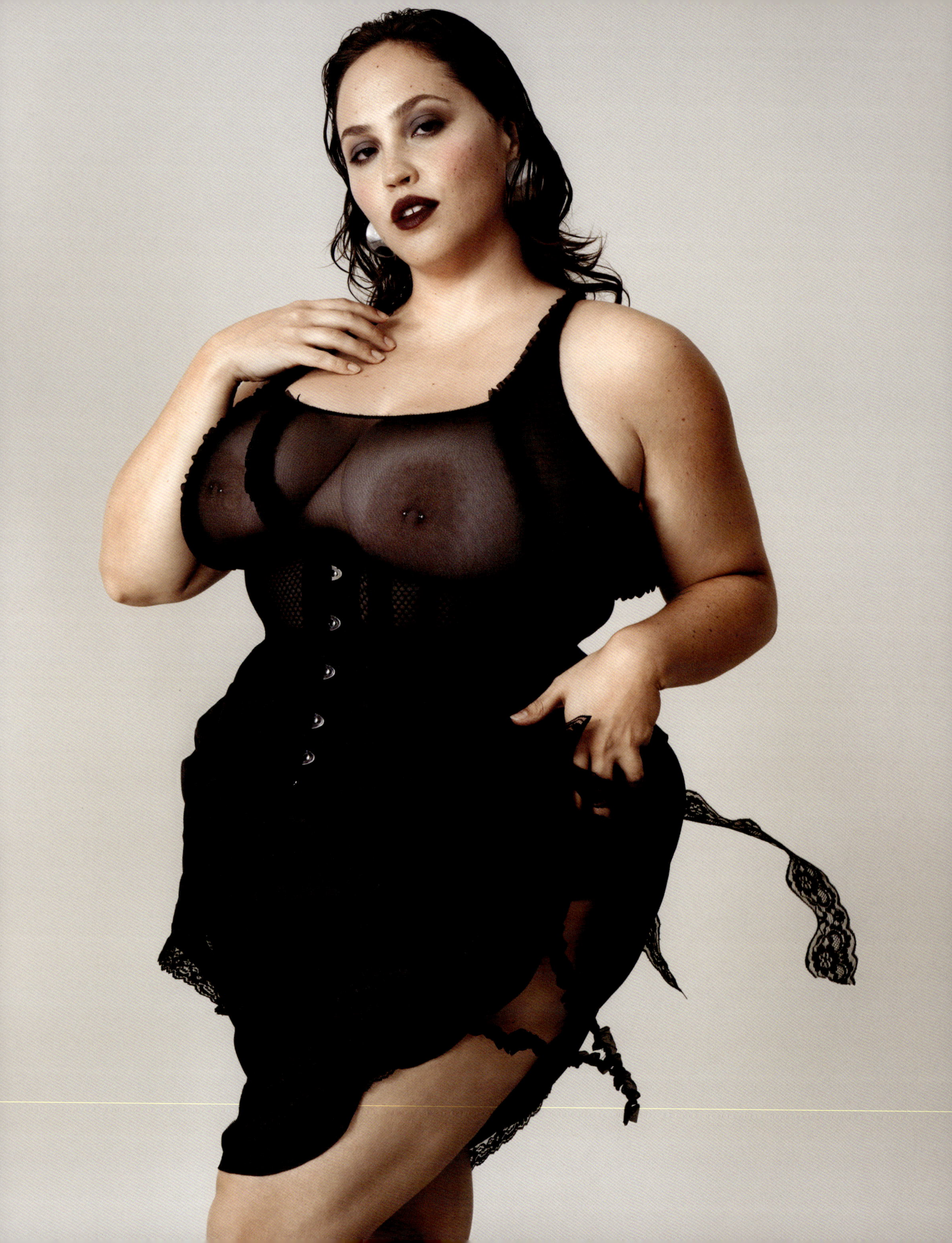

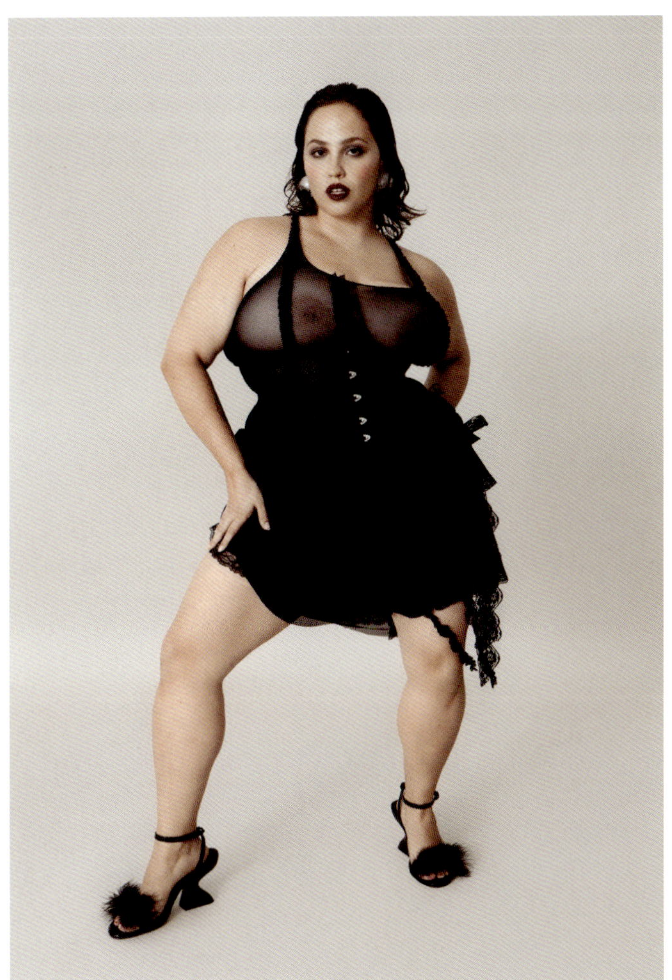

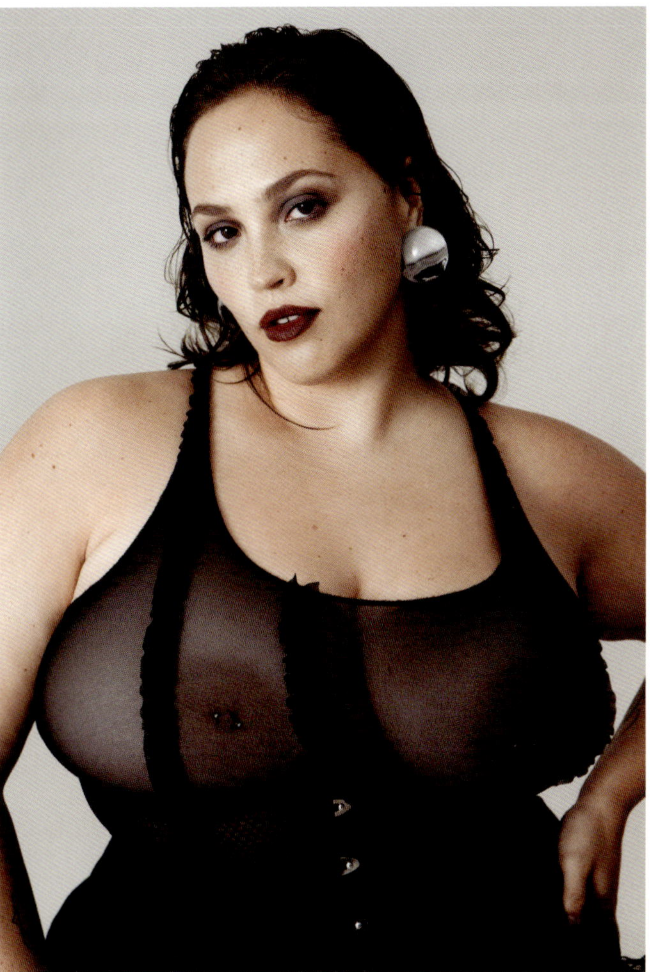

Sam Welsch wears Greta Garmel dress; Meadowland skirt; Circus NY by Sam Edelman shoes; Alexis Bittar earrings.

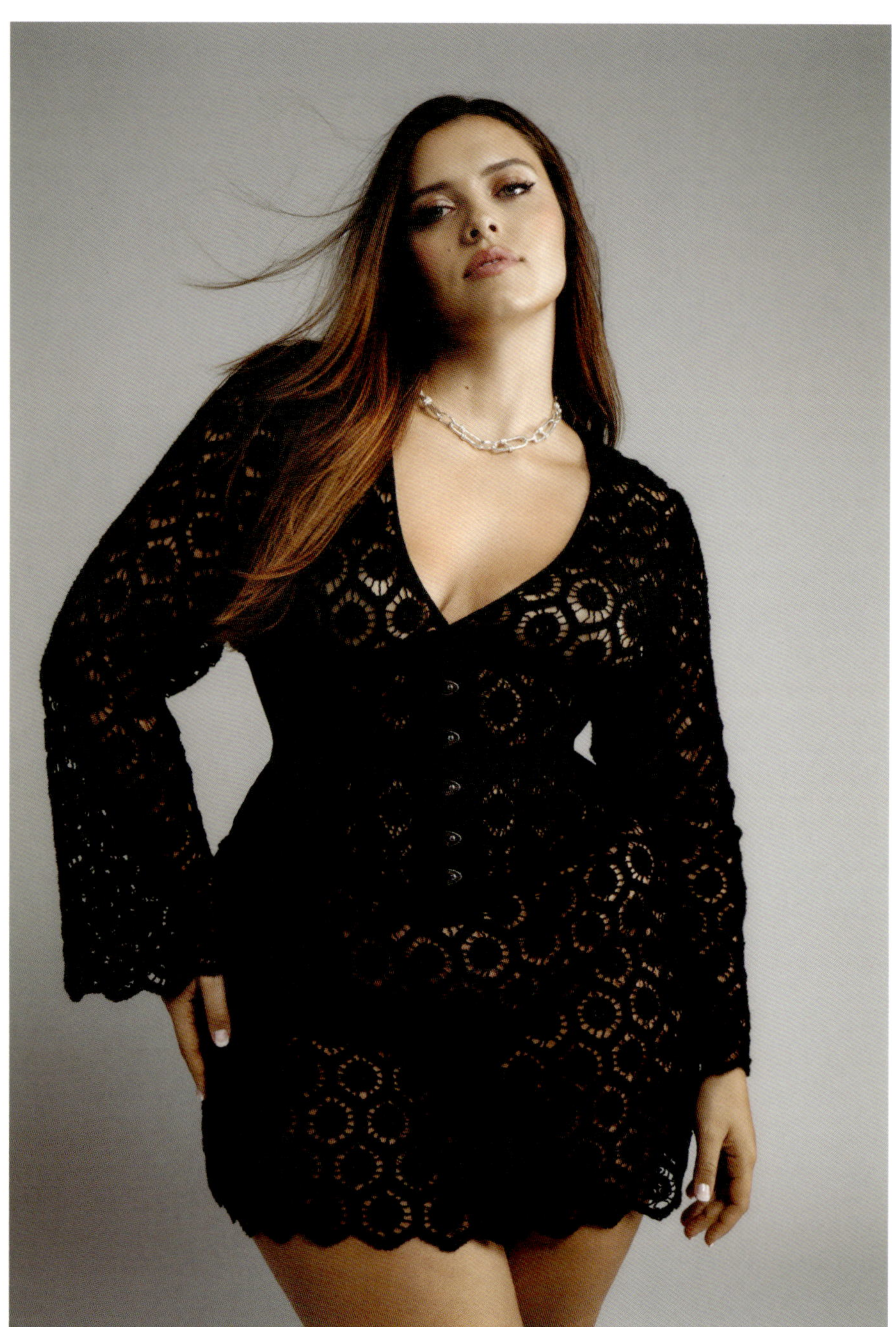

Wren Parker wears Tanya Taylor dress; corset from Lydia Hudgens' closet; Y/Project x Melissa shoes; CRZM jewelry.

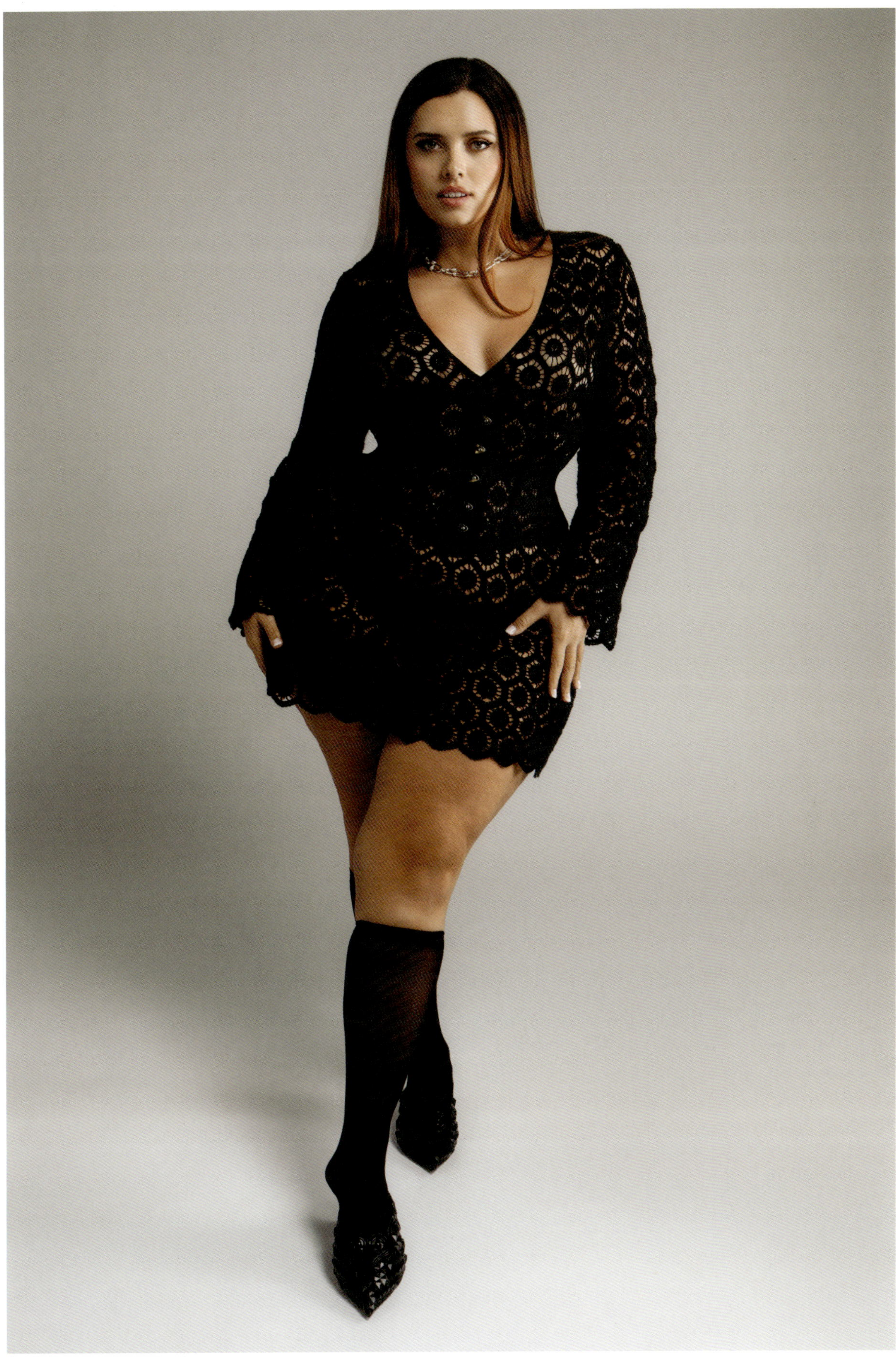

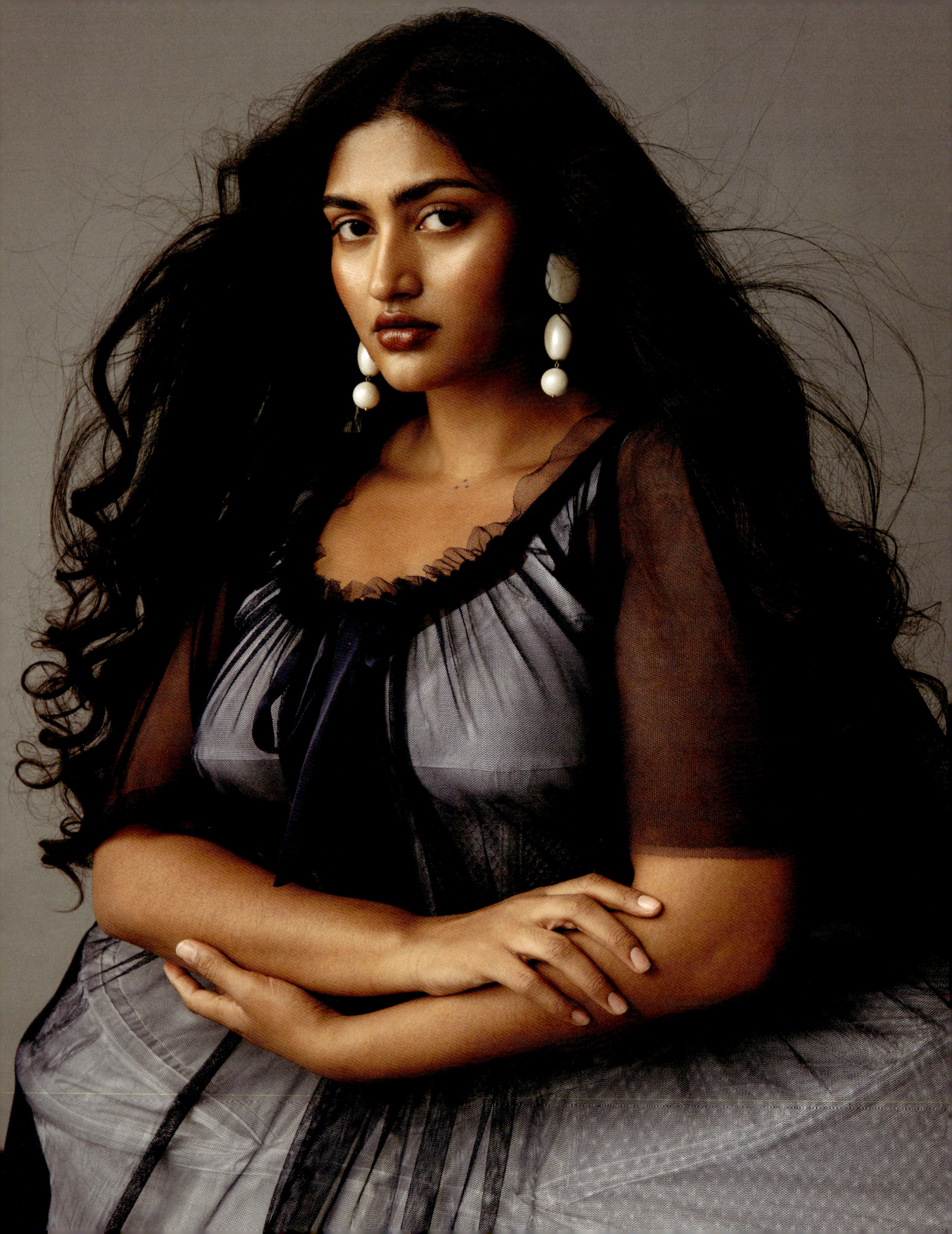

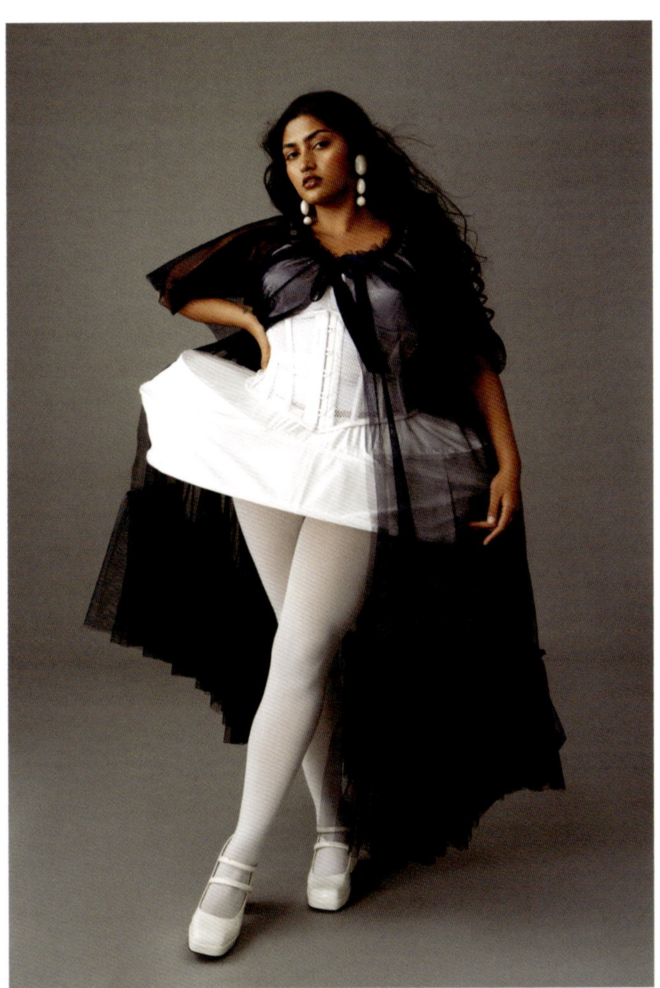

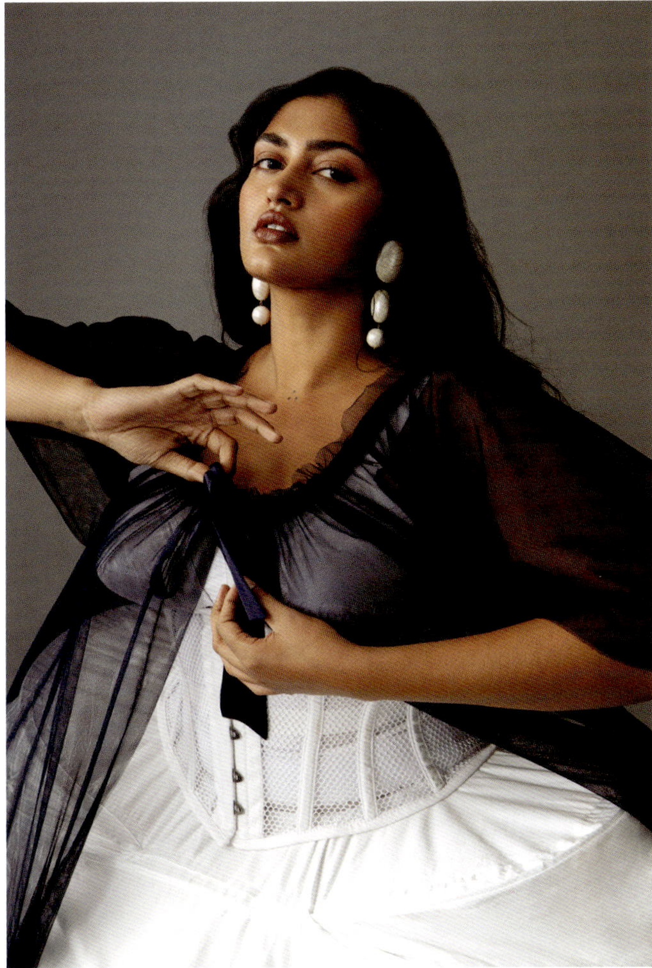

Shreya Navile wears Hill House Home robe; pannier from Lydia Hudgens' closet; Lele Sadoughi earrings.

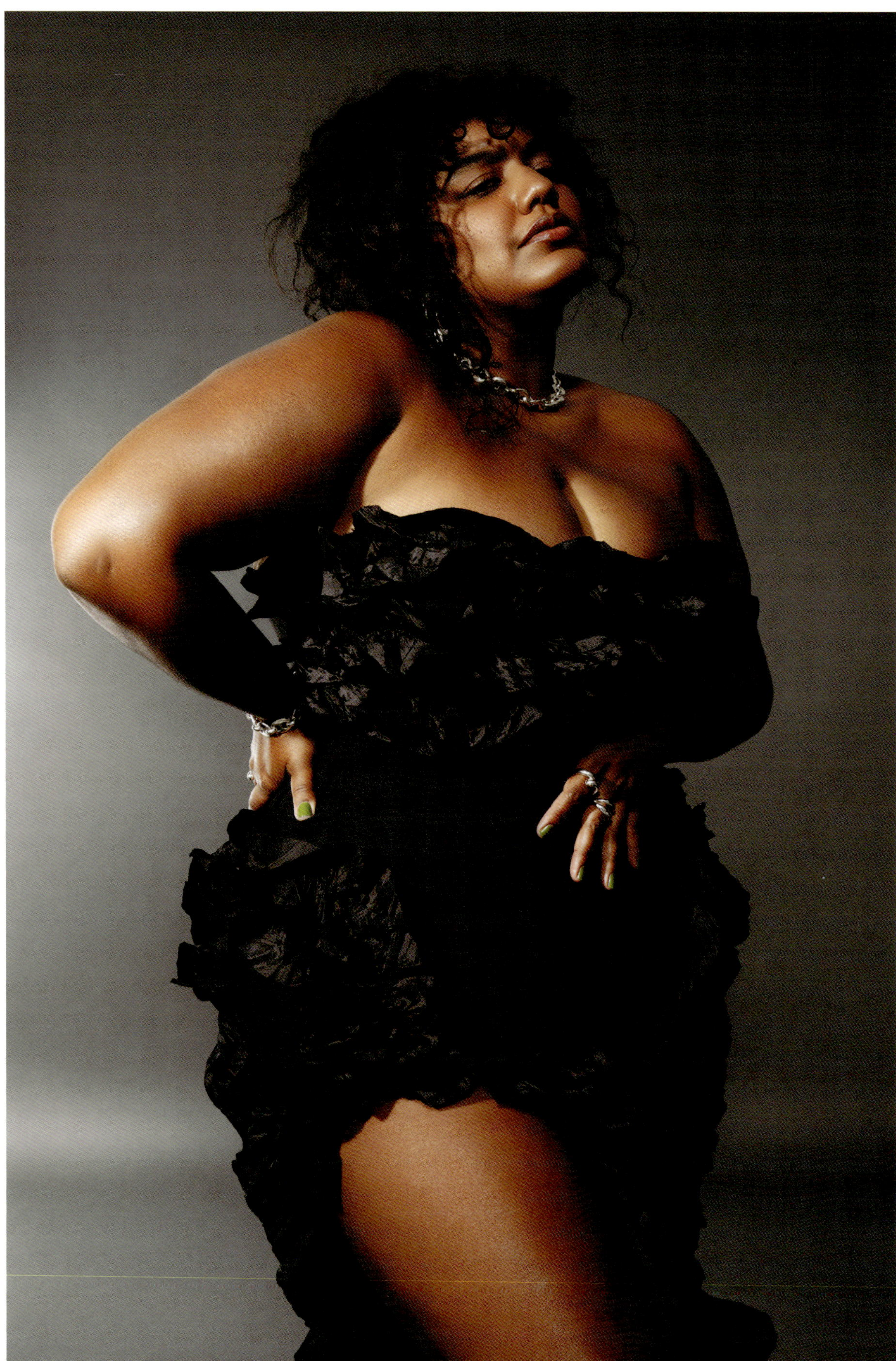

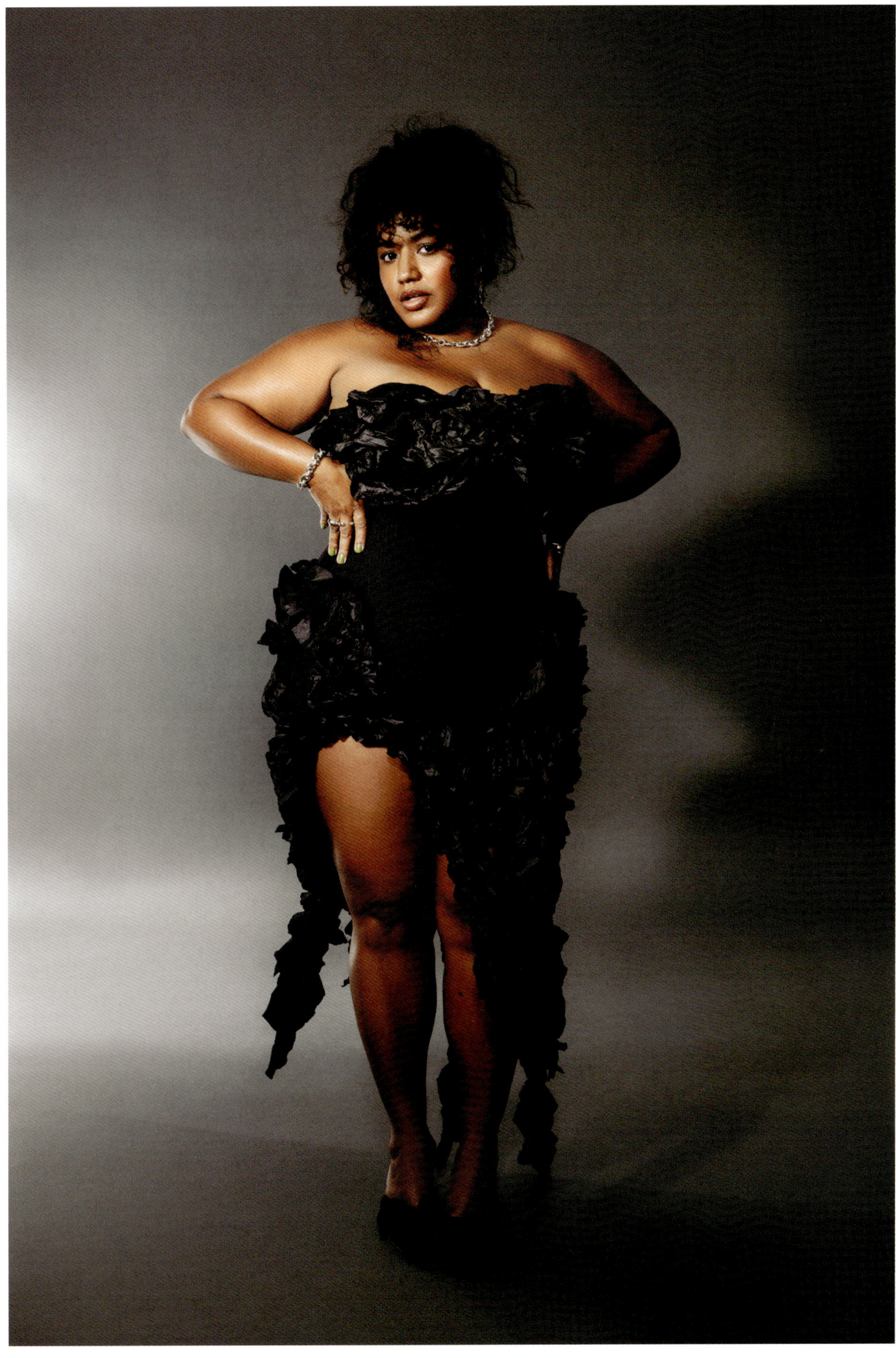

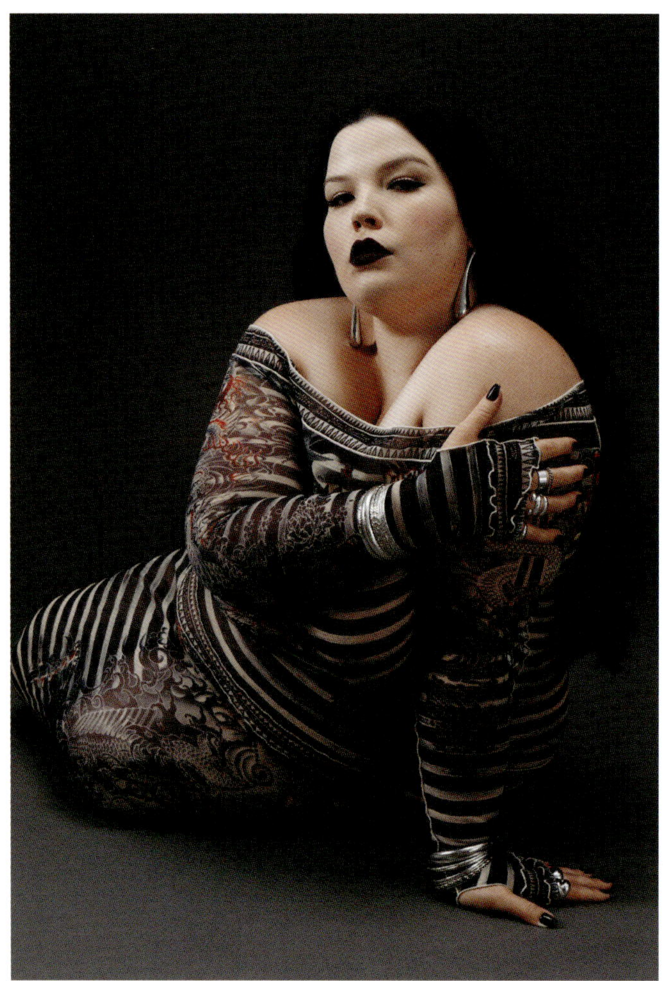

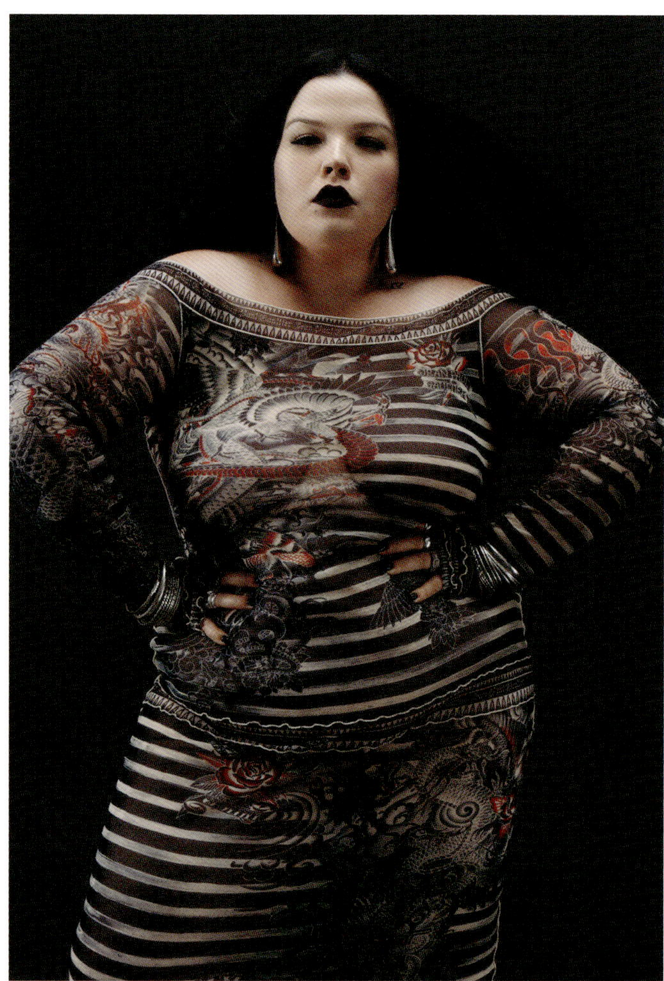

Previous pages: Veronica Campos wears dress from Lydia Hudgens' closet; Dolce Vita shoes; CRZM jewelry.

Emma Evans wears Jean Paul Gaultier dress.

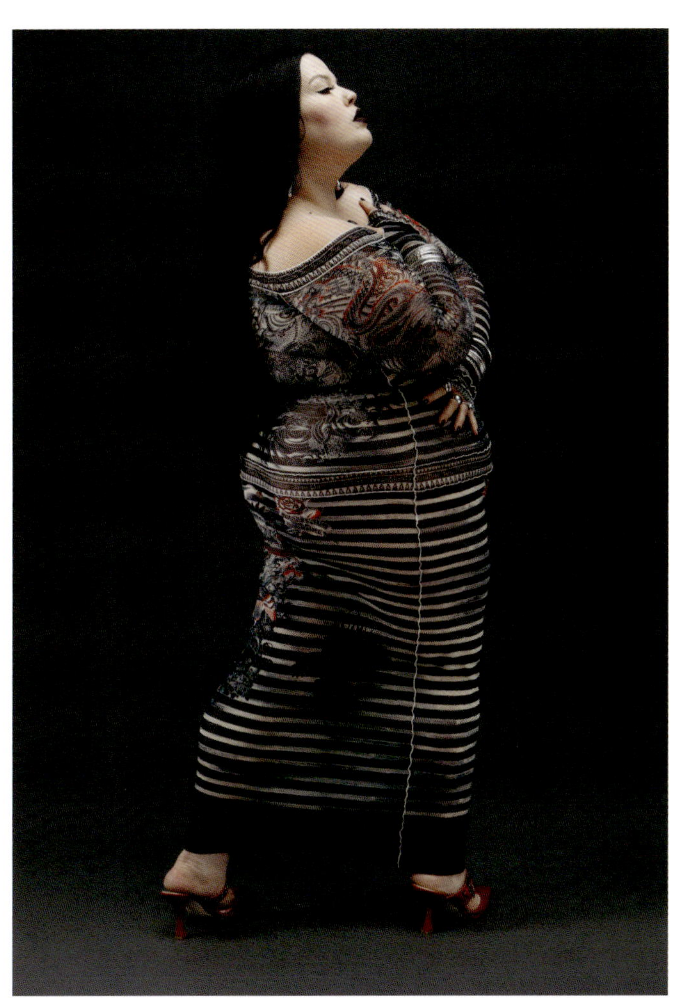

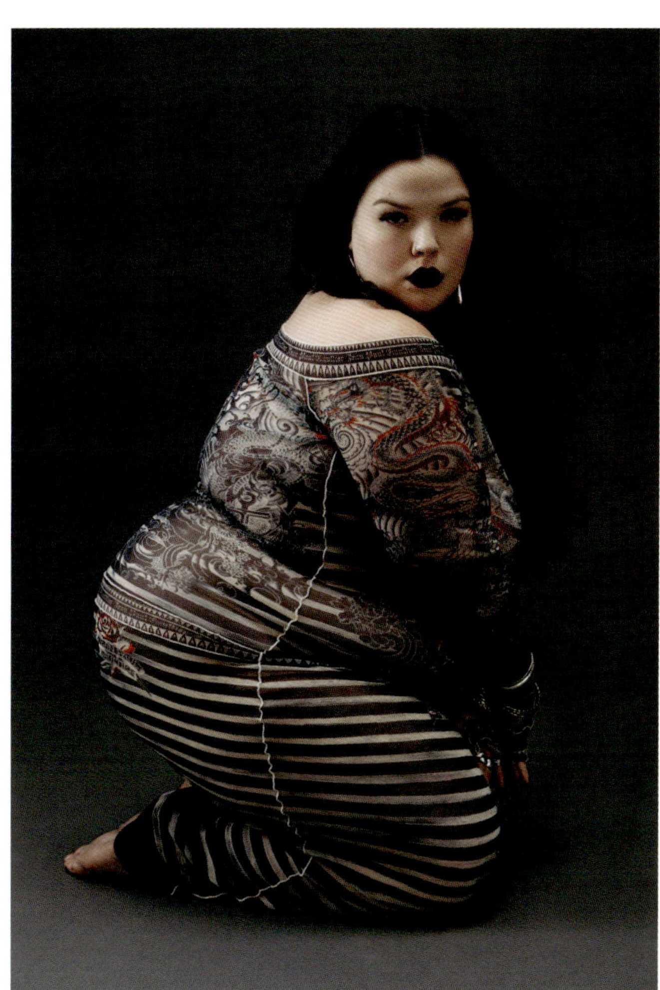

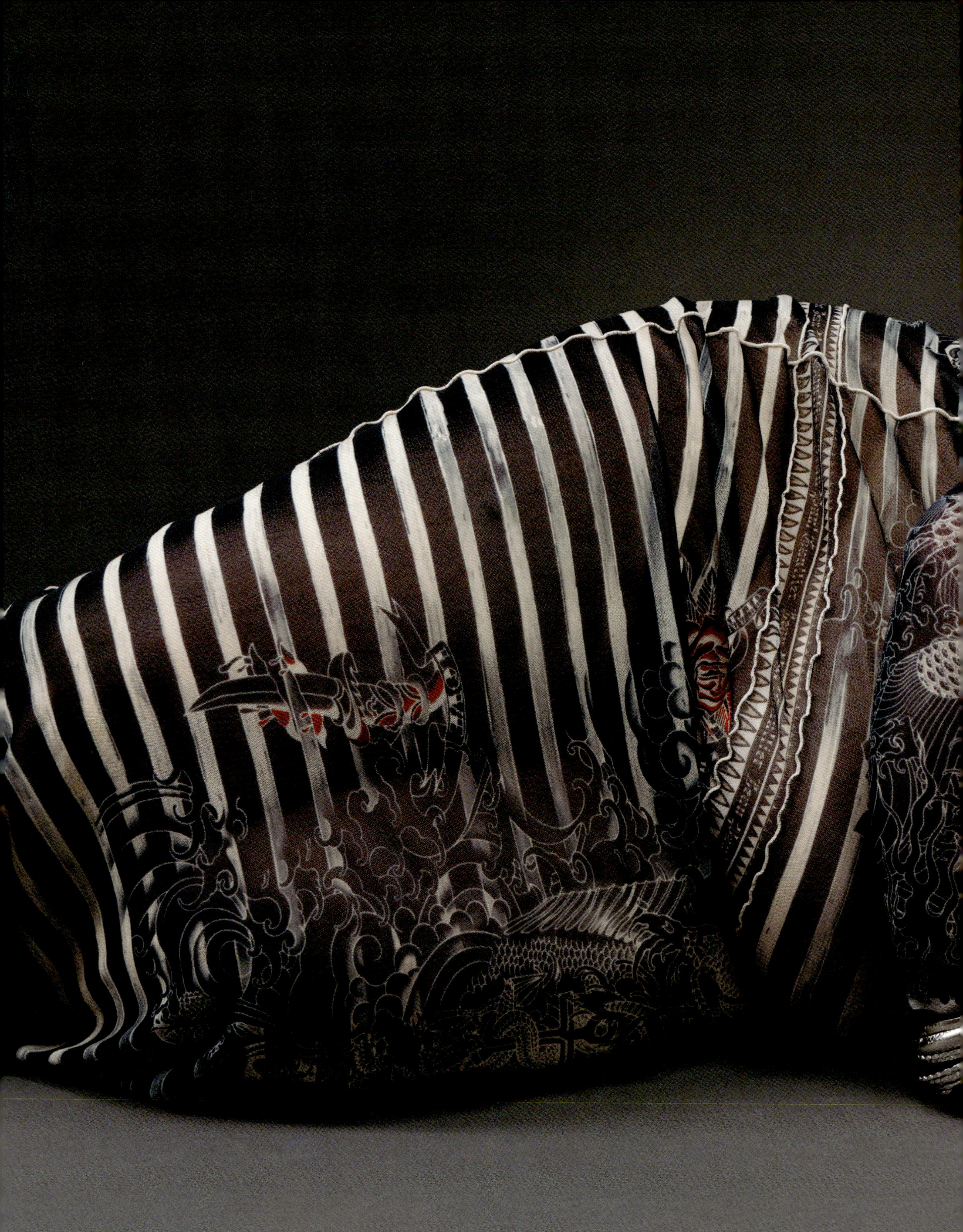

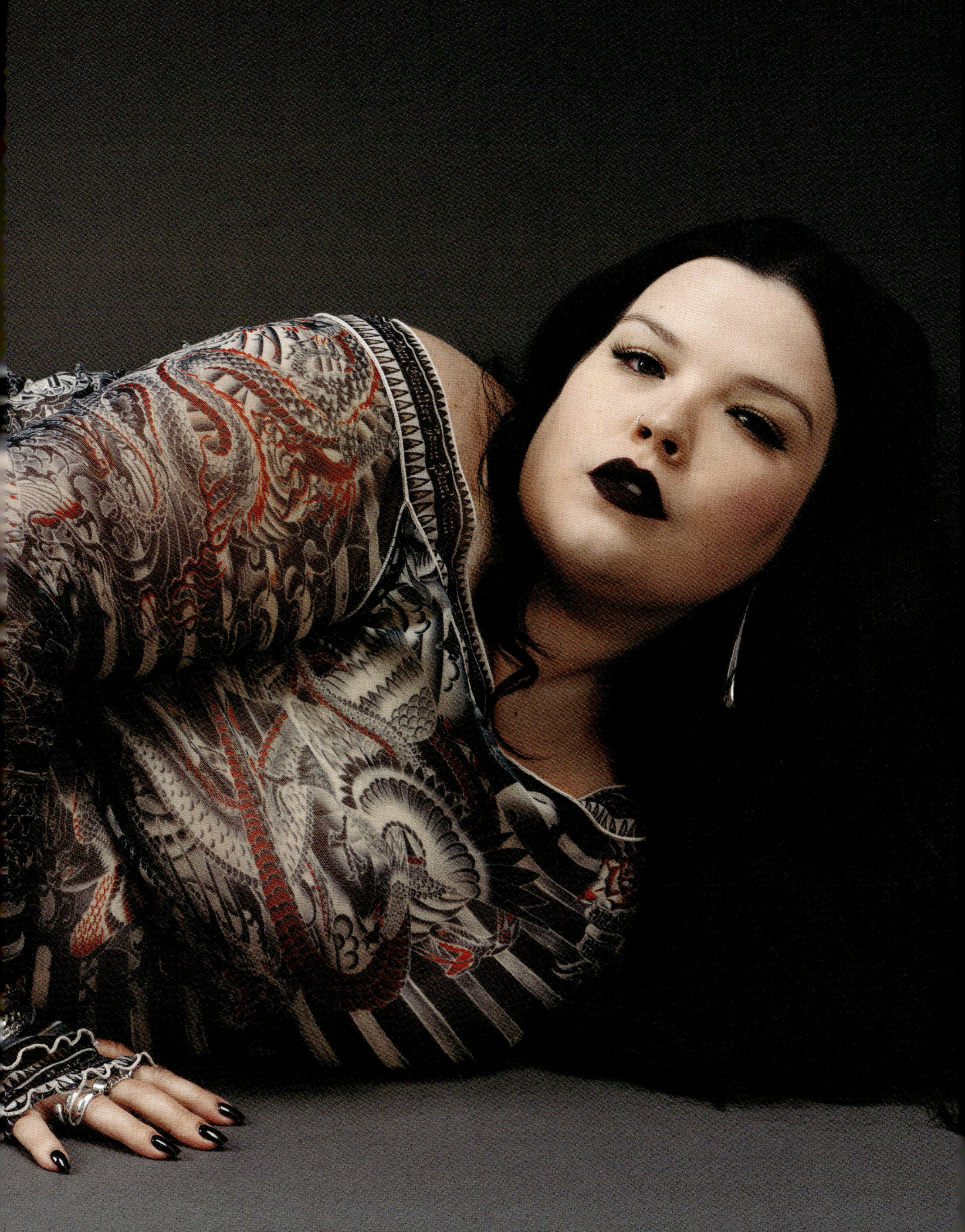

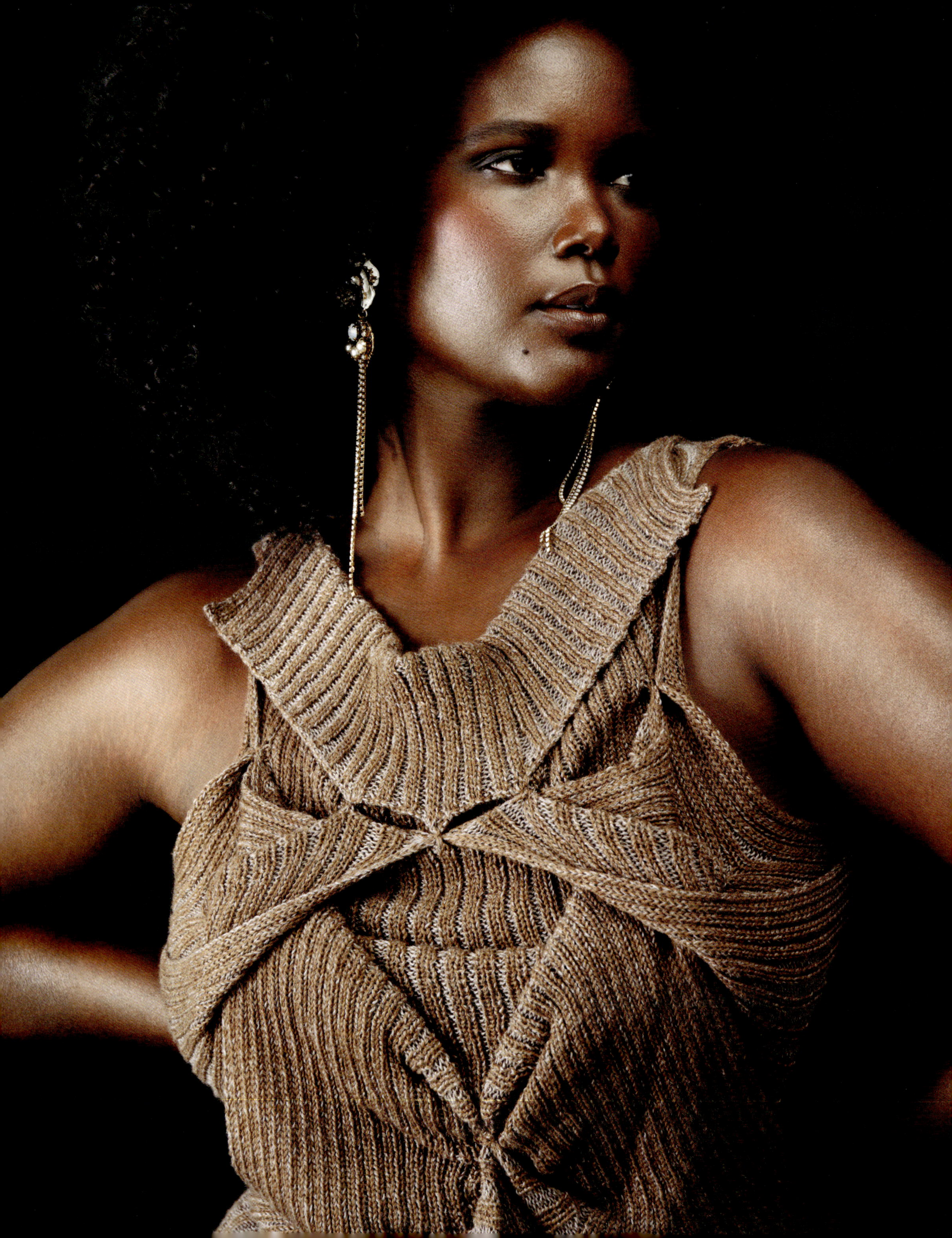

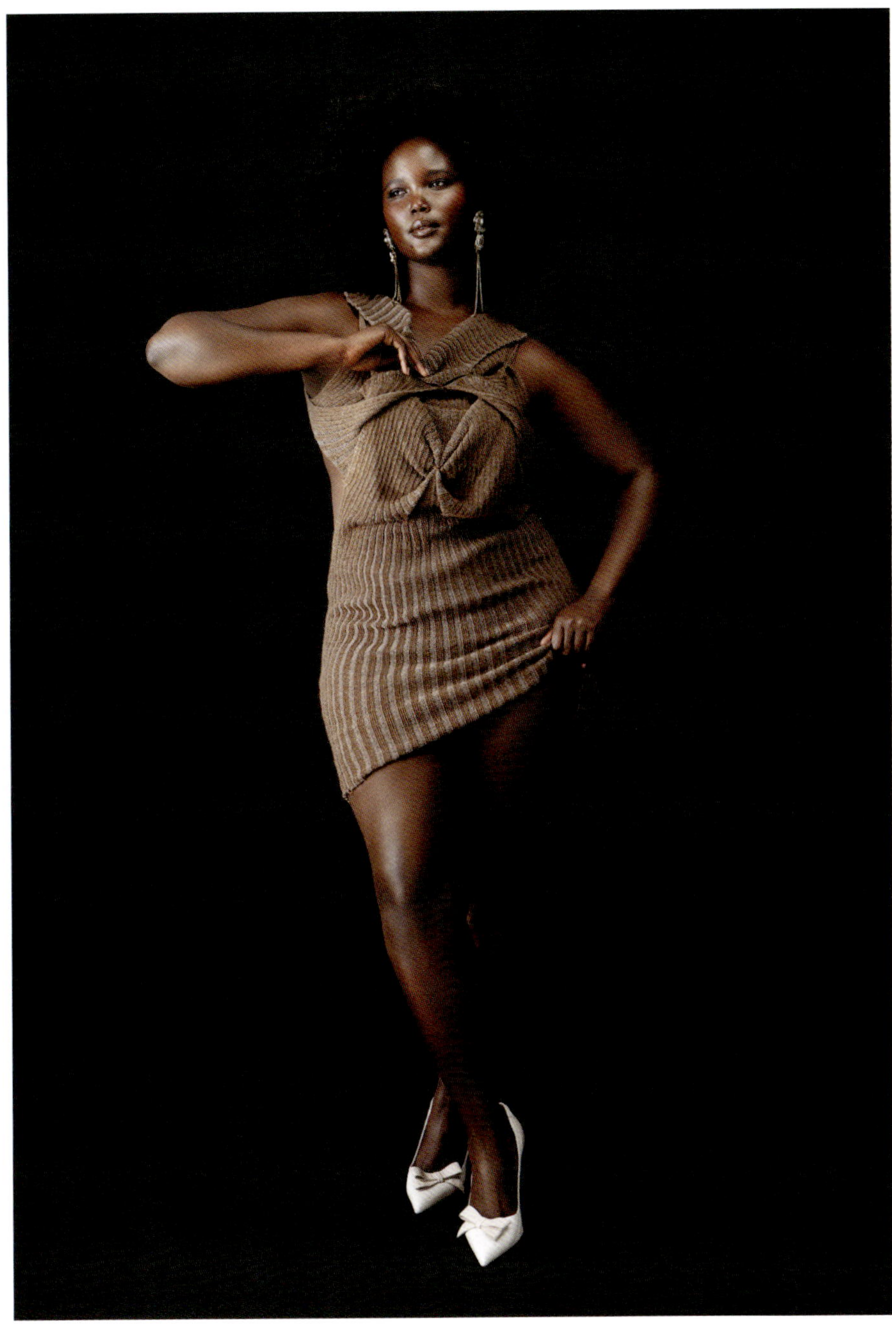

Sabey Dantsira wears Noah Kantrowitz
dress; Erickson Beamon earrings.

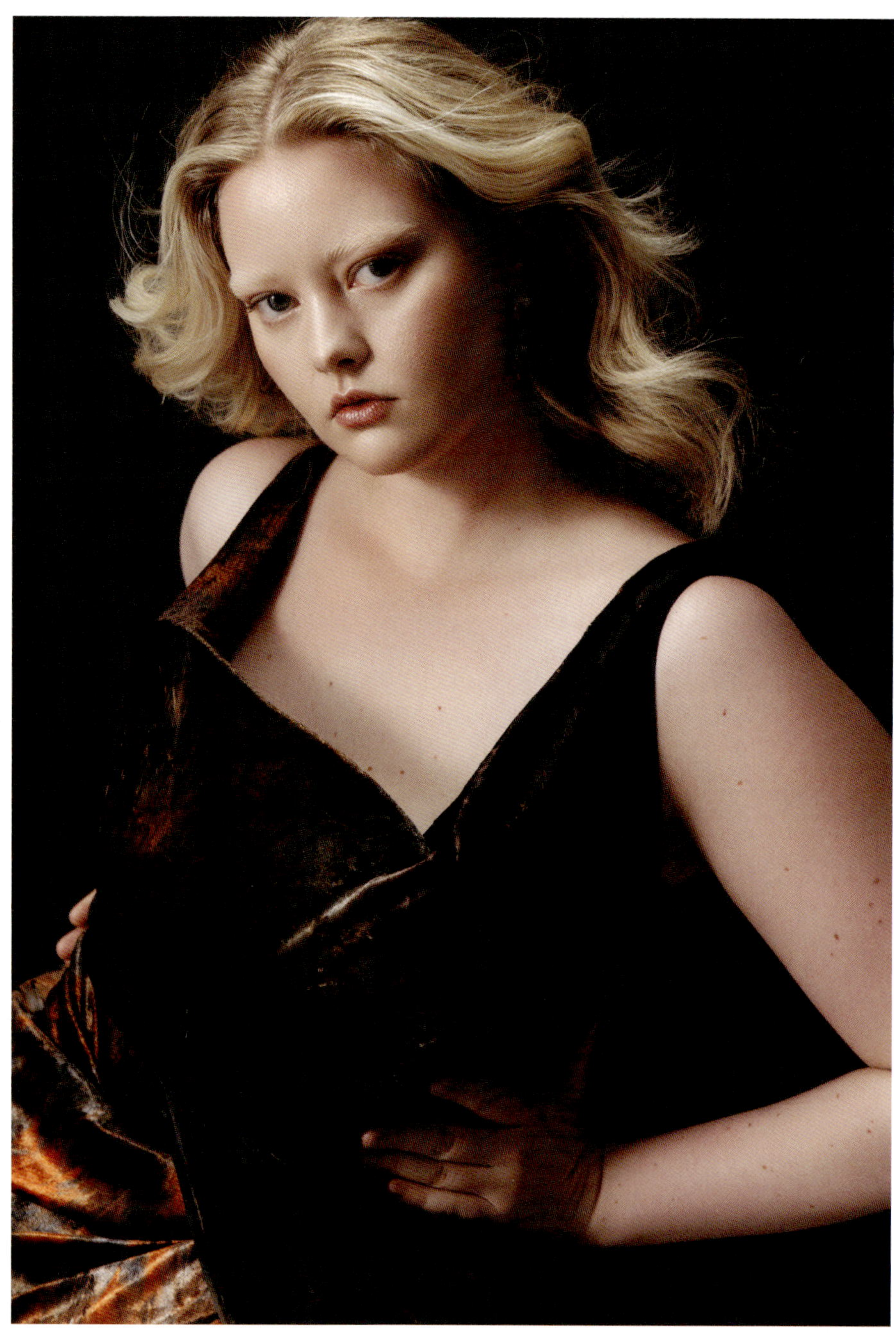

Delphine Clowe wears Theo Banzon dress.

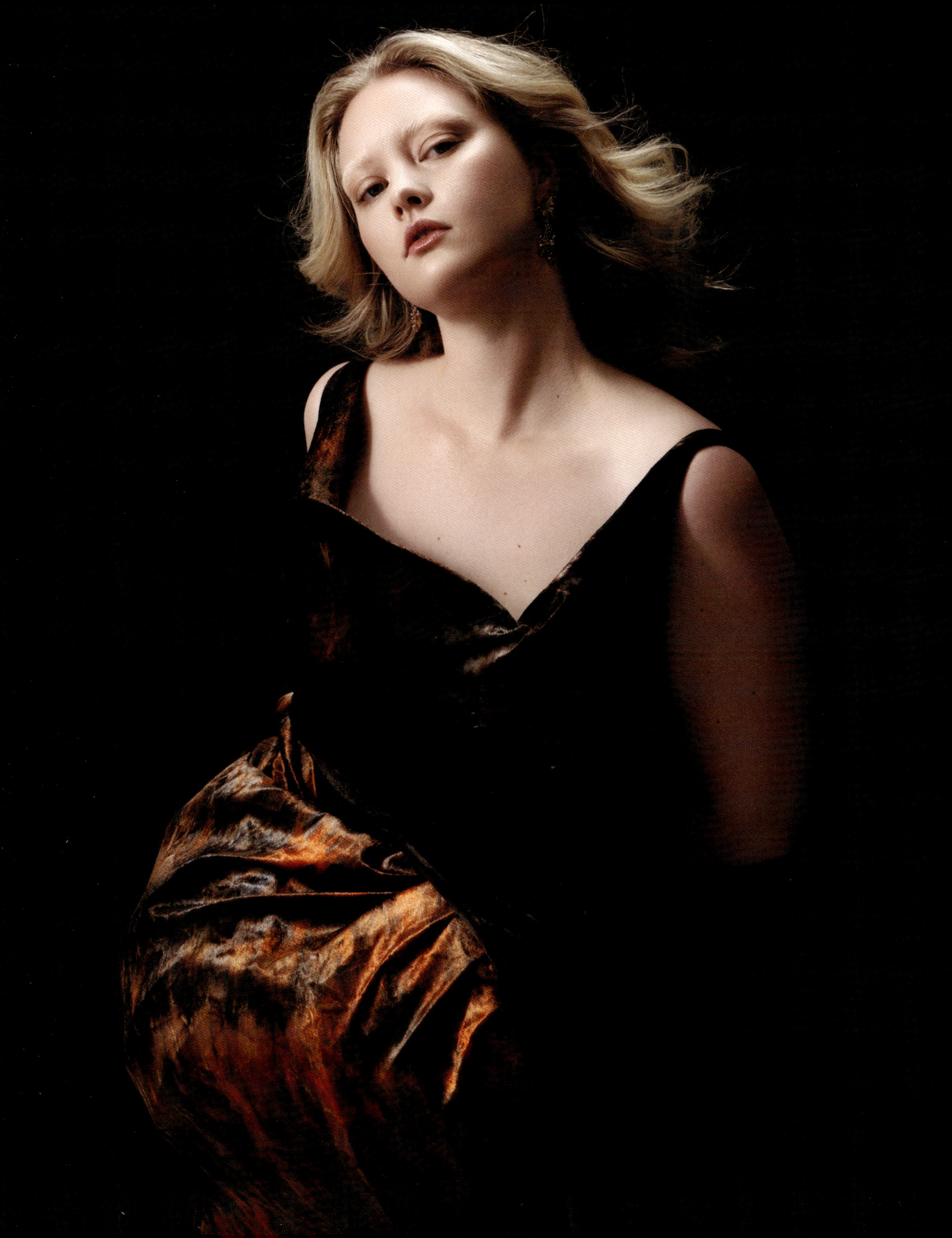

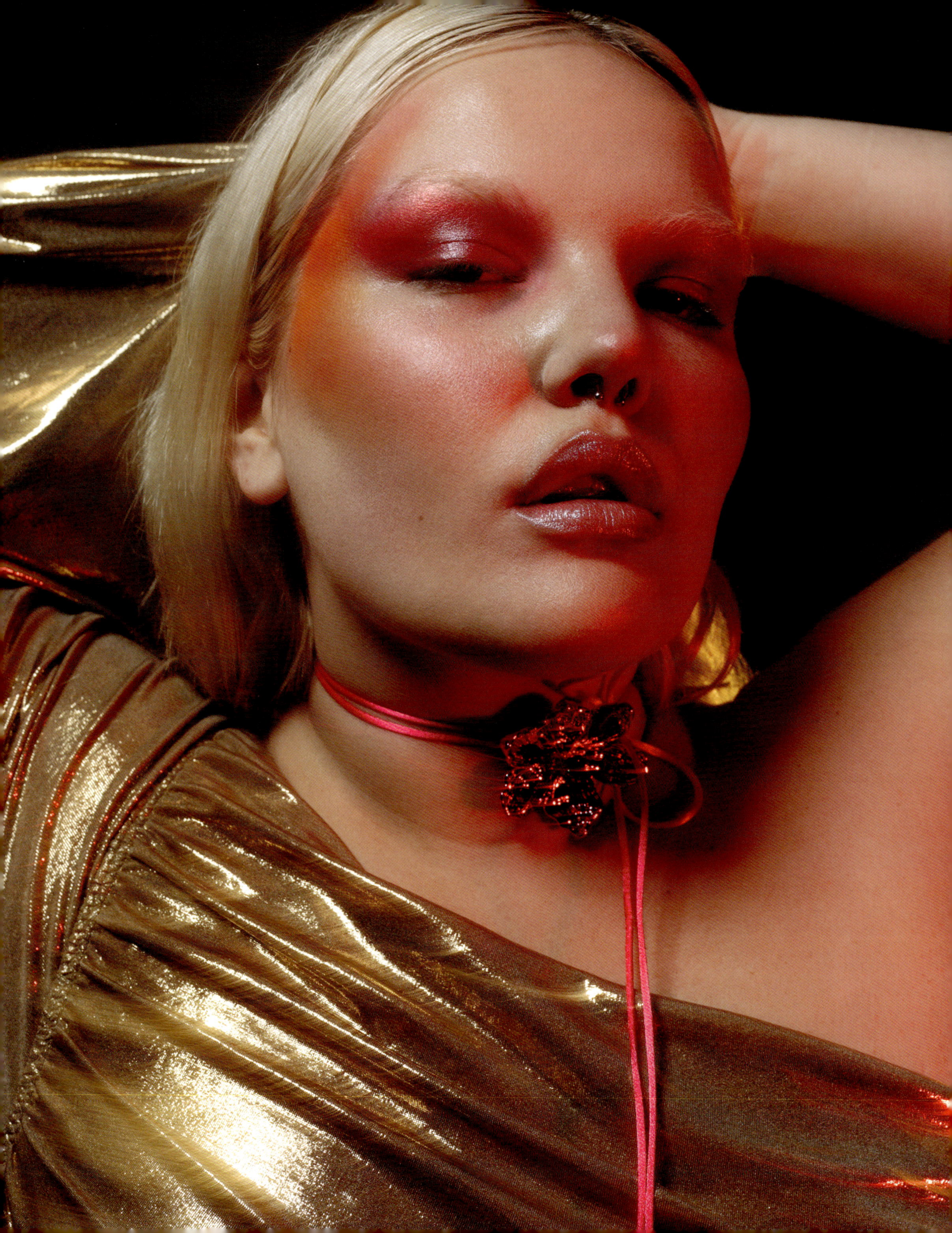

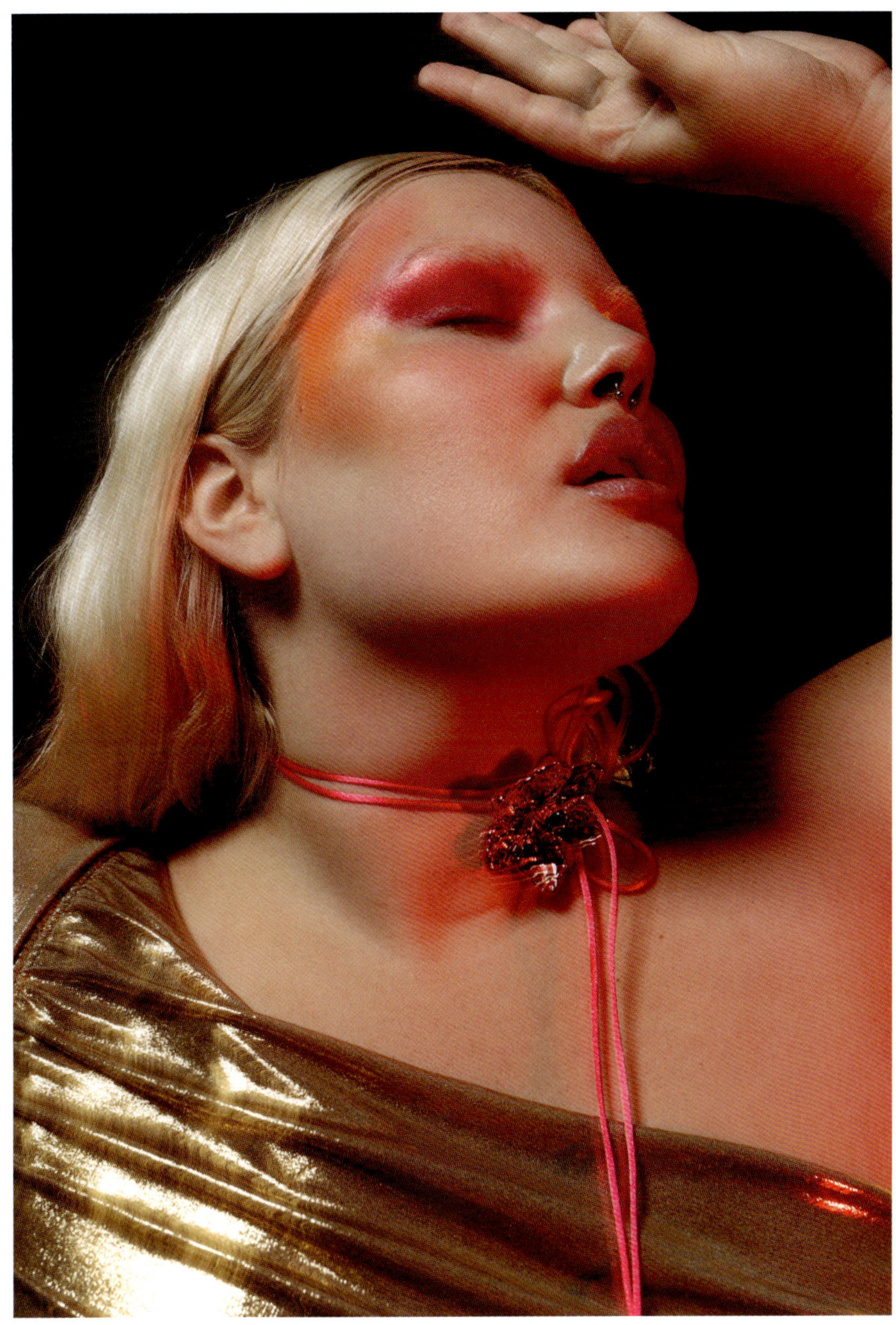

Kyrsten Sinclair wears dress from Emma Zack's closet.

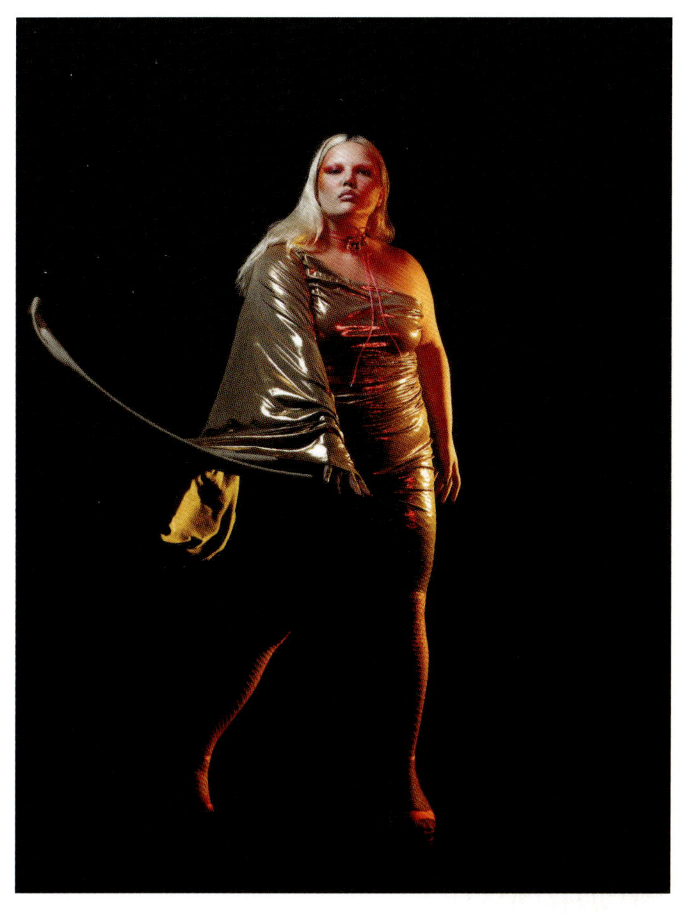
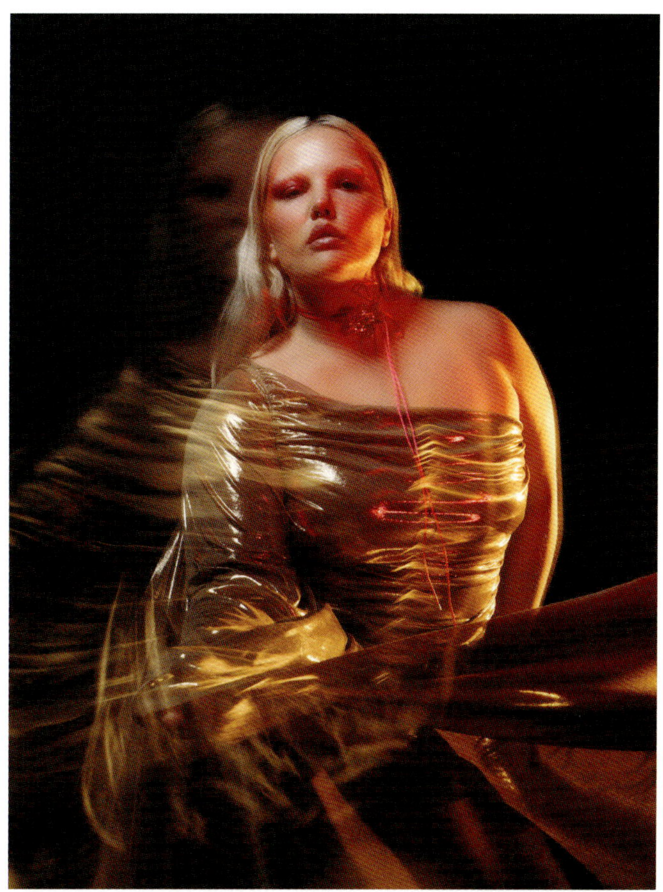
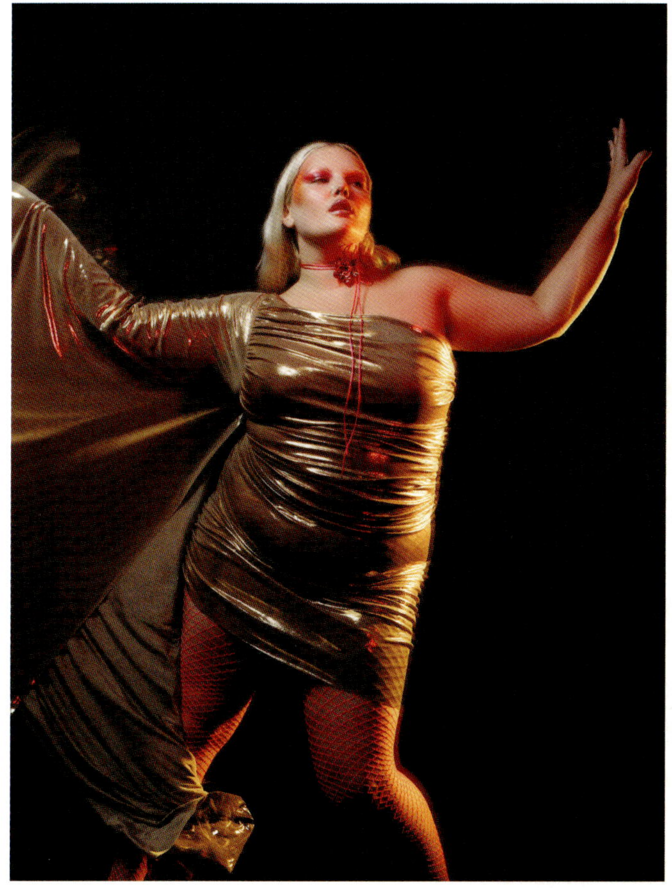
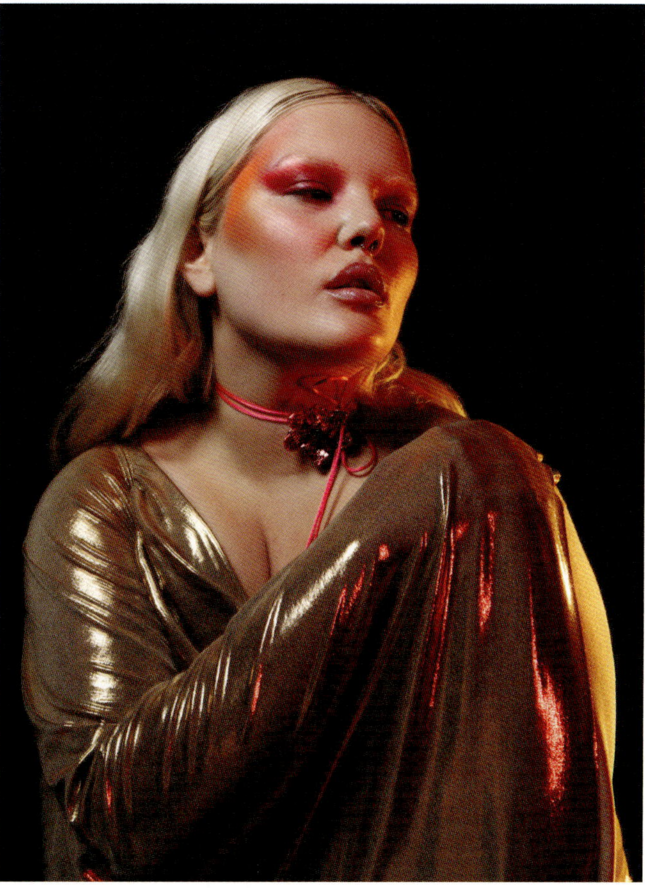

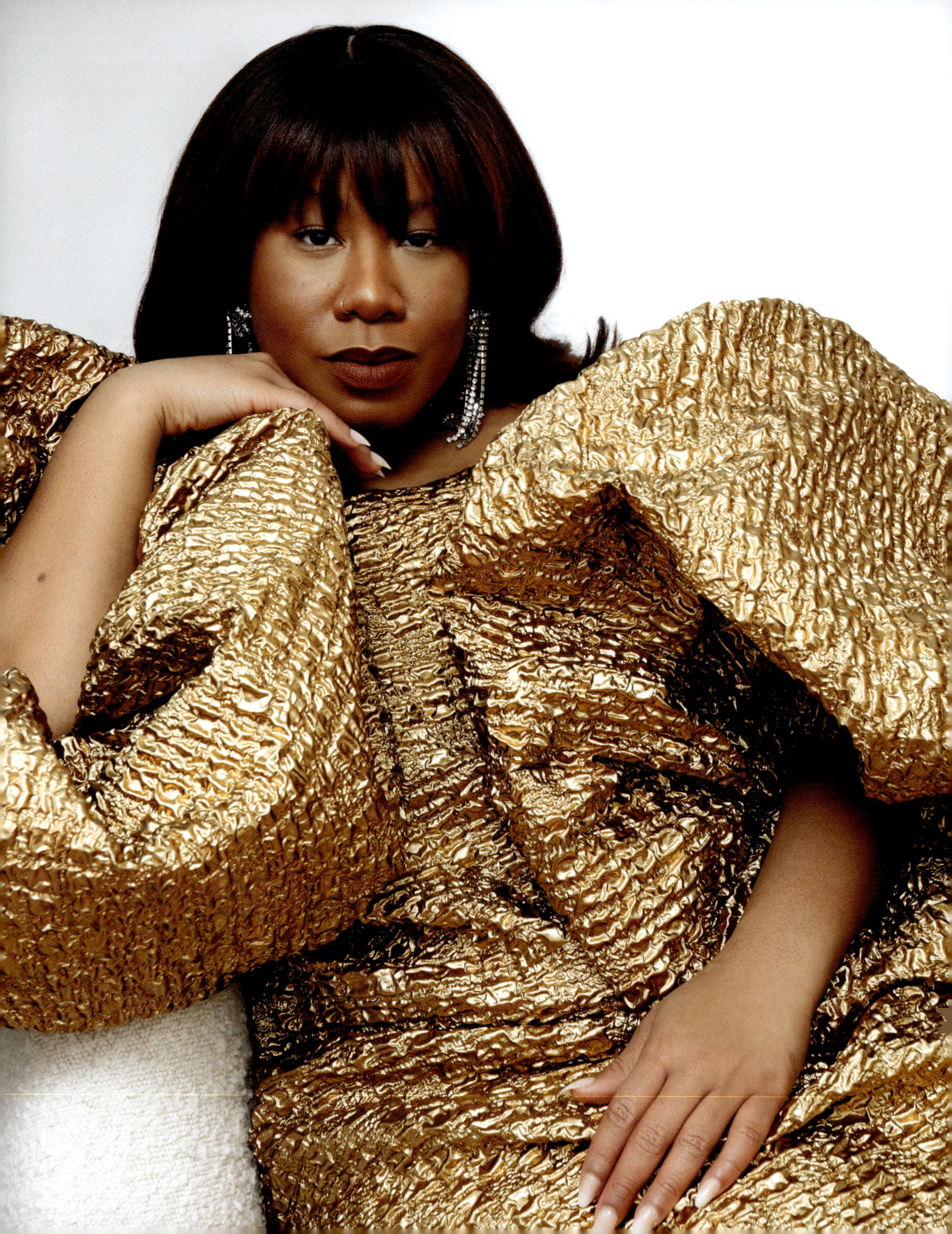

Kelly Augustine

A visionary in inclusive styling

As a plus-size influencer and stylist, Kelly Augustine's work has moved the needle toward inclusivity in fashion. I first met her during a Catherines campaign, and we quickly bonded over the creative process, spending time shooting and photographing each other during my brief time as an influencer. Since then, Kelly has made a name for herself styling high-profile clients like Amari, one of Beyoncé's dancers.

"My entry into the plus fashion space was really by circumstance—I just happened to be a plus person that wanted to look cute. I didn't set out to become an advocate in any way, I was simply sharing my life in New York City as a 20-something creative. The tables turned once I realized that me living in my truth was helping other people do the same, and I haven't looked back since."

Asked about the main challenges Kelly faces styling plus-size individuals—especially with the lack of options on offer in mainstream fashion—she shares that "... there are a number of limits, the biggest being access and finance. For celebrity clients, it comes down to relationships and whether you have the budget to hedge a custom look. With personal styling clients, there's just not a wide variety and assortment of style types."

One of the biggest hurdles for stylists in plus fashion is avoiding repetition. With a limited number of brands catering to extended sizes, it can be difficult to find fresh, distinct looks. "As a stylist, you don't want everyone looking the same," she explains. "But there are only so many brands available to shop from before you have to spend extra money for custom—especially once you extend beyond a 3X."

Despite this lack of resources, Kelly still manages to excel at styling thanks to her knack for creative solutions. "I'm all about thinking outside the box and finding unique combinations that still create standout looks for my clients.

I like to be in spaces where love and respect are in abundance, and would rather not put energy into chasing designers to prove we as a community are worth working with.

My job is to make sure the client feels like the best version of themselves."

To navigate these challenges while maintaining the integrity of her work, Kelly has made it her mission to work with independent designers. "More often than not, [they] are size-inclusive and more willing to do custom. The energy is also much more free and creative in the indie space."

While most stylists aim for relationships with luxury brands, Kelly focuses on designers who already prioritize plus-size clients. "I think it's much more interesting to find … designers that align with a client's style. Working with indie designers is a personal choice I've made because I think it's important to champion those who champion us."

Kelly's commitment to these collaborations is not just about accessibility—it's about building relationships where respect is mutual. "I like to be in spaces where love and respect are in abundance, and would rather not put energy into chasing designers to prove we as a community are worth working with."

This dedication to fostering inclusive spaces is a cornerstone of Kelly's career, both as a stylist and a voice for the plus-size community. In a world where cracking fashion open is still a work in progress, Kelly is all about finding that balance—advocating for more plus-size options while achieving her clients' vision.

Her approach to her work is a testament to her ingenuity and resourcefulness. "I go into every project with an open mind," she says. "Anything can become a garment with a bit of imagination! I'm always keeping an eye out for texture, color, and shape." For Kelly, though, "The sharpest tool in a shed is your measurements—the size on a tag is not law." By focusing on fit rather than label sizes, Kelly is able to transform simple pieces into custom, show-stopping looks that speak to her clients' individuality.

Kelly also works with emerging designers and supports size-inclusive education in fashion schools, helping to push plus fashion forward. Reflecting on how these relationships have shaped her direction as a stylist, she says, "It's been lovely to see the work of students coming out of Parsons, FIT, SCAD, etc. become more and more size-inclusive without sacrificing vibes or aesthetics. It's brilliant to see the fruits of those labors."

She's also been particularly inspired by the resurgence of plus-size brand collaborations, especially from celebrities who have long championed inclusivity. Her excitment about these is paired with an interest in emerging brands whose clothes are produced domestically, helping to create a sustainable, size-inclusive future for fashion.

Despite the setbacks and limitations that still exist, Kelly remains optimistic. "I see moments of slowdown as opportunities to reassess and innovate." Right now, she's especially energized by Gen Z plus-size designers and content creators who are reinventing fashion through upcycling, thrifting, and custom pieces. "I love to see Gen Z plus creators work their magic on sewing machines and thrifting to craft unique looks." Another shift giving her hope? The push from educators to implement more inclusive design practices: "It will be brilliant to see the fruits of those labors."

With her commitment to pushing styling boundaries and her dedication to supporting the plus-size community, Kelly is undoubtedly a key player in the fashion industry's ongoing evolution. Through her work with independent designers, her advocacy, and her creative vision, she continues to lead the charge in ensuring style is for everyone.

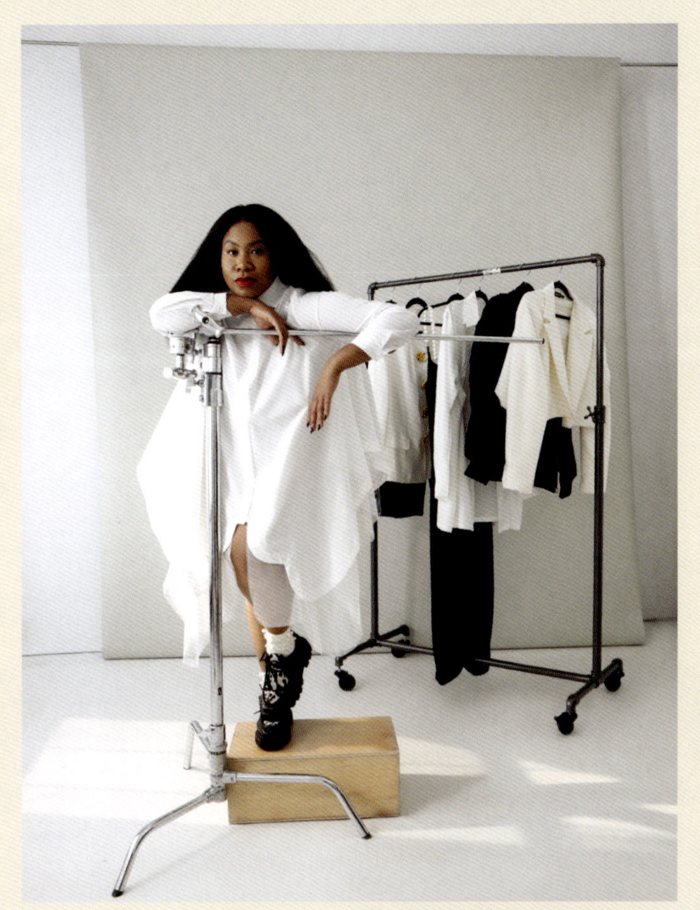

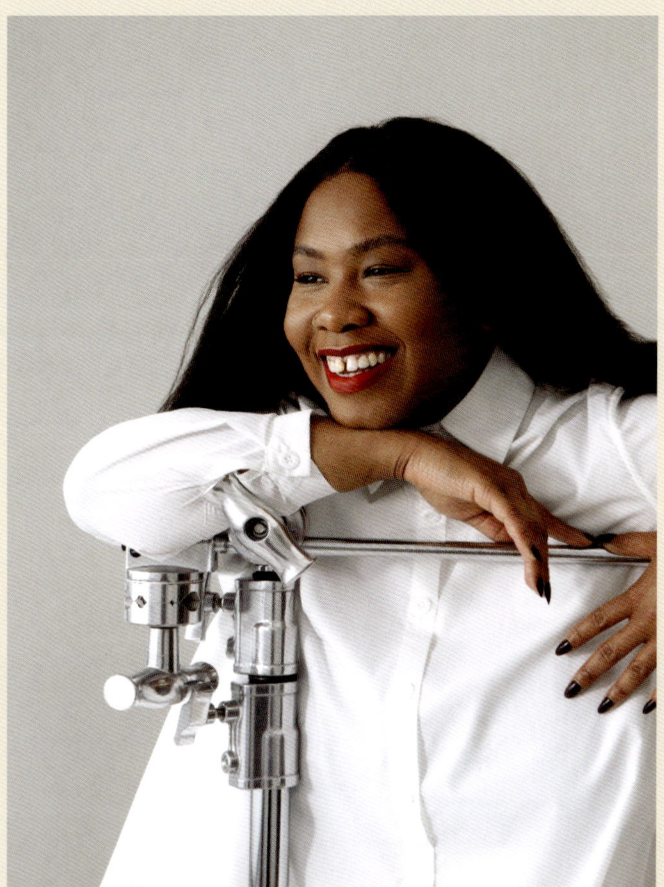

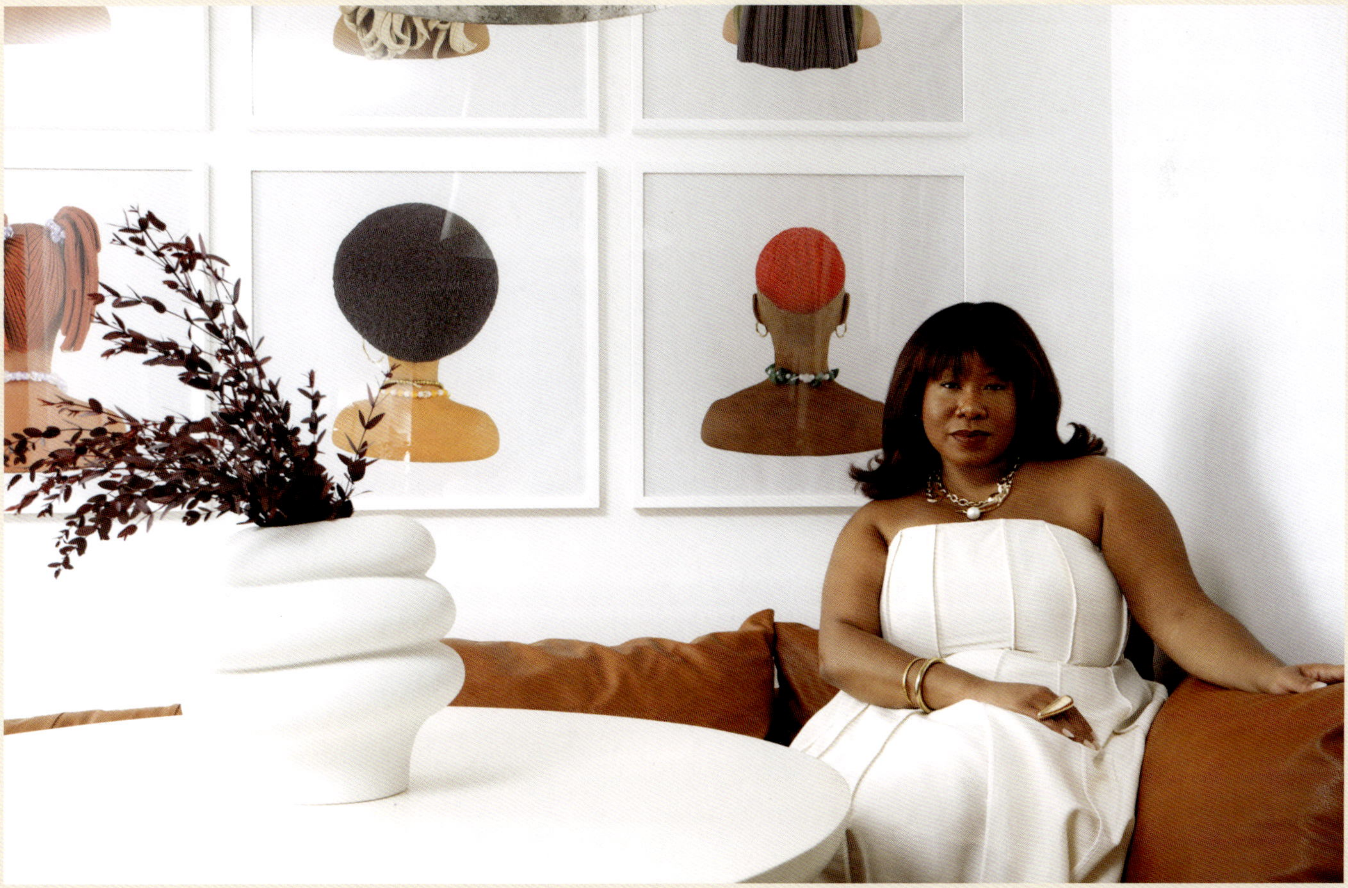

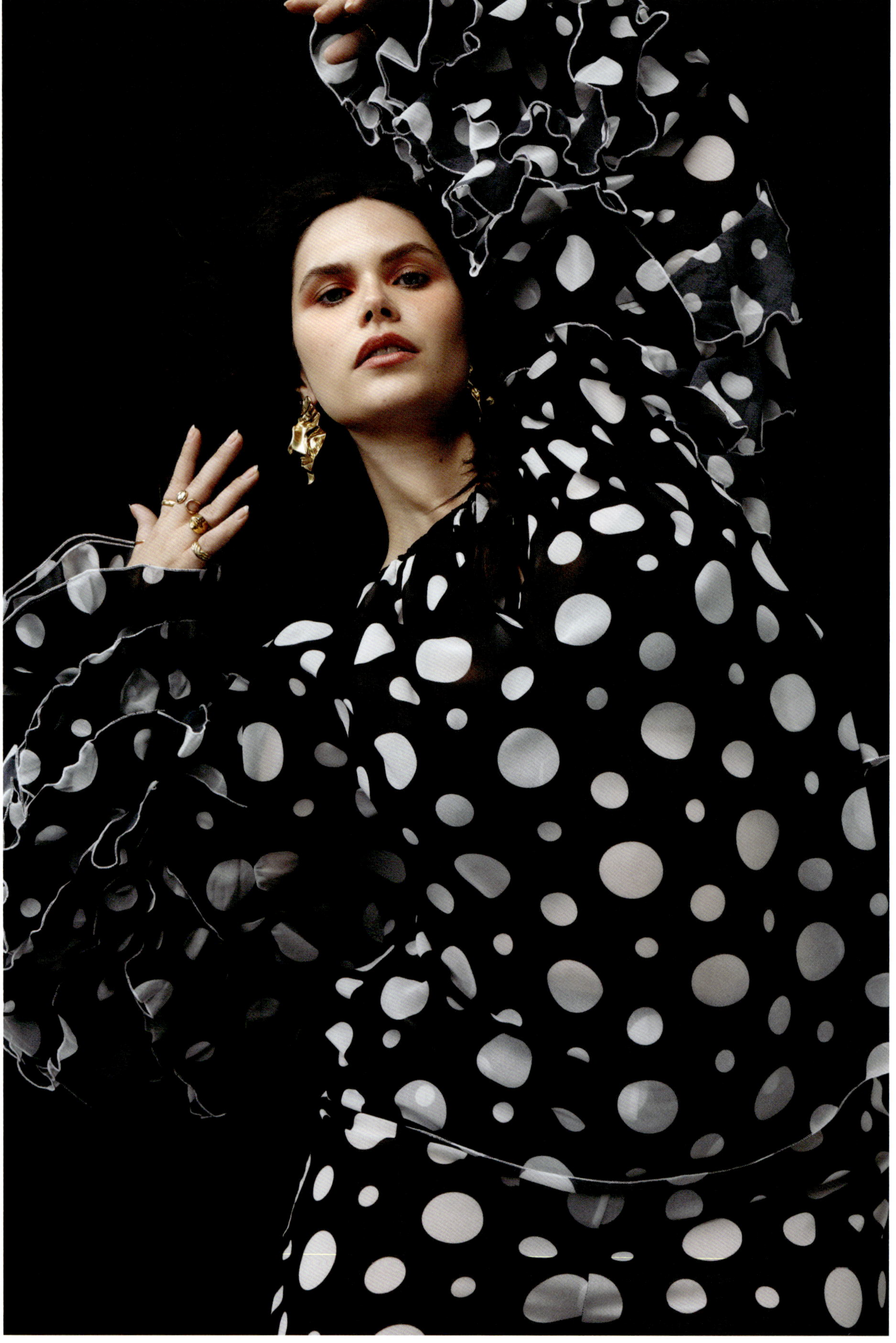

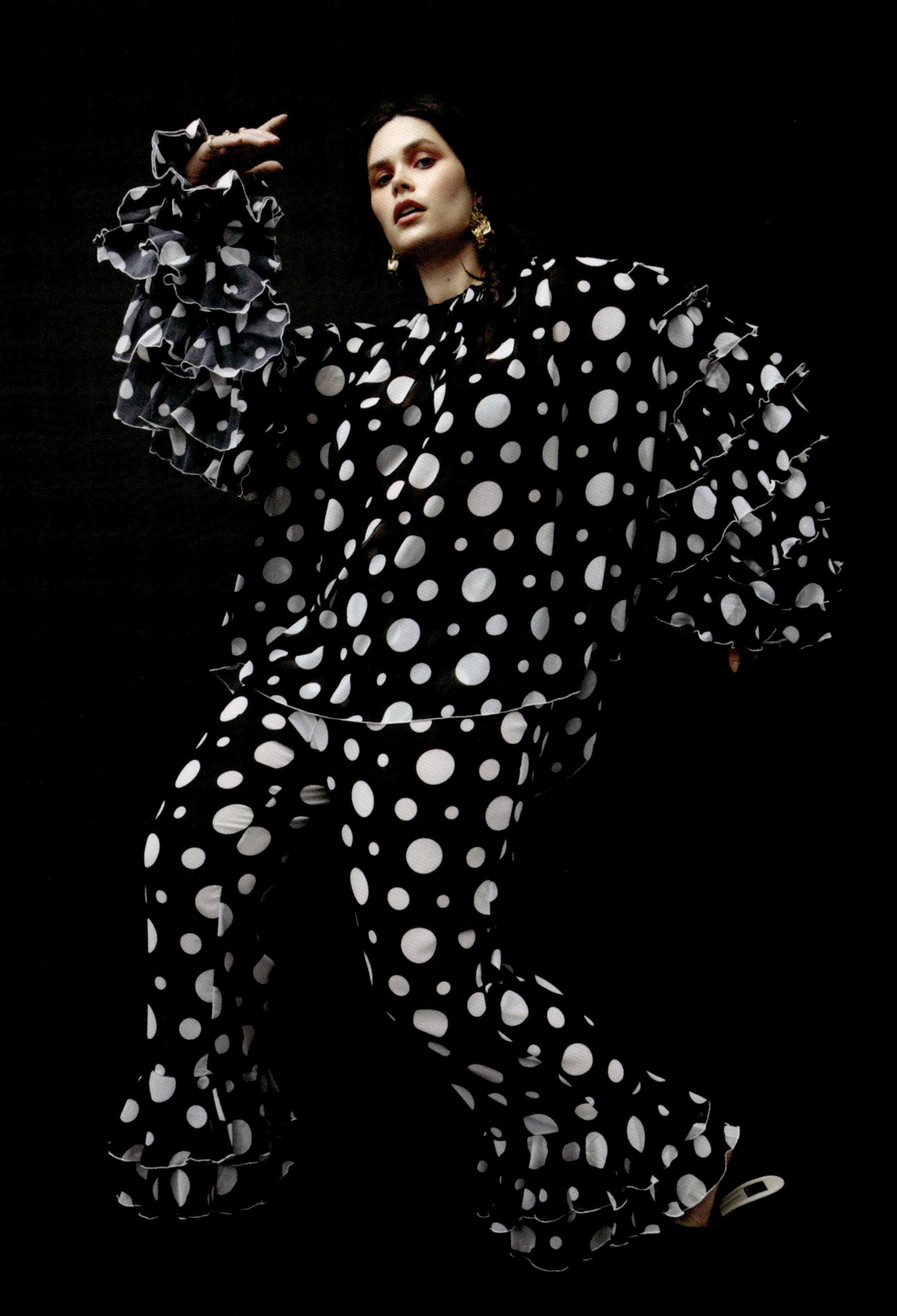

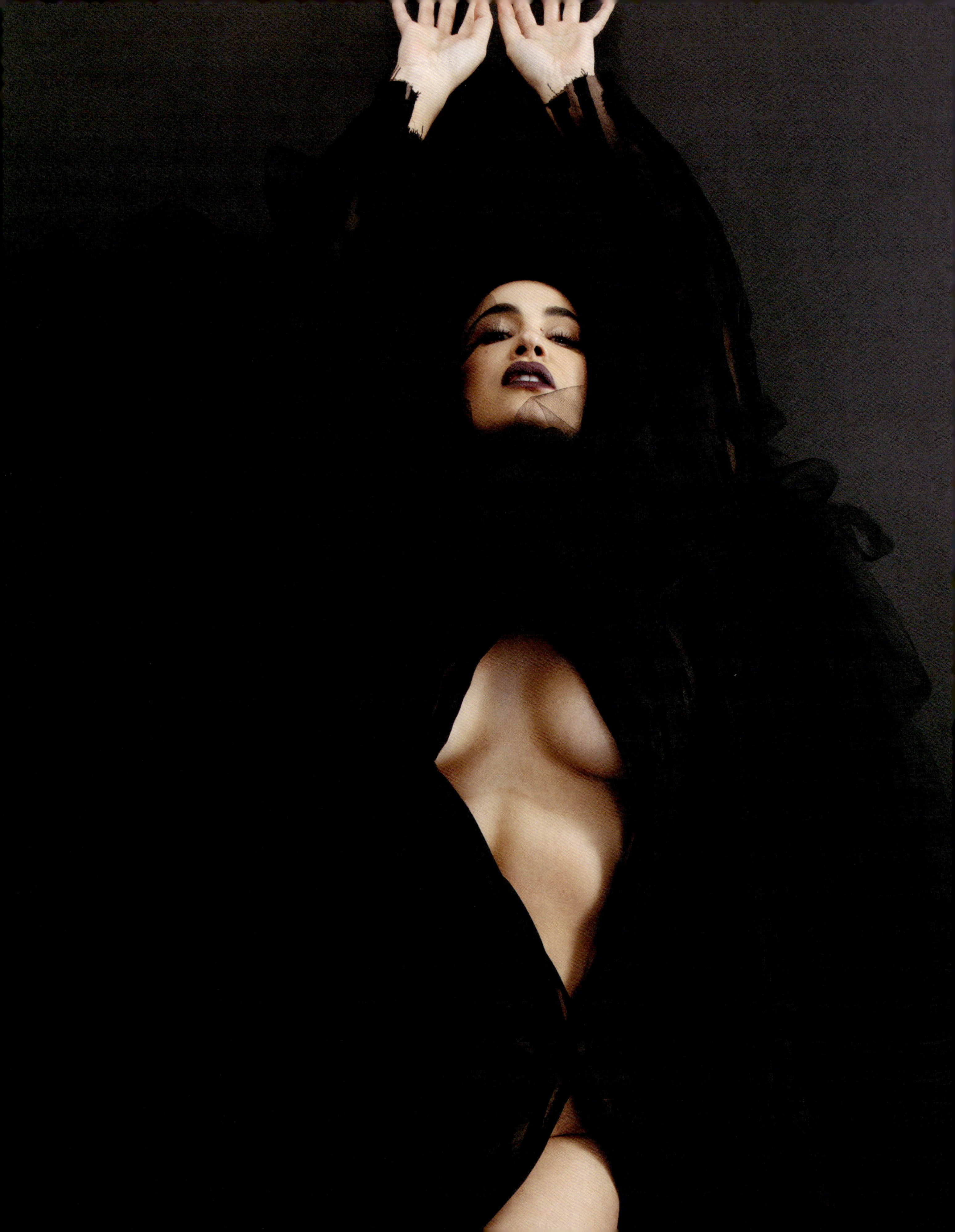

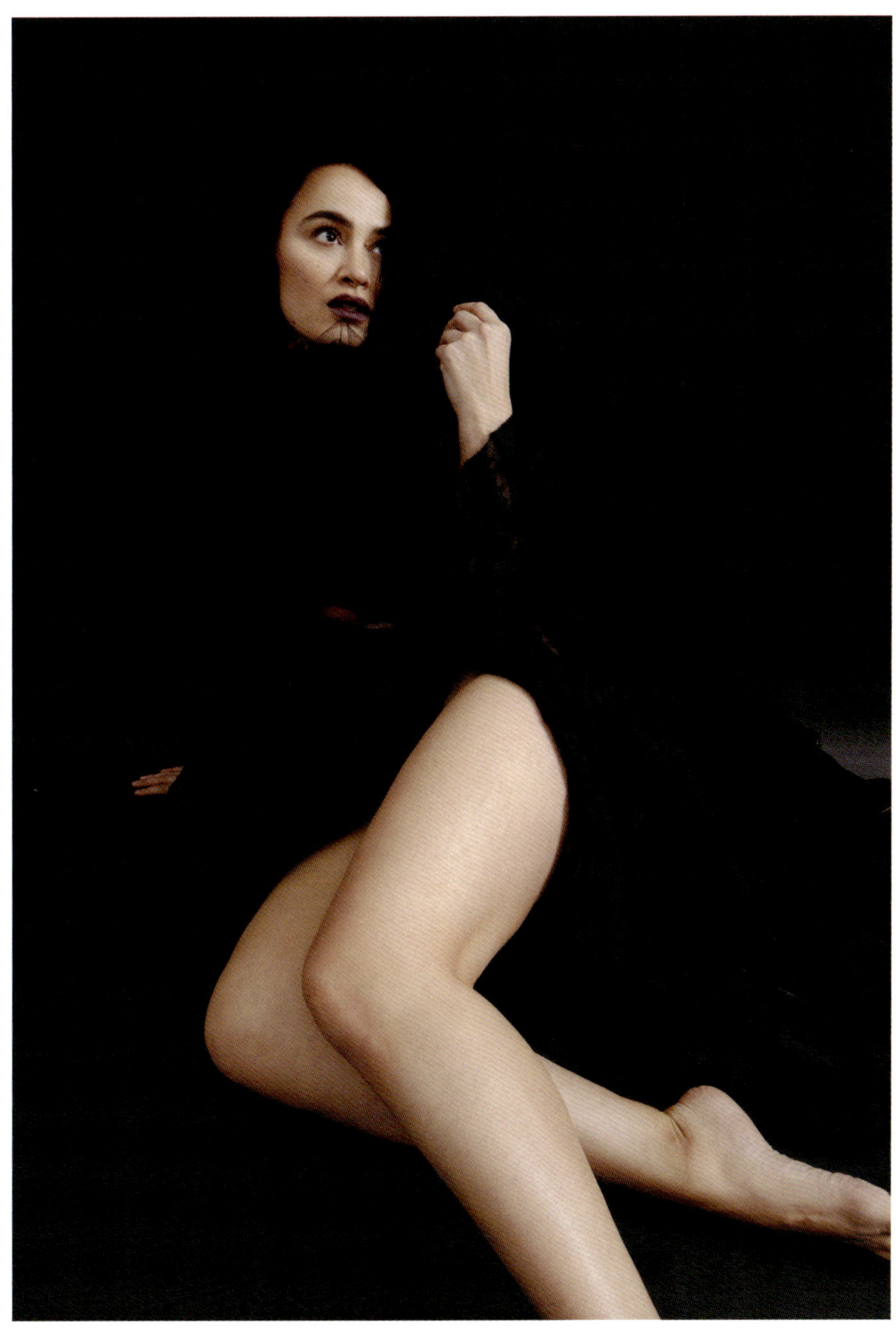

Previous pages: Chloe DeCleene wears Sleeper set; Dolce Vita shoes; Alexis Bittar earrings.

Denka Obradovic wears Caycee Black.

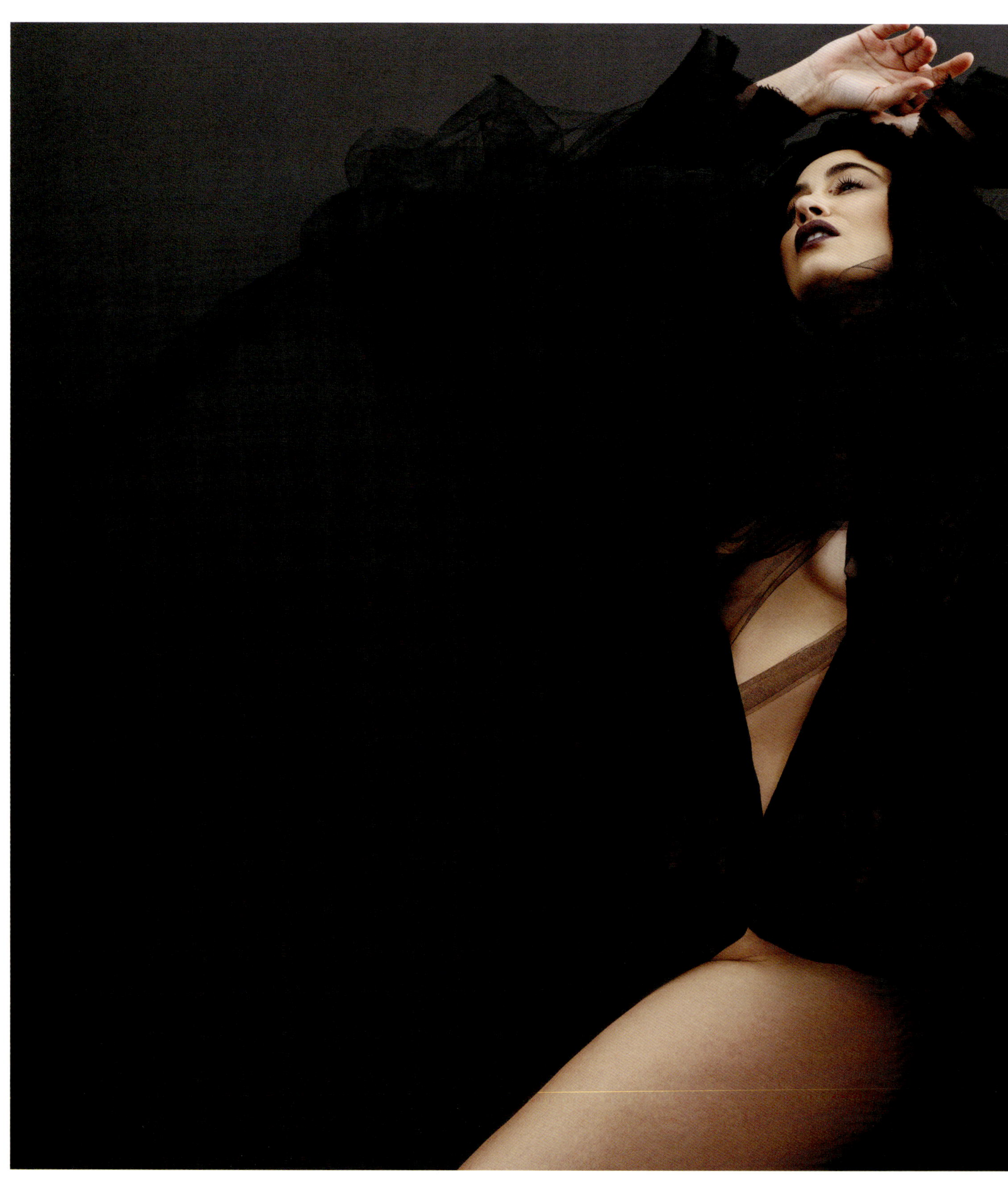

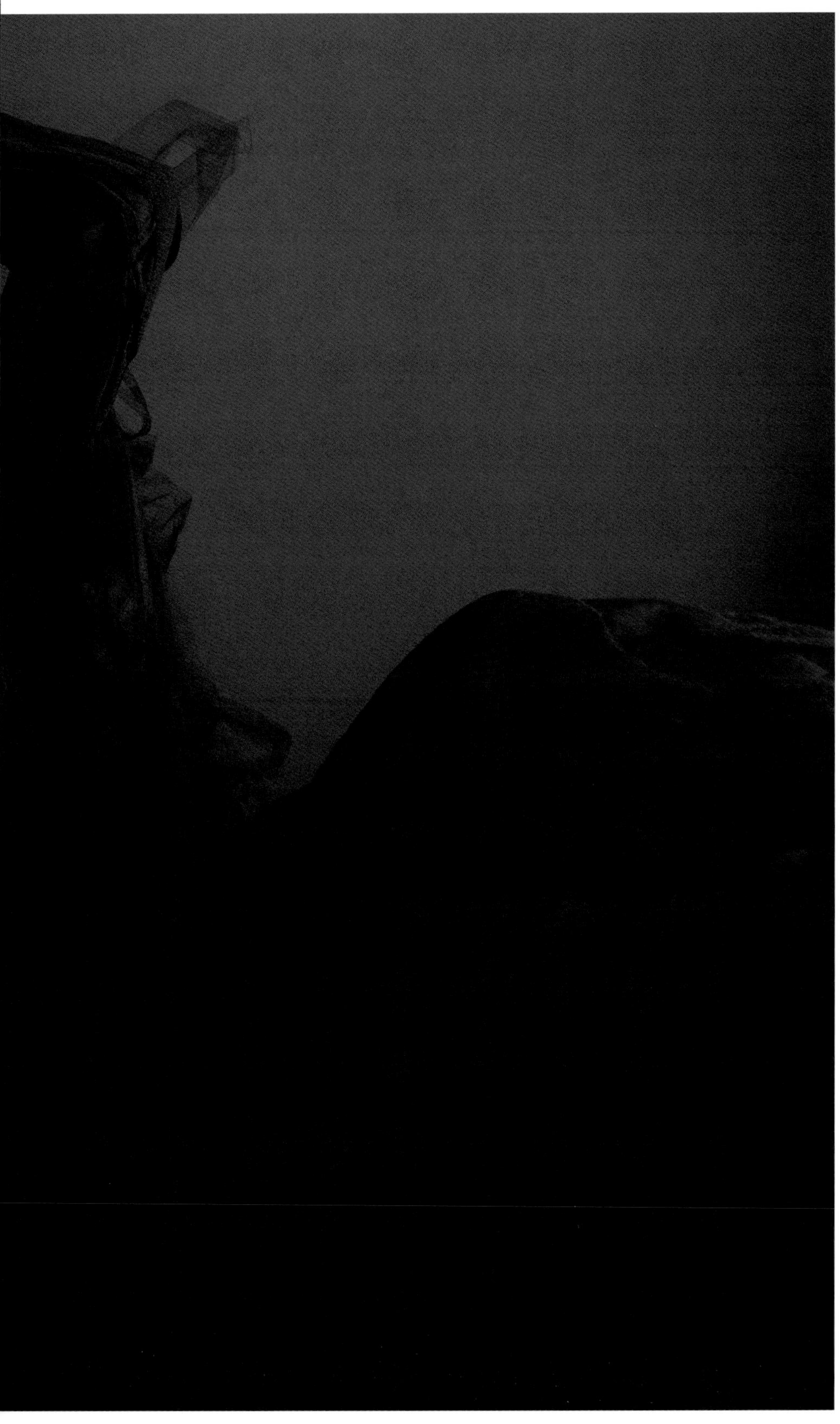

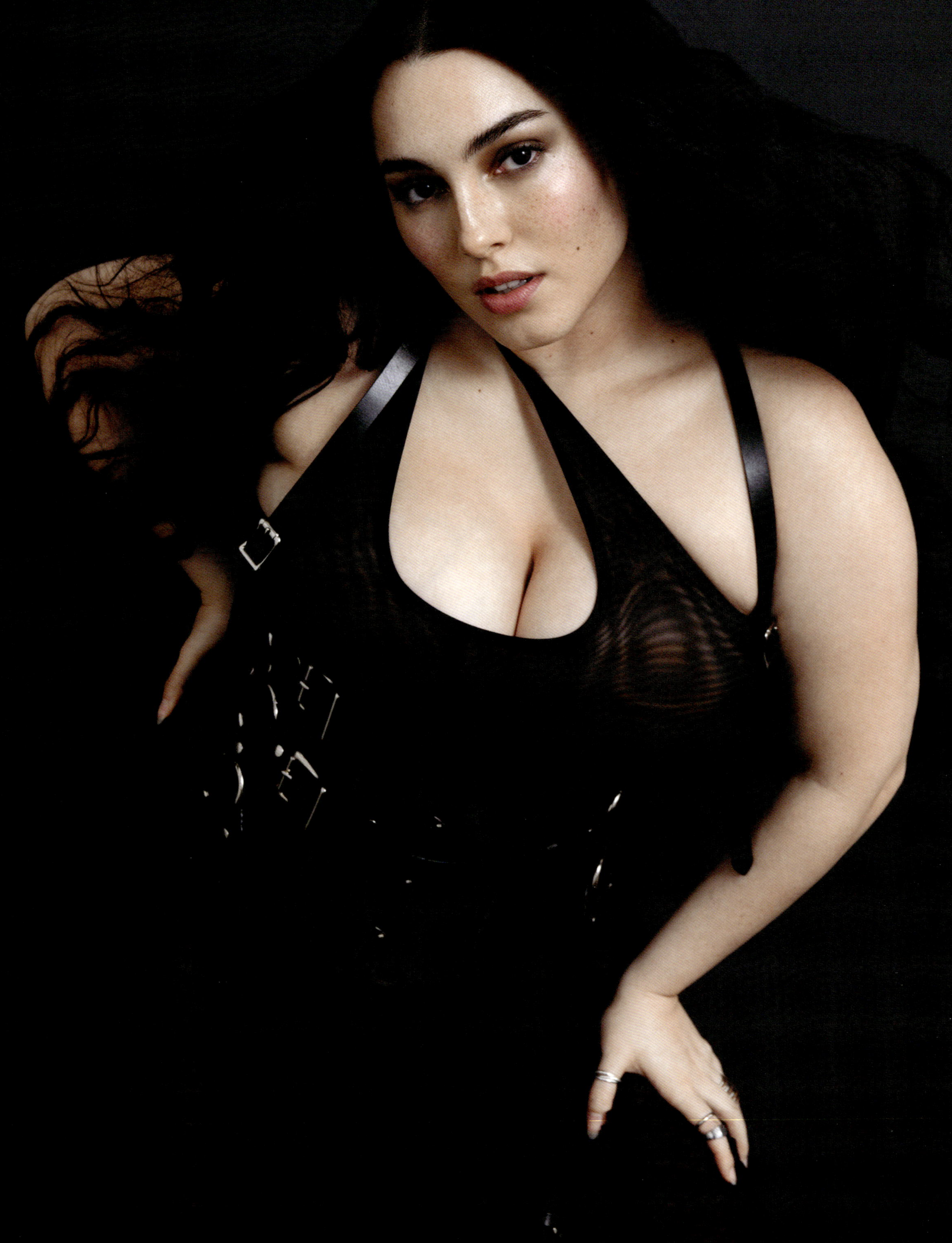

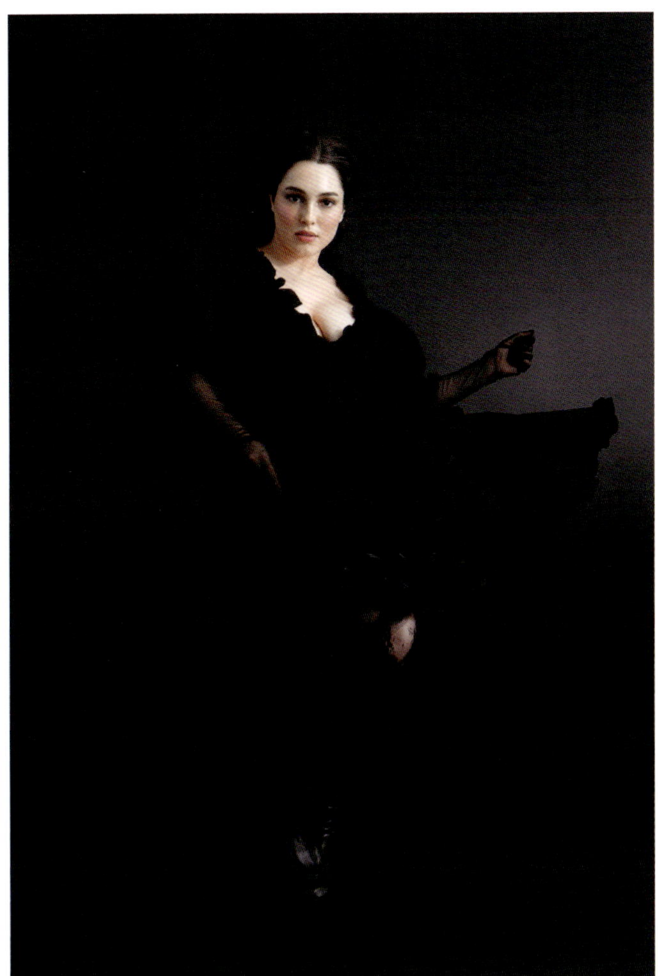

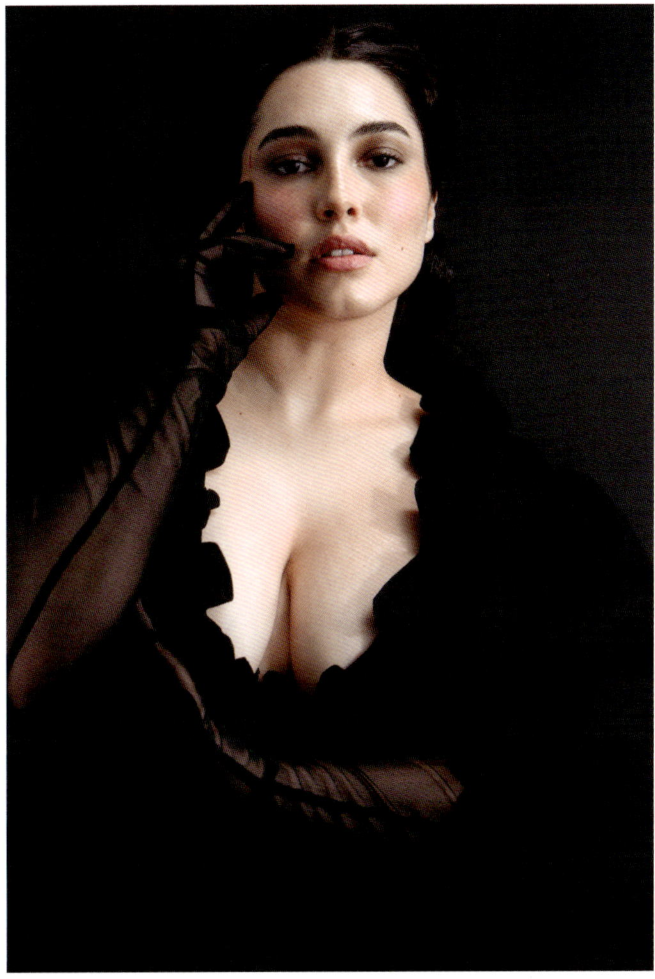

Kristen Alvarenga wears Curvy Couture bodysuit and Zana Bayne harness (left); Selkie dress (right).

Overleaf: Sabey Dantsira wears Pipenco Lorena.

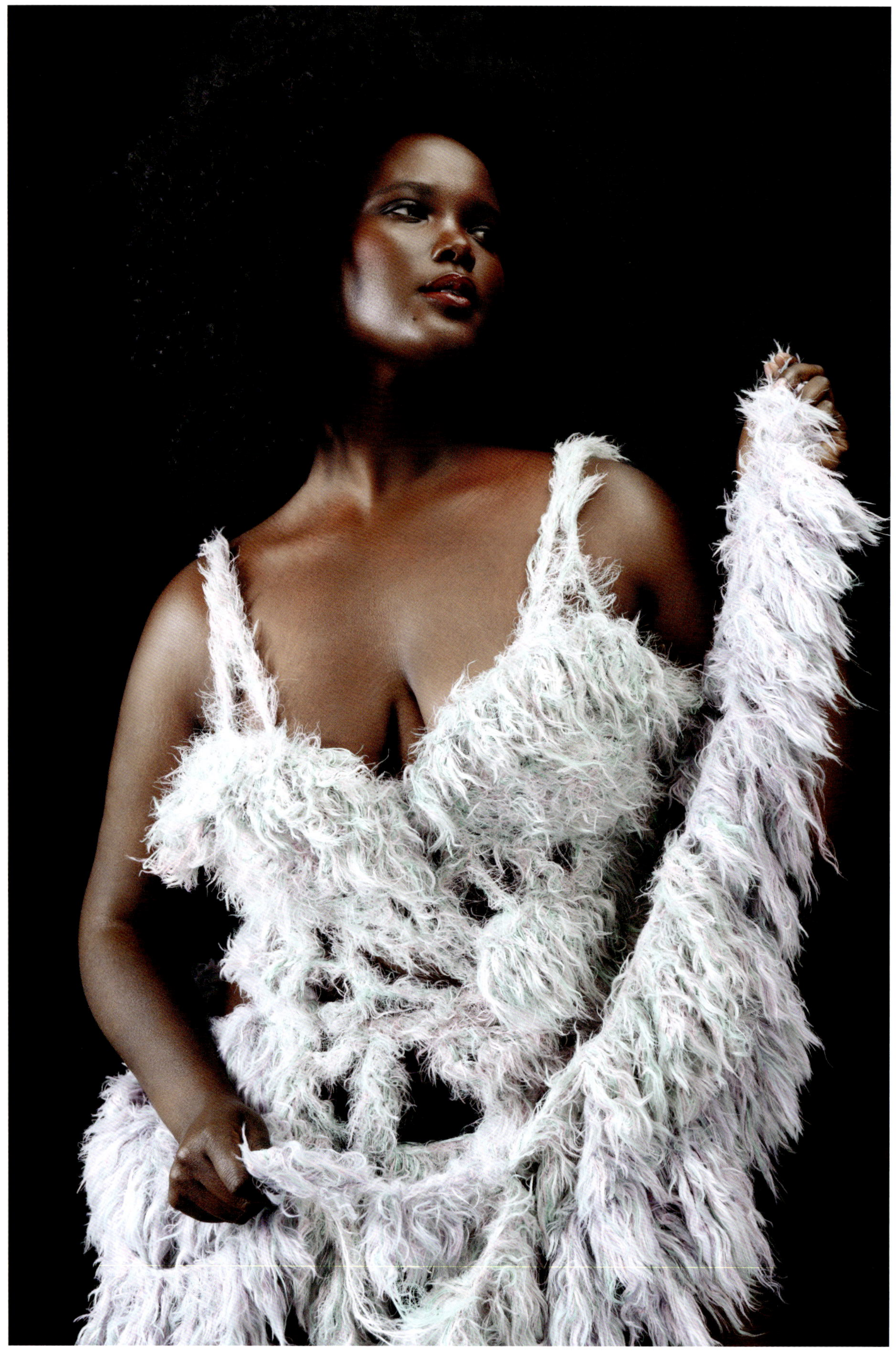

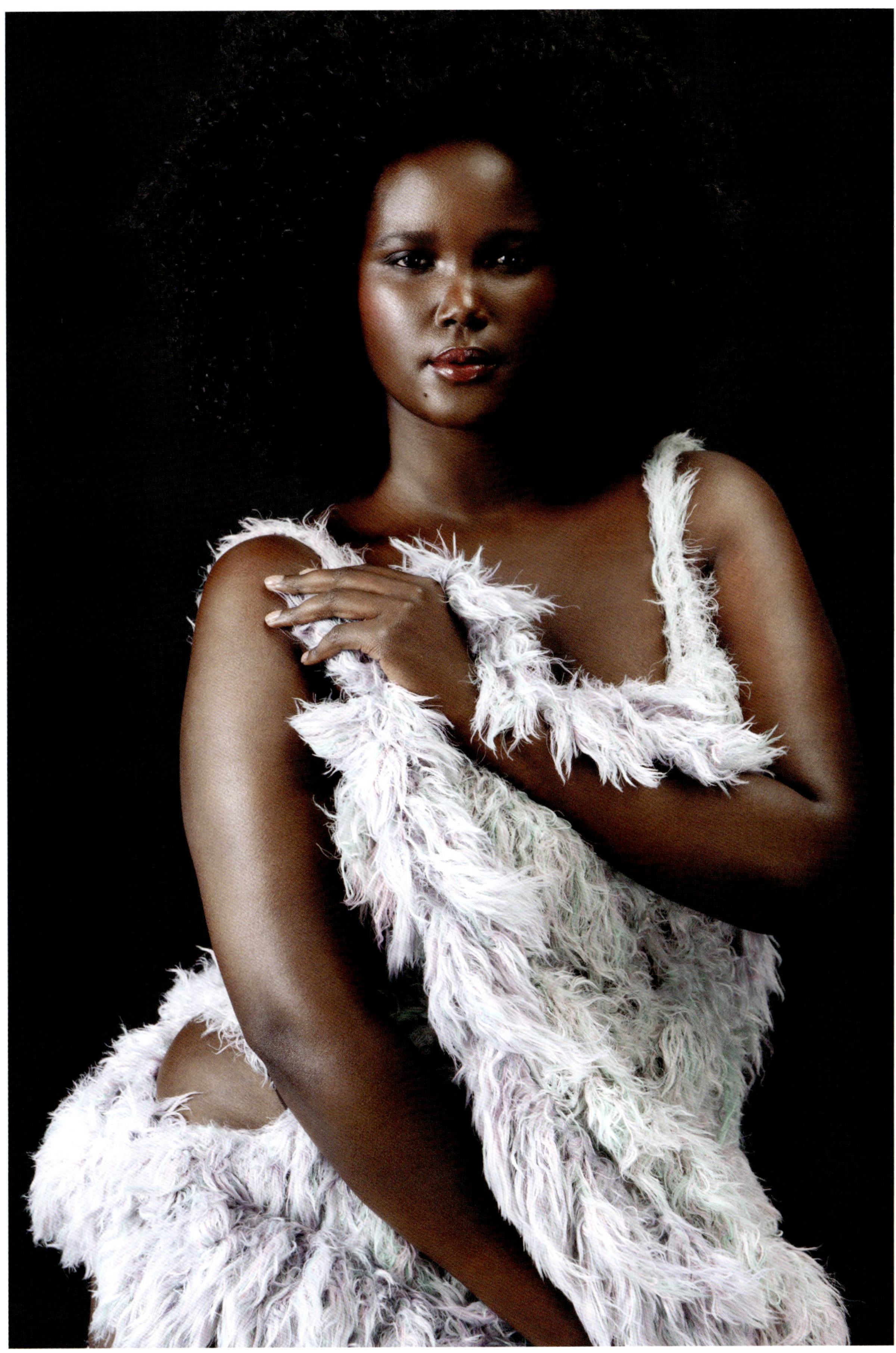

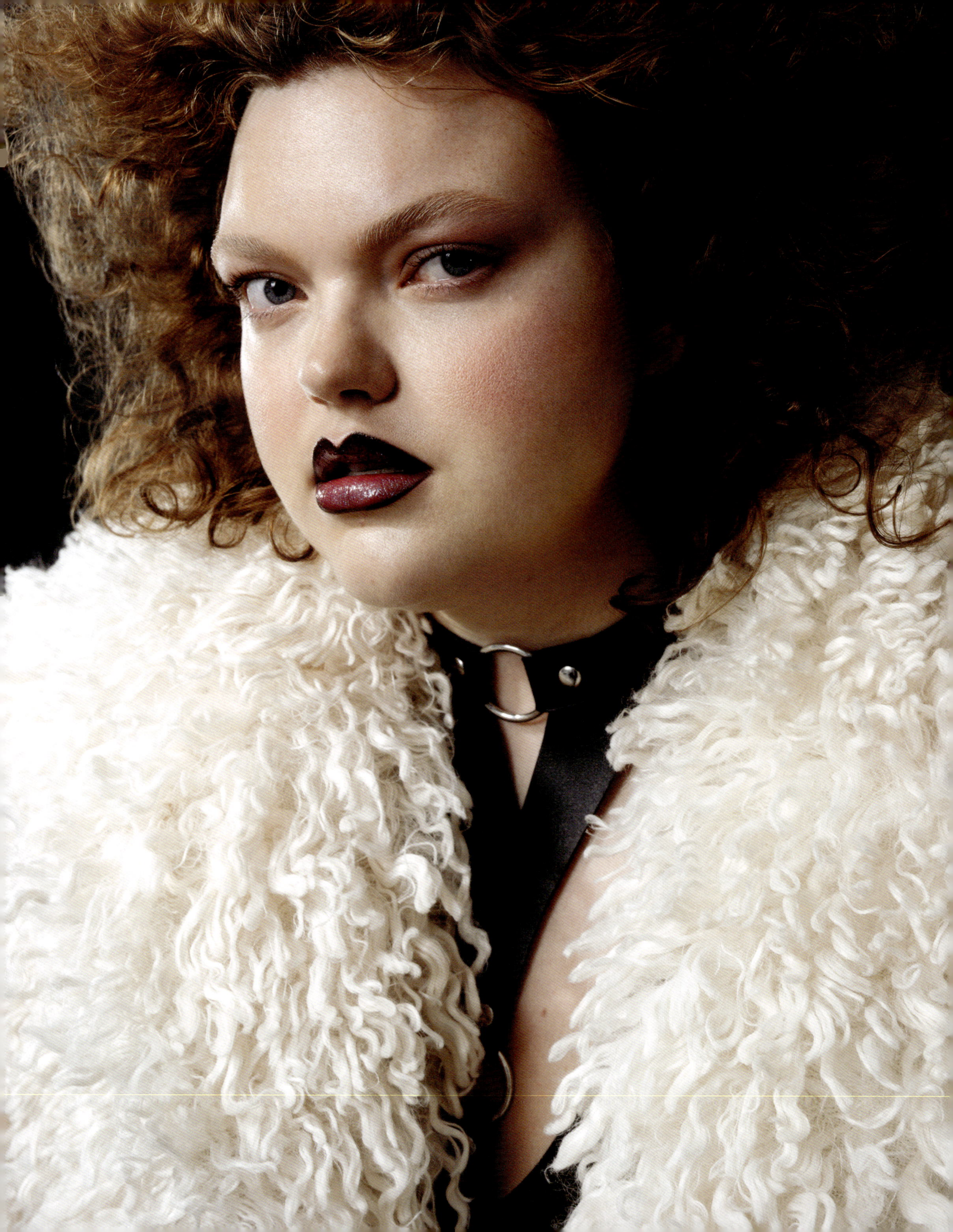

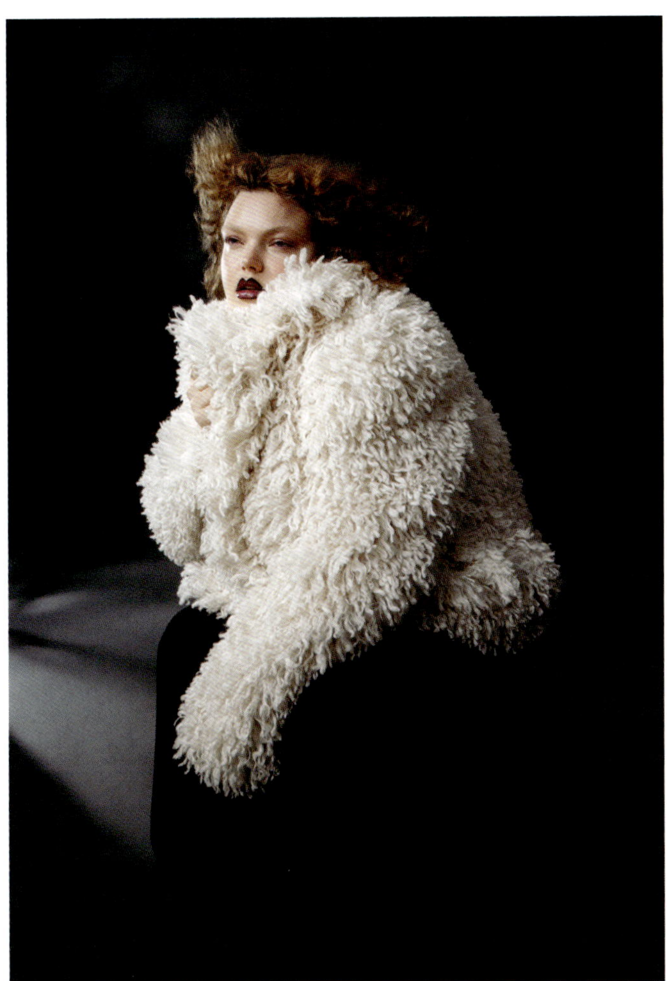

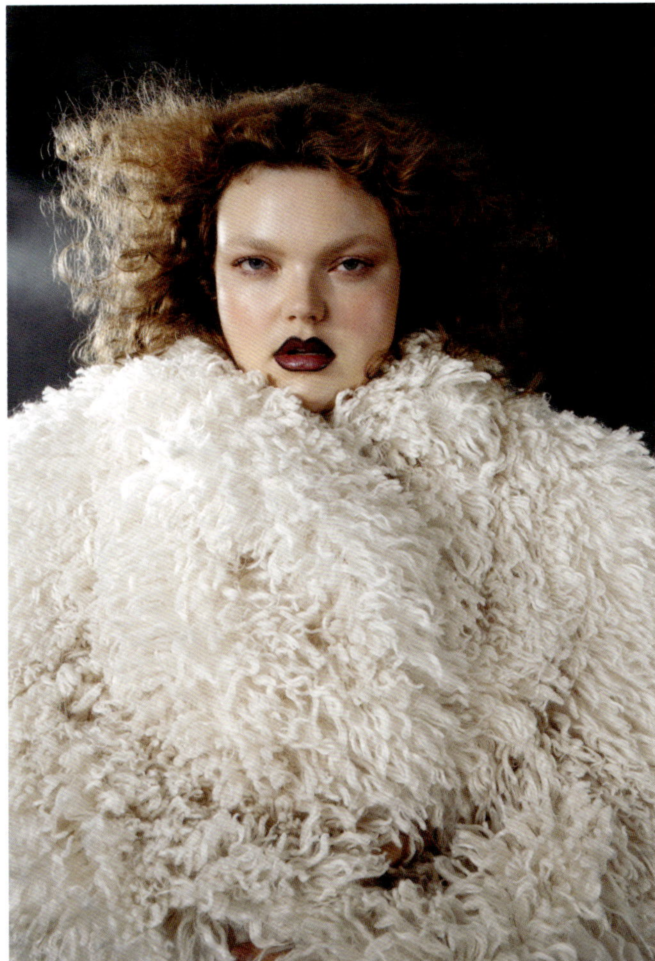

Charlie Reynolds wears coat and skirt from Lydia Hudgens' closet; Thistle and Spire harness.

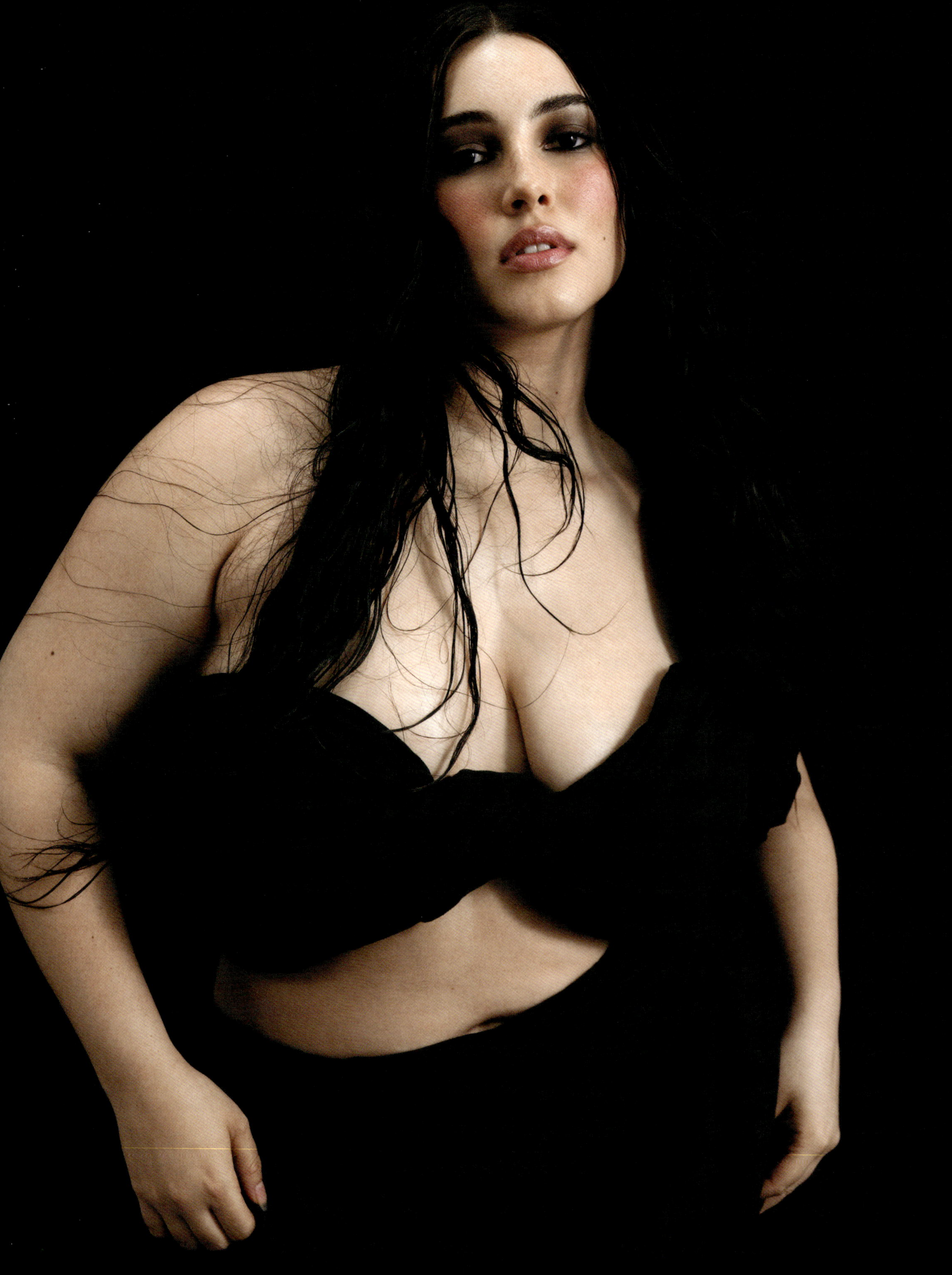

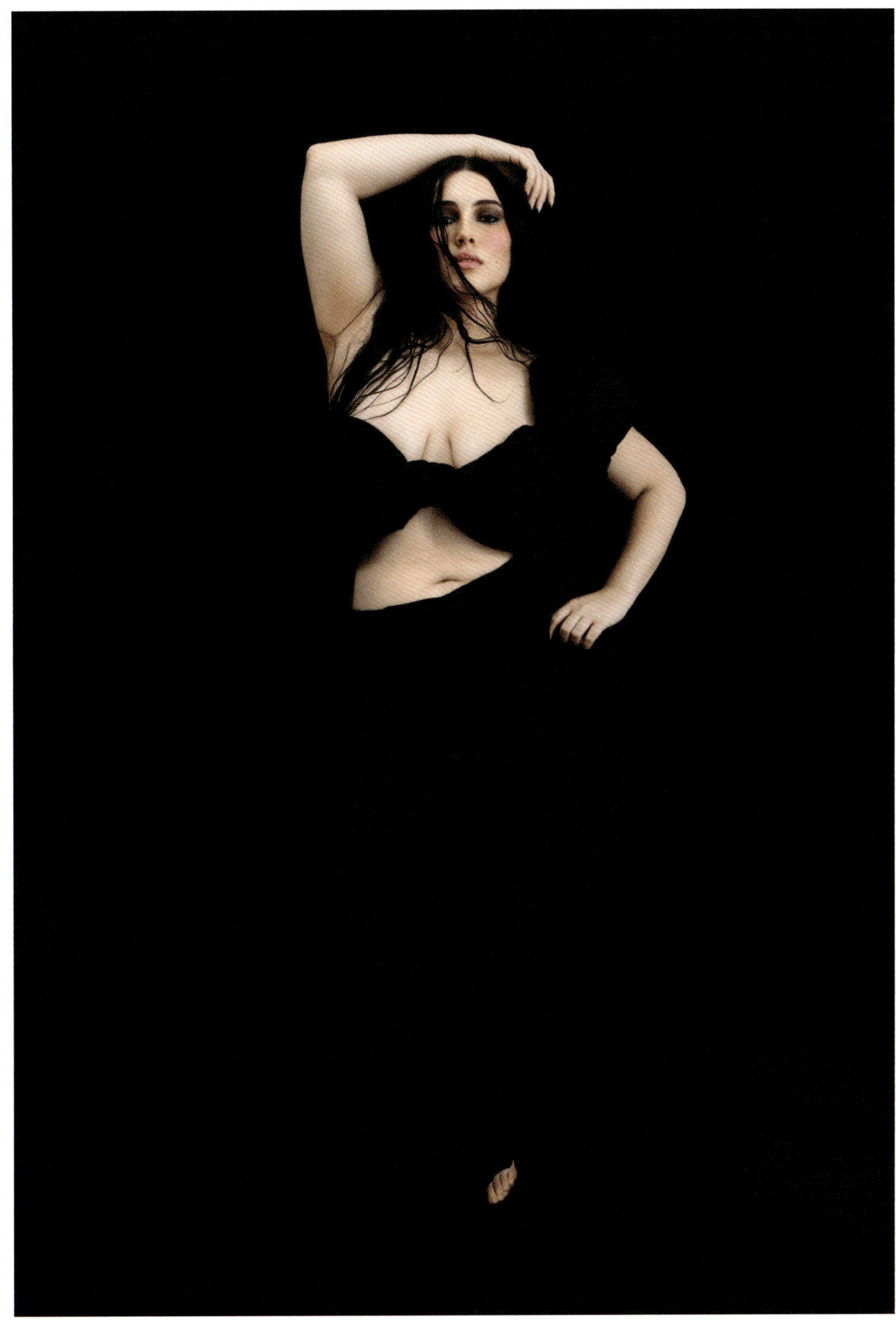

Kristen Alvarenga wears fabric draped by Lydia Hudgens.

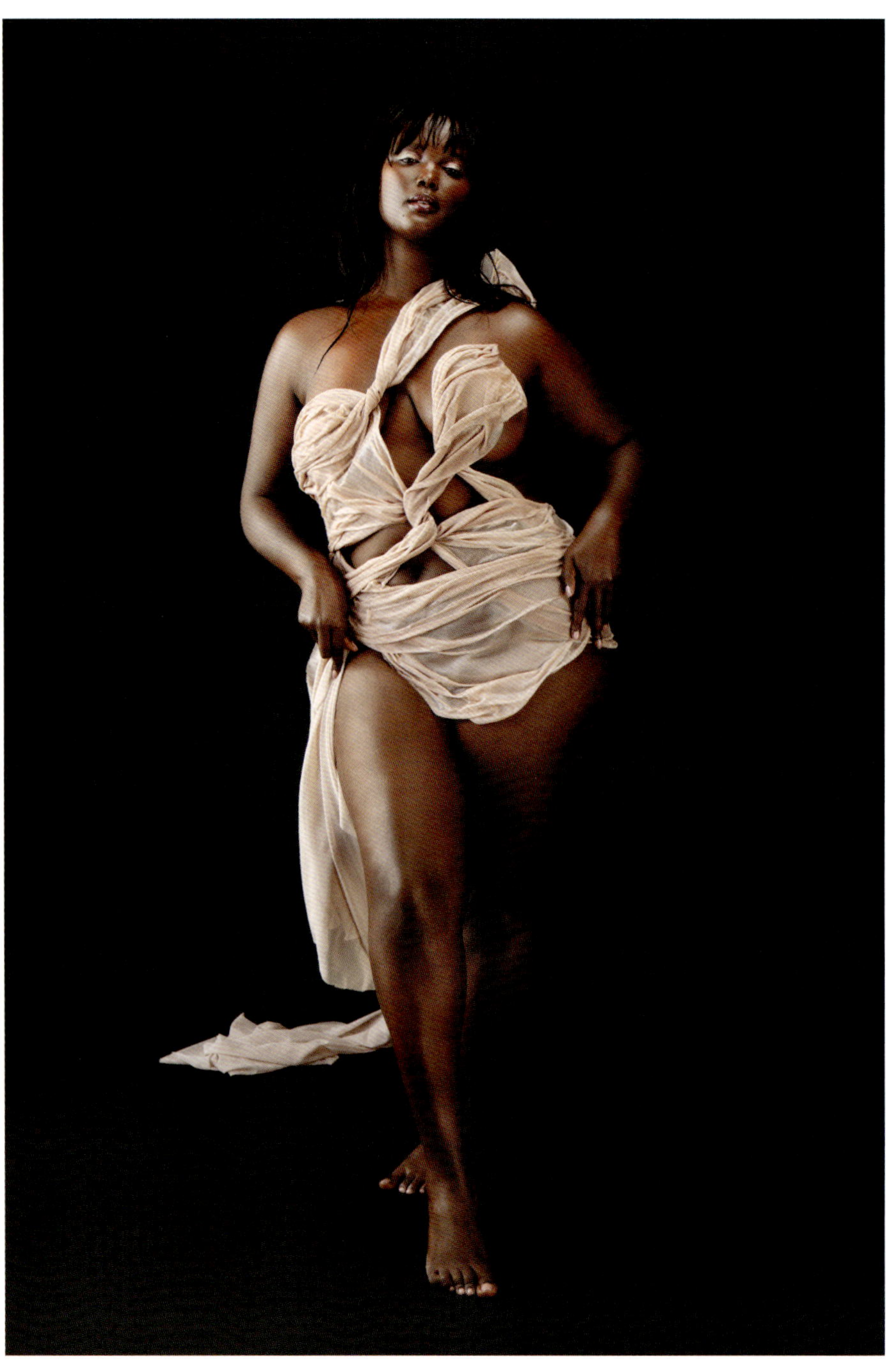

Sabey Dantsira wears Kim Mesches.

Overleaf: Delphine Clowe wears Theo Banzon.

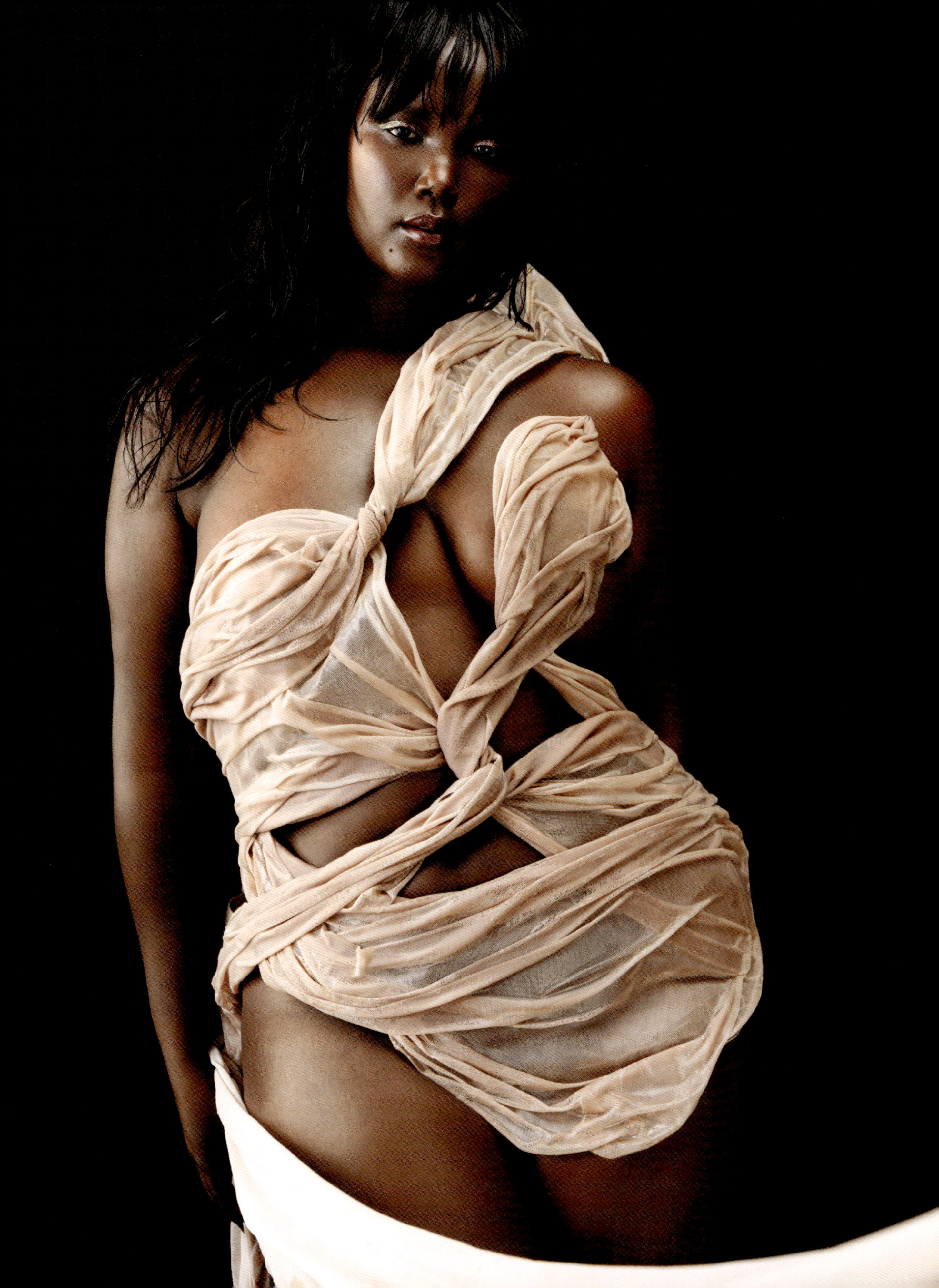

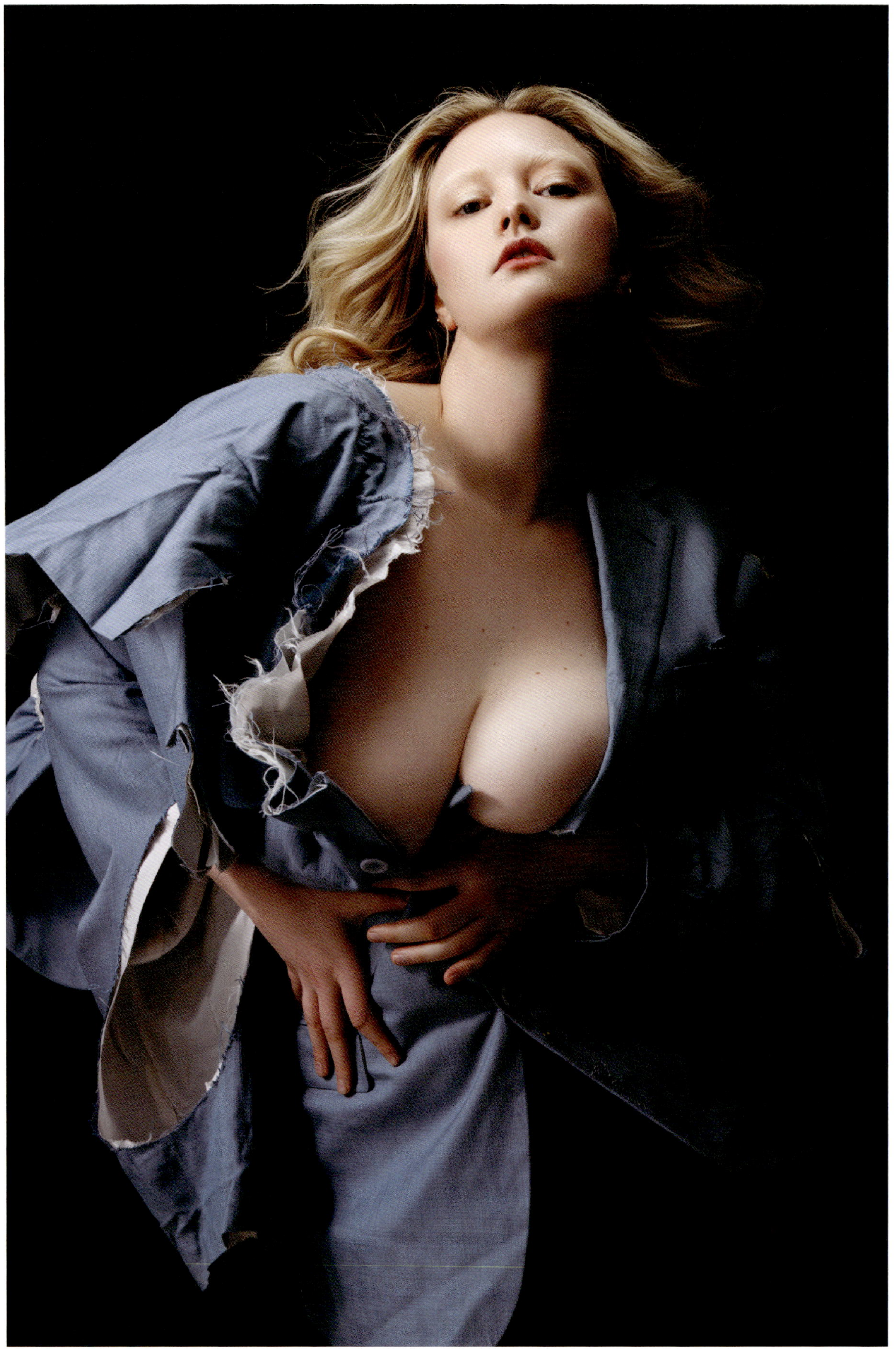

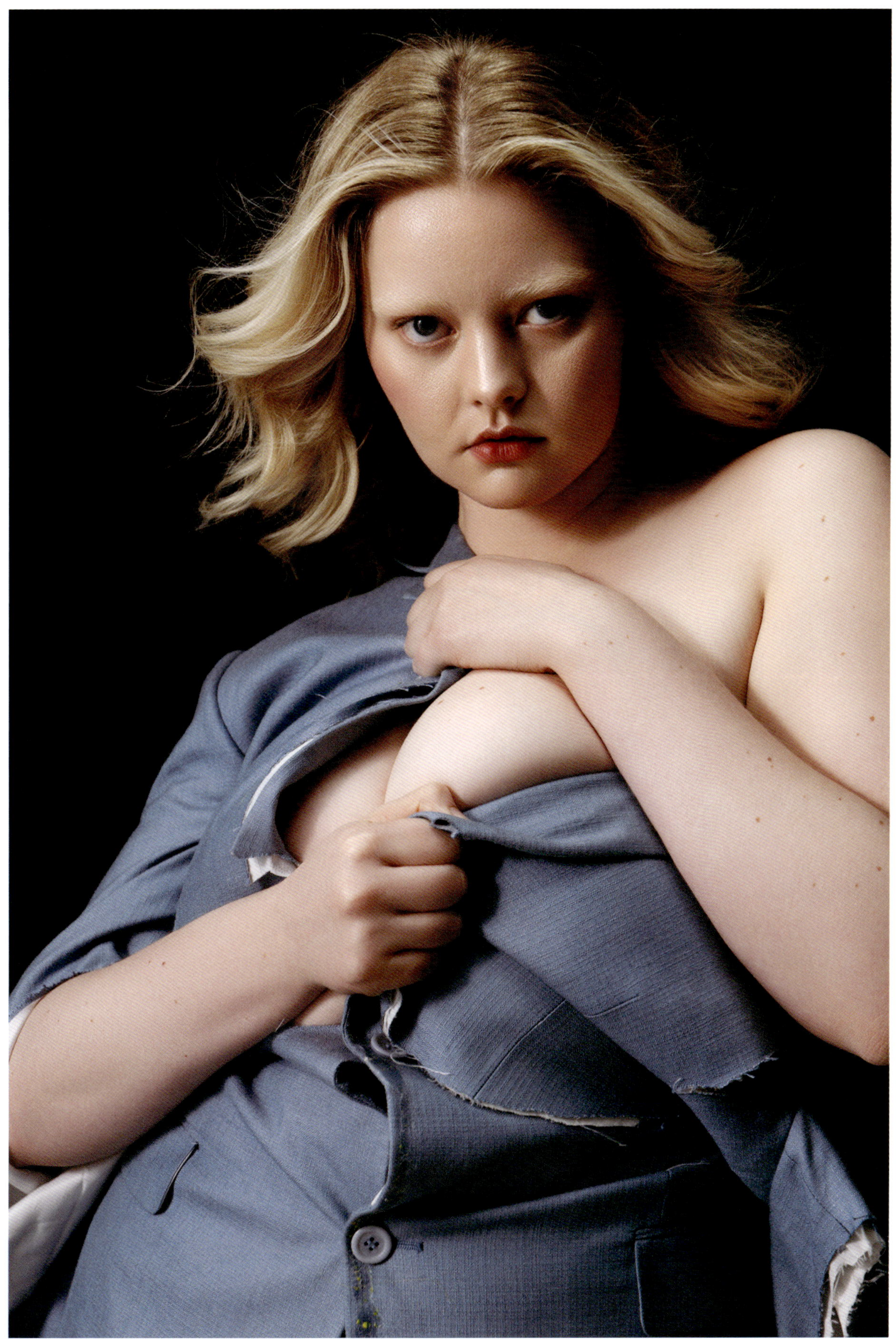

Beauty

For people who grow up plus-size, beauty often feels like an unattainable standard. From a young age, we're conditioned to believe that it's something we can only earn if we lose a little weight, if we change something about ourselves. Compliments like "You have such a pretty face" feel backhanded, implying that our beauty is conditional, that our bodies somehow negate our worth.

The truth is plus-size people are rarely allowed to feel beautiful without qualifiers or caveats. Even now, in an era when representation in beauty campaigns is slowly expanding, plus-size models are still expected to meet narrow standards. The ones who gain the most visibility often have features that align with conventional beauty ideals, whether that's sharper bone structures or slimmer faces—traits that make them appear thinner.

The erasure and obsession with perfection have only grown more intense in the years following 2020. We live in a time when the cultural focus on thinness has resurged, fueled by diet culture, Ozempic, and the push for "youthful" plastic surgery. The faces we see most often right now on screens and in ads—that we idealize—are transformed into something impossibly smooth, ageless, and altered. The natural parts of ourselves—wrinkles, softness, and double chins—are dismissed as undignified, as though beauty can only exist when we minimize, hide, and reshape ourselves.

But beauty is not about erasure. It is not about shrinking into society's mold of acceptability. Beauty is about radiating creativity and individuality in a world that often tries to dim our light. There is beauty in aging. There is beauty in discovery—in learning to love the parts of ourselves we've been told to hate, from the lines that mark our smiles to the softness that reflects a life lived fully. Even something as ordinary as a double chin deserves to be seen, to be celebrated, because it's part of who we are.

This chapter is a celebration of individuality. My goal while creating these images was not just to capture flawless hair or makeup—though those elements can be stunning—but to focus on the essence of each model. Some images are bold and editorial, leaning into the aspirational energy of high-fashion beauty campaigns. Others are stripped back and raw, placing the focus on expression, emotion, and presence. Across all of them, I aimed to amplify the unique qualities of each model and tell a story that radiates beyond the frame.

In these pages, beauty isn't about compromise. It's about showing up fully, unapologetically, and embracing the parts of ourselves that society often asks us to hide. While these portraits are a celebration of beauty, they are also a reclamation of what it means to feel seen, powerful, and whole.

Kristen Alvarenga wears own shirt.

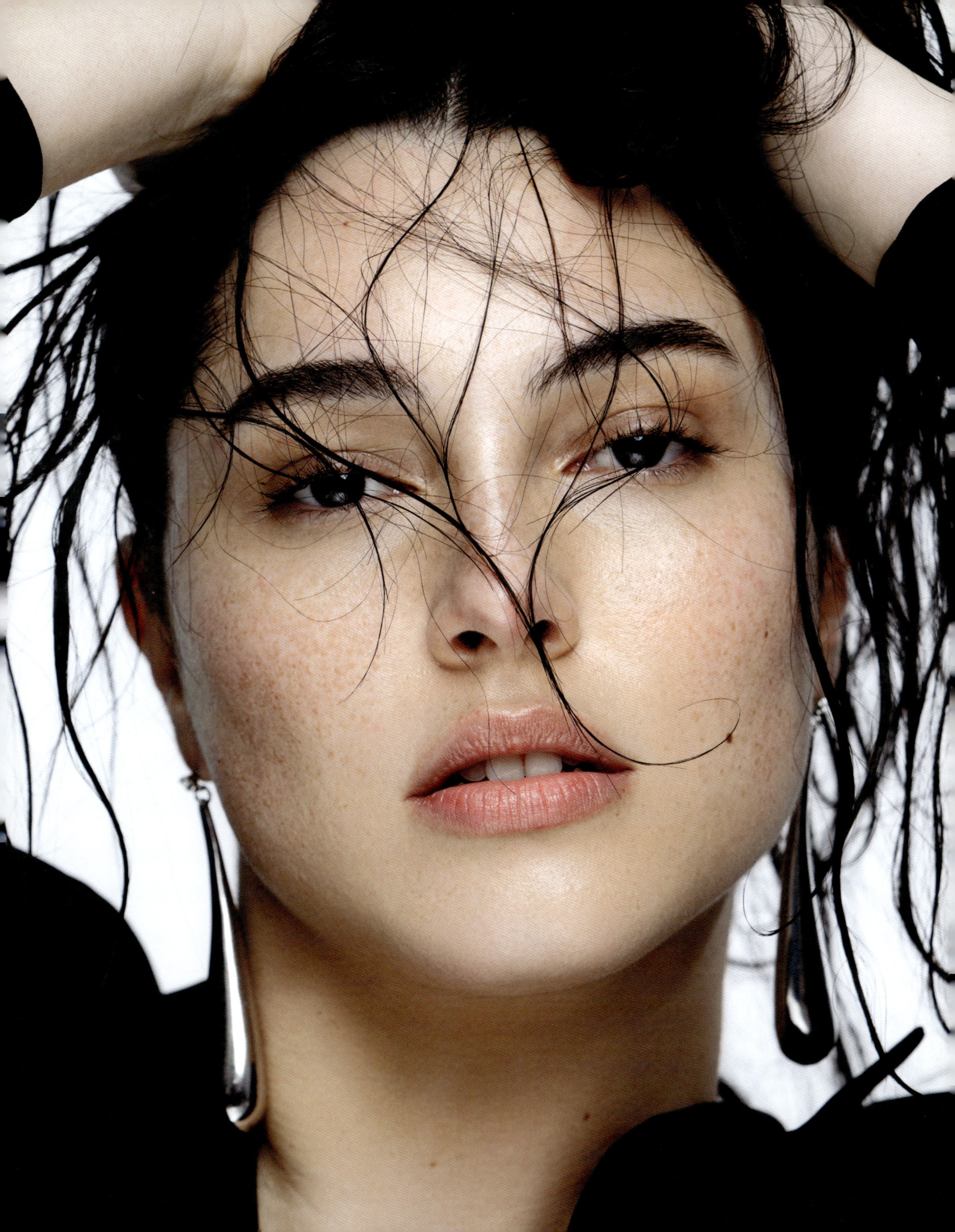

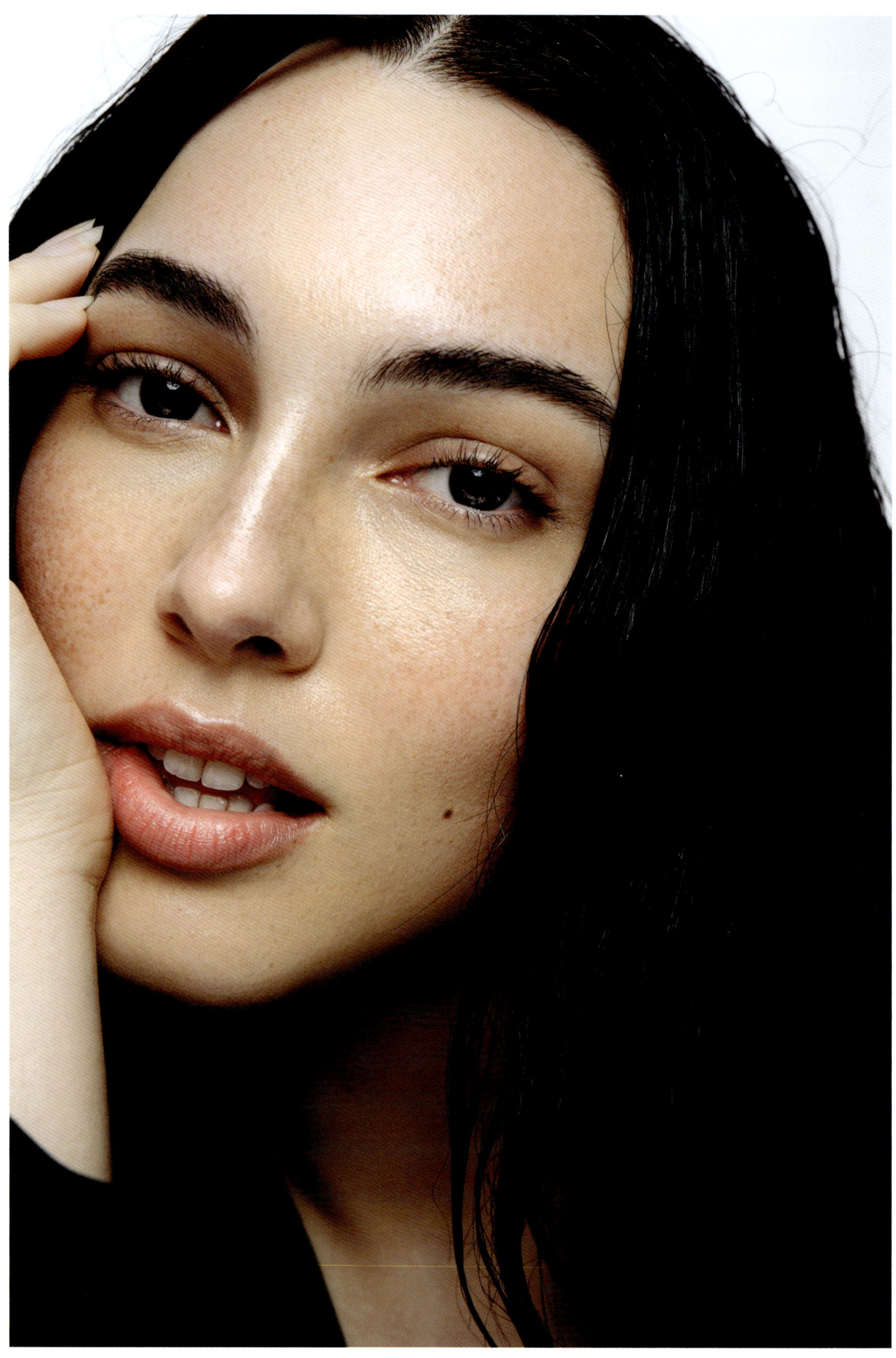

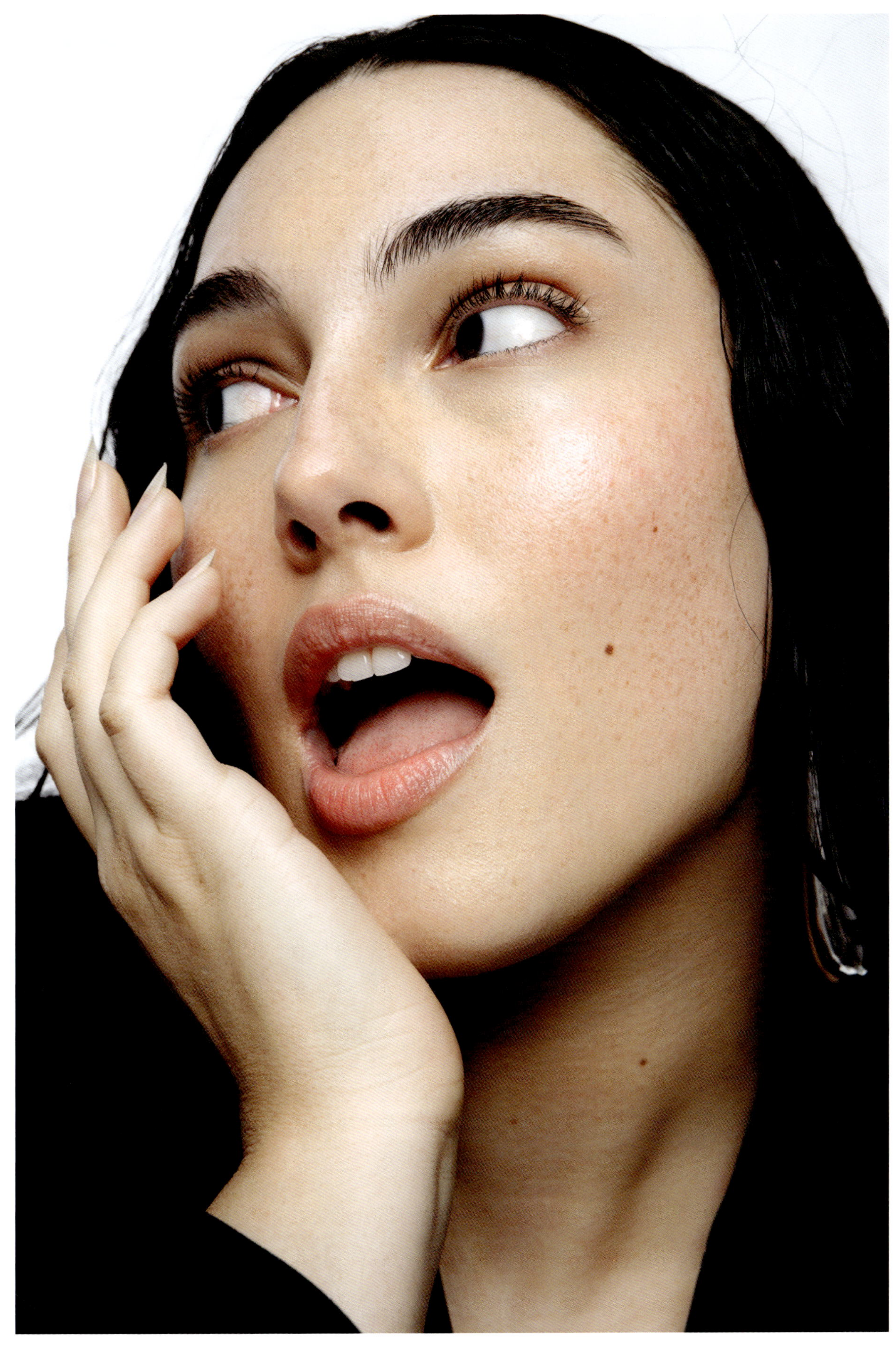

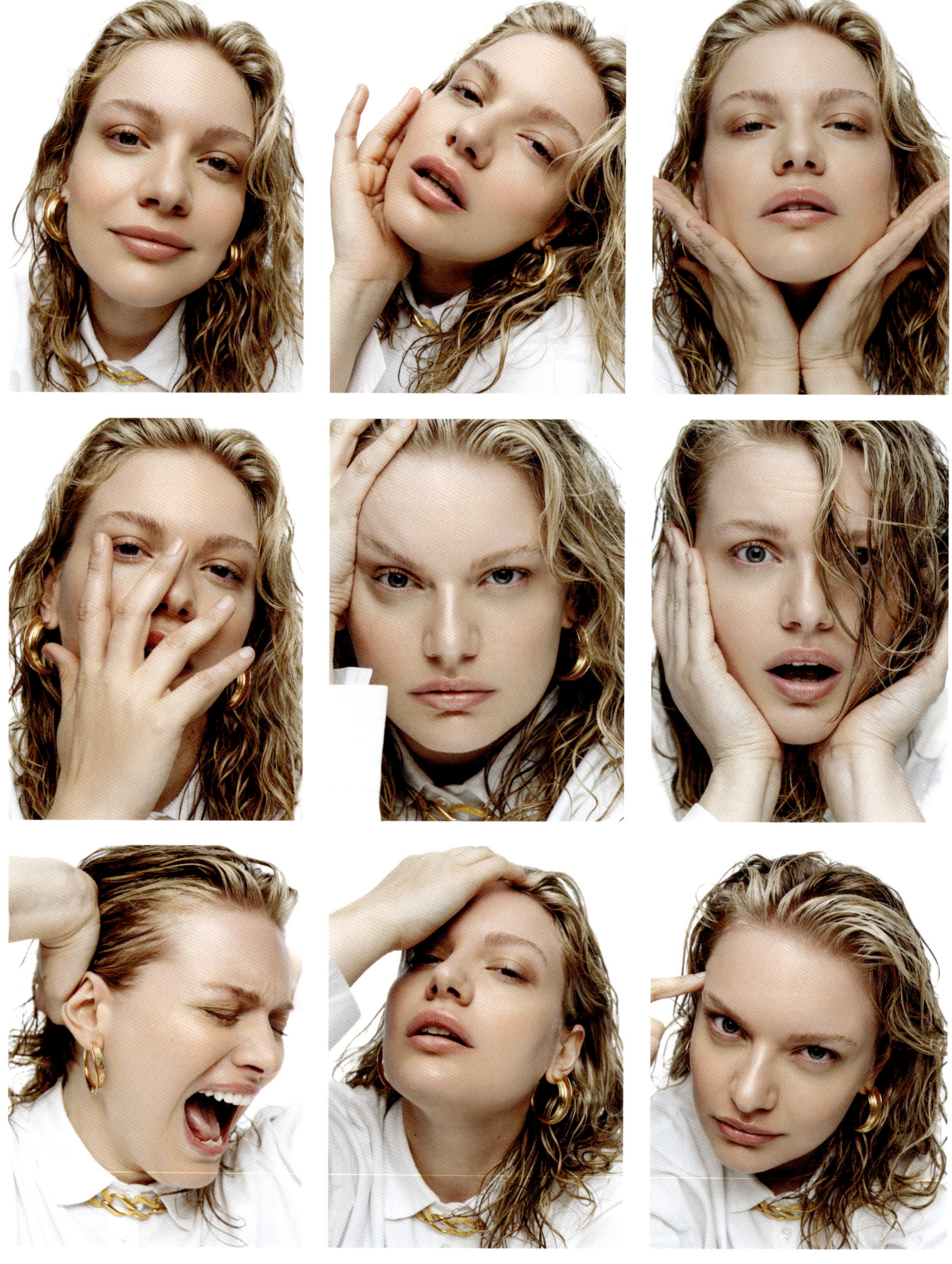

Ariana Corrao wears own shirt.

Overleaf: Melonee Rembert

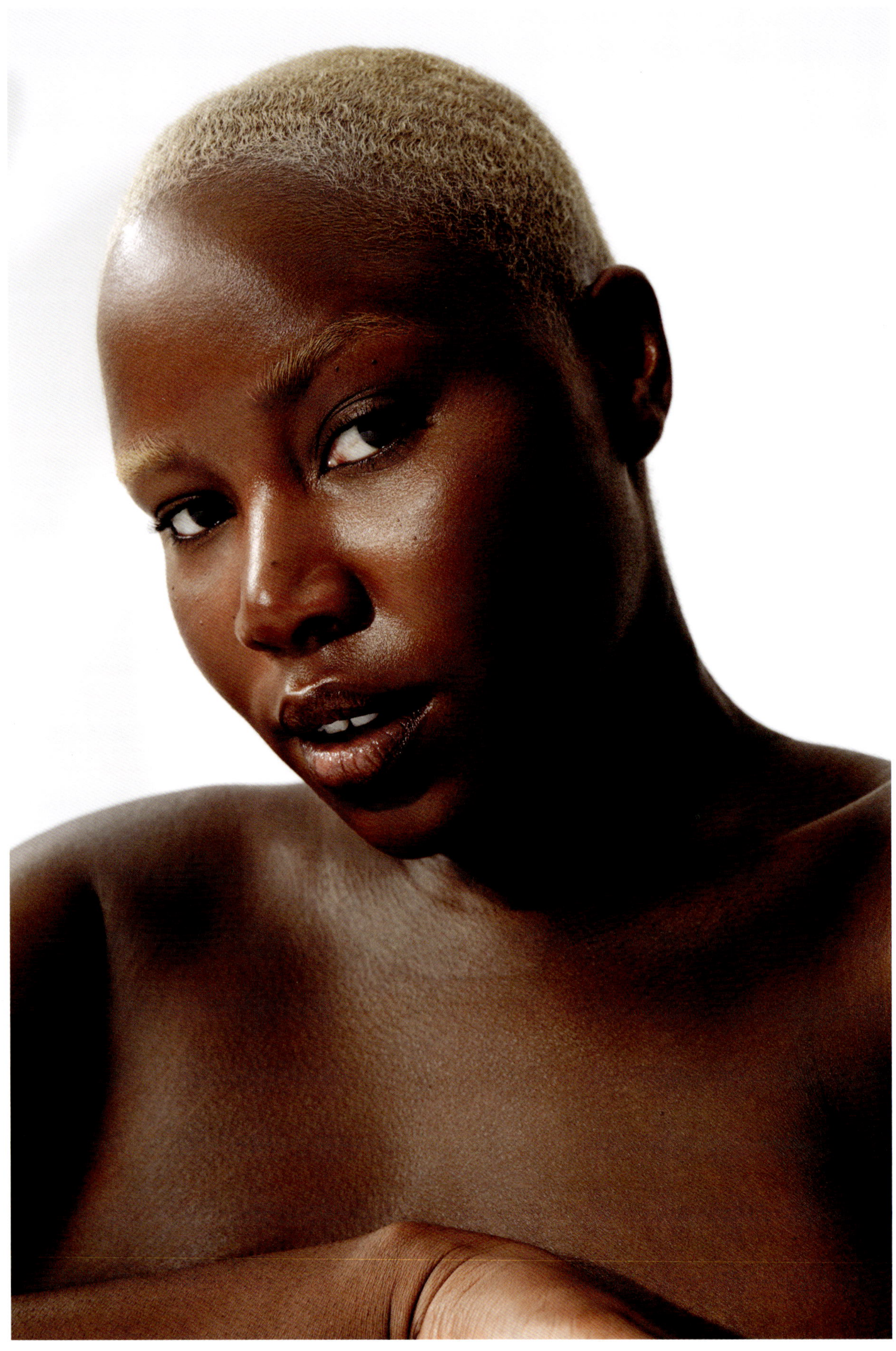

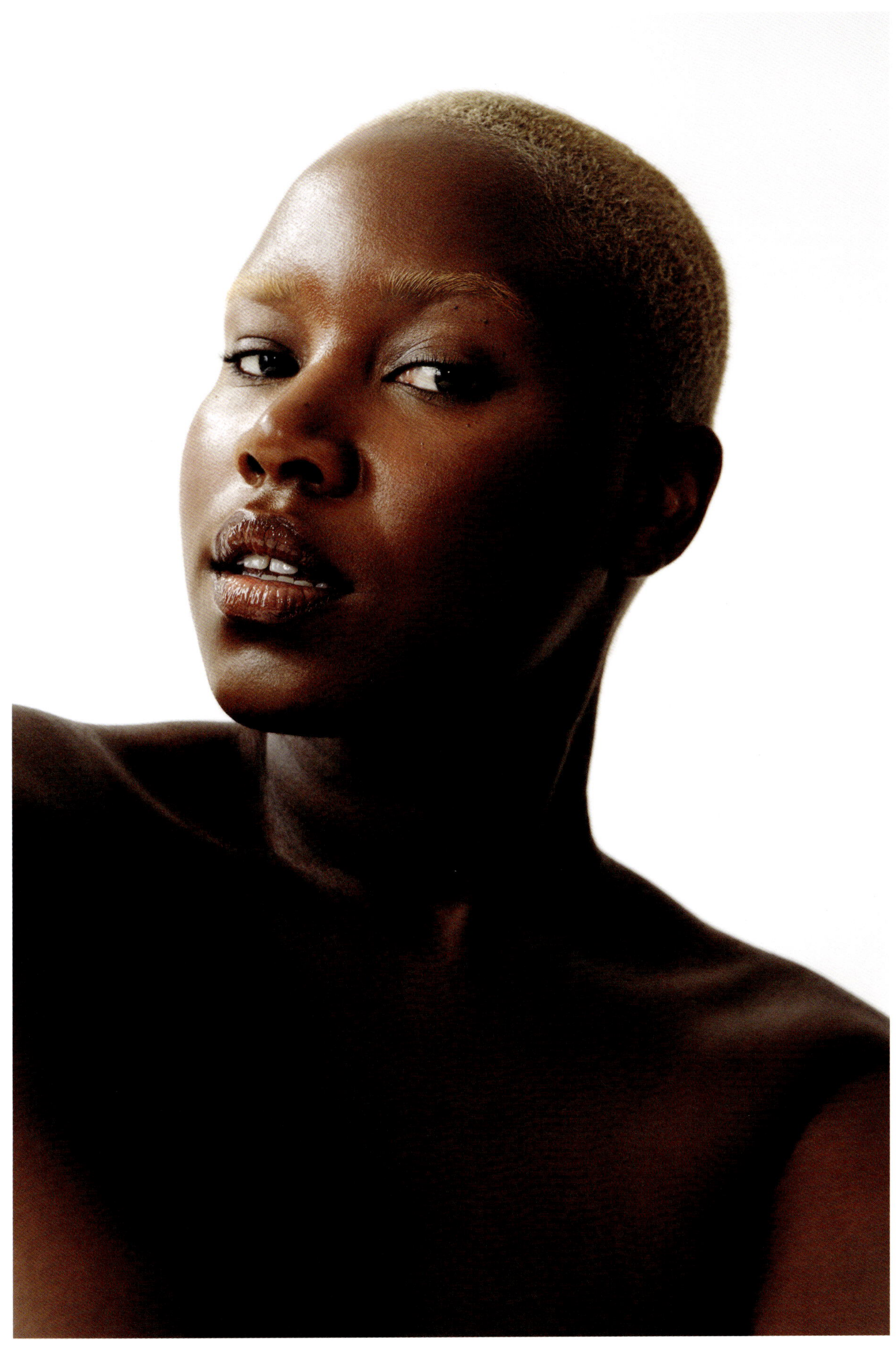

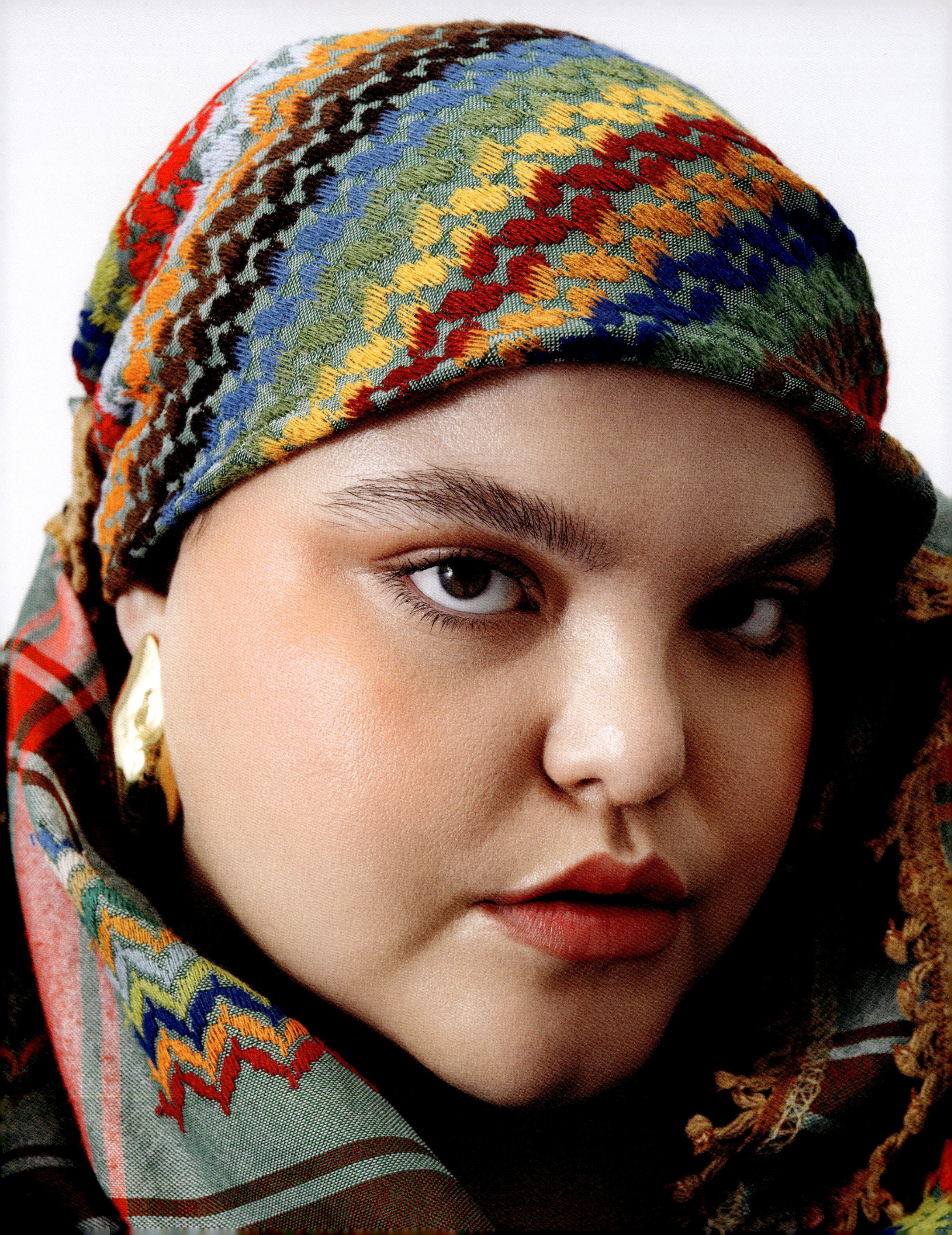

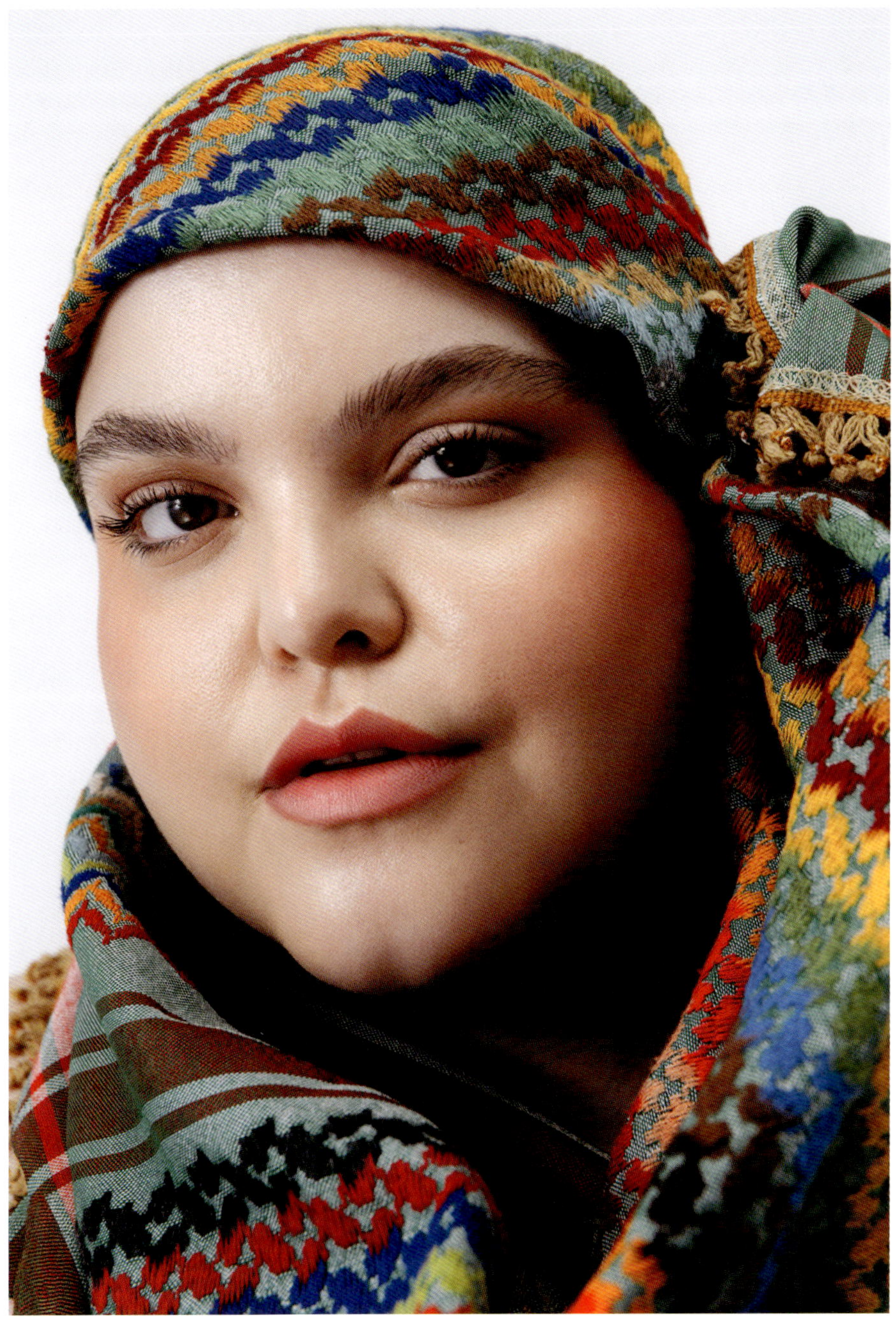

Isabel Ebeid wears own keffiyeh.

Maria Diaz

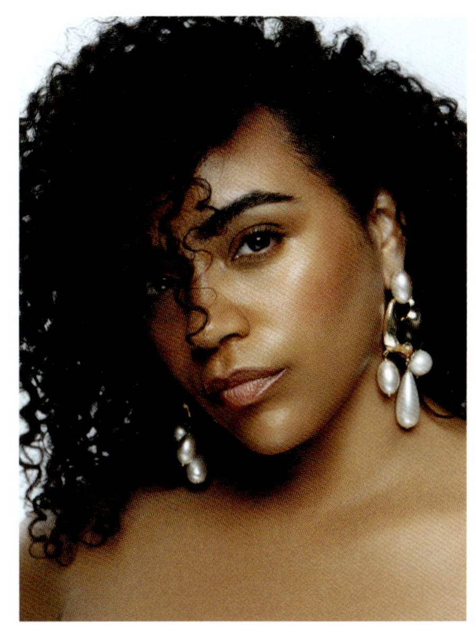
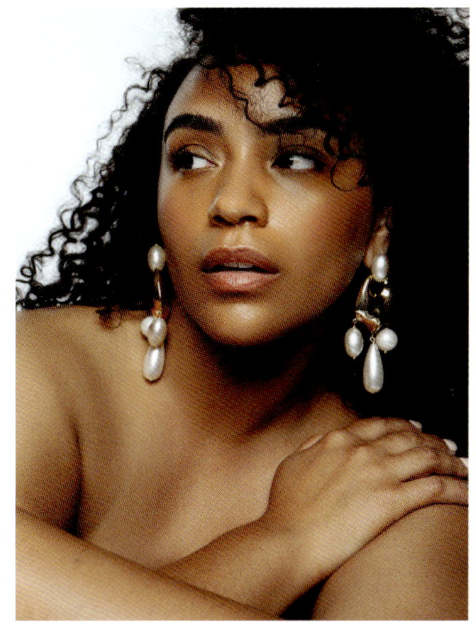
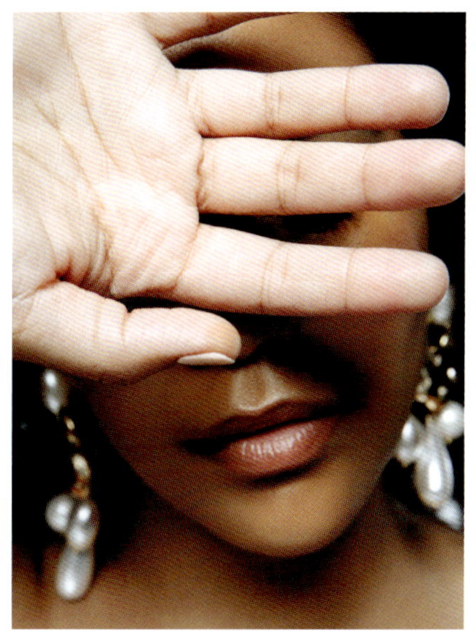
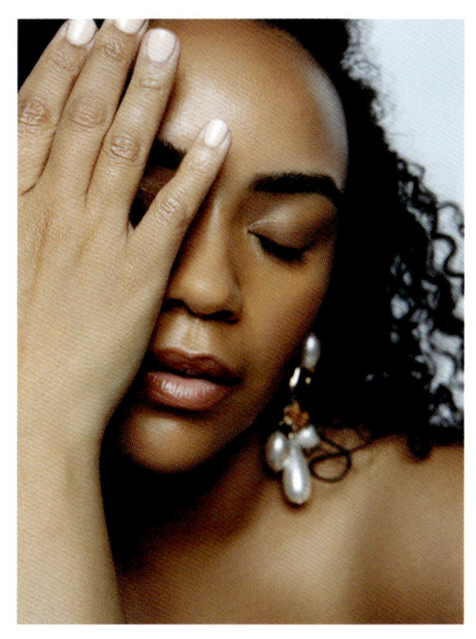
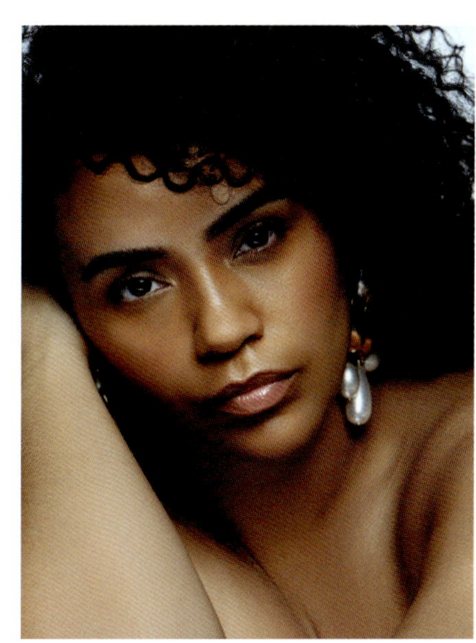
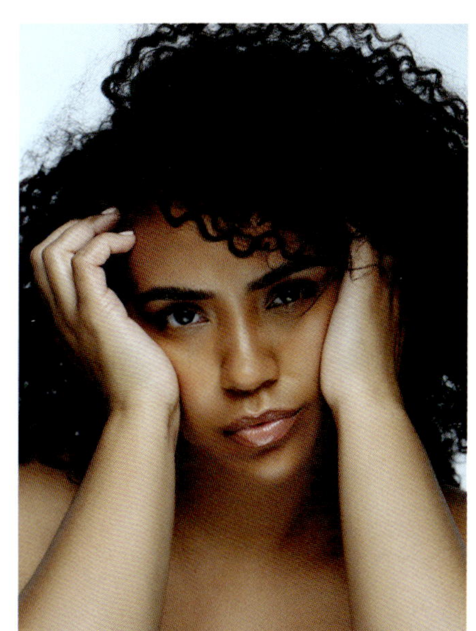
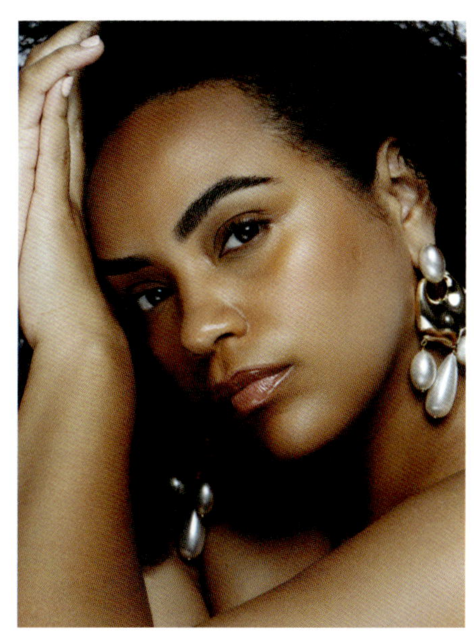
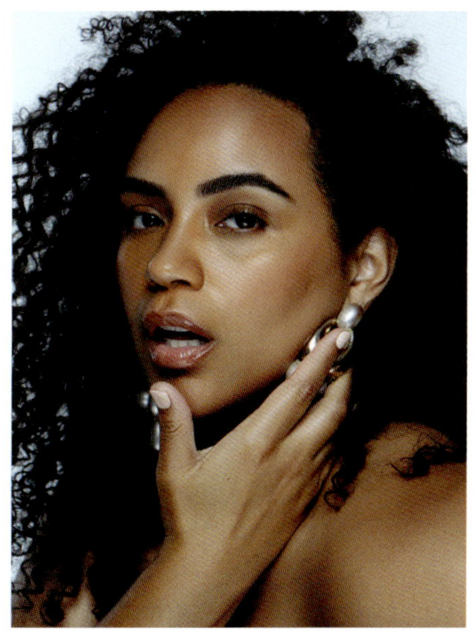
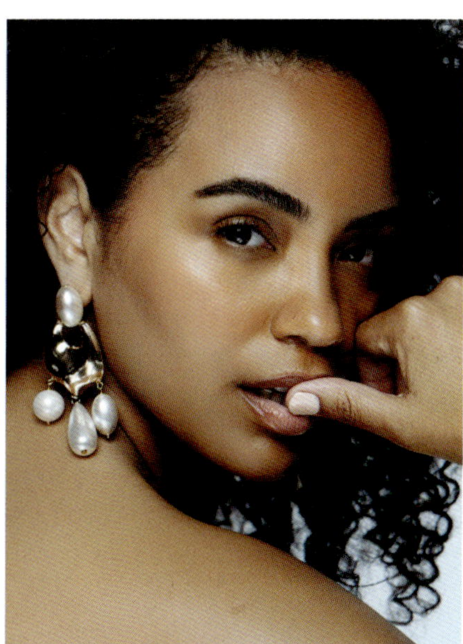

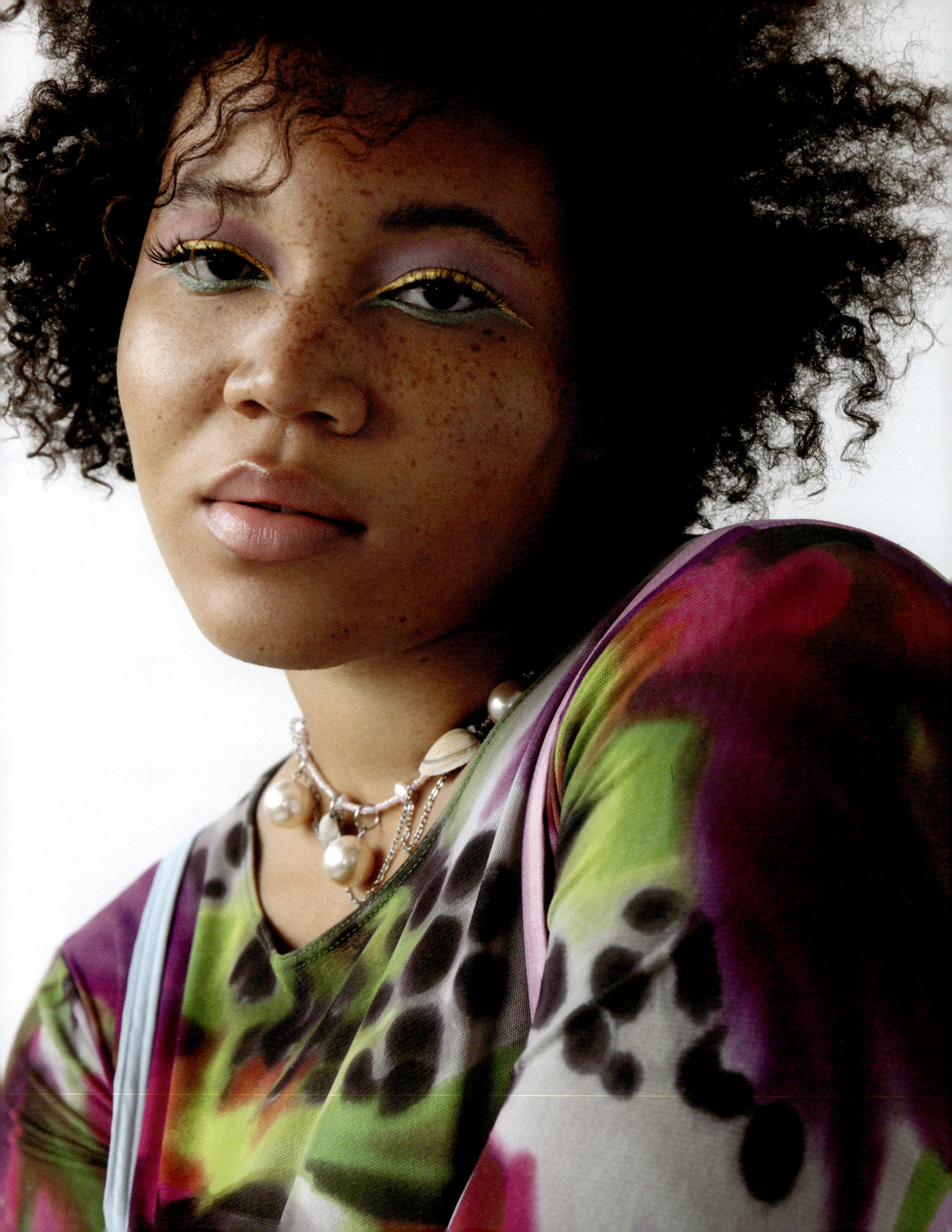

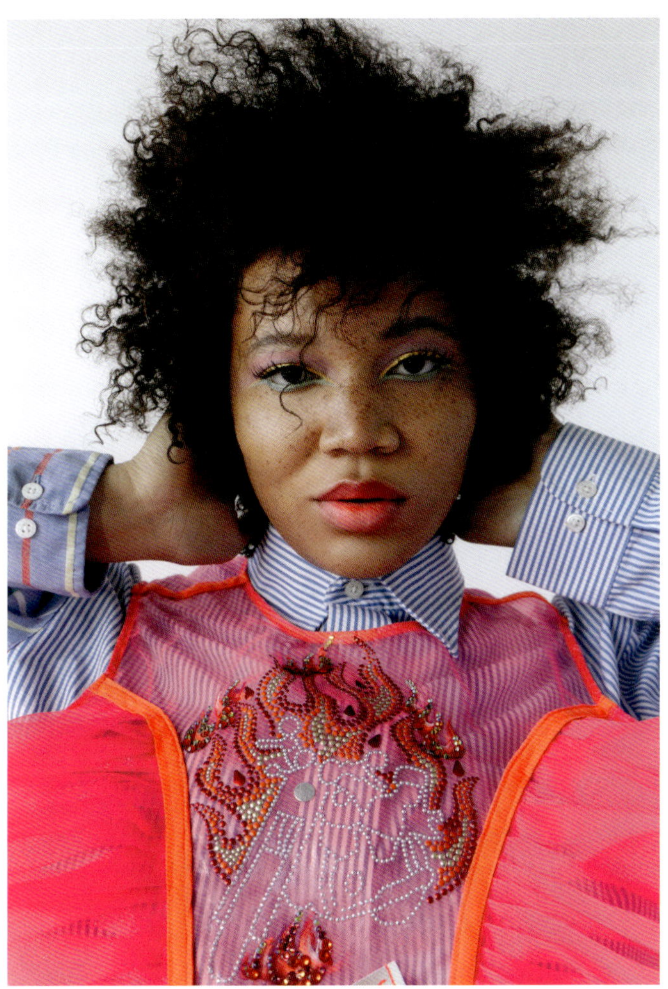

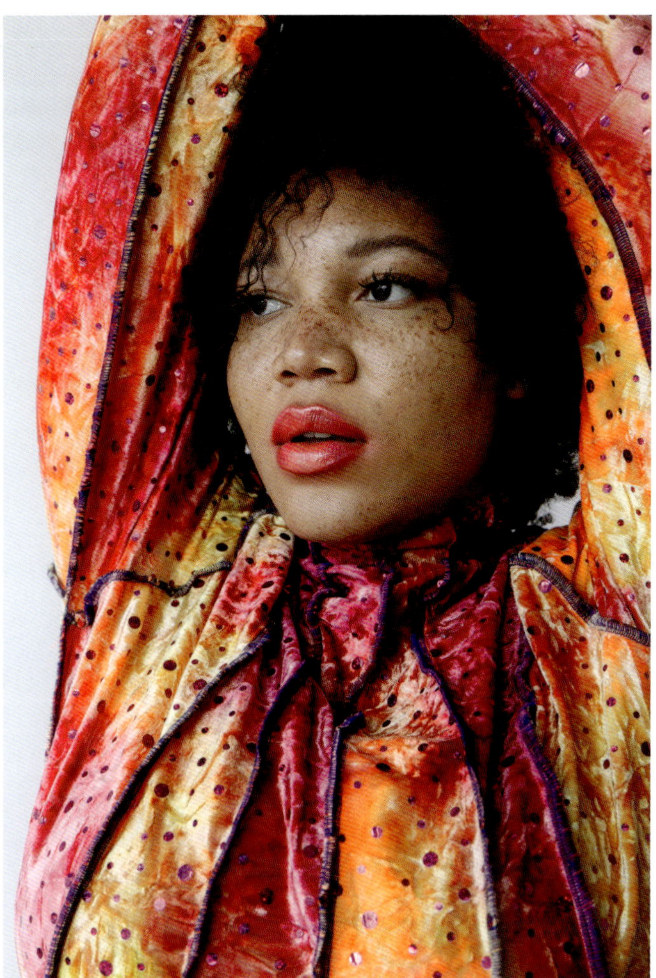

Noni Cyngor wears Jazz by Jazz blouse (left), dress (middle and right), and necklace; House of Tame shirt (middle); vintage undershirt from Shop Berriez.

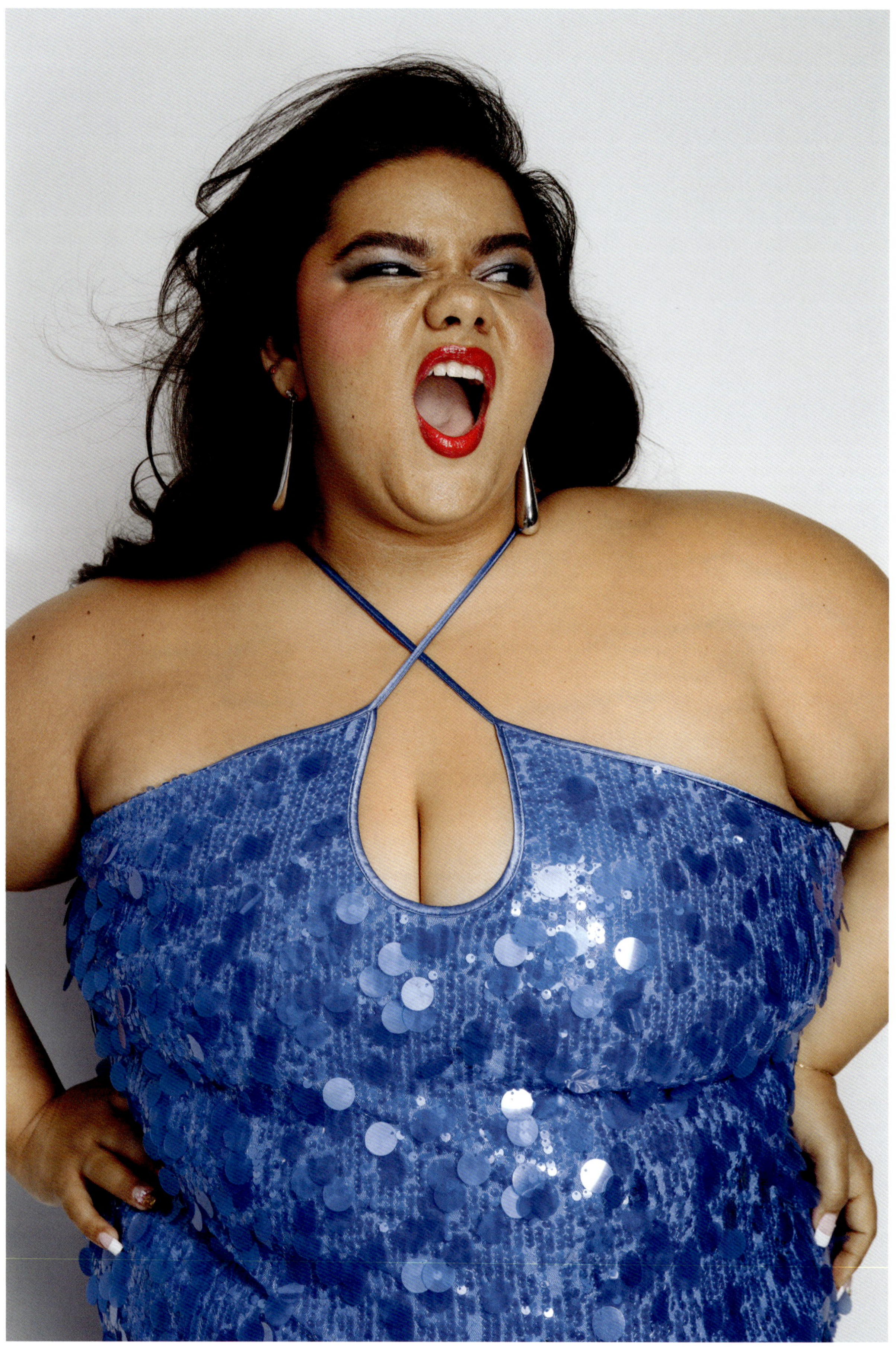

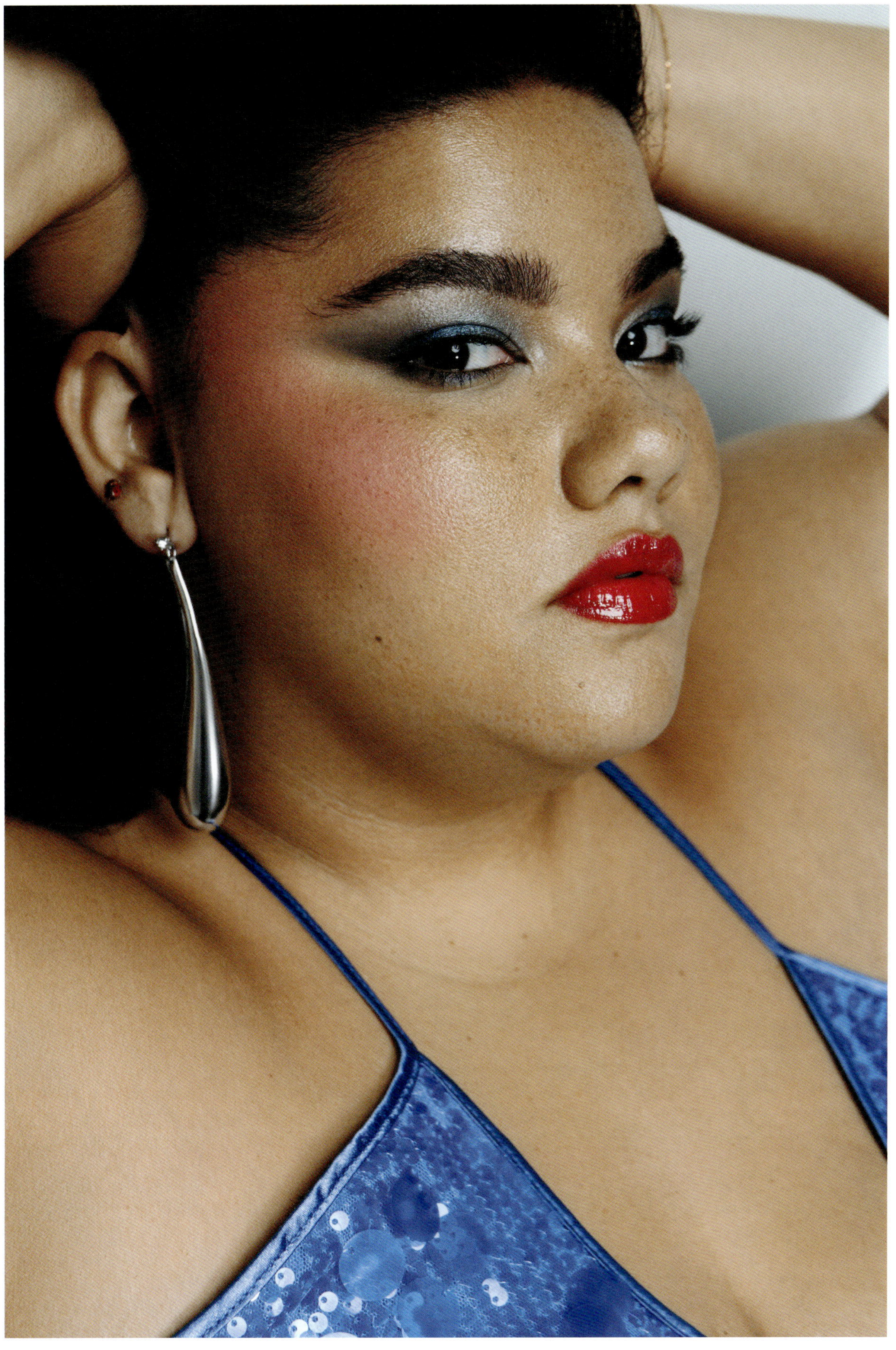

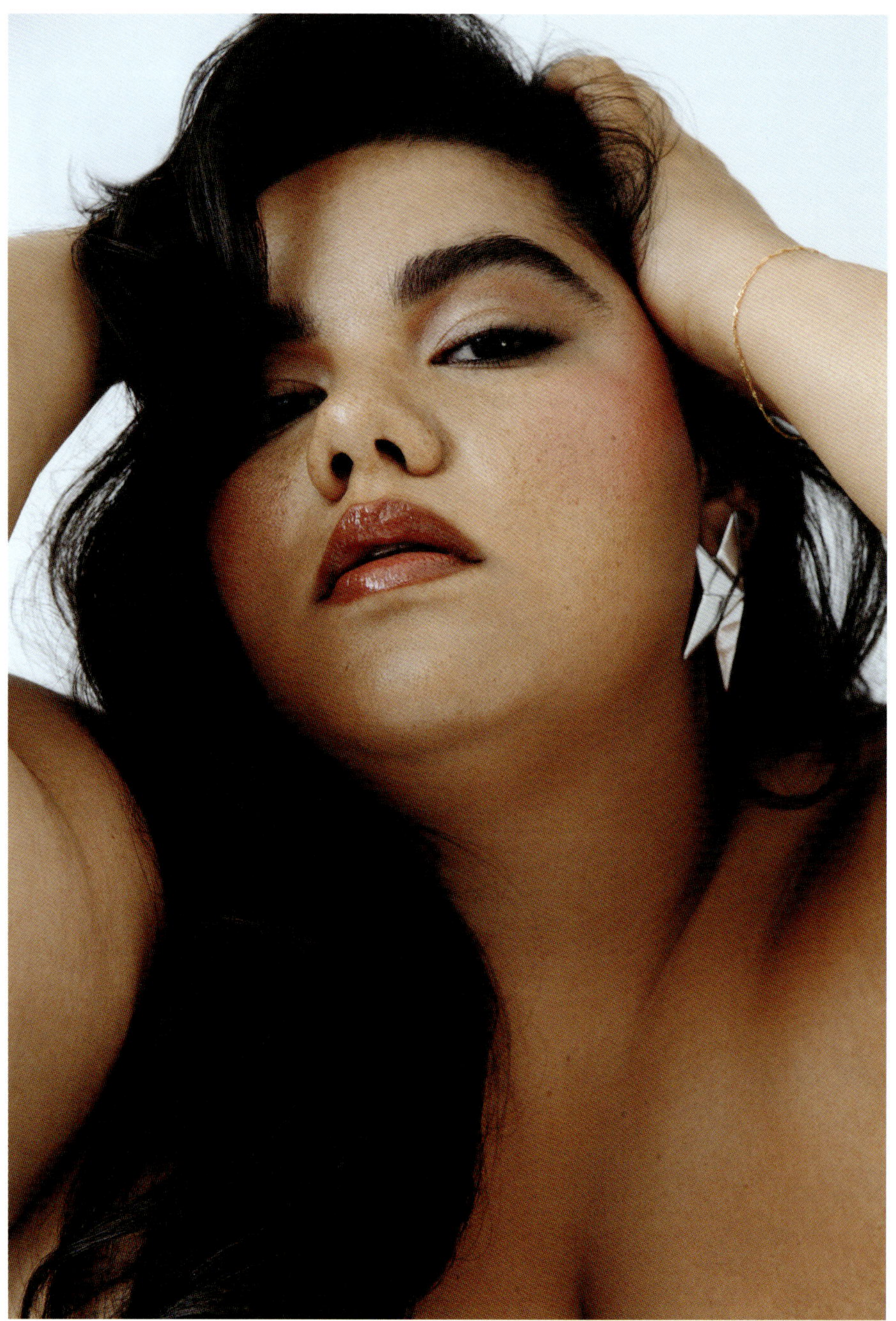

Priscilla Del Castillo wears Eloquii dress
(previous pages); Selkie corest.

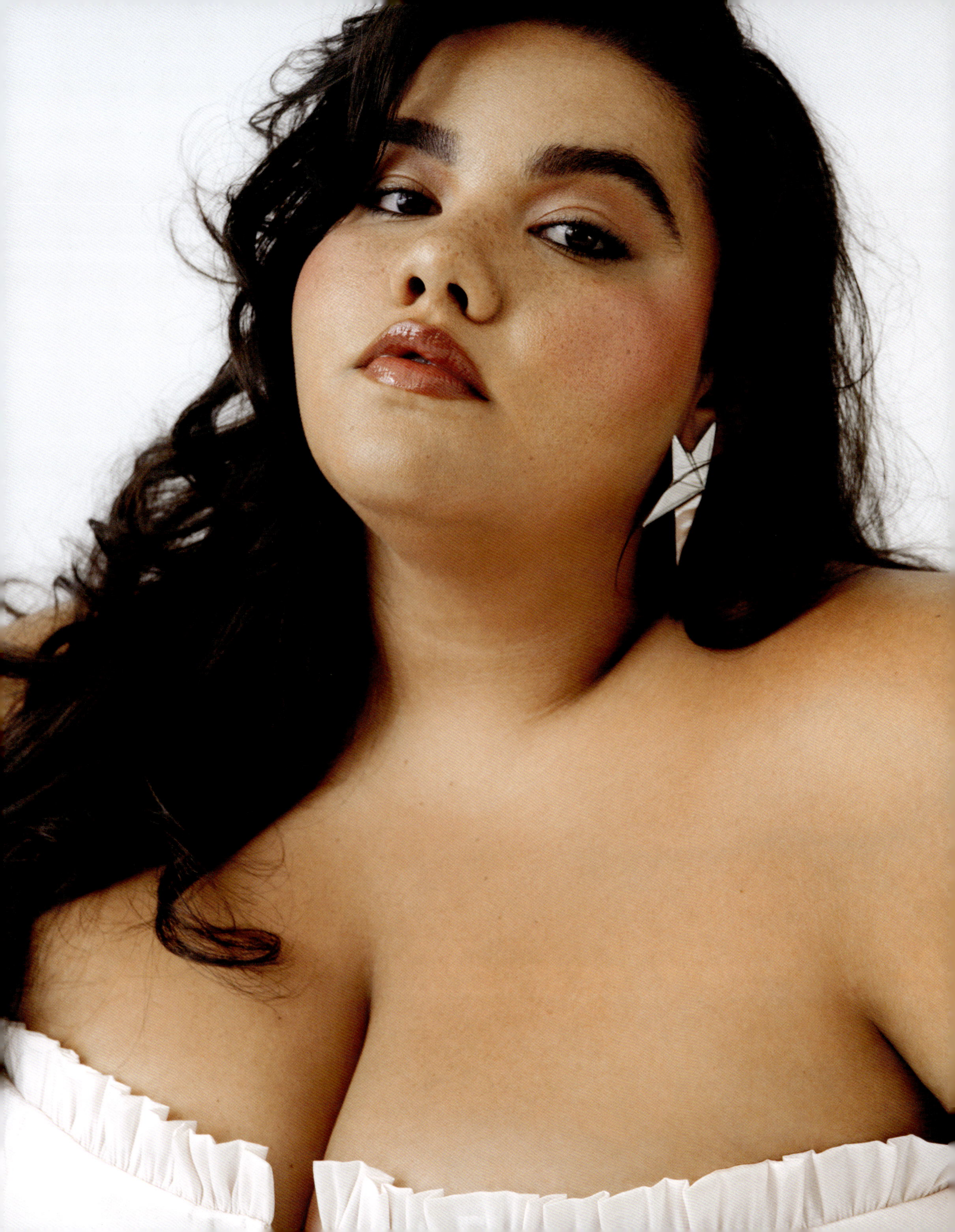

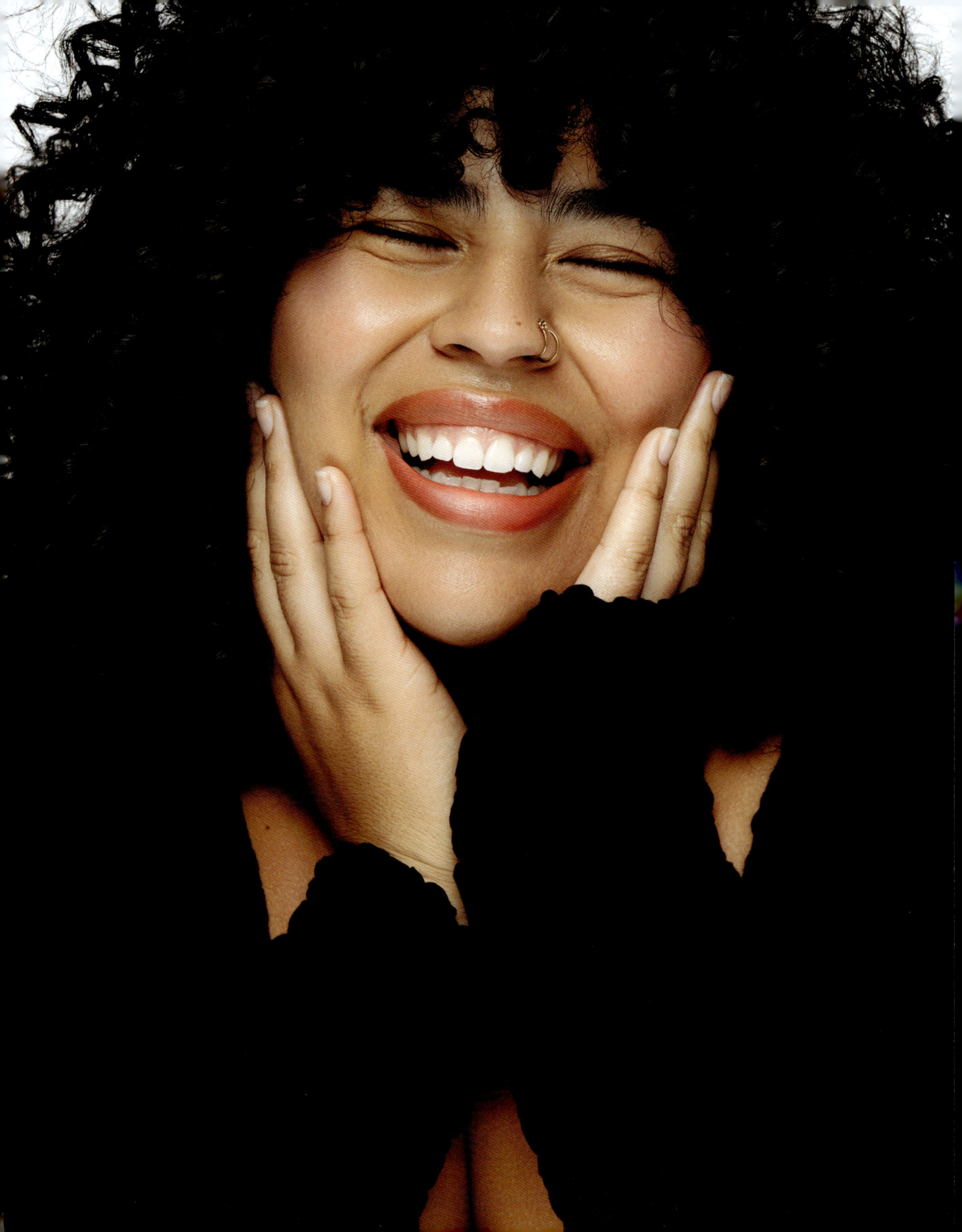

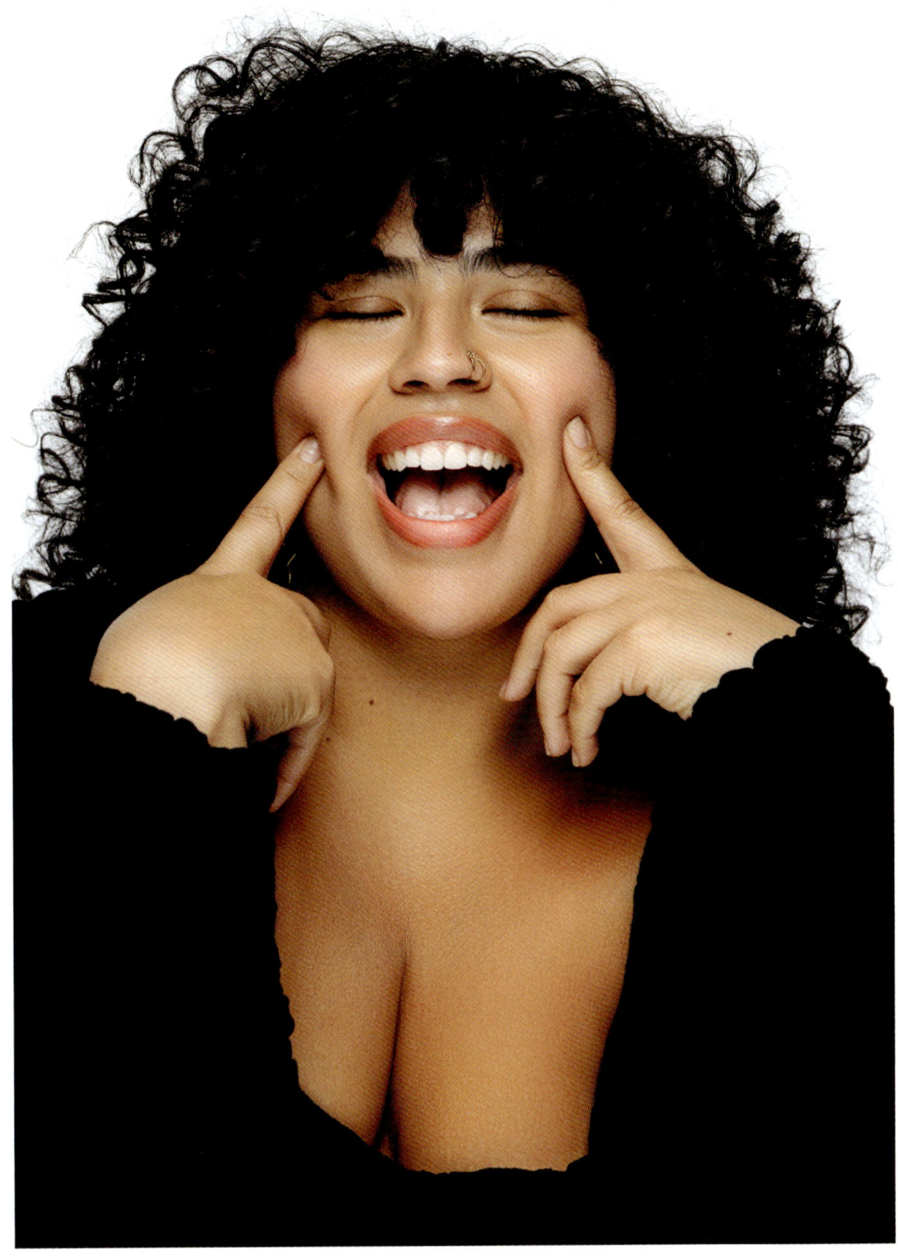

Naomi La Crespa wears Mara Hoffman.

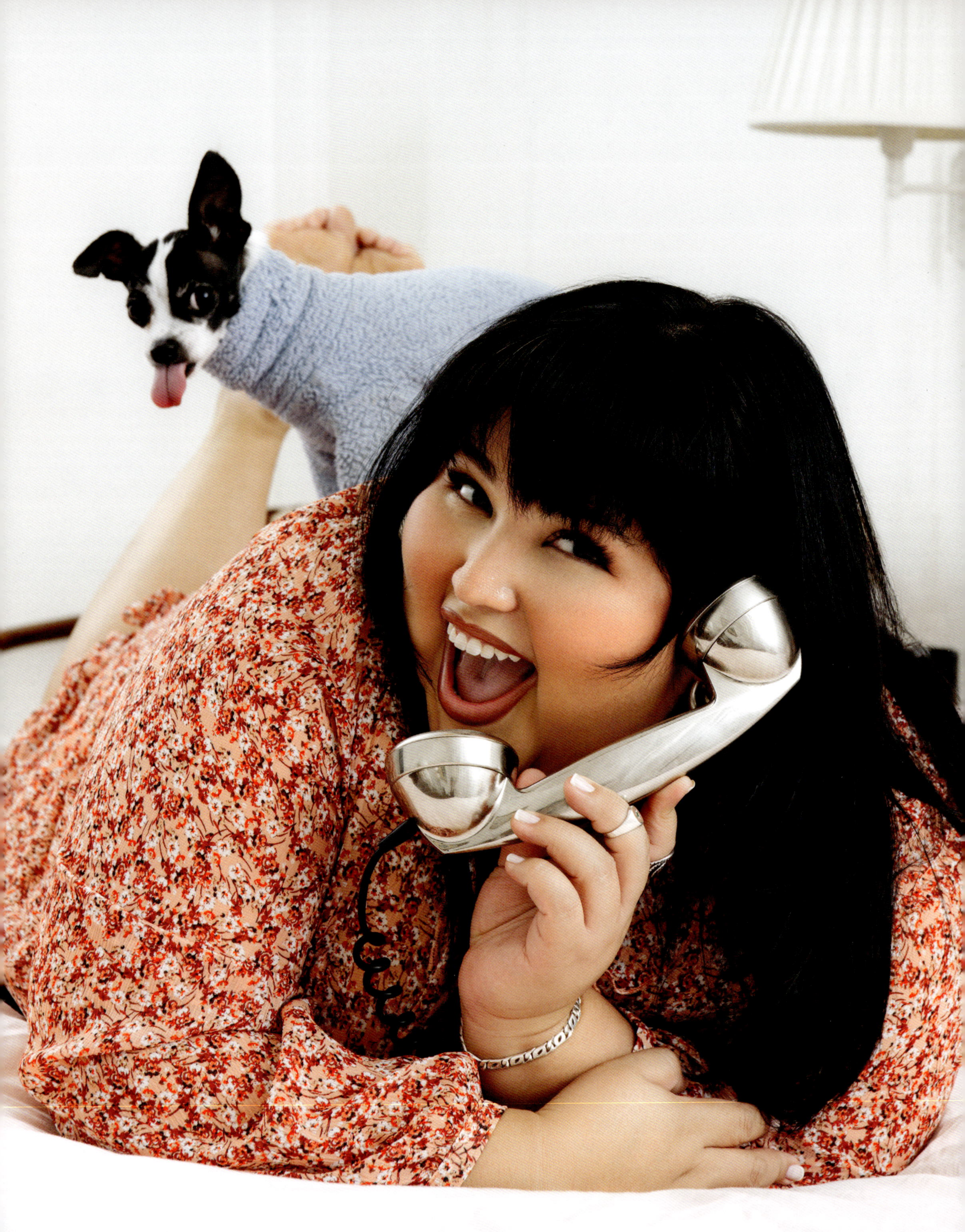

Jessica Torres

A pioneering voice in body positivity

I first met Jessica Torres on a Catherines trip: a chance to travel that the brand offered influencers. It was one of the early opportunities of its kind that included plus-size creators, and it must have felt significant to receive that kind of exposure at a time when almost every collaboration was given to straight-size counterparts. Reflecting on the trip, Jessica acknowledges the stark differences in the resources that were available, along with gratitude that she was included in such a unique experience that allowed her to explore new places.

Jessica's rise to prominence as an influencer and a key voice in the body positivity movement started with her work at Revelist. She began creating engaging video content for them in 2016 and later did the same at BuzzFeed, starting in 2021. Her work focused on fashion and the experience of being plus back when the community was even more severly underrepresented, this period laying the groundwork for her future success. "Creating videos allowed me to express myself and connect with others," she shares, thankful for the journey and the growth it provided.

Her work since her start at Revelist includes her first shoot in lingerie for Catherines, which I shot and which Jessica admits she found both exhilarating and vulnerable. She wanted her audience to share in that moment with her, which created a connection that felt genuine. "In that moment, I was stripped bare, both literally and figuratively," she recounts. "I never want to feel like I'm an 'expert' because that could stunt my growth. Instead, I want to be open about my journey and allow others to see the real me, imperfections and all."

Jessica's style has always been a celebration of boldness, filled with vibrant colors and unique patterns that reflect her personality. She says discovering her distinctive sense of style began with a desire to break free from the discomfort she felt about her appearance. Growing up, she often wanted to hide

Body activism became almost instinctive. I felt like I had to use my voice for something bigger.

her body, but that all changed when she began creating plus-size fashion content; it was through this exploration that she found her true self. "I draw inspiration from everything around me—architecture, the vibrant hues of strangers in the street, and the eclectic styles of the 70s and 90s," she explains. Her passion for color and creativity shines through in her work, showcasing an aesthetic that is both eye-catching and deeply personal.

Her YouTube channel, ThisIsJessicaTorres, covers everything from fashion to beauty to lifestyle. When asked what inspired her to start this channel in 2015, and how it allows her to connect with her audience differently, Jessica says that she initially felt the pressure to be on every platform, fearing her audience would forget about her. As social media rapidly evolved, though, she needed to step back from the fast pace of the Internet. "I decided to focus more on creating slower content."

As one of the top body-positive voices in the influencer industry today, Jessica has received recognition that carries significant weight. Reflecting on what this recognition means to her and how it's shifted the conversation around inclusivity in fashion and media, she says her initial goal was simply to be seen and hopefully land a job at a magazine. However, as her social media presence grew, she realized the impact she could have. "Body activism became almost instinctive. I felt like I had to use my voice for something bigger."

The landscape Jessica works in now has progressed since she started, thanks, in part, to the massive boost in visibility TikTok has offered content creators, straight and plus size alike. When it comes to this explosion in access to exposure, Jessica emphasizes that social media acts as a great equalizer, enabling people to share their talents and connect with like-minded individuals. However, she also highlights the downside: the oversaturation of creators has allowed companies to exploit inexperienced influencers, complicating the landscape further.

Tied to this are questions around fair pay, particularly for plus-size content creators, which is essential to their growth and sustainability. As to her own experiences with compensation, Jessica has concerns over the number of plus-size creators who lack awareness of their worth: an industry shift that has made it increasingly challenging for anyone in her field to sustain a living. "We were barely compensated fairly before, and now it's close to impossible."

To ensure plus-size influencers receive the same opportunities as their straight-size counterparts, Jessica emphasizes that real change will come when companies start including actual fat people in their campaigns, rather than just those who fit narrow beauty standards. In 2025, plus-size representation is still extremely limited, and with brands backsliding in their sizing, it is all the more important for influencers to make their voices heard.

Despite these uncertainties, though, Jessica's full of excitement for the future. "I hope to create content that resonates and makes people think about the discrimination of fat bodies. I would love to experiment with this through a book in the future. Fingers crossed!"

Jessica continues to break barriers, using her voice to advocate for inclusivity and body positivity while inspiring others. Her journey reflects not only her personal growth but also the evolving landscape of plus-size representation in media. With her bold style and unwavering commitment to her community, she is truly a pioneer in this movement.

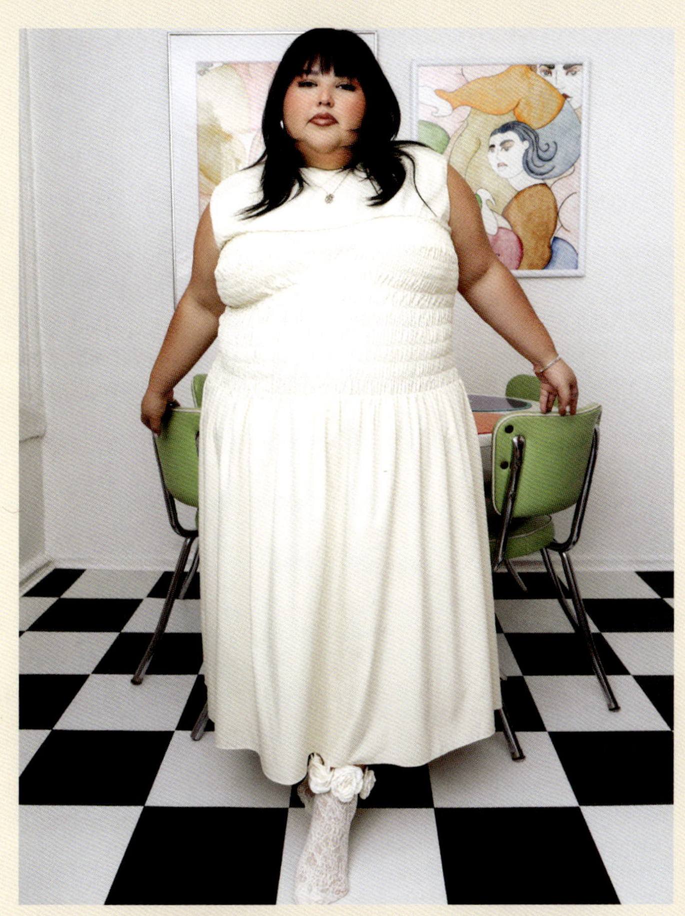
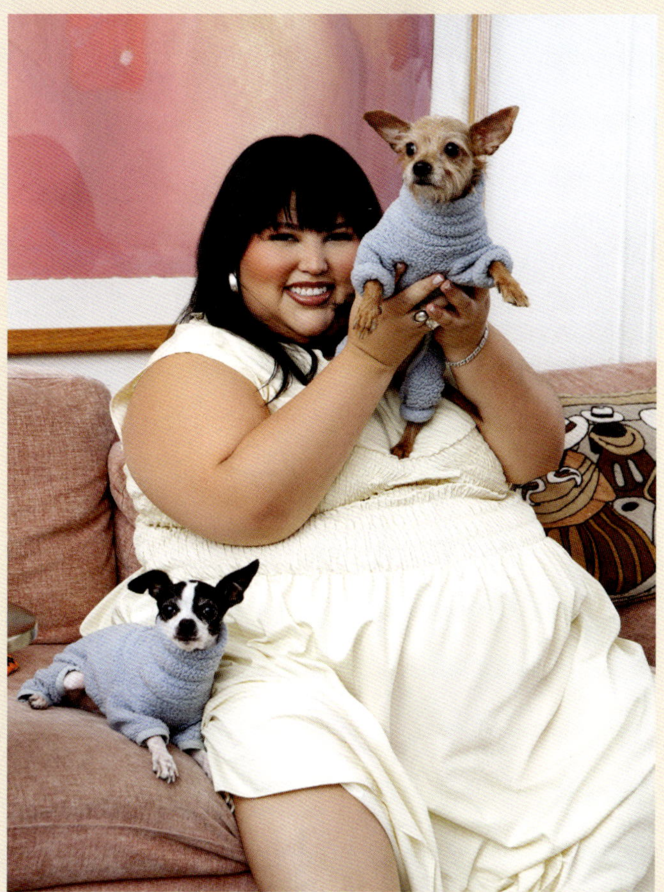
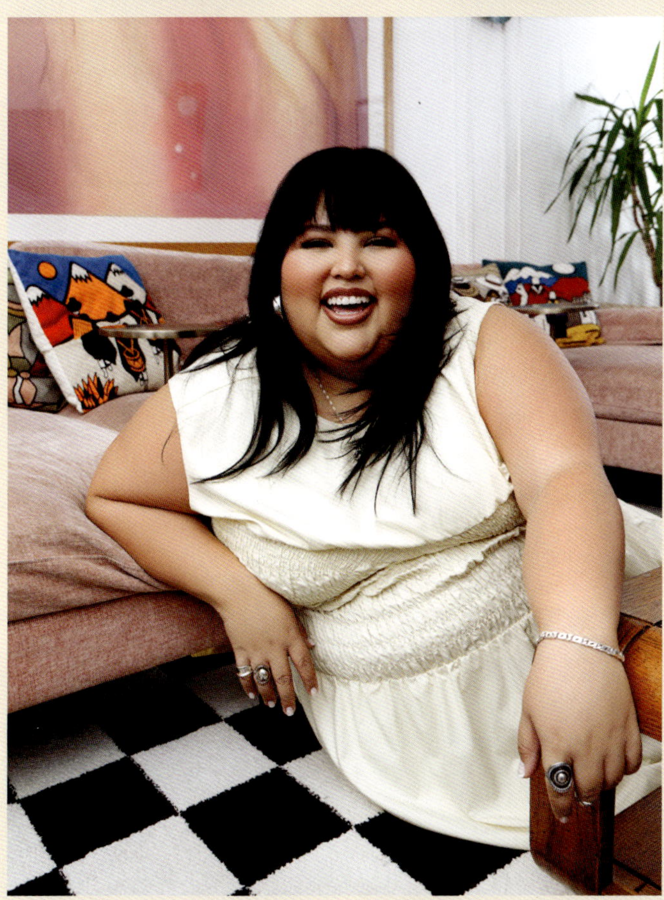
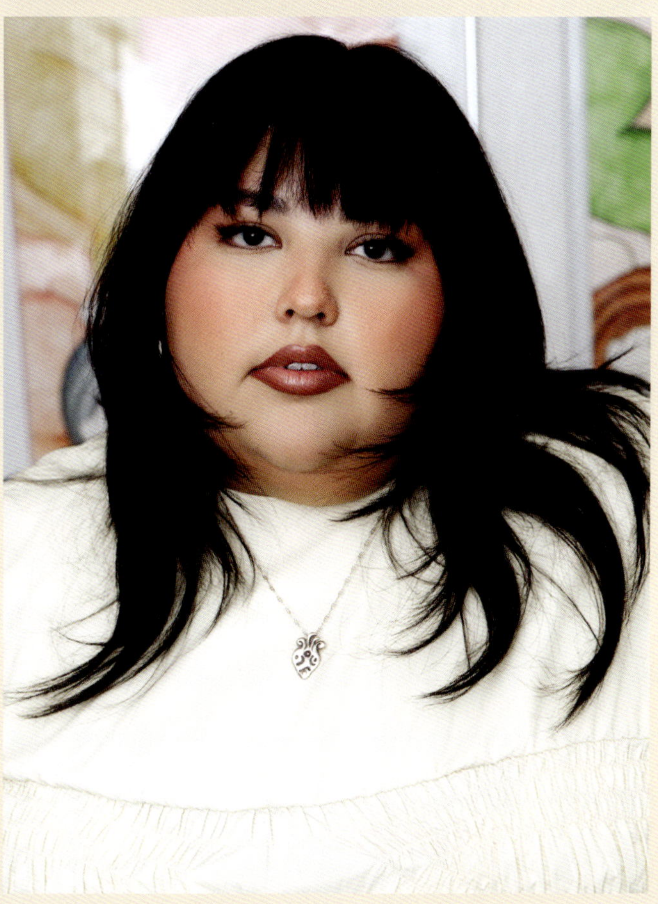

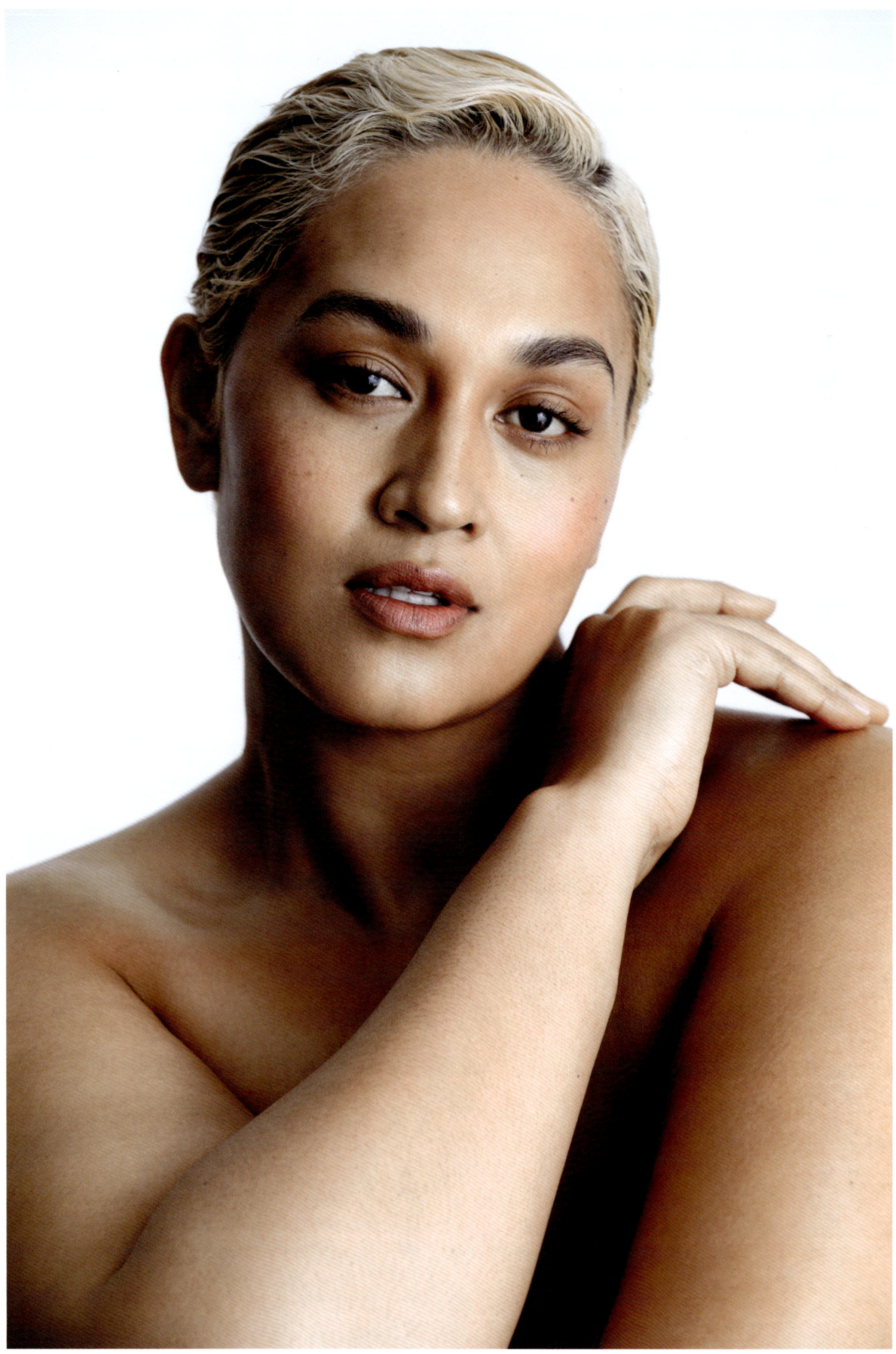

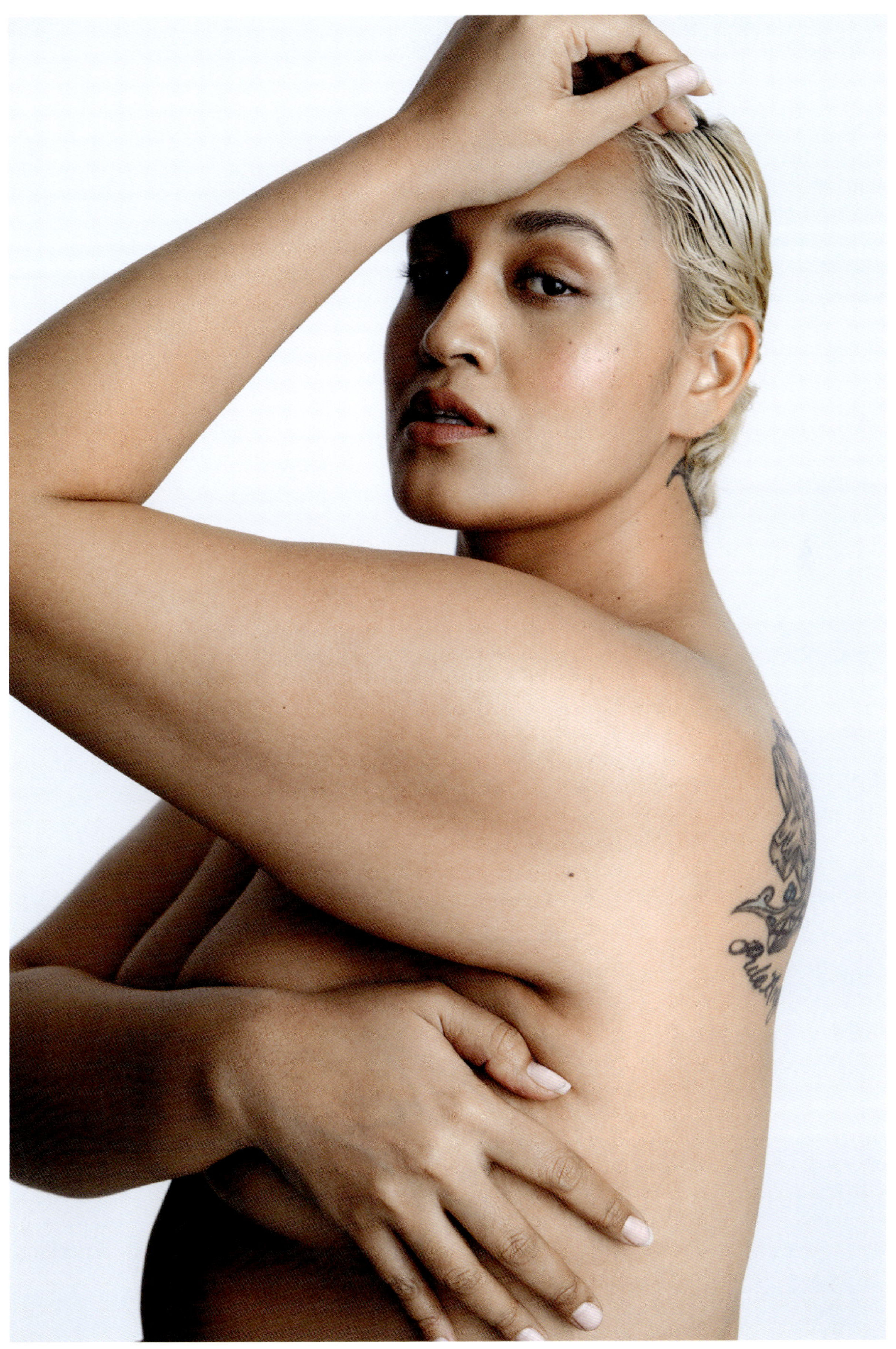

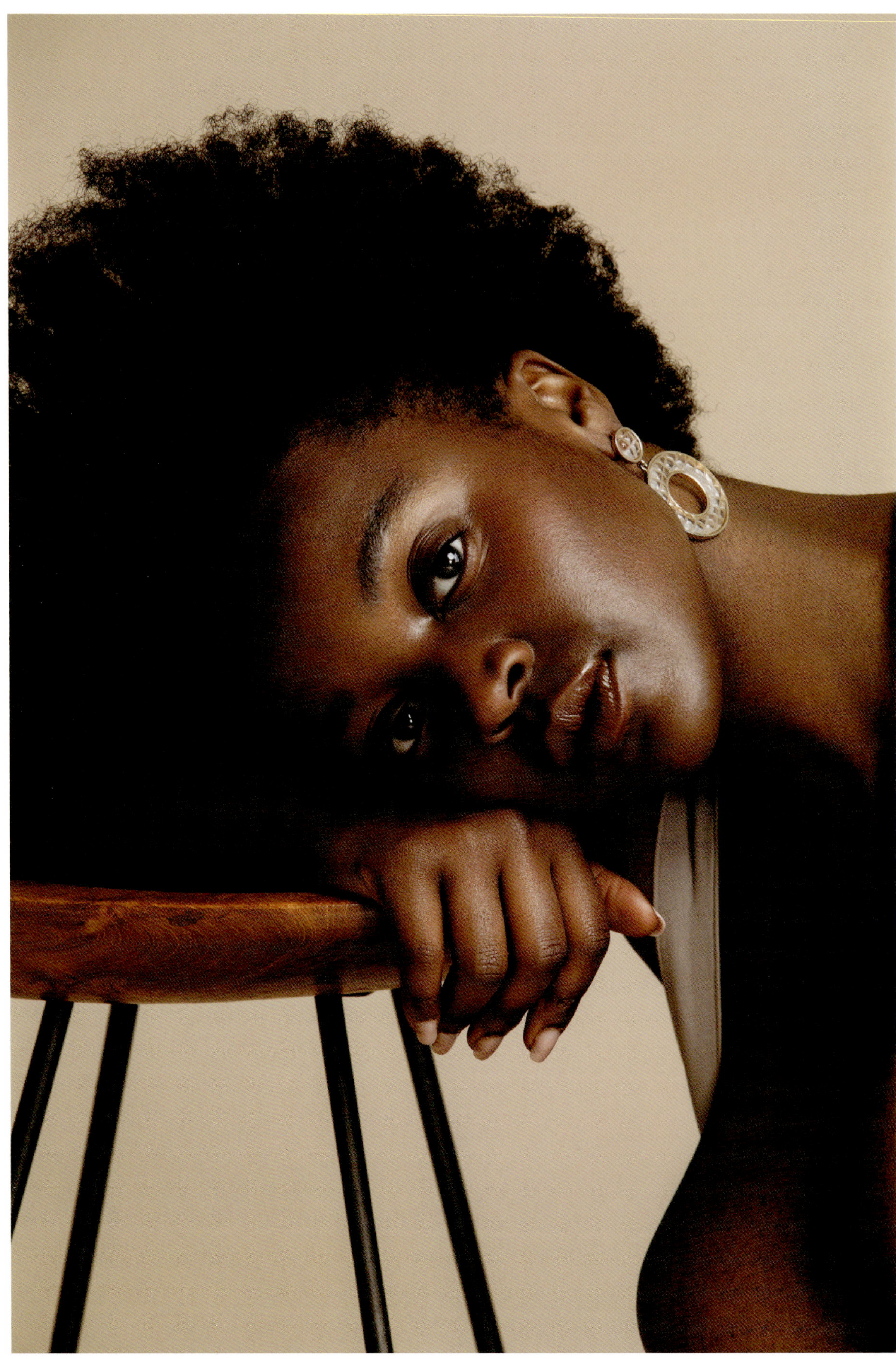

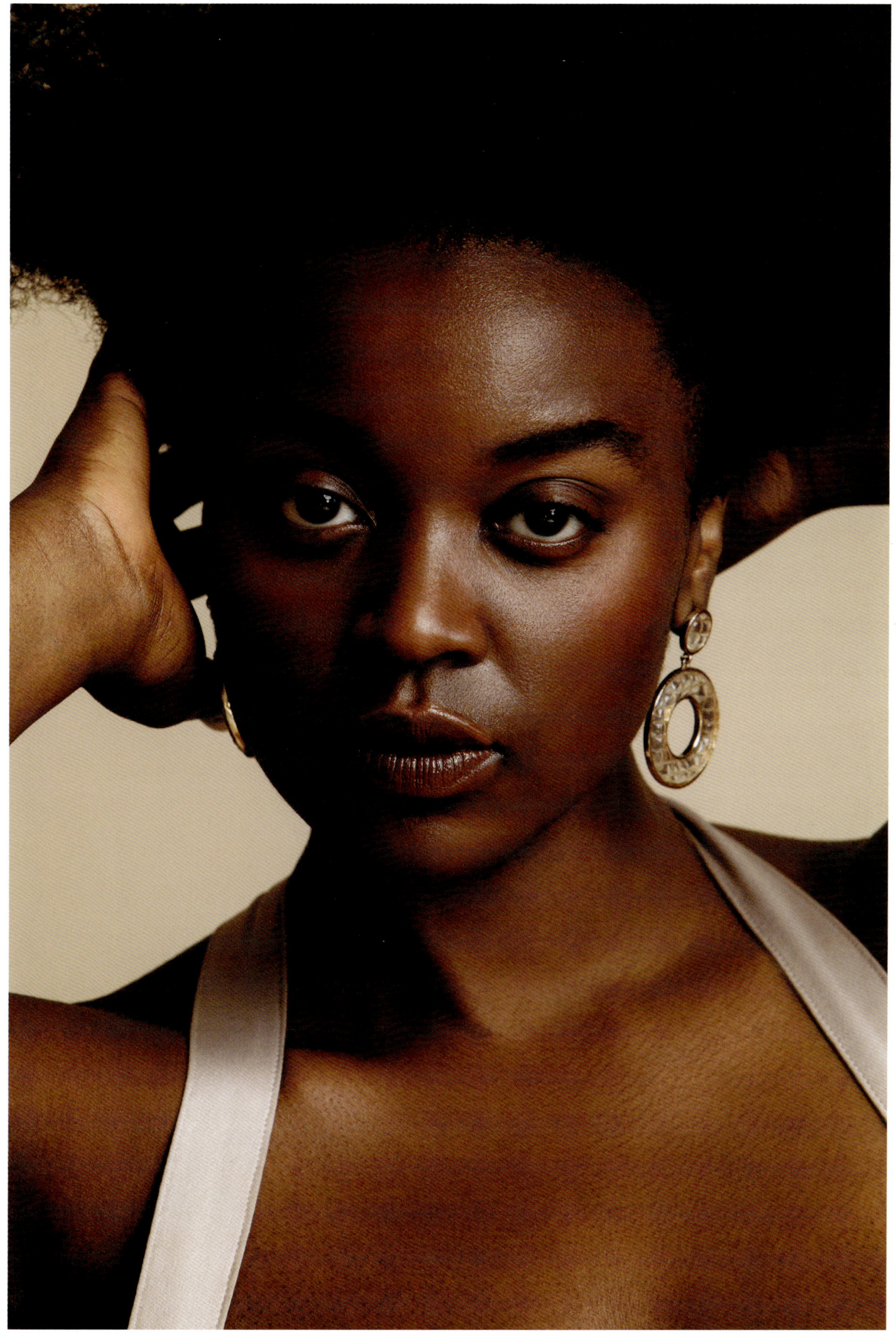

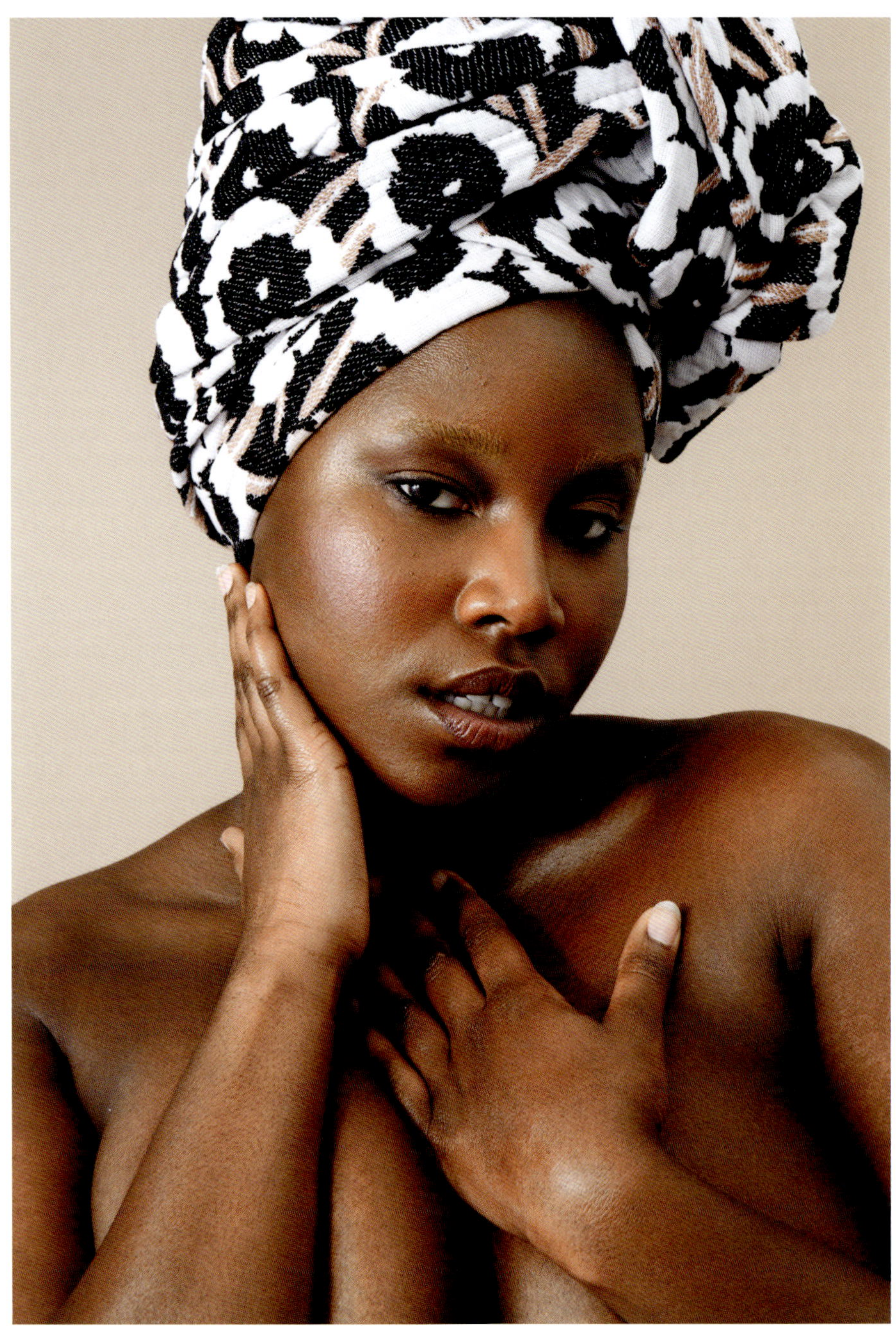

Pages. 156–157: Velonika Pome'e

Pages 158–159: Carri Murphy wears own corset.

Melonee Rembert wears cloth headpiece
draped by Yoko J.

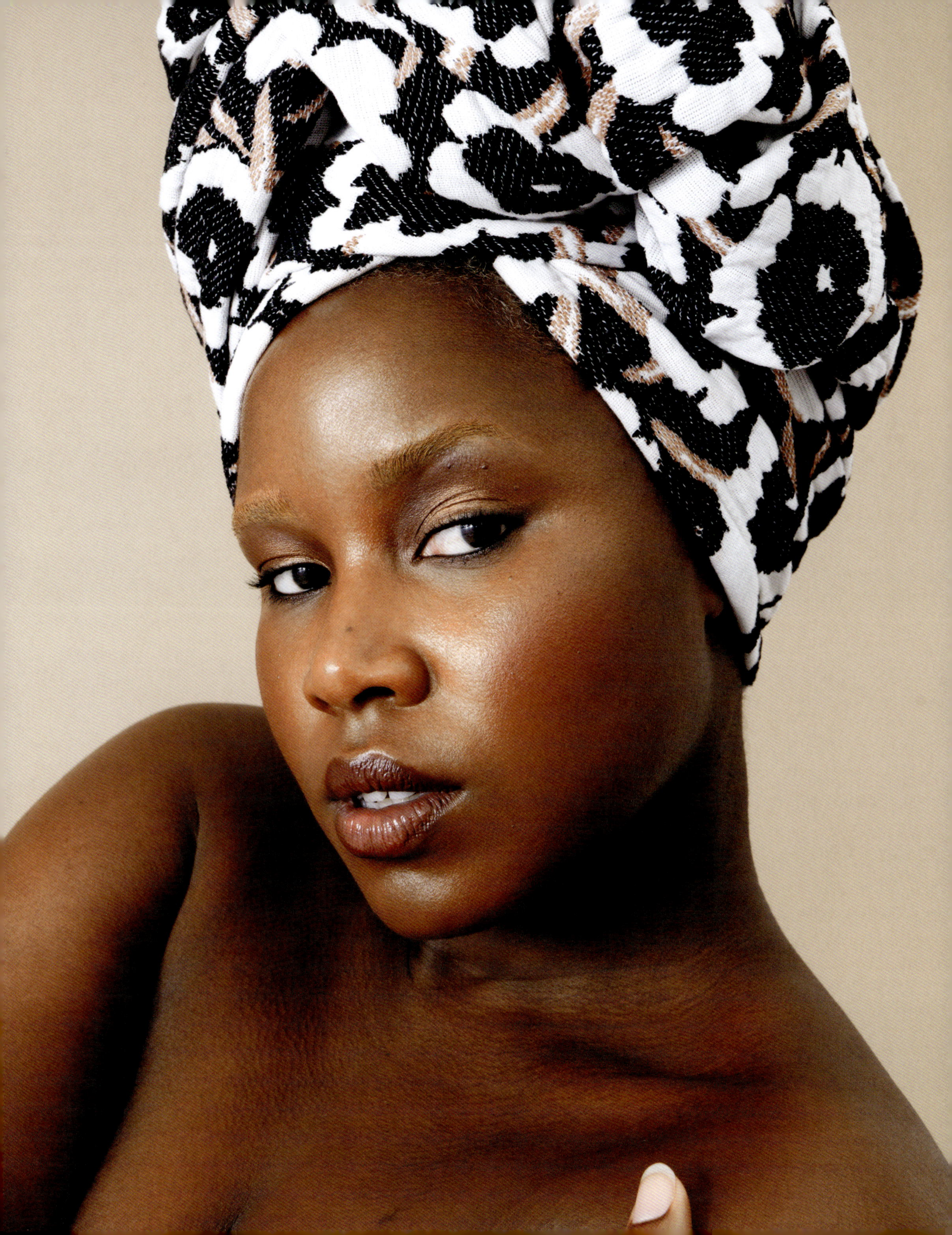

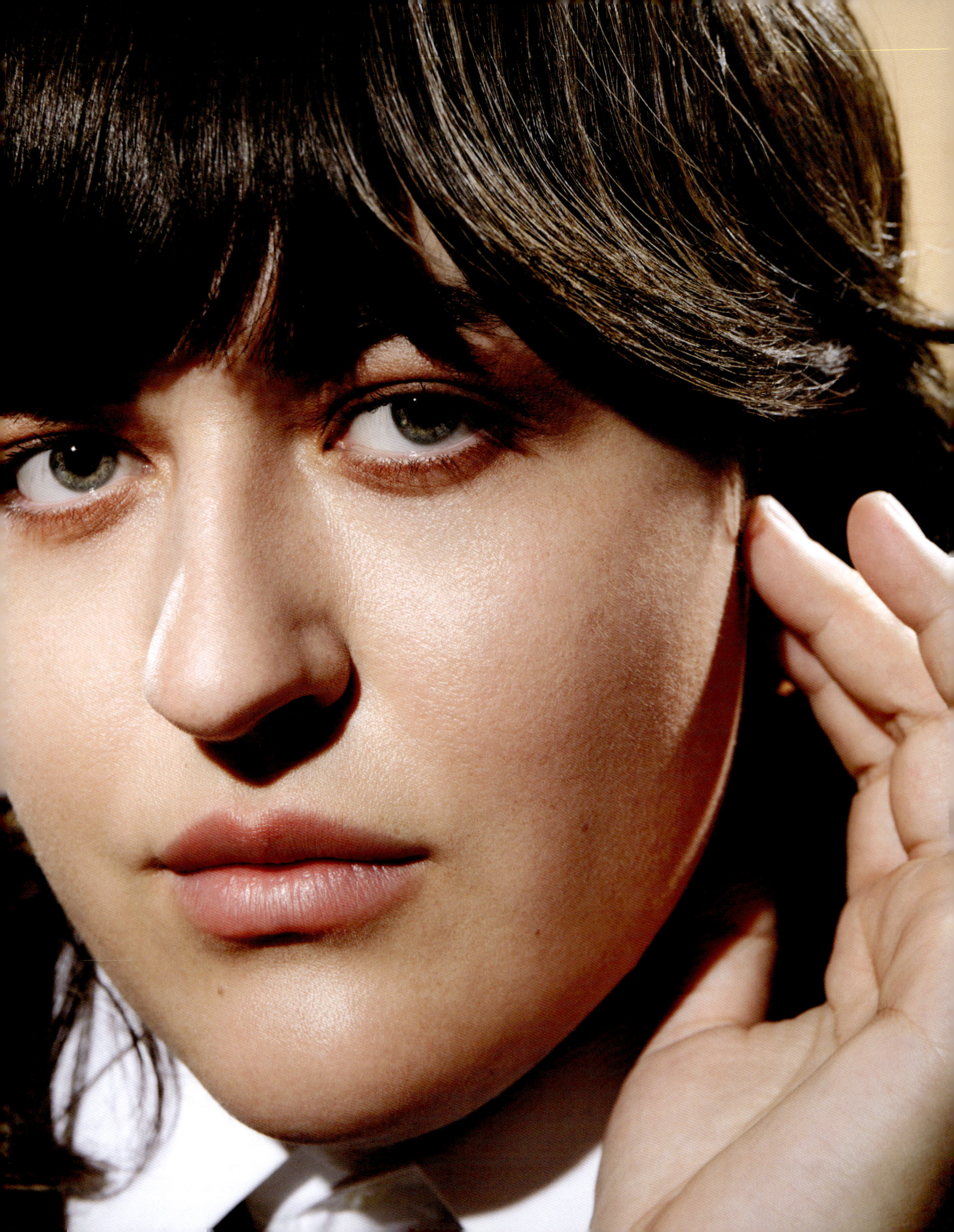

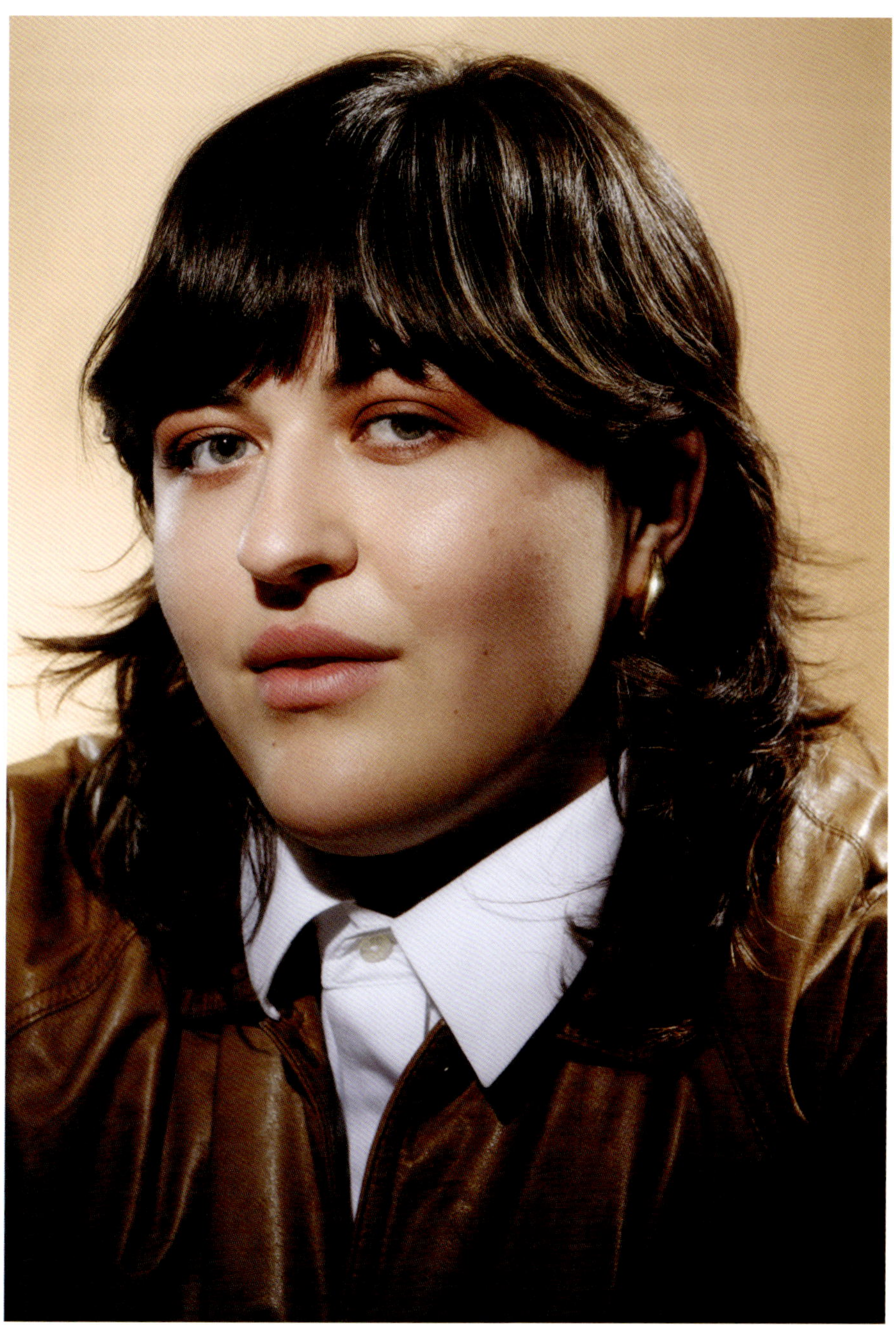

Tayler Smith wears vintage jacket from Shop Berriez.

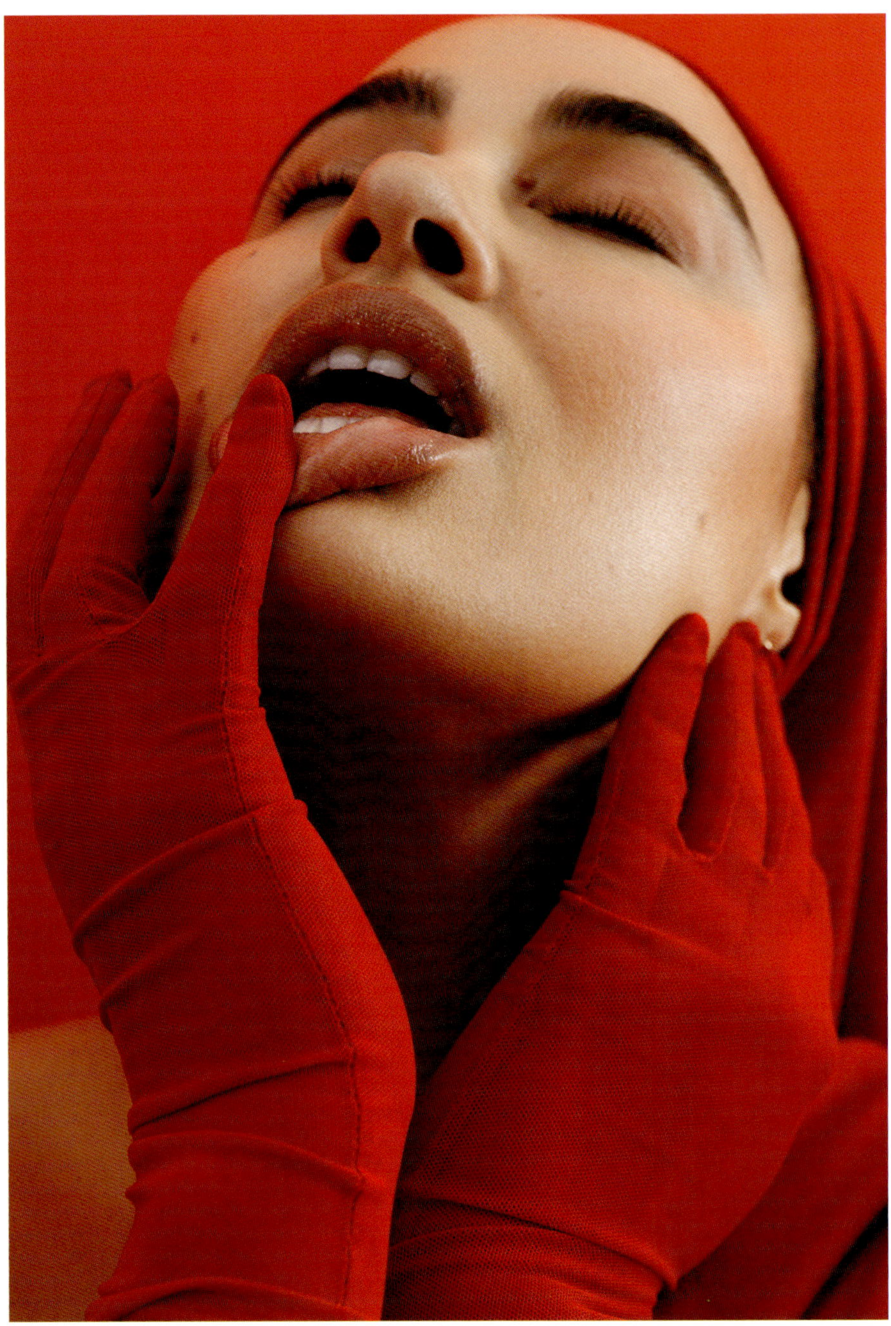

Denka Obradovic wears fabric draped by Yoko J.

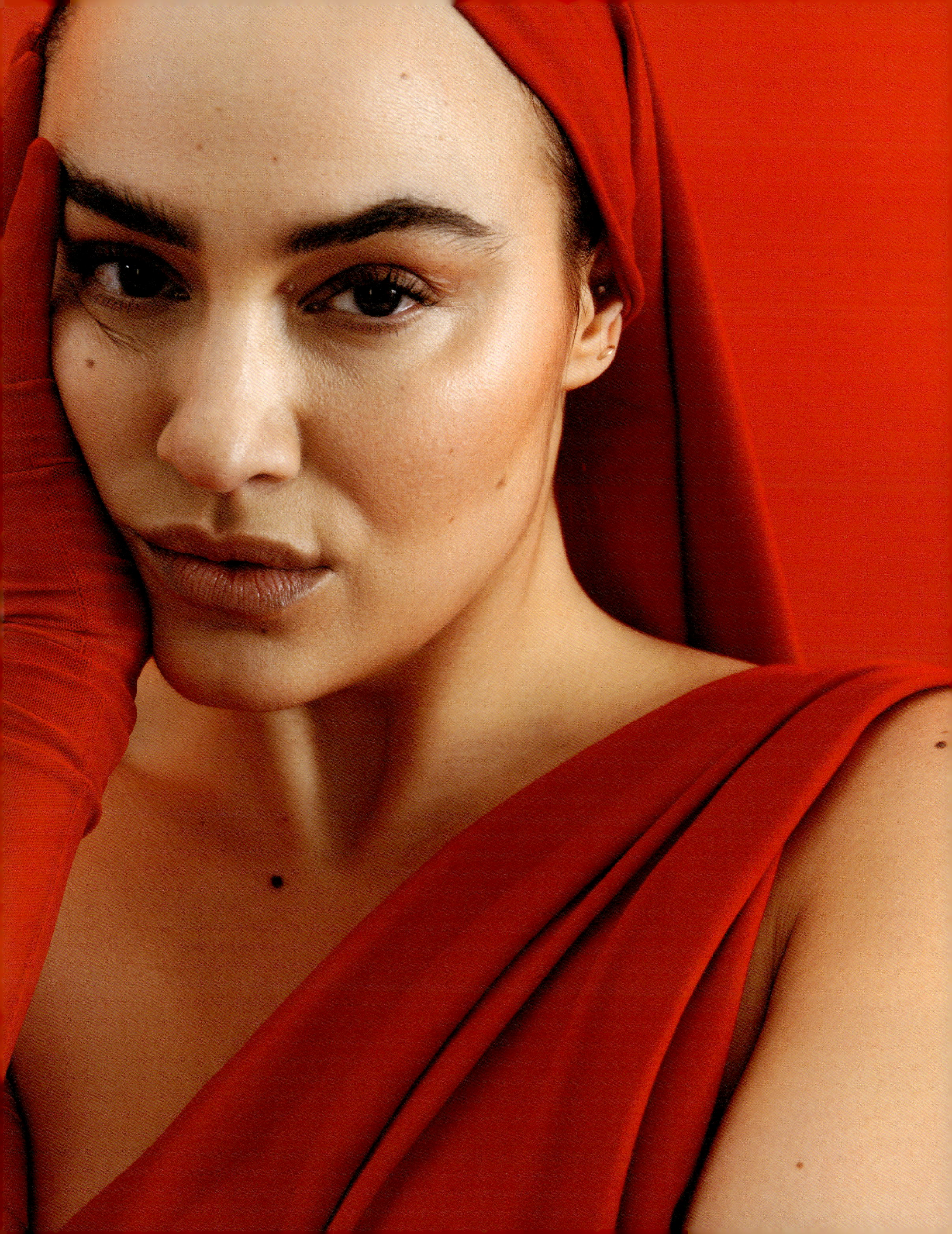

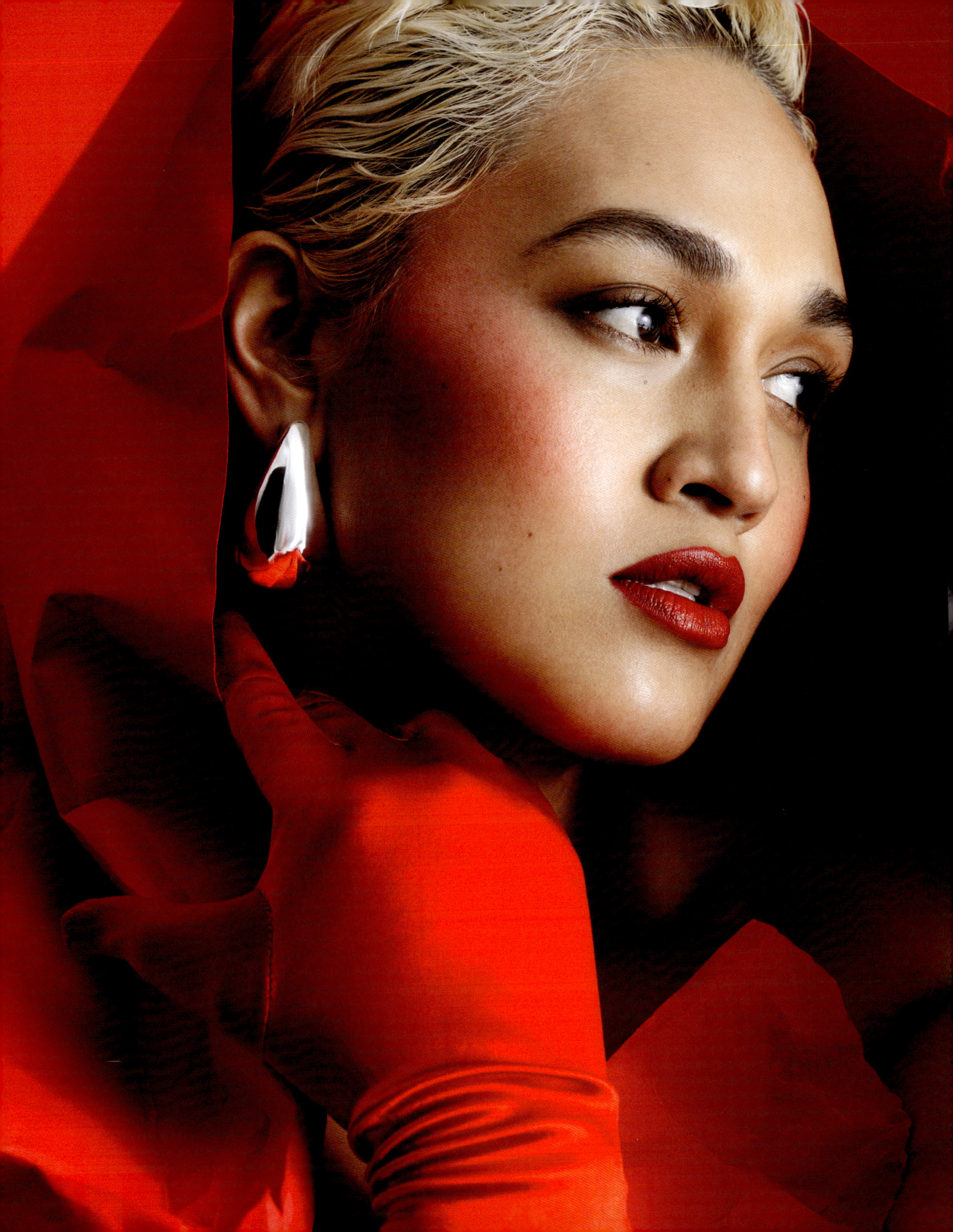

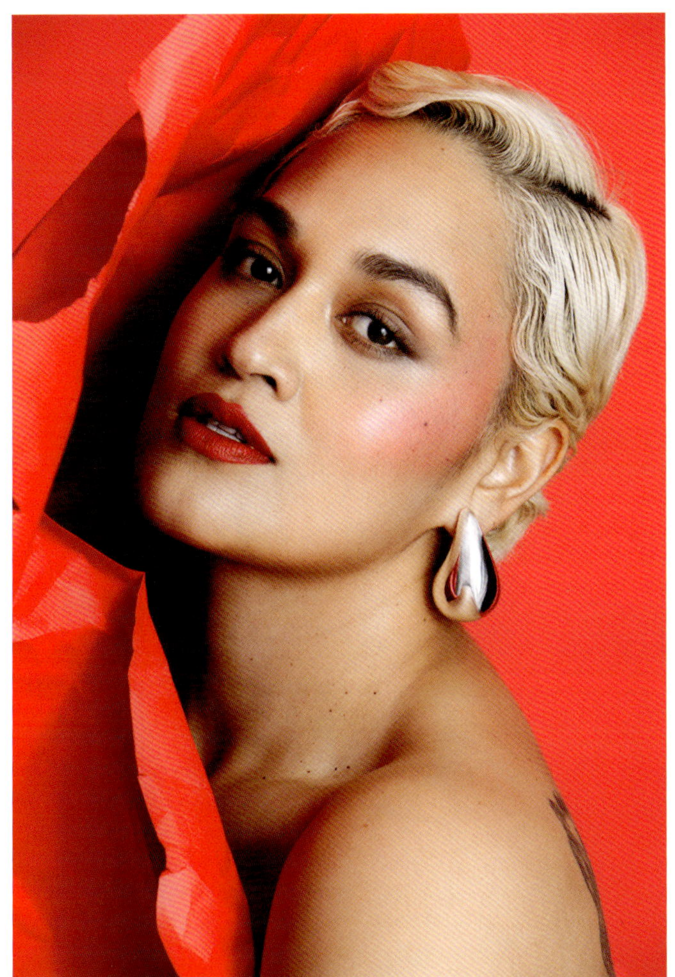

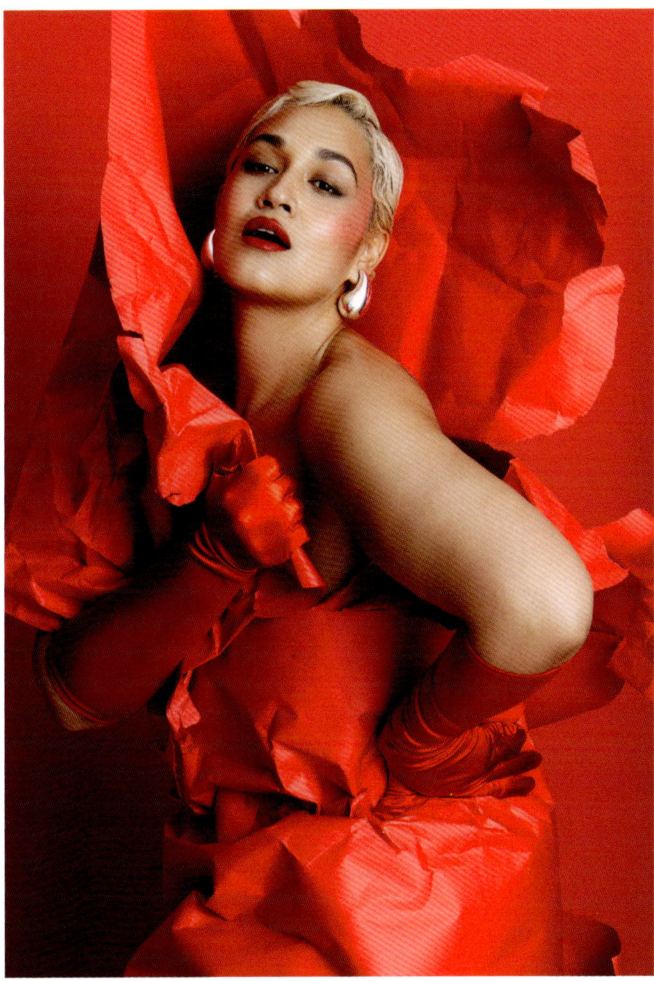

Velonika Pome'e wears paper sculpted by
Lydia Hudgens.

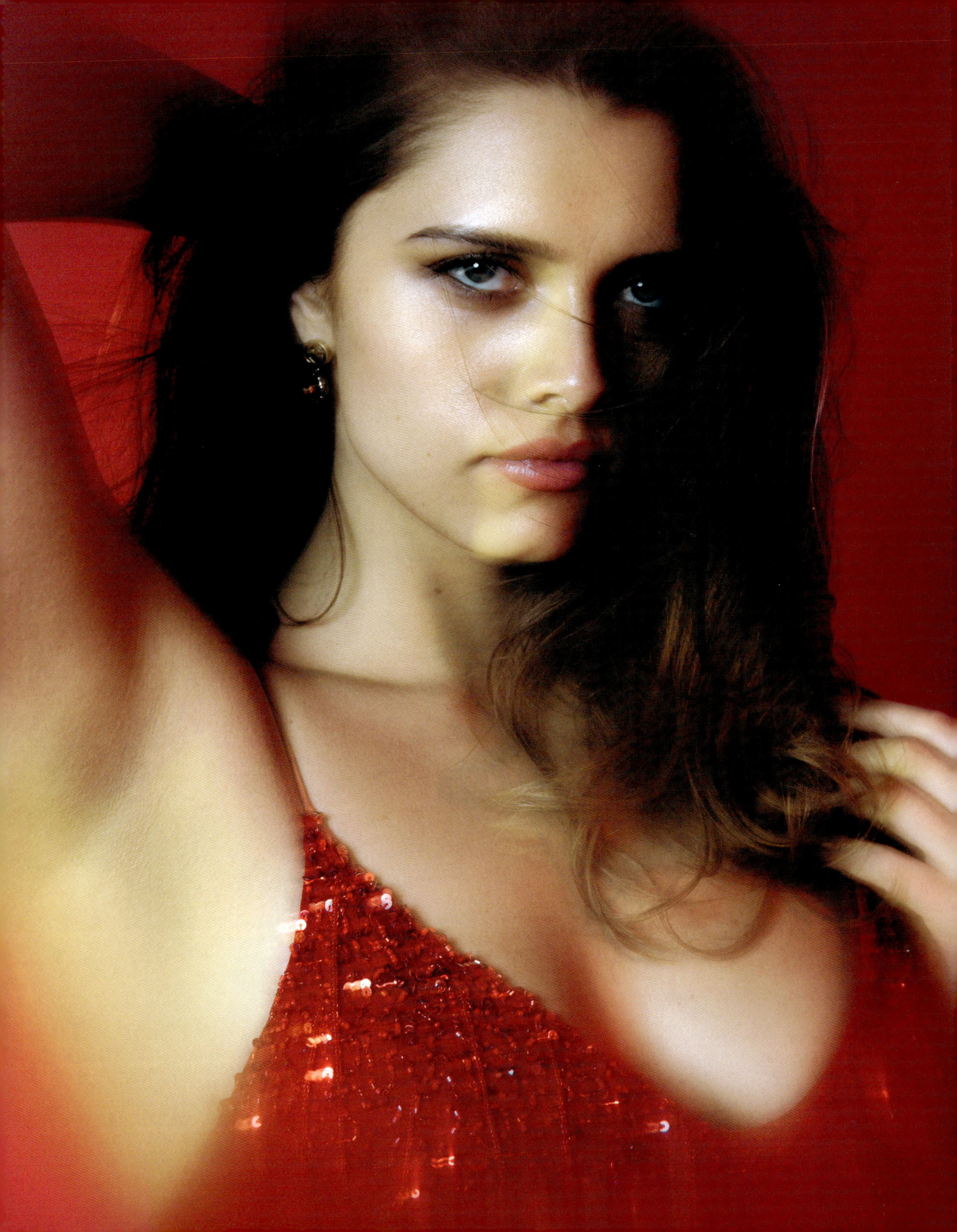

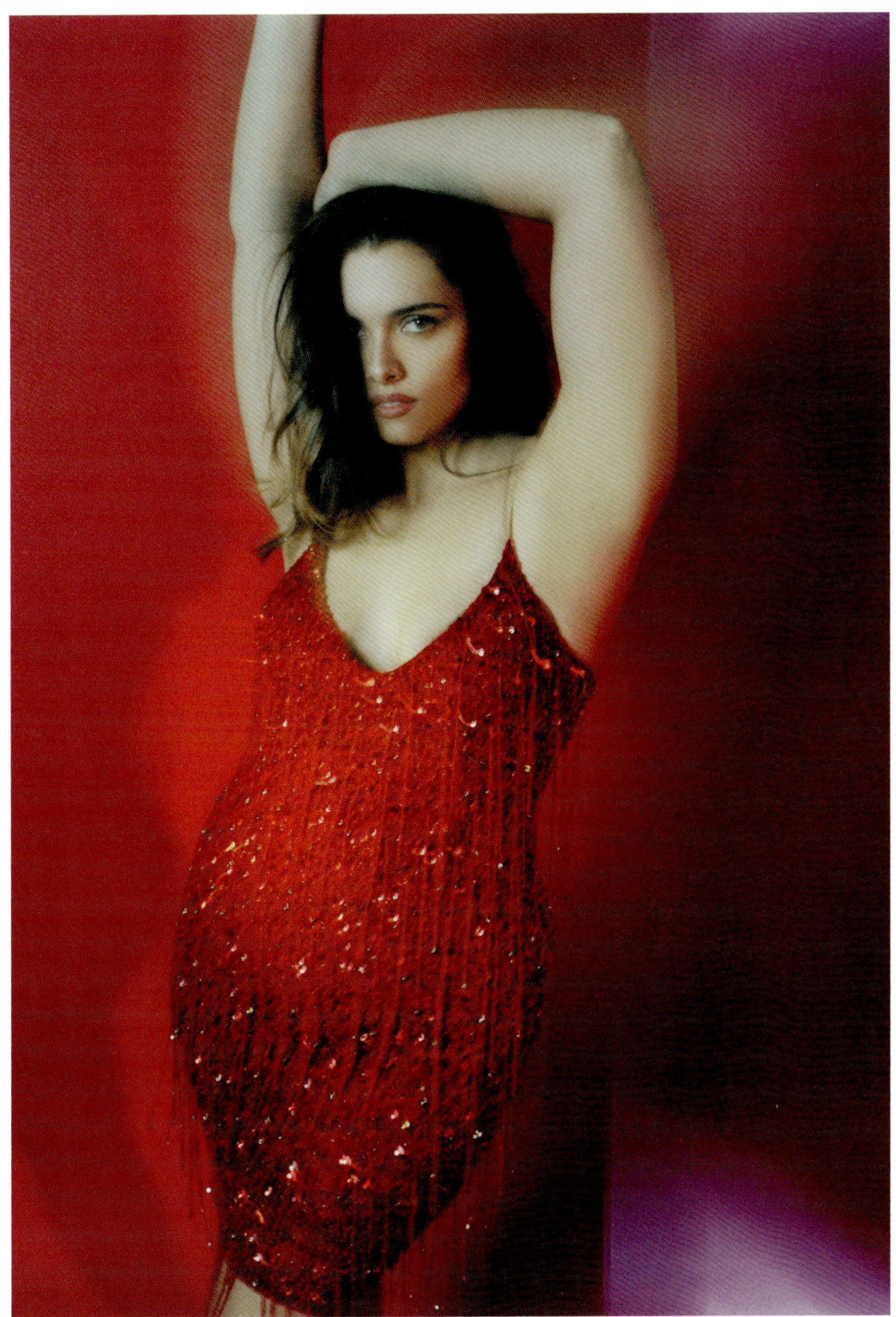

Wren Parker wears Retrofête dress.

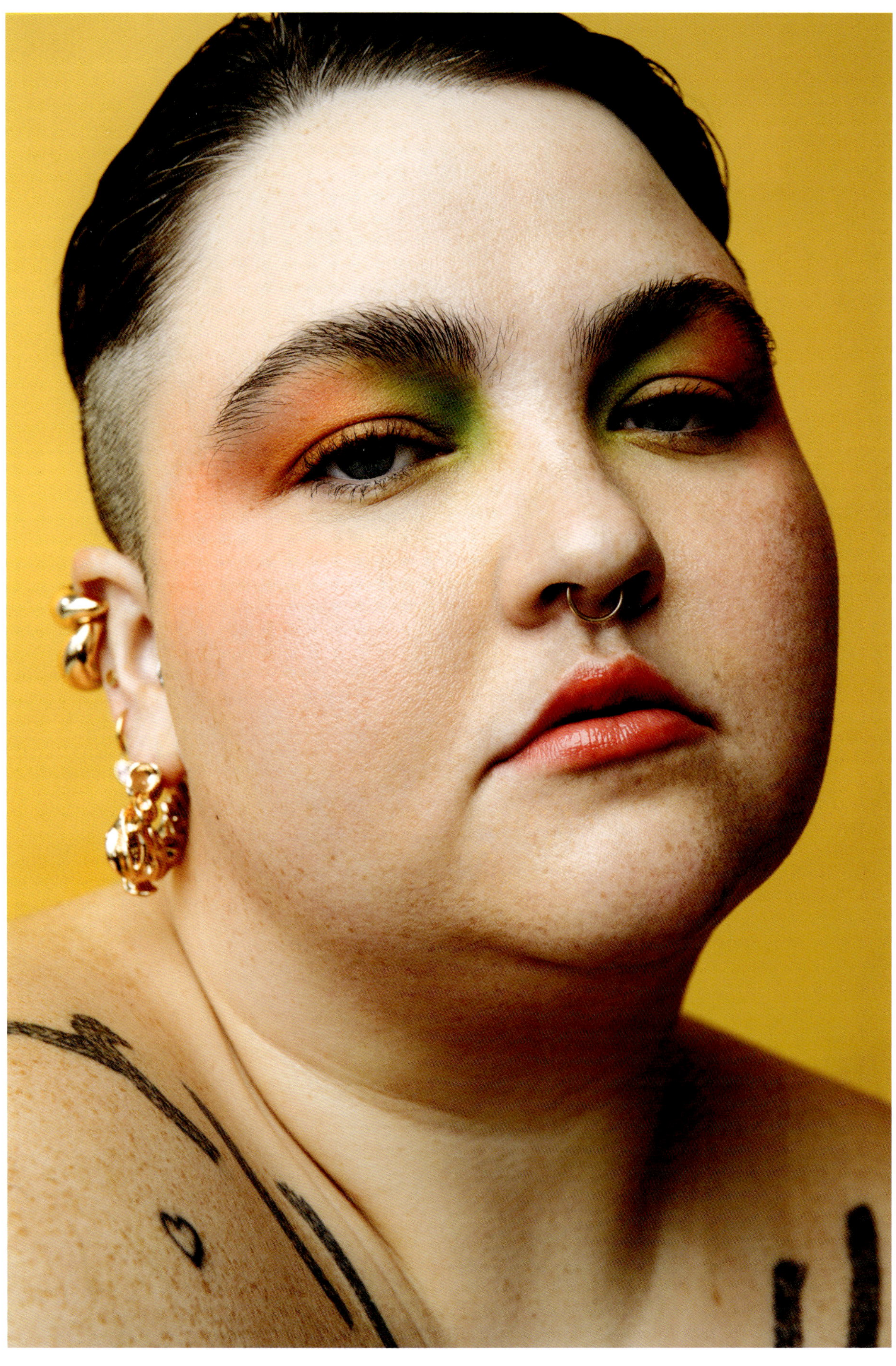

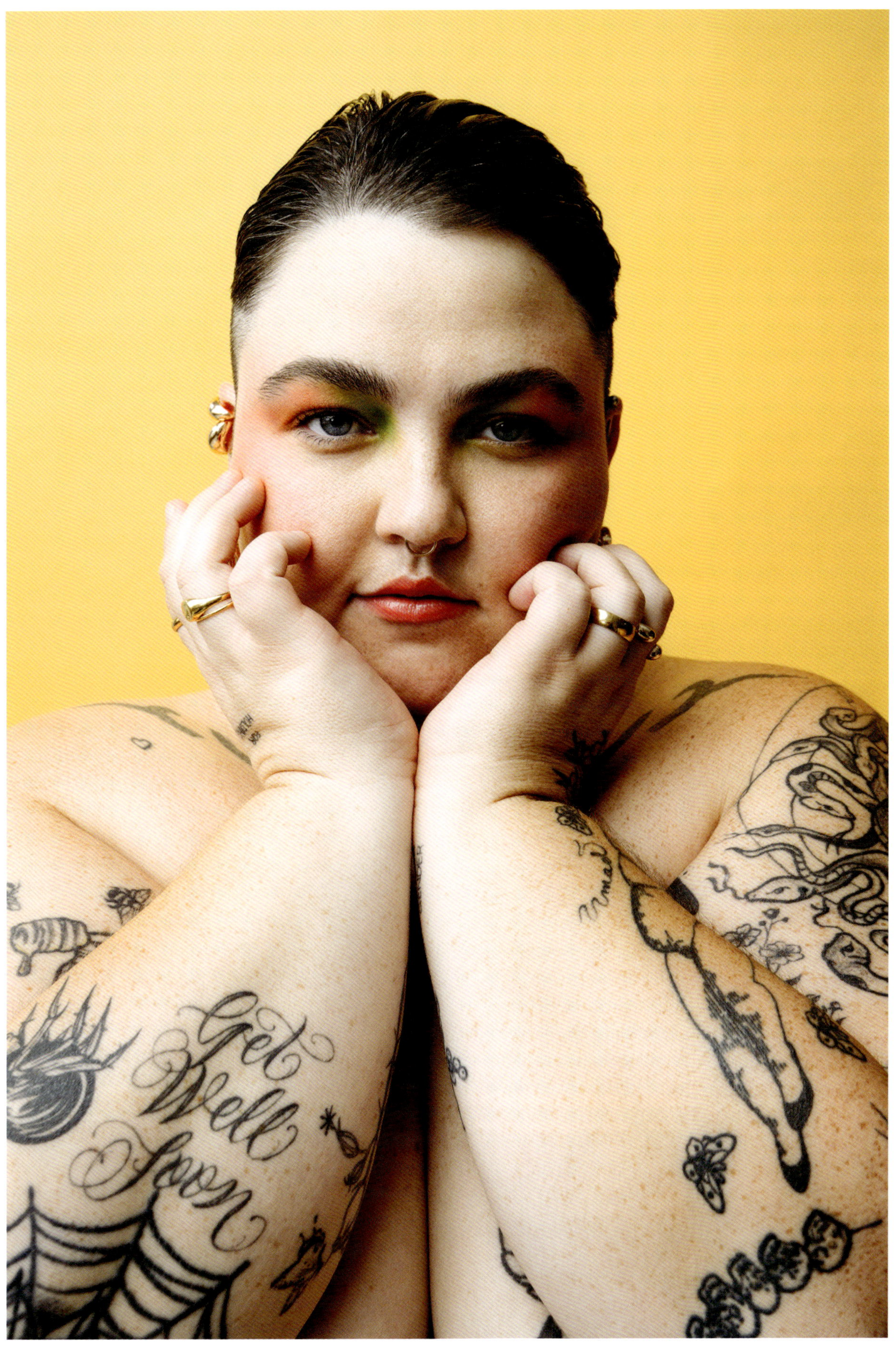
Get Well Soon

Previous pages: Jordan Underwood

Veronica Campos wears Nicole Miller dress;
Sachin & Babi earrings.

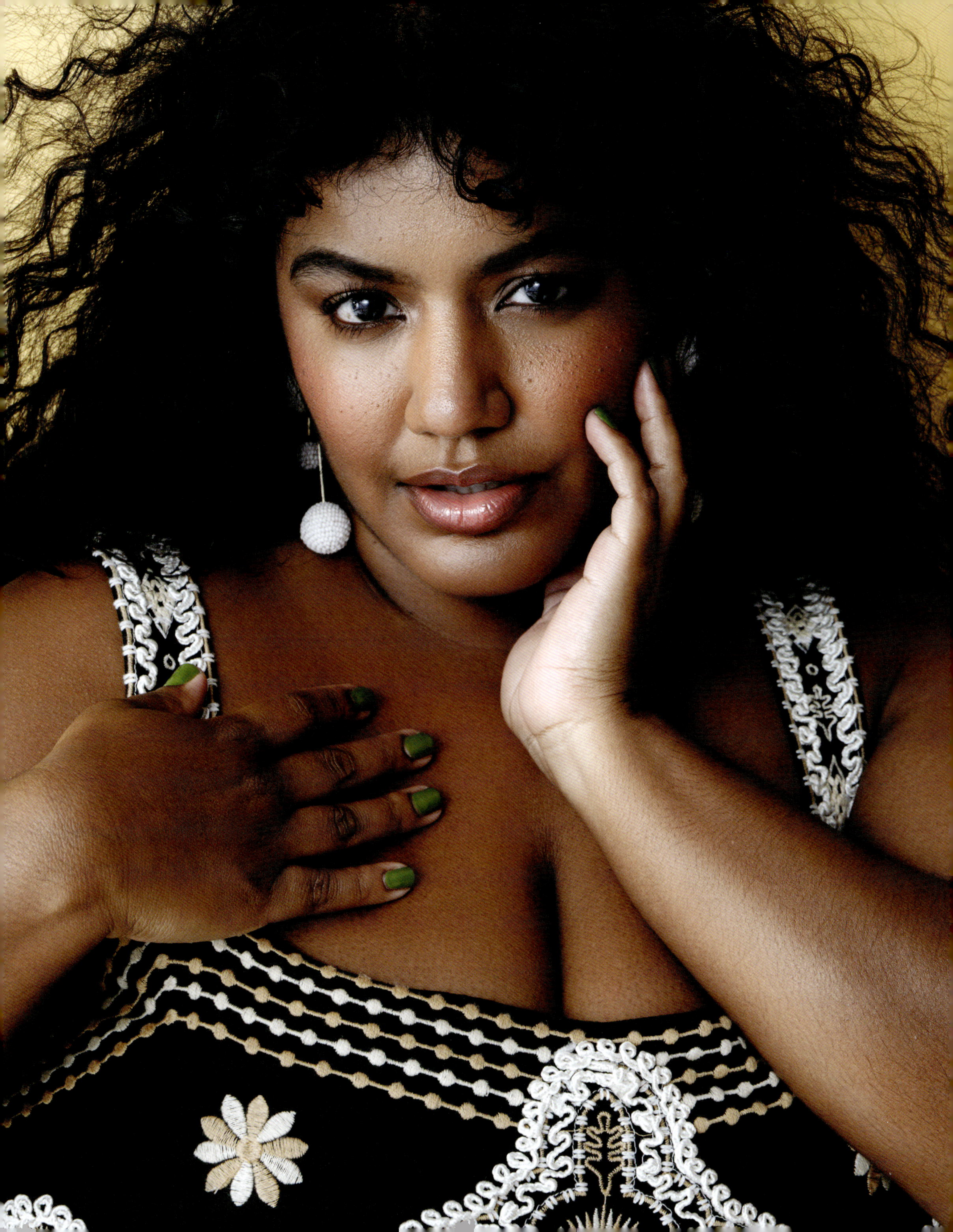

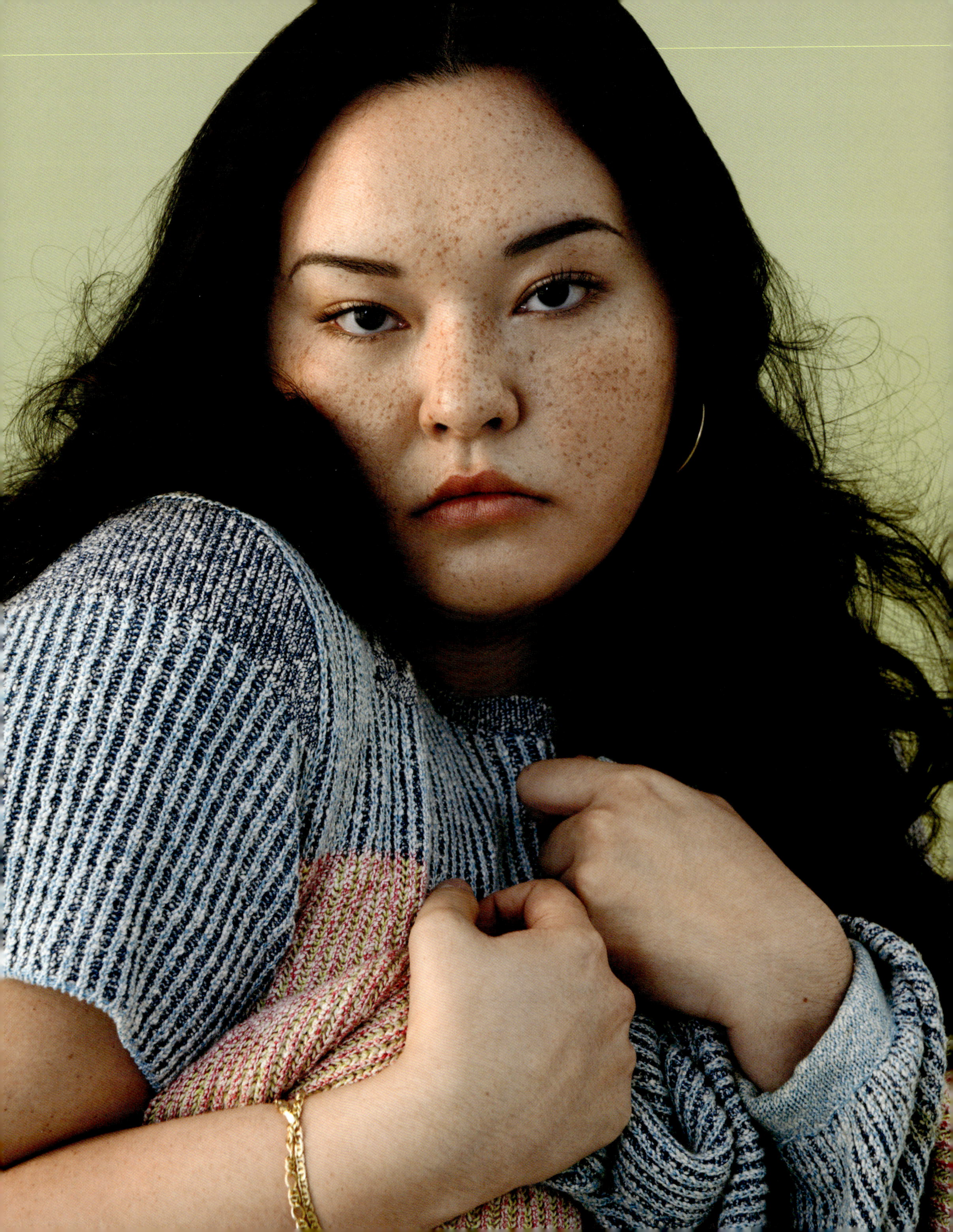

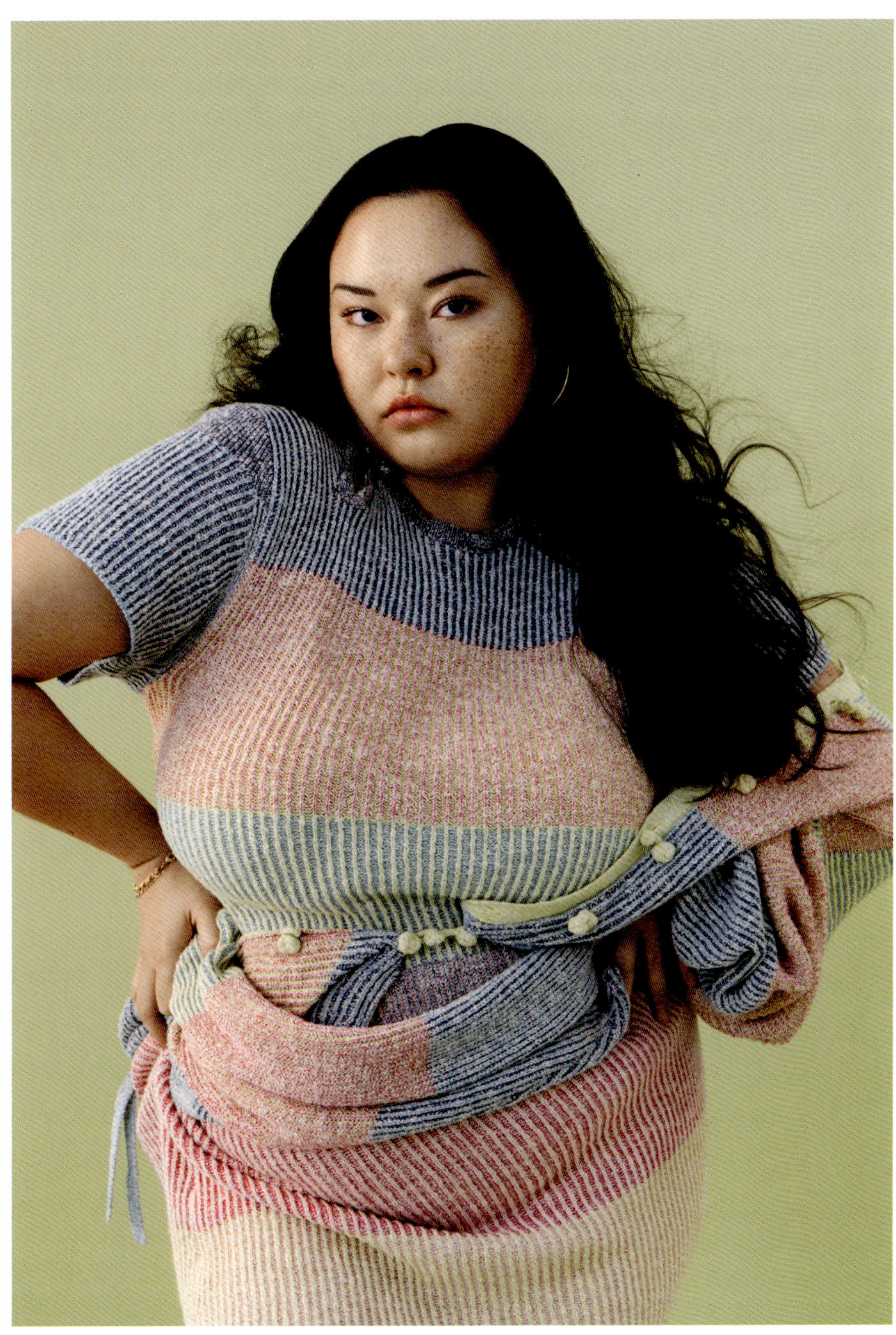

Madison Z. McNally wears vintage set from Shop Berriez.

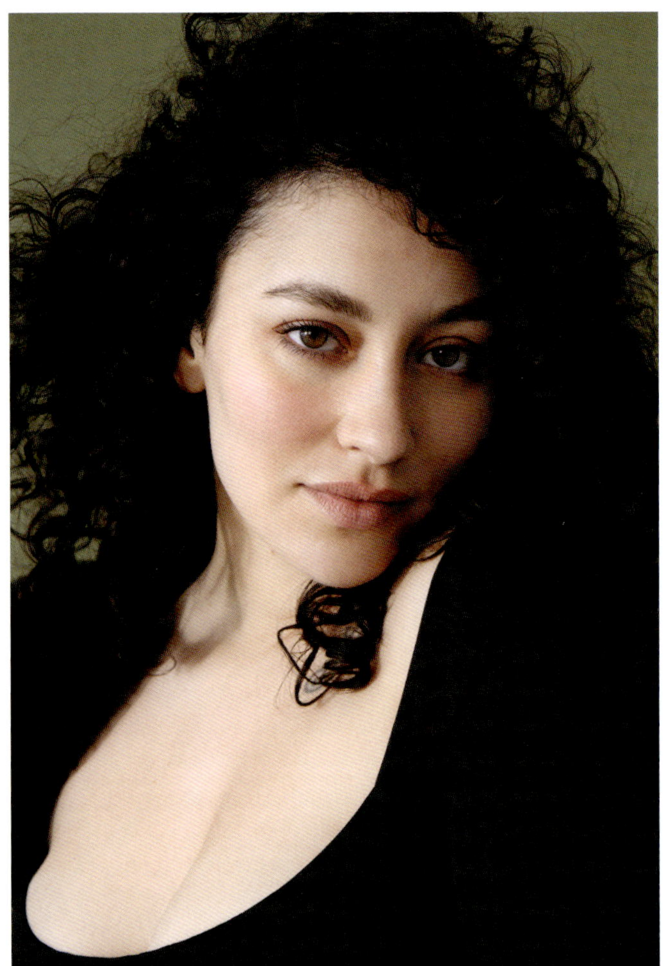

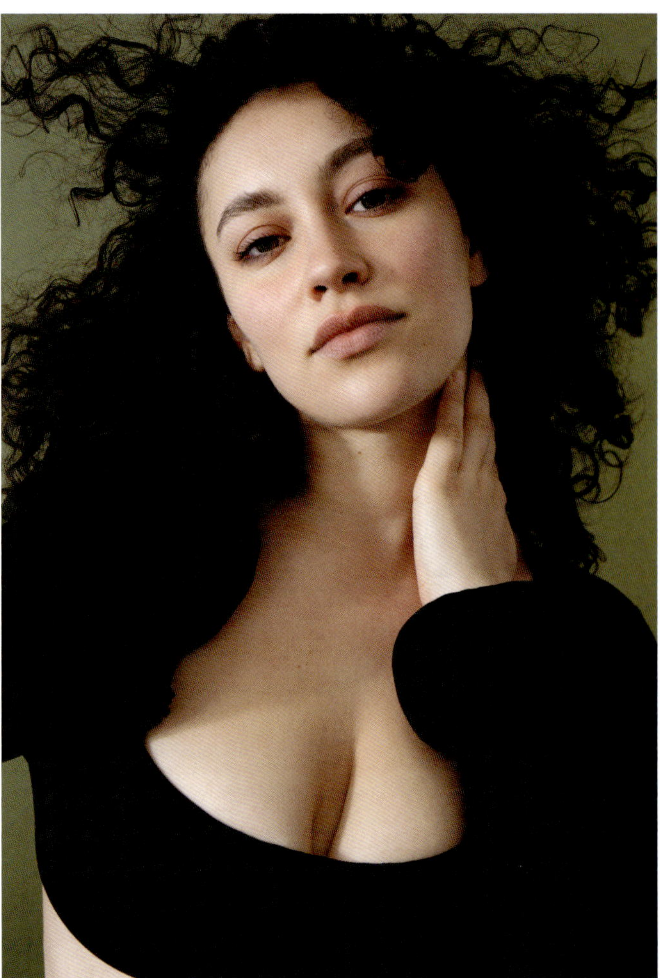

Cearah Peck wears shirt
from Kelly Augustine's closet.

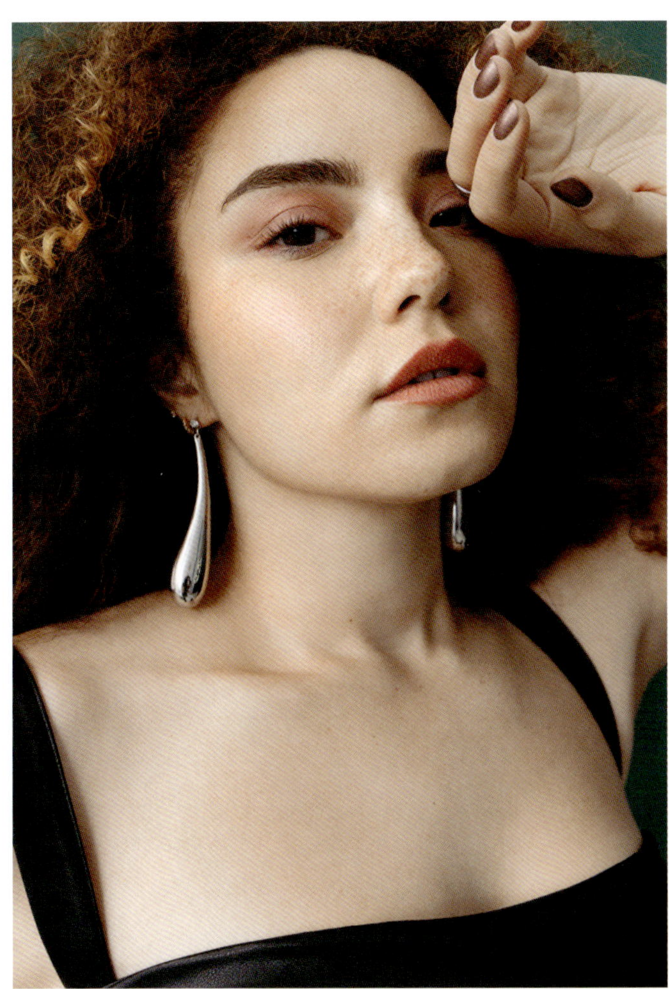

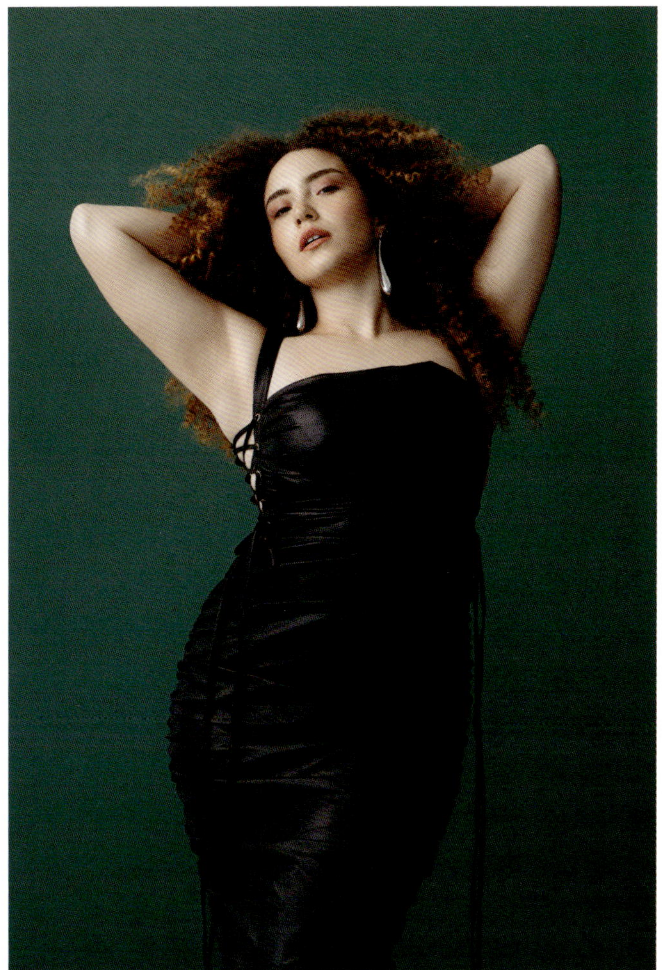

Katarina Tsokolati wears dress
from Lydia Hudgens' closet.

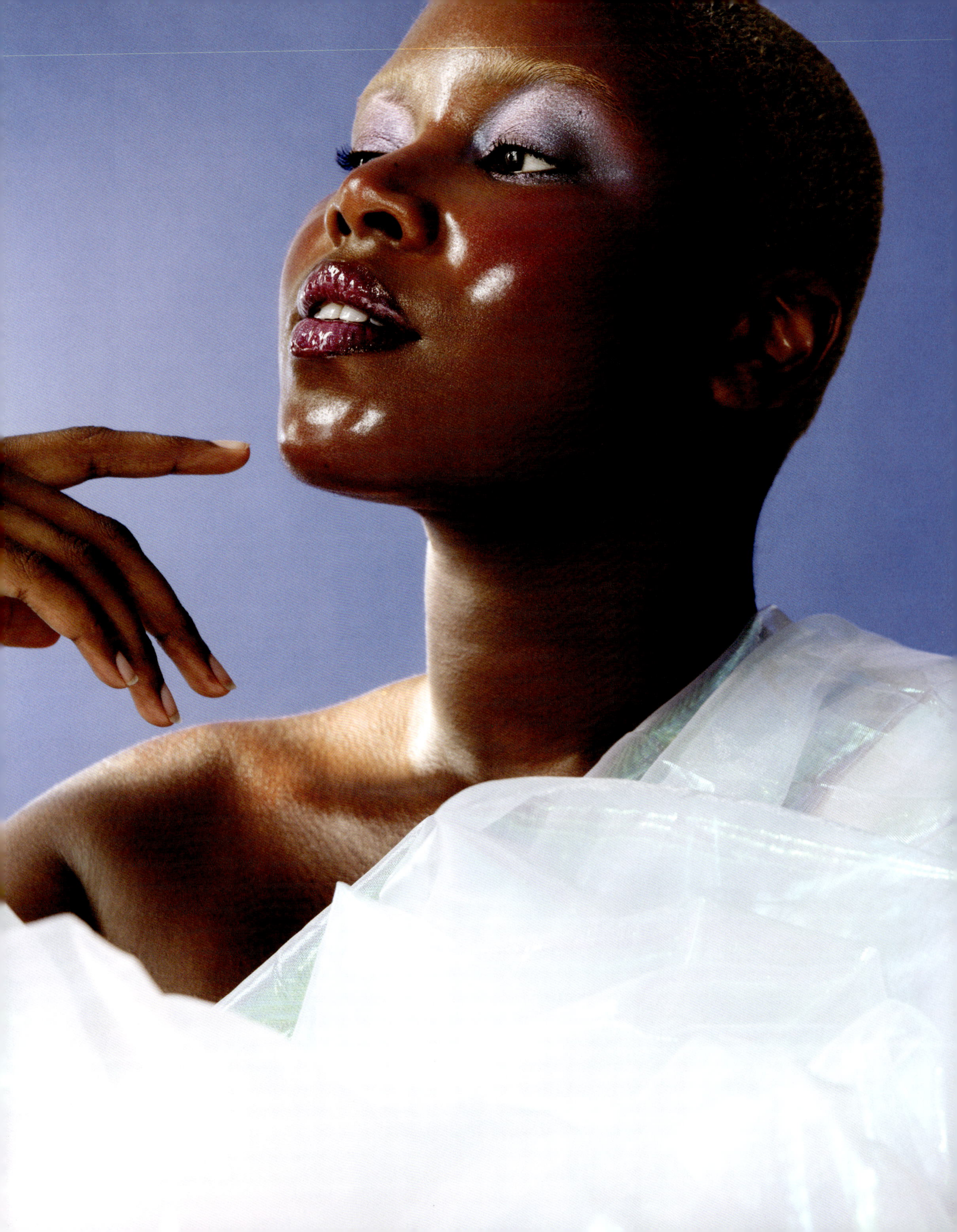

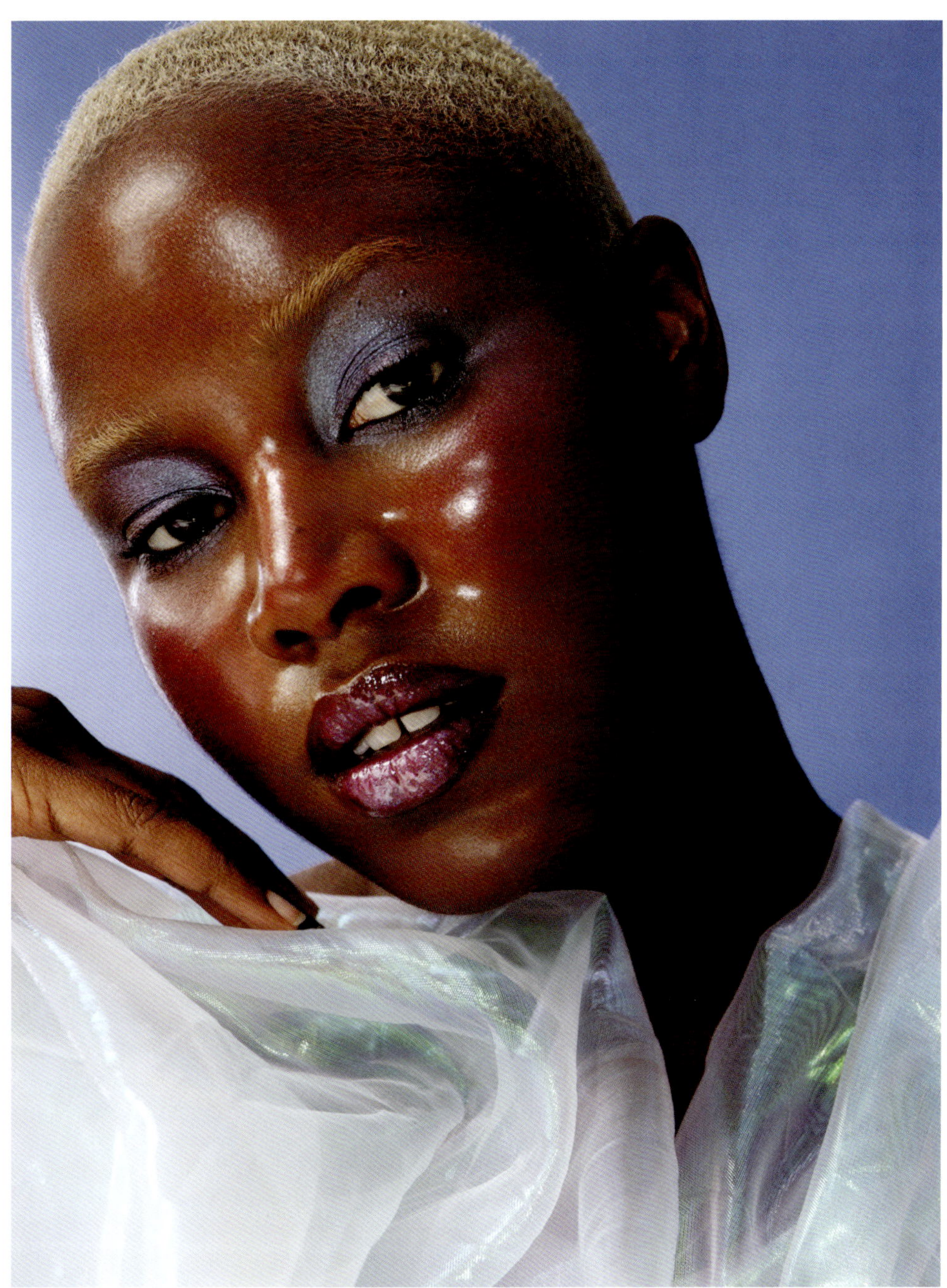

Melonee Rembert wears fabric draped by Lydia Hudgens.

Overleaf: PJ Nyambok wears Highdive NYC.

Pages 182–183: Roseline Lawrence wears CRZM jewelry.

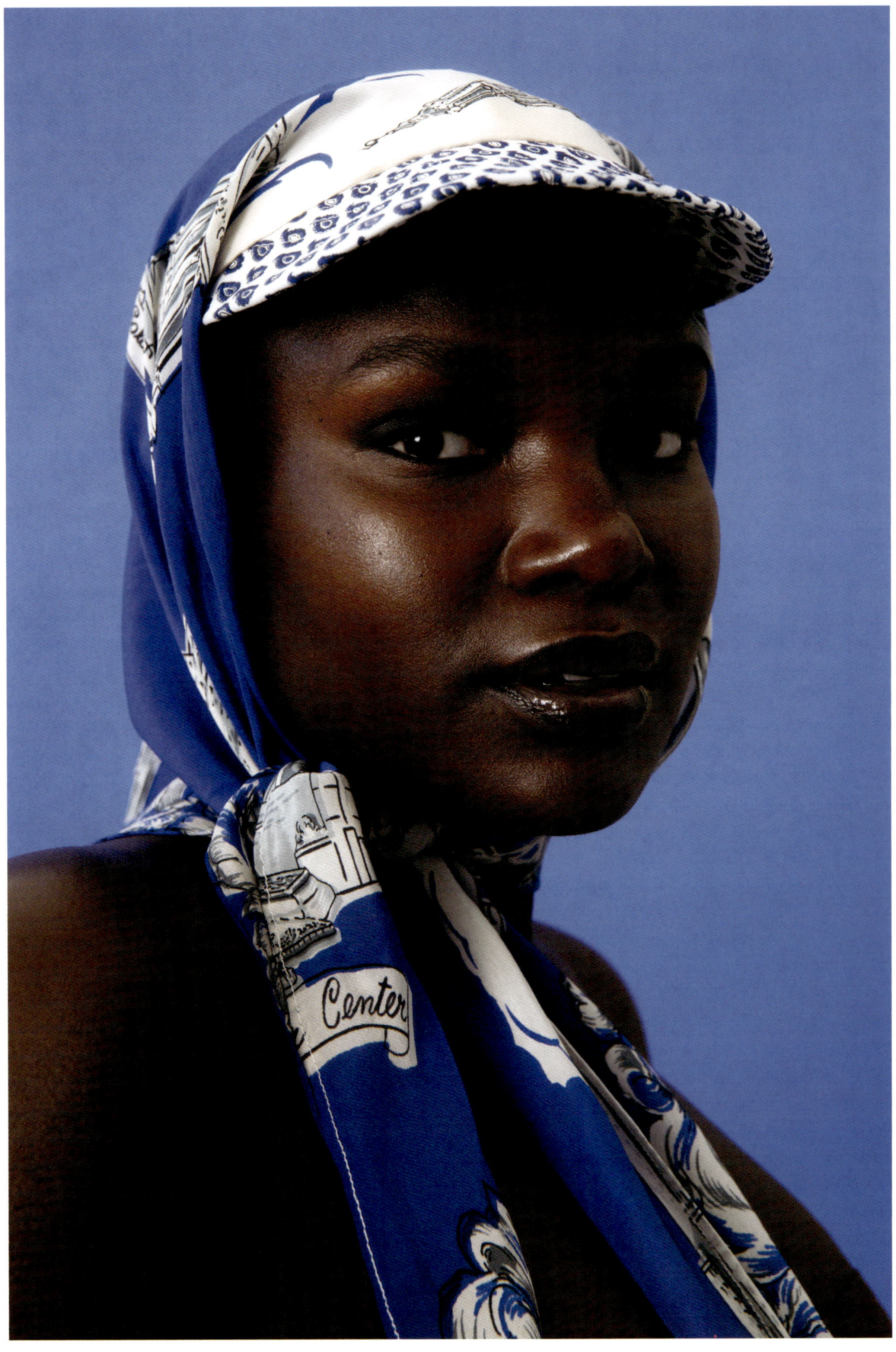
Center

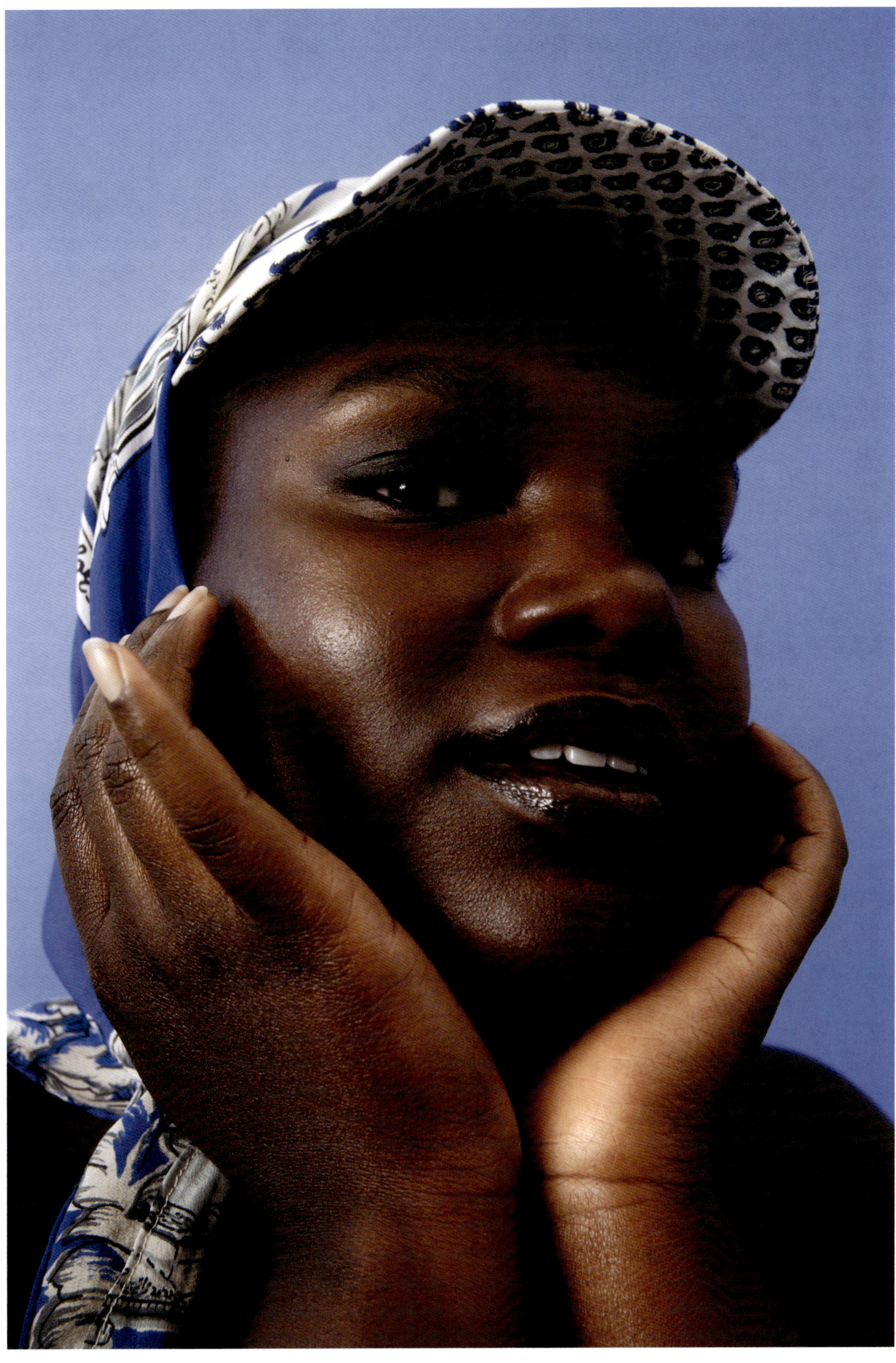

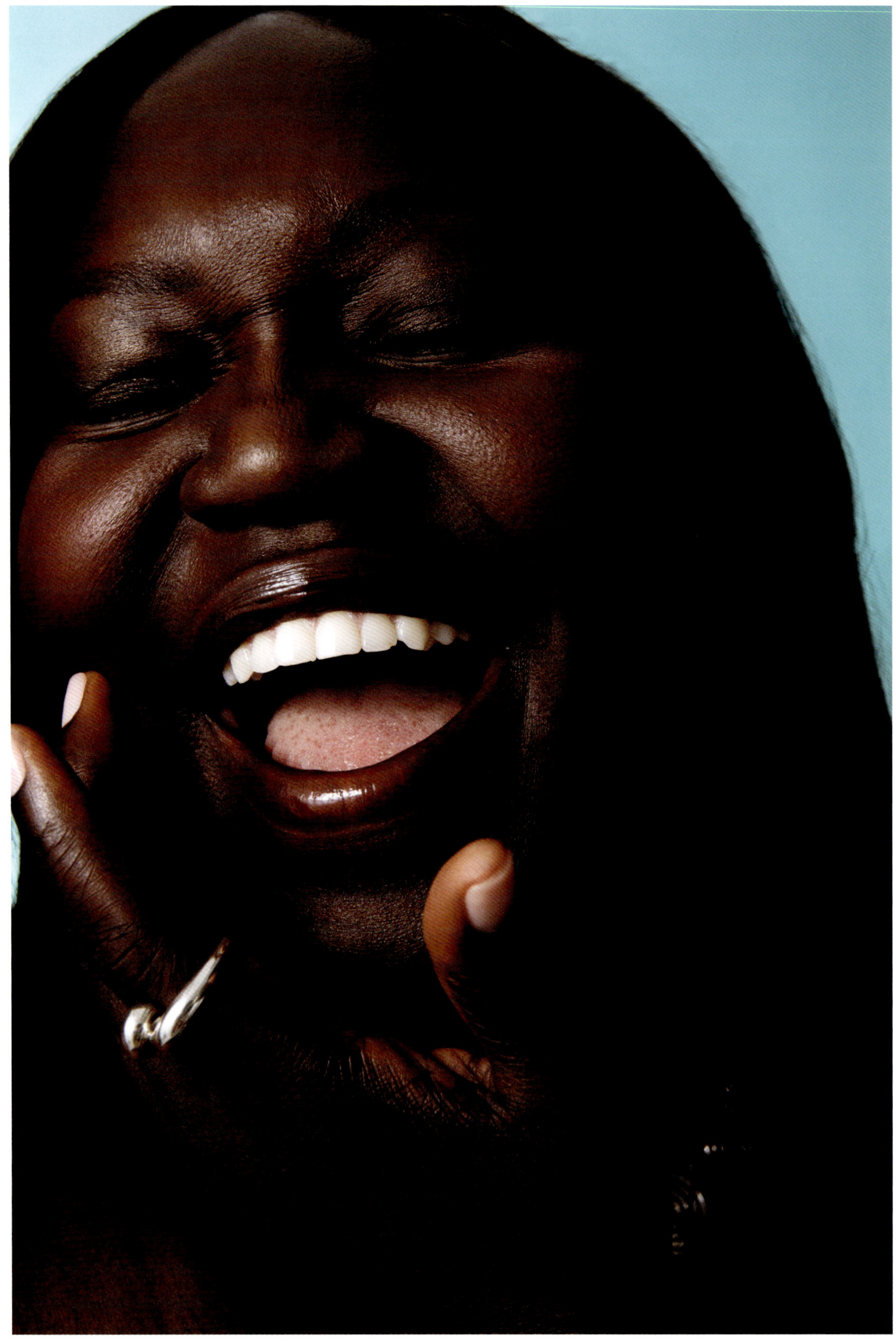

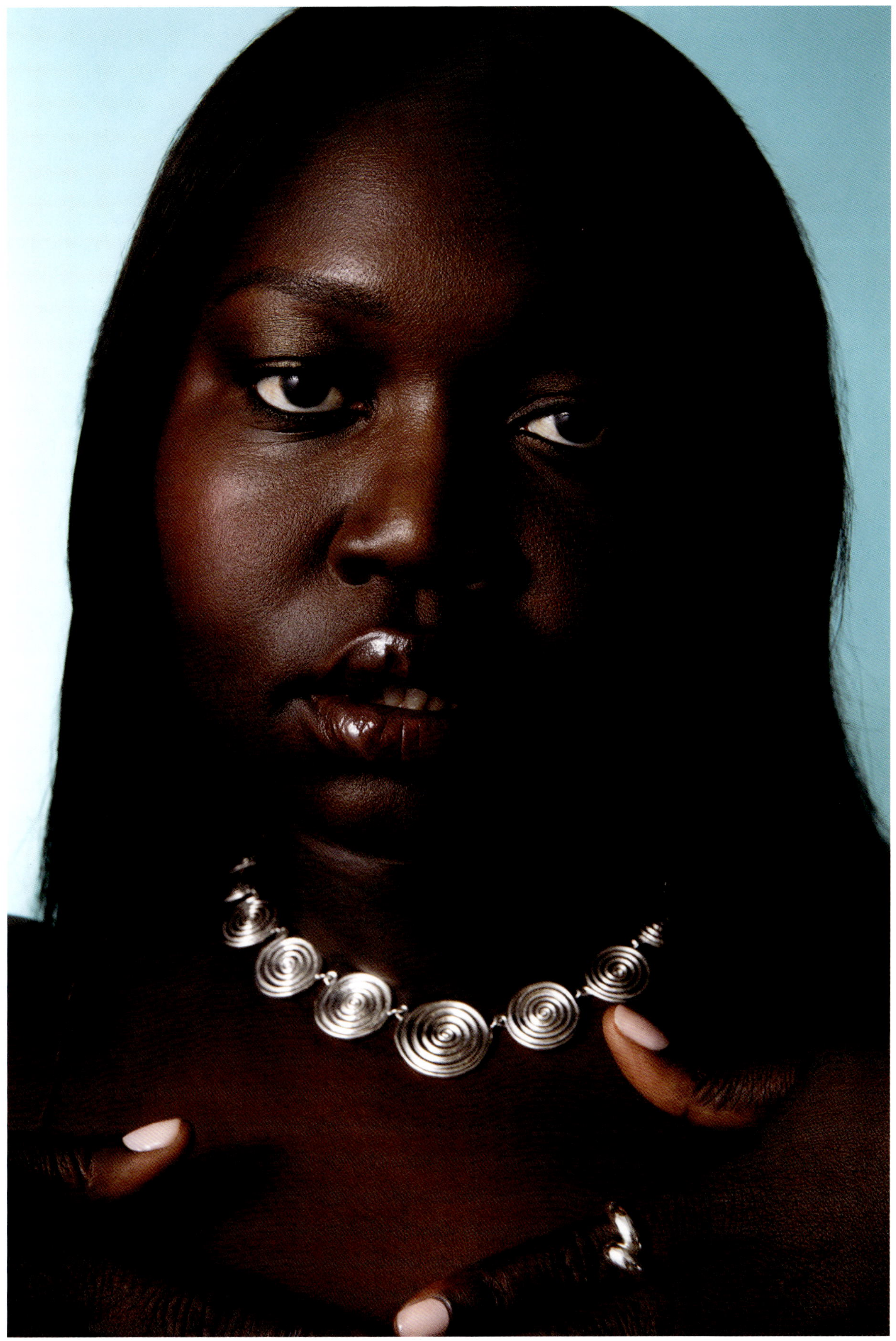

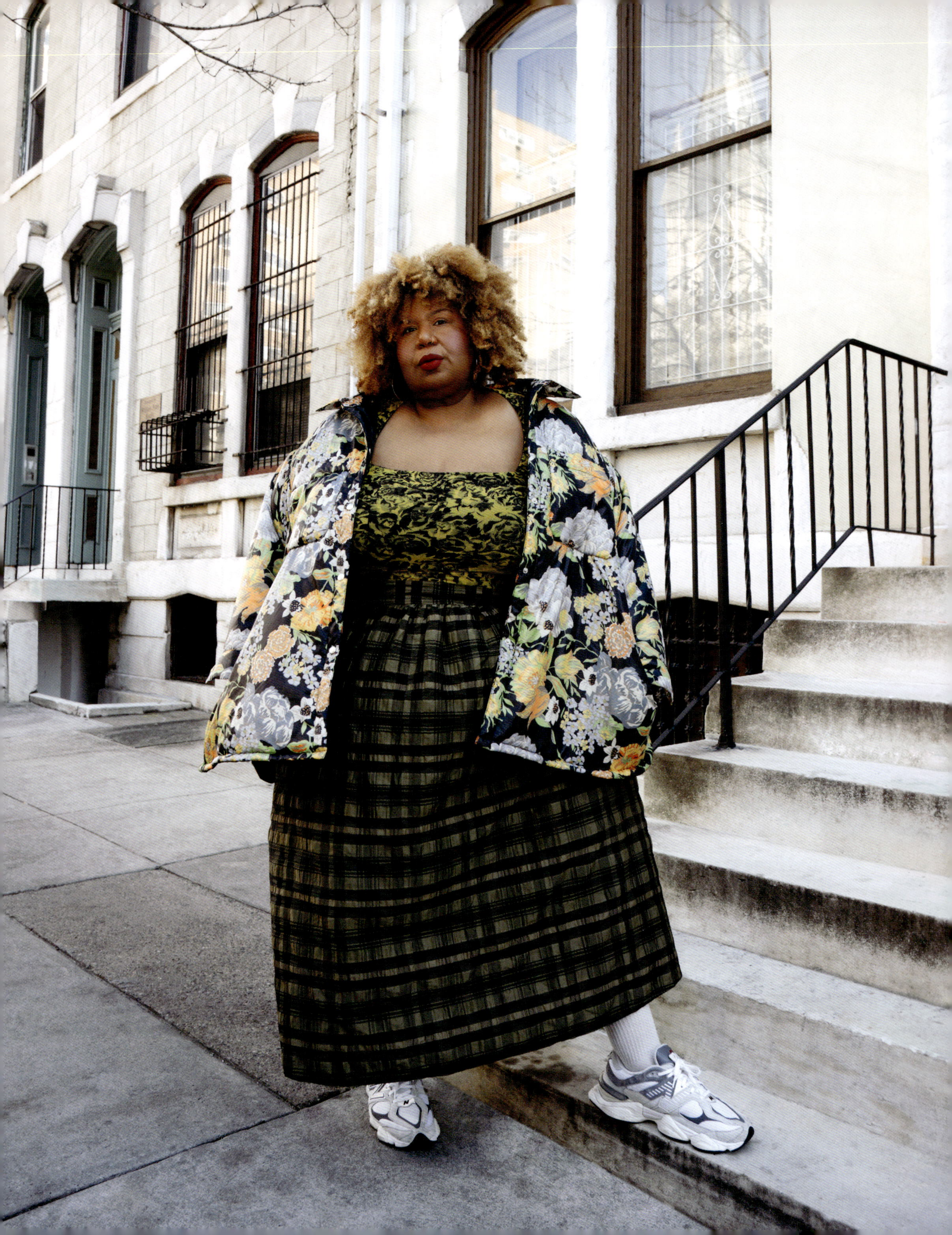

Kellie Brown

A leader in plus-size fashion and advocacy

From our first shoot together nearly 15 years ago, it was clear that Kellie Brown was a force to be reckoned with. A pioneer in plus-size fashion, she has helped brands understand the power of this community and has created opportunities for influencers who had long been excluded from the conversation. Throughout the years, she has used her platform to prove these influencers have the same business-building impact as their straight-size counterparts, all while advocating for stylish and bold fashion choices for more bodies.

Kellie was one of the first to push for the inclusion of plus-size influencers in campaigns. Her work with Catherines is a prime example: She helped the brand take creators around the world for two years running, offering opportunities that had never been available before. Reflecting on the significance of this early work, Kellie notes, "It's hard to watch things revert back to a less inclusive space, because what we did not only gave plus-size influencers opportunities… it also created space for us to demand more from brands."

Kellie's influence today stretches across many facets of fashion, including swimwear. In 2012, she played a pivotal role during her time as a consultant for Swimsuits for All in launching the fatkini with Gabi Fresh: a collaboration that forever changed the swimwear landscape.

"It was the early days of fashion blogging, and I had noticed a young woman making serious waves." Kellie had seen Gabi posting what she was calling a "fatkini," and she knew she had to reach out. "Her idea for a galaxy print bikini at a time when options were limited to styles your grandmother might wear was revolutionary."

This collaboration ended up becoming one of the most impactful, visionary moments in plus-size fashion history. "It not only affected the swim industry, but it showed brands that plus-size customers wanted actual fashion that was on-trend, and it

I looked around at all these powerful creatives—makeup artists, models, designers, editors—and we were all plus-size. If my younger self could see this room, it would have been life changing.

changed the game. Further proof that Black, plus-size women behind the scenes, in rooms that challenge the status quo, create opportunity for other Black women—and thus, create opportunity for all."

Beyond swimwear, Kellie has been instrumental in driving some of the most noteworthy campaigns in the plus-size space. While she acknowledges that her work sometimes goes unrecognized, she remains proud of the role she's played. "I've had people take credit for my work," Kellie admits. "I've had people attempt to leave me out of the history of things that came from my brain, but I know the impact I've had, as do many others. Often when you're on the early side of change, the people who stand on your shoulders might be more seen, but that doesn't mean we don't still hold them up, just as I am held up by the many women who came before me."

In 2019, Kellie created the hashtag #FatAtFashionWeek to raise awareness about the lack of plus-size representation at the event. Kellie didn't just want to highlight the absence of representation, though; "it was to honor the many people in this industry who exist in bodies outside of the fashion norm … It was a call to action to be seen. It was an invitation. I looked around at all these powerful creatives—makeup artists, models, designers, editors—and we were all plus-size. If my younger self could see this room, it would have been life changing."

It isn't just her peers who recognize Kellie's influence; her name has appeared across major platforms like *Vogue*, *Architectural Digest*, and *Good Morning America*. "It's been incredible to see myself in places where I used to work so hard to put clients. The funny thing is, I've never pitched myself to media. It was organic. It was people seeing me create and it resonating—and that feels good."

Kellie's creative presence is felt beyond fashion, extending into interior design. With a keen eye, she has cultivated a true passion for creating spaces that reflect her unique aesthetic and values. Her approach aligns closely with the principles that define her work in fashion: inclusivity, creativity, and authenticity. Kellie explores this connection through her Substack, *Deeply Madly*, blending her fashion background with her passion for interiors to offer her perspective on how design can be both beautiful and inclusive.

As a creative professional, Kellie uses a range of tools, including photography and video. Her work with both captivates with its humor, honesty, and genuine expression. Her authentic presence resonates with her audience, making them feel seen and understood, while her charm, energy, and refreshing honesty draw people in. Whether through content creation or her PR and consulting work, Kellie deftly shapes how inclusivity is presented and embraced across the industry.

Looking ahead to the future of plus-size fashion and the opportunities for continued inclusivity, Kellie says, "Every industry has peaks and valleys, and I like to look at valleys as opportunities for growth and expansion." In particular, she sees potential in the new generation of creators and the continued work of educators in teaching inclusive patternmaking and fitting. While there is still work to be done, Kellie remains excited about the industry's evolution.

For Kellie, fashion goes beyond clothes—it's about confidence, represenation, and visibility. "I'm just trying to make the things younger me needed to see," she says. "I hope my journey to wholly loving myself and my desire to help others see their full beauty shines through in everything that I do."

Kellie's work reflects this hope as she continues to lead by example, pushing the boundaries of style and representation for plus-size individuals everywhere.

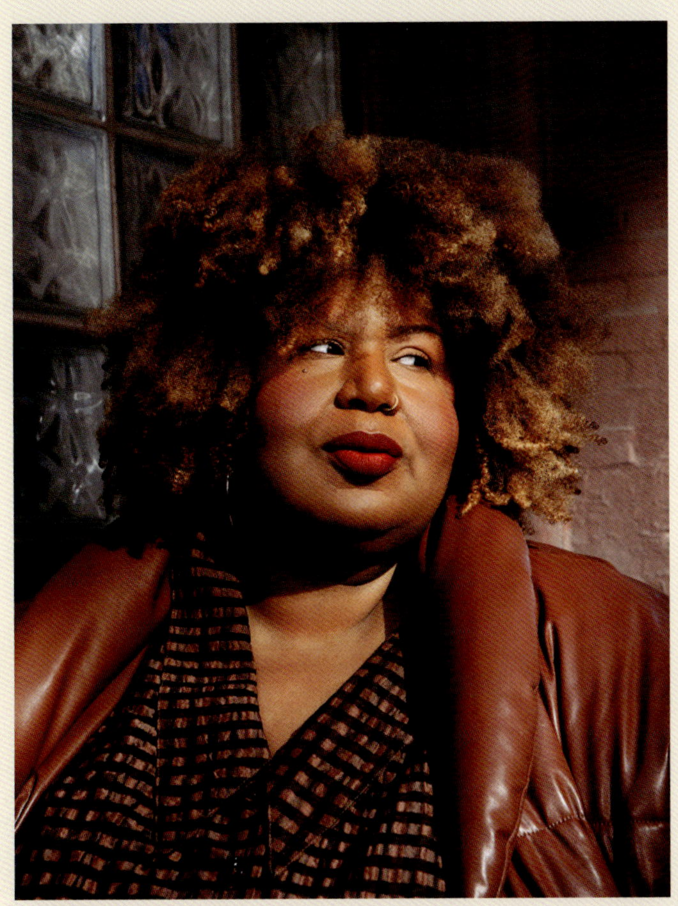

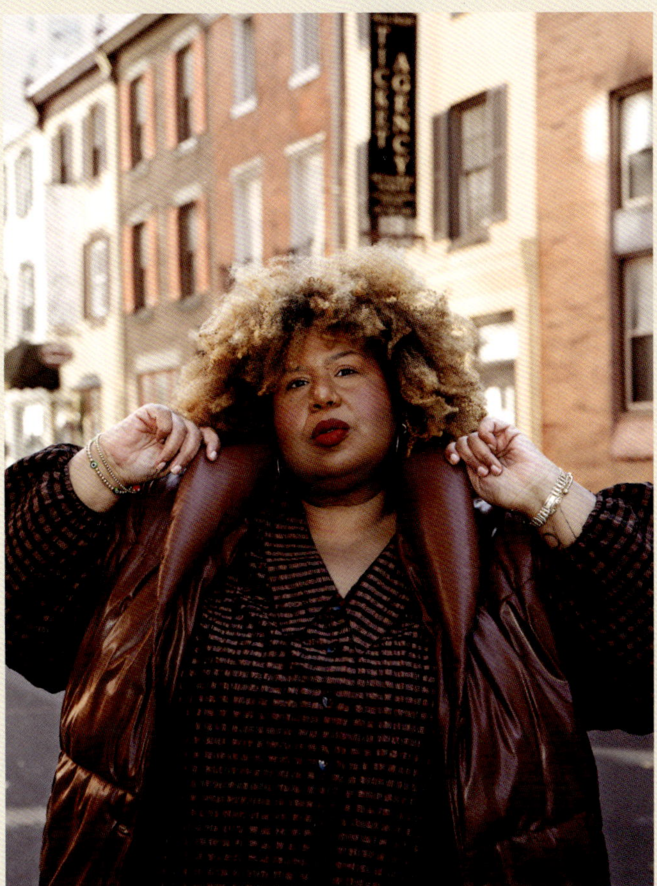

TICKET
AGENCY

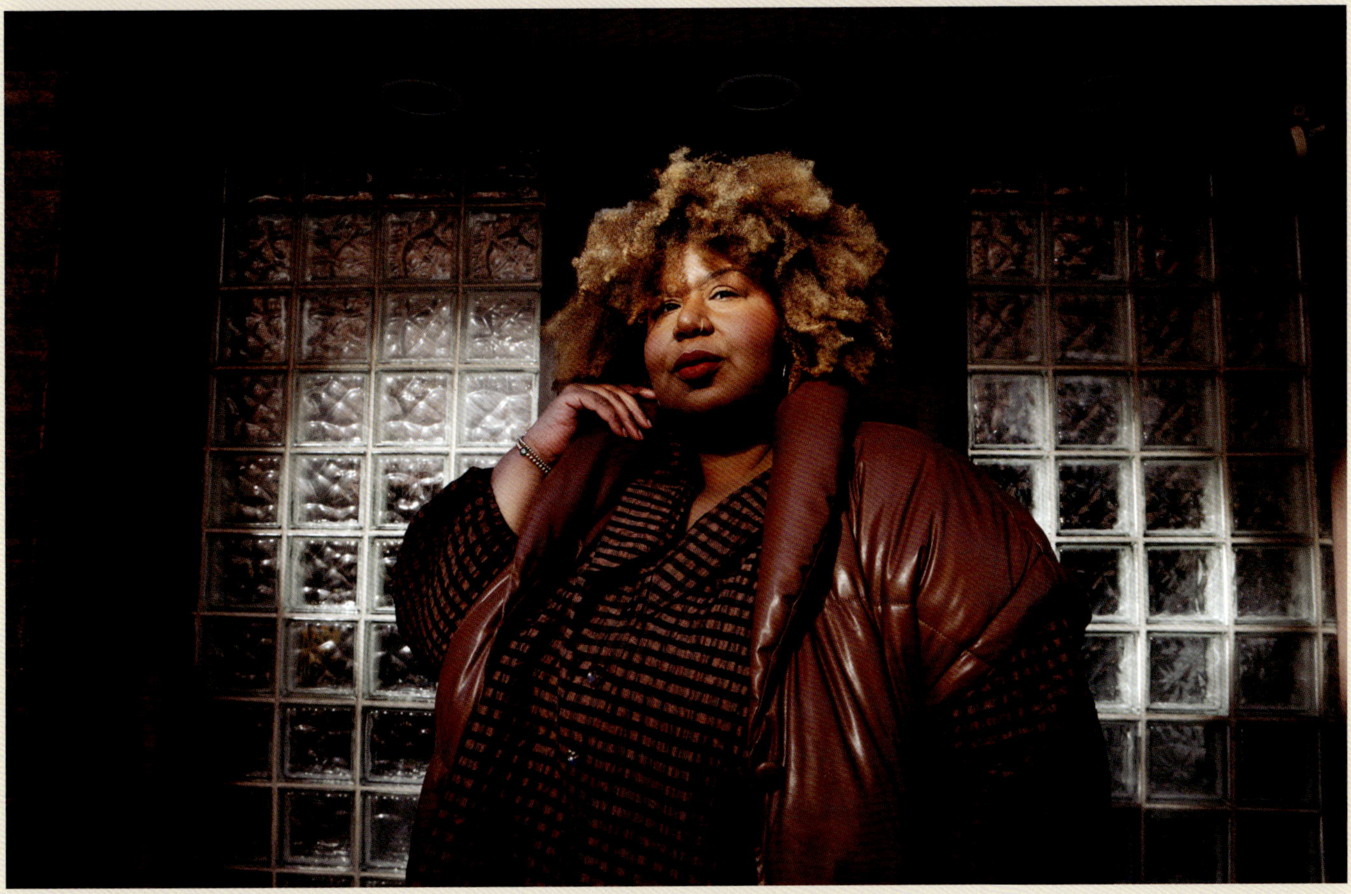

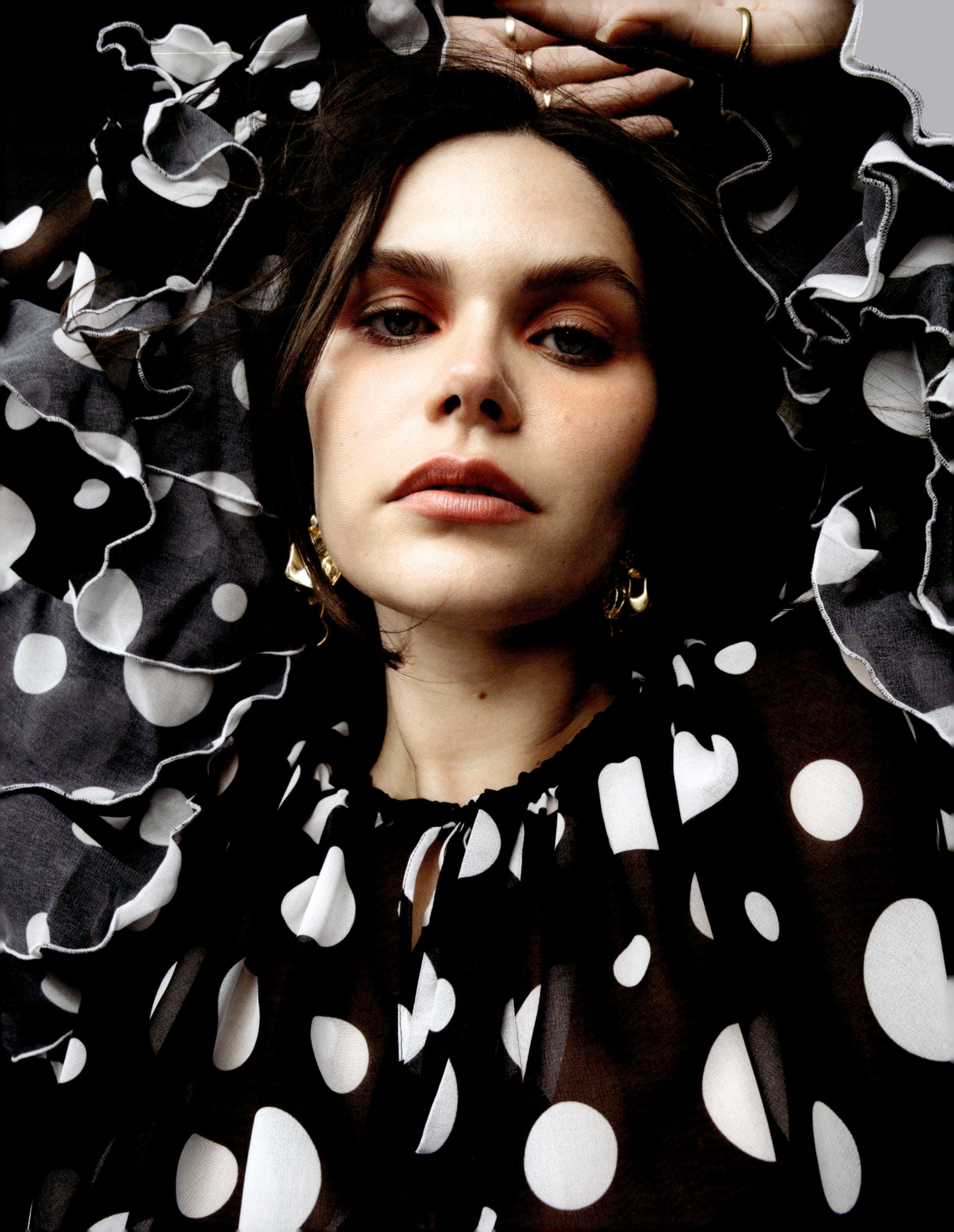

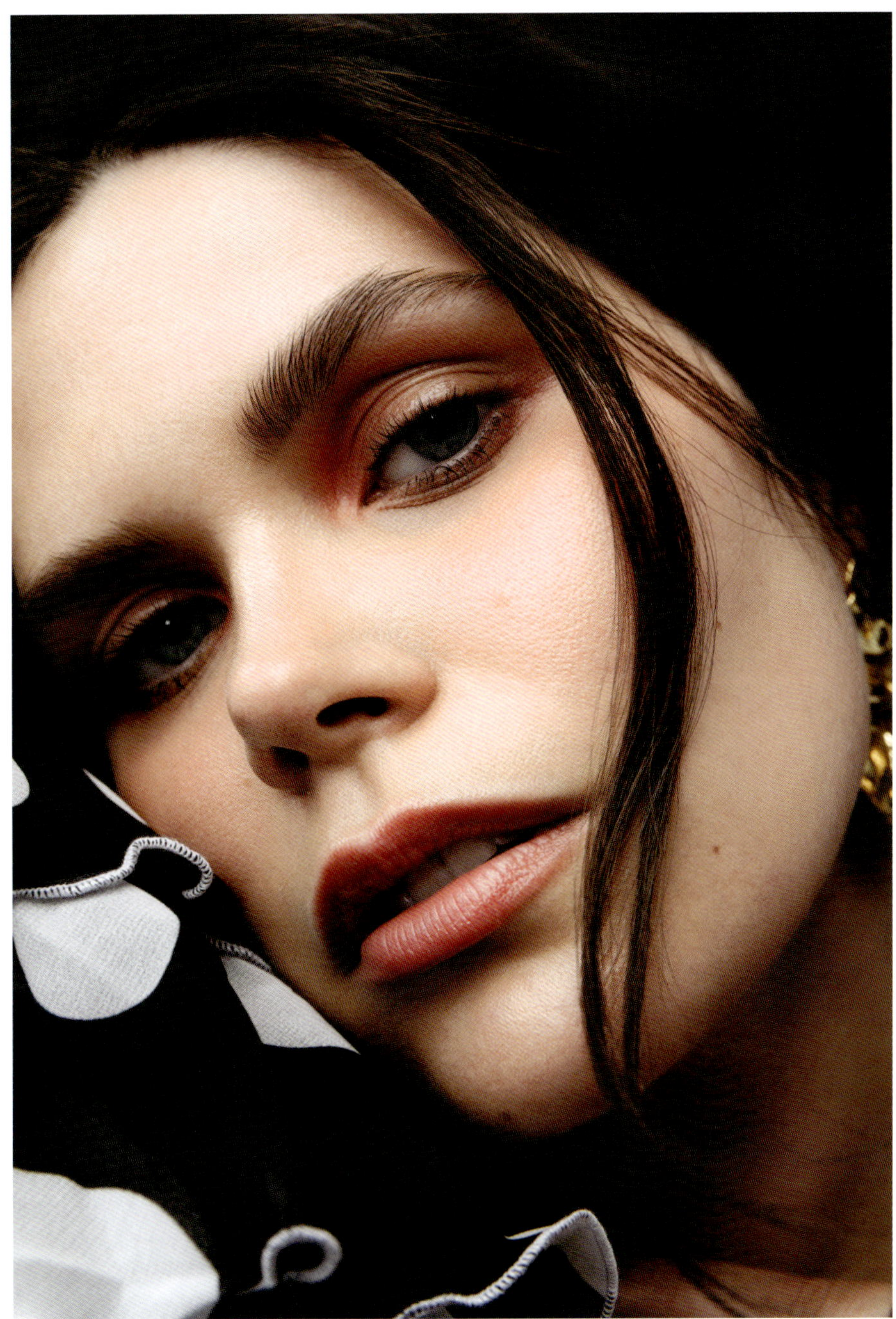

Chloe DeCleene wears Sleeper set; Alexis Bittar earrings.

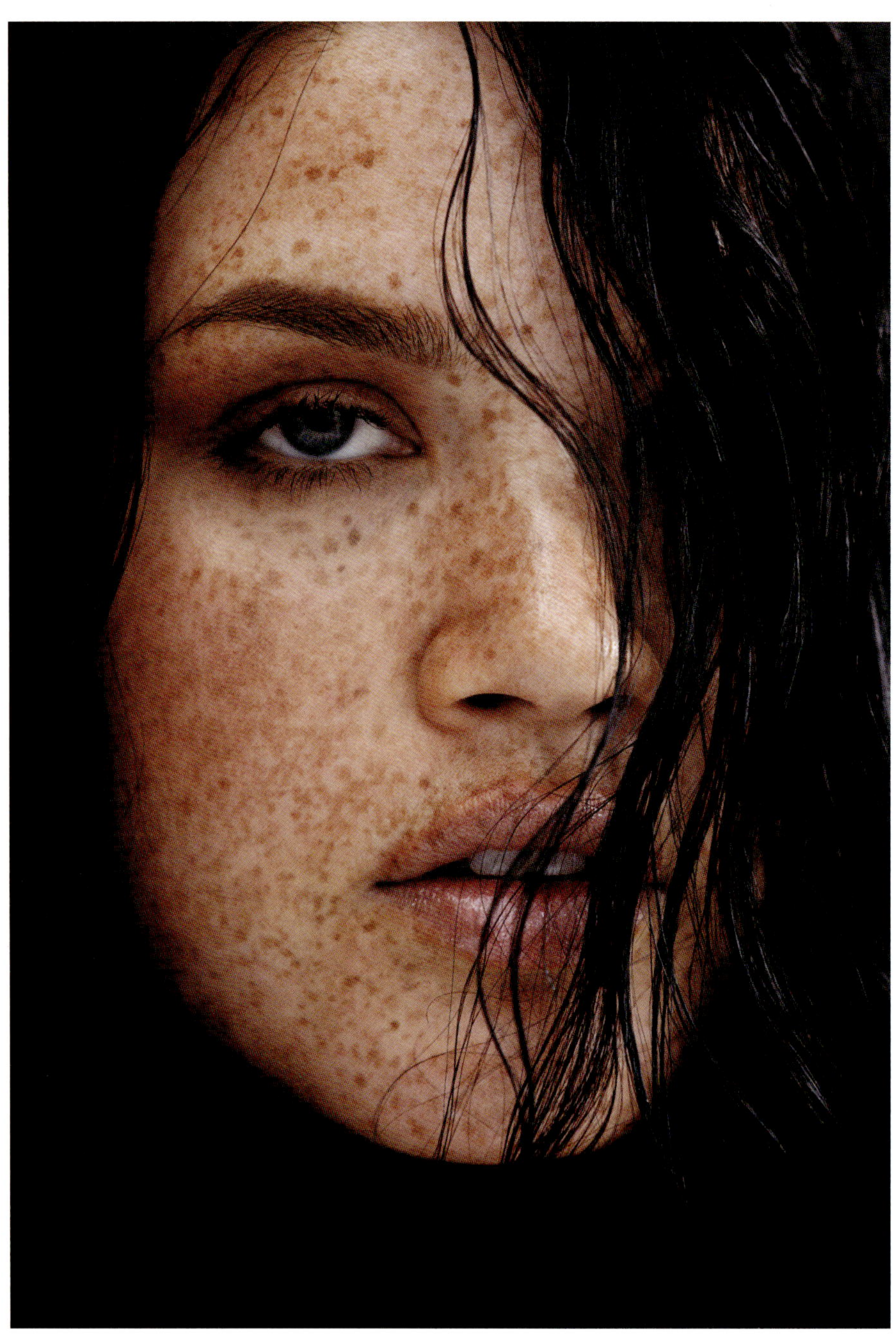

Mariah Sun

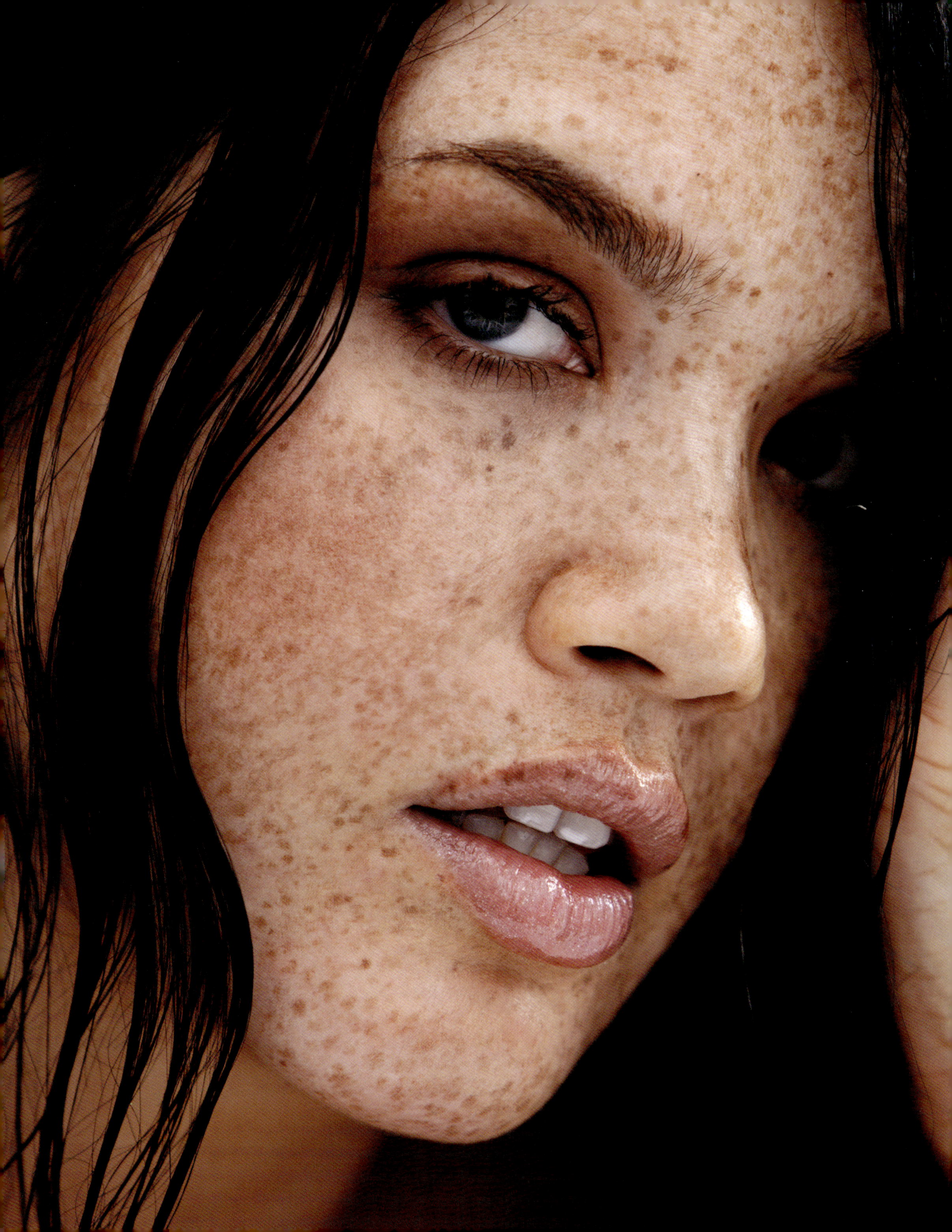

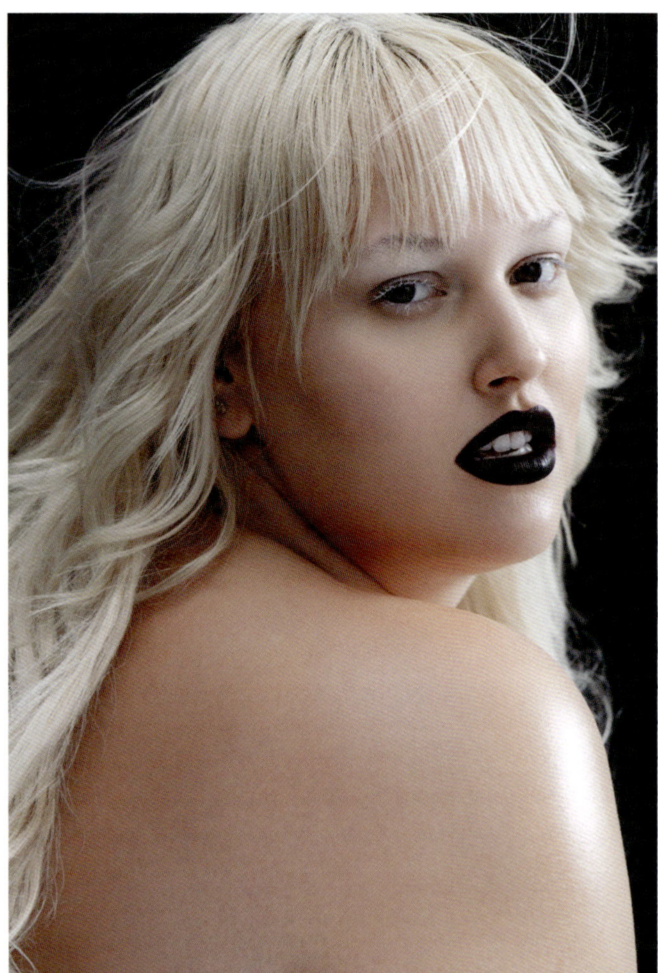

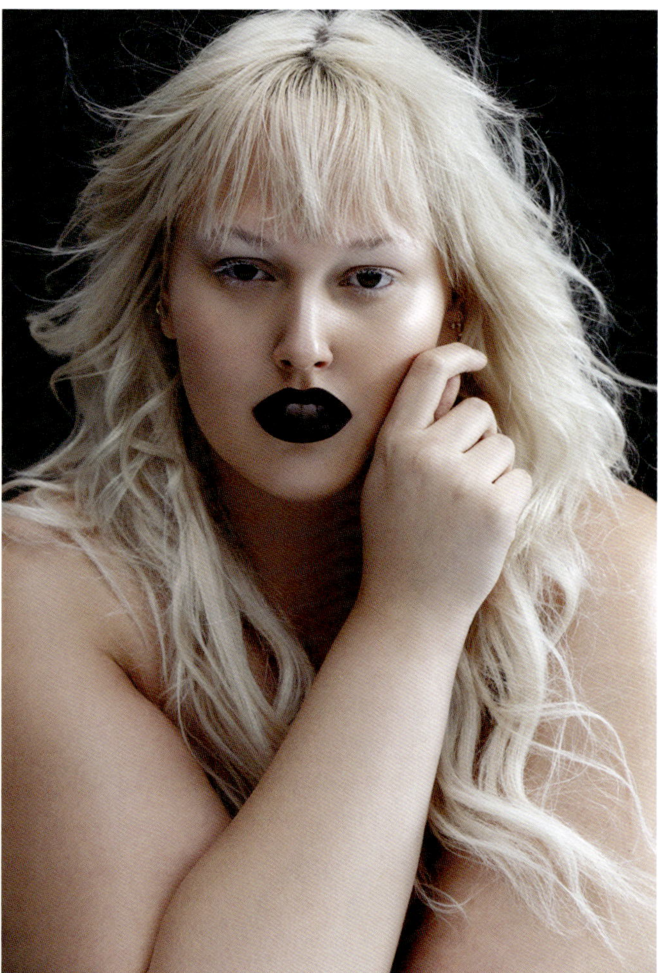

Isabella Salvucci

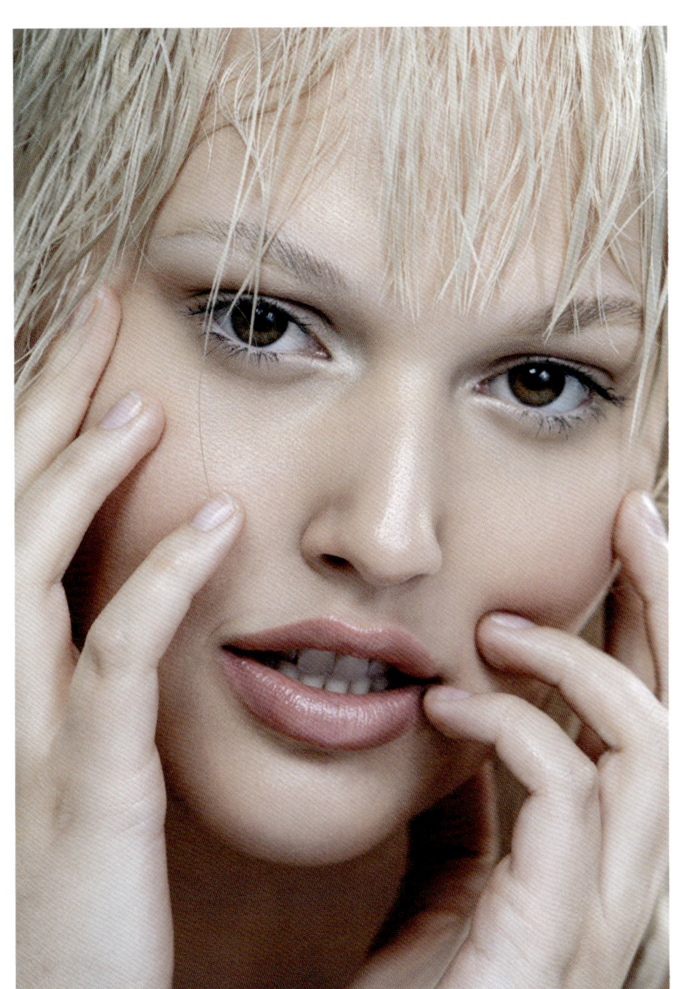

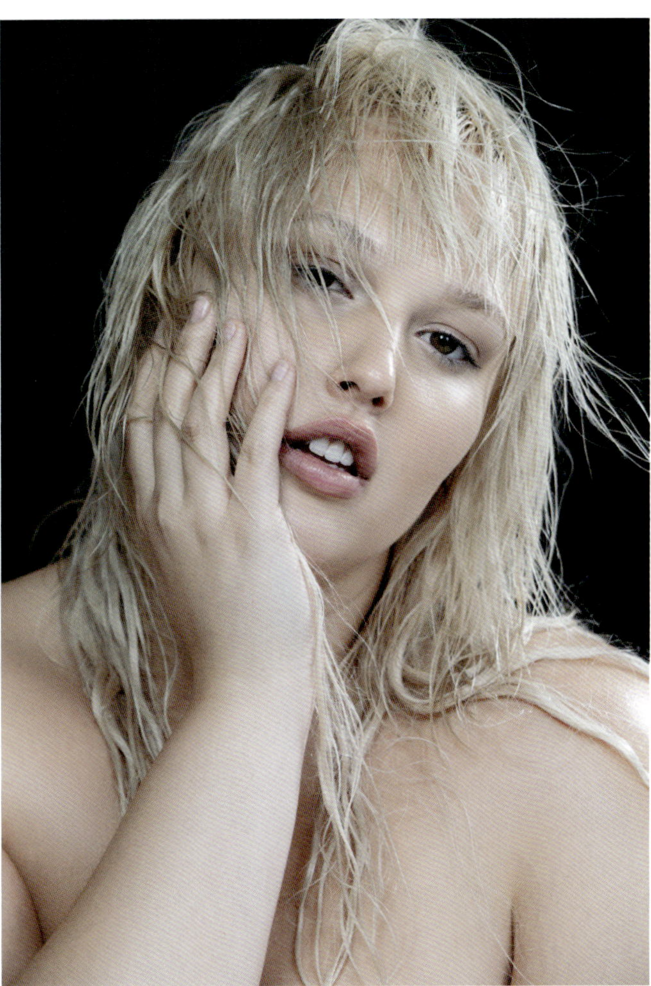

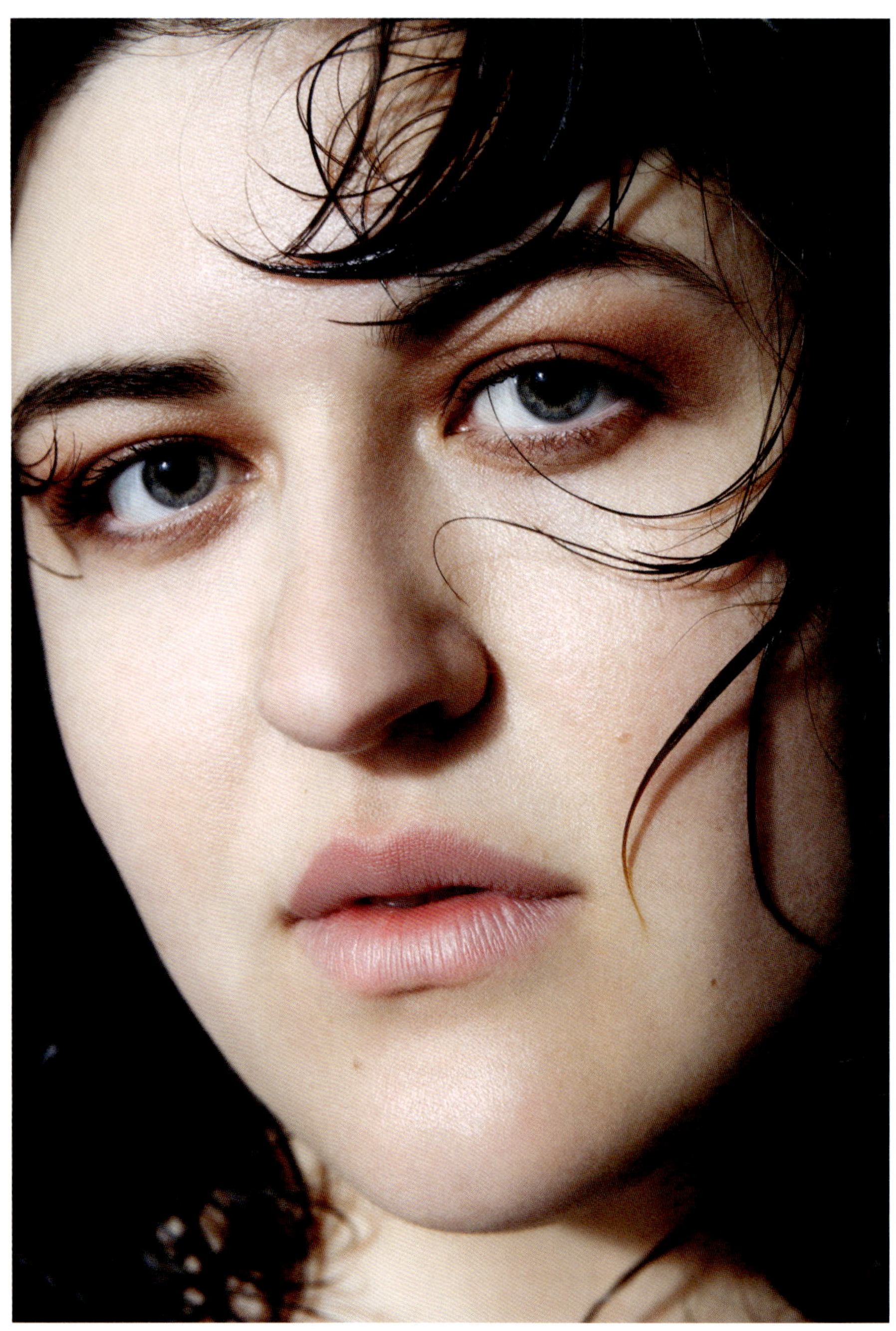

Tayler Smith

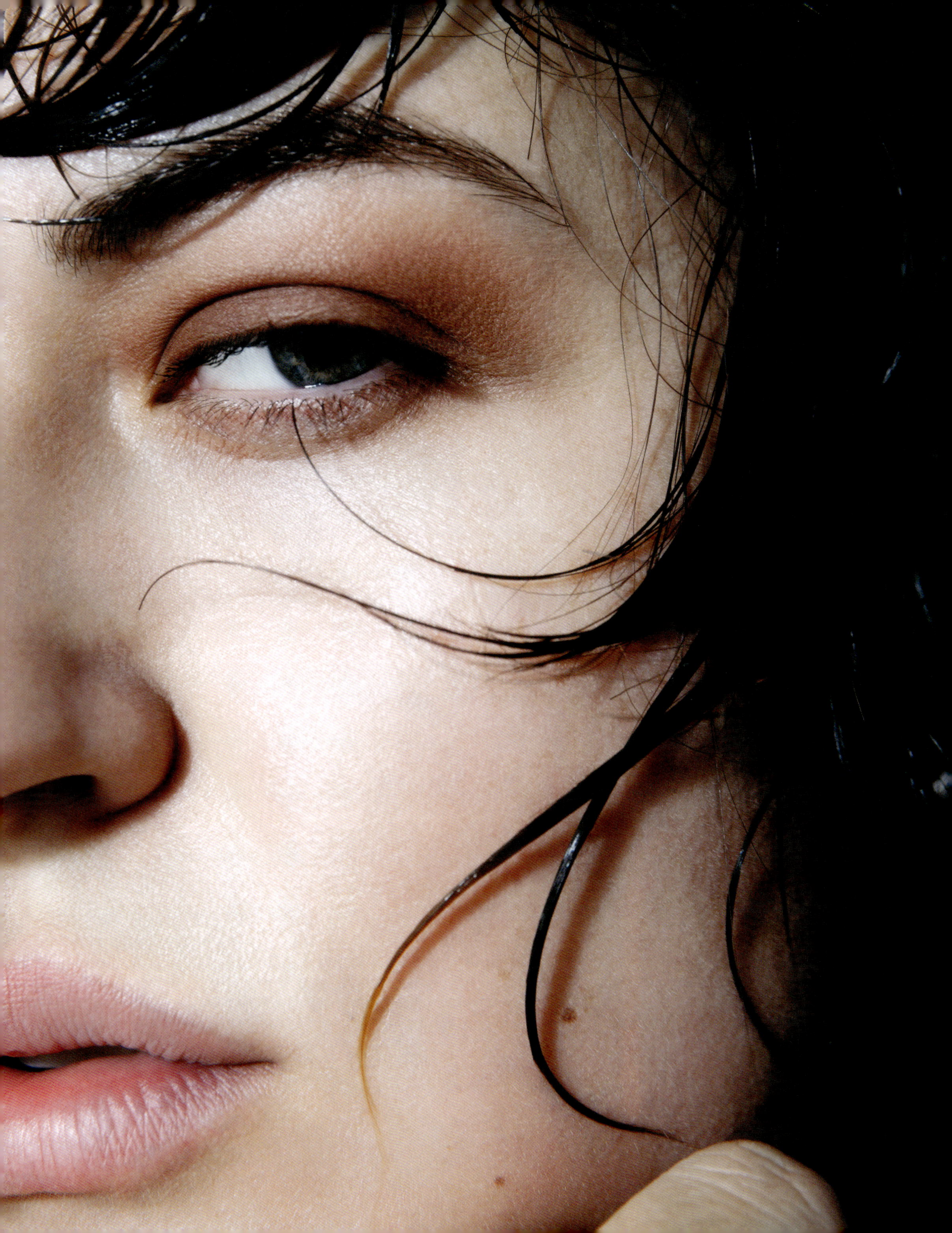

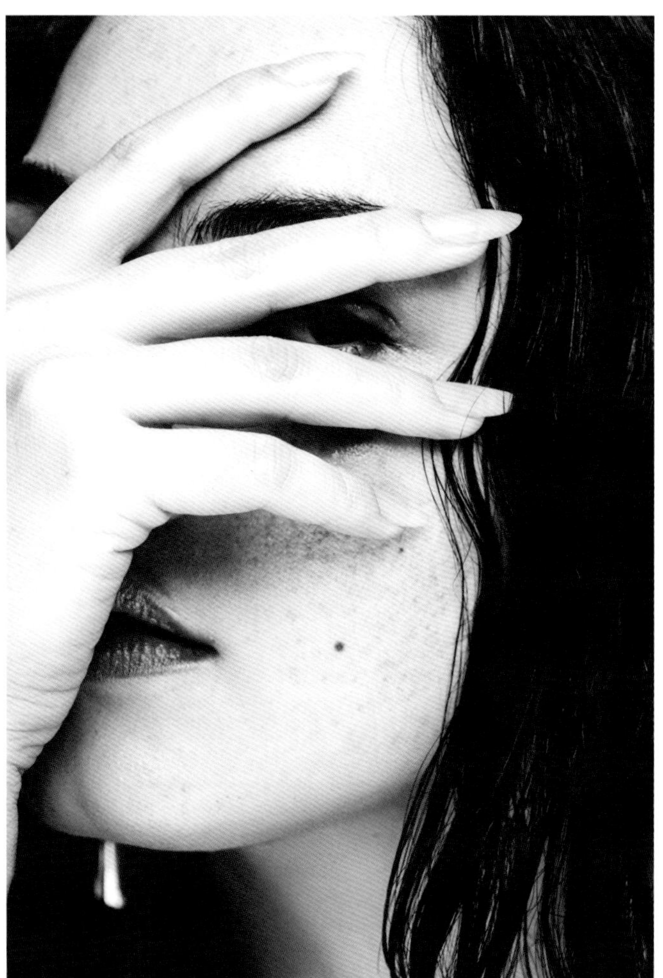

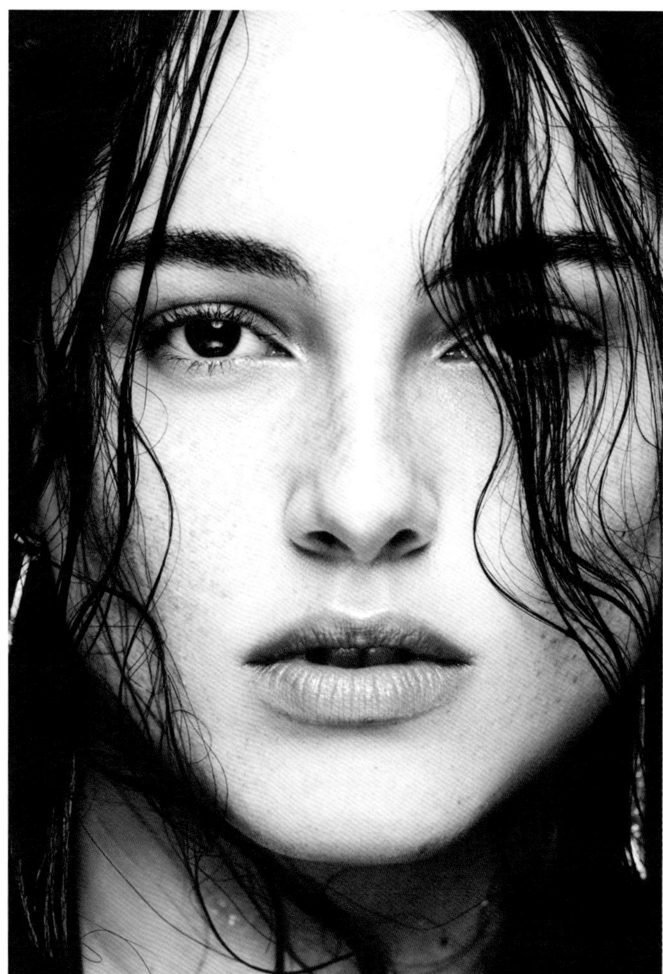

Kristen Alvarenga

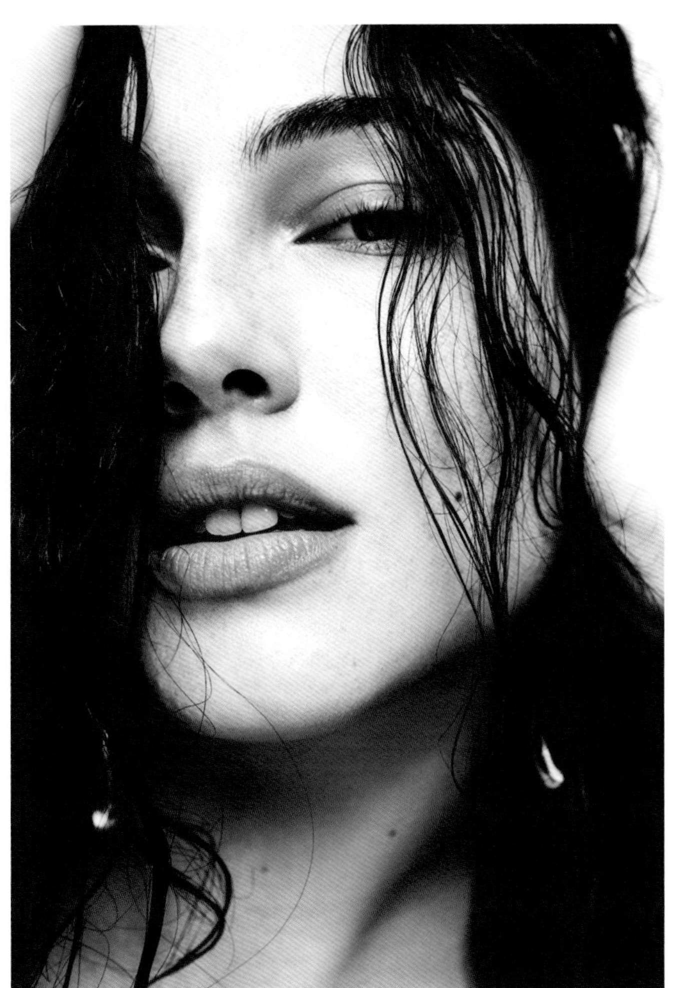

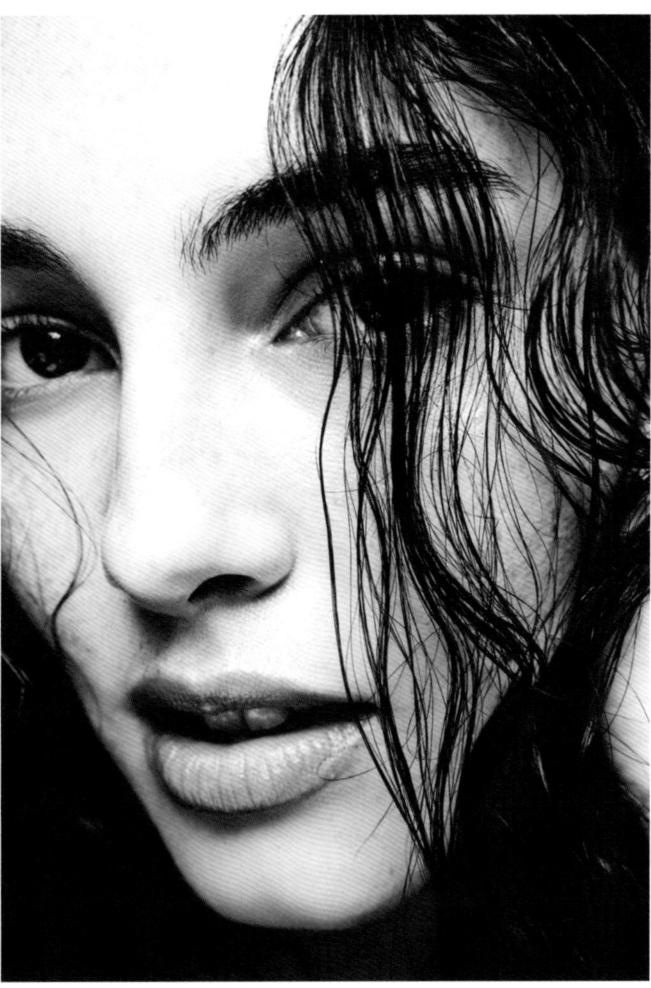

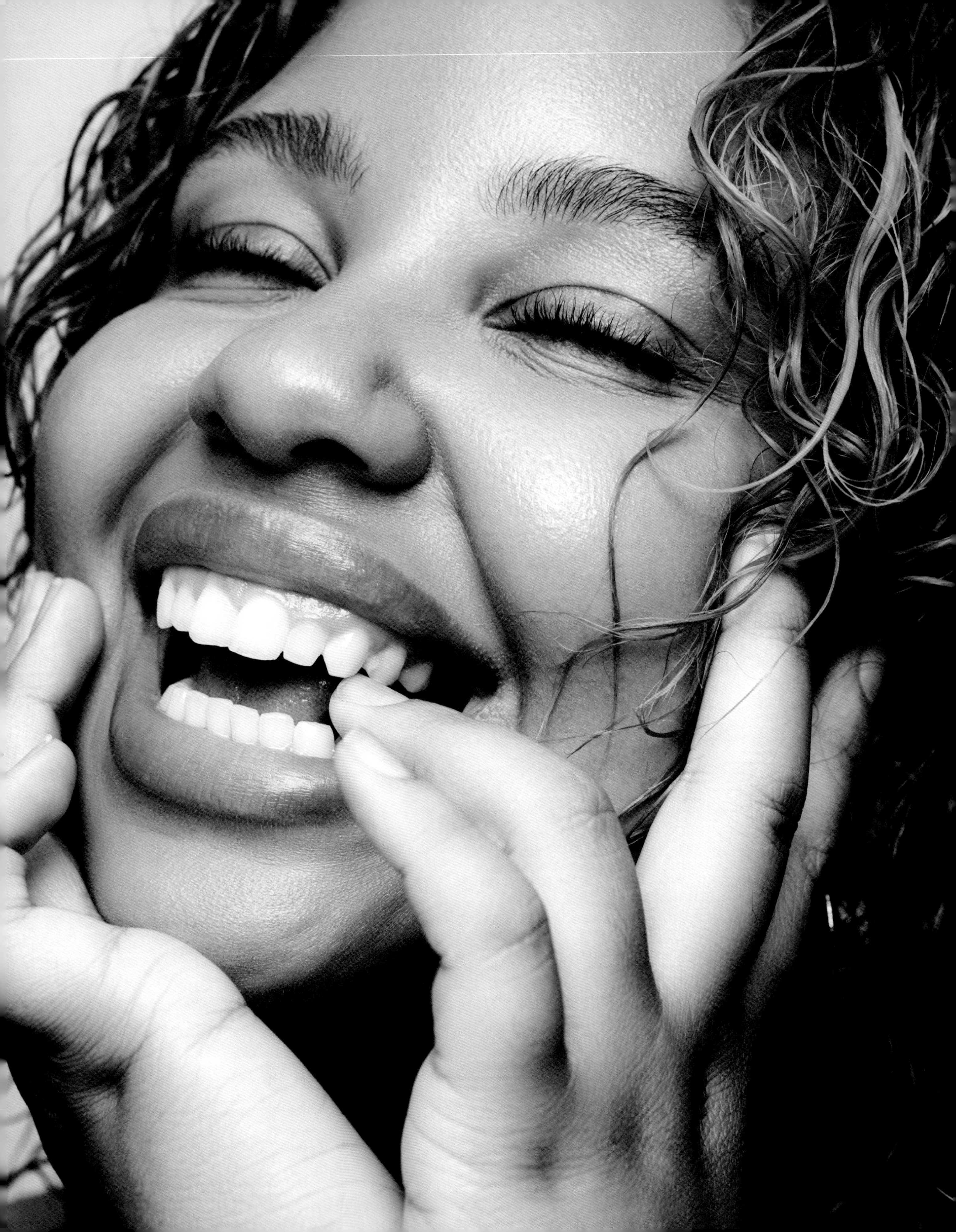

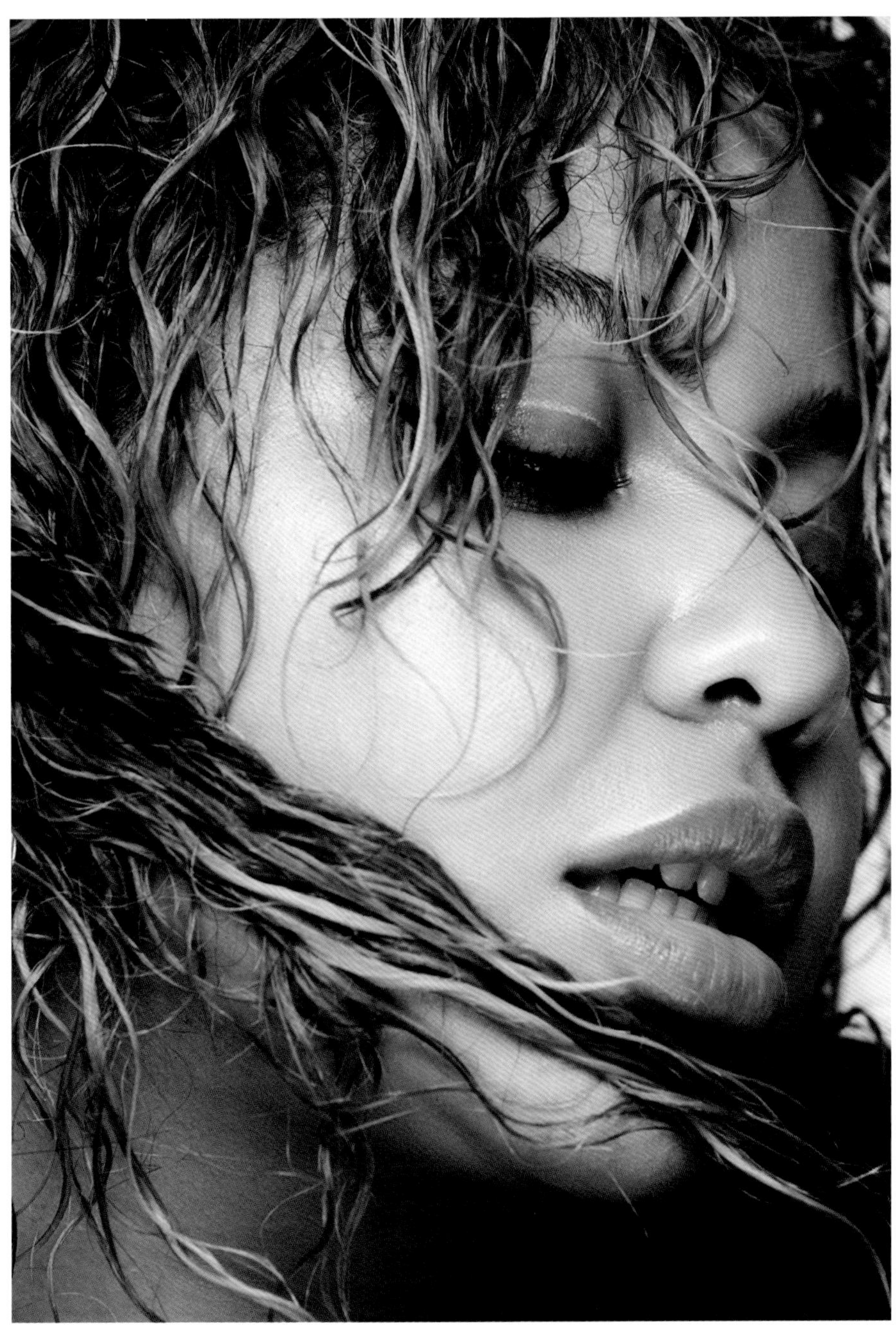

Annchristine Velazquez

Kali Renae wears 11 Honoré shirt.

Overleaf: Crisdanil

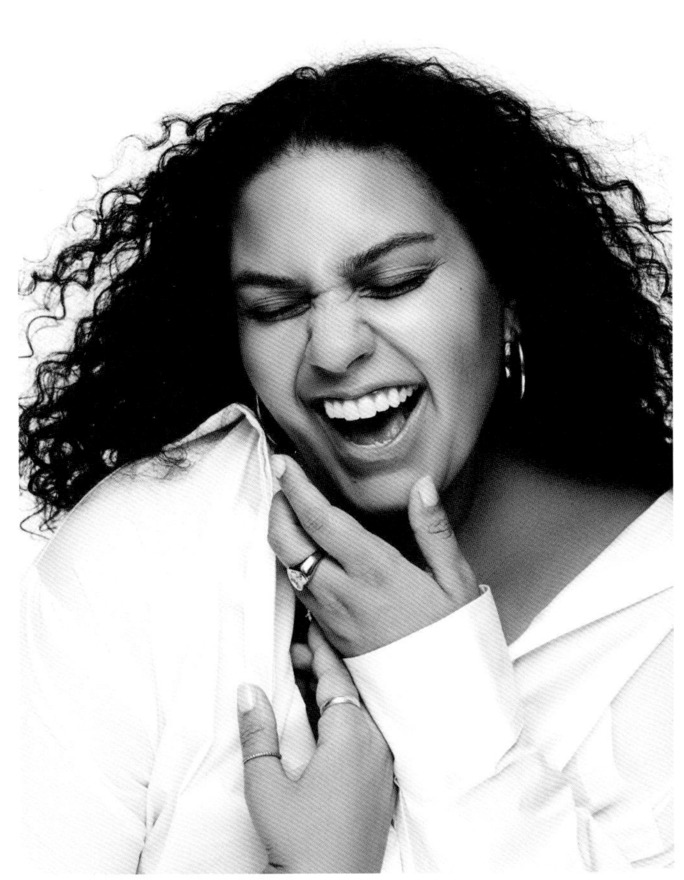
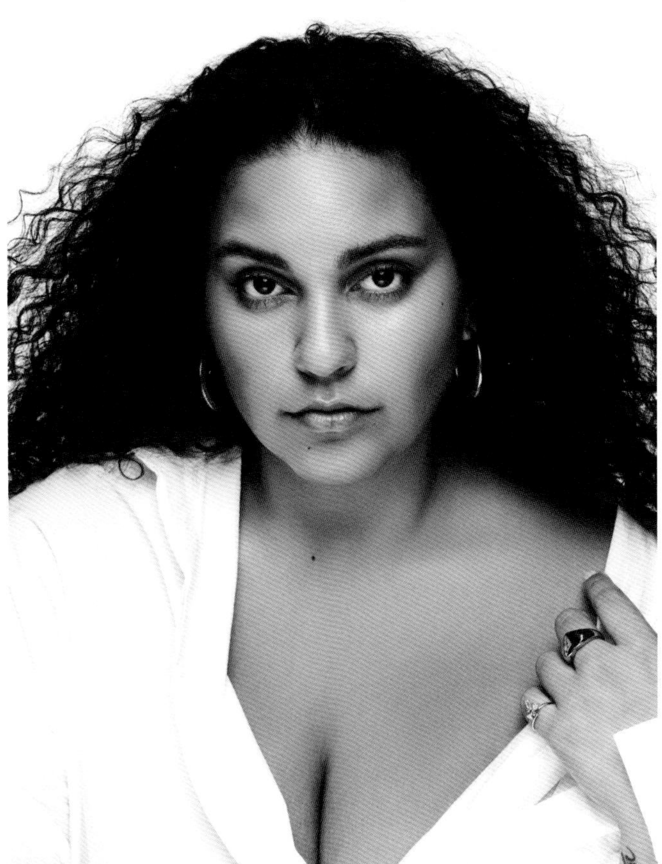
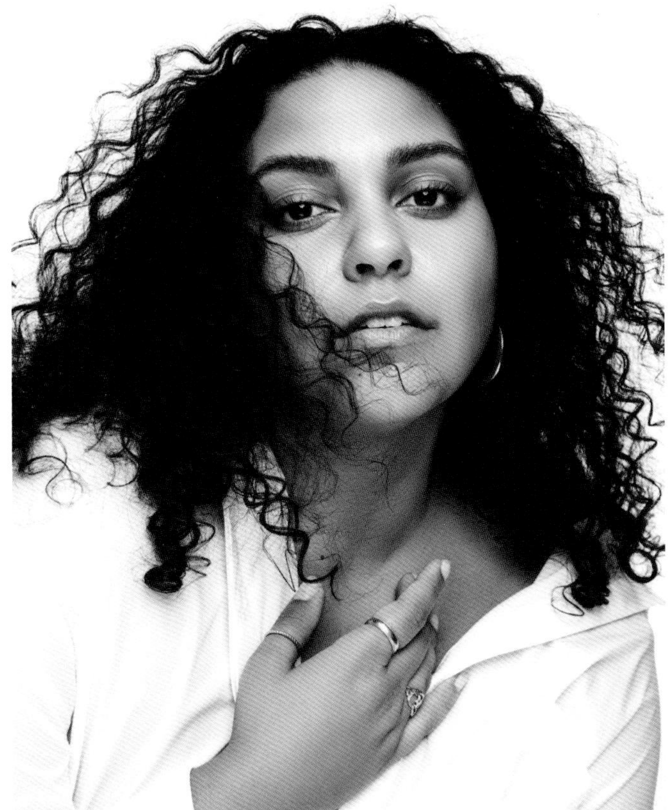
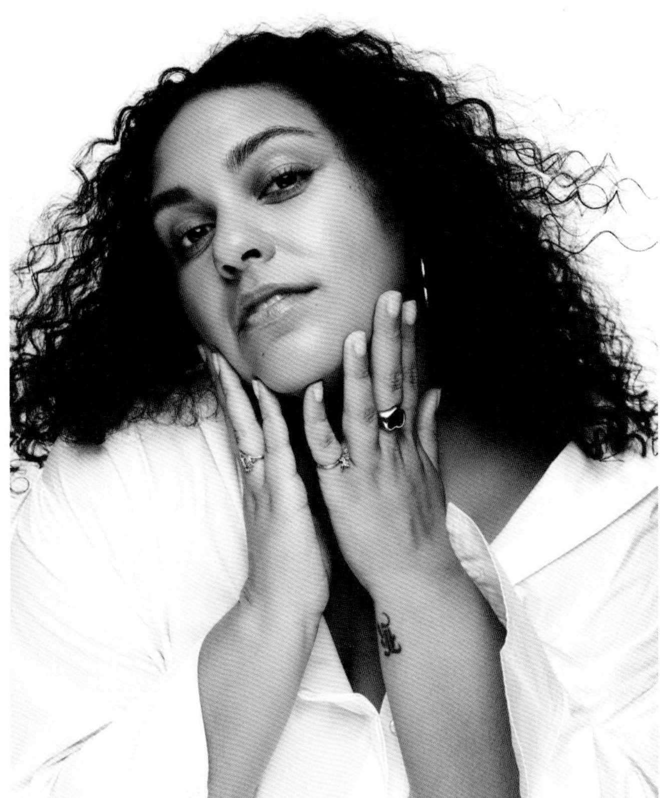

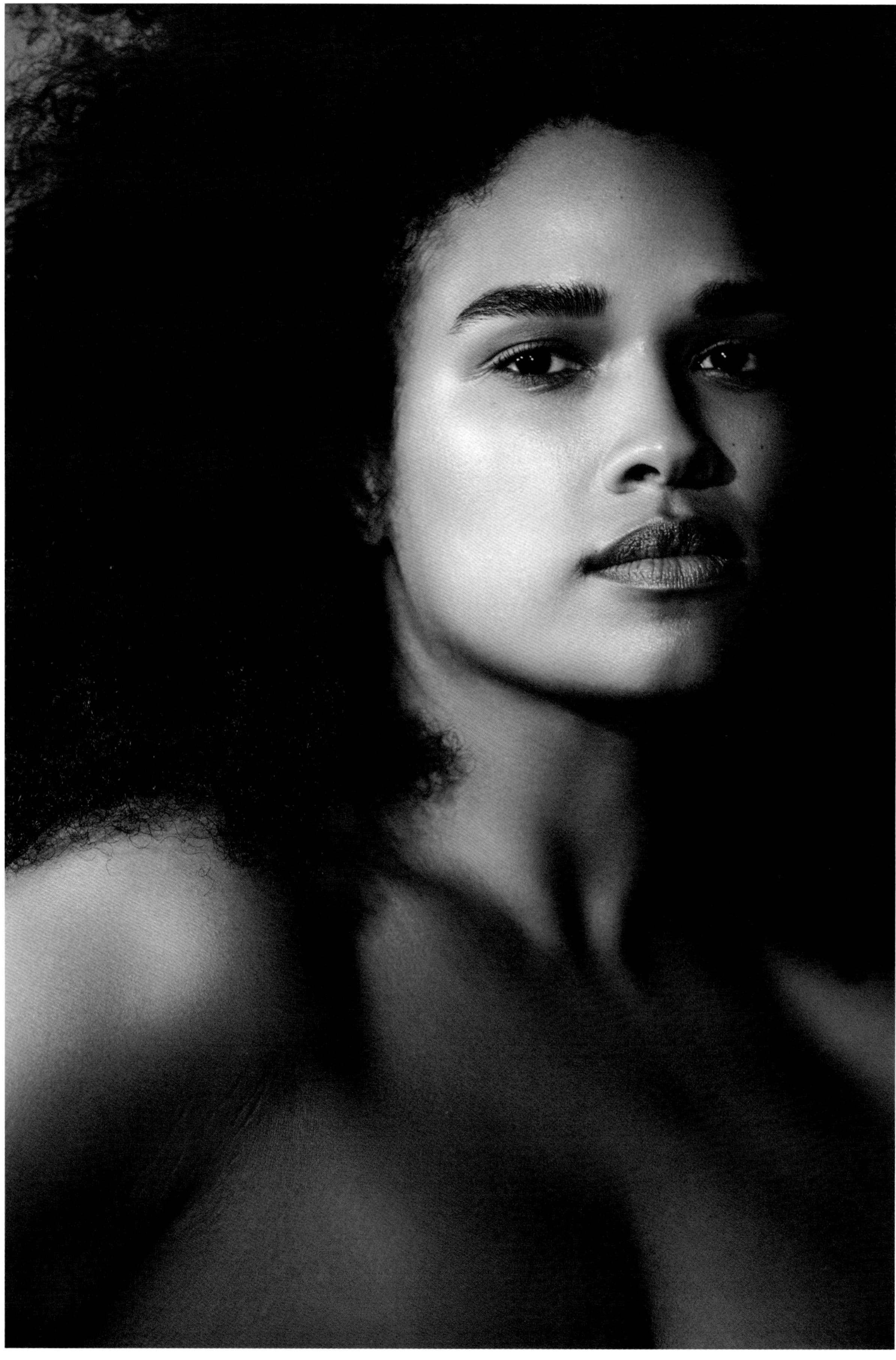

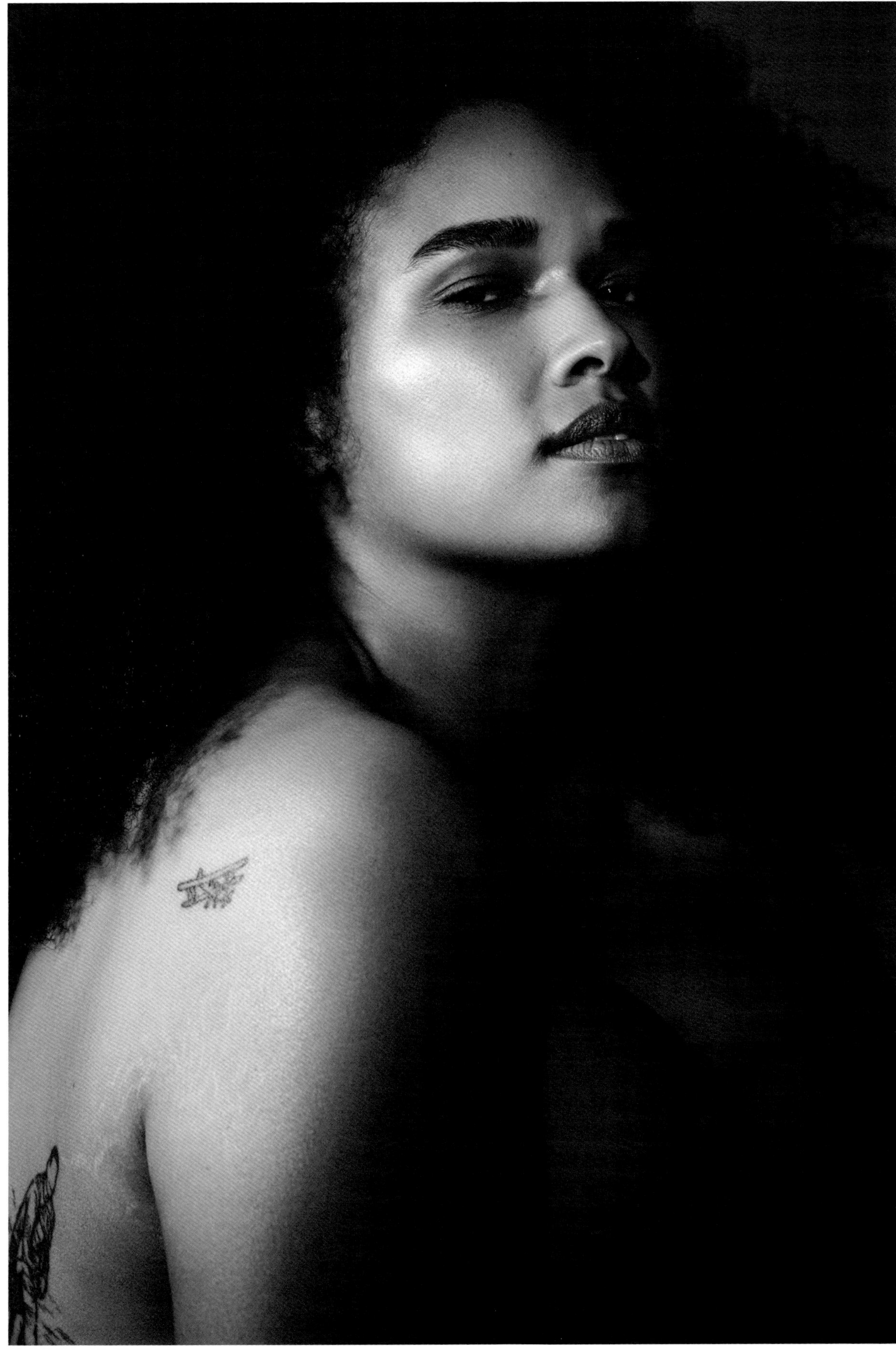

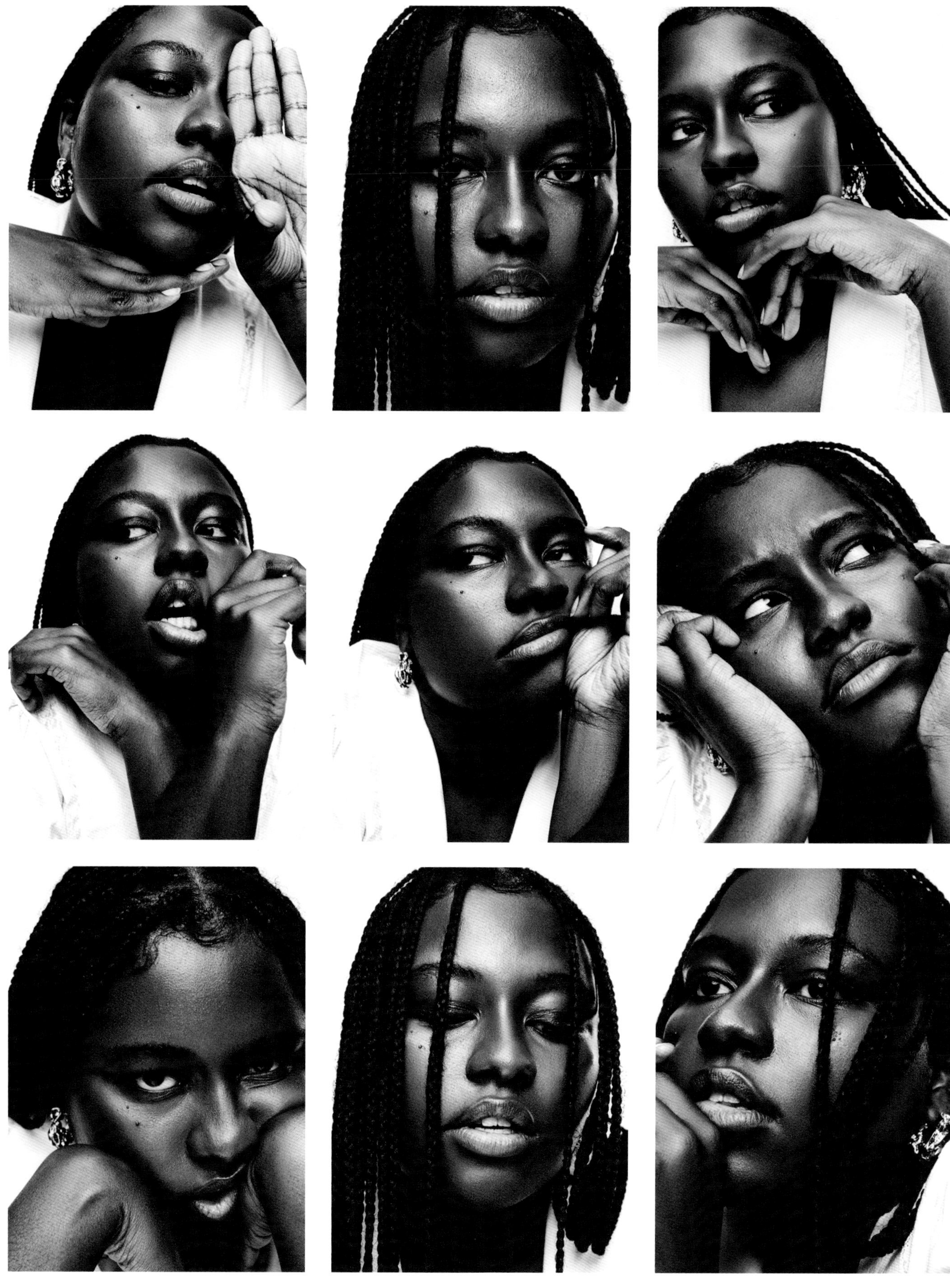

Marly Lake wears shirt from Shop Berriez.

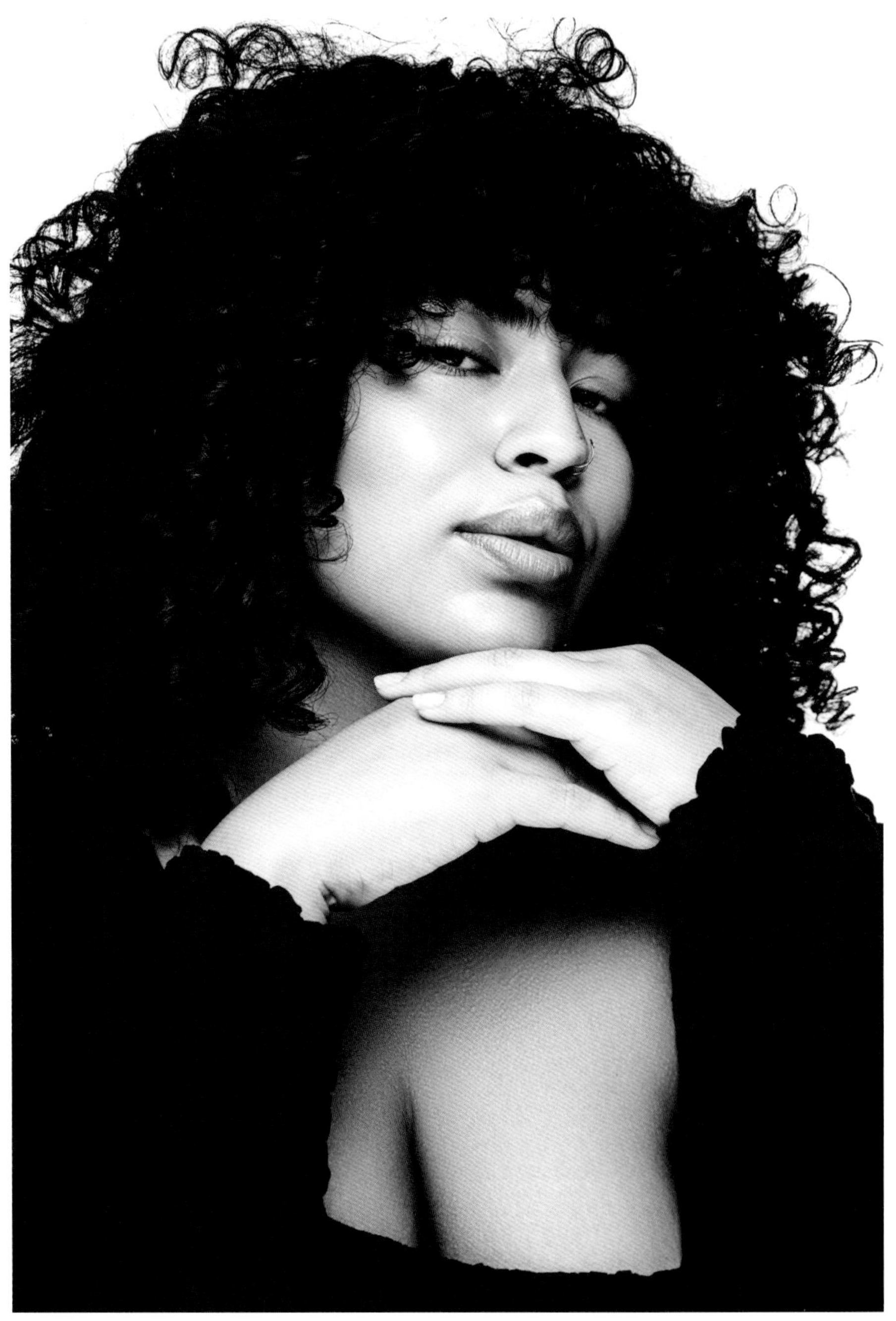

Naomi La Crespa wears Mara Hoffman top;
Alexis Bittar earrings.

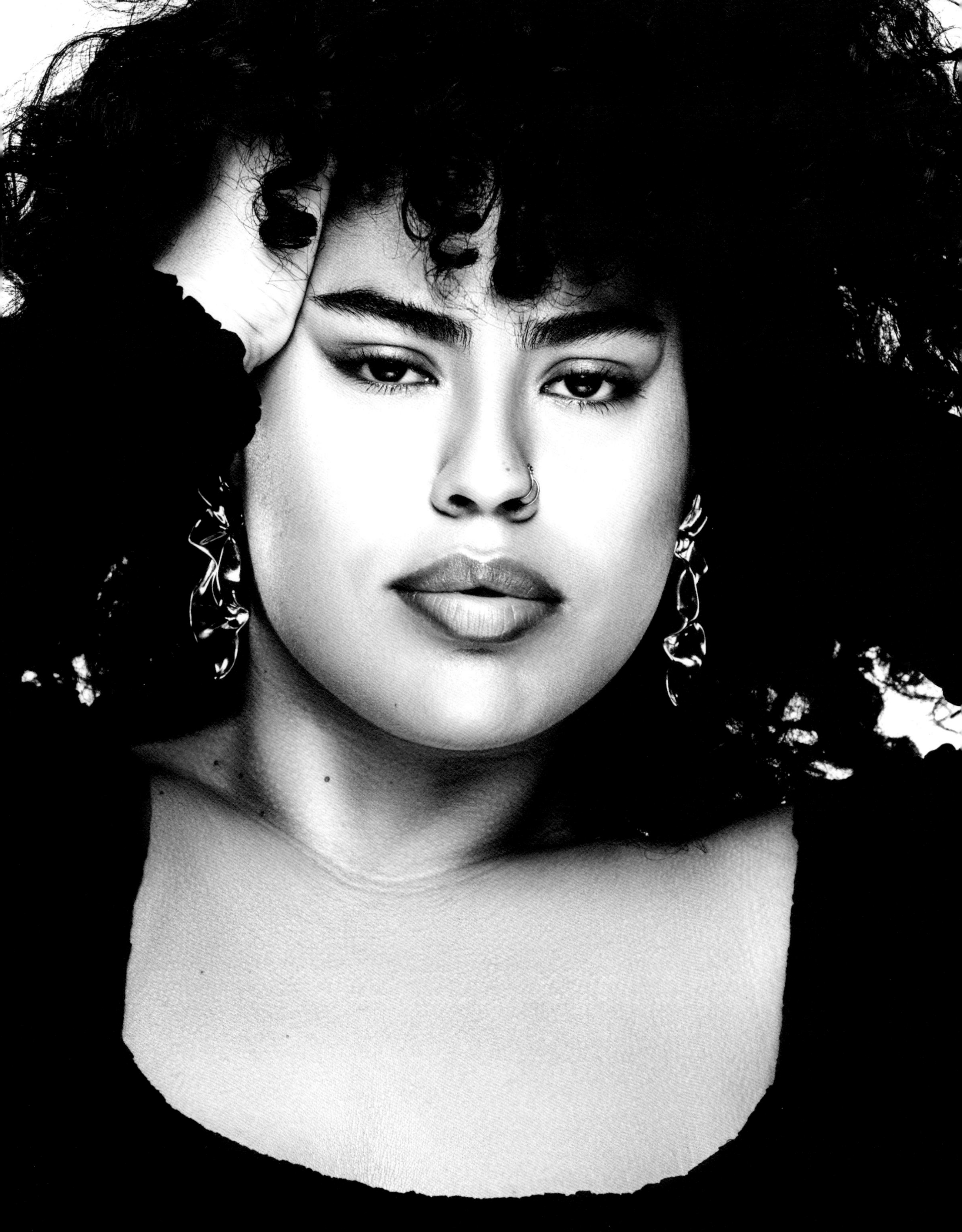

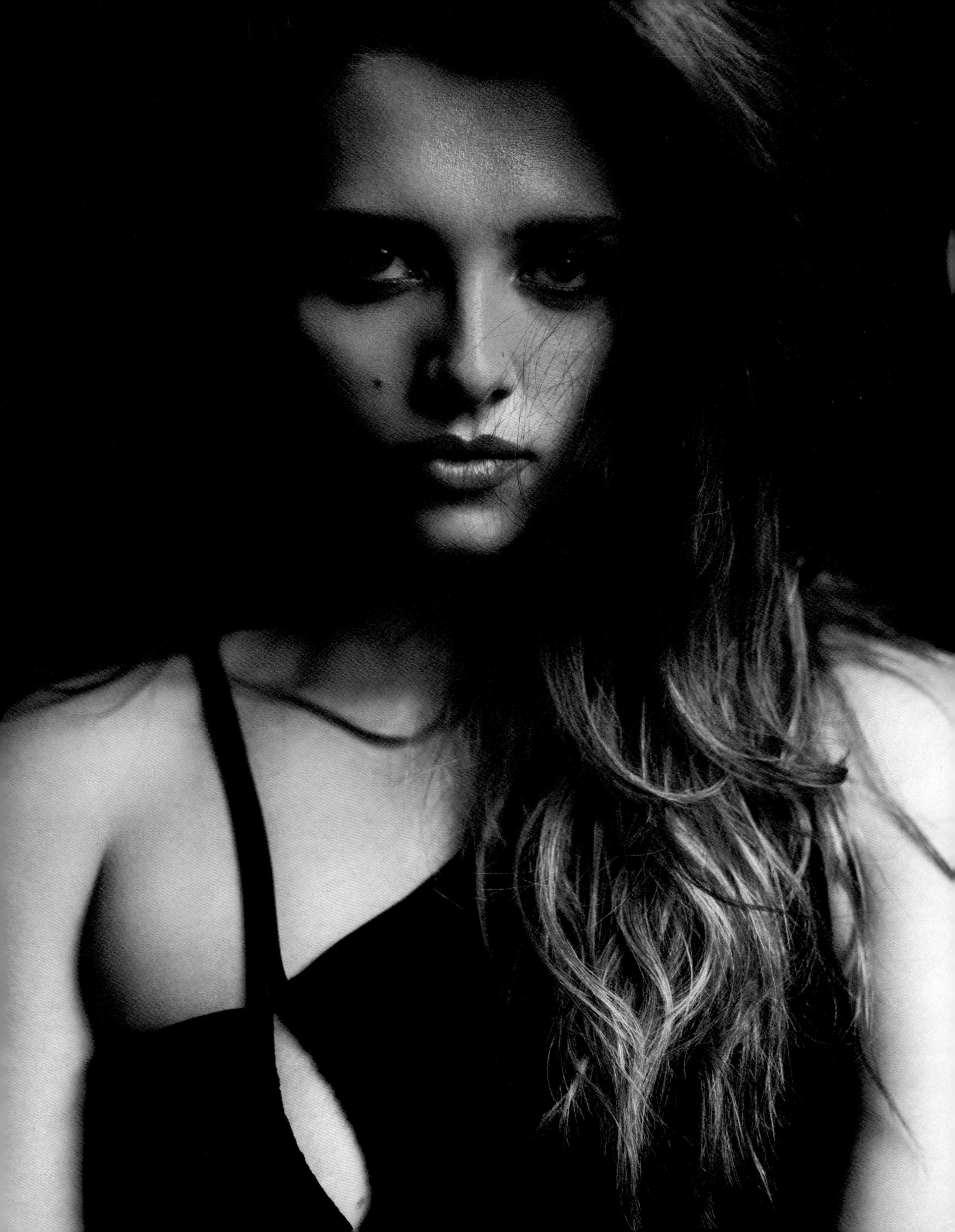

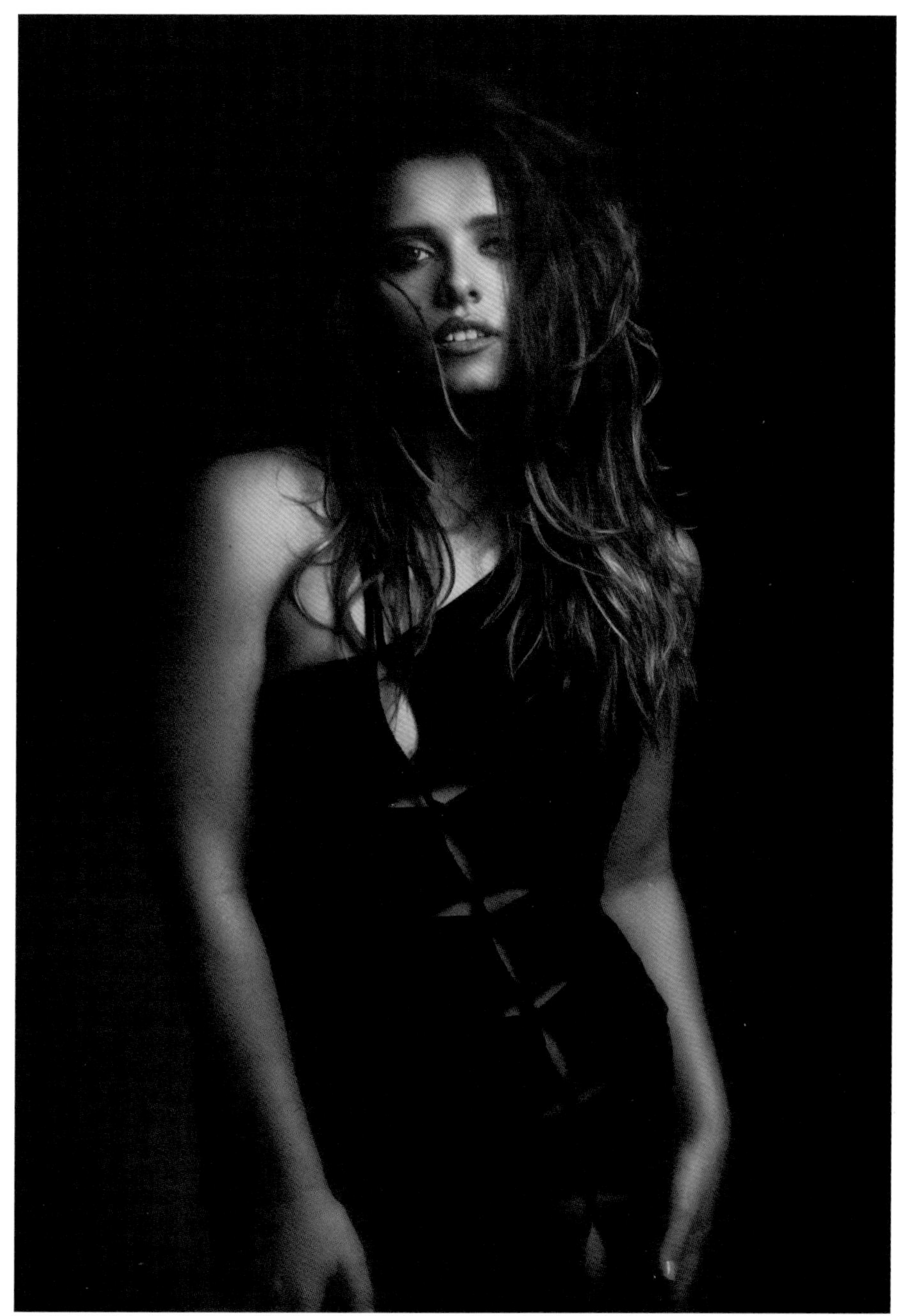

Wren Parker wears dress from Lydia Hudgens' closet.

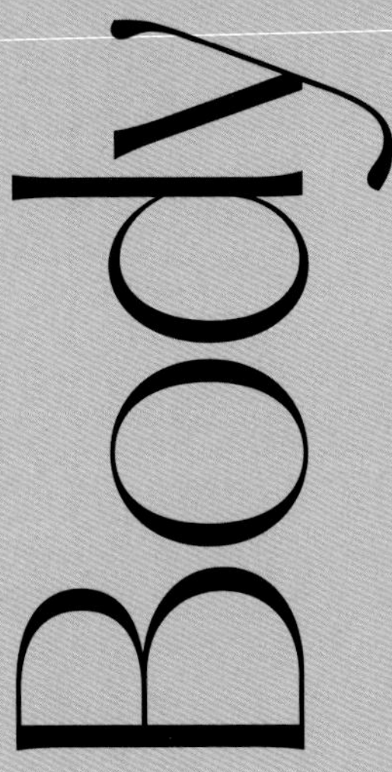

Body

This chapter is especially meaningful to me, as it captures the beauty and power of the human form—a subject I've always found fascinating.

My journey as a photographer started with a deep appreciation for the body, especially in its rawest and most unfiltered moments. In college, I spent countless hours capturing self-portraits, often in the nude, out of the belief that the human form, in all its natural states, deserves to be celebrated. This exploration continued over the years, leading to a focus on lingerie and swimwear to showcase models in ways that felt intimate and full of power.

Before the COVID-19 pandemic, I began a personal nude series as an opportunity to capture something more private, just for myself, exploring the body in a way that felt deeply personal but also artistic. However, for *Plus*, I wanted to take a different approach, returning to swimwear and lingerie to capture images that were raw, real, and unapologetic.

Initially, I hadn't considered including nudes at all, but as I continued working, it felt like a natural yet subtle extension of my vision and important to the book's overall message. I believe there is a tendency, especially in the fashion industry, to oversexualize plus-size bodies. It's something I've witnessed often: models labeled as "sexy" simply because of their size, even when they're posed exactly the same way as a thinner counterpart.

This is an issue that goes beyond fashion: a reflection of the way society imposes assumptions on bodies. Too often, people with curves—whether they have a bigger bust or fuller hips—are automatically labeled as sexual simply because they exist. Instead of viewing larger bodies as beautiful and powerful, we attach labels.

This chapter is about embracing the body in all its forms and allowing it to express itself in ways that are both grounded and bold. Its fashion represents a balance of strength and fluidity, the body's power framed through choices that lean into both structure and freedom. This exploration is not about hiding or covering up, but rather about showcasing what is already there. It is about allowing models to take up space, capturing the full potential of their beauty and presence.

I want to thank the models who trusted me to capture these intimate moments. Their openness, their willingness to be in front of my lens, and the dedication they brought to this project made it all possible. These photos are a reflection of both themselves and their resilience in this industry, and I am incredibly grateful.

Jordan Underwood wears knit from Lydia Hudgens' closet.

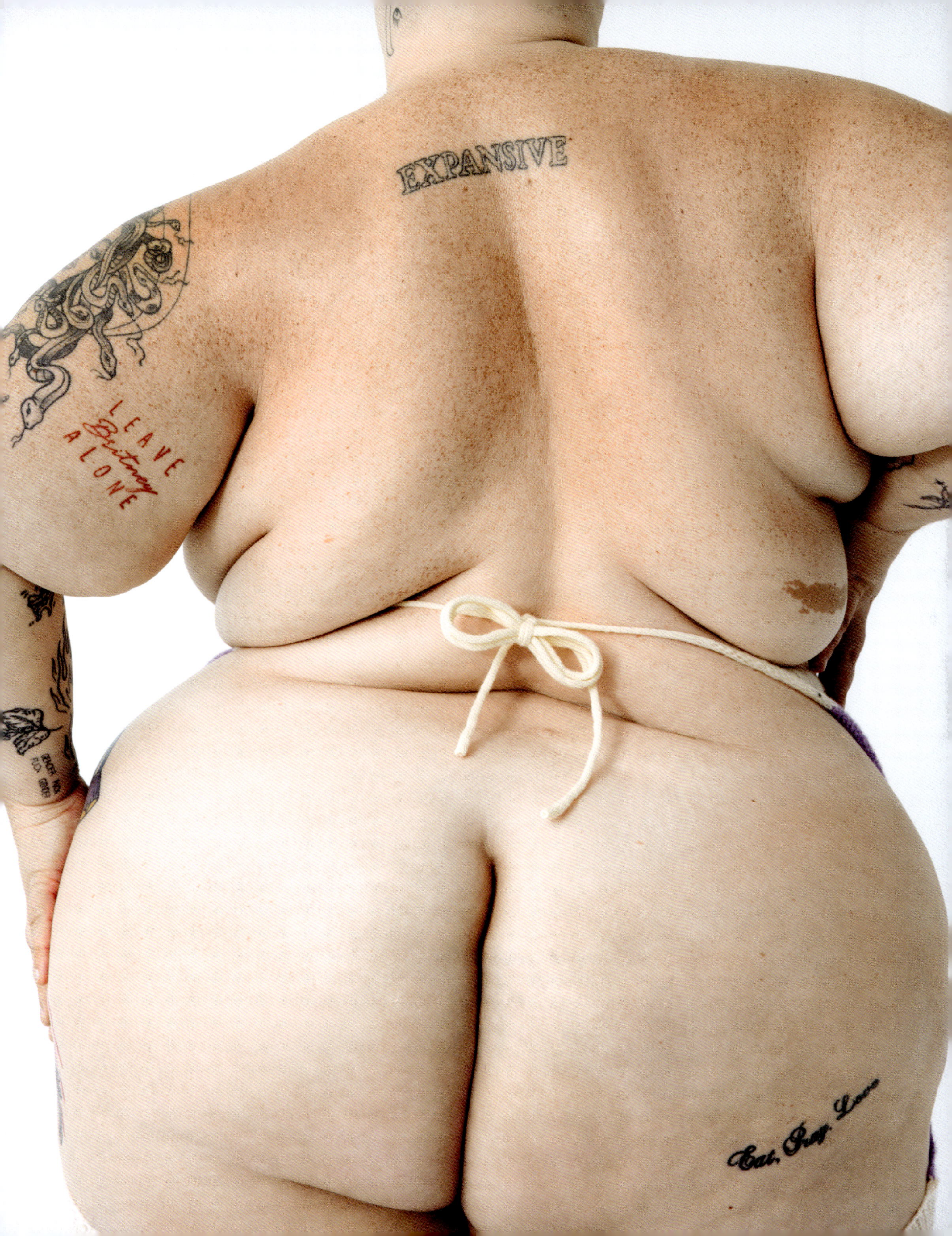
EXPANSIVE
LEAVE
Britney
ALONE
Eat, Pray, Love

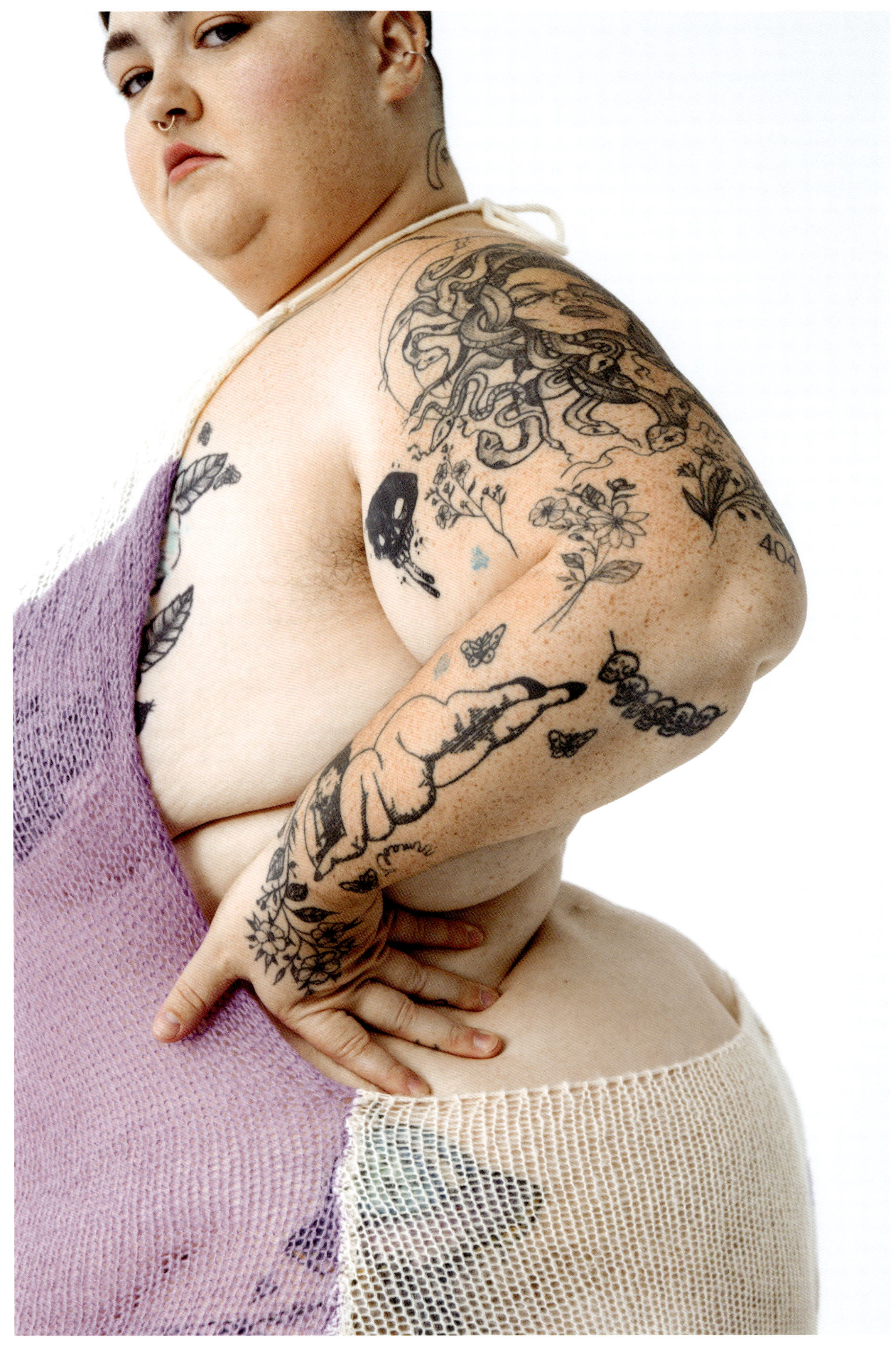
404

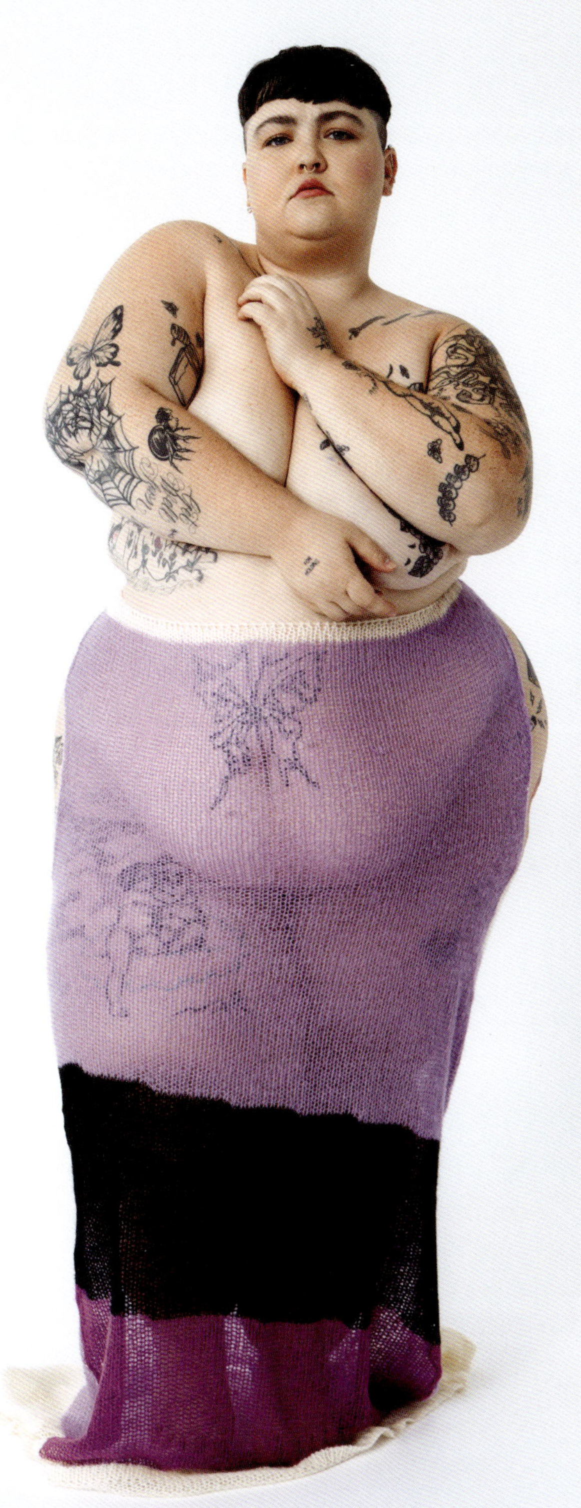

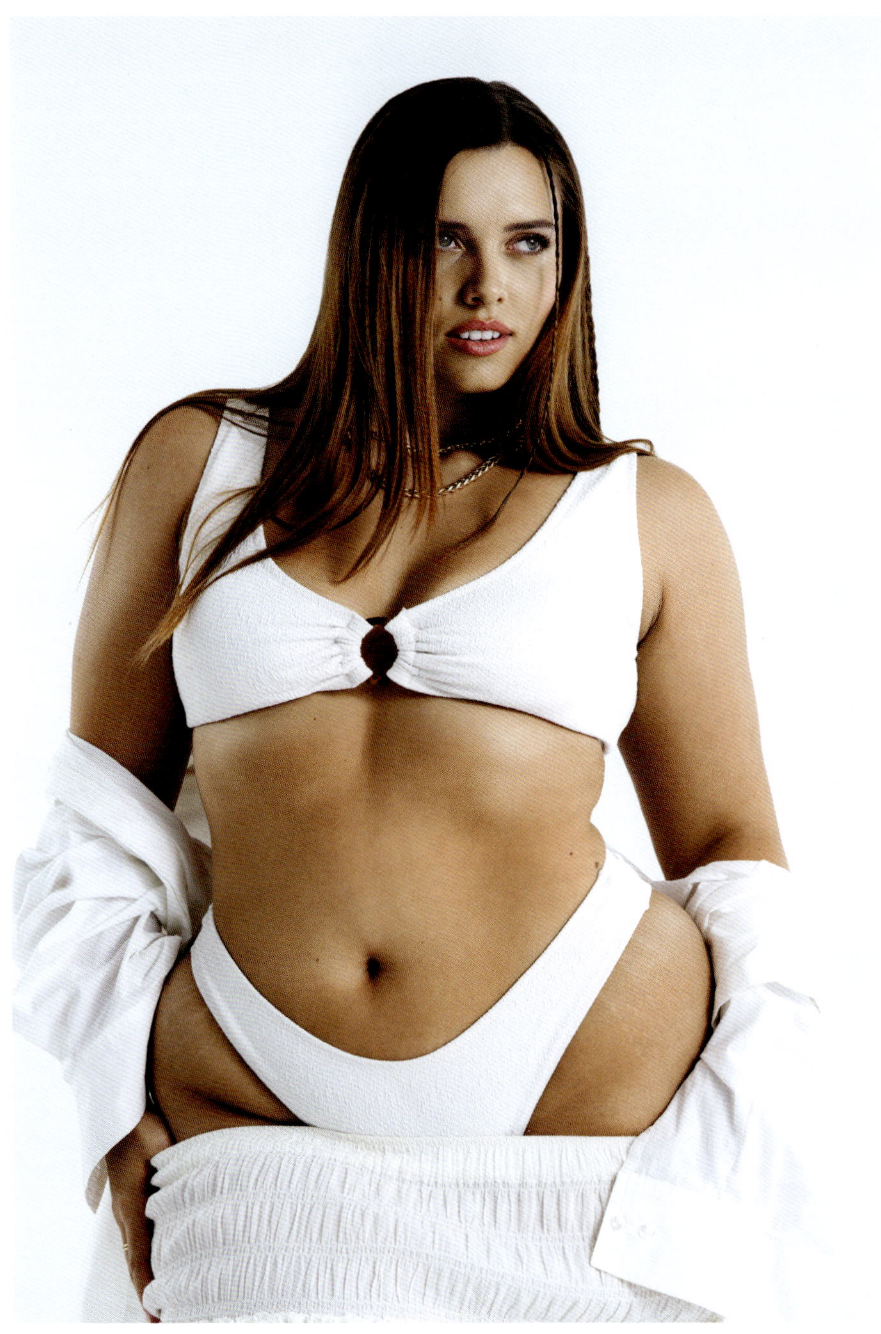

Wren Parker wears 11 Honoré shirt; swim set
from Lydia Hudgens' closet; Mara Hoffman skirt.

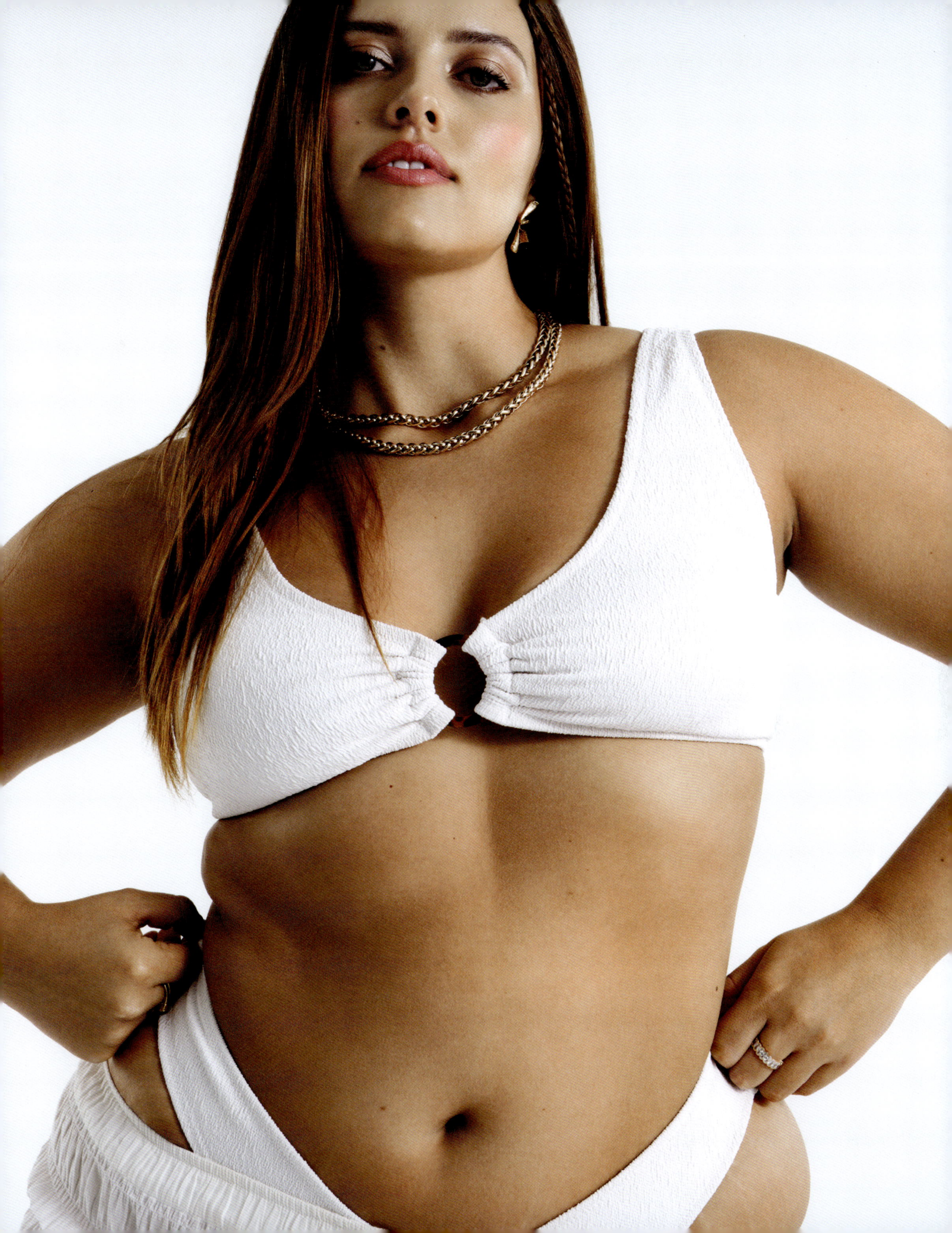

Ariana Corrao (right) and Charisse Nicole Thompson (overleaf) wear swimwear from Yoko J's closet.

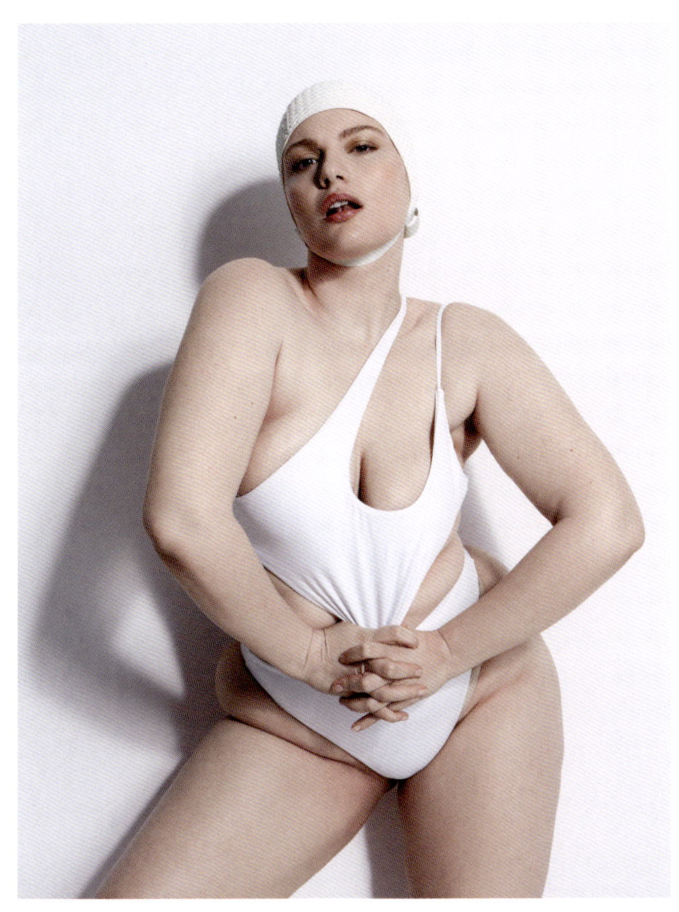
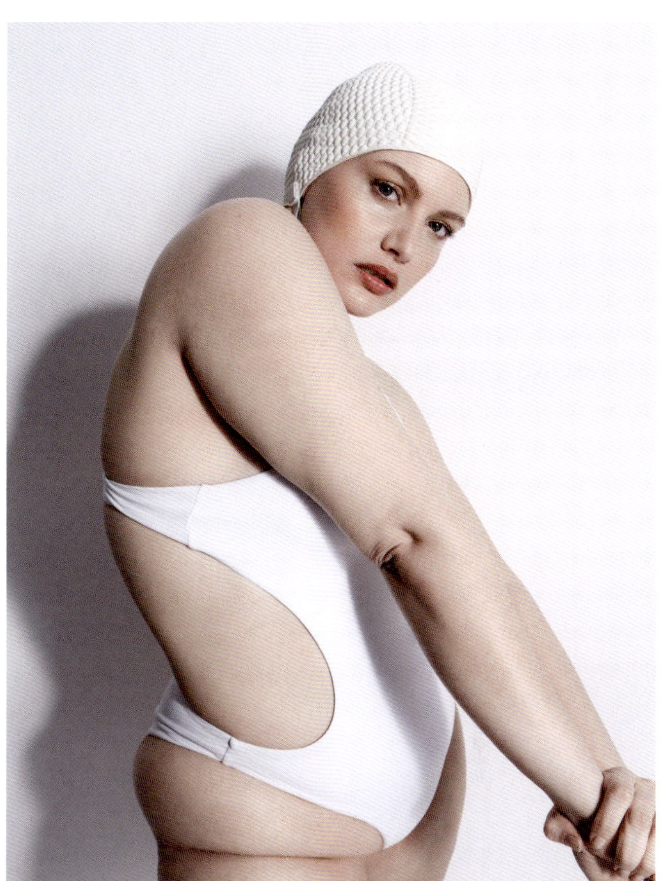
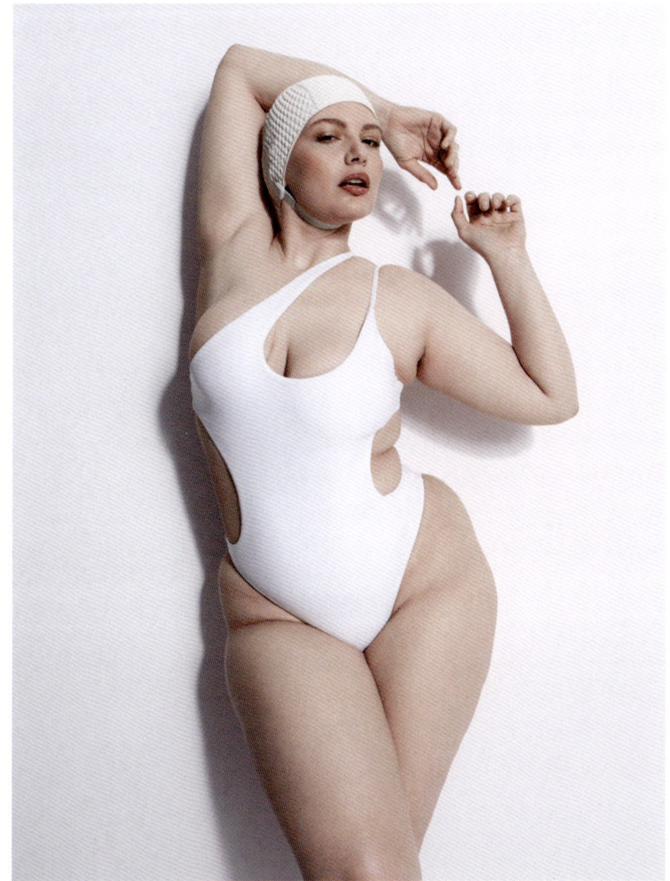
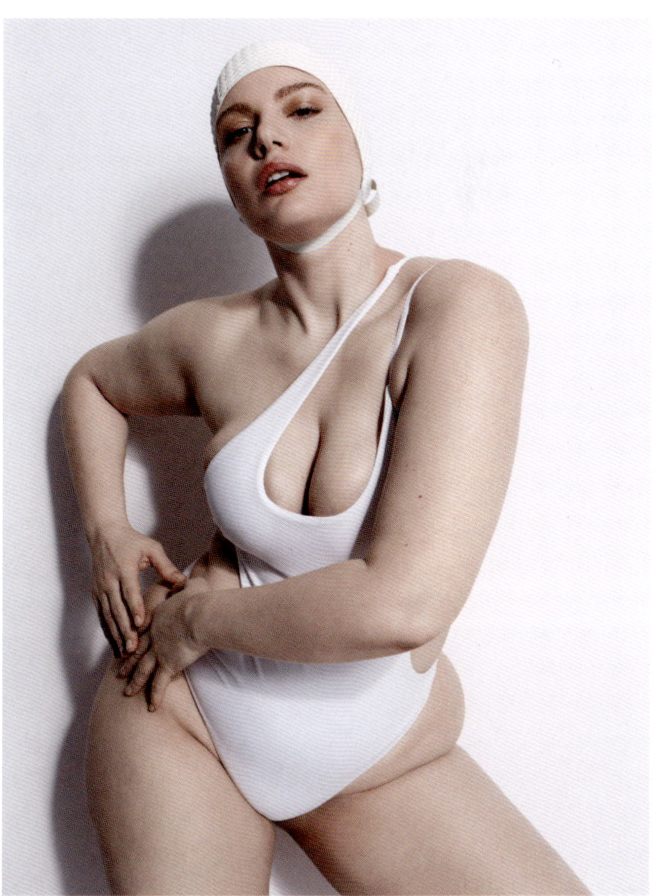

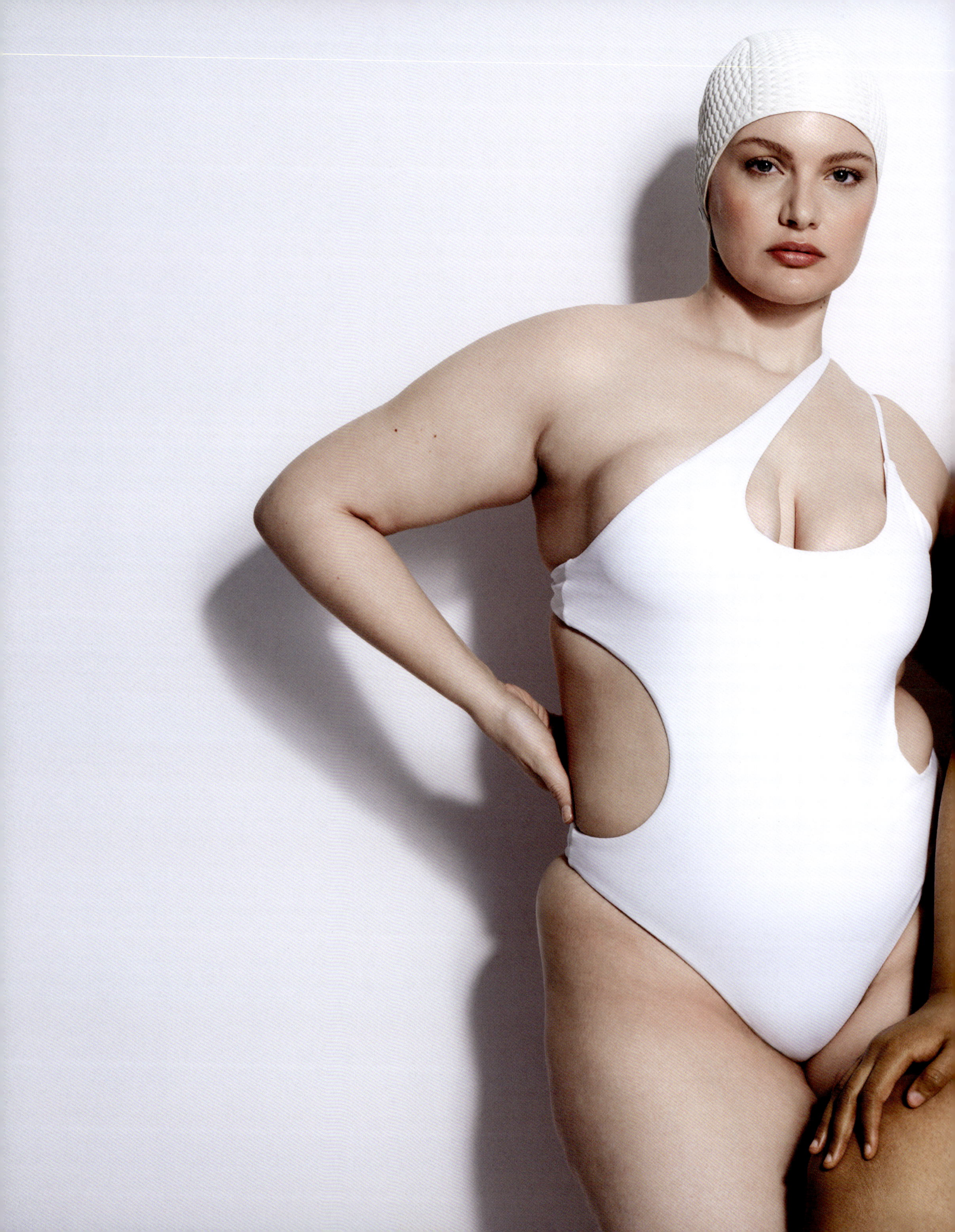

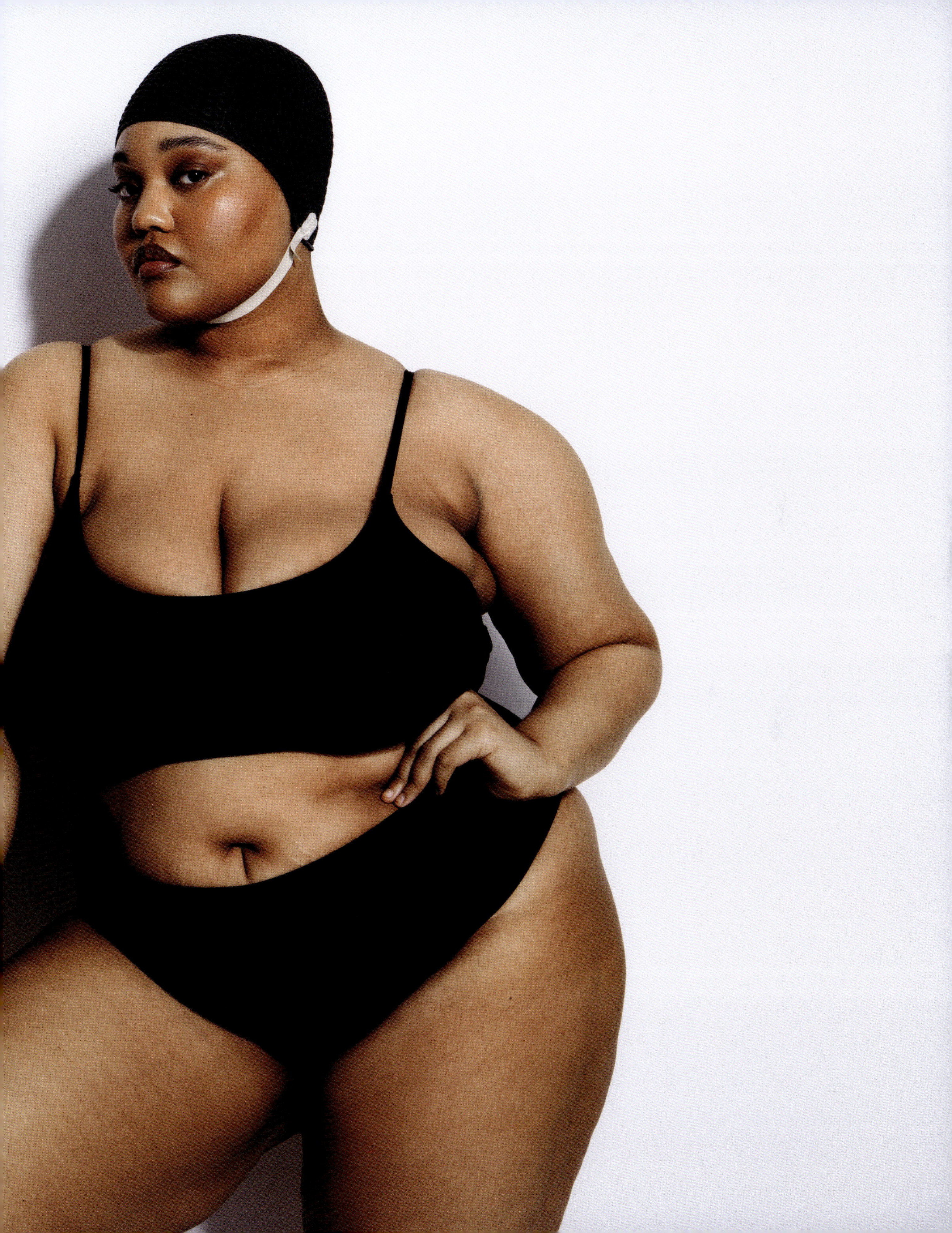

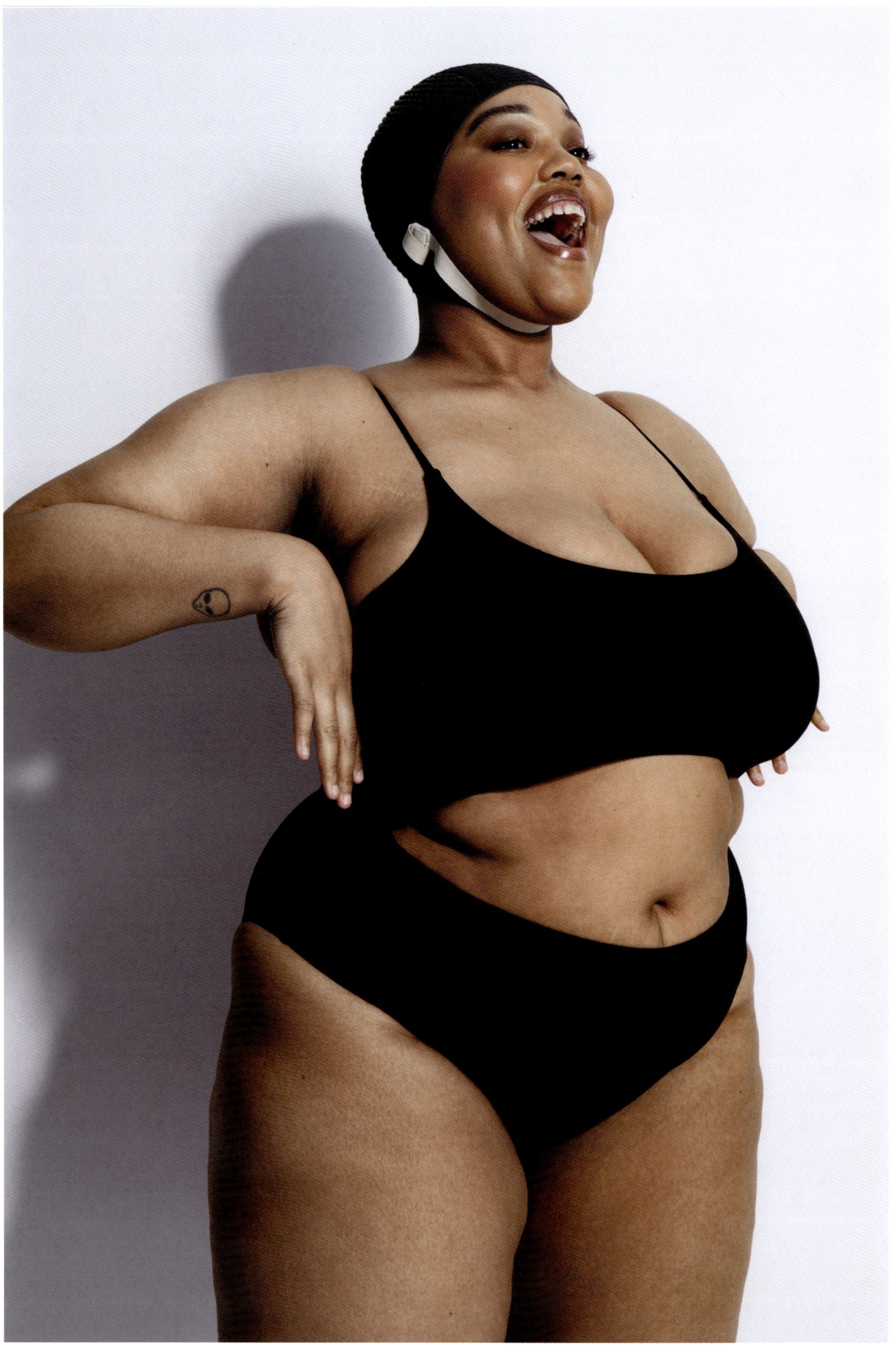

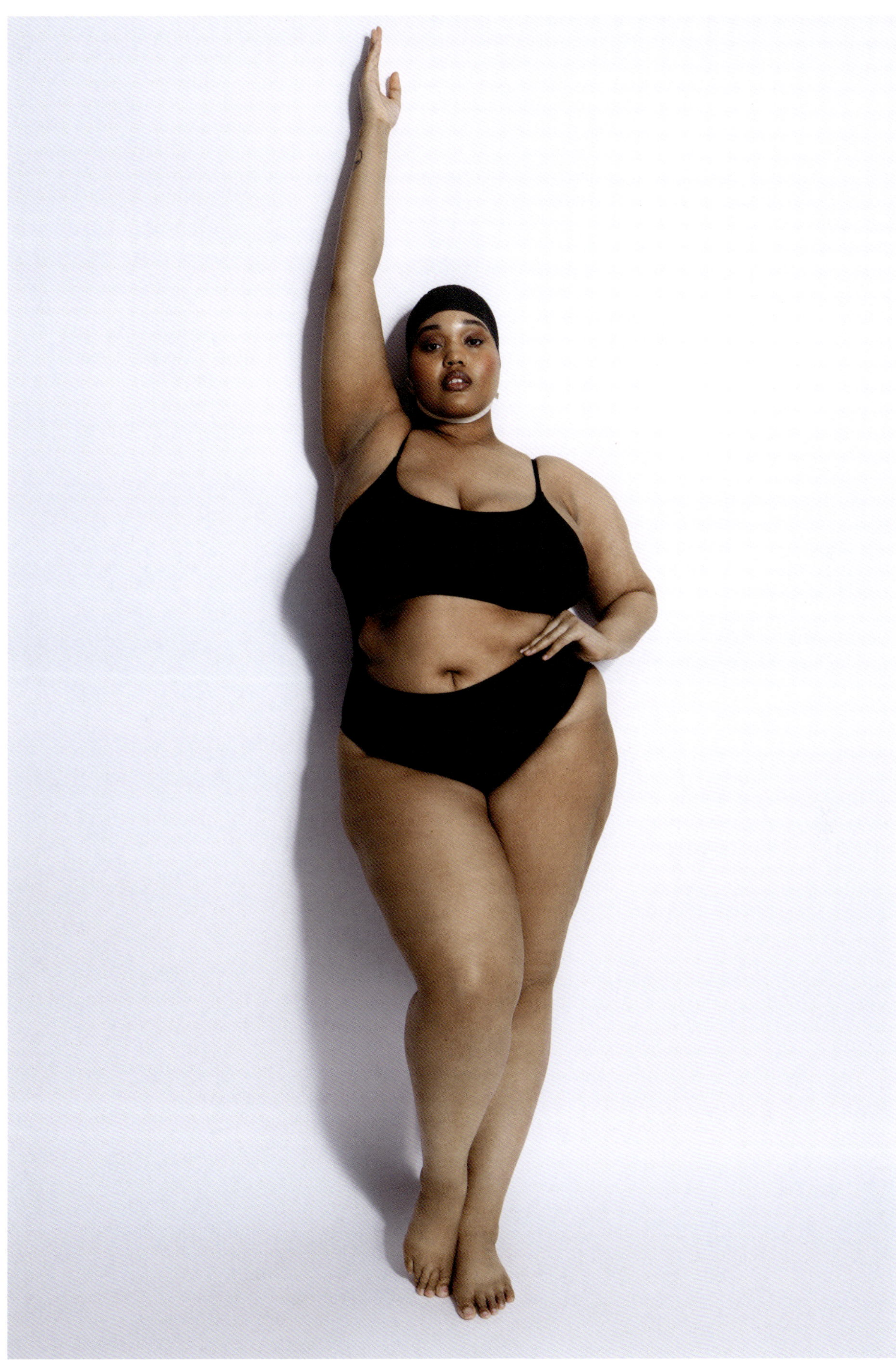

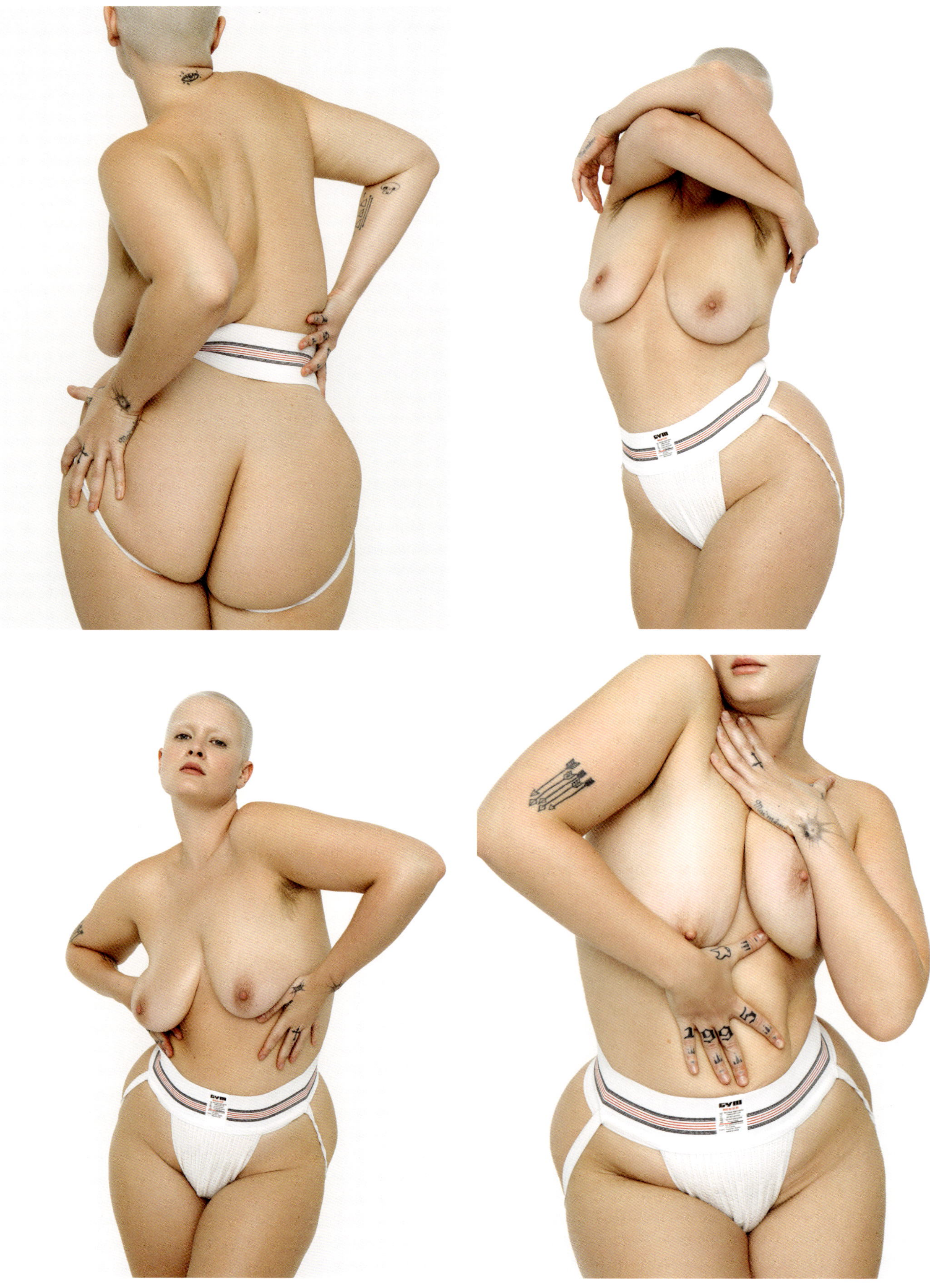

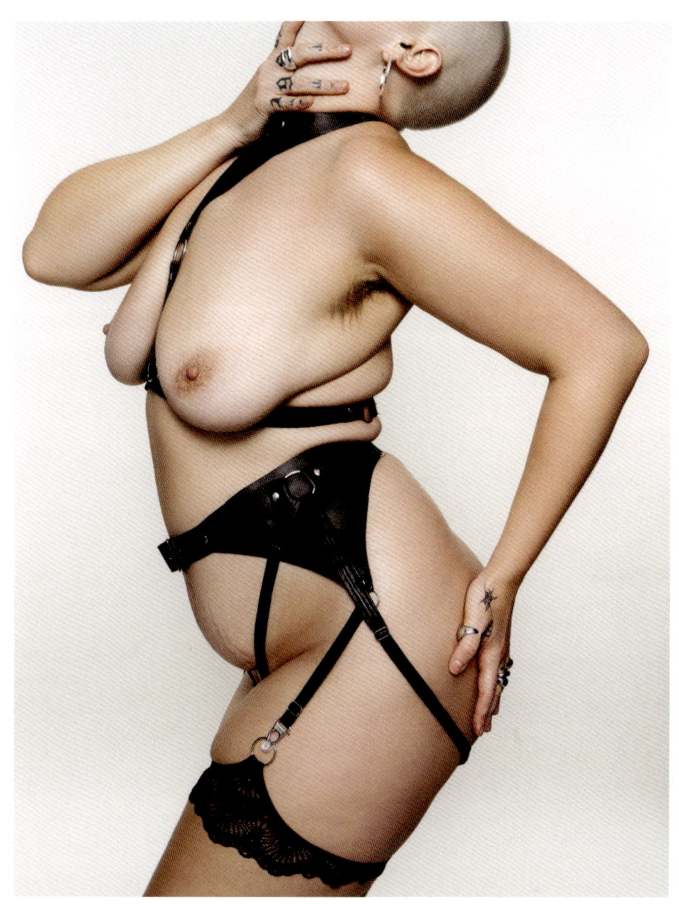
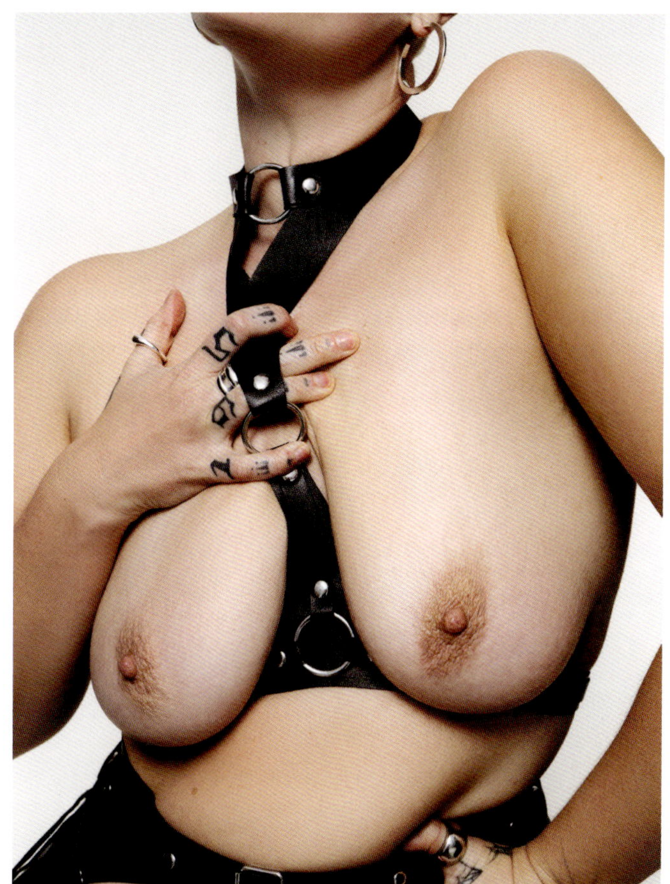
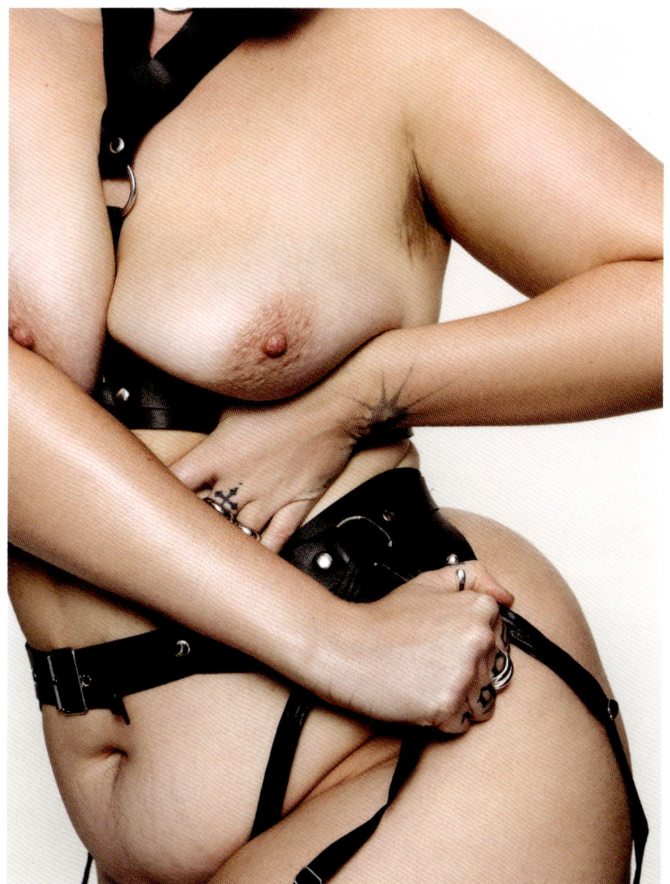
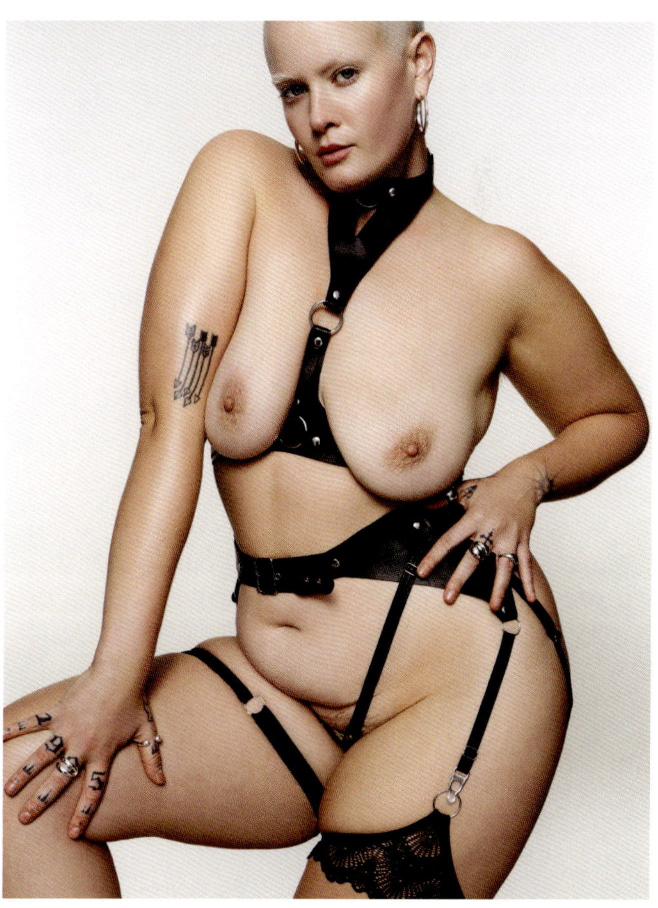

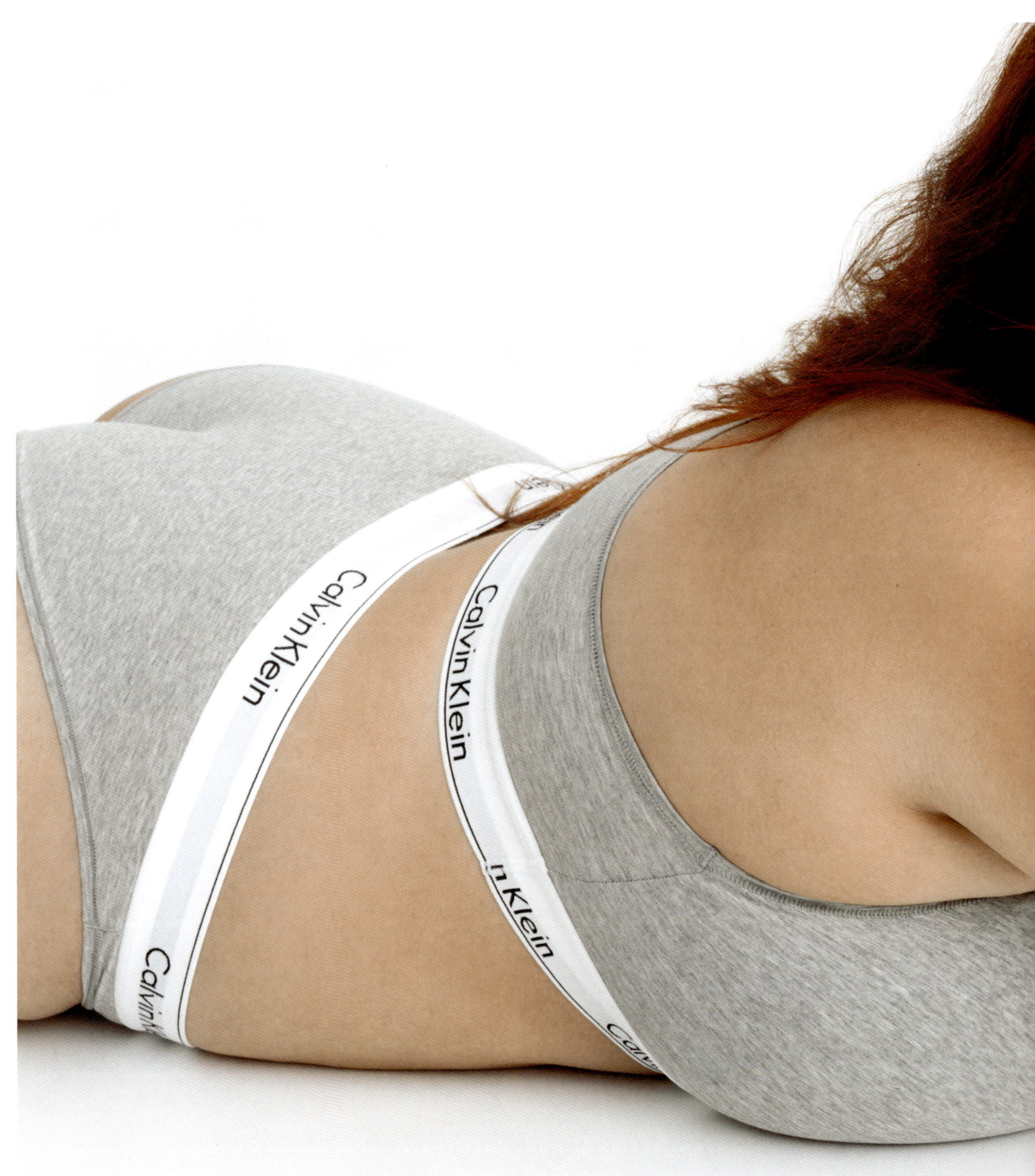
Calvin Klein
Calvin Klein

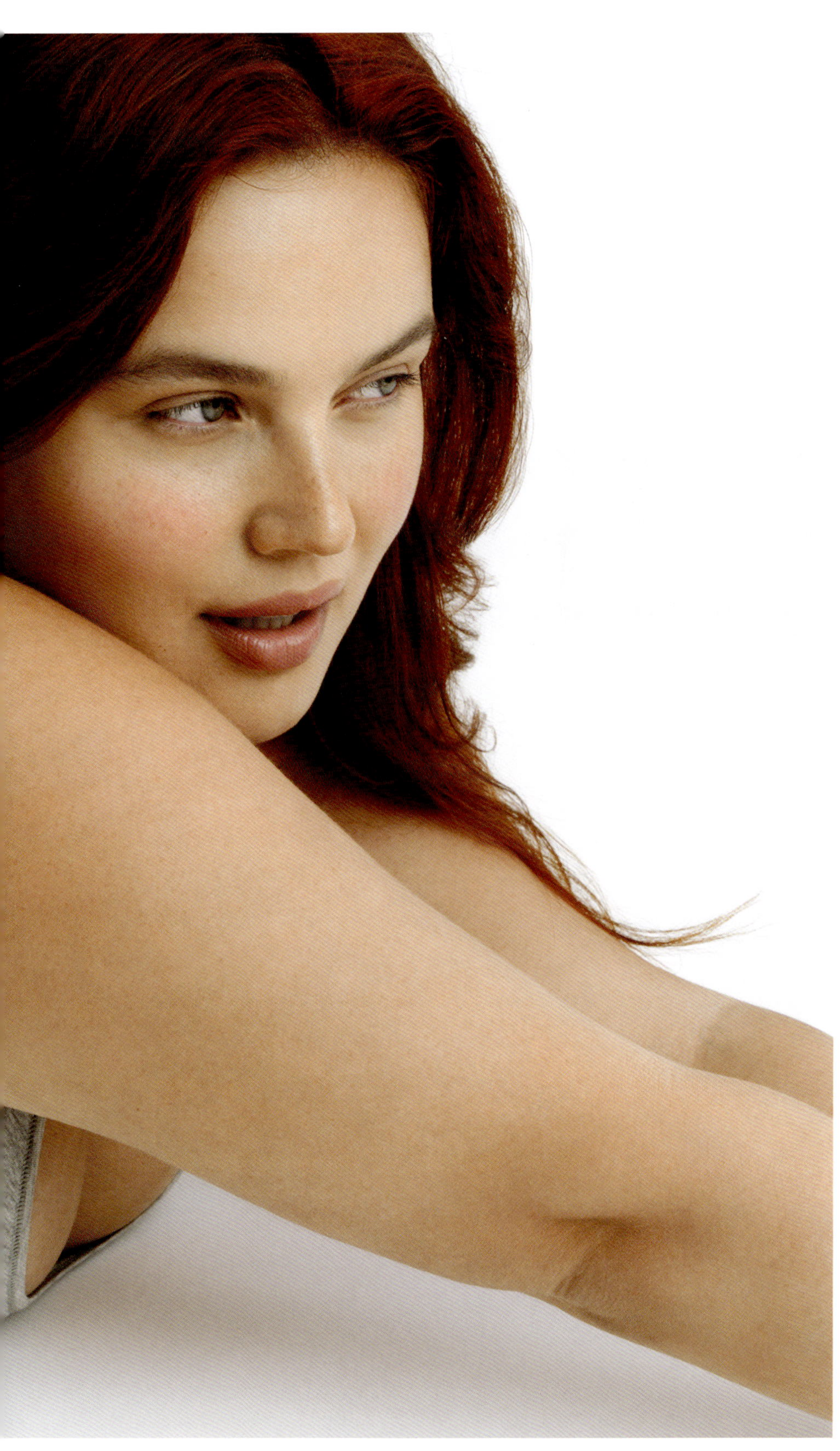

Previous pages: Apollo wears own underwear (left); Thistle and Spire harness set (right).

Bruna Lapinskas wears Calvin Klein.

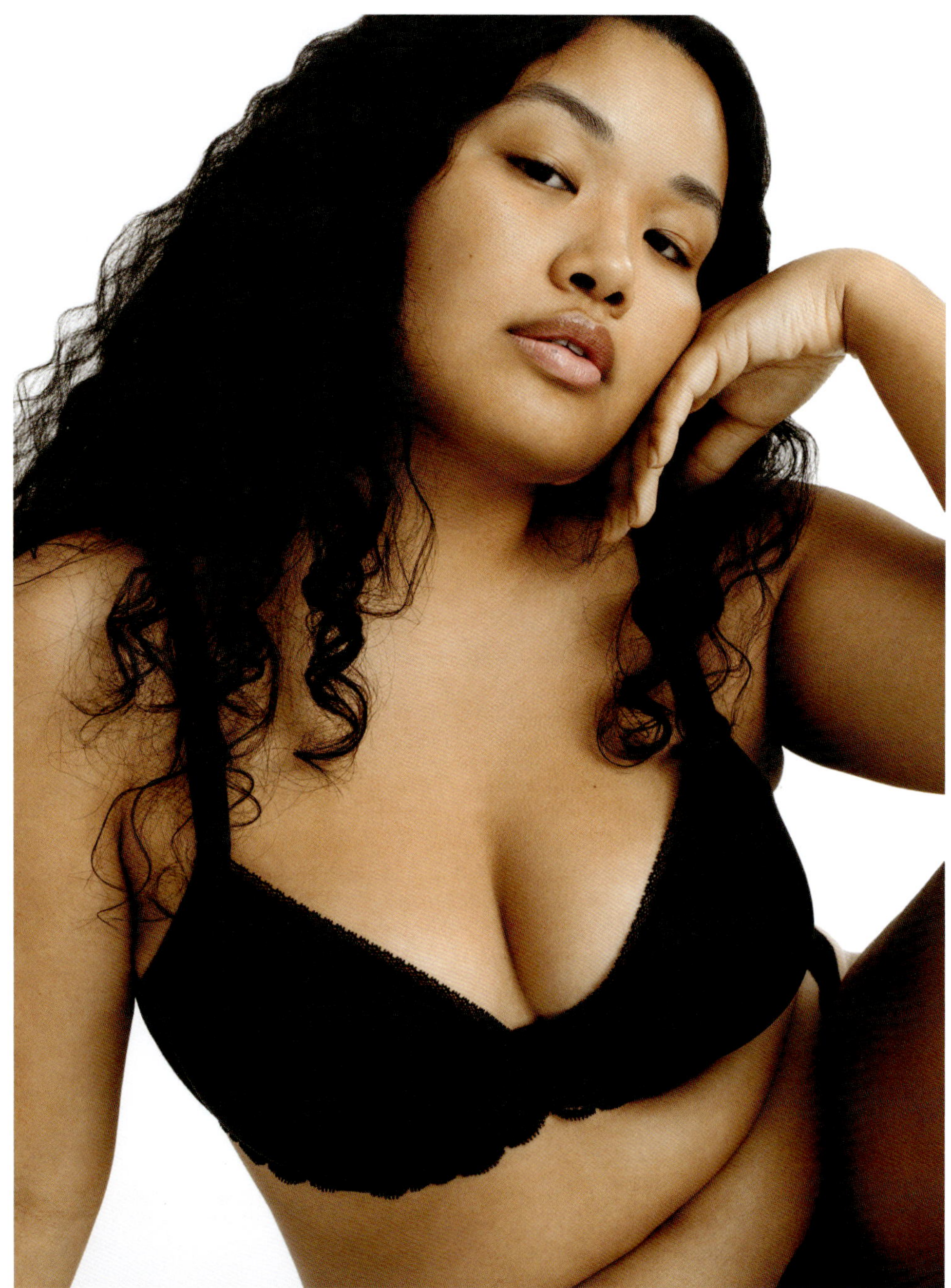

Isadora Satie wears own lingerie.

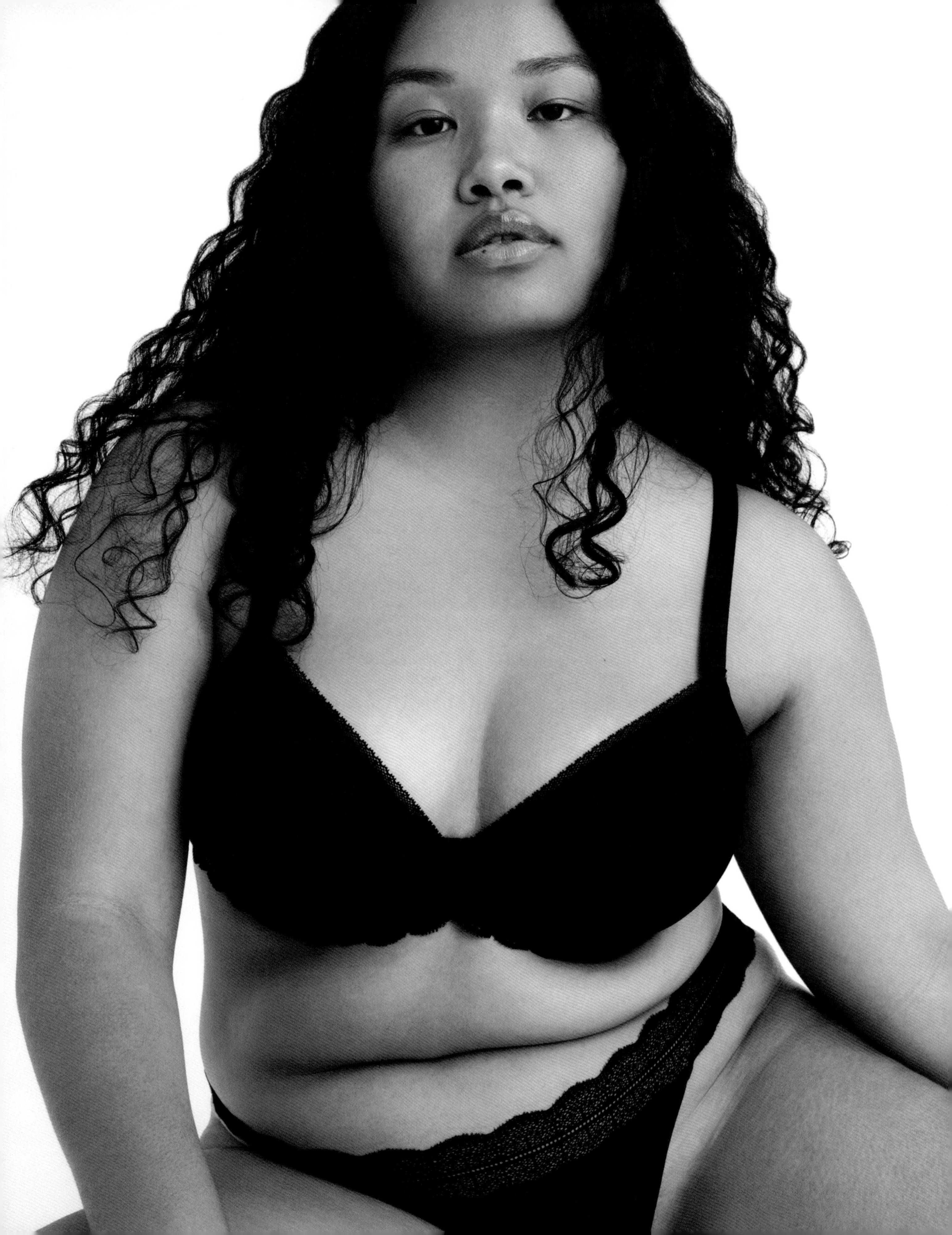

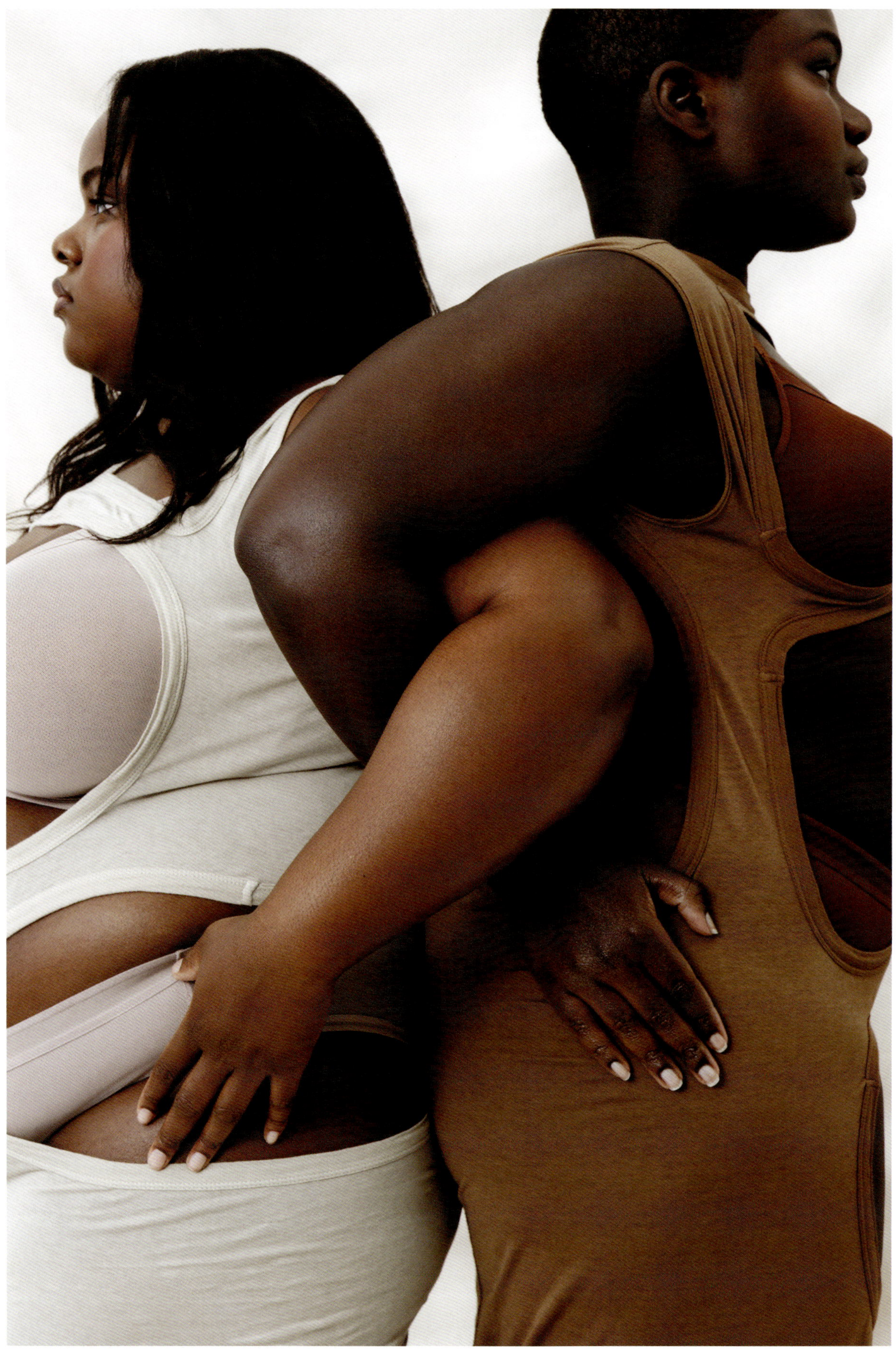

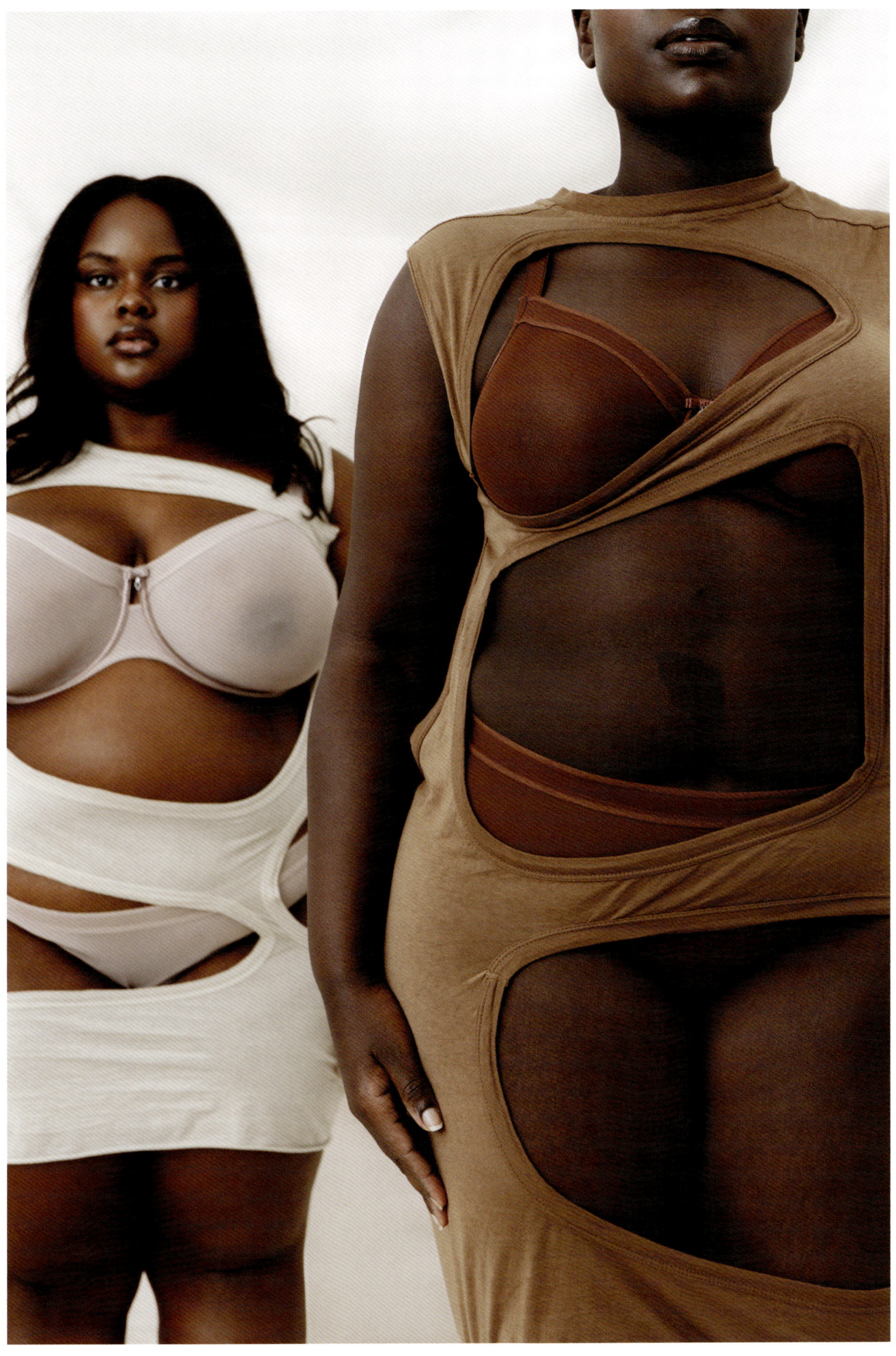

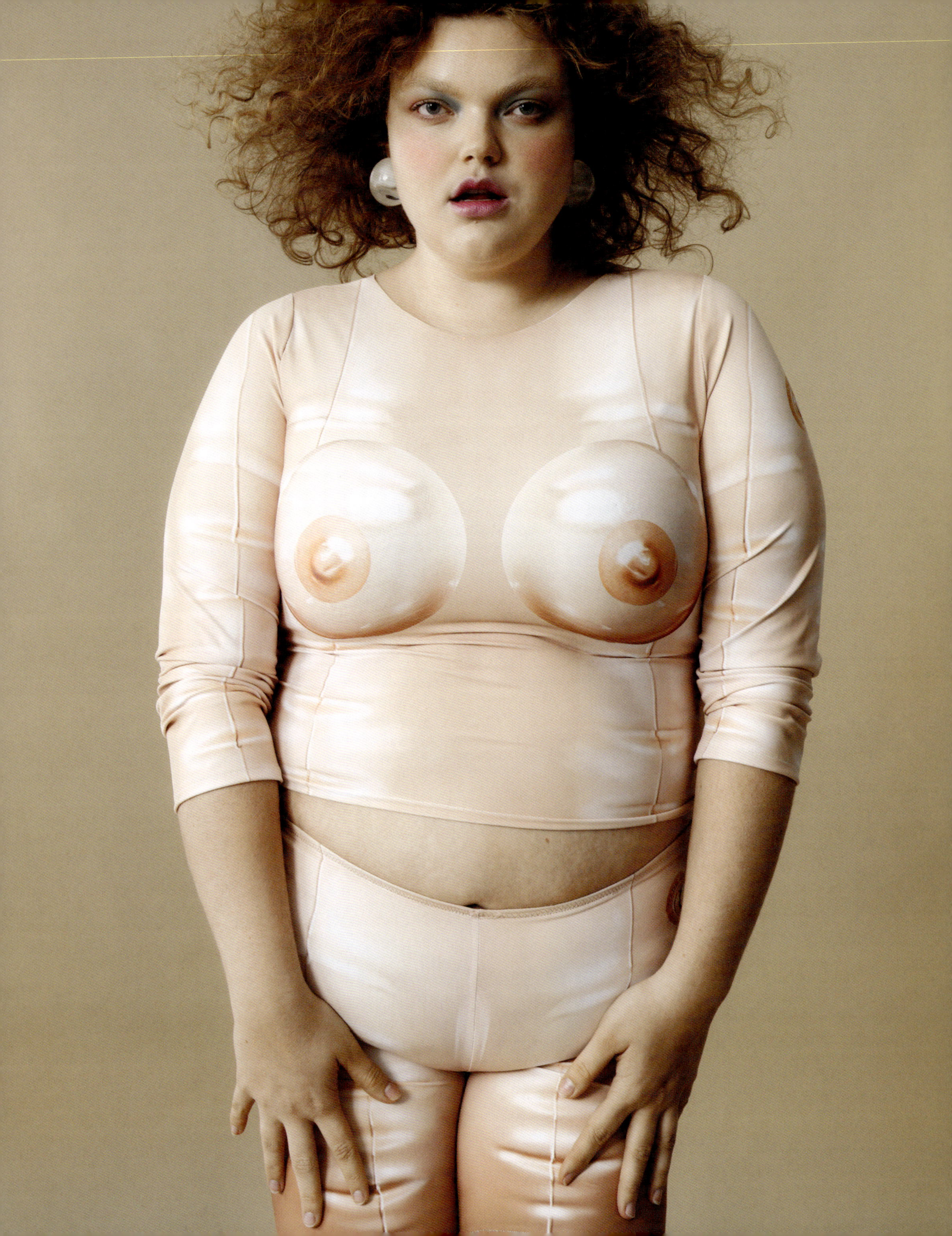

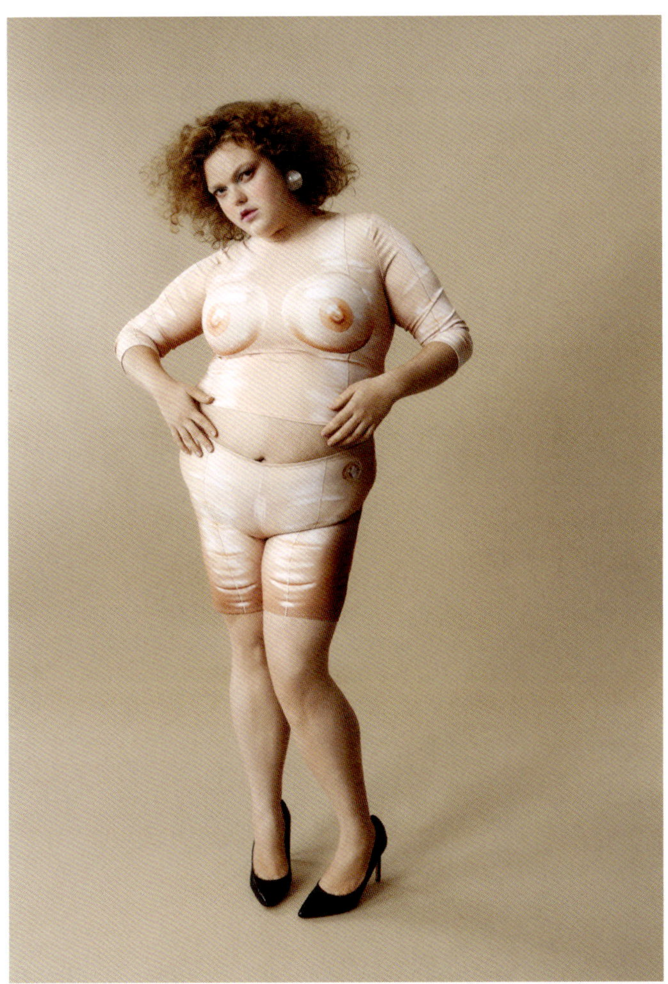

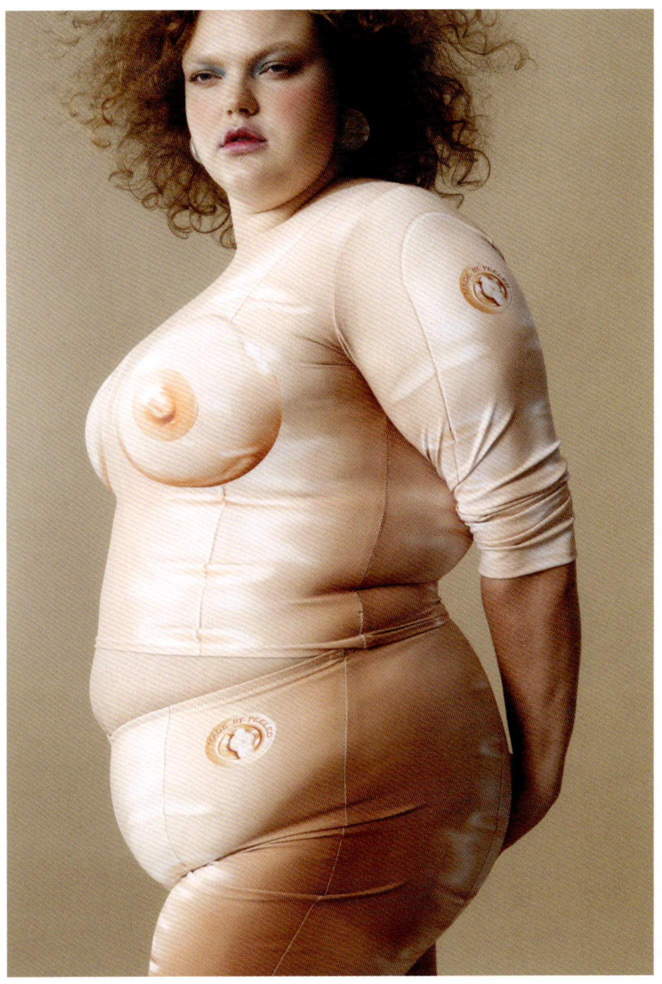

Previous pages: Manni Amoah (left) and PJ Nyambok (right) wear Rick Owens knitwear; Curvy Couture lingerie.

Charlie Reynolds wears Mariee Riee set; Alexis Bittar earrings.

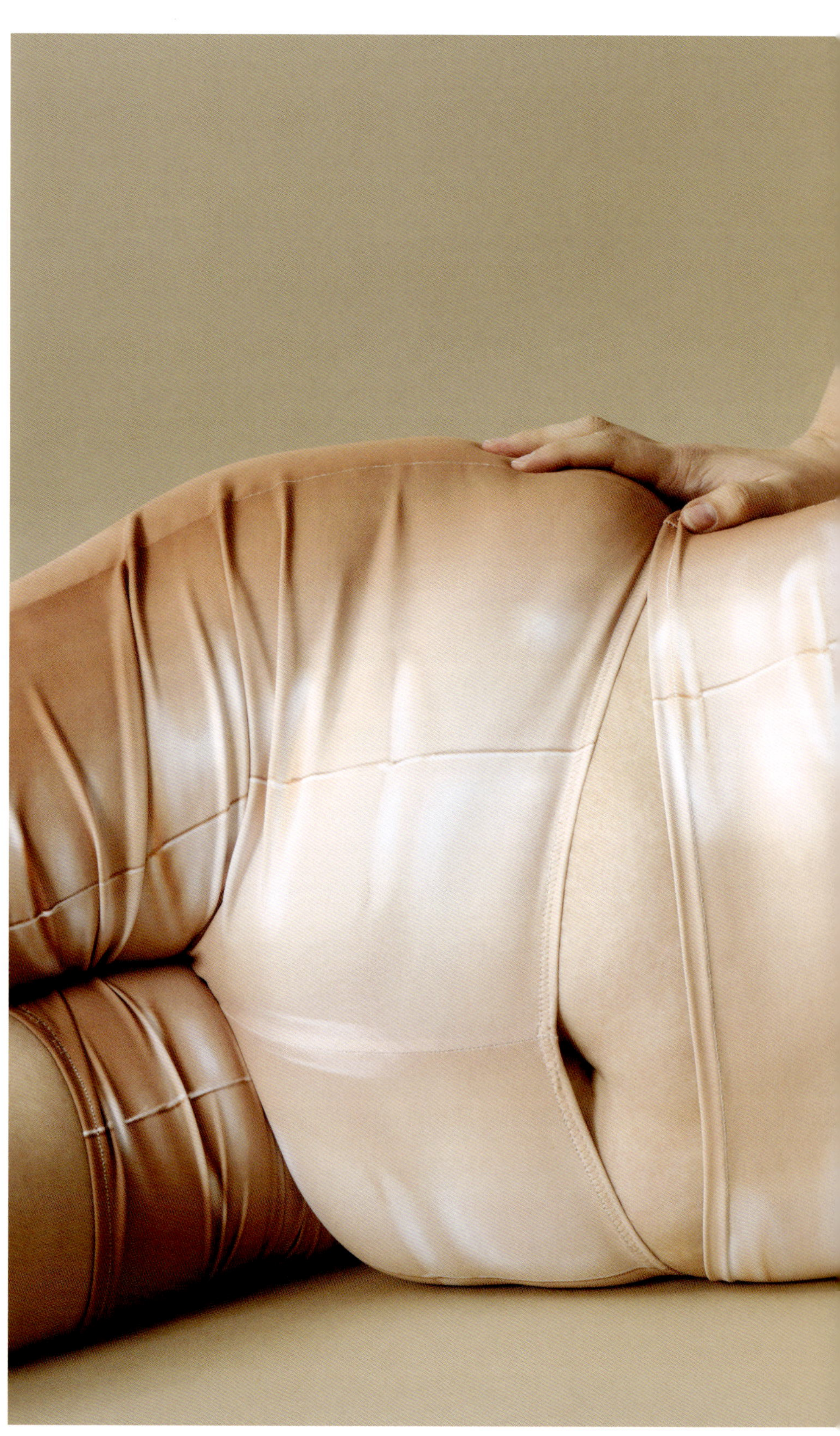

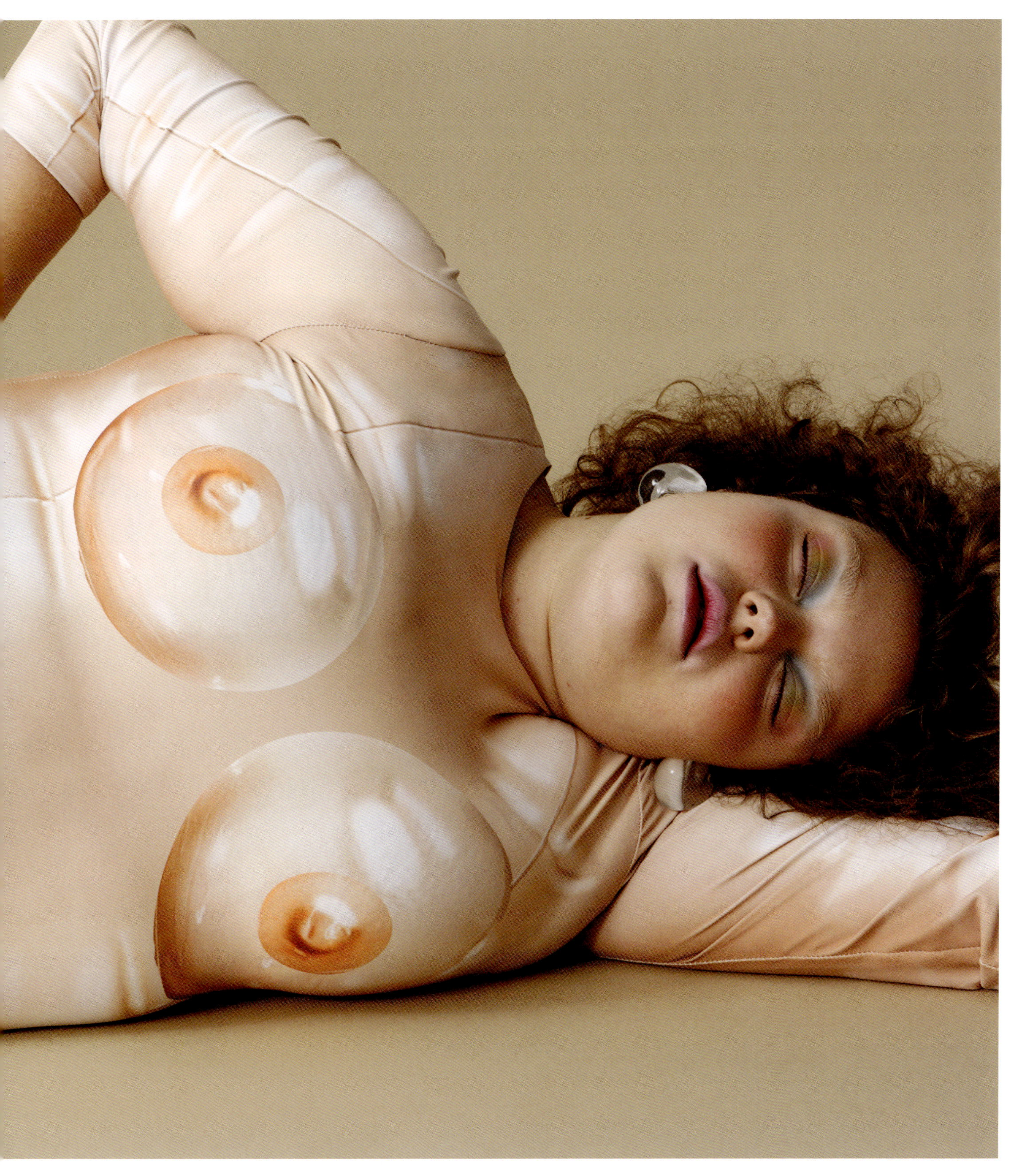

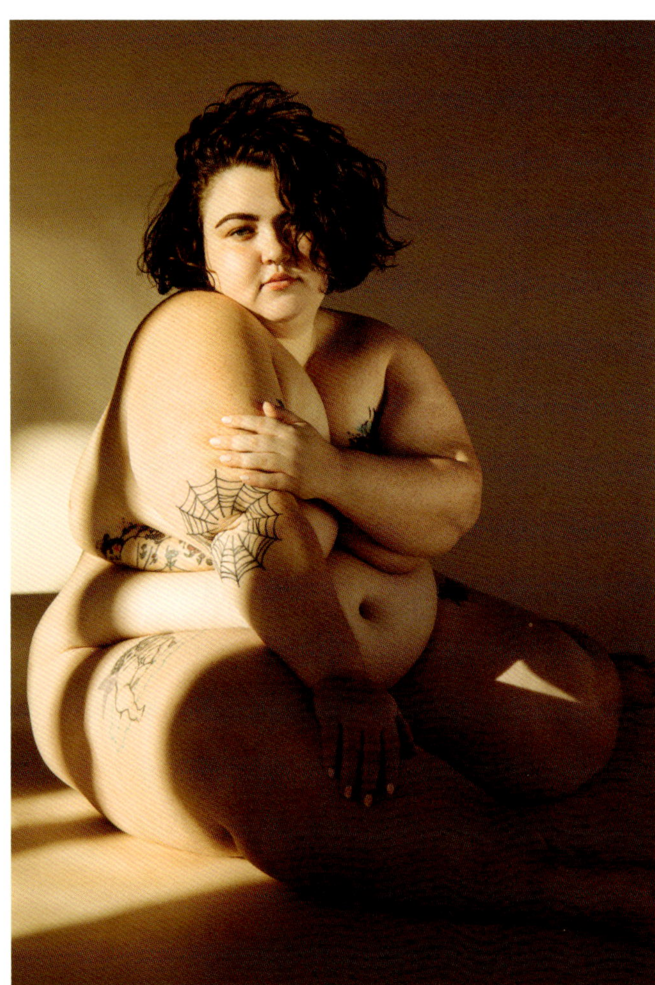

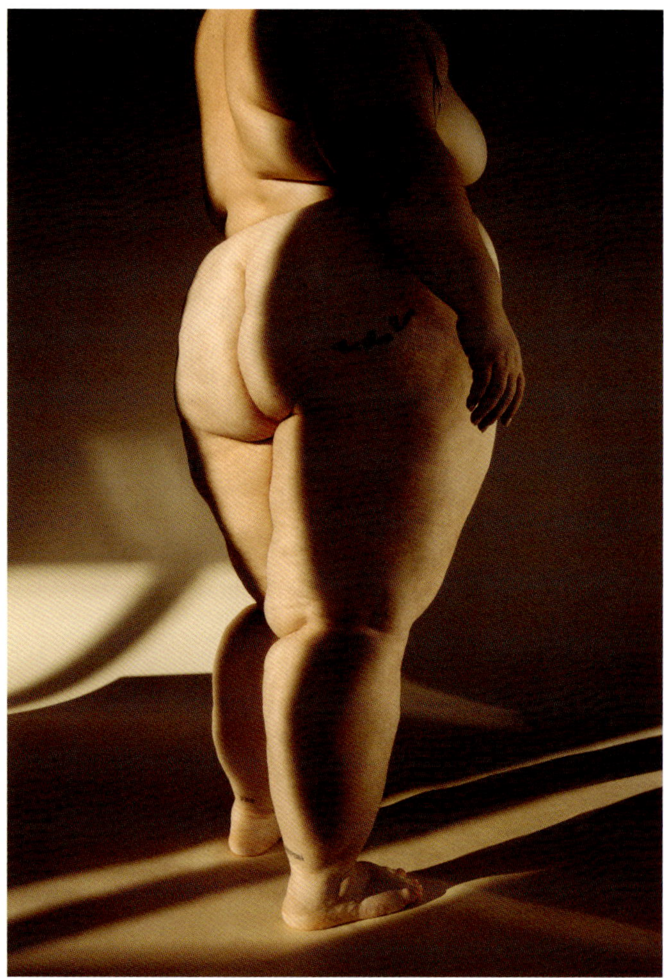

Jordan Underwood

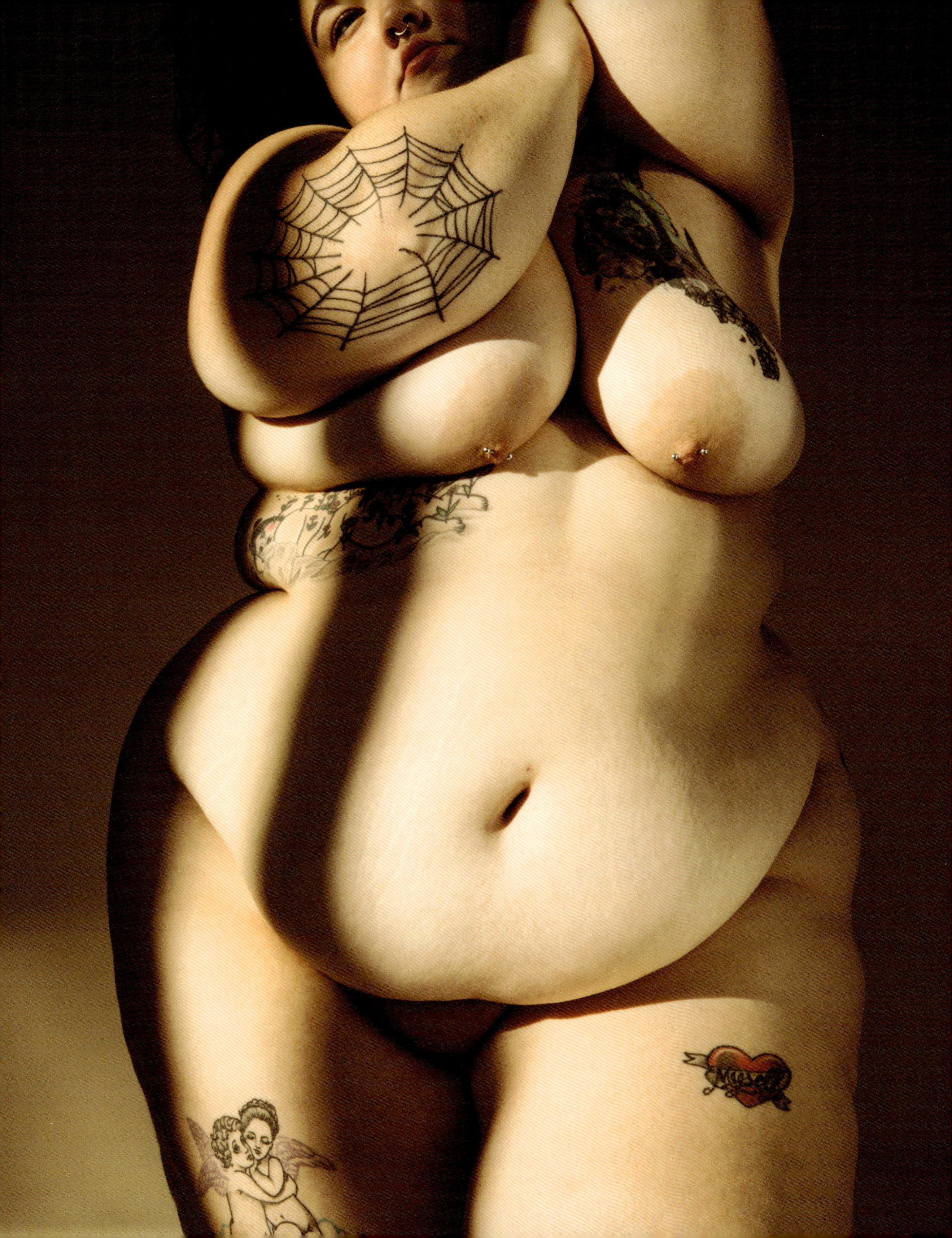

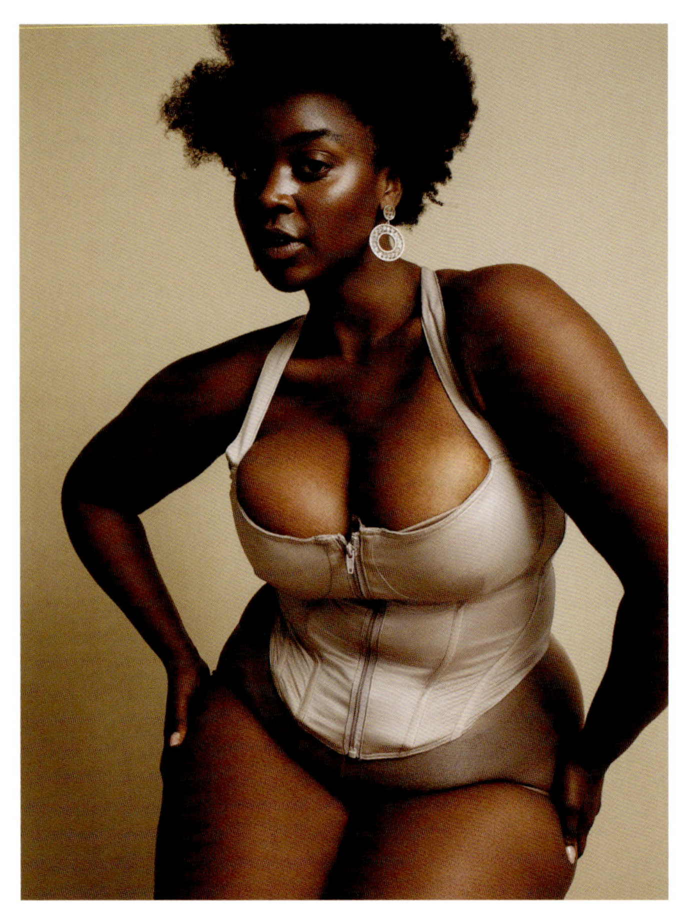
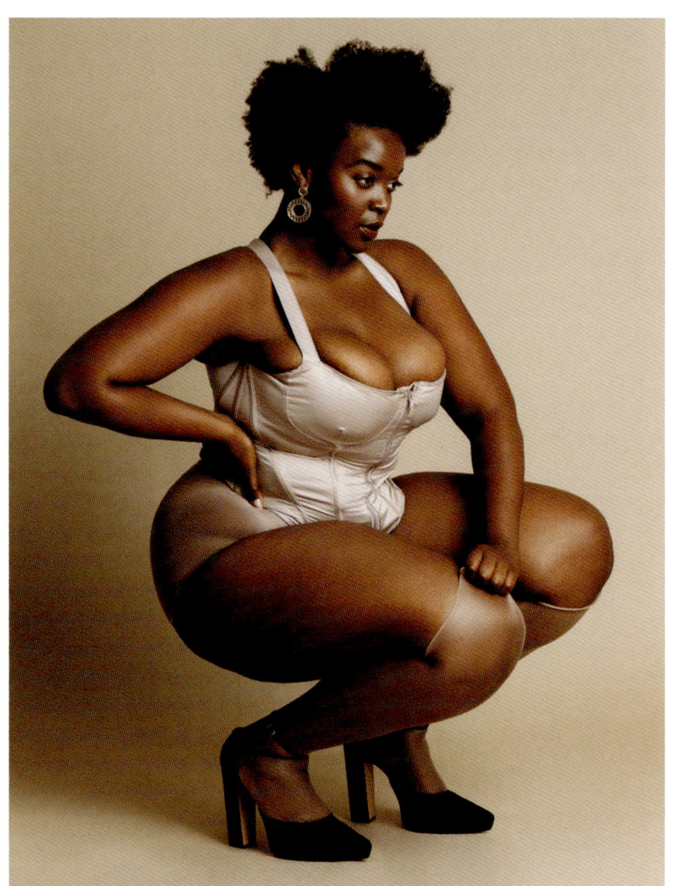
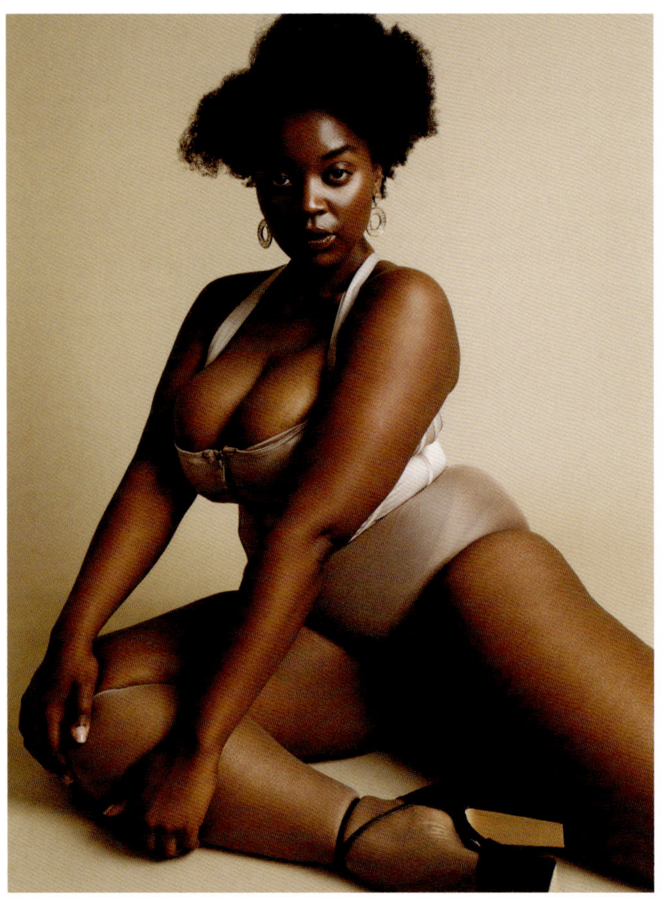
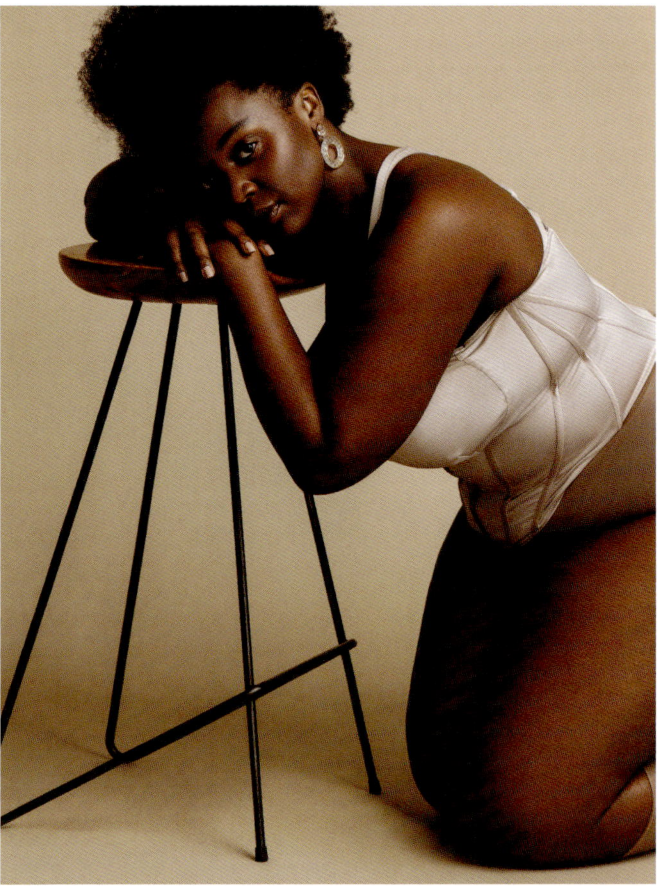

Carri Murphy wears own lingerie.

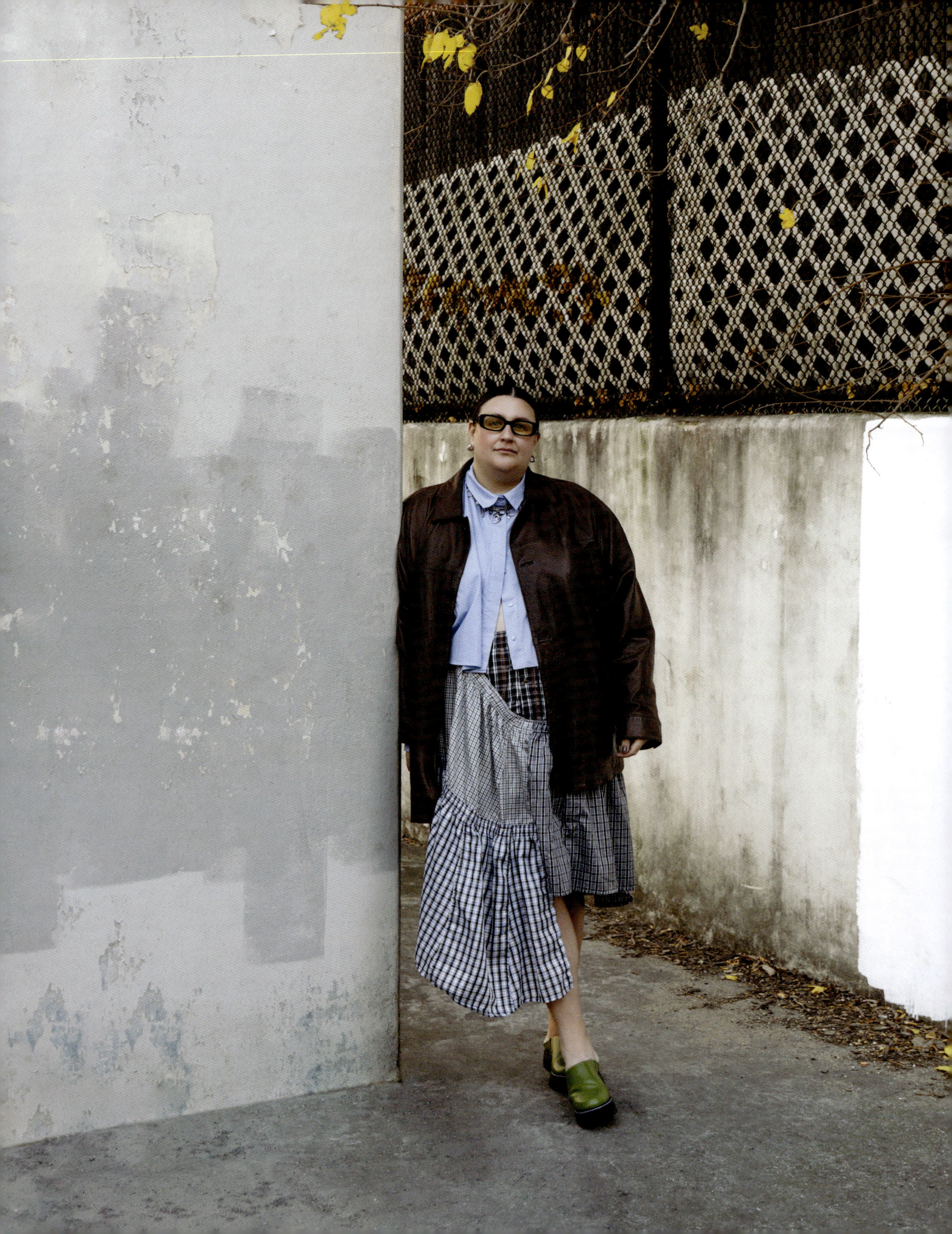

Amanda Richards

A trailblazer in fat fashion journalism

I first collaborated with Amanda Richards while working with her on *InStyle*'s inaugural plus-size street style gallery in 2019 for New York Fashion Week. That experience was not just a professional milestone for me; it was a turning point in my appreciation for diverse voices in fashion. It was a joy to see how passionate Amanda was about the project, and her dedication inspired me to focus even more on inclusivity in my own work. These days, we live in the same building, and I often get to see her and her two adorable dogs, which adds a delightful personal touch to our professional relationship. Our chats over coffee in the morning have turned into meaningful conversations about fashion, identity, and the importance of representation.

Amanda made a name for herself by writing for major publications like *InStyle*, *Bustle*, and *Travel + Leisure*. When asked what initially drew her to focus on fat fashion and body image, and how those topics have shaped her career, she shares, "I've always been interested in clothing. When I was younger, my interest was very much as an outsider. Like many other fat 12-year-olds, I pored over the pages of the Delia's catalogue and was absolutely desperate to look as cool as they did." This deep-rooted passion led her to focus on fat fashion in her writing, in which she emphasizes how significantly clothing can impact a person's self-perception and emotional well-being.

The street style gallery was particularly meaningful for both of us; it felt important to not only showcase plus-size representation, but to create a space where individuals could celebrate their unique styles. Amanda recalls, "When I was first hired at *InStyle* as an editor, I thought, 'Wait, this is a legacy fashion and lifestyle magazine. How did I, a fat gay from Cleveland, arrive in this role?'" Her vision was clear: She wanted to ensure that plus-size individuals were more than an afterthought among fashion week galleries filled with

Any intersectional space is going to be more interesting than one that caters to a single aspect of our identities. Fashion could use more of it, that's for sure.

thin models. "It felt important to showcase the real diversity of bodies at such a prestigious event."

These days, Amanda shares her insights on her Substack, *Fat Hell*. Asked about how the conversation around fat fashion has evolved over time, and what keeps her motivated to continue writing about it, she says, "We're currently in a phase of reckoning. The feel-good, 'body positive' marketing from a handful of years ago is no longer resonating with our demographic, and plus-size clothing doesn't have the same momentum behind it that it once did." This candid insight marks Amanda's commitment to authenticity. She continues to provide an honest perspective on the complexities of existing in a fat body: a refreshing approach in the fashion industry, which often favors superficial narratives. "I want to show the nuance that comes with being fat and trying to get dressed in the morning."

One thing I love about Amanda is her adventurous approach to style and her ability to tackle fashion with limited options. She acknowledges, "I have a lot of privilege in the sense that I've worked in the fashion industry and have a good sense of what's on offer, along with the disposable income to buy it." Yet, there is also the challenge of being thoughtful about style rather than just buying something because it fits.

"I'm really inspired by Emma Zack at Shop Berriez. Emma manages to find unique pieces for a huge range of plus-size bodies and encourages people to experiment with their style. My own aesthetics have certainly gotten a bit more fun since I met her."

As we discuss the current state of the fashion industry, Amanda says that while there has been significant shifts in plus-size representation, many of the same challenges persist. As to whether she believes any real progress has been made: "The fashion industry was never going to save us. It felt powerful when brands acknowledged fat people's existence, but that was just novel. The real power comes from fat people who utilize what's available and turn it into style, culture, and a movement."

Amanda has often expressed frustration with the cyclical nature of the inclusivity conversation. To stay motivated to continue pushing for change, she says, "We need to inspire and support each other in figuring out how to navigate this space. Real change happens on an individual level and through community building." Her words resonate as a call to action to those working to achieve inclusivity and representation: an effort which needs to be enriched by welcoming diverse voices. "Any intersectional space is going to be more interesting than one that caters to a single aspect of our identities. Fashion could use more of it, that's for sure."

With fashion trends coming and going, Amanda reflects on how we can shift to a long-term commitment to body diversity. "We're never going to be satisfied if we use the fashion industry as a metric for our worth," she says. "It's about figuring out how to carve out our own spaces and supporting each other in that journey."

This sentiment captures the essence of her mission: fostering a community where everyone feels valued and represented. As a vital voice in the realm of fat fashion journalism, Amanda provides insights, passion, and a dedication to inclusivity in her writing that offer a much-needed perspective to inspire change.

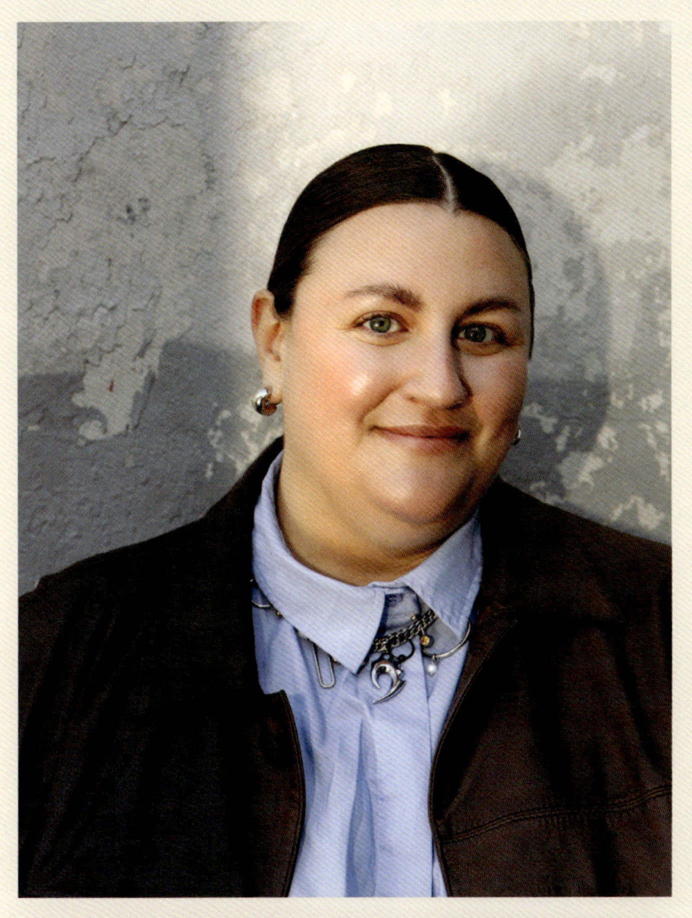

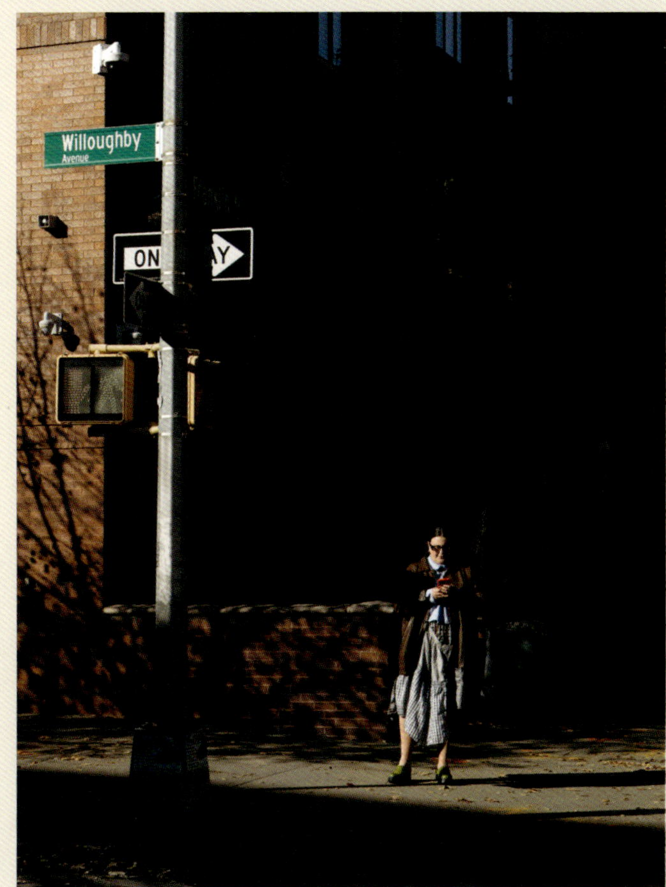
Willoughby
Avenue

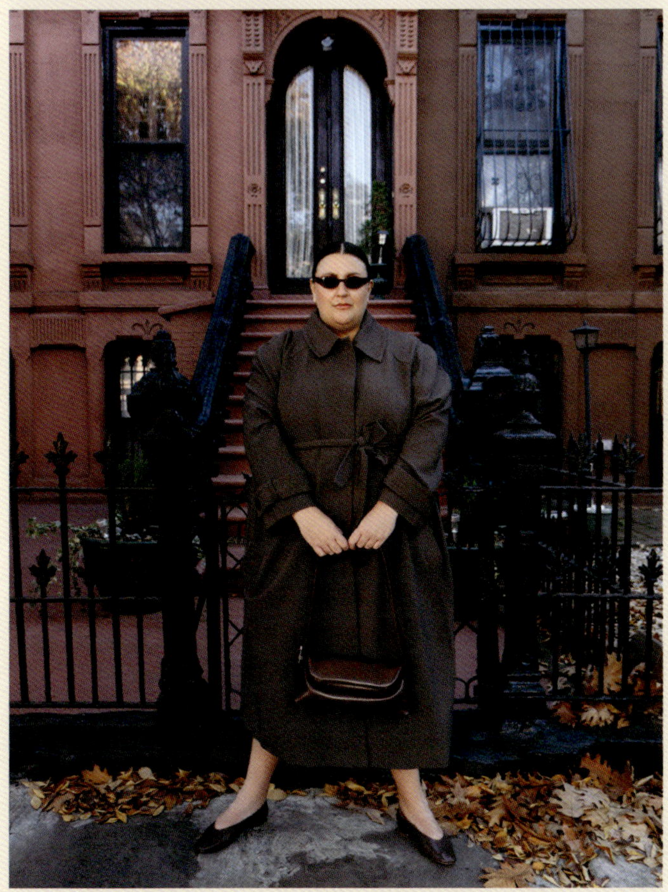

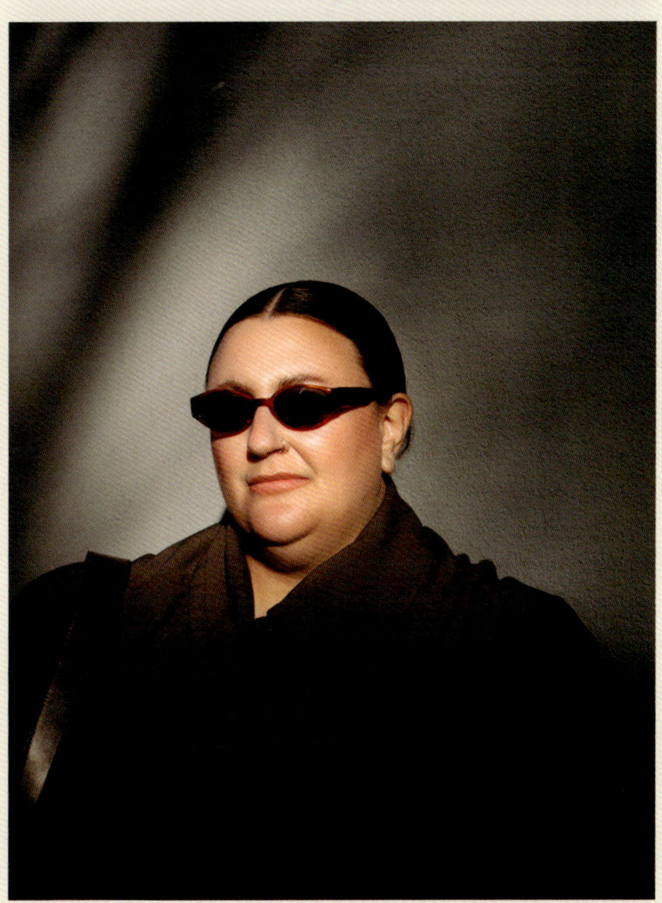

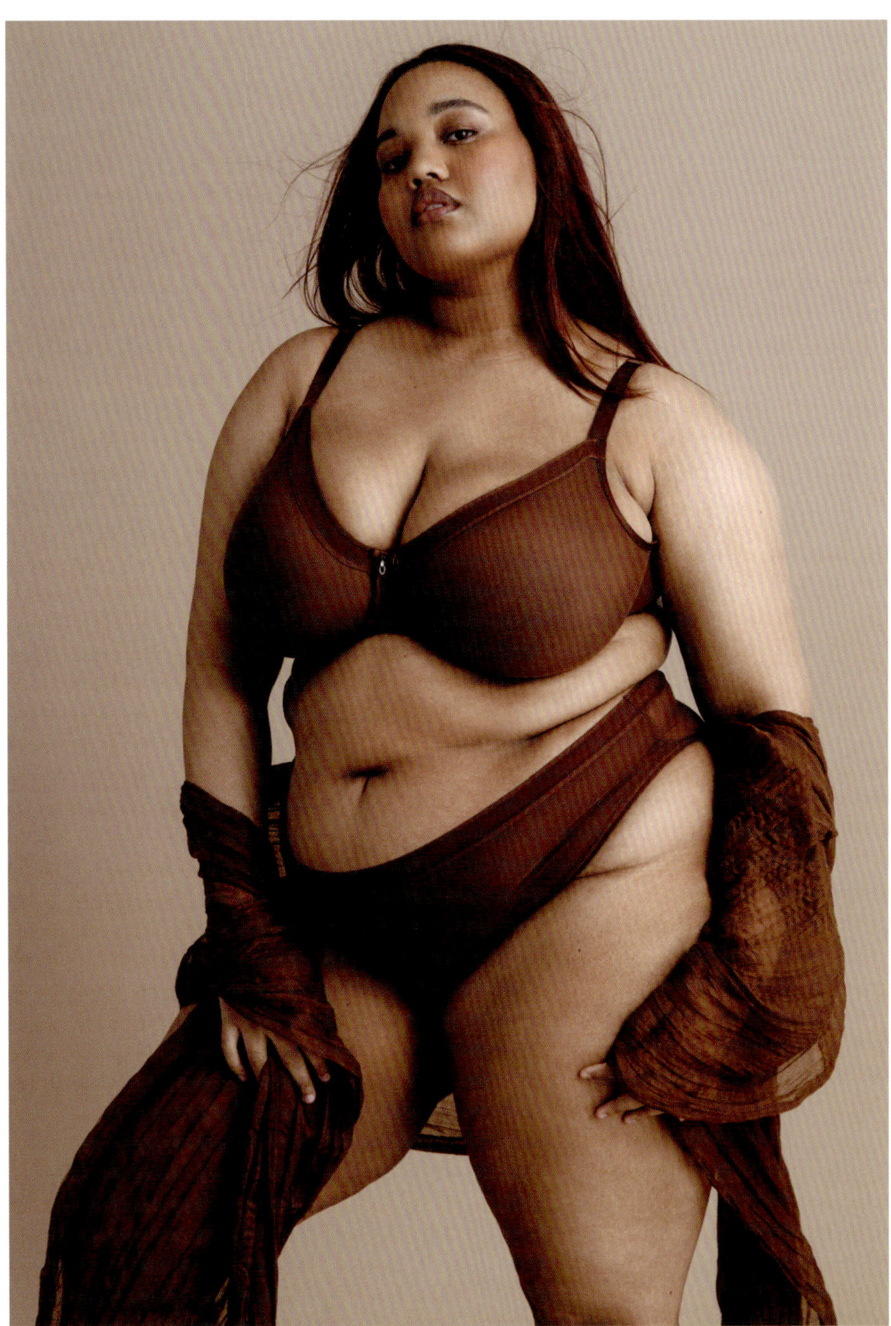

Charisse Nicole Thompson (above) and Ariana Corrao (right) wear Curvy Couture lingerie.

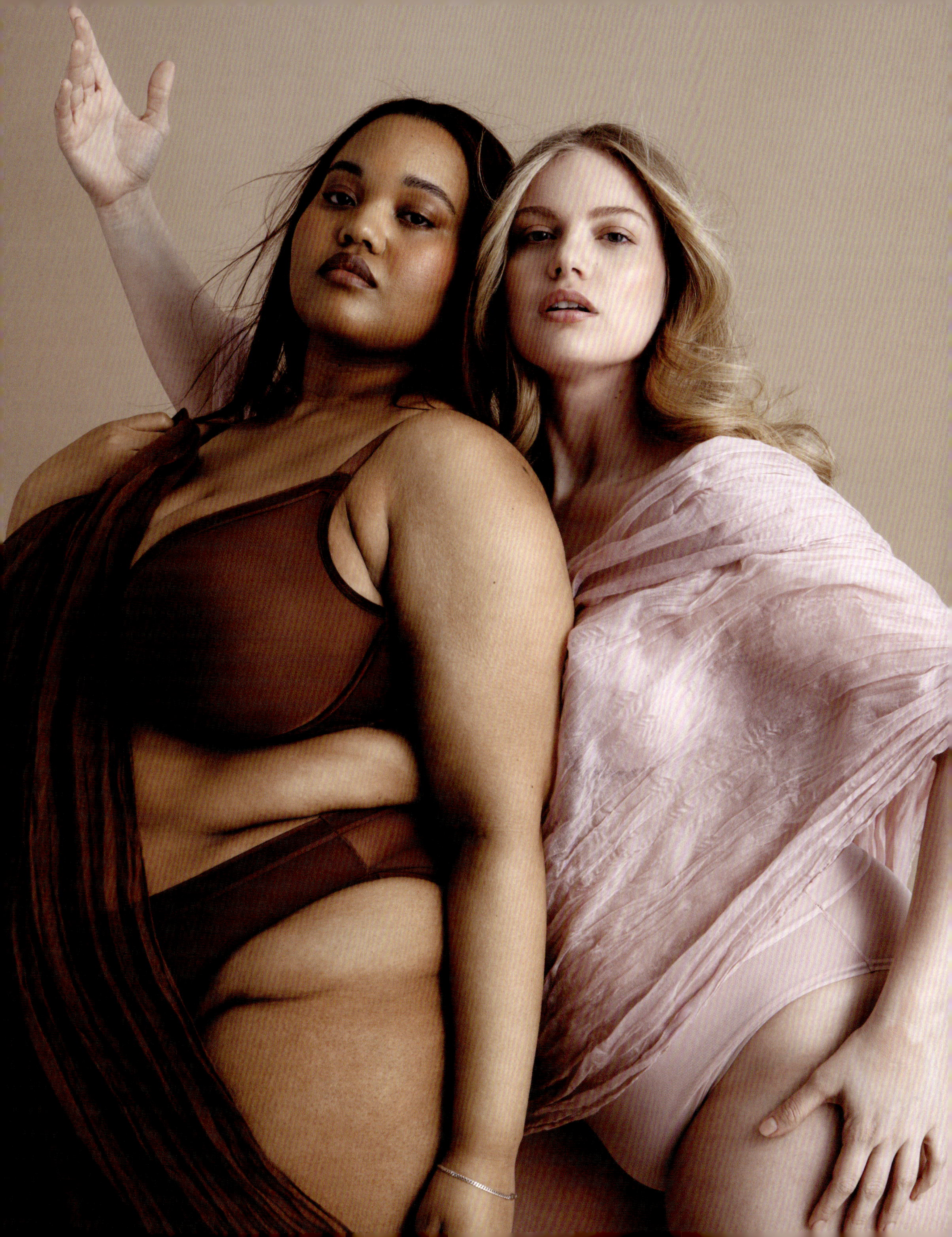

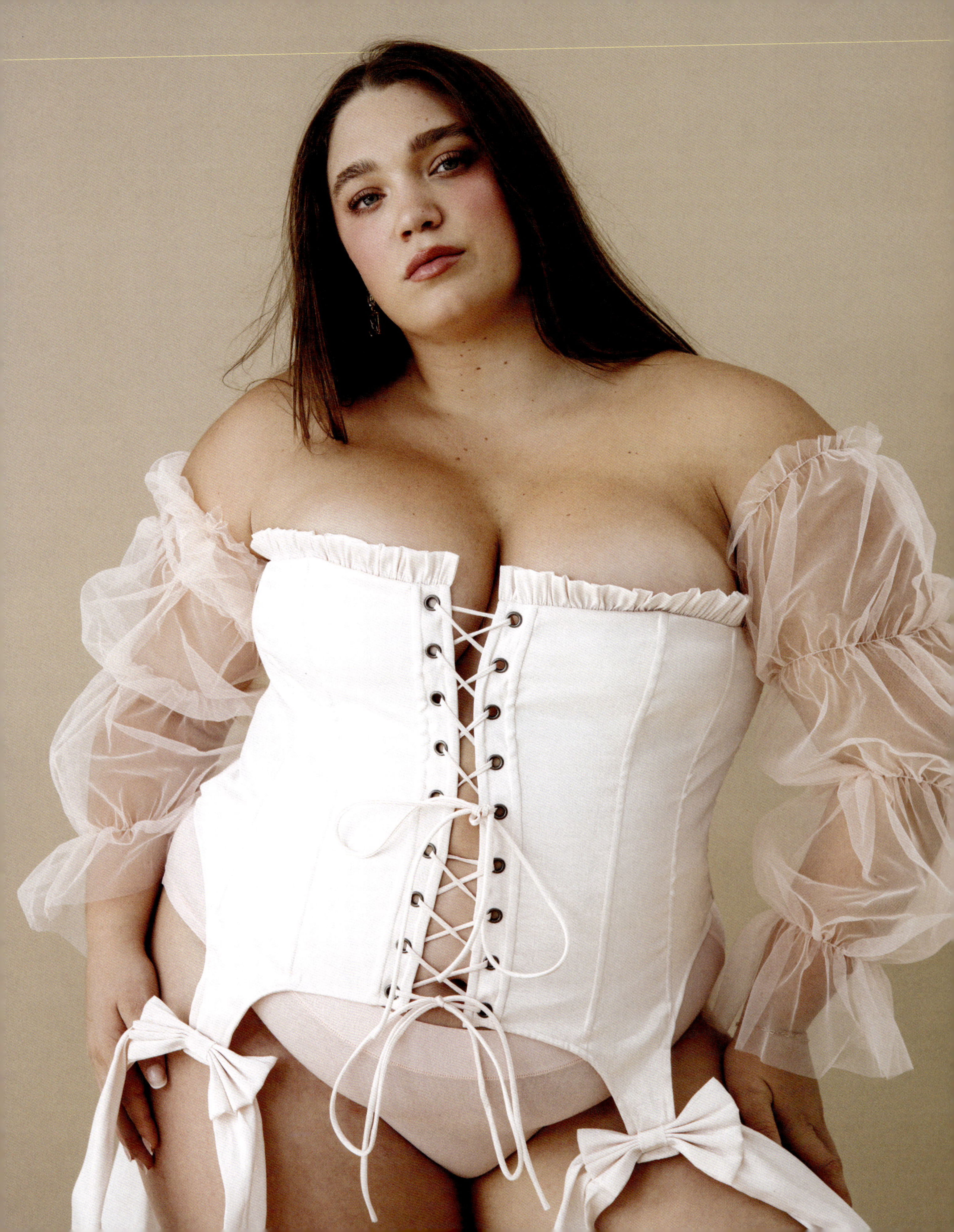

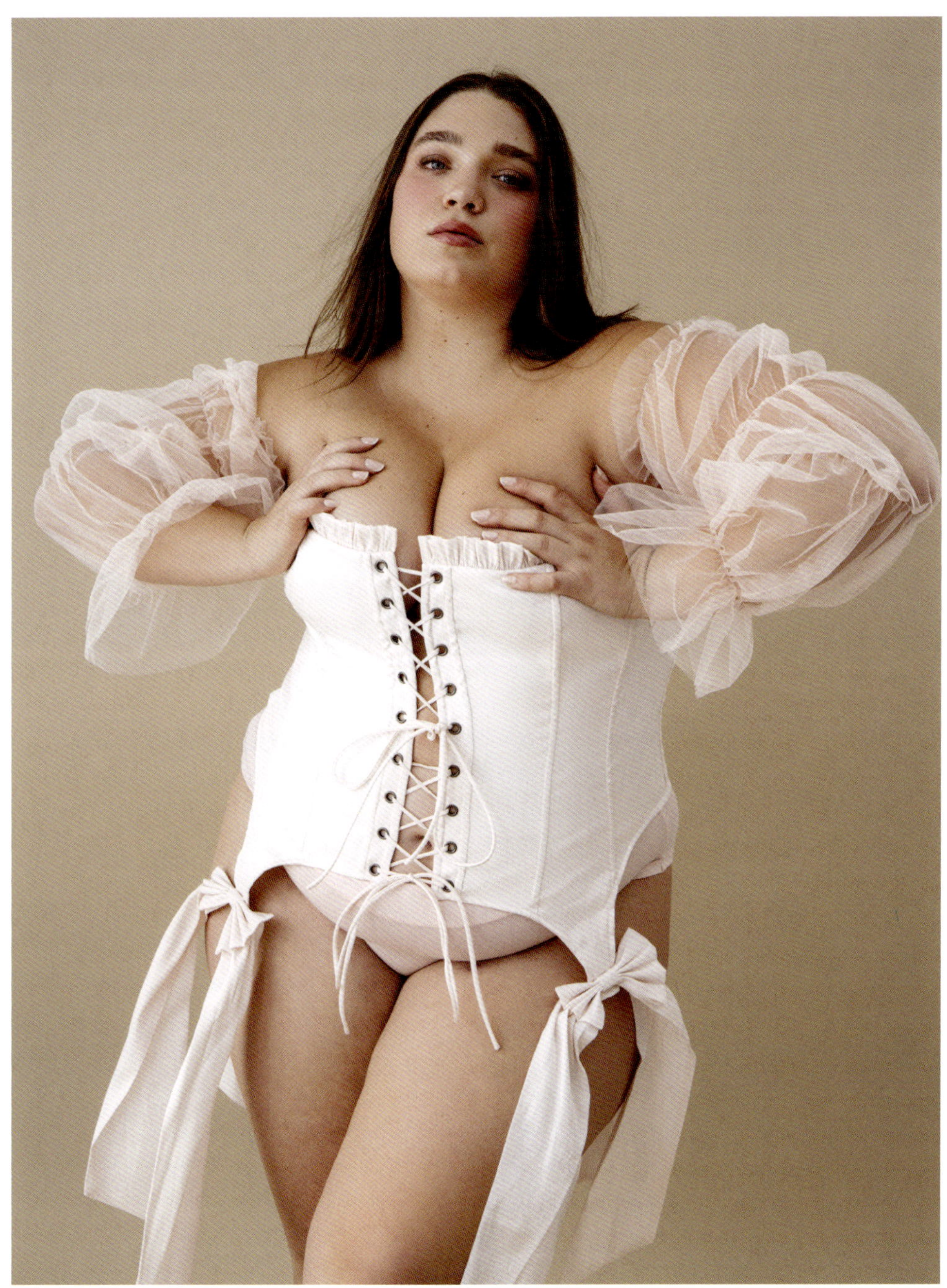

Danielle Lucker wears Selkie.

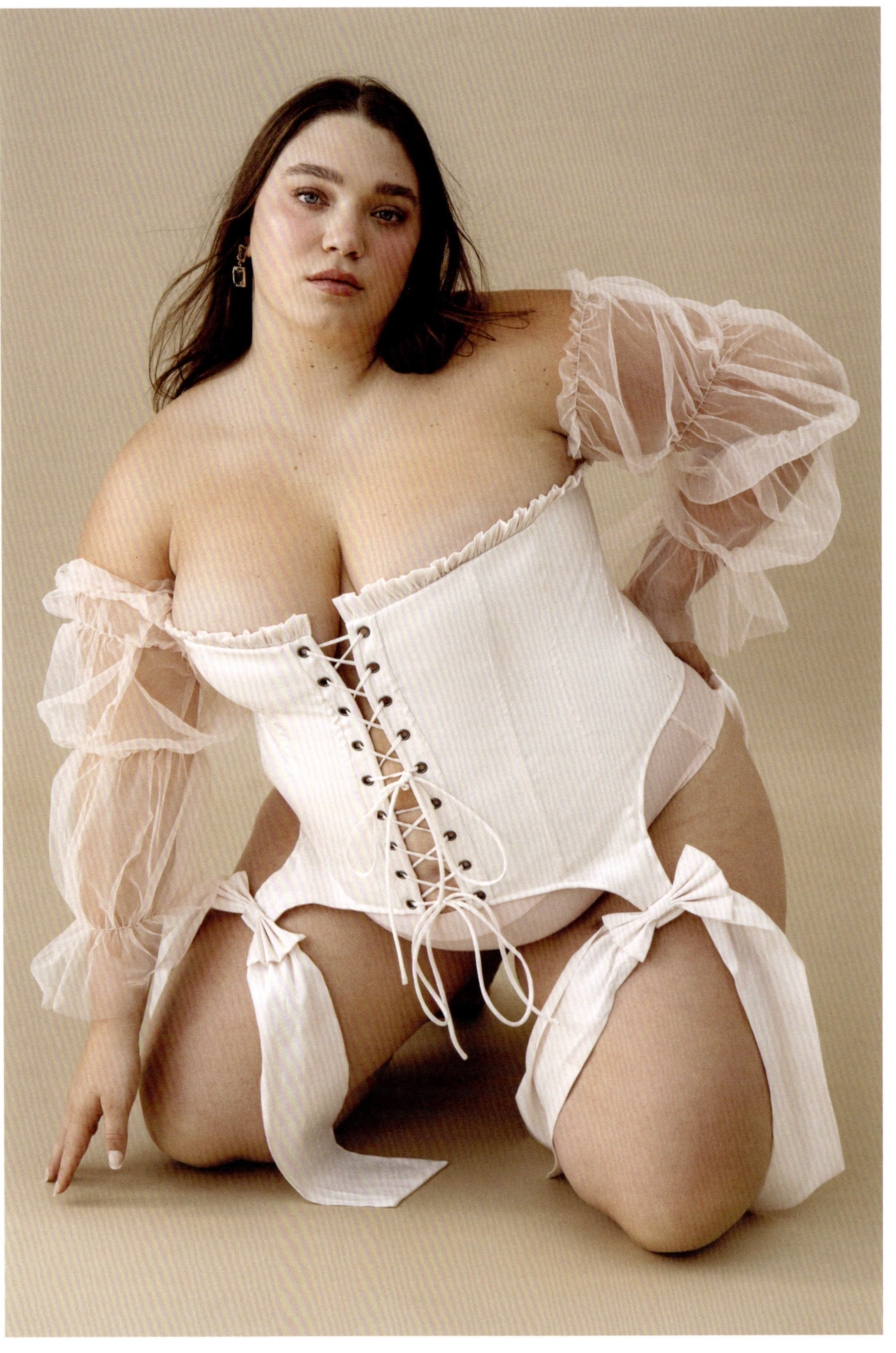

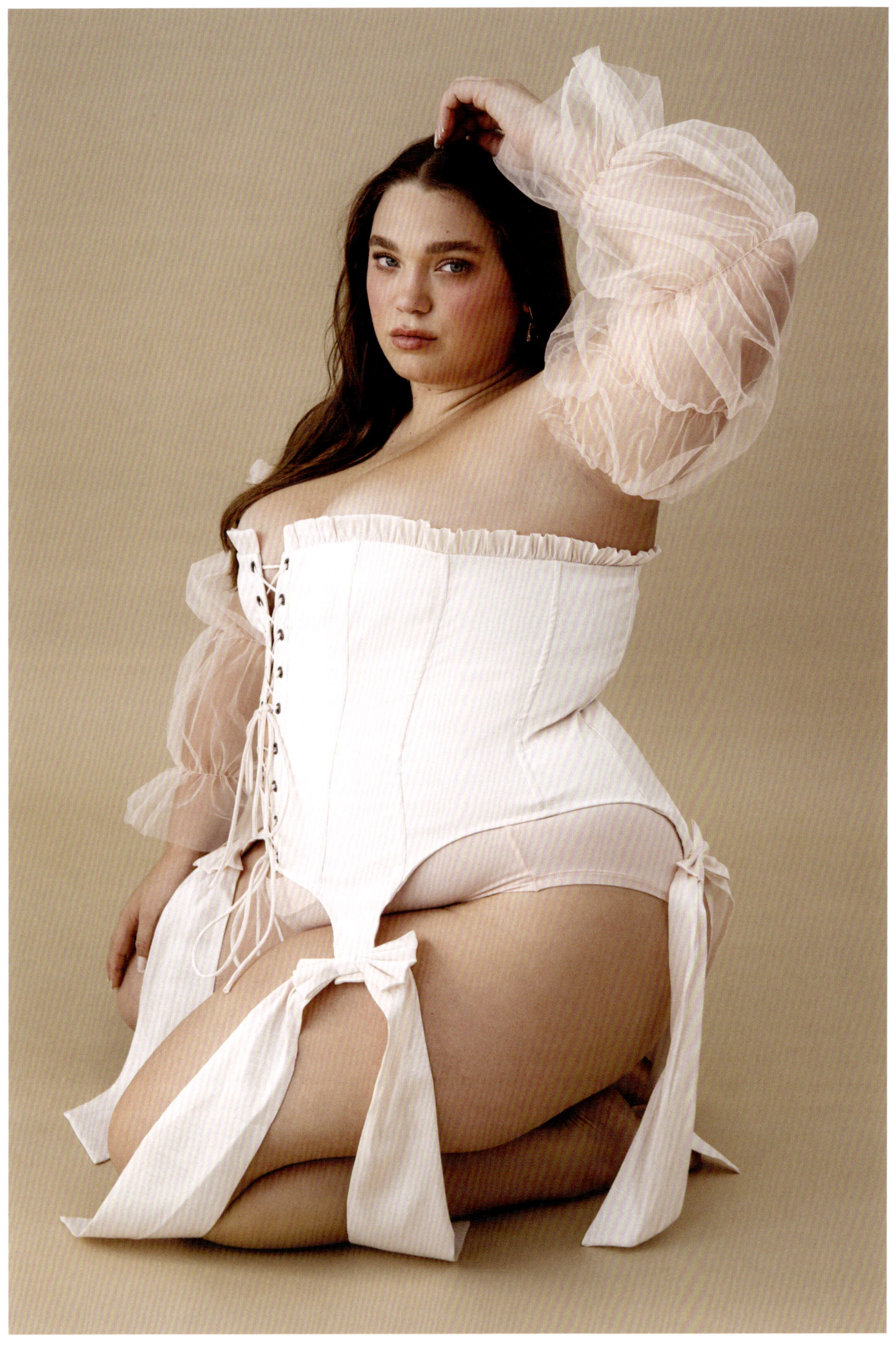

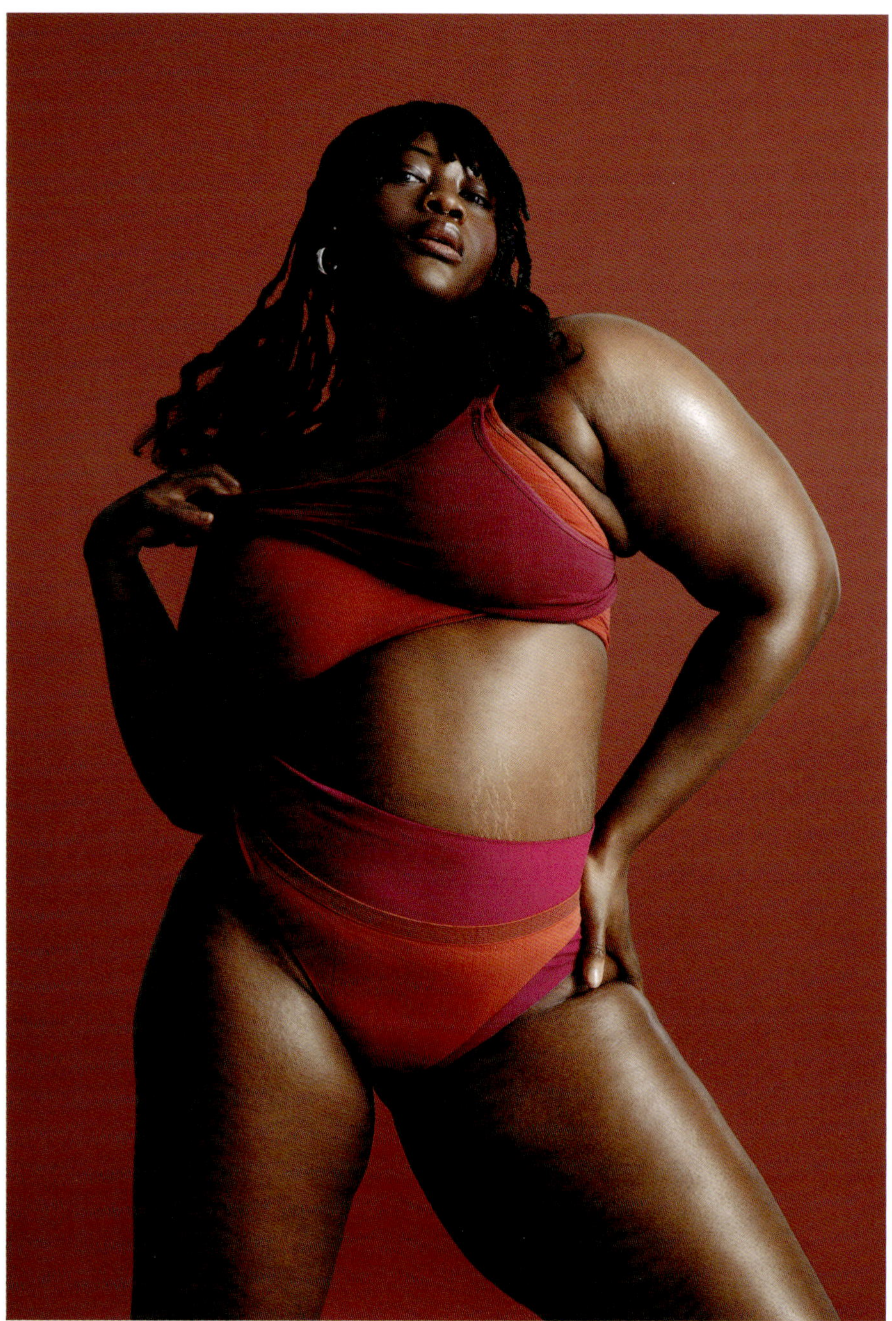

Oskar Sinclair wears Bombas set.

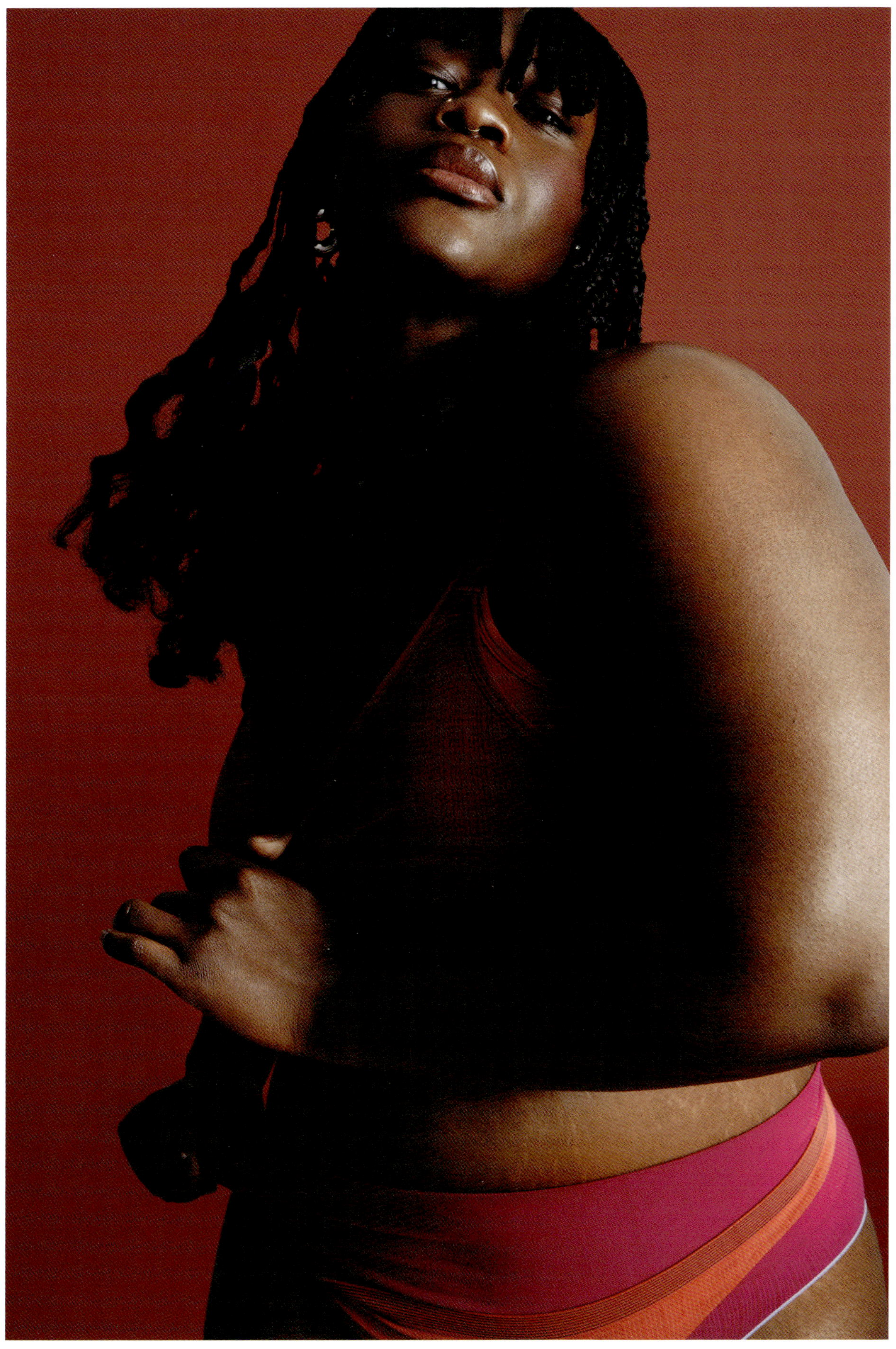

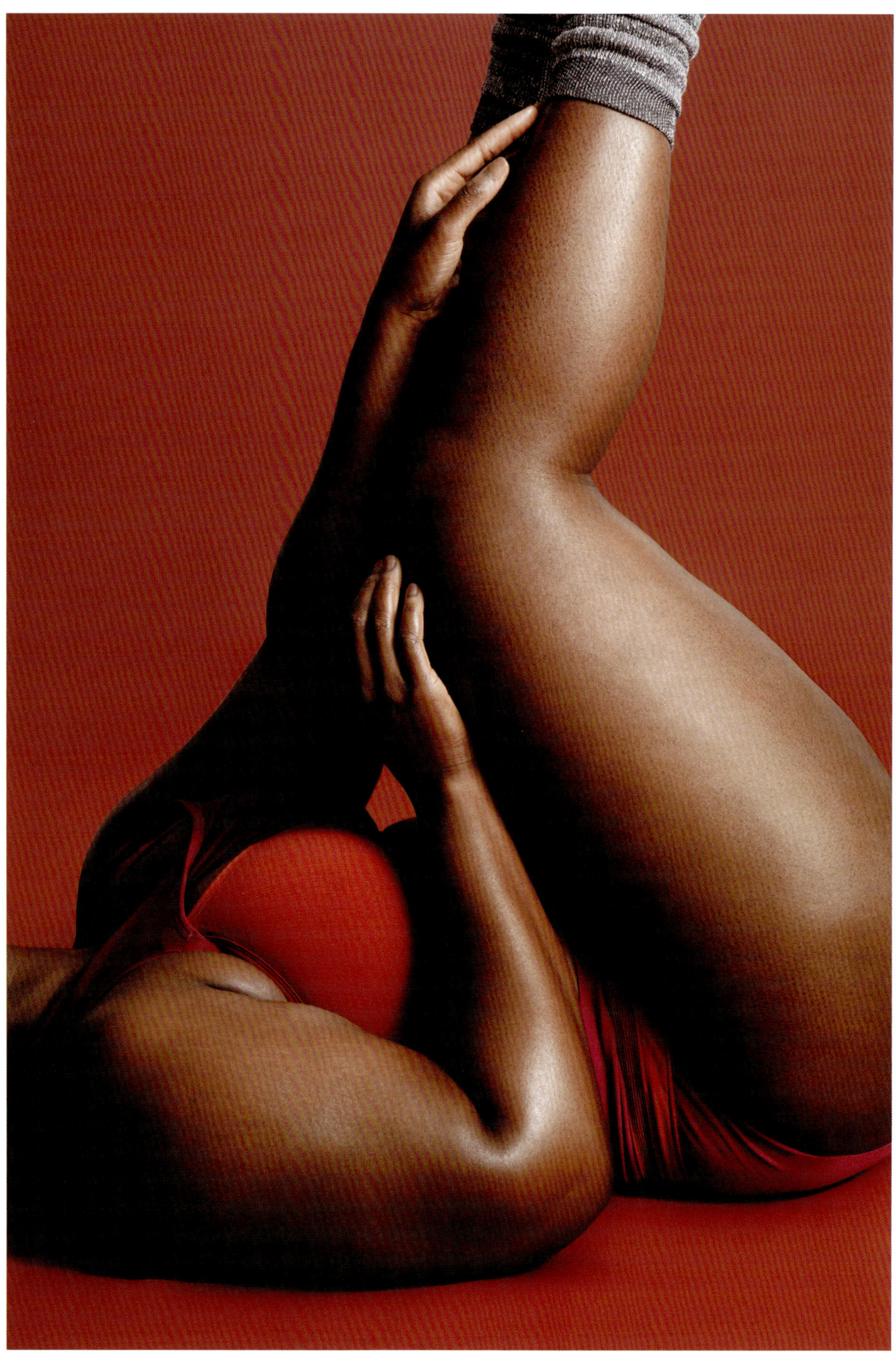

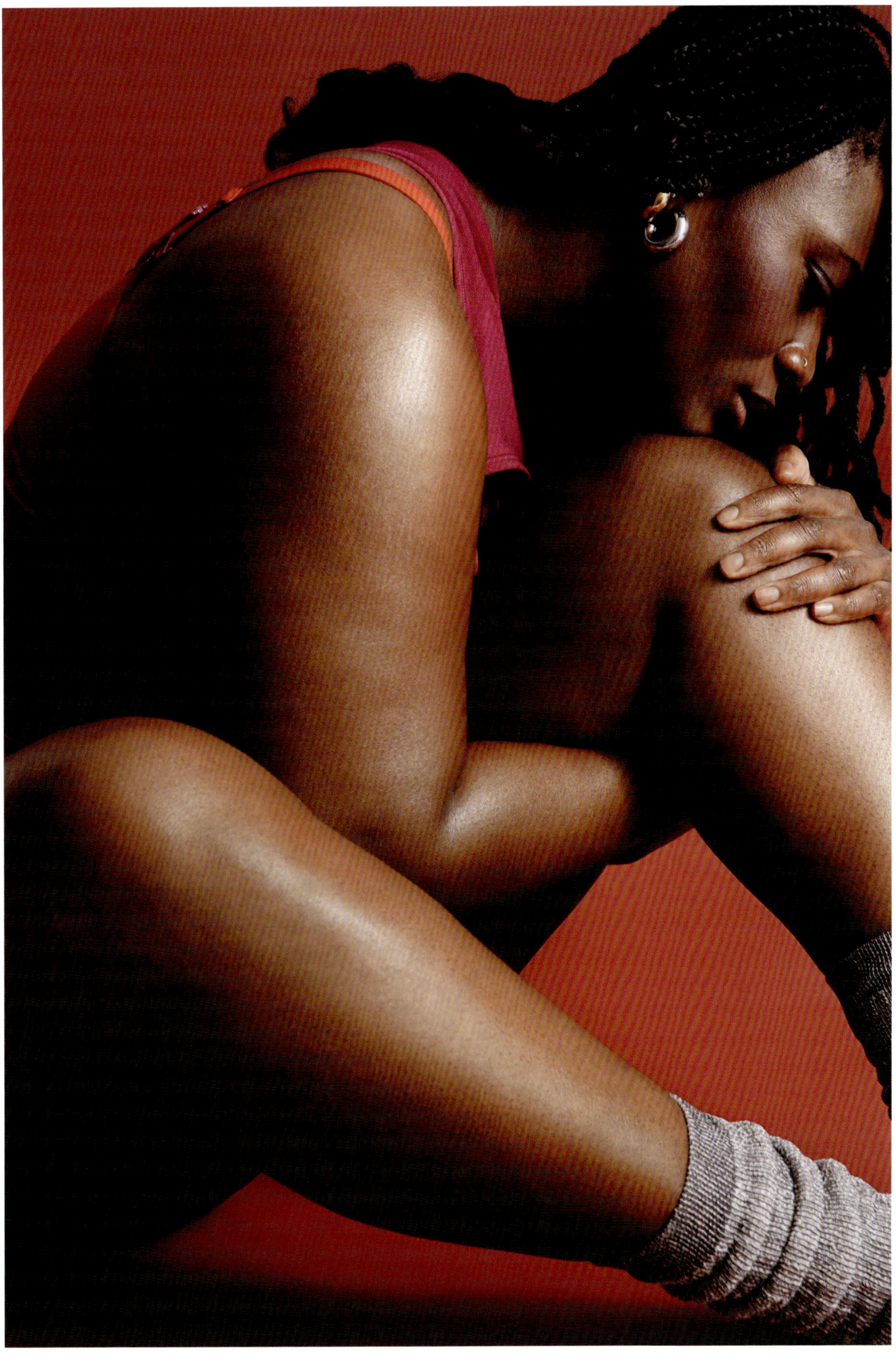

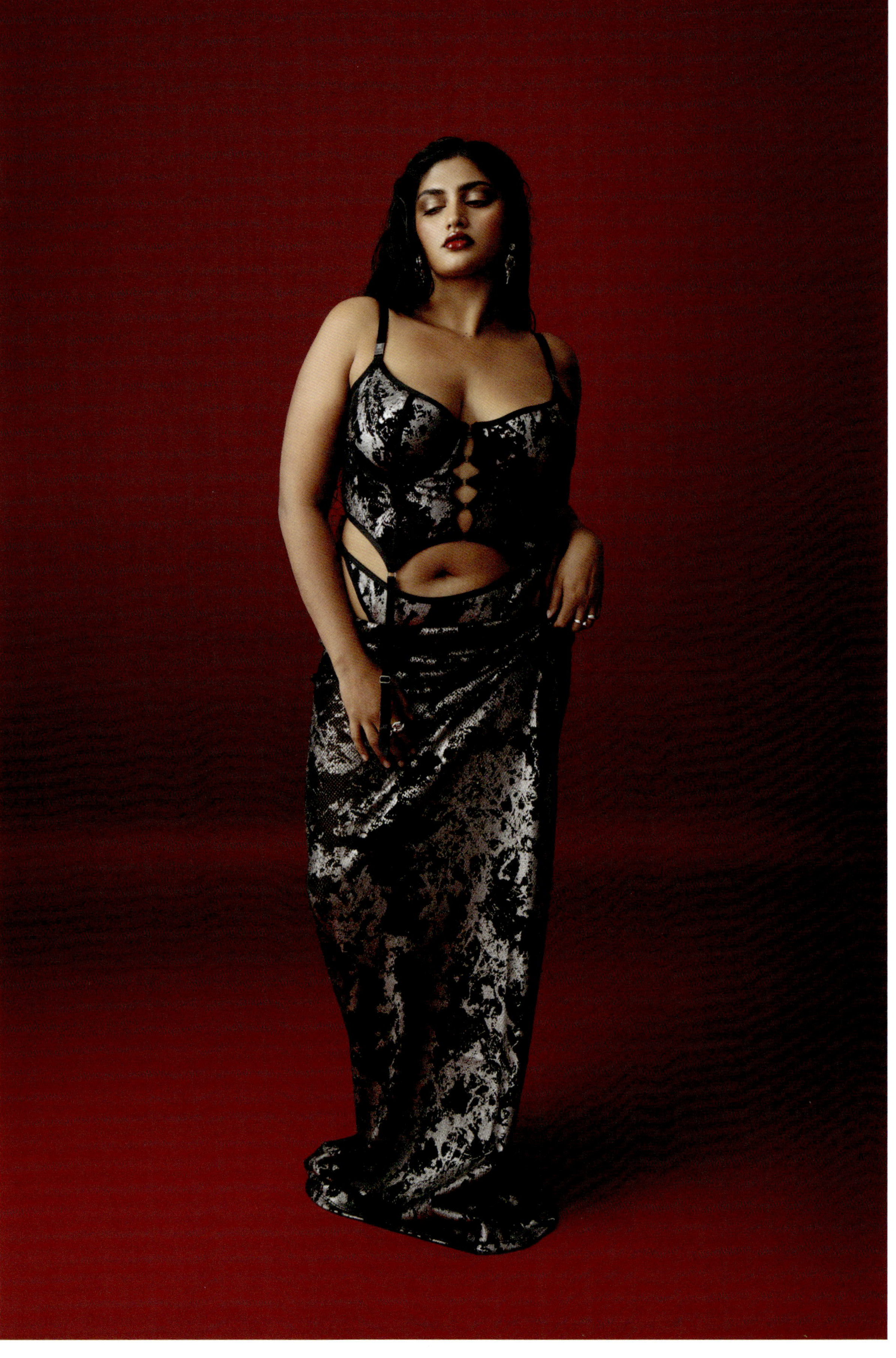

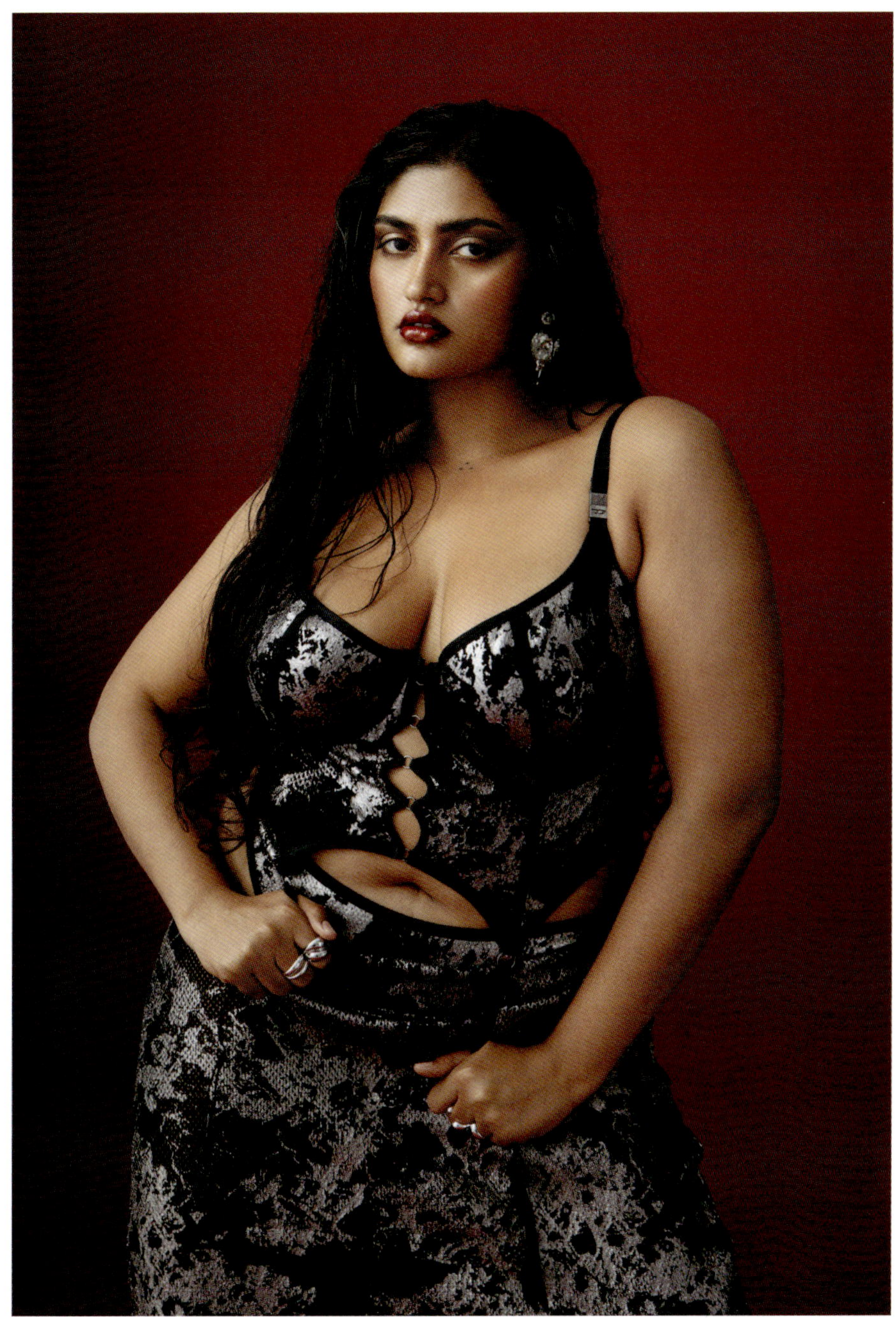

Shreya Navile wears Diesel x Savage x Fenty set.

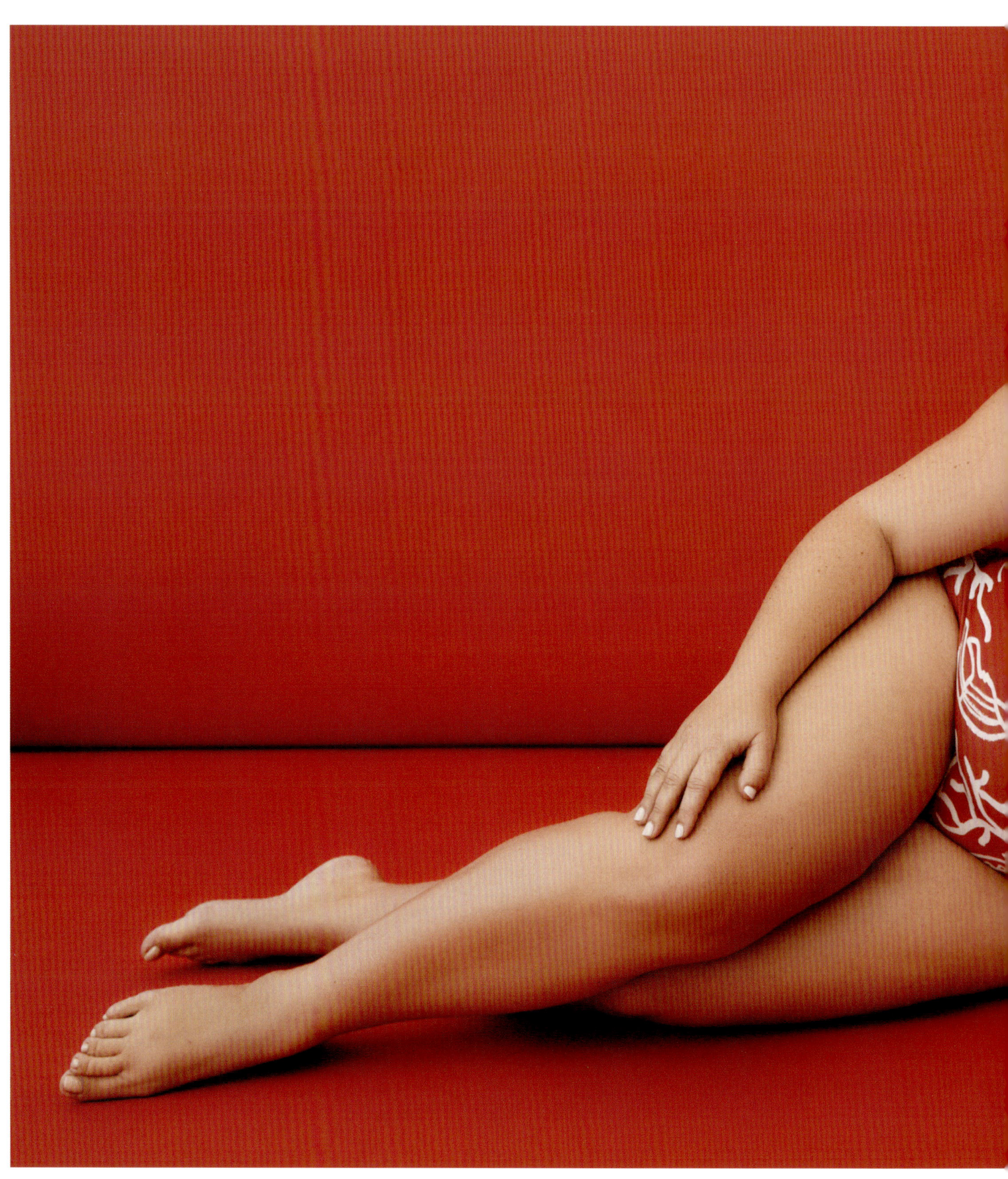

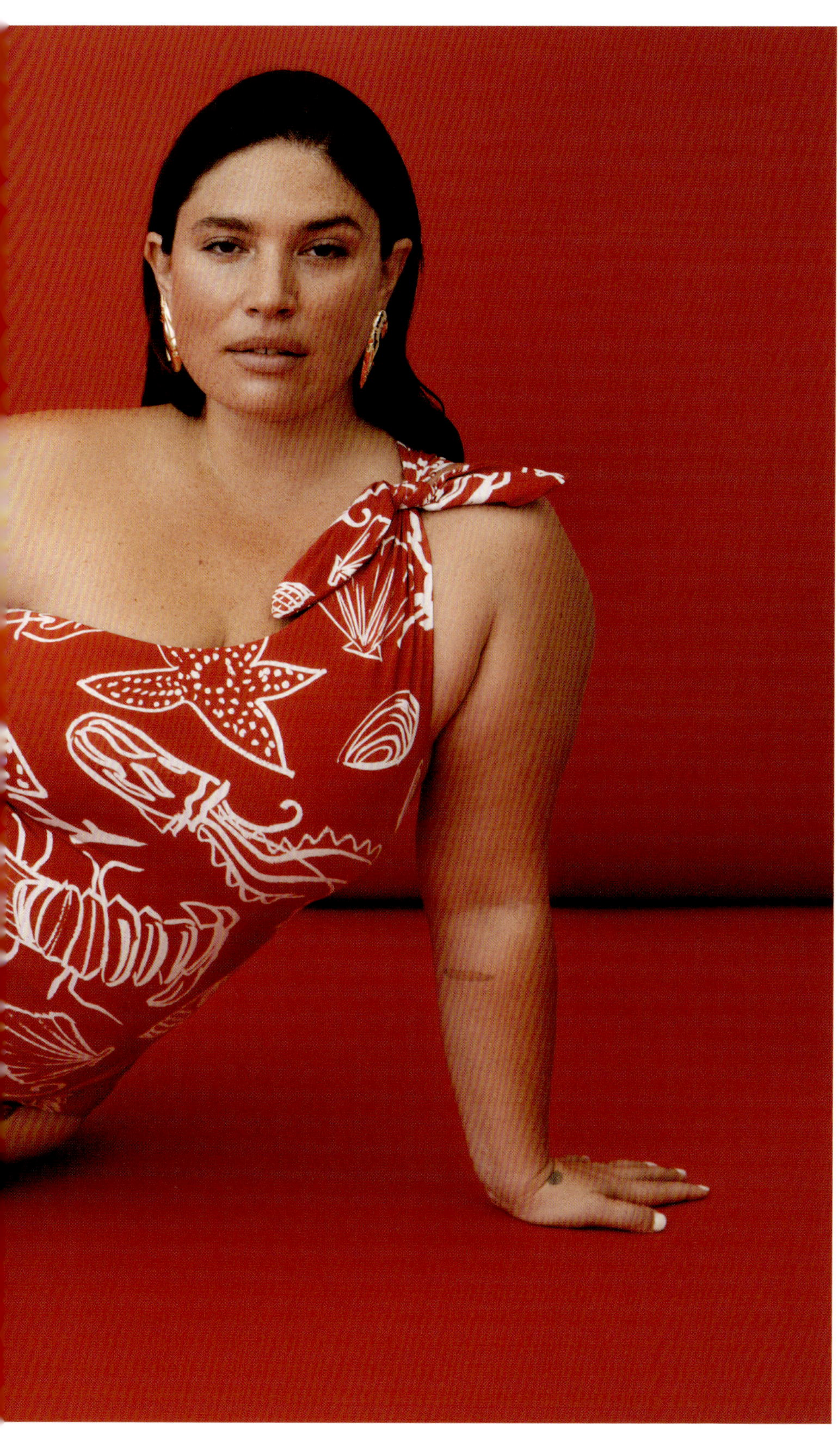

Clémentine Desseaux wears own swimwear.

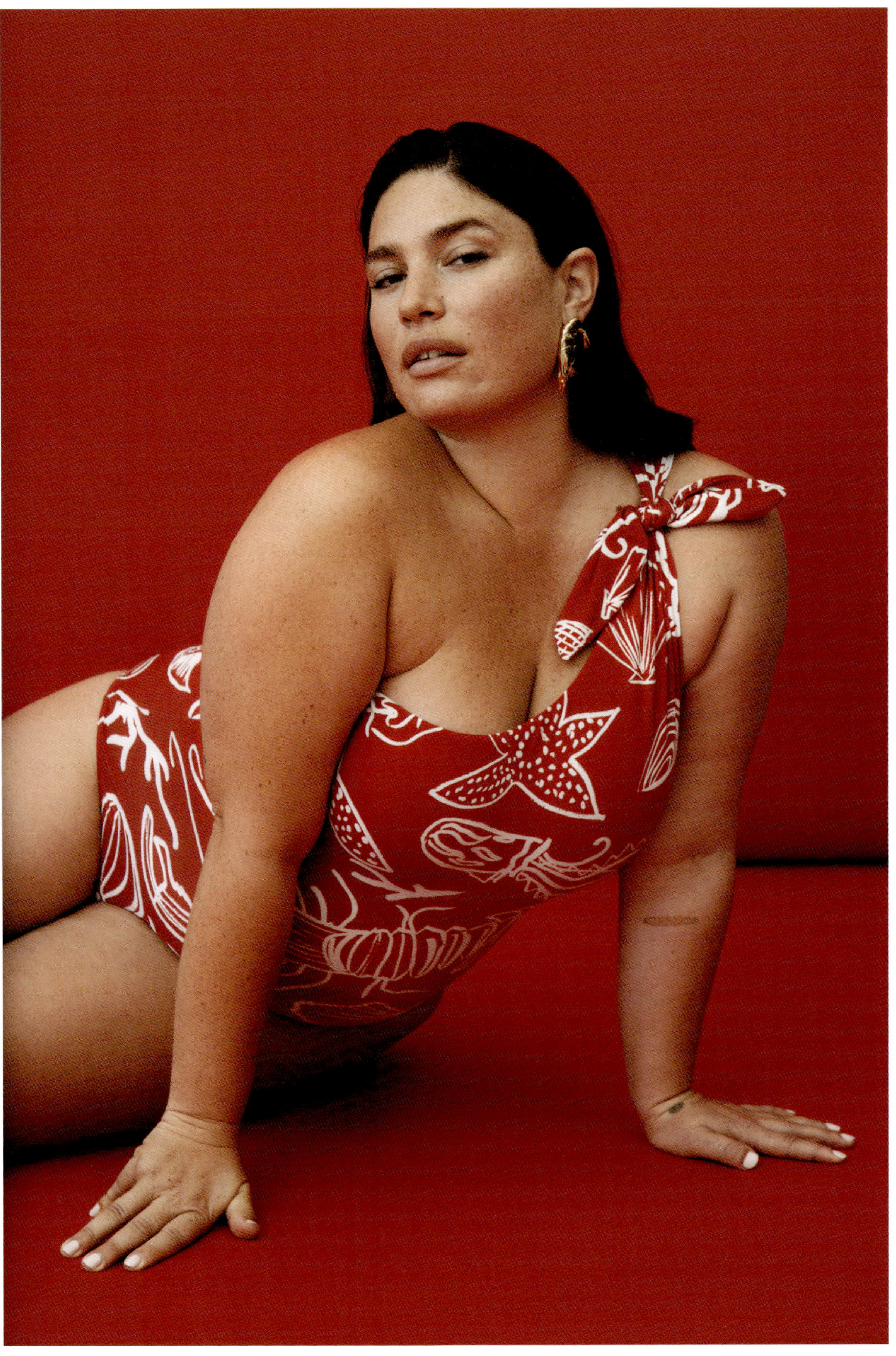

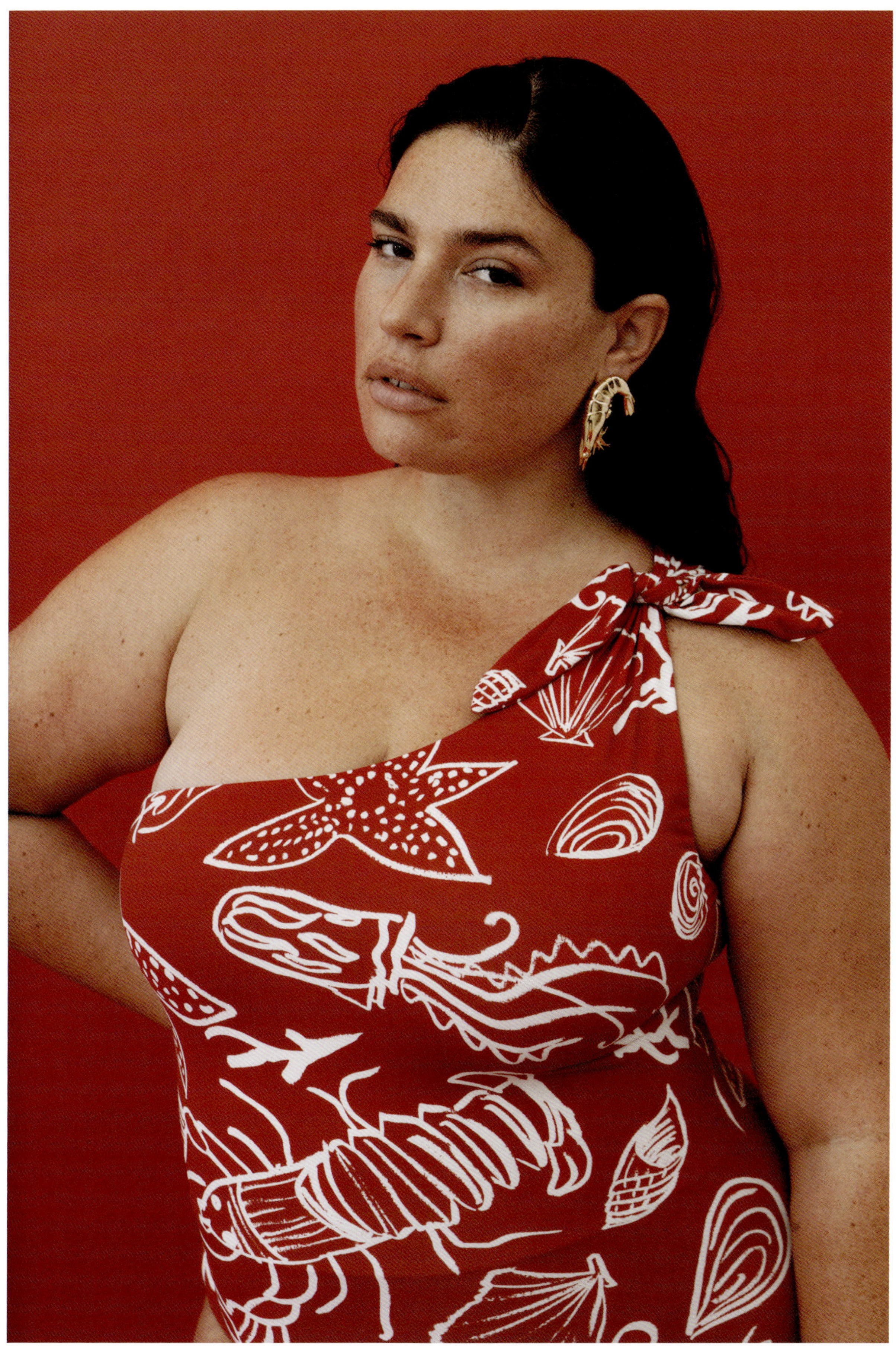

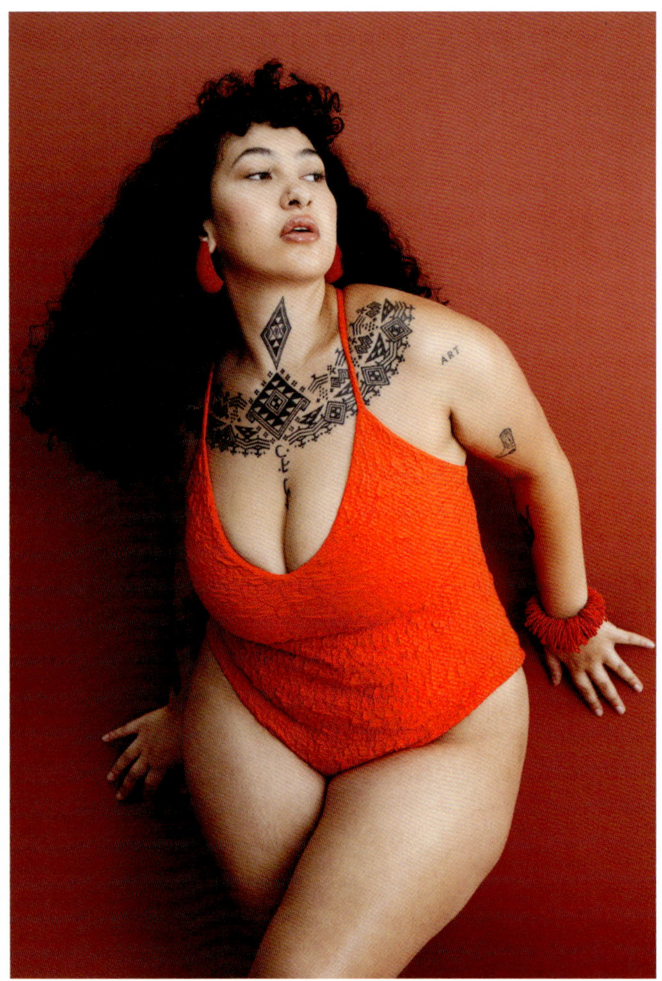

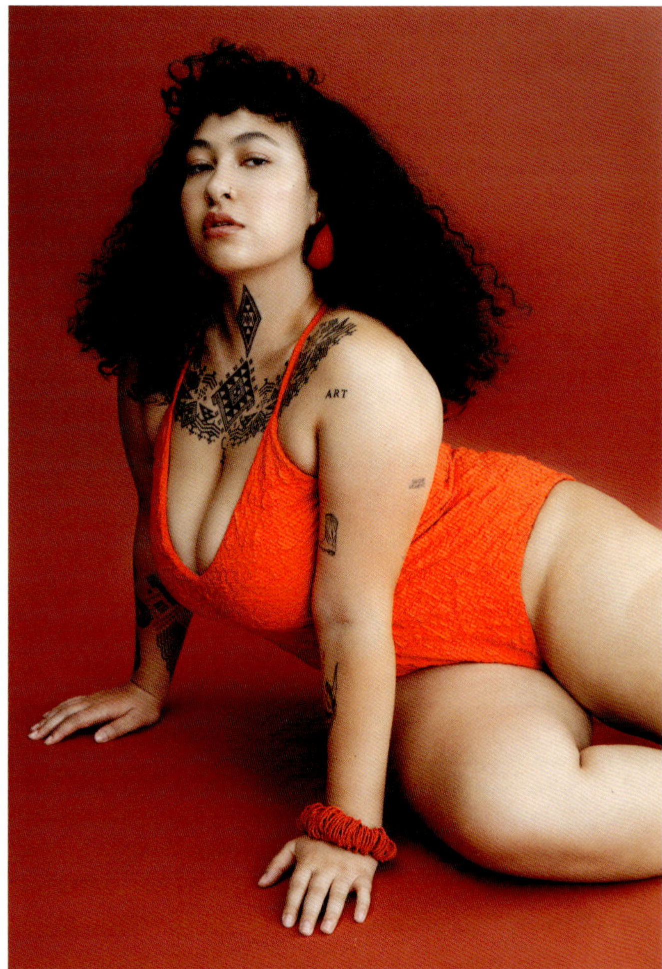

Ashley Emiko wears Mara Hoffman swimwear.

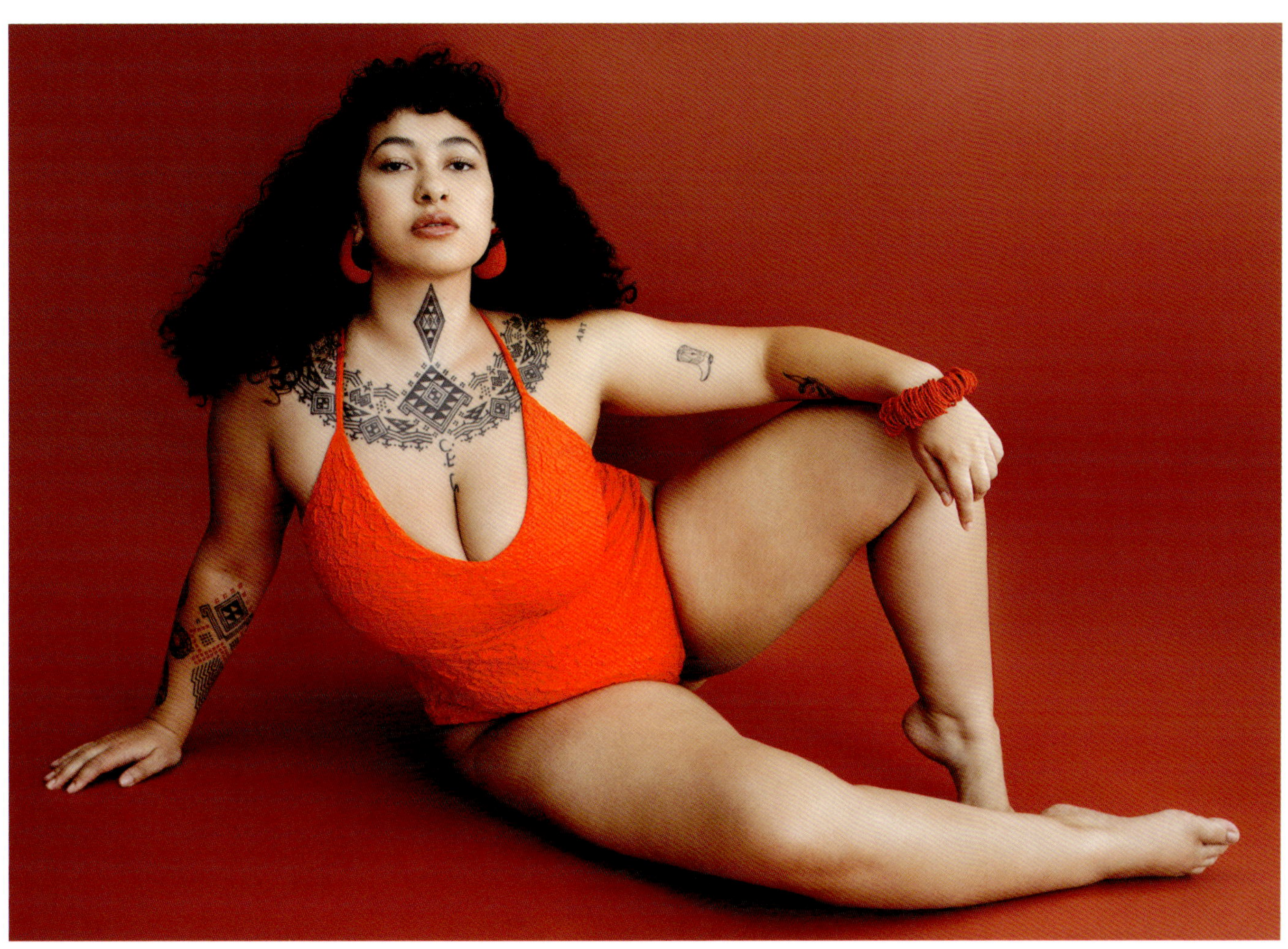

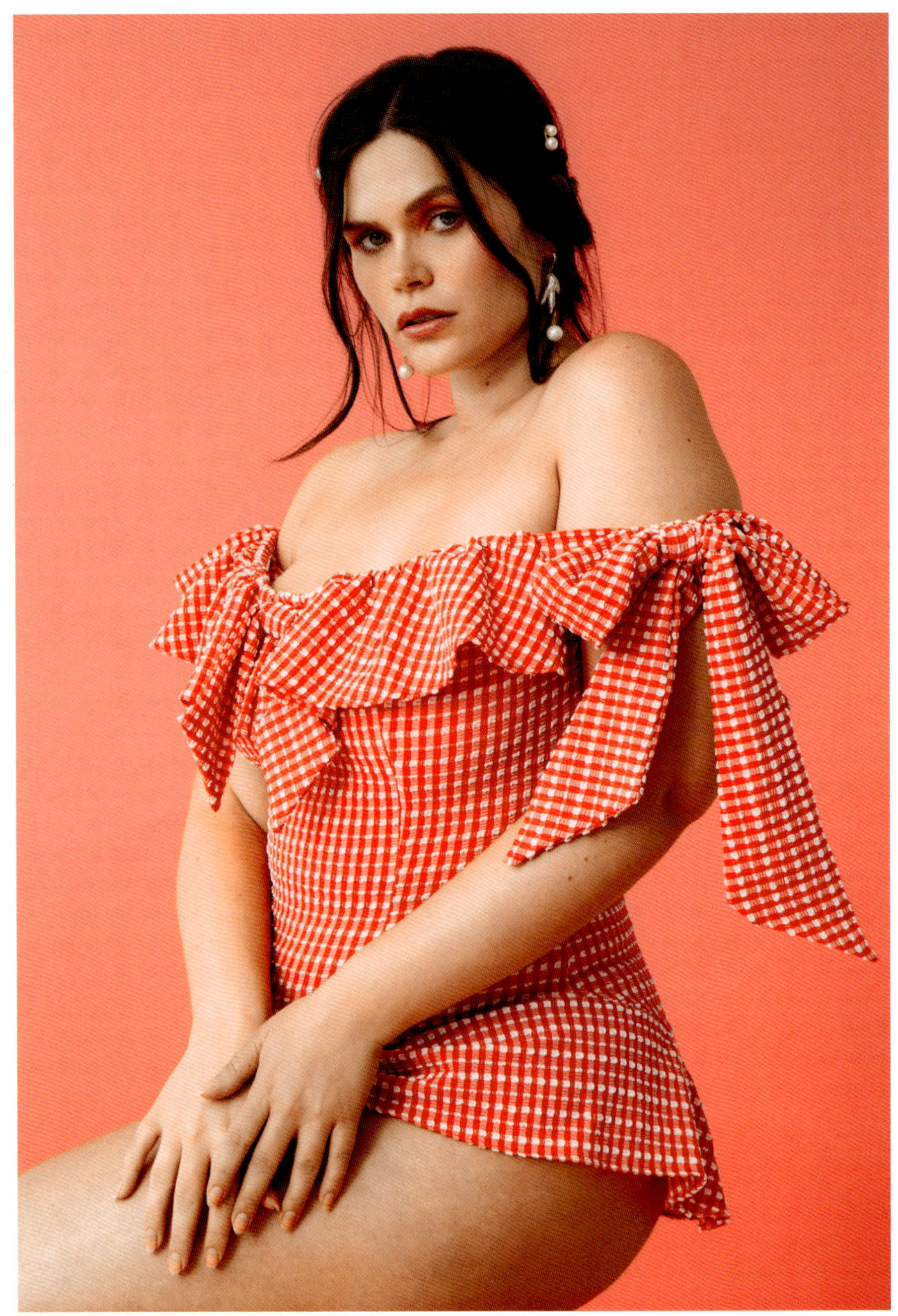

Chloe DeCleene wears Alpine Butterfly swimwear.

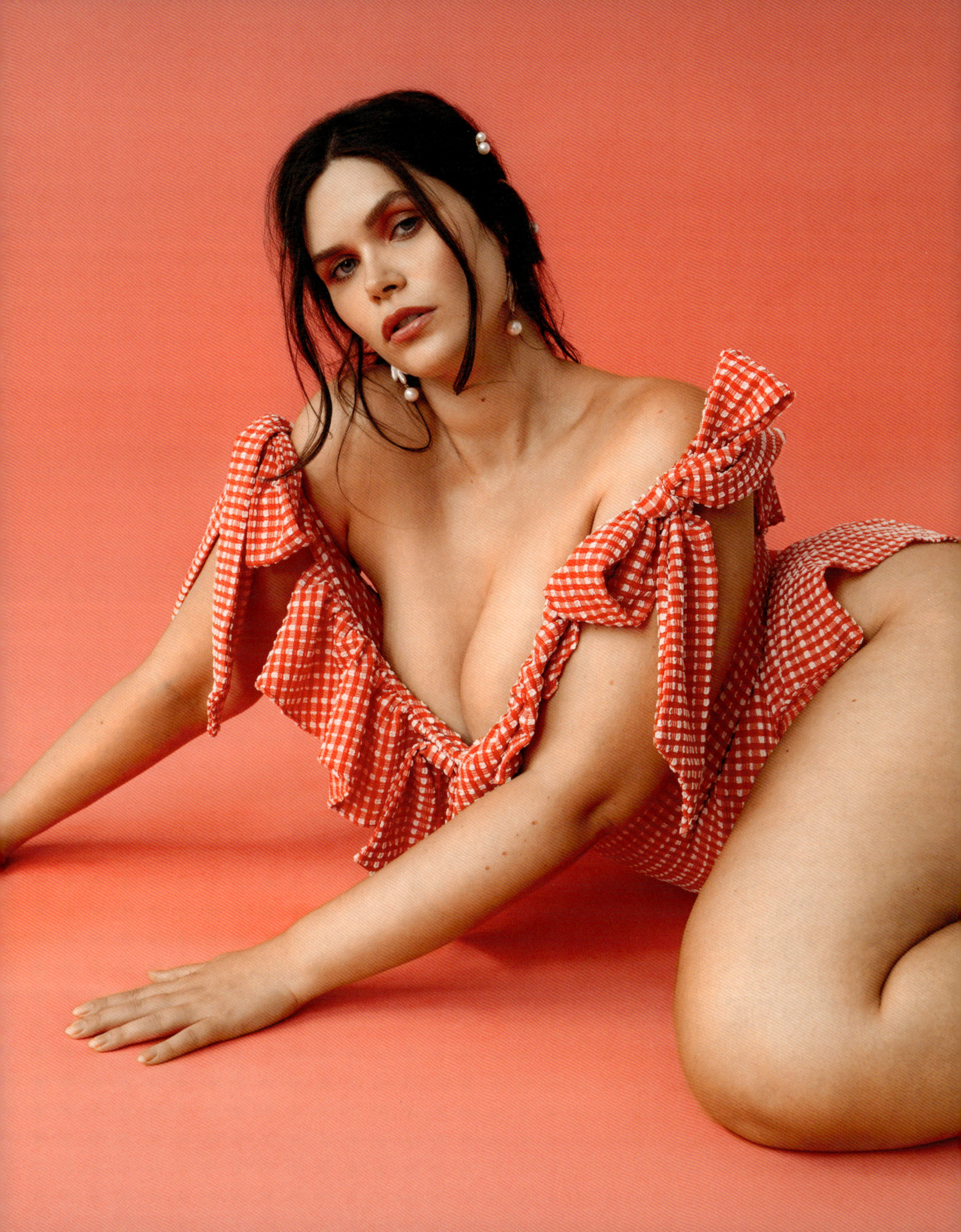

Madison Simone wears Shop Berriez top.

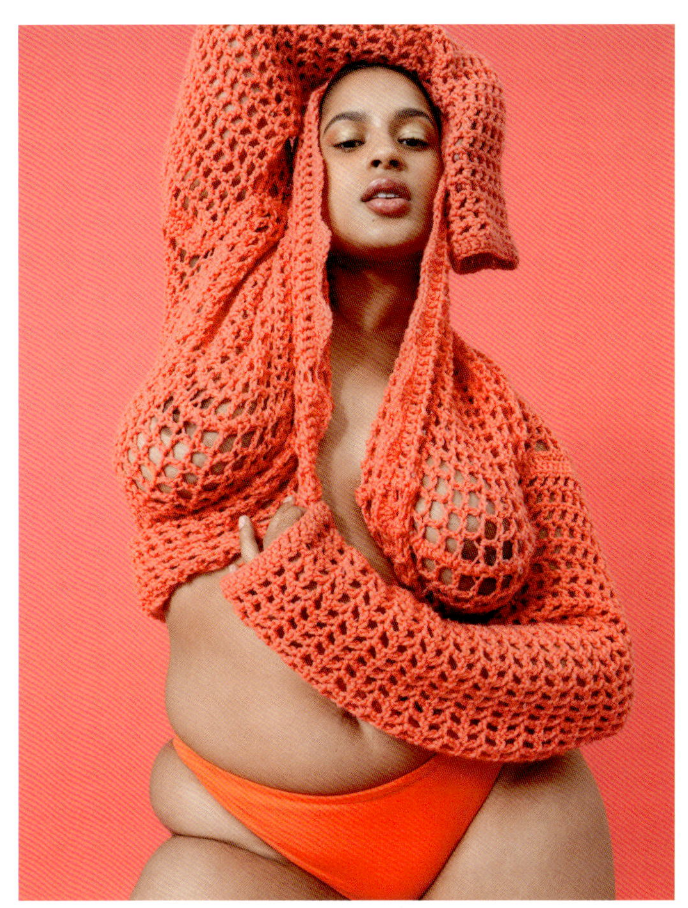
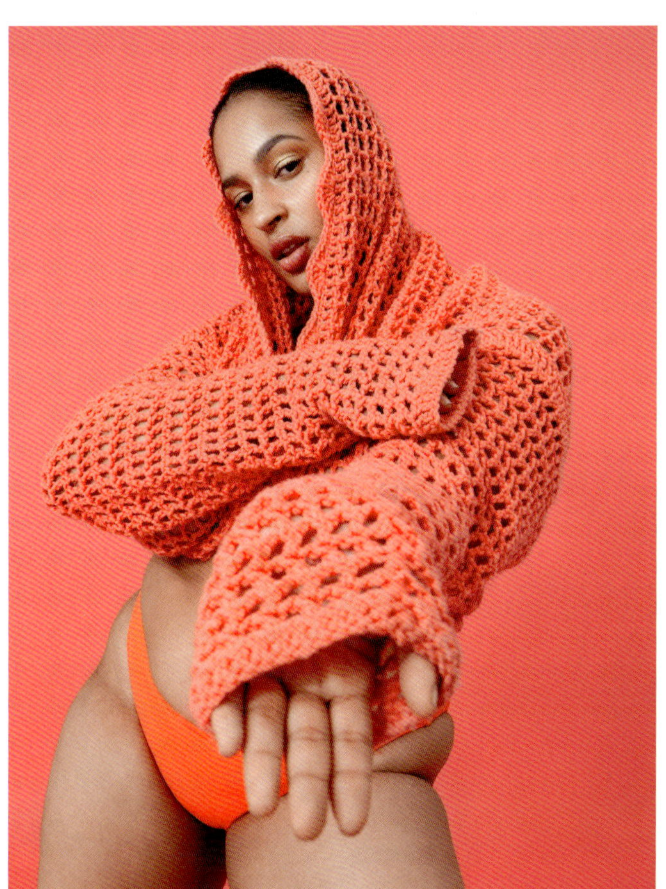
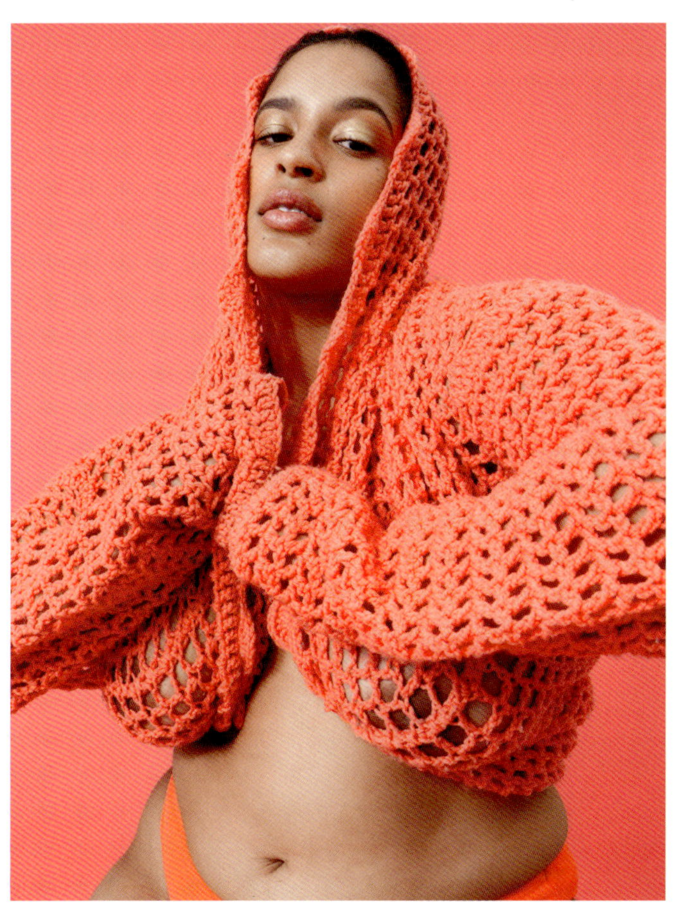
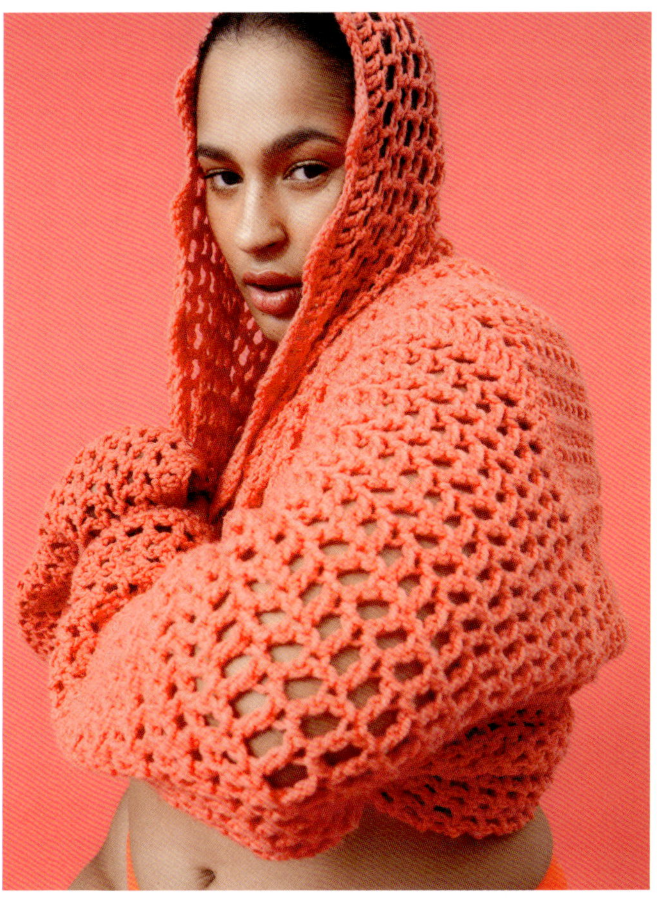

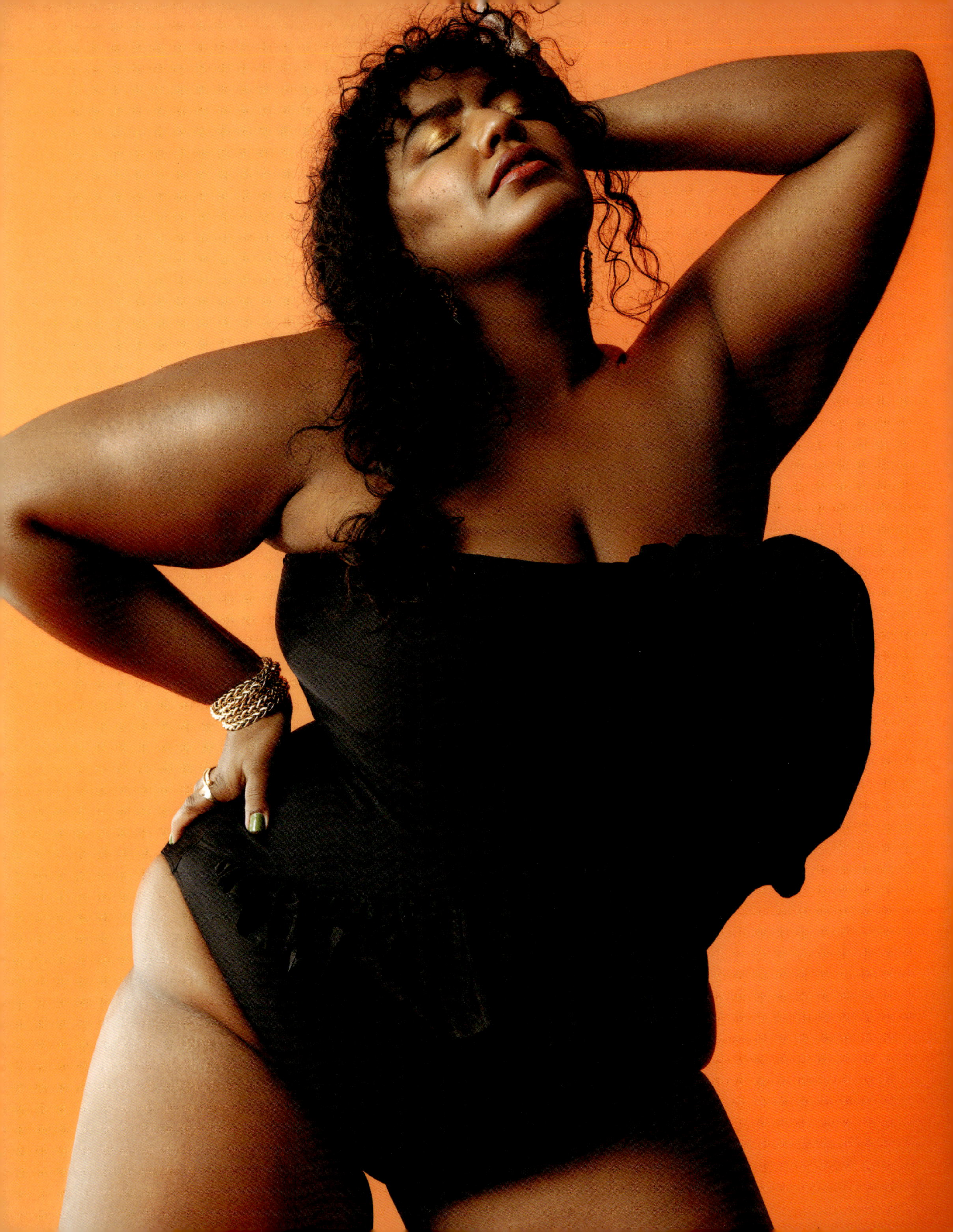

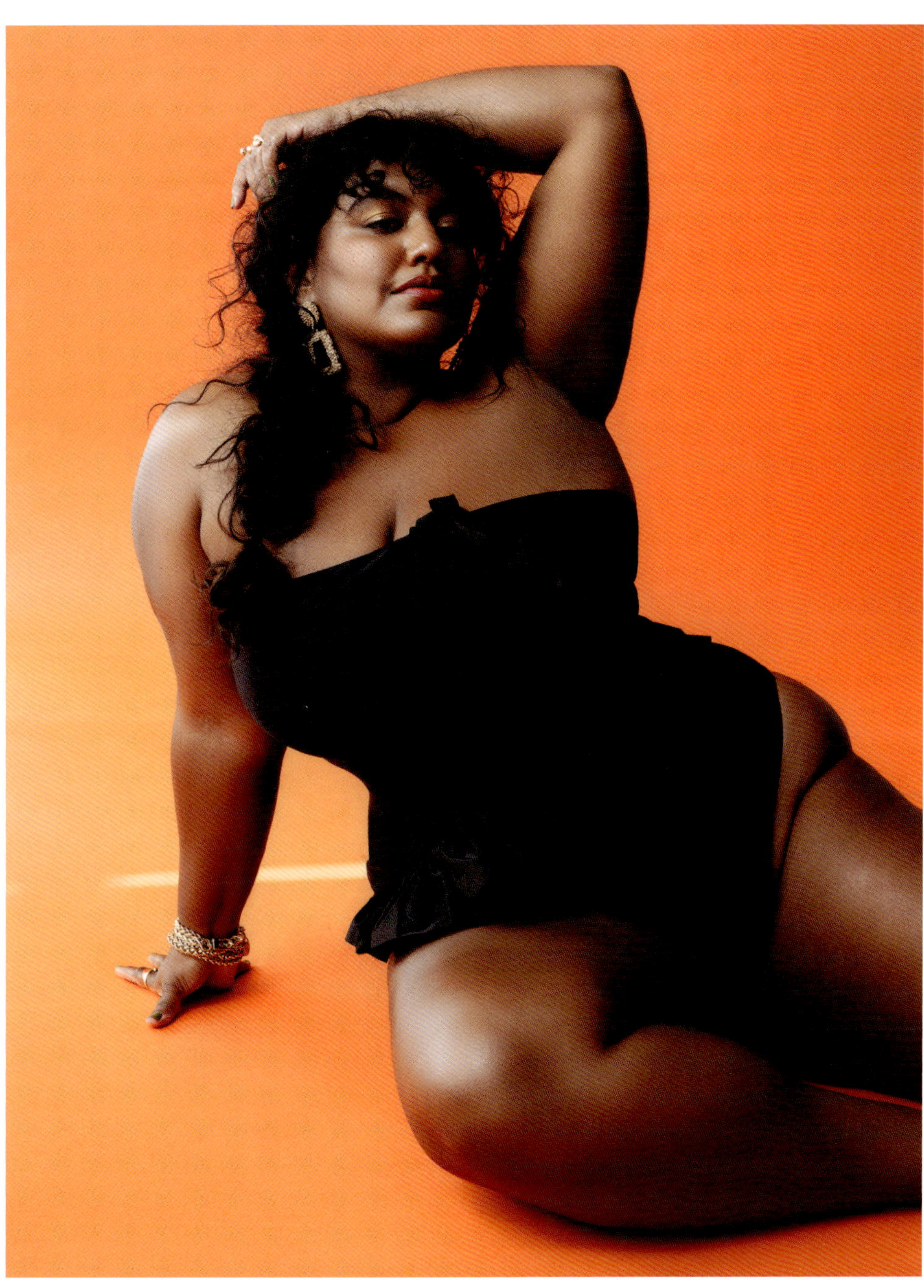

Veronica Campos wears Tanya Taylor swimwear.

Overleaf: Jordan Underwood wears Softcore swimwear.

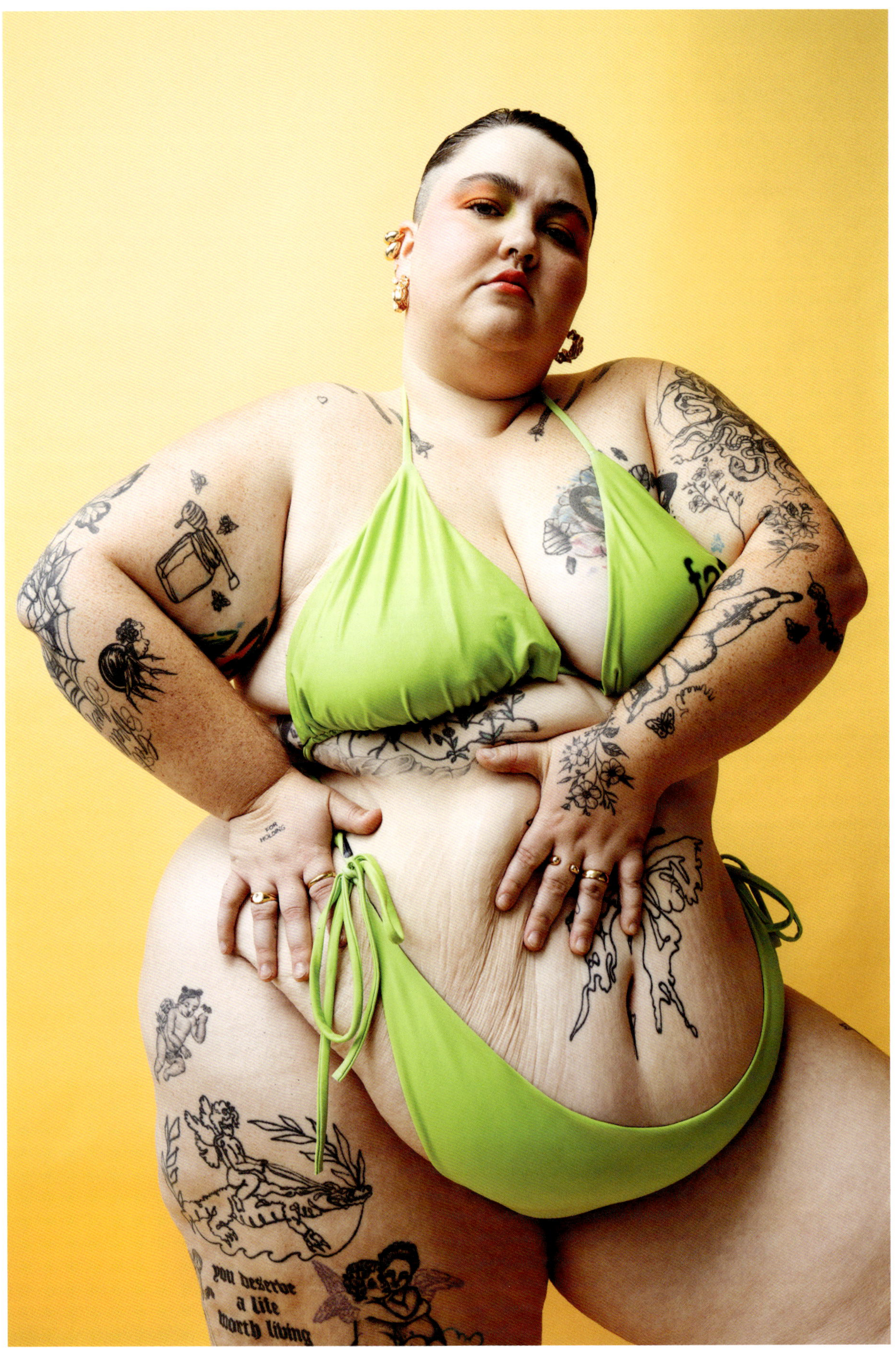
FOR HOLDING
you deserve a life worth living

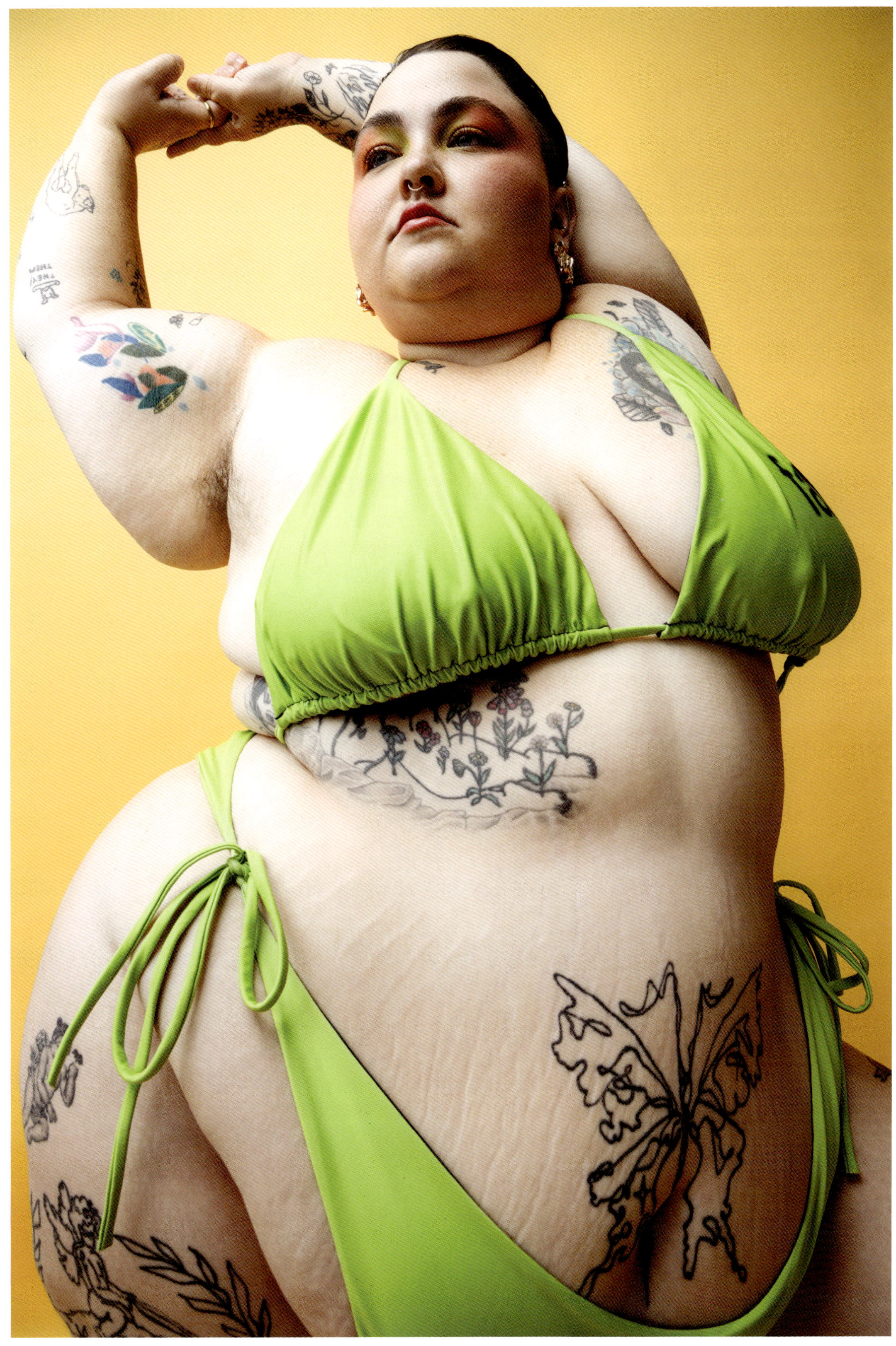

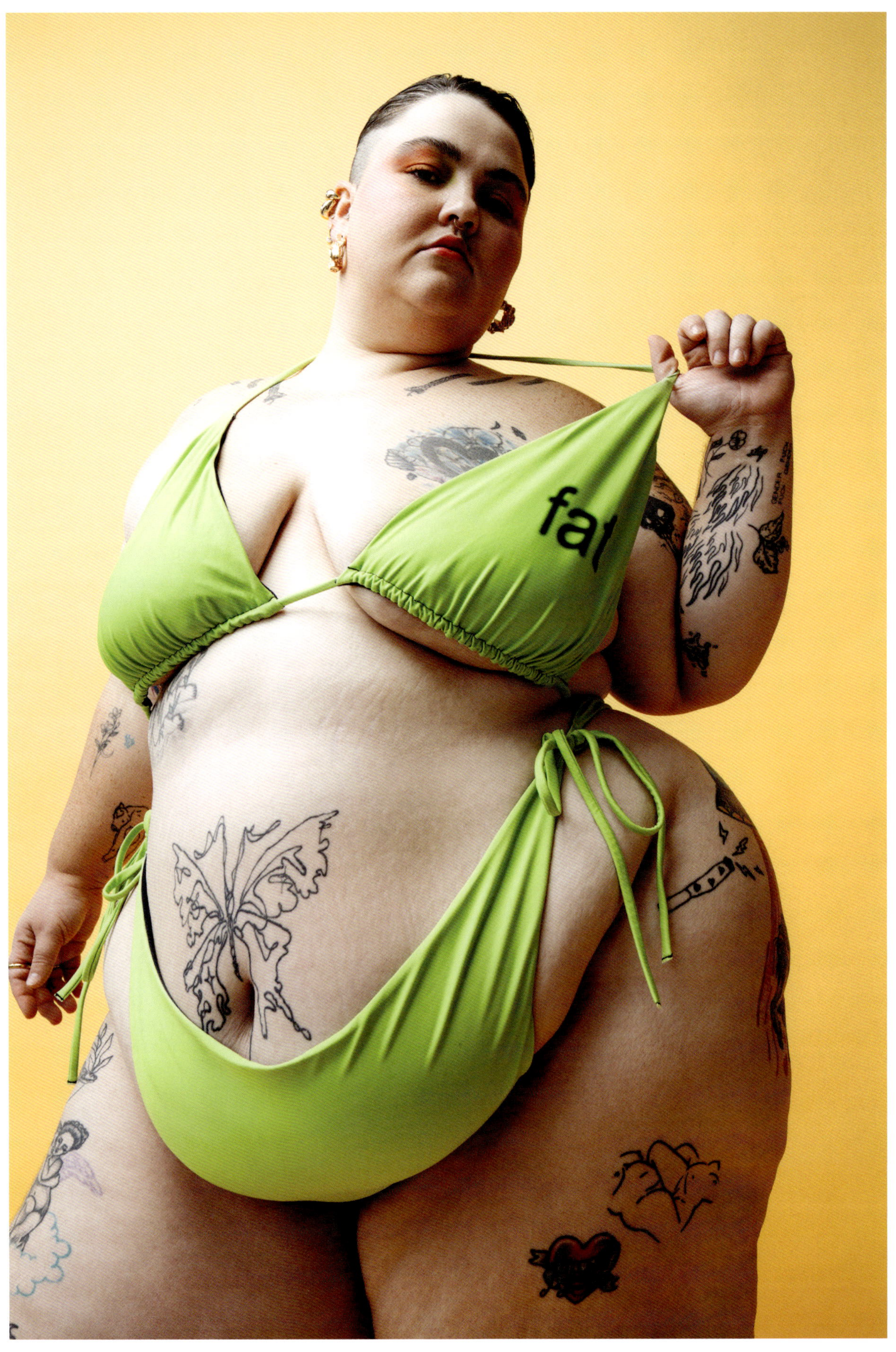
fat

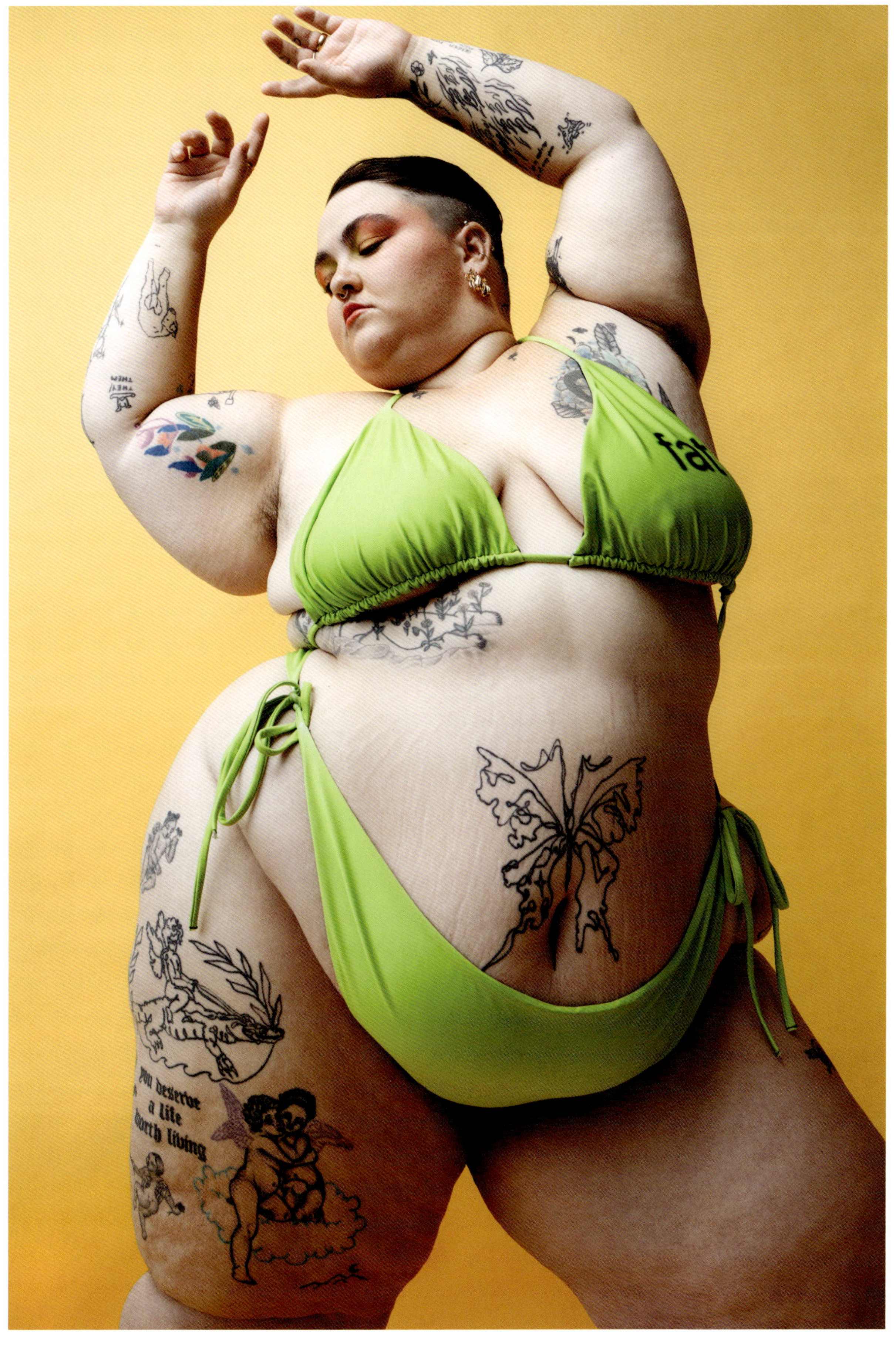
fat
you deserve
a life
worth living

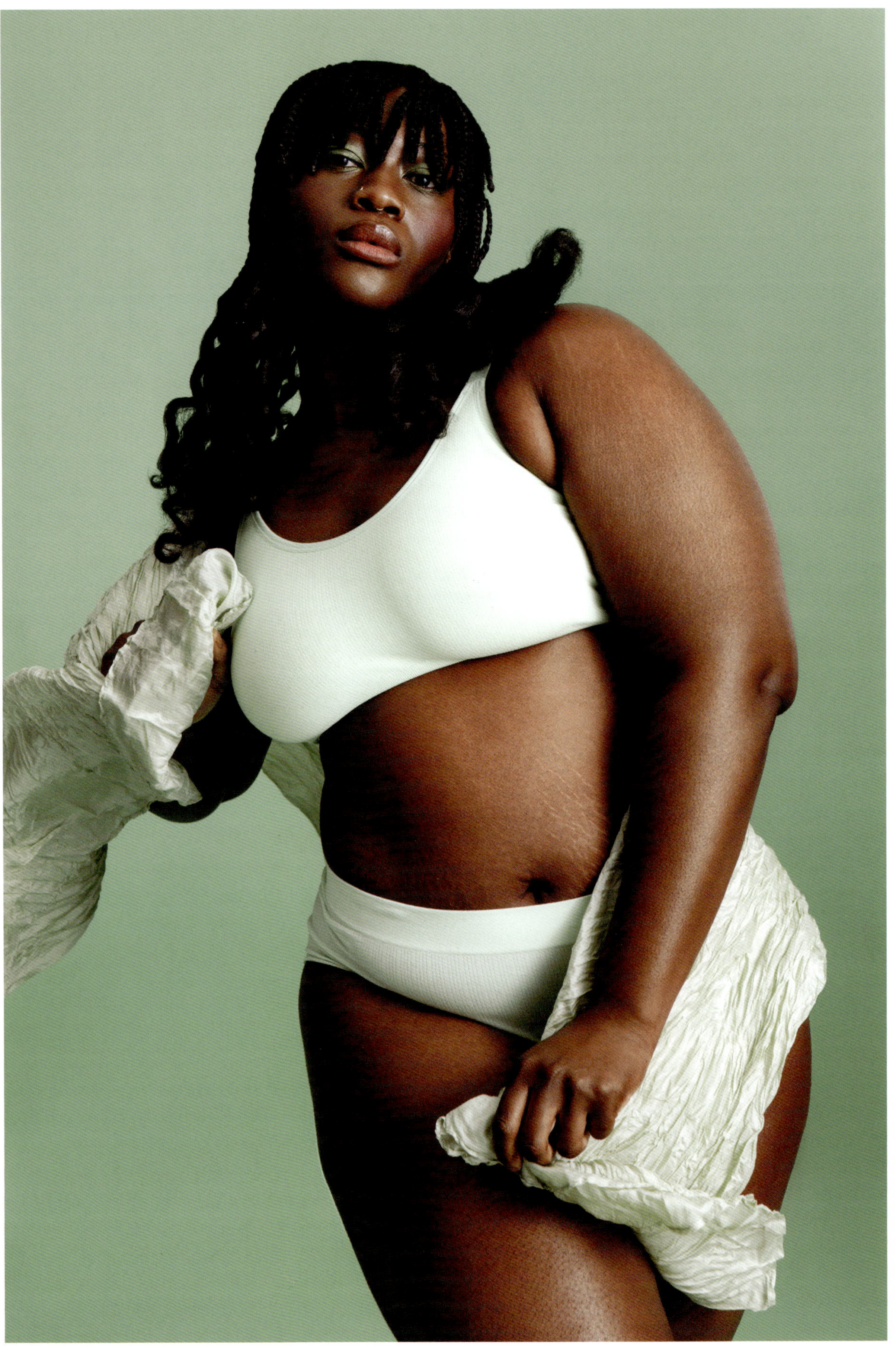

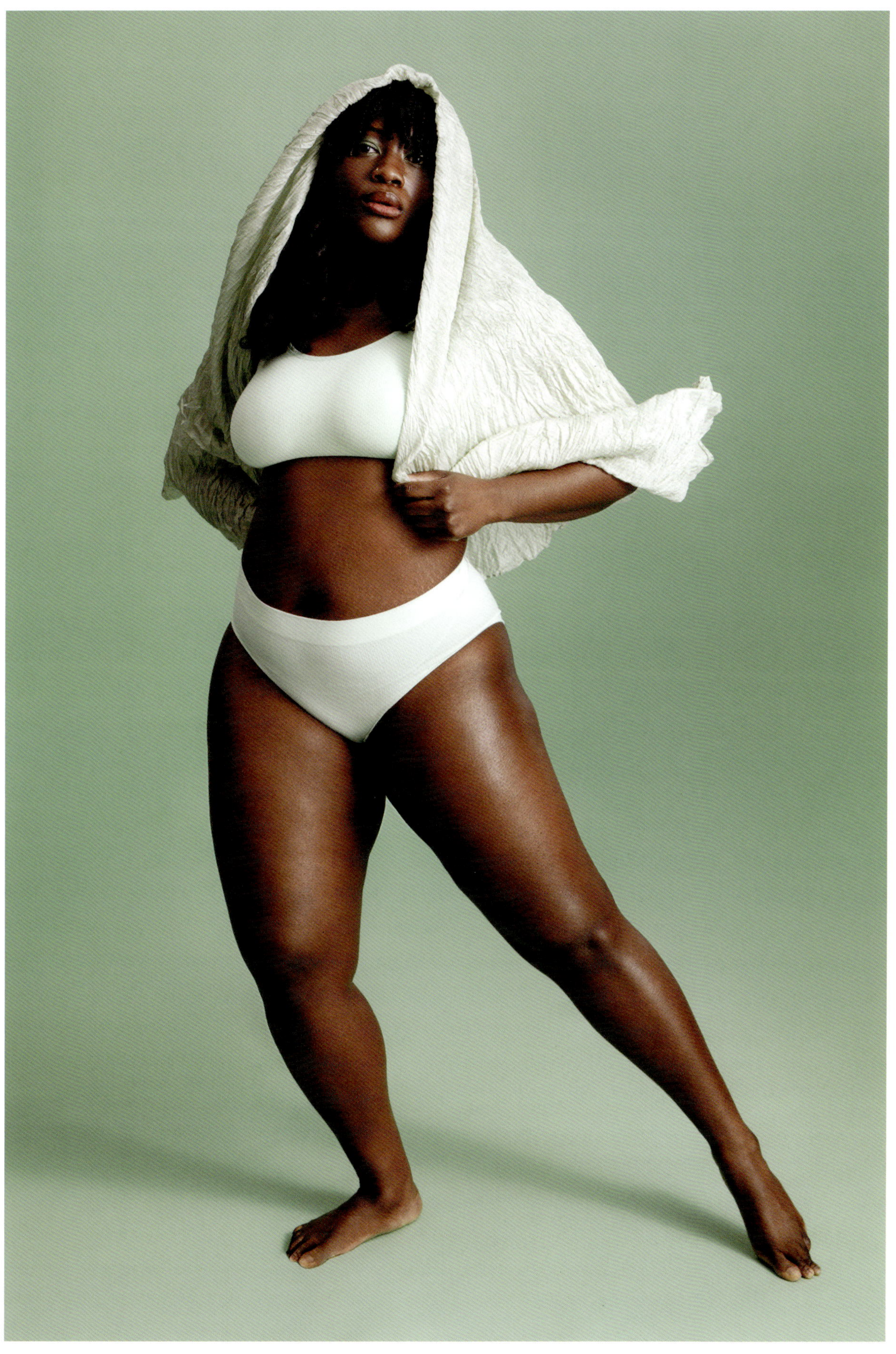

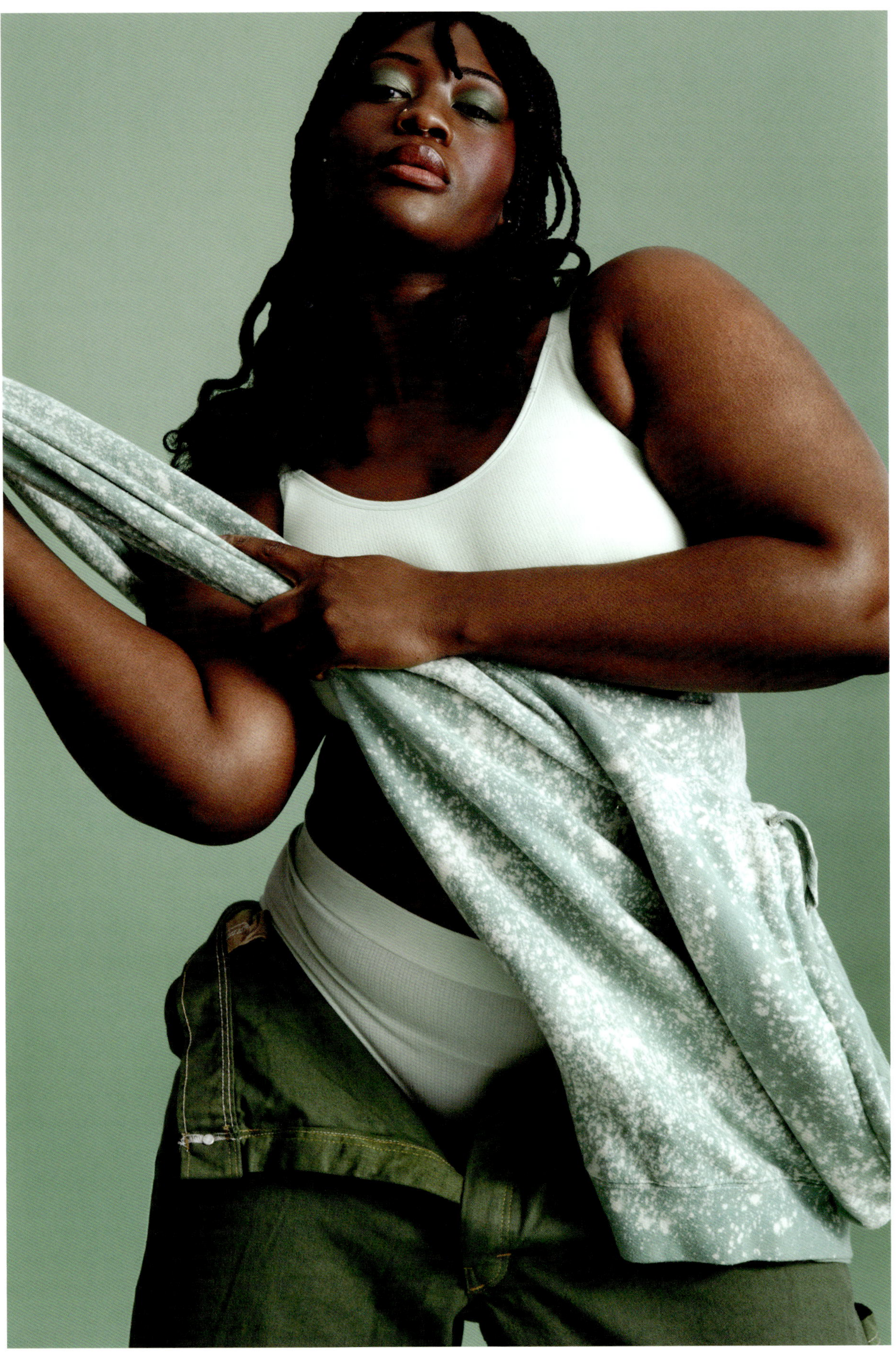

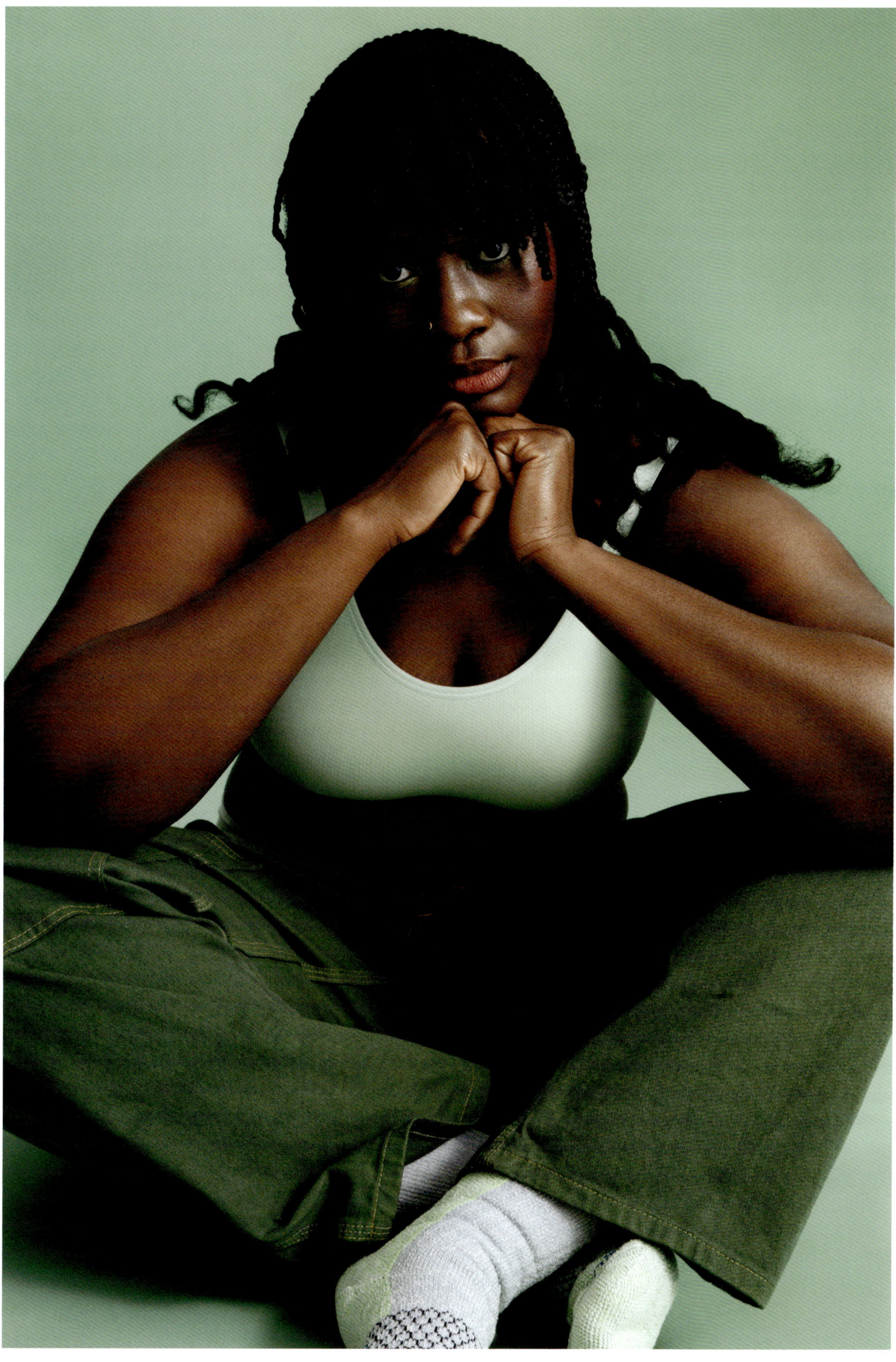

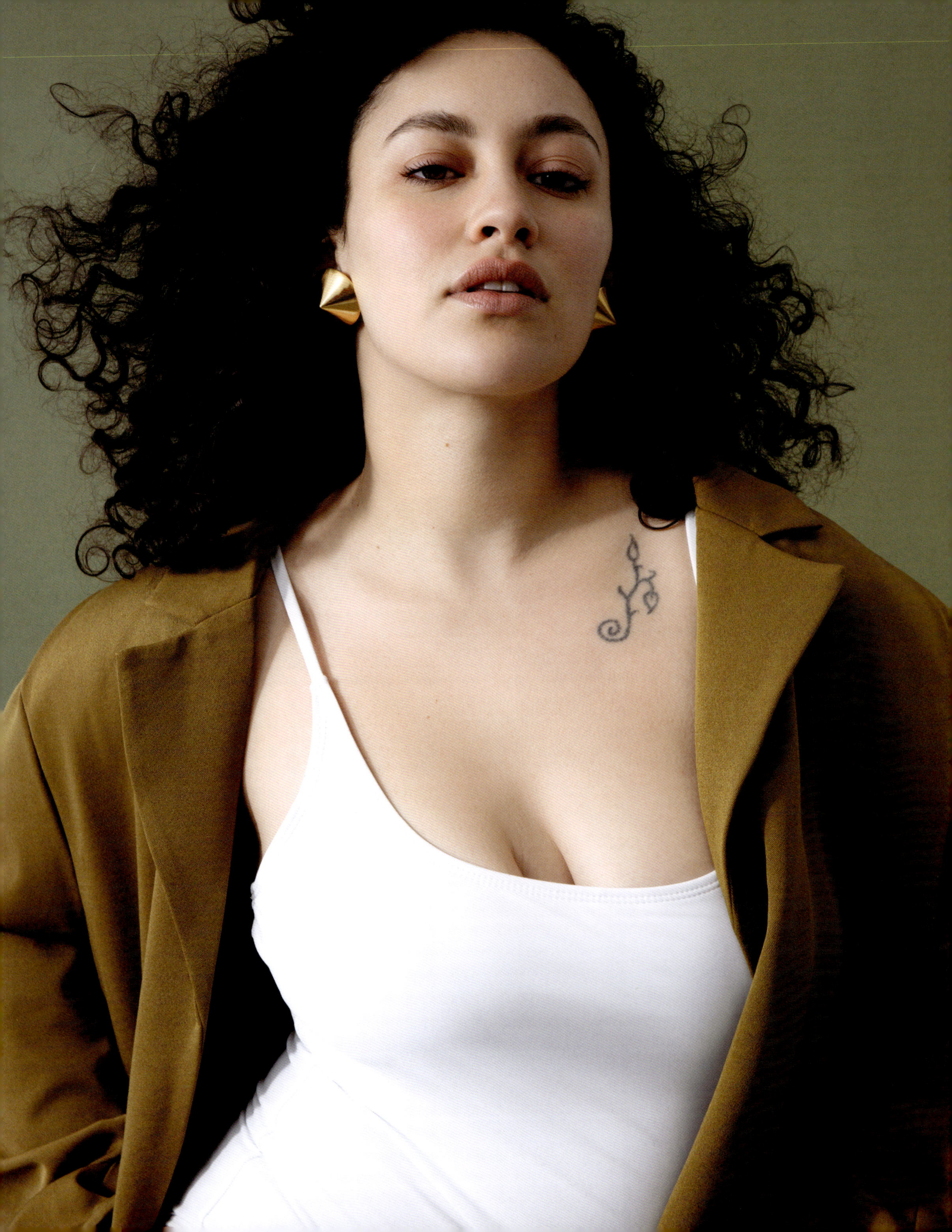

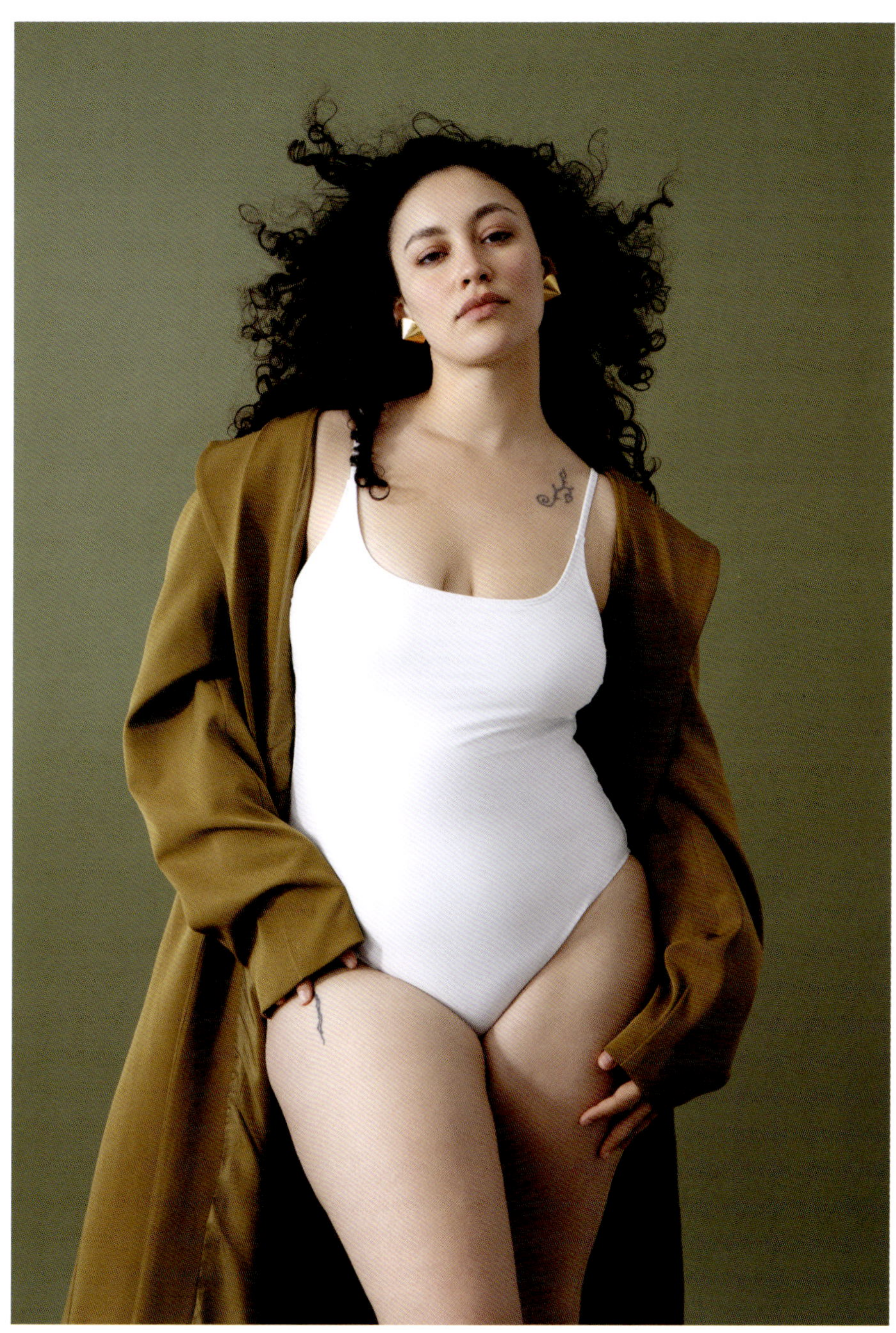

Pages 280–283: Oskar Sinclair wears Bombas set; vintage jeans and skirt repurposed into scarf from Shop Berriez.

Cearah Peck wears outfit from Kelly Augustine's closet.

Ashley Emiko wears Tanya Taylor swimwear.

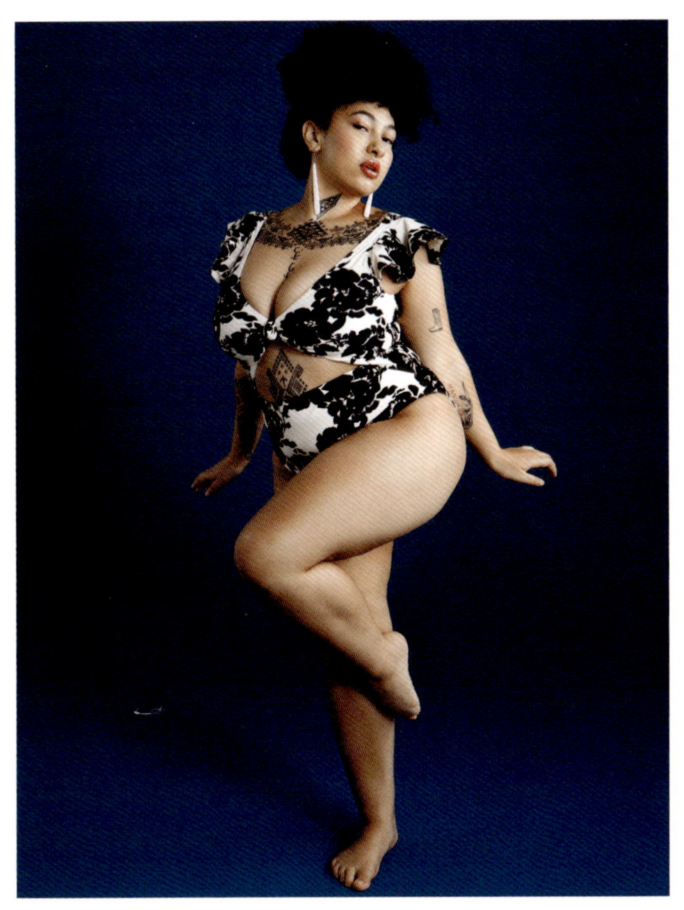

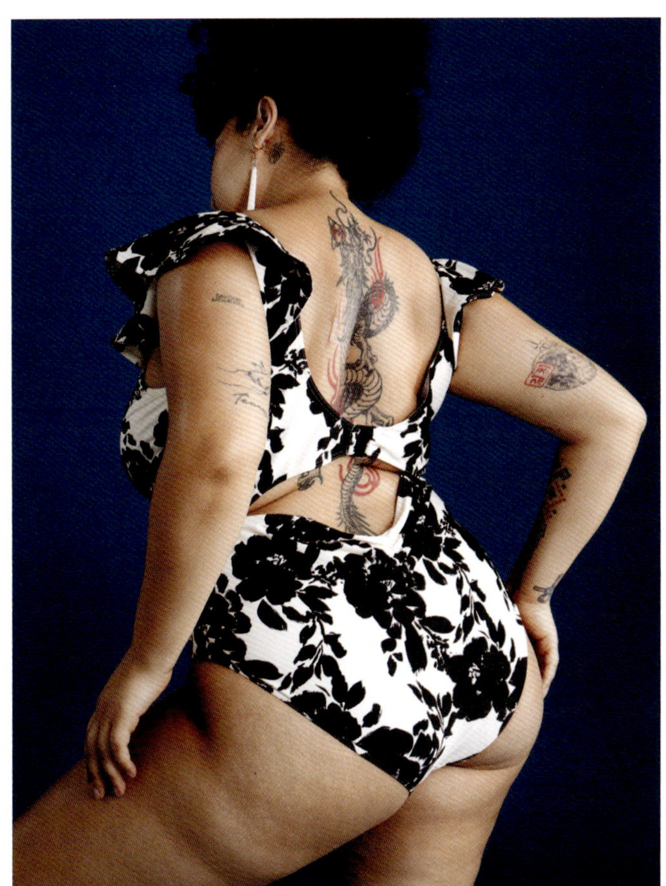

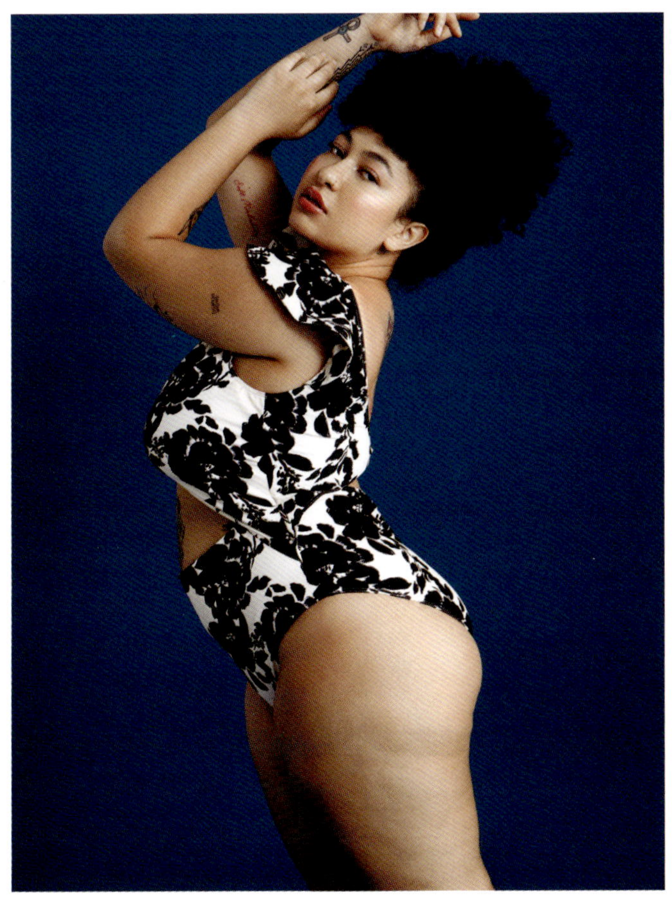

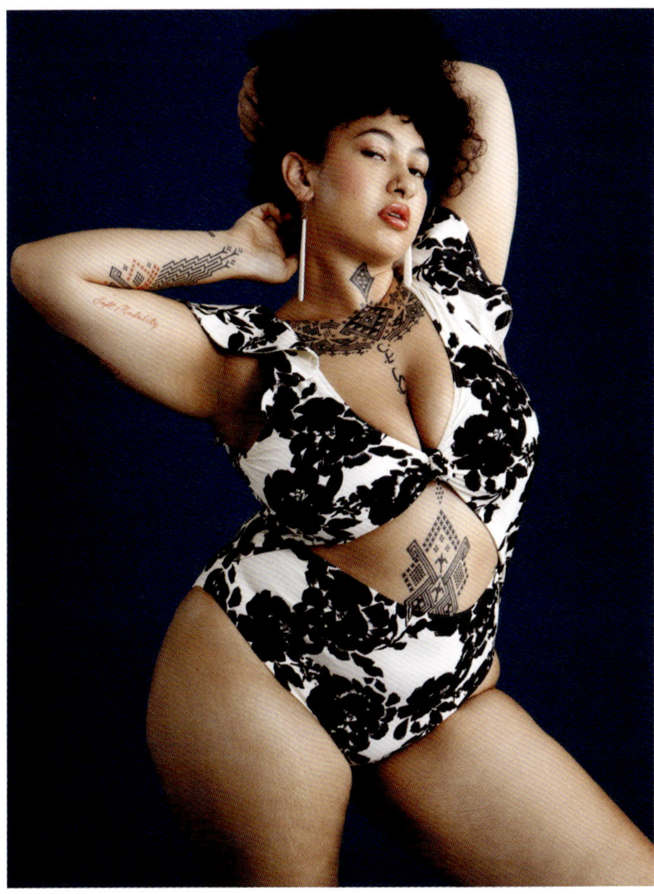

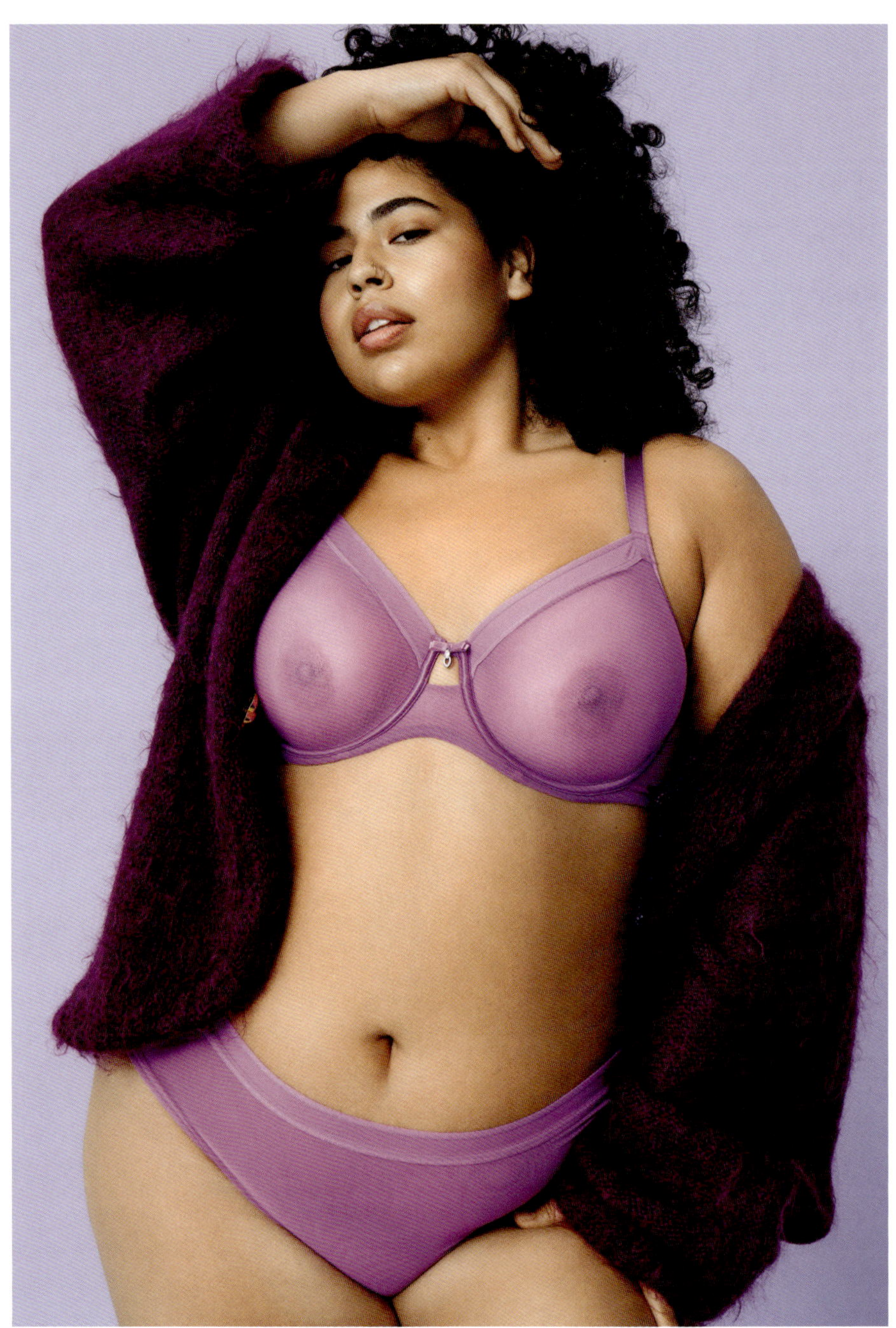

Naomi La Crespa wears Curvy Couture;
vintage cardigan from Shop Berriez.

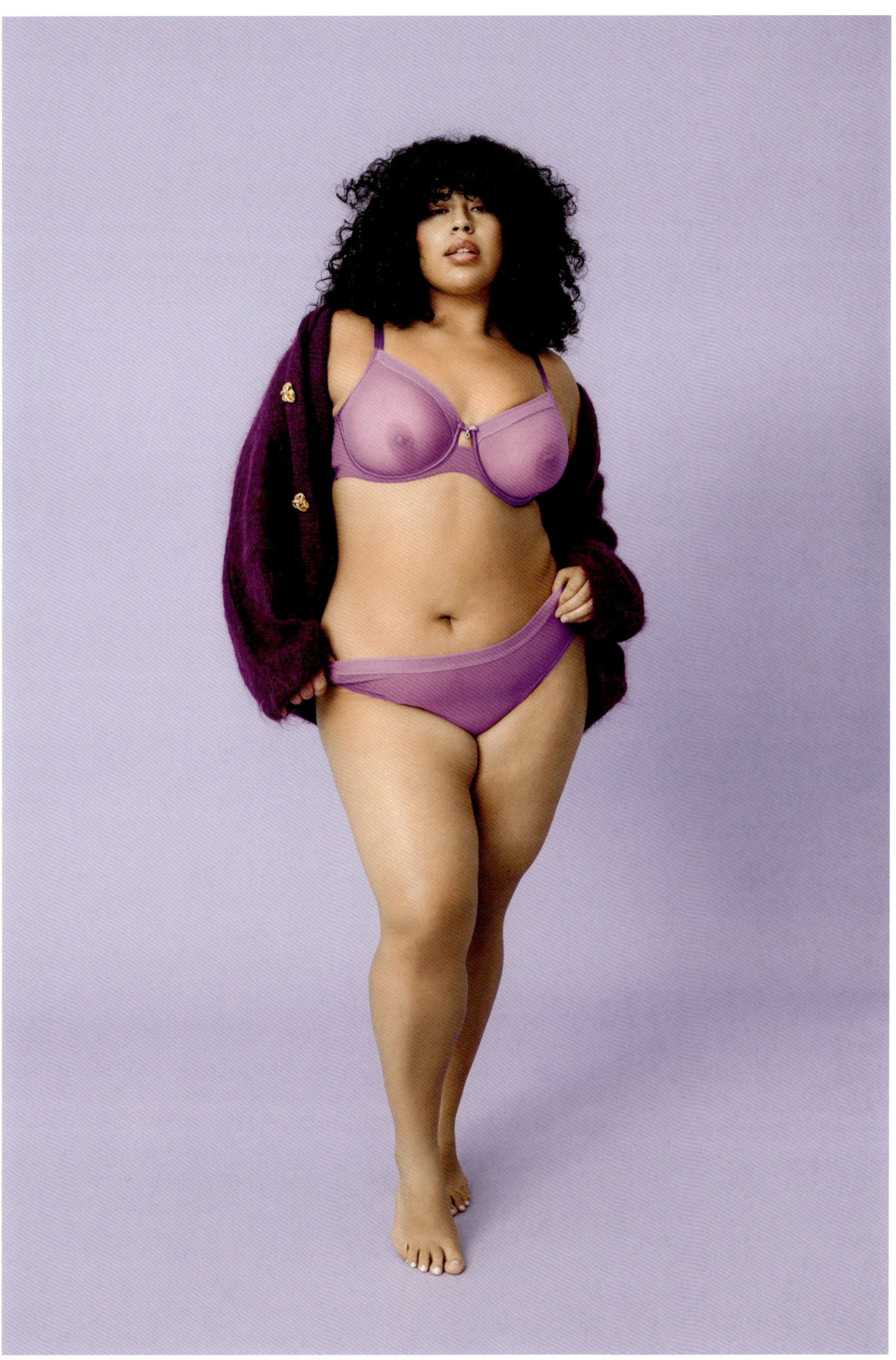

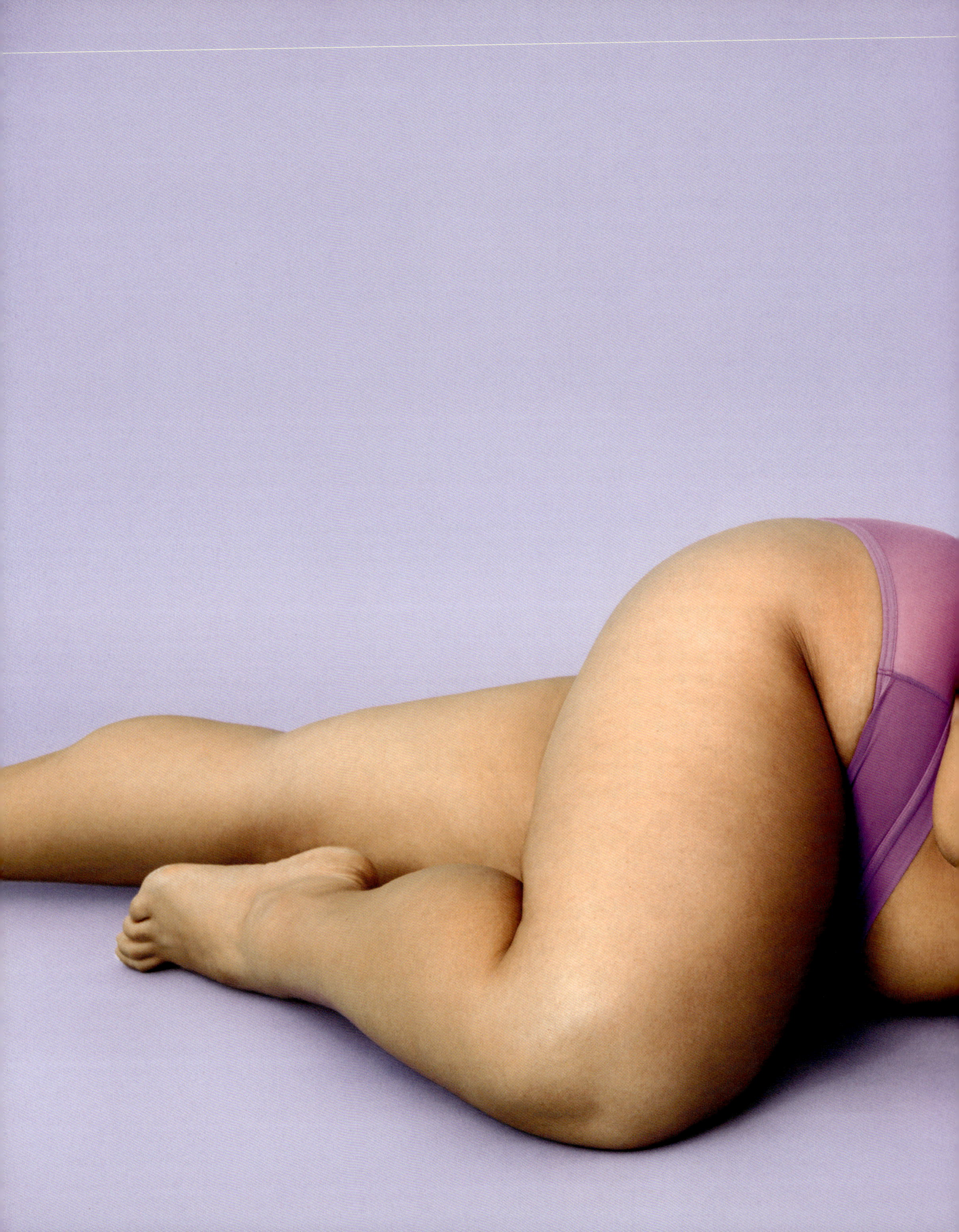

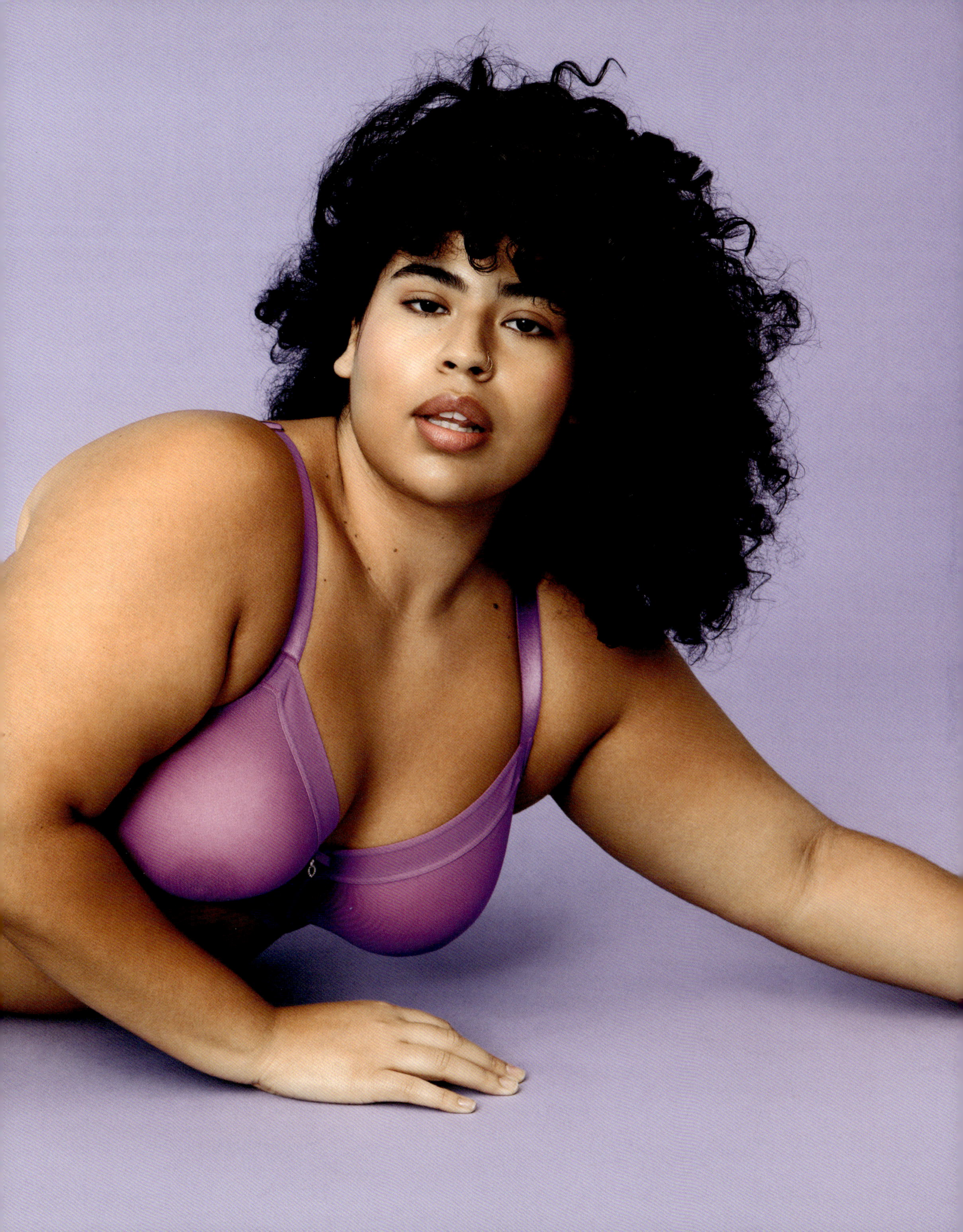

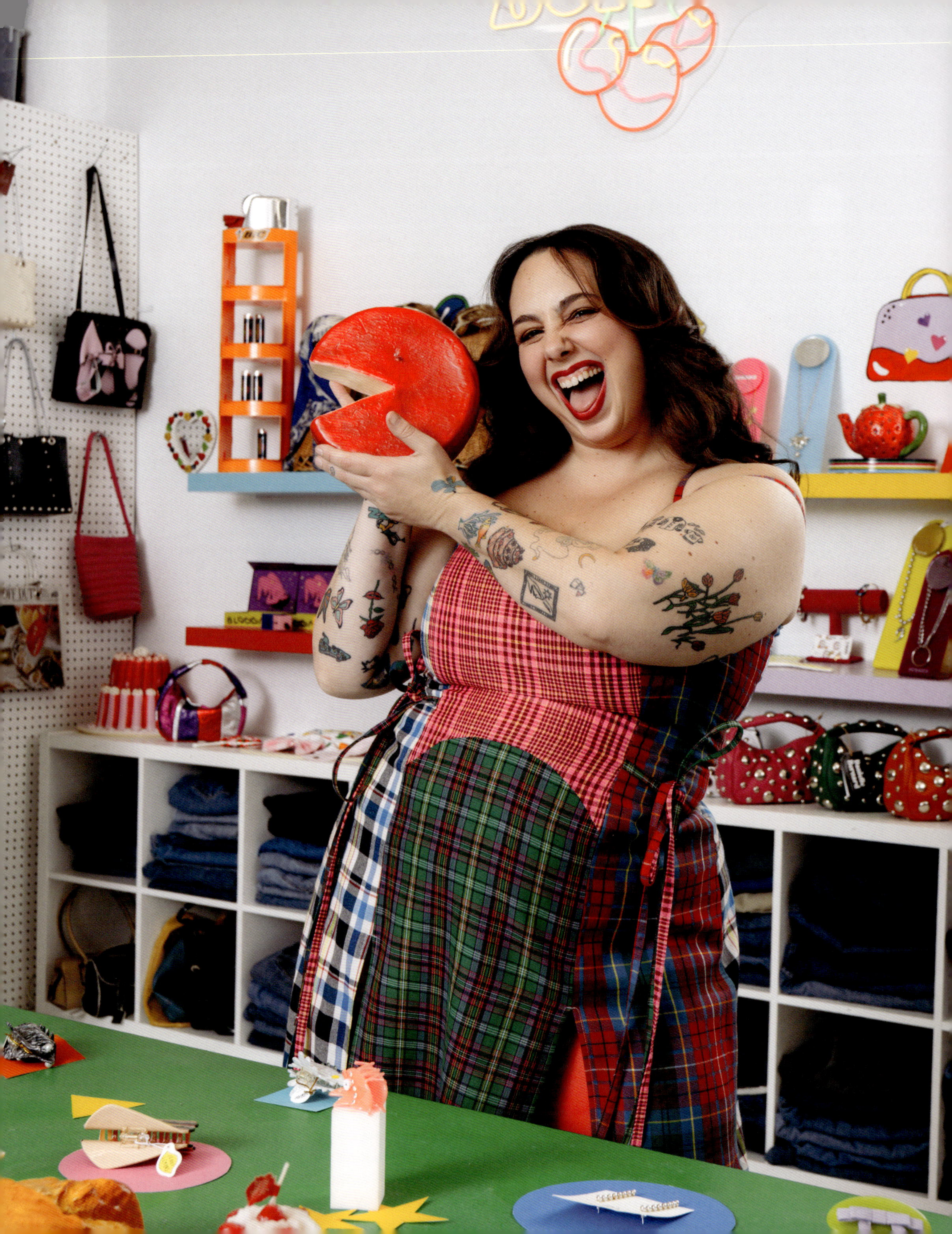

Emma Zack

A champion for plus-size style

I discovered Shop Berriez during the pandemic and was instantly captivated by the stylish, inclusive options it offered for plus-size women. Emma later hired me to shoot for her brand in Soho, and when we realized our studios shared the same building, we began collaborating more often. Over the past four years, we've worked together on everything from e-commerce to campaign shoots, and I've seen firsthand how talented Emma is at styling—particularly for plus-size clients.

Emma's journey began when she noticed a gap in the market. She started Berriez as vintage shopping on Instagram became popular, but she struggled to find pieces that fit her as a size 12/14. This experience fueled her passion to create a brand that puts plus-size individuals at the forefront, using fashion to celebrate a community that is often overlooked and undervalued. Today, Berriez is a showroom and online shop that focus on plus-size and inclusive vintage, reworked vintage, and independent designers.

When asked what sparked Berriez's traction in the fashion world, Emma emphasizes the importance of community, both in person and on social media, noting how rare similar spaces are when so few brands carry larger sizes in-store. "We've created a space for plus-size folks to gather, shop, and celebrate each other—all while looking fabulous." This sense of belonging has been instrumental to the brand's growth, with Berriez offering plus-size shoppers opportunities often available only to their thin counterparts.

As a woman-owned independent business, Berriez has thrived even as many larger brands reduce their offerings. Against this backdrop, Emma acknowledges the challenges posed by societal pressures and the current weight-loss craze, but she remains committed to her vision and her approach to business. "I'm going to continue to find stylish, elevated pieces for my customers and center plus-size bodies in my brand,"

I'm also inspired by my friends and what they wear. If they like what I curate, then I know I'm doing something right.

Emma asserts, emphasizing her focus on what truly matters to her.

That focus includes a commitment to upcycling and collaborating with smaller independent labels. Emma explains that she chooses which designers to partner with by considering fit, quality, popularity, and alignment with the Berriez aesthetic. This thoughtful approach ensures that every piece in her collection resonates with her mission of inclusivity.

Emma's personal closet is eclectic, colorful, and filled with unique pieces that tell a story. However, she says that her fashion journey didn't begin with confidence; rather, it was shaped by her desire to blend in and hide her body. However, once she began creating plus-size fashion content on Instagram and TikTok, she discovered her authentic self. "I wear what I like and what makes me happy," she explains, noting her influences, which range from vintage jazz posters and thrift store art to the vibrant colors of 1980s Miami interiors. Emma embraces clothing that sparks conversation and often finds nostalgia in prints and patterns.

Her styling expertise truly shines through in projects like her work on the "Vices" fashion show: a size-inclusive show she put on during Fall 2022's New York Fashion Week. In response to my question about how she balances styling for events while keeping her brand's inclusive values intact, she answers that representation is key, ensuring each size is considered in her styling choices, even if it means creating custom pieces. "I want to show plus-size bodies in the same pieces that straight-size bodies are wearing."

When it comes to sourcing vintage, working with designers, and collaborating with artists on one-of-a-kind pieces, Emma says that while she looks at trends, her priority is to always think about what plus-size people want to wear. "I'm also inspired by my friends and what they wear. If they like what I curate, then I know I'm doing something right."
In a fashion landscape that's always shifting, Emma manages to steer Berriez through cultural changes by letting authenticity drive her vision. "I'm just trying to find the best clothes for plus-size people and make clothing that doesn't already exist for us."

Recently, Berriez has gained significant attention, with *Vogue* even naming it a top shopping destination in New York. I ask Emma what this kind of recognition means to her, and she shares that while it brings more customers, it also adds complexity to her business. "Recognition is a double-edged sword," she says, but she "is so grateful for it, because without it, Berriez wouldn't be where it is today."

Emma isn't done yet, though. She shares her ambitious goals for the future, which include opening a ground-floor retail location in either NYC or Los Angeles. "I'm also working on a clothing line for Berriez. I also want to start personal styling and closet cleanout services. There are so many things I want to do, and I am excited—and nervous—about what the future holds. I know deep down that as long as I remain authentic and stay true to my core values, I will succeed."

Emma's journey with Berriez exemplifies the strength and creativity of independent, woman-owned businesses in a landscape that often overlooks plus-size representation. Her commitment to inclusivity and authentic expression has not only helped her to carve out a space for herself but has inspired many others to embrace their true selves through fashion.

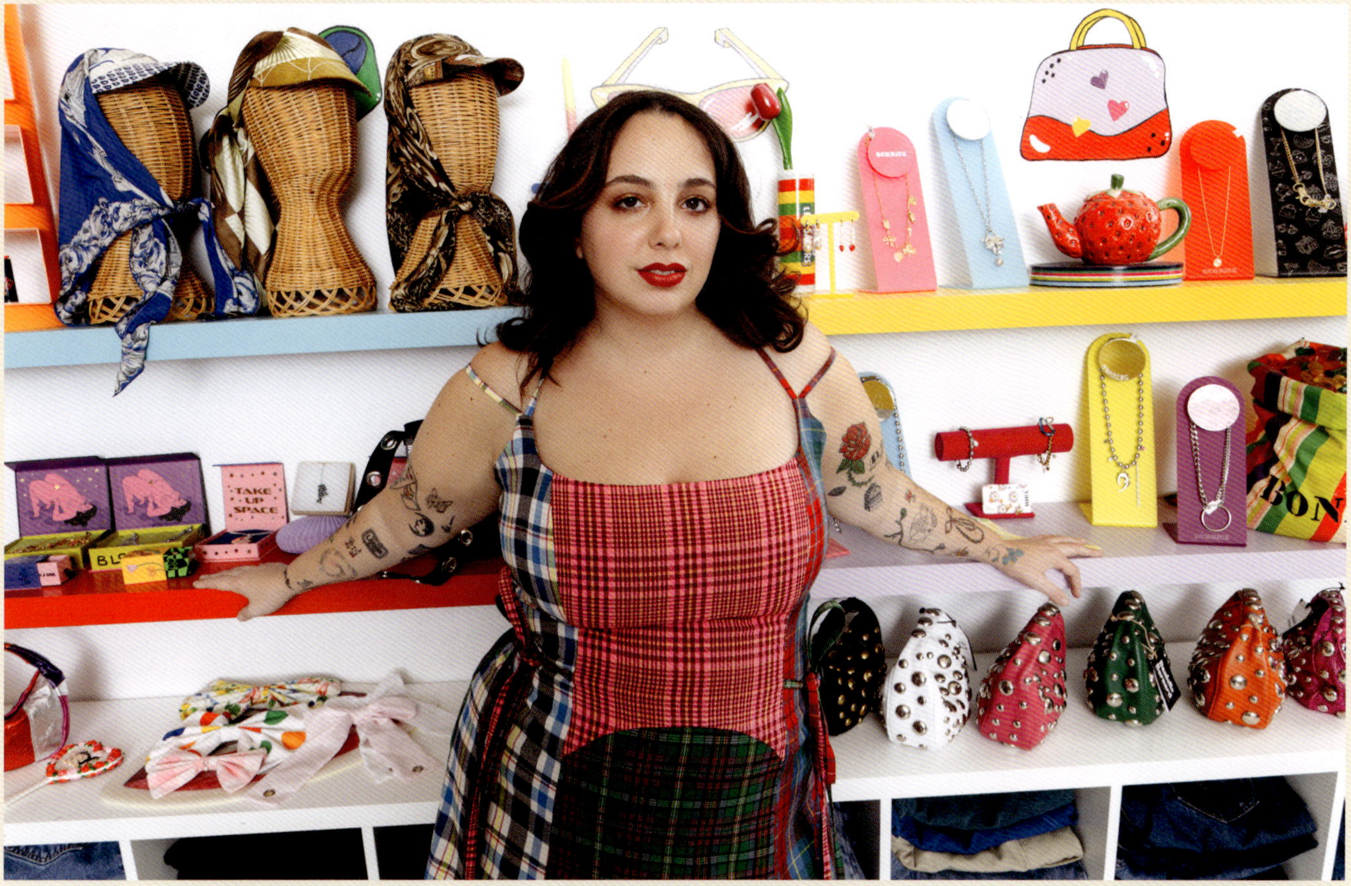

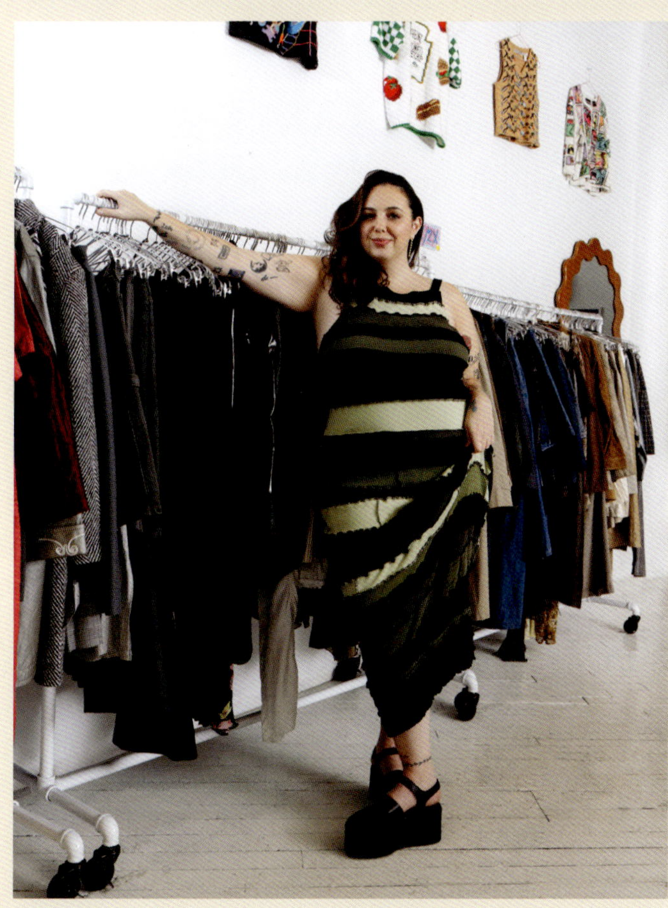

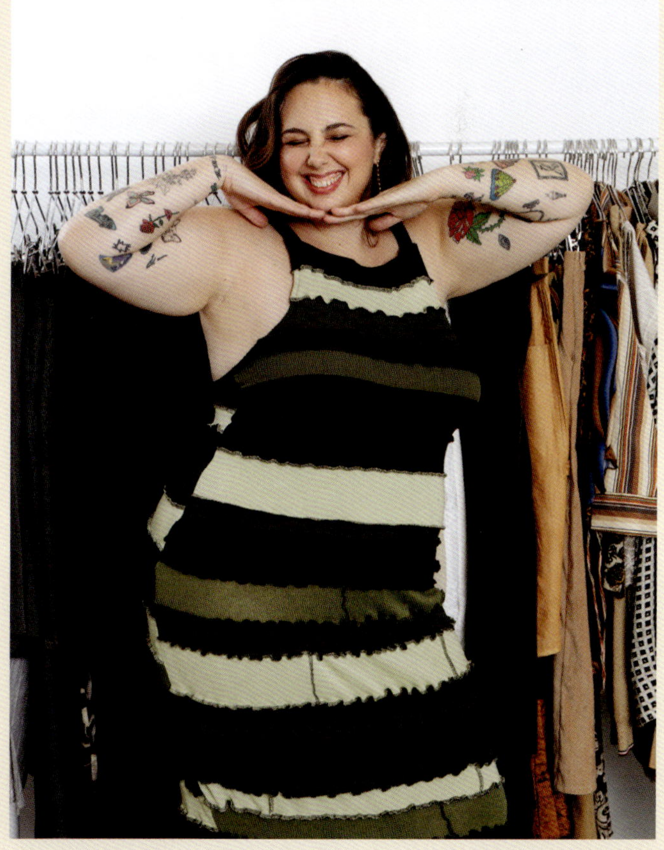

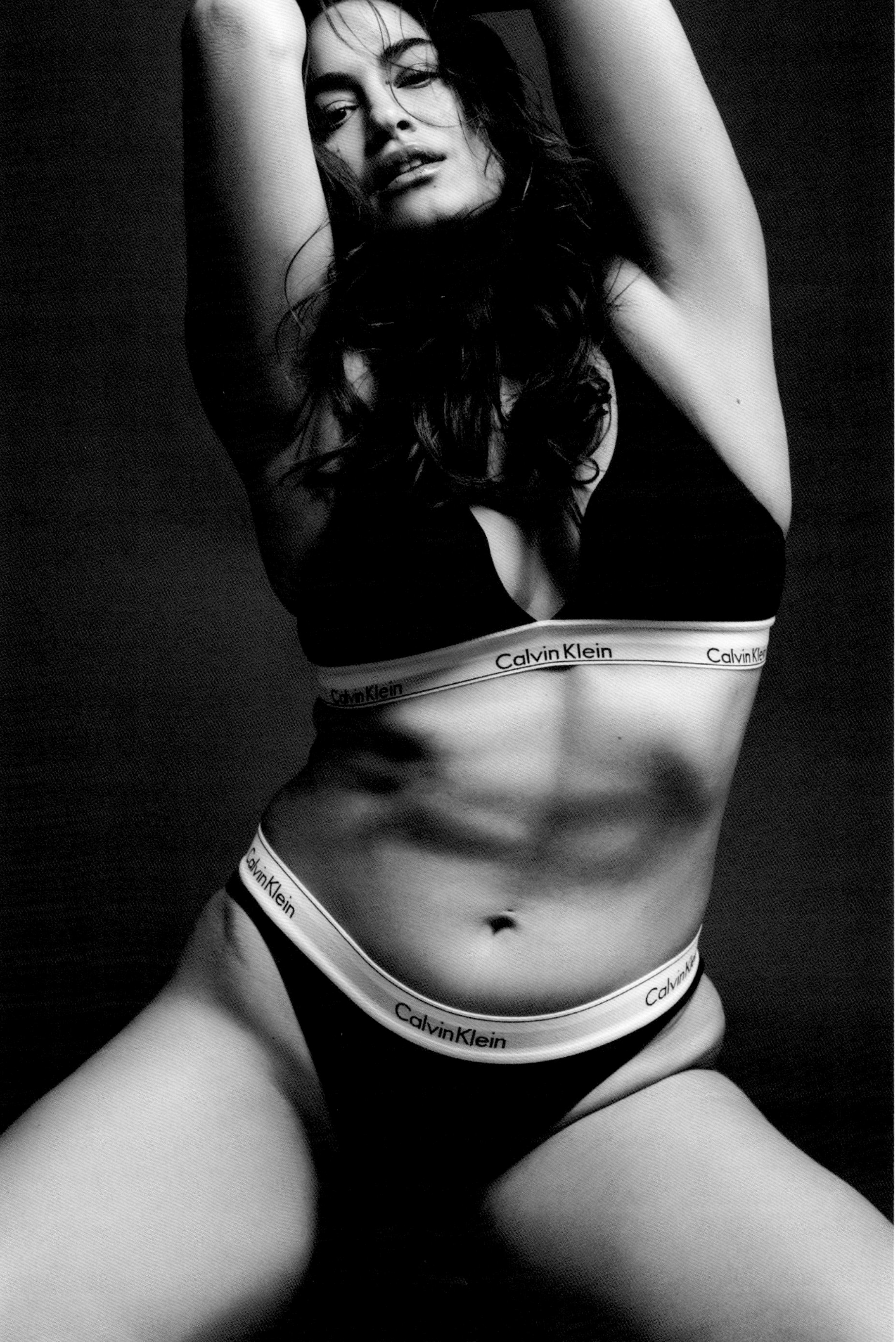

Calvin Klein
Calvin Klein
Calvin Klein
Calvin Klein

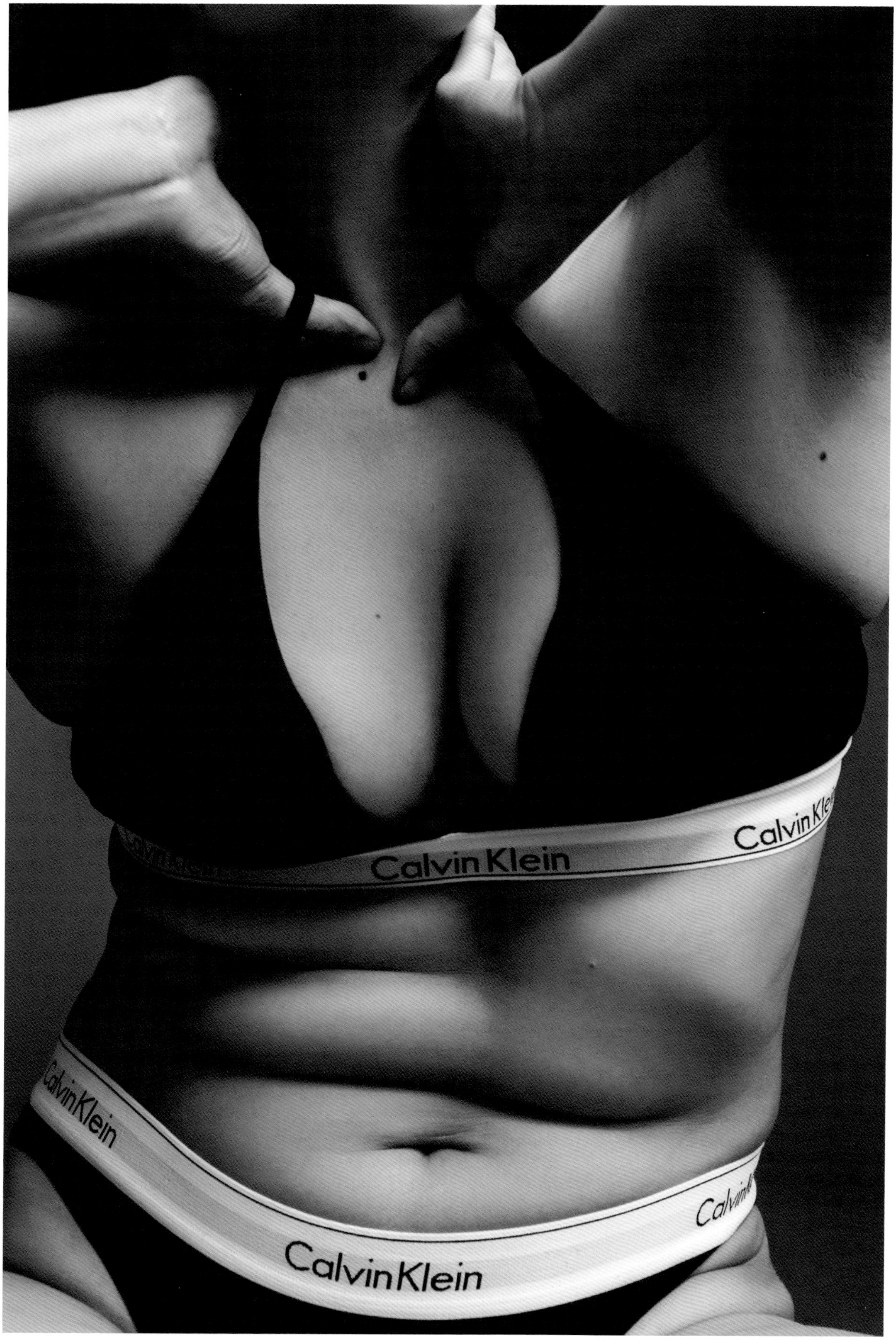

Calvin Klein
Calvin Klein
CalvinKlein
CalvinKlein

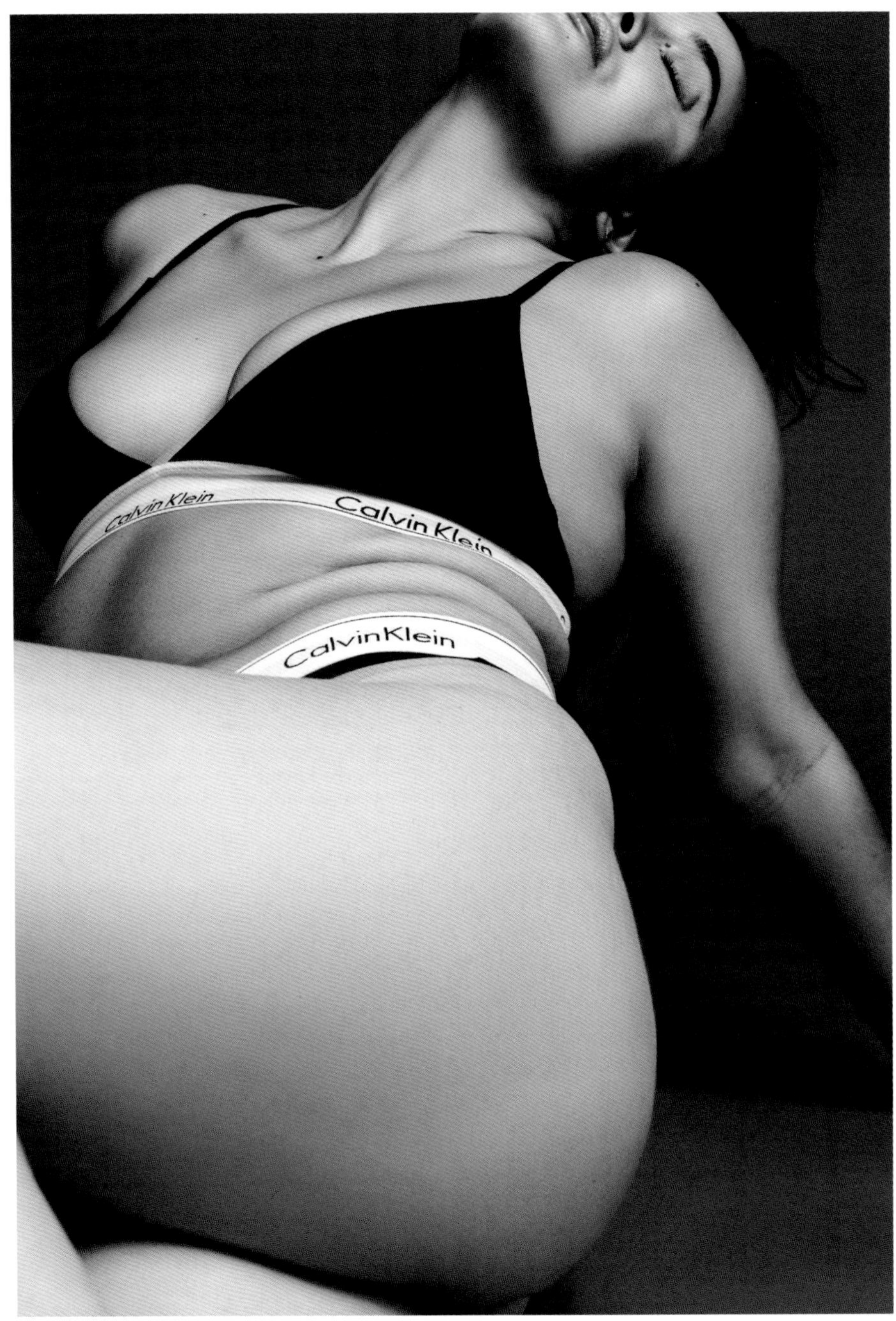
Calvin Klein
Calvin Klein
Calvin Klein

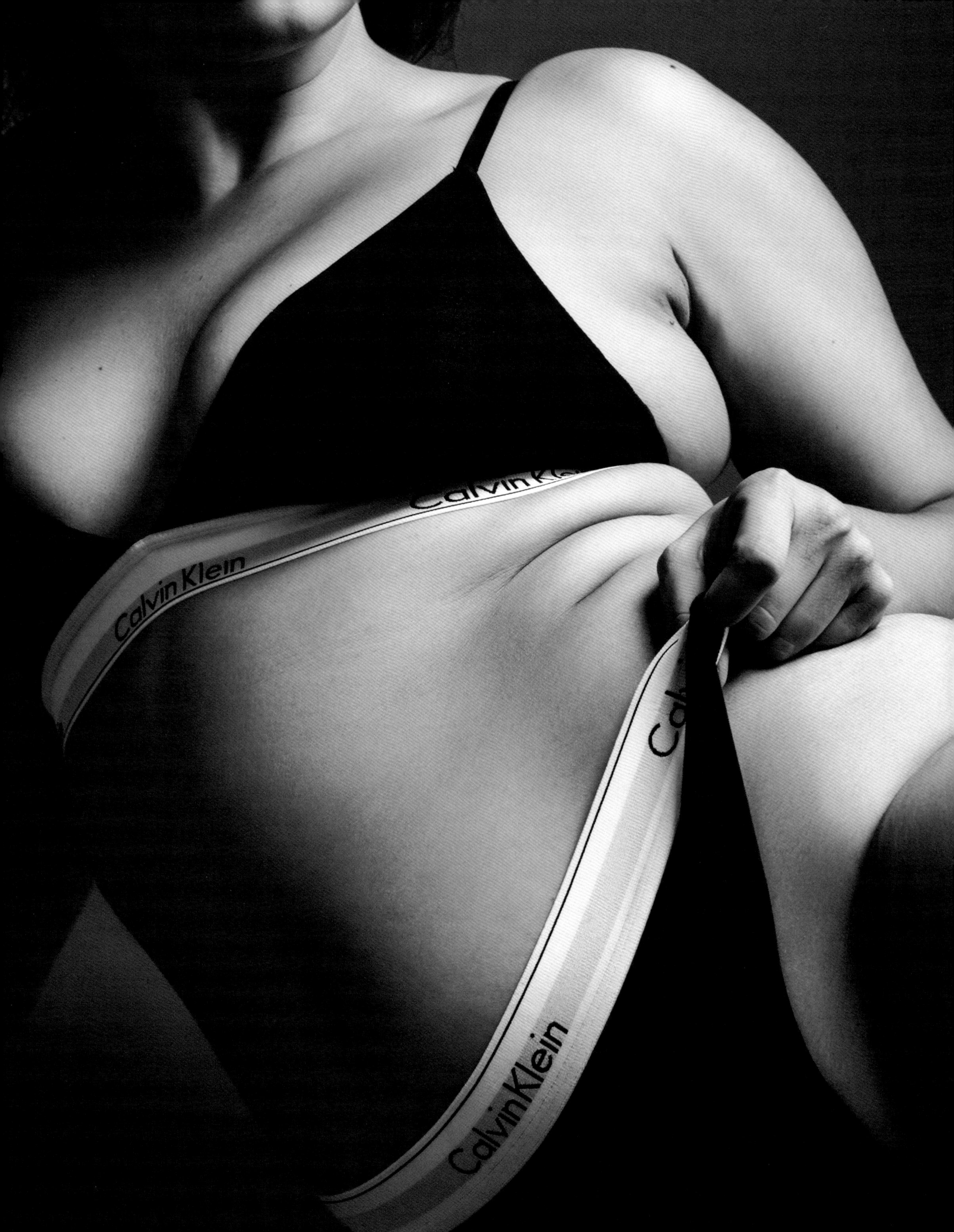
Calvin Klein
Calvin Klein

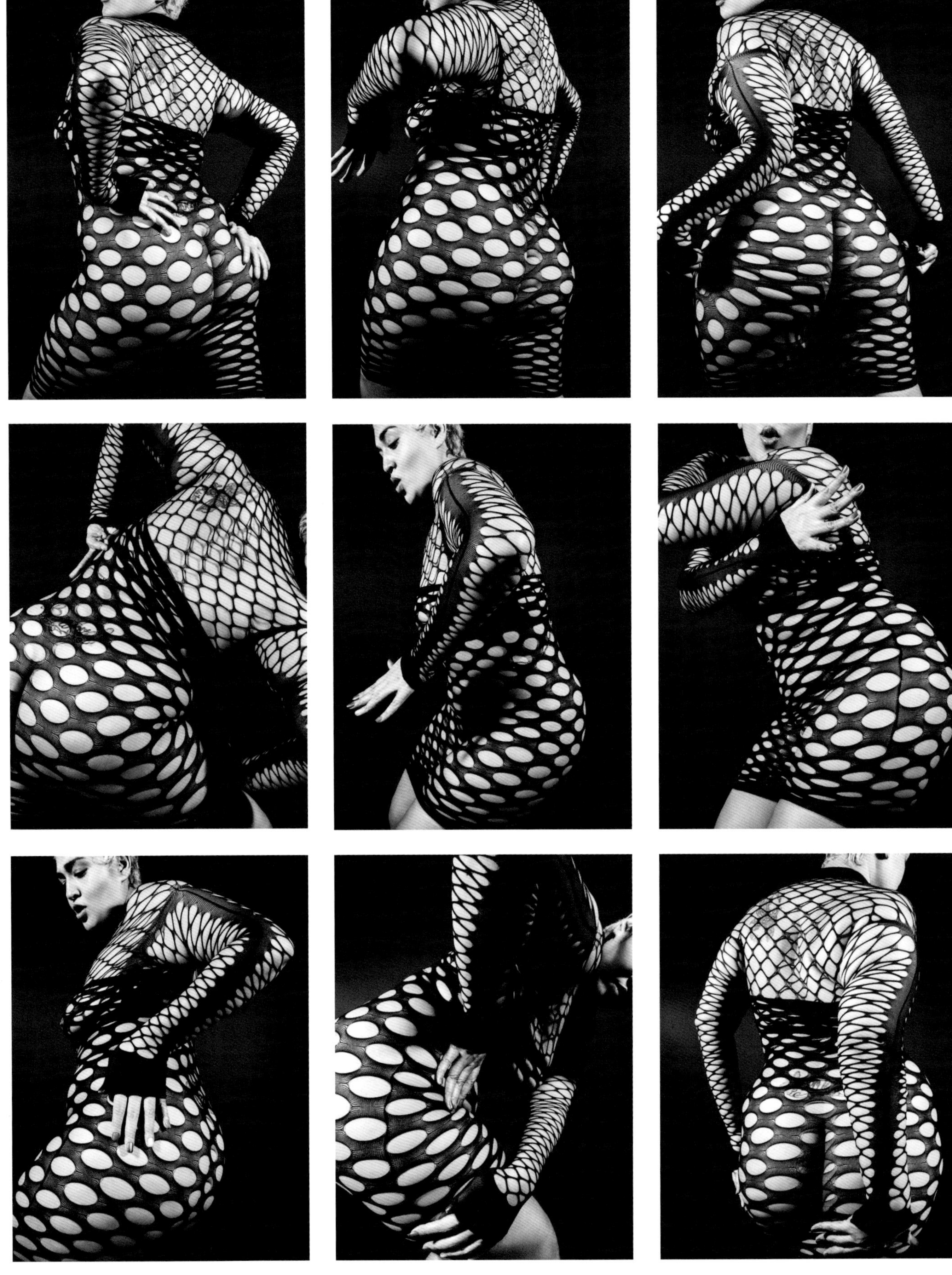

Pages 286–289: Denka Obradovic wears Calvin Klein.

Velonika Pome'e wears own bodysuit.

Apollo wears outfit from Lydia Hudgens' closet.

Overleaf: PJ Nyambok wears metallic set from Lydia Hudgens' closet; Dolce Vita boots; Alexis Bittar cuff.

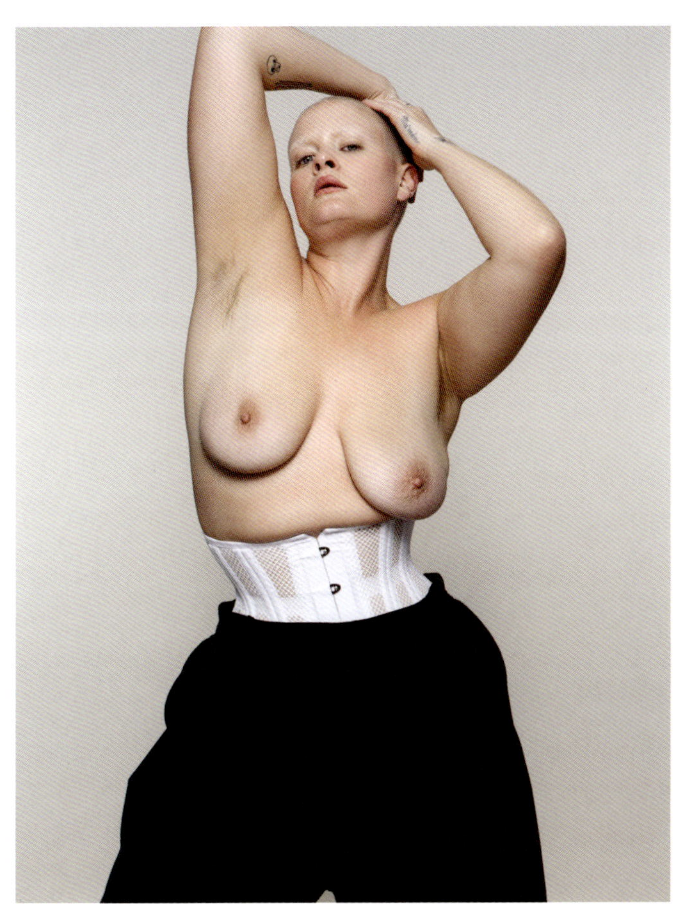
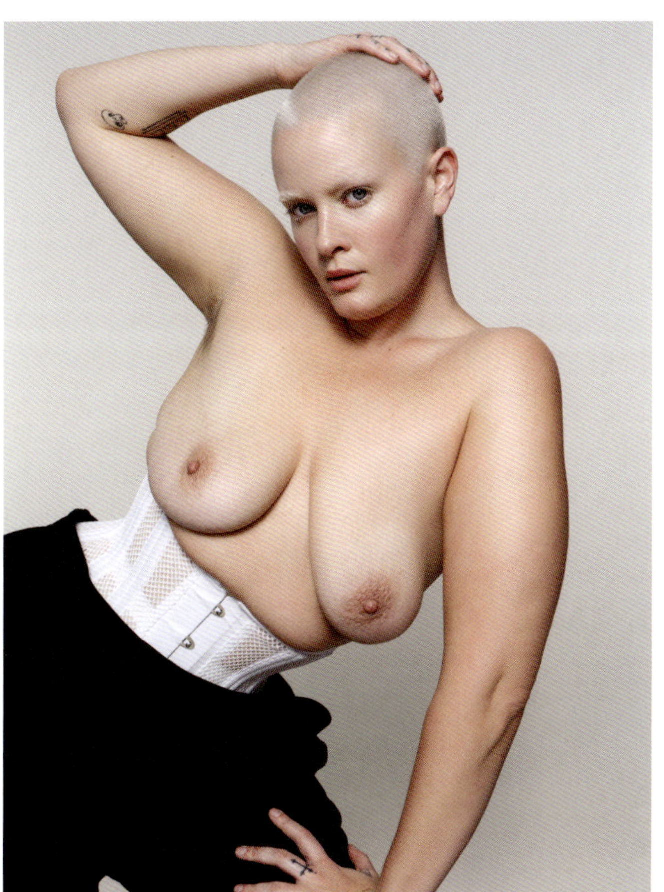
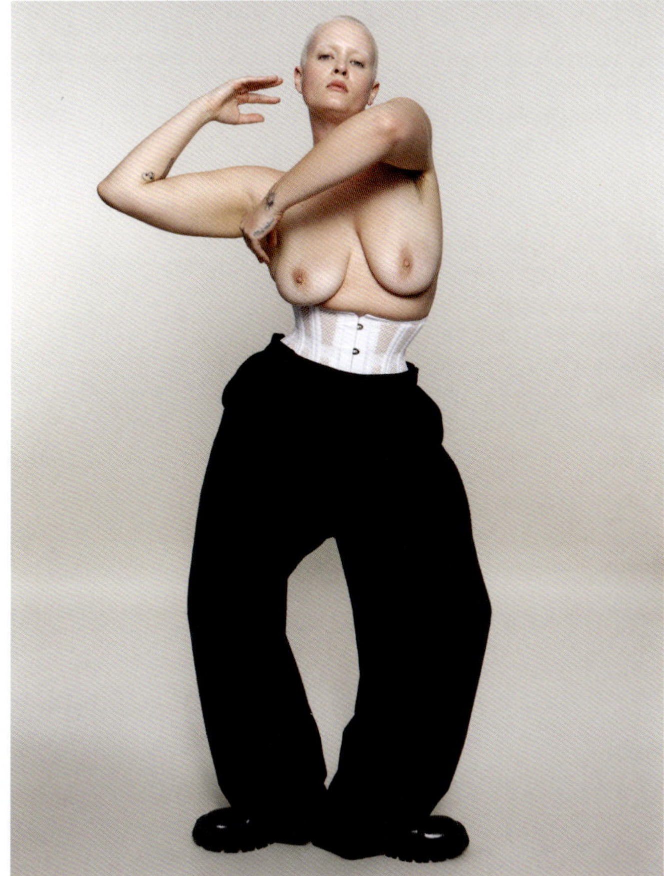
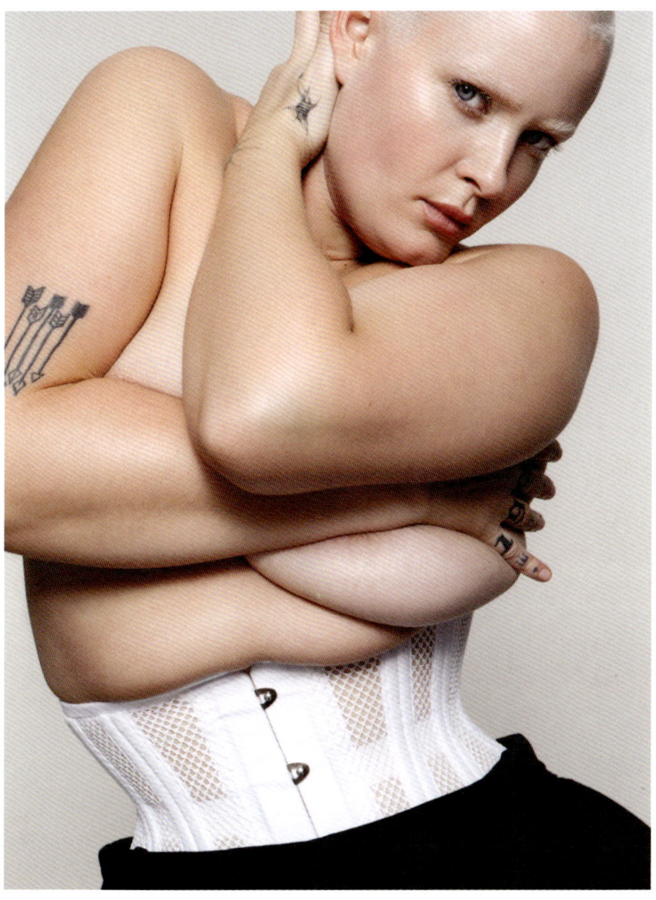

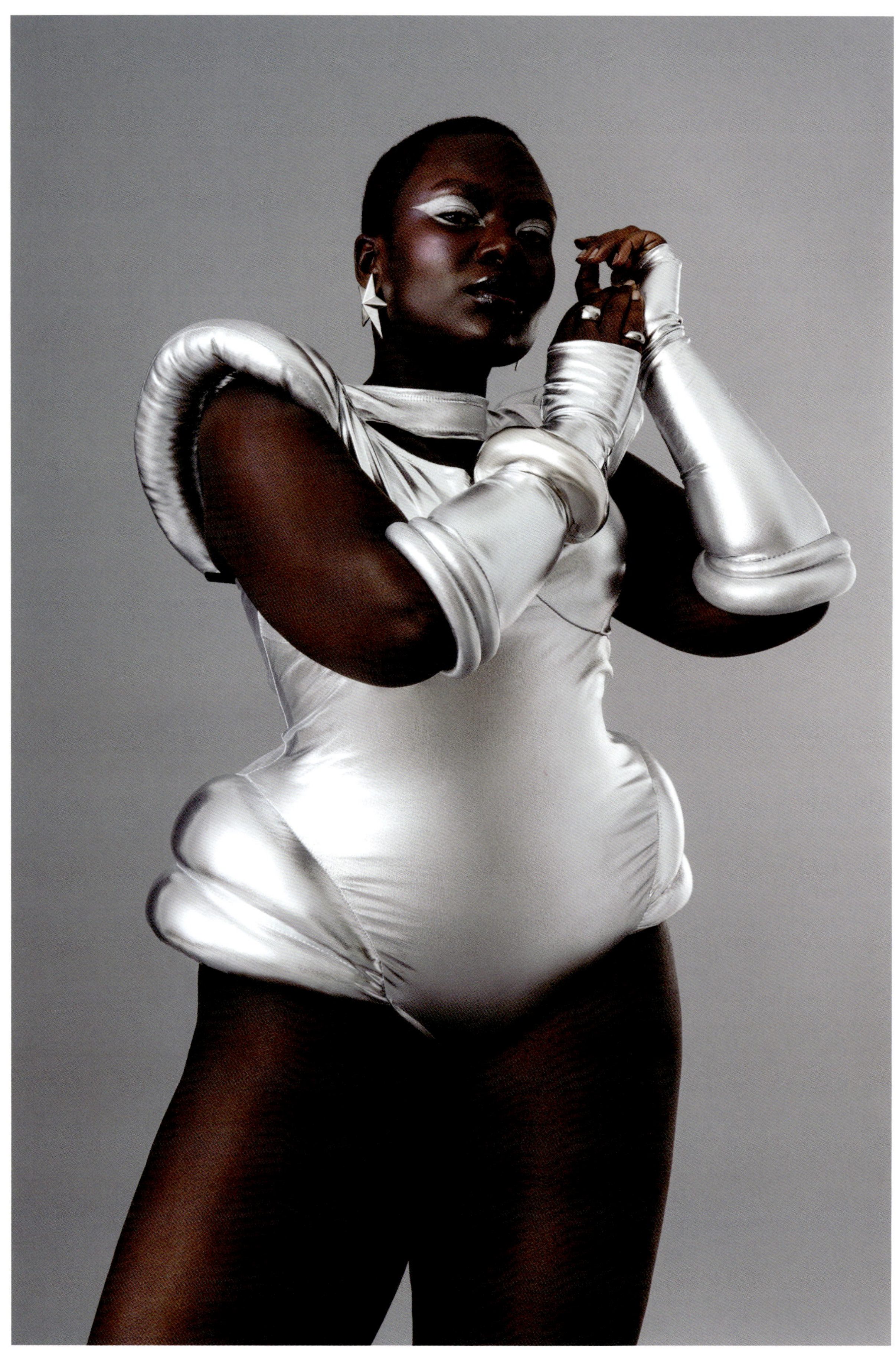

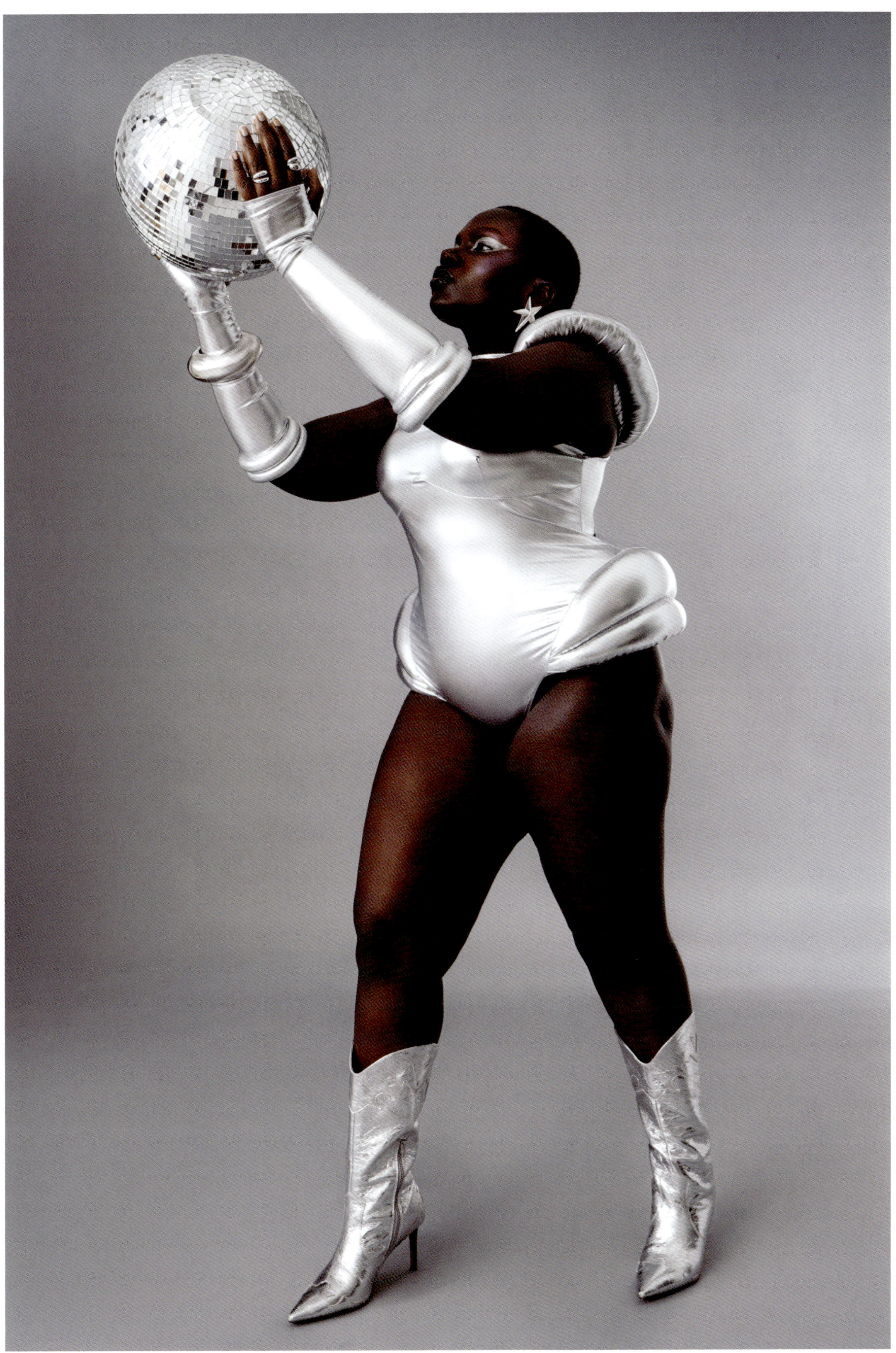

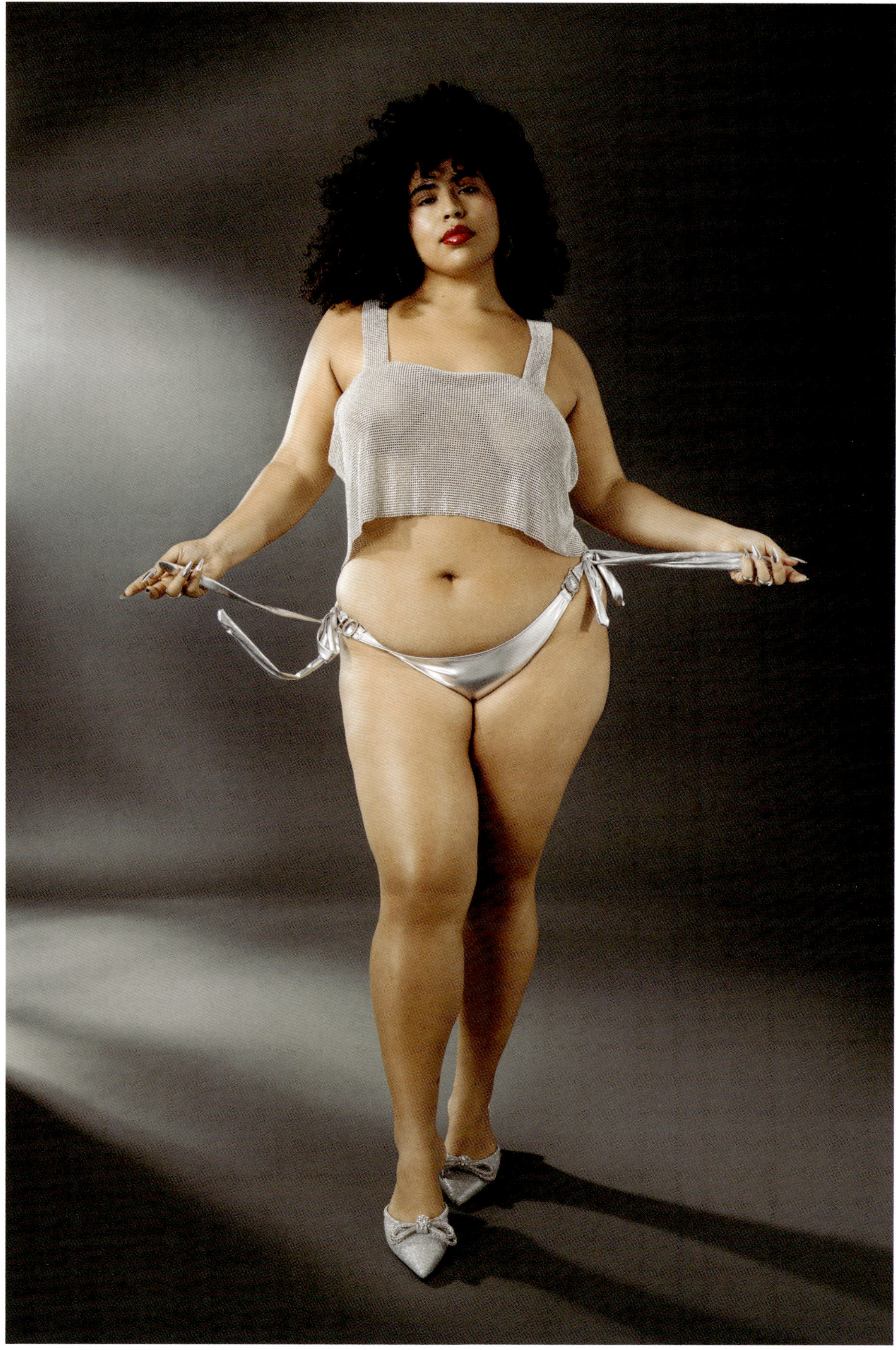

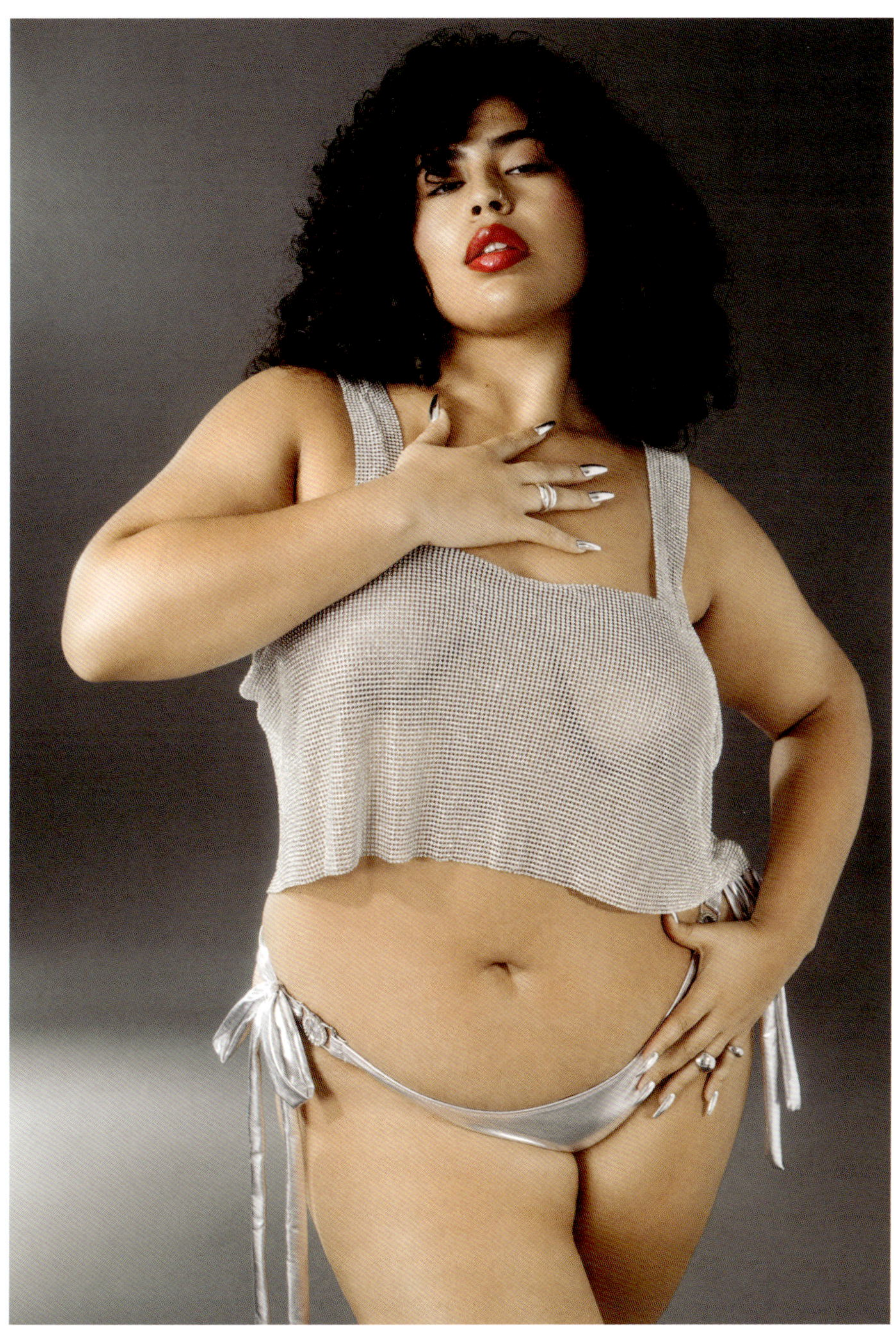

Naomi La Crespa wears vintage top and bottom.

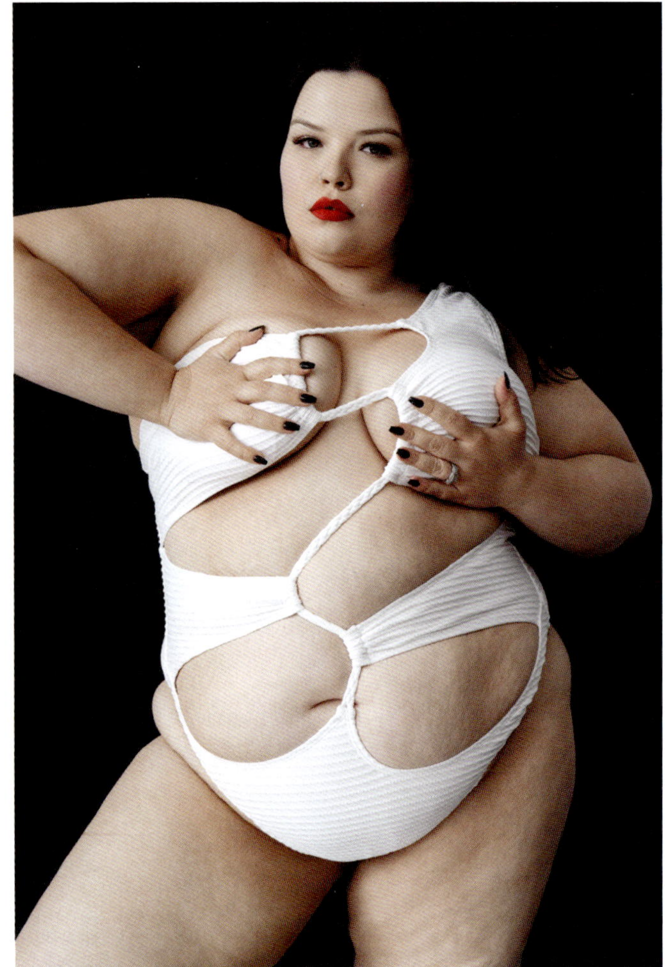

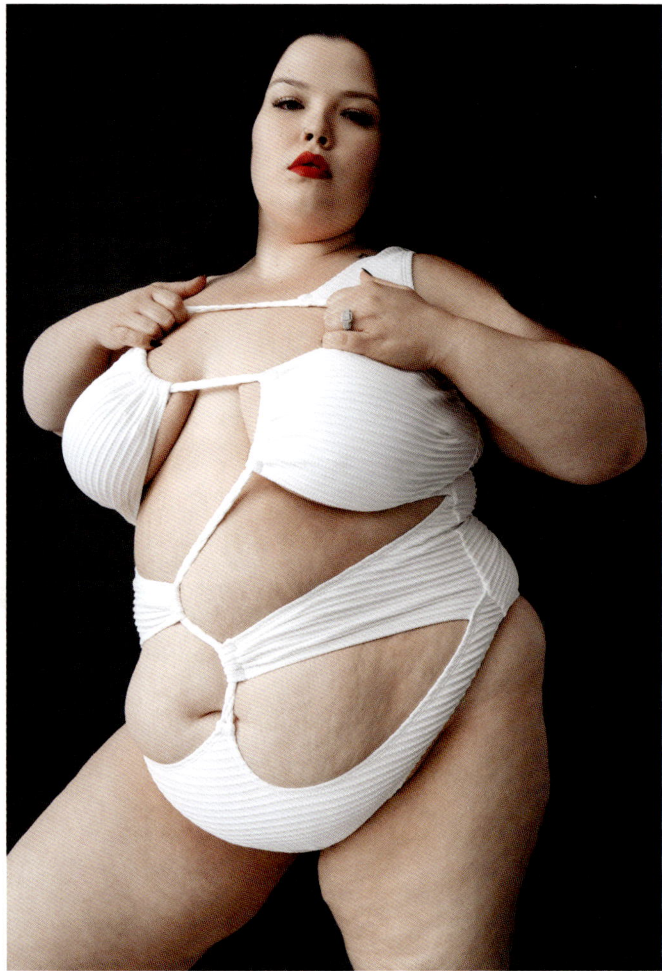

Emma Evans wears swimwear from Lydia Hudgens' closet.

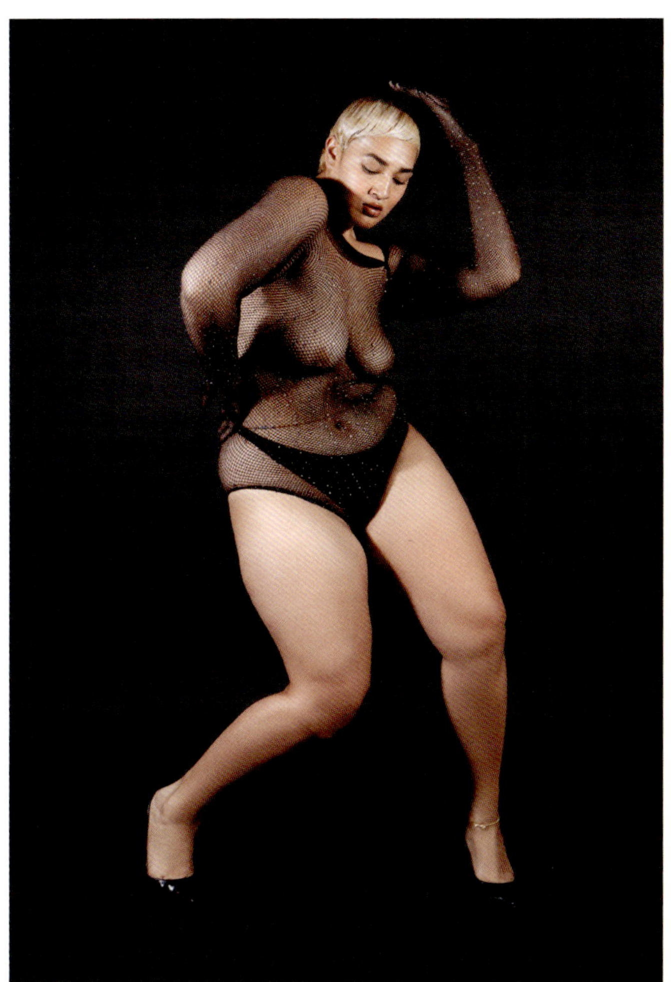

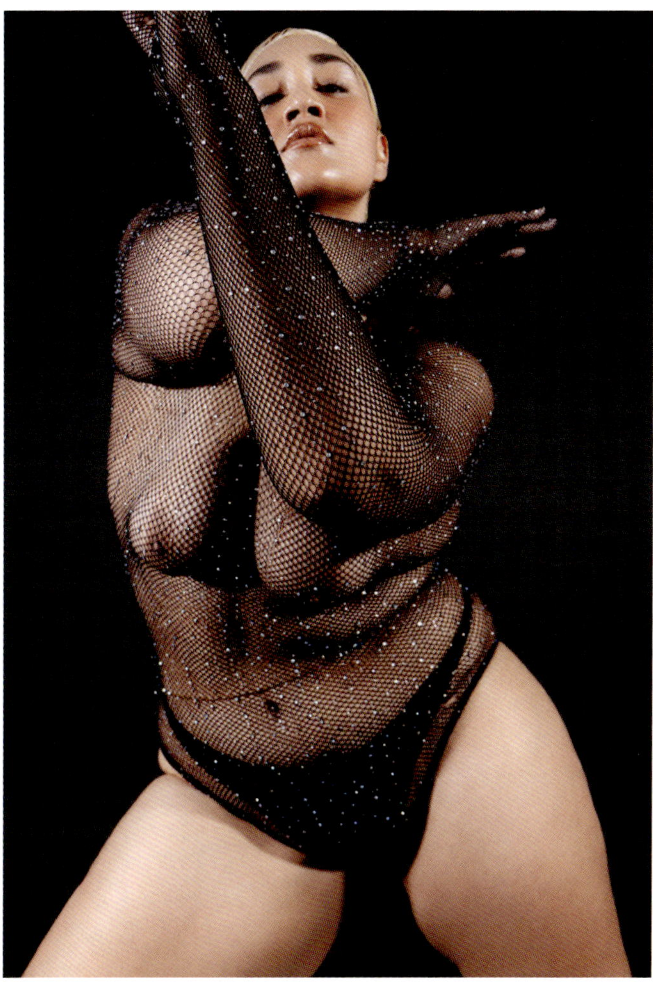

Velonika Pome'e wears own bodysuit.

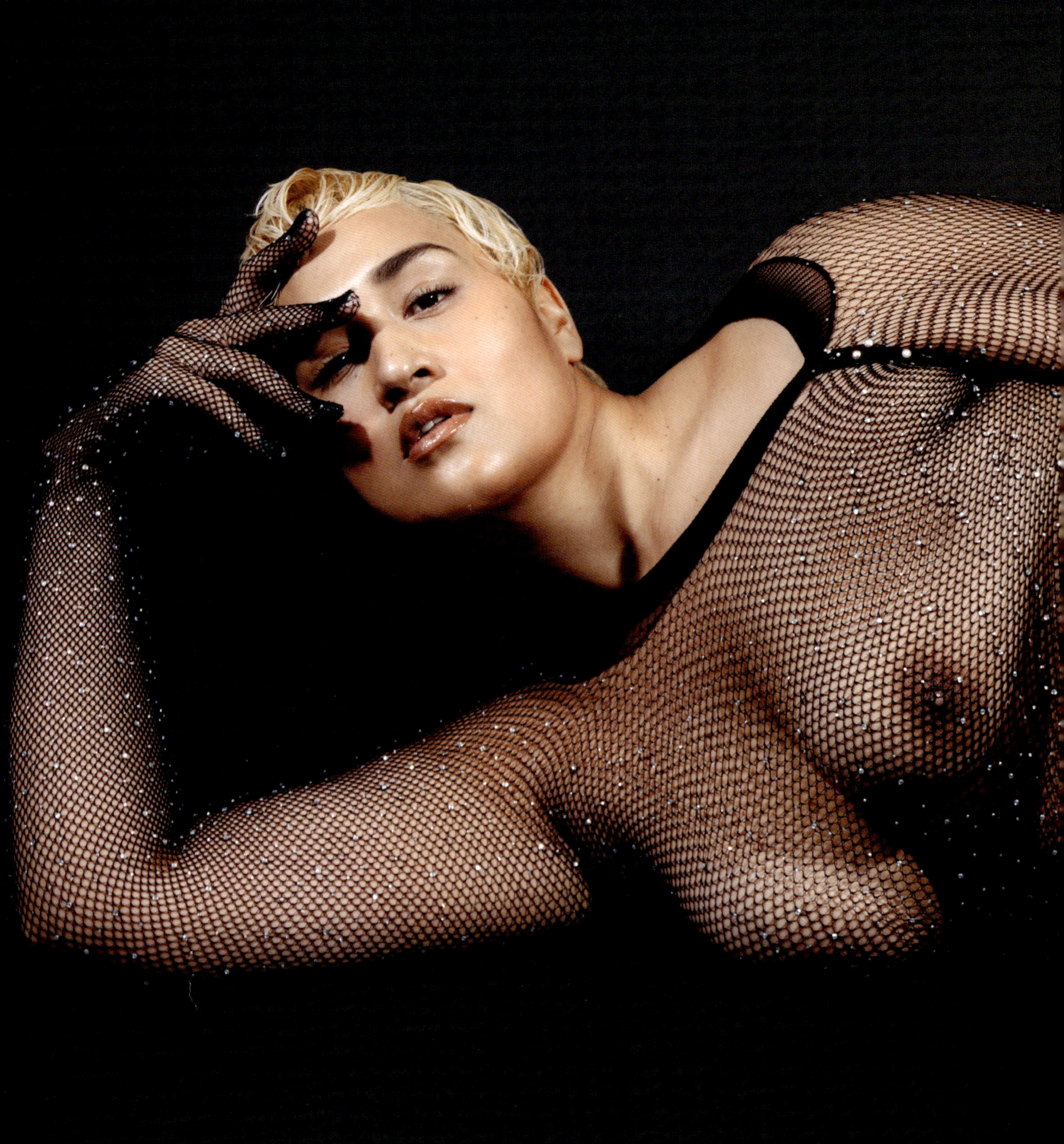

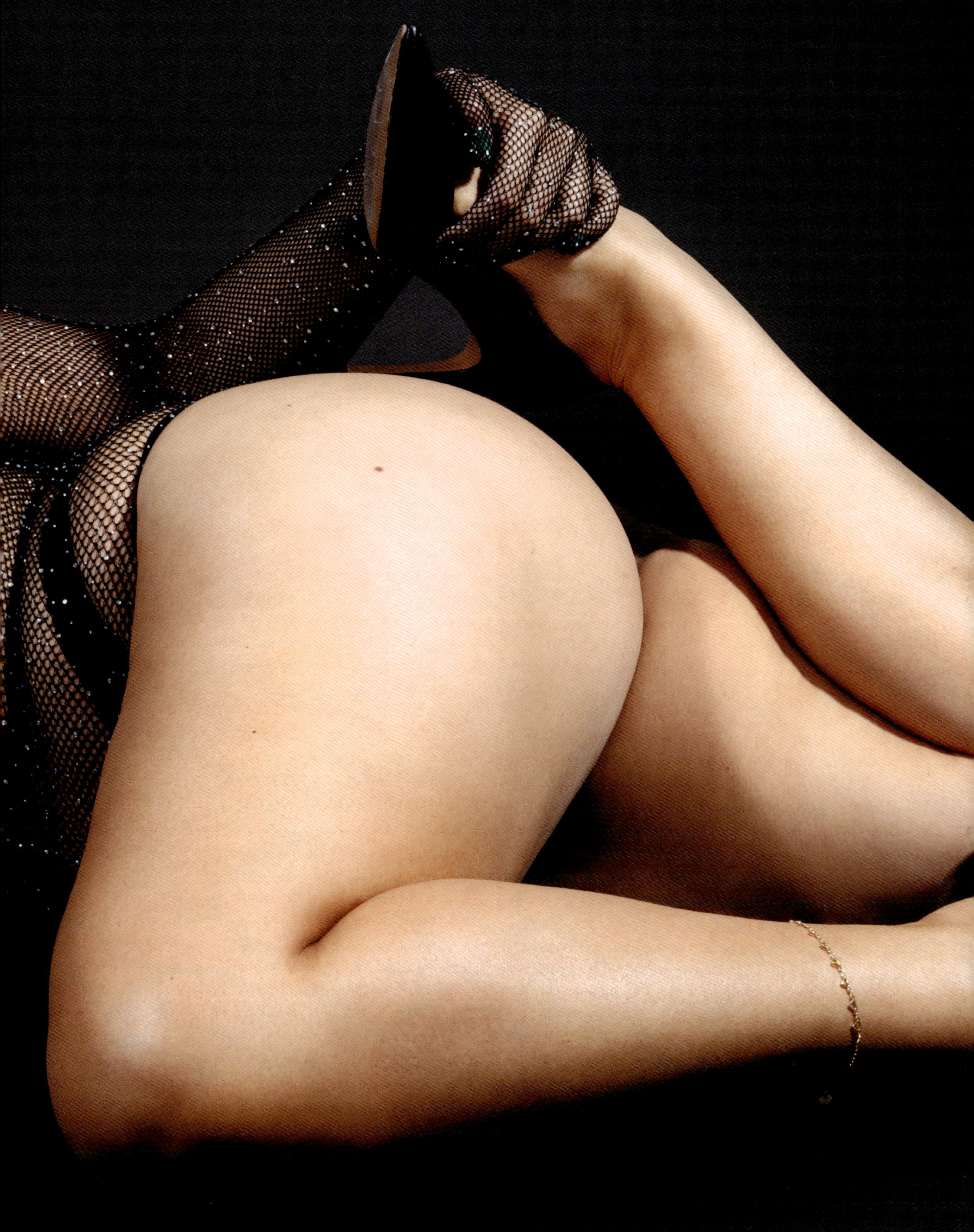

Credits

PHOTO RETOUCHER
Tatiana Lia

PAGE 6 PHOTOGRAPHER
Lalo Torres

PAGE 4
STYLIST Kingsley Osuji
BEAUTY Kelly Mazzini
HAIR Kelly Mazzini

PAGES 11–13
STYLIST Kelly Augustine
BEAUTY Kelly Mazzini
HAIR Kelly Mazzini

PAGE 15
STYLIST Kelly Augustine
BEAUTY Cearah Peck
HAIR Cearah Peck

PAGES 16–19
STYLIST Theo Banzon
BEAUTY Kelly Mazzini
HAIR Kelly Mazzini

PAGES 20–25
STYLIST Emma Zack
BEAUTY Will Metivier
HAIR Noni Cygnor

PAGES 27
STYLIST Lydia Hudgens
BEAUTY Kelly Mazzini
HAIR Auralis Flores

PAGES 28–29
STYLIST Lydia Hudgens
BEAUTY Kelly Mazzini
HAIR Auralis Flores

PAGES 30–31
STYLING Yoko J
BEAUTY Kelly Mazzini
HAIR Madison Simone

PAGES 32–33
STYLIST Theo Banzon
BEAUTY Kelly Mazzini
HAIR Kelly Mazzini

PAGES 34–35
STYLIST Lydia Hudgens
BEAUTY Kelly Mazzini
HAIR Kelly Mazzini

PAGES 36–37
STYLIST Lydia Hudgens
BEAUTY Kelly Mazzini
HAIR Kelly Mazzini
SET Lapoze

PAGES 38–39
STYLIST Yoko J
BEAUTY Crisdanil
HAIR Crisdanil

PAGES 44–47
STYLIST Lydia Hudgens
BEAUTY Kelly Mazzini
HAIR Auralis Flores

PAGES 48–49
STYLIST Lydia Hudgens
BEAUTY Kelly Mazzini
HAIR Auralis Flores

PAGES 50–51
STYLIST Lydia Hudgens
BEAUTY Tayler Smith
HAIR Tayler Smith

PAGES 52–53
STYLIST Wren Parker
BEAUTY Wren Parker
HAIR Wren Parker

PAGES 54–55
STYLIST Kelly Augustine
BEAUTY Maggie Rodriguez
HAIR Maggie Rodriguez

PAGES 56–57
STYLIST Aylah Karine
BEAUTY Aylah Karine
HAIR Aylah Karine

PAGES 58–59
STYLIST Lydia Hudgens
BEAUTY Kelly Mazzini
HAIR Auralis Flores

PAGES 60–63
STYLIST Theo Banzon
BEAUTY Kelly Mazzini
HAIR Kelly Mazzini

PAGE 64
STYLIST Aylah Karine
BEAUTY Aylah Karine
HAIR Aylah Karine

PAGES 66–67
STYLIST Lydia Hudgens
BEAUTY Kelly Mazzini
HAIR Kelly Mazzini

PAGES 68–69
STYLIST Lydia Hudgens
BEAUTY Kelly Mazzini
HAIR Auralis Flores

PAGES 70–73
STYLIST Lydia Hudgens
BEAUTY Kelly Mazzini
HAIR Kelly Mazzini

PAGES 74–75
STYLIST Lydia Hudgens
BEAUTY Kelly Mazzini
HAIR Auralis Flores

PAGES 76–77
STYLIST Lydia Hudgens
BEAUTY Angel Gabriel
HAIR Angel Gabriel

PAGES 78–81
STYLIST Lydia Hudgens
BEAUTY Apollo

PAGES 82–85
STYLIST Lydia Hudgens
BEAUTY Kelly Mazzini
HAIR Auralis Flores

PAGES 86–89
STYLIST Lydia Hudgens
BEAUTY Kelly Mazzini
HAIR Auralis Flores

PAGES 90–91
STYLIST Lydia Hudgens
BEAUTY Kelly Mazzini
HAIR Kelly Mazzini

PAGES 92–93
STYLIST Lydia Hudgens
BEAUTY Angel Gabriel
HAIR Angel Gabriel

PAGES 94–95
STYLIST Lydia Hudgens
BEAUTY Kelly Mazzini
HAIR Auralis Flores

PAGES 96–97
STYLIST Lydia Hudgens
BEAUTY Kelly Mazzini
HAIR Auralis Flores

PAGES 98–101
STYLIST Lydia Hudgens
BEAUTY Emma Evans
HAIR Emma Evans

PAGES 102–103
STYLIST Kingsley Osuji
BEAUTY Kelly Mazzini
HAIR Kelly Mazzini

PAGES 104–105
STYLIST Theo Banzon
BEAUTY Kelly Mazzini
HAIR Kelly Mazzini

PAGES 106–109
STYLIST Emma Zack
BEAUTY Sarah Hart
HAIR Sarah Hart

PAGES 114–115
STYLIST Lydia Hudgens
BEAUTY Kelly Mazzini
HAIR Auralis Flores

PAGES 116–119
STYLIST Yoko J
BEAUTY Crisdanil
HAIR Crisdanil

PAGES 120–121
STYLIST Lydia Hudgens
BEAUTY Kelly Mazzini
HAIR Auralis Flores

PAGES 122–123
STYLIST Kingsley Osuji
BEAUTY Kelly Mazzini
HAIR Kelly Mazzini

PAGES 124–125
STYLIST Lydia Hudgens
BEAUTY Kelly Mazzini
HAIR Kelly Mazzini

PAGES 126–127
STYLIST Lydia Hudgens
BEAUTY Kelly Mazzini
HAIR Auralis Flores

PAGES 128–129
STYLIST Kingsley Osuji
BEAUTY Kelly Mazzini
HAIR Kelly Mazzini

PAGES 130–131
STYLIST Theo Banzon
BEAUTY Kelly Mazzini
HAIR Kelly Mazzini

PAGES 133–135
STYLIST Kelly Mazzini
BEAUTY Kelly Mazzini
HAIR Kelly Mazzini

PAGE 136
STYLIST Ariana Corrao
BEAUTY Kelly Mazzini
HAIR Kelly Mazzini

PAGES 138–139
BEAUTY Kelly Mazzini

PAGES 140–141
STYLIST Kelly Augustine
HAIR Kelly Mazzini

PAGE 143
STYLIST Maria Diaz
BEAUTY Kelly Mazzini

PAGES 144–145
STYLIST Emma Zack
BEAUTY Will Metivier
HAIR Noni Cygnor

PAGES 146–149
STYLIST Lydia Hudgens
BEAUTY Kelly Mazzini
HAIR Auralis Flores

PAGES 150–151
STYLIST Kelly Mazzini
BEAUTY Kelly Mazzini
HAIR Naomi La Crespa

PAGES 156–157
BEAUTY Kelly Mazzini
HAIR Kelly Mazzini

PAGES 158–159
BEAUTY Carri Murphy
HAIR Carri Murphy

PAGES 160–161
STYLIST Yoko J
BEAUTY Kelly Mazzini

PAGE 162–163
STYLIST Tayler Smith
BEAUTY Tayler Smith
HAIR Tayler Smith

PAGES 164–165
STYLIST Yoko J
BEAUTY Crisdanil

PAGES 166–167
STYLIST Lydia Hudgens
BEAUTY Kelly Mazzini
HAIR Kelly Mazzini

PAGES 168–169
STYLIST Wren Parker
BEAUTY Wren Parker
HAIR Wren Parker

PAGES 170–171
STYLIST Lydia Hudgens
BEAUTY Kelly Mazzini
HAIR Auralis Flores

PAGE 173
STYLIST Lydia Hudgens
BEAUTY Kelly Mazzini
HAIR Auralis Flores

PAGES 174–175
STYLIST Lydia Hudgens
BEAUTY Kelly Mazzini
HAIR Auralis Flores

PAGE 176
STYLIST Kelly Augustine
BEAUTY Cearah Peck
HAIR Cearah Peck

PAGE 177
STYLIST Lydia Hudgens
BEAUTY Kelly Mazzini
HAIR Auralis Flores

PAGES 178–179
STYLIST Lydia Hudgens
BEAUTY Kelly Mazzini
HAIR Kelly Mazzini

PAGES 180–181
STYLIST Lydia Hudgens
BEAUTY Kelly Mazzini
PAGES 182–183
STYLIST Lydia Hudgens
BEAUTY Kelly Mazzini
HAIR Auralis Flores

PAGES 188–189
STYLIST Lydia Hudgens
BEAUTY Kelly Mazzini
HAIR Auralis Flores

PAGES 190–191
BEAUTY Kelly Mazzini
HAIR Kelly Mazzini

PAGES 192–193
BEAUTY Kelly Mazzini
HAIR Kelly Mazzini

PAGES 194–195
BEAUTY Tayler Smith
HAIR Tayler Smith

PAGES 196–197
STYLIST Lydia Hudgens
BEAUTY Kelly Mazzini
HAIR Kelly Mazzini

PAGES 198–199
BEAUTY Kelly Mazzini
HAIR Kelly Mazzini

PAGE 201
STYLIST Lydia Hudgens
BEAUTY Kelly Mazzini
HAIR Kali Renae

PAGES 202–203
BEAUTY Kelly Mazzini
HAIR Kelly Mazzini

PAGE 204
STYLIST Lydia Hudgens
BEAUTY Kelly Mazzini
HAIR Marly Lake

PAGES 206–207
STYLIST Lydia Hudgens
BEAUTY Kelly Mazzini
HAIR Naomi La Crespa

PAGES 208–209
STYLIST Lydia Hudgens
BEAUTY Angel Gabriel
HAIR Angel Gabriel

PAGES 211–213
STYLIST Lydia Hudgens
BEAUTY Kelly Mazzini
HAIR Auralis Flores

PAGES 214–215
STYLIST Lydia Hudgens
BEAUTY Angel Gabriel
HAIR Angel Gabriel

PAGES 217–221
STYLIST Yoko J
BEAUTY Kelly Mazzini
HAIR Auralis Flores

PAGES 222–223
STYLIST Lydia Hudgens
BEAUTY Apollo

PAGES 224–225
STYLIST Bruna Lapinskas
BEAUTY Bruna Lapinskas
HAIR Bruna Lapinskas

PAGES 226–227
STYLIST Isadora Satie
BEAUTY Isadora Satie
HAIR Isadora Satie

PAGES 228–229
STYLIST Lydia Hudgens
BEAUTY Kelly Mazzini
HAIR Kelly Mazzini

PAGES 230–233
STYLIST Lydia Hudgens
BEAUTY Kelly Mazzini
HAIR Kelly Mazzini

PAGES 234–235
BEAUTY Jordan Underwood
HAIR Jordan Underwood

PAGE 236
STYLIST Carri Murphy
BEAUTY Carri Murphy
HAIR Carri Murphy

PAGES 242–243
STYLIST Yoko J
BEAUTY Kelly Mazzini
HAIR Auralis Flores

PAGES 244–247
STYLIST Danielle Lucker
BEAUTY Danielle Lucker
HAIR Danielle Lucker

PAGES 248–251
STYLIST Lydia Hudgens
BEAUTY Kelly Mazzini
HAIR Oskar Sinclair

PAGES 252–253
STYLIST Lydia Hudgens
BEAUTY Kelly Mazzini
HAIR Auralis Flores

PAGES 254–257
STYLIST Clémentine Desseaux
BEAUTY Clémentine Desseaux
HAIR Clémentine Desseaux

PAGES 258–259
STYLIST Lydia Hudgens
BEAUTY Kelly Mazzini
HAIR Auralis Flores

PAGES 260–261
STYLIST Lydia Hudgens
BEAUTY Kelly Mazzini
HAIR Auralis Flores

PAGE 263
STYLIST Yoko J
BEAUTY Kelly Mazzini

PAGES 264–265
STYLIST Lydia Hudgens
BEAUTY Kelly Mazzini
HAIR Auralis Flores

PAGES 266–269
STYLIST Lydia Hudgens and Jordan Underwood
BEAUTY Kelly Mazzini
HAIR Auralis Flores

PAGES 270–273
STYLIST Lydia Hudgens
BEAUTY Kelly Mazzini
HAIR Oskar Sinclair

PAGES 274–275
STYLIST Kelly Augustine
BEAUTY Cearah Peck
HAIR Cearah Peck

PAGE 277
STYLIST Lydia Hudgens
BEAUTY Kelly Mazzini
HAIR Auralis Flores

PAGES 278–281
STYLIST Lydia Hudgens
BEAUTY Kelly Mazzini
HAIR Kelly Mazzini

PAGES 286–289
STYLIST Denka Obradovic
BEAUTY Kelly Mazzini
HAIR Kelly Mazzini

PAGE 290
STYLIST Velonika Pome'e
BEAUTY Velonika Pome'e
HAIR Velonika Pome'e

PAGE 293
STYLIST Lydia Hudgens
BEAUTY Apollo

PAGES 294–295
STYLIST Lydia Hudgens
BEAUTY Kelly Mazzini
HAIR Kelly Mazzini

PAGES 296–297
STYLIST Lydia Hudgens
BEAUTY Kelly Mazzini
HAIR Kelly Mazzini

PAGE 298
STYLIST Lydia Hudgens
BEAUTY Emma Evans
HAIR Emma Evans

PAGES 299–301
STYLIST Velonika Pome'e
BEAUTY Velonika Pome'e
HAIR Velonika Pome'e

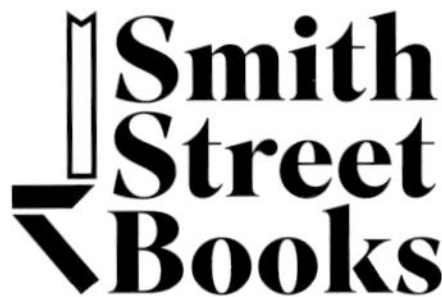

Published in 2025 by Smith Street Books
Naarm (Melbourne) | Australia
smithstreetbooks.com

Distributed outside of ANZ, North & Latin America by
Thames & Hudson Ltd., 6–24 Britannia Street, London, WC1X 9JD
thamesandhudson.com

EU Authorised Representative: Interart S.A.R.L.
19 rue Charles Auray, 93500 Pantin, Paris, France
productsafety@thameshudson.co.uk; www.interart.fr

ISBN: 978-1-9232-3936-4

Smith Street Books respectfully acknowledges the Wurundjeri People of the Kulin Nation, who are the Traditional Owners of the land on which we work, and we pay our respects to their Elders past and present.

Publisher: Paul McNally
Commissioning editor: Avery Hayes
Photo retoucher: Tatiana Lia
Proofreader: Pam Dunne & Penny Mansley
Design concept & layout: Claire Orrell
Production manager: Aisling Coughlan

Printed & bound in China by C&C Offset Printing Co., Ltd.

Book 402
10 9 8 7 6 5 4 3 2 1

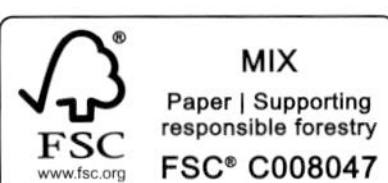

Thanks

This book is my love letter to the plus-size space—a testament to the beauty, strength, and individuality of bodies that have too often been overlooked or marginalized by the fashion industry.

Photography has given me a platform to challenge these narratives, to create images that honor the depth and complexity of plus-size individuals, and to envision a future where representation isn't an afterthought but a foundation.

Representation isn't just about visibility—it's about reframing beauty and power in ways that resonate. With this book, I hope to contribute to that ongoing conversation and to create something that feels revolutionary in its quiet, confident defiance of what the industry has long dictated.

Plus is a culmination of years spent pushing myself to create work that feels honest and powerful, but it is also a statement of gratitude. These images wouldn't exist without the incredible people who brought them to life.

To the models: Thank you for your trust, your vulnerability, and your strength. Your presence in this book reflects the beauty and power that has always existed in the plus-size space, and it's been an honor to work with each of you.

To my team: To the stylists, hair and makeup artists, assistants, and everyone who worked tirelessly behind the scenes, your creativity and dedication are woven into every image. This book is as much yours as it is mine.

To the brands: Thank you to the companies and designers who believed in this vision and contributed to its realization. Your support has helped pave the way for a more inclusive and representative industry.

To the collaborators: To the creatives who helped guide the direction of this book, your input has been invaluable.

And finally, to everyone who has supported me on this journey—thank you. This book is a celebration of all that we've accomplished together and a reminder of the work that still lies ahead.